From Appleton to Atlanta:

The Institute's First 75 Years

Author, Lead Historian
Megan Murray Wilhoit

Production Editor
Cindy Warden Bowden
Megan Sheppard

Research Historian
Bonnie Sue Boyd

Editor
Peter Hopkins

Graphic Designers
Gina Fontana-Siepierski
Julie Sanders

Research
David Hamilton
Qingfen Pan

Photography
David Bell
Tom Bowden
Robert Hill
Kara Kynast
Karl Warden

Printing
Printed in China by
Sun Fung Offset Binding Co. Ltd.

Publisher
Sun Fung Museum Catalogs & Books,
Sarasota

We would like to extend our gratitude to everyone who contributed to the Institute's 75th Anniversary Book Project through oral history interviews, donations of photographs and other memorabilia, monetary gifts, and general good wishes.

Production
Connie Adams
George Atkins
Charles Andry
David Bell
Christina Bowden
Charles Brookshire
Juan Chevere
Bob Davies
Perry Dear
Owen Dundee
Lavon Harper
Farnaz Jafari
Patrick Johnson
Jessica Kirk
Megan Kirk
David Pena
Fran Rottenberg
Santiago Santamarina
Laurie Sedicino
Megan Sheppard
Doug Stone
Matt Tennihan
Teresa Williams
Robin Young

Museum Advisory Board
Wayne Daniels
Rick Fisher
Gus Giebelhaus
Joan Giordano
Peter Hopkins
Mariana Kaplun
Charles Liotta
Sam Marks
Kate Martinson
Steve Miller
Woody Rice
Peter Sowiski
Doug Stone
Lynn Sures
Robert Williams
Sarah Morgan Wingfield

SUN FUNG
Museum Catalogs & Books

Table of Contents

BOOK SPONSORSHIPS

Legacy Donors

George W. Mead

IPC Foundation

IPST Alumni Association

Georgia-Pacific Corporation

Platinum Level

William A. Finn

J. Carter Fox

Woody Rice

Sondra and Charles Gilman, Jr.
  Foundation, Inc.

Gold Level

William R. Haselton

Robert W. Hisey

David G. McMaster

Richard E. Olson

Richard W. Roberts

William H. Trice

Silver Level

A. Nurhan Becidyan

Steven L. Edwards

David Fary, Jr.

William J. Frederick, Jr.

Arthur J. "Ben"Haug

Carl A. Jentzen

Joseph V. Koleske

Aarre Metsavirta

W. Thomas Myers, Jr.

Paul Saueracker

John M. Vaughan

Bronze Level

Peter Balousek

Richard G. Barker

John S. Barton

C. Nevin Betts

Robert L. Boehm

Keith E. Bradway

Alan Button

Jeffrey and Gail Carels

Jacinta Castellino

Thomas E. Crozier

Thomas P. Czepiel

Roy L. Davis

Arthur Dreshfield

Richard C. Erickson

James C. Farrand

James D. Freiberg

Margaret S. Gander

David P. Graves, Jr.

Brenton S. Halsey

Gerald R. Haw

Thomas W. Johnson

Robert L. Jones

Daniel Kane

Stuart E. Lebo

Ismo Lepola

James E. Macklem

George Martin

Victor F. Mattson

John M. McEwen

Timothy McIlvenna

David McIntyre

Jer Fei Mih

John Parkinson

John Rogers

Vincent Russo

SAPPI Fine Paper

S.D.Warren Company

Harry Seamans

Harry L. Spiegelberg

James S. Street

Donald W. Theisen

Nick Triantafillopoulos

Karen Turnboom

Larry W.Wanamaker

William H.Wiseman

Dear Institute Family And Friends,

We are pleased and proud to present to you *From Appleton to Atlanta: The Institute's First Seventy-Five Years*. This product of labor and love is the result of hundreds of hours of oral history interviews with former and current Institute students, faculty and staff members, administrators, and friends as well as a myriad of Institute memorabilia from the museum's archives.

This project would not have been possible without the time and effort of many interested and invested parties. Megan Murray Wilhoit, the book's author and lead historian, has worked on this project for more than three years and has done a wonderful job transforming interviews, photographs, and a wide-ranging series of documents pertaining to the Institute's history into what you now hold in your hands. Cindy Bowden, the director of the Robert C. Williams Paper Museum at Georgia Tech, has dedicated endless hours to the book's production, campaigning tirelessly for the support needed to complete the project. To Megan and Cindy, as well as to the rest of the museum staff and others at the Institute who have supported this project, we extend our deepest gratitude.

I would also like to thank our Legacy Donors - George W. Mead, the IPC Foundation, the IPST Alumni Association, and the Georgia-Pacific Corporation – as well as all of the other Institute alumni and friends whose financial contributions have made this project possible. Your support will ensure that the Institute's rich and proud legacy will be forever remembered.

Sincerely,

DR. WILLIAM J. FREDERICK, JR.
Director
Institute of Paper Science and Technology at Georgia Tech

INTRODUCTION

1920-
1929

The 1920s was a decade renowned for gaiety and flamboyance, an era of unparalleled prosperity and rapid change. American women, emboldened by their newfound right to vote, embraced the fashion of the "Flapper" and could be found dancing the Charleston with young World War I veterans as jazz tumbled out of nightclubs and speakeasies across the country. Prohibition, brought on by the 1919 Volstead Act and codified by the Eighteenth Amendment, ushered in the legendary and oft-romanticized era of gangsters making substantial livings controlling the flow of illegal liquor in cities across the country. American consumerism reached a fevered pitch and manufacturers raced to keep pace with the ever-increasing demand for automobiles, telephones, refrigerators, and radios.

And then it was over.

Americans crowded around their newly-purchased radios and listened, stunned, as news of a stock market crash, the worst in the nation's history, raced across the airwaves. That fateful day, "Black Tuesday," October 29, 1929, marked the end of the lavish splendor of the Roaring Twenties and ushered in one of the most challenging eras in United States history. The Great Depression, which cost some thirteen million jobs within the first two years, wreaked havoc on the American economy. Businesses folded at an alarming rate and plans for new ventures were abandoned for lack of capital.

Except for one.

Westbrook Steele

Milwaukee was the site of Wisconsin's first paper mill. On March 7, 1848, three months before Wisconsin was officially granted statehood, papermakers at a mill located at the junction of the Milwaukee and Menomonee Rivers used recycled cotton rags to produce paper for the *Milwaukee Sentinel and Gazette* newspaper. Production eventually climbed to ninety reams per week.

Westbrook Steele arrived in Appleton in 1928 to assist Lawrence College in its ambitious reorganization program. He left twenty-seven years later as President Emeritus of the Institute of Paper Chemistry, the graduate school to which he had contributed enormous amounts of time, energy, and plain, old-fashioned sweat.

BUT SOUTHERN WISCONSIN was not to become the center of the state's papermaking industry. Papermakers, following the bountiful supply of fresh water from the Fox, Wisconsin, Chippewa, Menominee, Peshtigo, Eau Claire, and Flambeau Rivers, began to move northward, transforming abandoned flour and lumber mills into paper mills.

Steele was no stranger to educational experiments. He had spent more than twenty years as general manager of National Systems, a company that directed the reorganization of schools and colleges. His record boasted the successful restructuring of more than seventy educational institutions.

In 1853, the Richmond brothers established the Fox River Valley's first paper mill in the town of Appleton. Its primary products were a coarse-grain rag paper and wrapping paper made from straw. The mill, like so many before and so many to follow, burned in 1859, but was rebuilt at once and began producing more than four tons of wrapper and manila paper per day. Within the next twenty-five years, additional mills were built at Kaukauna, Neenah, and Fond du Lac, establishing the Valley's reputation as the papermaking center of Wisconsin.

Steele's contributions to the Institute are legendary. It was he who persuaded local paper manufacturers to donate equipment for the original pulping laboratory. He convinced allied industries to furnish the money needed to complete the Institute's first building, and, in one of his final acts as the Institute's President, arranged the acquisition of the Dard Hunter Collection of paper and paper-related artifacts. Institute alumni will forever remember the welcoming tea party held each September in the Steeles' home and the cheerful holiday parties for all the Institute children hosted by Mrs. Steele each Christmas.

1872 proved a turning point for what was quickly becoming Wisconsin's chief industry. In the latter part of that year, Col. H.A. Frambach, a Civil War veteran, introduced to the state the Keller Groundwood Process. Developed in Germany in 1844 by Friedrich Keller, the process involved pressing logs against a grinder and adding water to create suitable fibers for papermaking, heralding the end of constant cotton rag shortages. The beautiful, untouched North Woods promised enough lumber to see the Wisconsin paper industry well into the next century. The Frambach and Stovekin Mill in Kaukauna, founded in 1873, was the first to install a machine for grinding pulpwood logs and others quickly followed suit.

During Steele's retirement celebration in September of 1955, Dean Harry Lewis, a long-time colleague and friend, aptly summarized Steele's Institute of Paper Chemistry experience:

His dreams have been realized in a very real way.

The Keller Groundwood Process connected Wisconsin's thriving paper industry with its other premier industry. Logging was slow to develop in Wisconsin, with the area's earliest white settlers preferring to bring lumber with them from the East. After 1836, however, when the Menominee Indians were forced to cede much of the land in central and eastern Wisconsin to the United States, the state's logging industry began to develop in earnest. Like the paper industry, logging was directly dependent on the state's numerous rivers and waterways, which provided convenient transport for pine logs from the wild forests of central and northern Wisconsin to the mills farther south. Dozens of new paper mills sprang up in central and northern Wisconsin in the years leading up to the dawning of the 20th century, including several still in operation today.

Even into the new century, papermaking was largely a pragmatic undertaking, with tried and true but self-limiting knowledge passed down from one generation of papermakers to the next. The science of papermaking was still in its infancy, with little real understanding of the chemistry of cellulose or the complexities of various paper properties. Papermaking was still a "feel-it, smell-it, taste-it" process.

But paper industry executives across the country began to recognize the need for concentrated research efforts within their own mills as well as within the industry as a whole. Several steps were taken in the early part of the 20th century, including the establishment of the USDA Forest Service's Forest Products Lab in Madison in 1910 and the development of the Technical Association of the Pulp and Paper Industry (TAPPI) and the American Pulp and Paper Mill Superintendents Management Association (PIMA) in 1915 and 1919, respectively. These organizations were formed to facilitate the exchange of scientific information and discuss possible solutions to the industry's technical challenges. Additionally, several notable research institutions, Syracuse University chief among them, began offering undergraduate courses in pulp and paper science. These efforts, though not well coordinated, were a vital step in the long path leading to the development of a graduate school fully devoted to the needs of the United States paper industry.

As paper industry executives pondered the challenge of advancing the industry in a technologically progressive age, a group of Wisconsin pulp and paper manufacturers came together to find a solution. The industry needed employees specifically trained in the scientific processes of papermaking. But who would train them? Individual mills lacked the resources needed to develop organized research programs and were unable to conduct a nation-wide search for men with adequate technical backgrounds to develop them.

In 1919, Dr. Samuel Plantz, President of Lawrence College, began to examine the possibility of organizing at Lawrence a pulp and paper curriculum similar to that at Syracuse University in New York. In April of that year, Plantz wrote a letter to Monroe A. Wertheimer, president of Thilmany Pulp and Paper Company and a trustee of Lawrence College, stating that "a school of this kind in our vicinity… would be of very great advantage to the men who are in the papermill industry." He did not envision a private graduate school of the magnitude that the Institute of Paper Chemistry would eventually become;

rather, Plantz visualized undergraduate classes that would provide technical training to local mill personnel. Espousing the idea of adding a practical dimension to Lawrence's liberal arts curriculum, he wrote: "I should like very much to see the college relate itself more practically to the industries of our community."

Dr. Plantz's 1919 letter to Wertheimer outlined his plan in great detail. Lawrence would offer evening classes so that men who worked in paper mills during the day would be able to attend. He determined that a new building "with sufficient paper

I dedicate this institution to the highest and most efficient use of language and to the economical manufacture of the product which carries the knowledge of the ages to all mankind.

— **Dr. John H. Finley,** Associate Editor, *New York Times,* September 23, 1931 mill machinery" would be needed and that skilled professors must be hired to give instruction. He suggested hiring men from local paper mills to teach special evening classes while supplementing this instruction with a partial liberal arts curriculum to produce a well-rounded individual, or what would later be called a "scientific generalist."

Dr. Plantz knew that a business venture such as the one he was formulating would

be much better received were it to be presented by, as he told Wertheimer, "the initiative of some paper men like yourself." He further observed, "I feel quite sure if I were to go to the paper mill men of the valley, they would look at it as a scheme of the college to get a larger work developed and would perhaps doubt the efficiency of the enterprise."

The idea of a school devoted to the education and training of young men specifically for work in the paper industry began to spread among the ranks of Wisconsin's premier paper manufacturers. In a letter to Plantz dated July 6, 1920, L.M. Alexander, president of the Nekoosa-Edwards Paper Company, called the idea "very commendable because it is not only furnishing what we call a dependable job; but also at very good remuneration… and as Wisconsin is the third largest producing state in the United States and probably will be for some time to come – it is something that is worthwhile looking into."

It would be another nine years before the institution Plantz had in mind would become a reality, with delays centering on the source of funds for the school. Plantz had estimated that between $200,000 and $250,000 would be needed to construct a building, buy equipment

and hire professors. Initially, none among Wisconsin's paper industry executives were willing to commit such an enormous amount of money.

Plantz remained an outspoken advocate of an institution dedicated to the training of young men for careers in the pulp and paper industry until his death in 1924. His immediate successor, Wilson Samuel Naylor, supported Plantz's plans, but his term as Lawrence's interim president proved too brief to act upon them. Then, in 1925, a professor of history at Connecticut's Wesleyan University was chosen by Lawrence's trustees to serve as the college's eighth president. Dr. Henry M. Wriston possessed, according to former Institute President John Strange in his 1979 publication *Fifty Years of Aspiration: An Abridged History of the Institute of Paper Chemistry*, "an uncompromising commitment to excellence" and though his tenure in Appleton was brief, his role in the founding the Institute of Paper Chemistry was significant.

Wriston did not act alone, however. His search among the ranks of Wisconsin's pulp and paper industry executives for a liaison, a man to link the technical with the educational and garner the support of his fellow "paper men," led Wriston to Ernst

Mahler, vice president and general manager of the Kimberly-Clark Corporation in nearby Neenah. Mahler was a Darmstadt man, distinguishing himself early on with his research in cellulose chemistry. His work caught the attention of Kimberly-Clark's top executives, who persuaded the Austrian to come to the United States and develop what would be one of the first research laboratories in the United States paper industry. Mahler's educational background – for it was intended that the new school model itself on the technical education philosophies of Darmstadt – combined with his experience and distinction in the industry, convinced Wriston that he would be the perfect candidate.

Wriston's choice of Ernst Mahler as the voice of the industry for the new school was a fine one. Mahler was both well-known and well-liked among paper industry executives of Wisconsin, and his voice was a strong one. By the early summer of 1929, Mahler delivered to Wriston a slate of nineteen pulp and paper companies – ninety percent of the paper manufacturers of Wisconsin – willing to support the new venture.

The Institute of Paper Chemistry was born.

Plans for the new school began in earnest.

Henry M. Wriston

In discussing the condition of liberal arts education in the United States, McGeorge Bundy, who, in addition to his role as an architect in foreign policy under the Kennedy and Johnson administrations, served as the Dean of the Faculty of Arts and Sciences at Harvard University, declared that, "we all go to school under Henry Wriston." His remark resonates with those fortunate enough to reap the benefits of Wriston's endless list of contributions to liberal arts education; indeed, Wriston certainly earned his title of the "American Educator."

Henry Merritt Wriston was born in Laramie, Wyoming, on July 4, 1889. He received his Bachelor of Arts degree in medieval history from Wesleyan University in 1911, followed by a Master's degree, also from Wesleyan, in 1912. Wriston pursued graduate studies in history and international affairs at Harvard University as an Austin Teaching Fellow, and in 1914, returned to Wesleyan as an instructor in history. In 1922, after Wriston had completed his dissertation and was awarded his PhD from Harvard, he was made a full professor at Wesleyan.

Wriston's leadership skills were evident even before his rise to several high-profile positions. As an undergraduate, he edited Wesleyan's newspaper, was a top debater, and won the senior oratorical contest. During World War I, Wriston served as the assistant manager of the Connecticut State Council of Defense. His success in this position led to his 1919 appointment as Executive Secretary of the Wesleyan Endowment Fund, which, in turn, greatly influenced Lawrence's Board of Trustees to select Wriston as the college's eighth president.

During his twelve-year tenure at Lawrence, Wriston earned national recognition for his numerous innovations in collegiate education, notable among them a program of educational and vocational guidance with experiments in adult education, art appreciation, and extensive reading programs. Upon Wriston's resignation from Lawrence in 1937, Appleton Mayor John Goodland acknowledged that the greatest strides in the history of Lawrence were made under Wriston's administration.

Most significant was his role in the founding of the Institute of Paper Chemistry. During Wriston's farewell banquet in late January of 1937, Ernst Mahler lavishly praised Wriston's vision, determination, and devotion in the Institute's development. "Indeed," he said, "the Institute has done more to put Appleton on the map than anything that has happened. The educational world had watched its growth and industries are fast realizing similar needs. Dr. Wriston, as director, has assembled most able educators, scientists, and administrators and leaves the personnel a solid foundation on which to build in the future... I believe Dr. Wriston will not stop as president of Brown University but is entitled by his abilities to the highest place the educational world has to offer.'

Wriston left Lawrence in 1937 to become the eleventh president of Rhode Island's Brown University. The farewell he received was a testament to the admiration bestowed upon him by both Lawrence University and the town of Appleton – more than three hundred students and townspeople gathered at the Chicago and Northwestern train depot on the day of Wriston's departure to wave goodbye as the eastbound train pulled away from the station.

Scholar, writer, educator, administrator, political advisor – Wriston was truly a Renaissance Man. "He was a complex personage," noted James Adams, who served as Brown's vice president during Wriston's tenure as president, "but he had a brilliant mind, a steady nerve, a provocative manner, and an unwavering determination."

Ernst Mahler

Many men have the gift of technical skill, but inventive and imaginative insight are seldom added to it. In you these powers are brilliantly combined, and you have used them devotedly for the cause of international industry. But in these busy years you have also shown a connoisseur's passion for art and a scholar's passion for the cause of education.

— *Lawrence College President Douglas M. Knight, in conferring upon Ernst Mahler an honorary Doctor of Law degree at the Institute's Silver Anniversary in 1954*

These were the attributes that convinced Dr. Henry Wriston that Mahler was the right man to help bridge the gap between industry and education. Mahler did not disappoint.

Ernst Mahler was born in Vienna, Austria, in 1887 and raised in a world of paper chemists; by the age of twenty, he had left Vienna for Darmstadt, Germany, to attend the world-famous Technische Hochschule de Darmstadt. There he studied industrial chemistry, specializing in cellulose chemistry and the scientific study of papermaking. Shortly after his graduation in 1912, Mahler immigrated to the United States to begin work at the Kimberly-Clark Corporation in Neenah, Wisconsin.

Mahler quickly distinguished himself within the Kimberly-Clark Corporation. The research and development department that he established was among the first – and the finest – in the United States paper industry. Mahler led a team that was responsible for the development of many products still in use today. Perhaps most significant among Mahler's many contributions to the American pulp and paper industry was the development of creped wadding, a wood-based material that was used as a substitute for cotton bandages during the first World War. After the war, Kimberly-Clark turned Mahler's product into a multi-billion dollar industry, creating many new products that would eventually be trademarked under now-familiar brand names such as Kleenex and Kotex.

By the time that Wriston approached him regarding the vision of a school dedicated to the needs of the United States pulp and paper industry, Mahler had advanced to the position of vice president at Kimberly-Clark. The proposition was of immediate interest to Mahler, who for several years had been lamenting the trend toward vocationalism in colleges across the country. "Unfortunately the results of this trend were unsatisfactory," Mahler noted in a speech several years later. "By substituting 'commercial' or vocational courses for fundamental instruction, educators lost sight of the fact that true education is a study of values and not an imitative process."

Mahler's role in the founding of the Institute was immeasurable. He spent countless hours in boardrooms across the state, persuading Wisconsin's paper executives to provide the financial backing for the new institution. When representatives from the Institute's member companies met for the first time to discuss the organization of the school, Mahler's contributions were acknowledged by his fellow industry executives as they elected him president of the Board of Trustees. He maintained this position until the restructuring of the Board in 1950; afterward, he served as the Chairman of the Board until 1957. He was then named Honorary Chairman, a title he held until his death in 1967. During Mahler's tenure as the Board's leader, the Institute experienced enormous growth – new buildings and facilities valued at more than $4 million, an annual operating budget increasing from $40,000 per year in 1929 to $1.8 million in 1957, and a staff increasing from four members in 1929 to more than two hundred and fifty.

Mahler's contributions to his industry and his country were many and varied. He played a large role in the founding of the Technical Association of the Pulp and Paper Industry (TAPPI) in 1915 and was awarded the TAPPI Gold Medal for contributions to the industry in 1933. During World War II, Mahler served as a member of the Purchase Policy Division of the Army Service Forces, where he aided in formulating policies, reviewing legislation, and implementing the utilization of small war plants. In 1945, he spent five months in Europe as a consultant in charge of paper production and organization rehabilitation of the paper industries of Belgium, Holland, Germany, and France. For his services as a member of the United States Reparations Commission in Russia, Berlin, and Potsdam, Mahler was awarded a certificate of appreciation from the War Department and the Presidential Medal of Freedom. Among the many honors bestowed upon Mahler during his long and distinguished career were an honorary Doctor of Science degree from Brown University, an honorary Doctor of Law degree from Lawrence College, and an honorary Doctor of Engineering degree from his Alma mater, Darmstadt. These honors, according to a speech delivered by Dr. Henry Wriston in 1937, were quite betting one who was "a leader in transforming an ancient art through modern scientific processes."

In his 1982 treatise on the American free market system, *The Economy of Mind*, economist Warren Brookes wrote of Ernst Mahler:

Mahler was an entrepreneurial genius whose innovative ideas and leadership, over a period of about twenty years, transformed a once-small, insular newsprint and tissue manufacturer into one of the largest paper corporations in the world, which gives prosperous employment to more than 100,000 and produces products – which Mahler helped to innovate – that are now used by more than two billion people... his personal fortune was insignificant when compared with the permanent prosperity he generated, not only for his own company but for the hundreds of thousands who work for industries which his genius ultimately spawned and which long outlived him... the revolutionary sanitary products that have liberated two generations of women, or the printing paper that completely transformed international publishing and communications for fifty years.

The Institute's First Home: Appleton, Wisconsin

THE FOX RIVER VALLEY, in which Appleton nestles, has a rich and diverse history. First settled by the Winnebago, Menominee, Mascoutine, Patawatami, and Fox Indians, the area also became home to Jesuit missionaries seeking to convert the "savages" and capitalize on the Valley's rich fur trade. In 1836, the valley's four million acres was ceded to the United States by the Treaty of the Cedars.

In 1847, Amos A. Lawrence, a wealthy Boston merchant engaged in the manufacture and sale of textiles, found himself in possession of more than five thousand acres of Wisconsin wilderness that had served as collateral on a defaulted loan. Lawrence, who was well known for his philanthropy, commissioned three Methodist ministers to establish a school on his land. Lawrence pledged a $10,000 endowment for the school on the condition that the Methodist Church do the same.

The school's charter, granted in that same year, was radical for its time, promising religious freedom to its students, faculty and staff, and opening admission to men and women. It thus became only the second coeducational college in the country.

As Lawrence's representatives searched for a site for the school, it was quickly determined that his holdings were inappropriate, as they were dangerously close to the Indian and French settlements in the area. The committee turned its sights to the Fox River Valley and ultimately selected a spot at Grand Chute, the home of the White Heron Trading Post. Classes began at Lawrence Institute, the "university in the wilderness," in November of 1849. The town of Appleton, named after Samuel Appleton, Lawrence's father-in-law who gave $10,000 for the school's first library, developed around the small education institution, growing steadily from the crude huts of the early settlers to the beautifully designed homes and buildings of the present.

The choice of Appleton as the home for the Institute of Paper Chemistry some eighty years after classes began at Lawrence was decidedly strategic. Many early Institute publications and speeches boasted that practically every type of pulp and paper manufacture in the world could be found within a seven-mile radius of the city, giving Appleton a unique status in the industry. The town's proximity to these mills provided the newly formed Institute

with access to much-needed paper machinery and to highly trained men with practical papermaking experience, several of whom were engaged as lecturers and guest speakers.

Appleton, according to Ernst Mahler, vice president of Kimberly-Clark Corporation and a founding trustee of the Institute, was certainly "paper mill conscious." The picturesque town located on the banks of the Fox River proved a comfortable home for the Institute, and the two enjoyed a mutually beneficial relationship for more than sixty years.

FOUNDING TRUSTEES

It was determined that the Institute would operate most effectively as a non-profit corporation and an independent entity, although it would maintain an affiliation with Lawrence College. The school would be governed by a Board of Trustees comprised of representatives from both Lawrence College and the Wisconsin paper industry in order to balance the academic and industrial missions of the Institute.

Financially, the Institute of Paper Chemistry would be supported by a membership structure. Companies producing pulp, paper, or paperboard would be eligible for membership and their dues – set at a yearly rate of $30 per ton of their daily paper production – would contribute to the school's operating budget. The original nineteen member companies brought in by Mahler pledged a total of $300,000 which, when augmented by funds from individuals and corporations allied with the paper industry, would guarantee the Institute's existence at a minimal operating budget for a period of five years.

The contributions of the Institute's member companies went above and beyond the financial. It was agreed that local mills would periodically send employees to the Institute to serve as guest lecturers. They also agreed to allow students access to their mills and provide them with hands-on experience not available in a classroom setting. Thus the pulp and paper mills surrounding Appleton became, in effect, laboratories for the Institute and its students.

Wriston, Mahler, and a handful of local paper executives dedicated to the school's development determined that the mission statement of the Institute of Paper Chemistry should focus on three specific functions. First and foremost, the school would provide postgraduate training to men who would then use that training to create and direct research laboratories in the nation's pulp and paper mills. The decision to develop the Institute as a graduate school was the subject of considerable debate throughout the summer of 1929. Other reputable institutions, such as Syracuse and North Carolina State, had well-established pulp and paper curriculums and the Institute's founders questioned the wisdom of simply duplicating those programs. It was ultimately decided that, though those undergraduate institutions were doing a fine job of instructing students in pulp and paper technology, the need for postgraduate training for men who had already completed their preliminary chemical or engineering training at the undergraduate level was immediate. Men with this training would be prepared to undertake the rigorous academic program the Institute would offer and, upon graduation, would ultimately possess the

qualifications to not only work in the United States' paper industry but to eventually guide its future as industry leaders.

The second purpose of the Institute would be to conduct research beneficial to the paper industry. As a result, the industry would greatly benefit from quality research and avoid duplication of staff and equipment. Most importantly, students would work alongside Institute staff, thereby receiving hands-on training in solving industry-related problems.

The founders determined that the Institute's third function should be to establish and maintain a complete library of pulp and paper science and technology. The library would support both the academic and research functions of the Institute by thoroughly covering the field and by

providing abstract and translation services, benefiting not only Institute faculty, students and staff, but the entire industry as well.

As the fall of 1929 approached, the Institute's founders had one more item on their organizational agenda: developing an educational philosophy upon which to base the school's curriculum. Since the early 1900s, graduate education – especially in the fields of science and engineering – had been treading a path of specialization. Professors were focusing much more on *how* something should be done rather than *why* it should be done and, to quote John Strange, "higher education was in danger of becoming too vocational." The Institute's founders saw in this new school a chance to veer off that path and return to a more old-fashioned teaching philosophy still en vogue at some of the more prestigious academies in Europe, such as Technische Hochschule de Darmstadt (Darmstadt Polytechnic). "Europe has long recognized the necessity of such schools," said Mahler in a speech delivered at the American Pulp and Paper Association Annual Meeting, "and they are existing today in every industrial country over there."

The plan was simple. The Institute of Paper Chemistry would apply a liberal arts philosophy to the teaching of science and technology. Students would receive a broad education in the disciplines relevant to the manufacture of pulp and paper. Faculty would encourage imagination and creative thinking, grounded in a thorough knowledge of fundamental research procedures. This educational philosophy would, according to Mahler, "turn out a student… who can go out into the industry and create the confidence of his employer to the point where he can be trusted with the technical problems that arise."

At last all was in place. On October 12, 1929, Articles of Incorporation were filed with the Wisconsin Department of the State, seeking approval to organize a graduate school in affiliation with Lawrence College in Appleton. Within

two weeks, the Articles had been granted and Wriston had called for a meeting to formally organize the Institute. On Monday, October 28, the Lawrence library was filled with paper industry executives from throughout the state of Wisconsin, all eager to take part in this revolutionary venture. Representatives from each member company cast their votes and selected L.M. Alexander of the Nekoosa-Edwards Paper Company, Dan K. Brown of the Neenah Paper Company, D.C. Everest of the Marathon Paper Mills Company, Ernst Mahler of the Kimberly Clark Corporation, Hugh Strange of the John Strange Paper Company, and Monroe A. Wertheimer of the Thilmany Pulp and Paper Company as the founding trustees. Dr. Henry Wriston was named Director of the Institute.

After a quick lunch break, those assembled elected Mahler President of the Board of Trustees. Everest was chosen as the board's Vice President and Wriston became Secretary. Westbrook Steele, a Lawrence College employee considered an expert in educational structuring and financing, was appointed Executive Secretary and Ralph J. Watts, Lawrence's business manager, was named Treasurer.

The meeting adjourned in the early evening of what would later be known as Black Monday, the day the stock market suffered a record one-day loss of close to thirteen percent. Although the newly elected officers and their fellow paper industry executives were warily watching the events in New York unfold, they found solace in the progress made that day. They had secured several rooms in Lawrence's new Alexander Gymnasium to conduct lectures and labs once classes began the following February. They had set basic entrance requirements for prospective Institute students – a bachelor of science degree with a major in chemistry and a satisfactory personal interview. They had set the tuition rate at $200 per year, which would include all laboratory fees. Finally, they had given approval to begin the search for the Institute's first two employees – a librarian and a technical director.

The next day the founders and trustees – and the entire country – awoke to worsening news from New York. To most historians, "Black Tuesday" – October 29, 1929 – was a watershed in American history, marking the point where the Roaring Twenties ended and the Great Depression began. Although the market fell slightly less than the previous day (about twelve percent), a record 16.4 million shares were traded, causing the ticker tape to fall almost two and a half hours behind. By the end of November, investors had lost more than $100 billion in assets and the value of the stock market had dropped by forty percent. It would continue dropping for another two years, finally bottoming out in July of 1932 with the Dow at 41.22, down from 381.17 in the months before the Crash. It was not until 1954 that the stock market fully recovered.

"How easy and forgiving it would have been," John Strange wrote in his *Fifty Years of Aspiration*, "for the original sponsors to take the position that a storm was gathering and that it would be circumspect to delay their commitments until a more propitious time."

Yet they persevered – and they succeeded.

THE WHITE HOUSE
WASHINGTON

October 19, 1929.

President Henry M. Wriston,
Lawrence College,
Appleton, Wisconsin.

Dear President Wriston:

I am glad to know of the organization of the Institute of Paper Chemistry at Lawrence College. The importance of sound technical processes based upon scientific research is becoming ever more important to American industry.

Through the association of institutions of learning with business the colleges will be in a position more adequately to serve present day needs. By associating themselves with institutions of learning the industries may keep abreast of scientific developments and make a sound contribution to the progress of the nation.

I hope that the success of this cooperative effort will point the way to other fruitful enterprises of like character.

Yours faithfully,

Herbert Hoover

CHAPTER 1 1930-1939

The world awakened to a solemn dawn in 1930. Even as politicians and the leaders of great American industries tried to sooth the dazed country with optimistic predictions and promises of "a brighter tomorrow," banks, factories, and thousands of other businesses closed their doors, leaving millions of Americans jobless and, in many cases, homeless and hungry. The American Dream had become, for many, a seemingly endless nightmare.

But in a small midwestern town on the banks of the Fox River, the dreams and visions of a group determined to shift the direction of higher education in the United States were quickly being realized…

"The Institute of 1930," remarked Harry Lewis in his August 1939 newsletter, " was largely Otto [Kress] at one end of the log and three students at the other."

WHAT MADE THIS COMMENT so humorous to anyone familiar with the Institute's humble beginnings was the element of truth it contained. Yes, there were a few – very few – other faces besides that of Dr. Otto Kress floating around in those early days. There were more than three students, but they were "special students" who worked in local paper mills and attended classes only part-time. And the few rooms in Lawrence's Alexander Gymnasium, modest though they were, were still more than simply a log. However, when compared with what the Institute would become, the mental picture Lewis's comment evoked did resonate, especially with those who had been around long enough to experience that growth first-hand.

Wriston, Mahler, and the other trustees elected at the October 28 board meeting wasted no time following up on the plans made that day. Memos flew back and forth from Appleton, Neenah, and surrounding areas as the Institute's founders debated course offerings, scholarship monies, administration, and a host of other issues associated with the development and management of a graduate school.

Dr. Otto Kress

Two positions needed to be filled immediately. The first was technical director. The position called for, as an early Institute academic brochure explained, "a man not only broadly trained in the various fields of pulp and papermaking but for one who also possessed wide contacts among the technical men associated with the paper and allied industries." No man fit the job description more perfectly than Dr. Otto Kress, who had been educated at New York's Columbia University and possessed more than twenty years of practical experience in the field of pulp and paper. It was, as Mahler once said, Kress's immediate and enthusiastic willingness to be the technical director, the only full-time teacher and the general factotum - including millwright and janitor - that formed one of the cornerstones of the Institute and made Kress a legend.

I had the privilege of visiting the Institute to recruit young engineers into the paper industry. I would go out to the Institute twice a year and talk to the boys out there. I was always impressed by the way new buildings came up and what started out as two buildings became three, four, five buildings. I was also impressed that they were still doing a good job with their training.

— Daniel Adams, entering class 1939

It was a happy time for me.

— Al Schenck, entering class 1938

I learned a lot. In essence, they made me a scientific generalist.

— Edwin Loutzenheiser, entering class 1939

Institute faculty meeting, c. 1931

The second position that required immediate attention was librarian. One of the three primary functions of the Institute of Paper Chemistry as discussed during the October 28 meeting was the establishment and maintenance of a complete library dedicated to the many aspects of pulp and paper science and technology to benefit the Institute students, faculty, and staff as well as the United States paper industry as a whole. On April 21, 1930, it was announced by Westbrook Steele, who was quickly becoming the Institute's chief promoter, that Hjordis Roseth had been chosen to fill the position. Miss Roseth, originally from Oslo, Norway, had attended New York State Library School in Albany, and at the time of her IPC appointment was working at the Riordan Research Institute of the Canadian International Paper Company. Although Miss Roseth only served as librarian for one year, it was she who first organized and arranged what would become the most comprehensive collection of pulp and paper reference materials in the country.

It is worth noting again that creating a "normal" graduate program is almost always difficult at best. To create a program

the likes of which had never before been seen in the United States made the task all the more complex. A case in point was the hiring of faculty and staff as February 3 – the date classes were scheduled to commence – drew near. According to Mahler, there were three possible courses of action that could be taken with regard to the hiring of faculty members: "The first is to secure a group of academically trained men, who are familiar with the processes of teaching and research in pure science. A second would be to take chiefly men of middle age who have long experience in the problems of productions but who have slight experience in the problems of teaching. A third would be to take a group of brilliant young men, just out of graduate school, and train them for our purposes." The beauty of developing such a unique institution was at once obvious. No one particular path was essential; the Institute's founders could, as Mahler suggested, "choose all three." And so they did. With the Institute's very first matriculation day so close at hand, little time was left to conduct a search for the type of men Mahler, Wriston, and others were looking for in an IPC professor and researcher. Since it was inconceivable that

Dr. Kress could teach all the classes on the proposed syllabus, it was suggested that the Institute "borrow" several professors from Lawrence College to ease Kress's teaching load. Lawrence professors Dr. Gottlob Cast, Dr. Stephen Darling, Mr. Walter Rogers, and Dr. Lewis Youtz answered the call. Although the positions were originally temporary, each of these four found a niche at the Institute of Paper Chemistry and eventually rounded out their prestigious careers as professors and researchers at the new institution.

Cast was recruited to teach a class in Technical German, deemed necessary due to the number of technical journals written in German. William Haselton, entering class 1949, recalls Cast as "strictly from the old school" but added that as long as you did your work, you would get along fine with him. George Ingle, entering class 1938, remembers with a laugh the difficulties

Technical German Class with Dr. Cast, c. 1931

"the guys from the southern schools who had never had a word of German in their lifetimes" had with Cast's course. "I tried to help them," he recalls. "But they were in a tough situation."

I remember it as a pleasant period in my life. I was busy and glad to be there, working to get my degree.

— Roy Davis, entering class 1930

Darling, who had received his doctorate from Harvard University in 1928 and thus was not much older than many of his students, was brought in to teach several areas of organic chemistry, including the chemistries of cellulose, carbohydrates, and lignin. Ingle, who describes Darling simply as "a likeable guy" remembers the fun times he and his fellow classmates had in the young professor's lab extracting rare

sugars from bales of various weeds and plants. "I think he sold them [the extracted sugars] and made some money for the Institute," Ingle said.

Rogers, who had spent much of his career in the paper industry, taught courses in wood chemistry and often accompanied the new entering classes on their bush trips, a facet of Institute life introduced

in September of 1930. Although he and Youtz, who was hired to teach technical analysis, did not spend quite as much time at Institute as did Cast and Darling, this Lawrence quartet removed a great deal of the teaching burden from Kress, who taught a total of four classes that first semester, and Miss Roseth, who taught a short course in technical abstracts and bibliography.

Acceptance letter to the Institute's
first entering class, 1930

At last the long-awaited day arrived. On Monday, February 3, 1930, coinciding with the commencement of Lawrence's second semester, Harold Bialkowsky, Roy Davis, and Ed Voightman, along with several other part-time men from local mills, joined Kress in a large room positioned directly over the lobby of the Alexander Gymnasium, where, according to Lewis, "any convenient tabletop, first cleaned of acid or alkali, formed the chair of the teacher, and other similar perches the resting places of the students." Roy Davis recalls not being fazed by the lack of available lab space or the makeshift laboratory equipment, much of which was developed by Kress himself. "We just accepted it," he stated good-naturedly. "That was the situation. We were getting the courses we needed."

That first semester was, by all estimations of those involved, truly an experiment in education. The students were guinea pigs,

cheerfully adjusting to changes in the curriculum, the crude equipment, and the living conditions of Brokaw Hall, the Lawrence College freshman dormitory that housed the first three Institute students at a rate of $350 per year. Those students,

Dr. Harry Lewis

according to Davis's recollections of that first semester, never minded Kress having to leave the classroom in order to answer a ringing phone or to clean up a mess in one of the labs. In fact, the students themselves often pitched in as well, doing their share of clean-ups, secretarial work, and library assistance. Perhaps it was the makeshift environment, or the double and sometimes triple-duties performed by Kress and others, or just simply the knowledge that something grand was happening, but,

as Lewis later noted, "the best teaching the Institute ever had was done that first semester beginning February 1930."

The first semester of classes at the Institute of Paper Chemistry, though hailed as an enormous success by all standards, was also a learning experience, carried out, according to Lewis, "more or less as a pilot plant study is utilized in the mill prior to a full-scale installation." As the special students returned to their respective mills and the three full-time students left for their summer jobs, Wriston, Mahler, and Kress began the process of evaluating progress made during the previous four months. There was, it was agreed, much to be done before the new class of students – a full class this time – came to Appleton in September.

The first order of business was to hire another faculty member. A graduate school needed a dean, it was decided. But for the Institute's purposes someone with only administrative skills would not suffice. The Institute needed a man who could aid Kress in the administration of the program, who was familiar with the paper industry, and who had some teaching experience under

Construction of the original General Activities Building, 1931

his belt. Kress found everything the newly formed graduate program needed – and a great deal more – in Dr. Harry Fletcher Lewis.

Lewis, who had received his PhD from the University of Illinois in 1916, joined the Institute staff as a professor of organic chemistry in June of 1930. Within a year, the Board of Trustees voted unanimously to appoint Lewis the dean of students; in Lewis's own words, "the budding organization needed someone who knew the educational language and rules and at the same time had some acquaintance with the descriptive phrases of the technical man." As dean of students, Lewis found himself in charge of admissions, academic organization, and supervision of the academic work undertaken at the Institute. It was, as it turned out, a job for which he was aptly suited. Like Kress, Lewis was soon recognized as a cornerstone of the Institute and, also like Kress, eventually achieved legendary status.

The summer of 1930 passed quickly and on September 15, 1930, seventeen students - graduates of fifteen colleges and universities across the country - met in Appleton to begin the first full year of classes at the Institute of Paper Chemistry.

Otto Kress

"In him, there is a combination of ripe technical experience, an interest in students, and an undying interest in anything at all that relates to pulp and paper."
- Dr. Harry F. Lewis, Dean of Students November 2, 1934

"I envy those young men who have the privilege of sitting at your feet. Through them you are making an impression on this grand industry, giving it a shape that will last for many years and form one of the important chapters in the history of pulp and paper."
- Mr. Ernst Mahler, President, IPC Board of Trustees
TAPPI Medal Presentation February 21, 1940

Born in 1884, Otto Kress received his PhD from New York's Columbia University in 1909. By the time he came to the Institute in 1930, he had gained more than twenty years of practical experience in the paper industry with positions at the Forest Products Laboratory at Madison, Badische Pulp and Paper Company, Consolidated Water Power and Paper Company, and Thilmany Pulp and Paper Company.

Known to his students as "Herr Professor," Kress was an invaluable contributor to the Institute's formation and development during its adolescent years. His colleagues and students often wondered why Kress, who was once described by Henry Wriston as a "genius in the paper industry," would leave his good position within the industry to join forces with the new and untested Institute of Paper Chemistry. During his acceptance speech of the 1940 TAPPI Gold Medal, Kress answered them: "It is this work in which I am presently engaged that I have found to be so satisfying, as the opportunity is presented not only to help in conducting suitable research work but, more important, to pass on to a limited group of intelligent men and interested young men the information which had been accumulated through the past ages and thus fit them for a career in their chosen field of pulp and paper manufacture."

Kress retired from his position as the Institute's Technical Director in 1948. He remained active in Institute life until his death in 1970, notably as the donor of more than $70,000 to a scholarship fund aptly named the Otto and Florence T. Kress Scholarship Fund.

Only a man of the vision of Otto Kress could have left his good position and helped to found the Institute. Other men could have given perhaps as much to the students and to the industry in the world of knowledge but no one else could have imprinted his character on the Institute and the students during the years like Otto Kress. As the graduates assume more and more executive responsibility in our industry, they and we owe an everlasting debt to Otto Kress.
- Ernst Mahler, President, IPC Board of Trustees, June 5, 1948

Otto Kress, we live in a part of the world where pioneers and pioneer virtues are held in high esteem. Pioneer member of a pioneer enterprise, the Institute of Paper Chemistry, before that, one of the pioneer doctors of philosophy to specialize in the problems of the pulp and paper industry, you have recently and, from our point of view, regrettably, pioneered again in becoming the first emeriti if the Institute you have so ably and loyally served. Inventor, teacher, equally at home in theoretical and applied aspects of chemical knowledge – in laboratory, classrooms, and the mill – you have been a great credit both to the Institute and to the pulp and paper industry.
- Dr. Nathan M. Pusey, President, Lawrence College, June 24, 1948

Miss Edith Stroschneider

As the first full school year came to a close, the Institute experienced its first staff rollover as the librarian, Miss Roseth, announced her resignation and her intention to return to Europe. She was replaced by Miss Edith Stroschneider, who, throughout the course of her twenty-fiveyear tenure at the Institute, brought the library recognition as one of world's most complete collections of materials relating to the production of pulp and paper.

Born in Vienna, Austria, in 1889, Miss Stroschneider attended the Studley Horticultural Institute in Birmingham, England. She came to the Institute in 1931 from the Abitibi Power and Paper Company in Canada, where she served as a librarian. Her experiences at Abitibi gave her a wide range of knowledge and a great appreciation of the paper industry, which proved quite useful as she commenced her duties at the Institute. Described as "intensely interested in her work," Miss Stroschneider held a myriad of responsibilities at the Institute, ranging from the organization of the library's materials to assisting students with research to teaching the course in Technical Bibliography. Most prominent among her duties, though, was the editorship and monthly production of the Abstract Bulletin, a forty-page publication listing recent additions to the library's collection and a compilation of abstracts of all important articles from the library's subscription list that was sent to all member companies and pulp and paper mills that provided support to the Institute.

Miss Stroschneider possessed unique talents as well as certain idiosyncrasies that made her one of the more memorable characters of the Institute's rst quarter-decade. She spoke seven languages well and had a rudimentary knowledge of several more, which allowed her to decipher the many technical publications published in a wide range of languages that came across her desk in the J.A. Kimberly Memorial Library. Her dedication to her work was immeasurable; a favorite expression around the Institute throughout the 1930s and 1940s (akin to the modern "when pigs fly") was "...when Miss Stroschneider takes a vacation."

Miss Stroschneider officially retired from the Institute in 1953 and was graced with the title of "Emerita," though she continued to serve as the editor of the Bulletin until her death in 1956. Dr. Lewis honored her best in his February 1957 newsletter:

"No one will have contributed more to the day-to-day program as well as to the permanent reputation of the Institute than Edith Stroschneider."

The librarian was very enthusiastic and she was very helpful in every way. Any information we wanted she knew where to find it.

— Joe Atchison, entering class 1938

The librarian, Miss Stroschneider, taught me a great deal – a real good old German gal. She was an excellent librarian. She taught me things about technical libraries that carried me through my days in Washington.

— George Ingle, entering class 1938

Edith Stroschneider - she was in charge of the library. She ran a tight ship in the library.

— Walt Bublitz, entering class 1941

I remember the librarian's little black poodle who spent the day in a basket under her desk.

— Ben Haug, entering class 1941

As those seventeen men settled in to the rigorous regime of the typical Institute of Paper Chemistry student, Wriston, Mahler, and Kress turned their attentions to a new problem: space, or, rather, the lack thereof. The makeshift laboratories and offices in the rooms on the second floor of Alexander Gymnasium were quickly becoming crowded and the library, which had grown enormously the previous year, was quickly running out of storage space. The answer was simple: the Institute of Paper Chemistry needed a home of its own. Construction began in the spring of 1931.

June 8, 1931, was an epic day for the Institute. During Lawrence College's 81st Annual Commencement Ceremony, ten men - Edward Amstutz, Harold Bialkowsky, Karl Buff, Wilbur Cassiday, Richard Crain, Roy Davis, Emanuel Foreman, Harry Irwin, Edwin Laughlin, and Carl Schroeder – were granted the first Master of Science degrees awarded by Lawrence College for graduate work completed at the Institute of Paper Chemistry. Later that afternoon, faculty, staff, and students from both institutions gathered in a large field across the street from the Alexander Gymnasium to witness the laying of the cornerstone of what would become the Institute's permanent home.

The day of the building's dedication – Wednesday, September 23, 1931, which coincided with the matriculation of the Institute's second entering class of students – was equally significant. The new General Activities Building, built at a cost of $250,000, was an architectural masterpiece. Designed by Orbison and Orbison Engineers, the building was two stories high with two deep wings attached. One wing was designed to house the thirty-foot by sixty-foot digester room used for the cooking of wood and rags and the production of pulp from the half-stock on the first floor and a variety of special labs on the floor above, including a large lab for strength testing and color matching and another for microscopic study of fibers and finished paper. The other wing was devoted to work in colloid chemistry, containing a small research lab and a large student lab as well as a dark room for optical work and another for photographic work. The first floor of the building's front section contained the Institute's offices and classrooms as well as the rapidly expanding library; the second floor consisted of two large student research labs for work in the general field of pulp and paper technology, a large student organic lab and weighing room, and a small research lab for work in cellulose chemistry.

The TRUSTEES and STAFF
of
The INSTITUTE of PAPER CHEMISTRY
REQUEST
the PLEASURE of YOUR COMPANY
at the
LAYING of the CORNER STONE
of the
NEW BUILDING of the INSTITUTE
at TWO O'CLOCK
MONDAY AFTERNOON
JUNE EIGHTH, NINETEEN HUNDRED
THIRTY-ONE
APPLETON, WISCONSIN

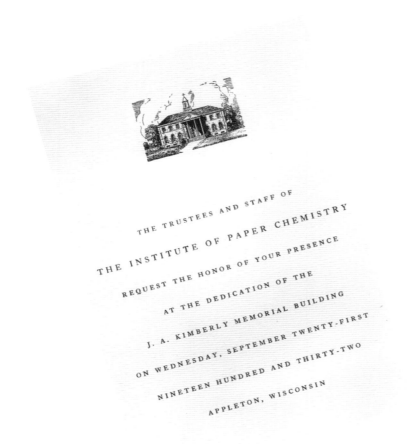

The Institute's First PhD class, 1933

Contributing to the excitement of the day was a special announcement made by Mahler during the key presentation ceremony. J.C. Kimberly, president of Neenah Paper Company, had donated $100,000 for a memorial to honor his father, Wisconsin pulp and paper magnate J.A. Kimberly who, after serving as president of the Kimberly-Clark Corporation for 56 years, had passed away in 1928. The gift was intended, according to Mahler's speech, "to erect contiguous to the present building, a library and laboratory to house the splendid collection of books we possess and to make provision for its growth and to provide additional laboratory space already shown desirable." Construction of the J.A. Kimberly Memorial Library began immediately.

Likes its sister building, the Kimberly Library was an architectural magnum opus. Resembling the General Activities Building with an exterior entirely done in Lannon stone, the building, in a classic colonial architectural style, was designed with a high-pillared porch and a cupola with a clock. Antique pine paneling covered the walls of the first floor, which hosted a spacious reading room, a recreational reading room, the librarian's office, and a stock room. The colloid chemistry labs, previously in the General Activities Building, were relocated to the second floor of the new building, along with a series of conference rooms. The building's basement contained optical and photographic dark rooms, a large optics lab, a research reading room, and the librarian's workroom.

The Institute's First Masters class, 1931

25

By the time the Institute's third anniversary rolled around, thirty-five students were attending classes in the General Activities Building. Seventeen of these students were in their first year, ten in their second year, and eight in their third year. The Institute's annual budget had grown to more than $100,000 and six paper companies had joined the Institute's membership, bringing the total to twenty-five. A press release circulated during the anniversary celebration in February of 1933 told the member companies that:

> *The aims of the Institute have been followed with some degree of success. Mills and individuals responded generously, and, as a result, buildings and equipment have been forthcoming. The reputation of the Institute is constantly spreading and the interest in it widening geographically. The foundation seems stable – its future, hopeful. It is especially gratifying to have found such a response to its aims in the midst of depression that has done so much to deaden activity in general.*

On Monday, June 12, 1933, four of the "stones" comprising the stable foundation upon which the Institute was built made Institute – and Lawrence College – history by receiving the first Doctor of Philosophy degrees ever granted by the college. One by one, Harold Bialkowsky, Roy Davis, Edwin

I'd say it's probably outdone Westbrook Steele's early vision of being a force in the industry.

— John McEwen, entering class, 1939

It was a good memory – an interesting period in my life.

— Joe Atchison, entering class 1938

Laughlin, and Ed Voightman took the stage during the commencement ceremony to be conferred by Dr. Wriston, presented by Dr. Lewis, and invested with a hood by Dr. Kress, thus culminating three and a half years of intense training in pulp and paper technology. The Institute was on its way.

The 1930s was a decade of colossal change; a dynamic situation heartily embraced by the Institute. Curricula were created, tested, revised, and tested again as the Institute's academic advisors searched for the best and most thorough way to fill a man's head with the knowledge he needed to become a major force in the United States pulp and paper industry. The original nine courses had expanded to more than thirty by the decade's end. A new division was created to keep up with the industry's emerging emphasis on physics. Work in fiber microscopy and photomicrography was emphasized, and the scope of work in pulp and paper

testing was greatly enlarged. Entrance requirements were tightened as more and more students throughout the country became familiar with the Institute and desired admission; by 1939, more than two thousand applications for admission had been received.

Dr. Ben Rowland

Harry Fletcher Lewis

Harry Fletcher Lewis was born on May 27, 1891, in Denver, Colorado. He spent his childhood and teenage years in Manhattan, then moved to Connecticut to attend Wesleyan University. Upon receiving his Master of Science degree from Wesleyan in 1913, Lewis transferred to the University of Illinois, where he received his PhD in organic chemistry in 1916.

Lewis held a variety of positions before arriving in Appleton to become dean of the Institute. He was a member of the research sta of the U.S. Department of Agriculture Bureau of Chemistry; then in 1919, he joined the research department of the National Analine and Chemical Company in Bualo, New York, where he aided in the development of the country's post-World War I dye industry.

He taught organic chemistry at several colleges and universities, including Iowa's Grinnell and Cornell colleges, the University of Maine, and Ohio Wesleyan University. He was serving as head of the department of chemistry at Ohio Wesleyan when he left that school to join the sta of the Institute of Paper Chemistry in 1930.

Though his duties as dean kept him busy, Lewis remained a scientist at heart and still found joy in his research in a variety of elds, including redwood chemistry, lignin and its conversion to useful products, the permanence of paper, chemistry of bark, and the structure and property of vegetable tanning. Cellulose chemistry remained his great passion; he was once quoted as saying, "the only denition one can give is that cellulose is a happy idea towards which everyone works but at which nobody ever arrives."

Lewis's career at the Institute was lled with awards, honors, and recognitions. He received two honorary doctor of science degrees, one from Ohio Wesleyan and one from Grinnell College. In 1955, he was awarded the Mitscherlich Medal, an award presented by the Vereinzellcheming, an association of pulp and paper chemists

and engineers in Germany. At the time of the award, Lewis held the distinction of being the only Mitscherlich Medal winner in the history of the award who was not in possession of a European education. In 1956, Lewis received the United States equivalent of the Mitscherlich Medal, the TAPPI Gold Medal, which was presented to him by one of his very rst students at the Institute, Dr. Roy Davis.

In late 1956, at age sixty-ve, Lewis announced his retirement from the nstitute of Paper Chemistry. He remained active in Ins titute life for several more years, serving for a period as the Institute's vice president, then, upon receiving emeritus status, working with Dard Hunter in the Dard Hunter Paper Museum as a curator. An article in the June 1956 issue of the Insti-Tooter summed up Lewis's retirement period perfectly: "to speak of him as being 'active' is weak – he will continue to serve as crusader."

He was active and he knew what was needed for this Institute to become a recognized educational institution.

— Roy Davis, entering class 1930

He was kind of a weird character, I thought, but at least he enthused me.
— George Ingle, entering class 1938

He was a very strong personality around the school. I don't recall him teaching, but he certainly was very evident and very much a part of the program.

— George Mead, entering class 1950

Harry Lewis was a small guy. In our class of fteen people, I think every one of us was bigger than he was.

— John McEwen, entering class 1939

He was a bubbly, cheerful guy. Always upbeat.
— Al Schenck, entering class 1938

Harry Lewis was a wonderful guy. He really cared about the students, as well as a number of companies and the quality of education and everything.

— Arthur Dresheld, entering class 1951

Dr. Henry M. Wriston

A steady stream of the country's brightest scientific minds came to Appleton to educate those fortunate enough to gain admittance. In December of 1930, Dr. Ben Rowland, who had received his PhD from the University of Wisconsin in 1925, joined the staff as a research associate and professor of colloidal chemistry. According to Dr. Lewis in a speech made some years later, "Dr. Rowland came in and overwhelmed them [the students] with the language of colloidal chemistry." Dr. Bertie L. Browning joined the staff in 1933 as an assistant to Lewis on the Rag Content Project; he became a full staff member in the analytical department a few months later. Two Germans, Dr. Friedrich (Fritz) Brauns and Dr. Emil Heuser, came on board in 1935 and 1938, respectively, and others – Dr. Johannes Van den Akker, Dr. Clarence J. West, John Graff and Sid Wells, to name just a few – rounded out the academic team.

In October of 1936, all in Appleton were dismayed to hear that Dr.Wriston, who had been so instrumental in the founding of the Institute, was leaving to assume the

presidency of Rhode Island's Brown University. Luckily, the Lawrence College board of trustees named as his successor Dr. Thomas Nicholas Barrows, who had served as Lawrence's dean since 1934 and who was very familiar with the Institute and its programs. According to a speech given by Mahler at Barrows' inauguration, "Under the guidance of Dr. Barrows, the educational program of the Institute will continue to be one of real substance and the balance between industry, research, and education will be maintained."

The J.A. Kimberly Memorial Library also grew by leaps and bound during the Institute's first decade. Edith Stroschneider, who took over the position of librarian after Miss Roseth resigned at the end of the 1930-1931 school year, often

Dr. Thomas N. Barrows

boasted of the completeness of the library's collection, which, by the Institute's fifth anniversary, contained some sixtyfive hundred bound volumes and subscribed to more than one hundred technical and scientific journals, fifty percent of which were foreign language publications. The Abstract Bulletin, a forty-page bound volume listing recent additions to the library's collection and a compilation of abstracts of all important articles from the library's subscription list, was published monthly and sent to all member companies and pulp and paper mills that provided support to the Institute.

As the drums of war were sounding in far-off Europe, the Institute of Paper Chemistry wrapped up its first decade. As Lewis said in his June 1940 newsletter, "in spite of wars and depressions, we can truthfully say that these ten years have been eminently successful in every respect...the wisdom of the organization of the Institute, its aims, and its programs, has been confirmed many times over."

The Summer Job Program

IN AN EARLY MEMO detailing the organization of the Institute of Paper Chemistry, Ernst Mahler developed a proviso requiring Institute students to forego their traditional summer holiday:

"During the summer months, the students are required to work in a pulp or paper mill, and in case they have not come to the Institute from other mills, positions will be secured for them at one of the local mills. In case, however, they have come from mills located elsewhere, it is to be expected that they will return to those mills during the summer months."

The Summer Job Program was born.

The program grew along with the Institute. In the earliest days, summer mill work was limited to upper classmen, but by the late 1930s, first-year students were participating as well, as faculty members stressed the importance of gaining as much practical experience as could be fitted into the four-year curriculum.

Here, Bob Miller, entering class 1936, describes his summer job experience:

The summer of my first year at the Institute, I worked for the Schmidt and Ault Paper Company in York, Pennsylvania. They made a variety of box-type stock on a cylinder machine, paten coated whites, etc.. They used a great deal of waste paper among which were the usual telephone books. When I wasn't running tests, I used to shoot the breeze with the beater operator. We would stand on a platform from which the beater was loaded. The favorite pastime was to feed the telephone books tossing them in. I gradually worked up to those from New York City, which were sometimes two inches thick. Try it sometime. There is a trick, of course, by flexing the book at the spine.

The second summer was at a similar mill in the Midway section between Minneapolis and St. Paul. That was a long, hot summer. I recall working behind the calendar stack of a paper machine feeding wax emulsion to a long tray that wet the paper, which was then ironed by the lower calendar rolls. The ironing action was achieved by the differential speed between two rolls. The friction set up a high-pitched screeching, which was deafening. This was before OSHA and ear plugs. My ears rang for a week after. Later, when I enlisted in the Navy, I barely made the hearing test.

The J.A. Kimberly Memorial Library

IN SEPTEMBER OF 1852, as the story goes, a young John Alfred Kimberly from Neenah paid tuition of $6.67 to become one of the very first students to matriculate at Lawrence University. From Lawrence, J.A. Kimberly moved easily into a sixty-yearlong career as one of the most successful pulp and paper manufacturers in the United States. Co-founder of the Kimberly-Clark Corporation and operator of a number of mills in Neenah, Kimberly, and surrounding areas, J.A. Kimberly was, according to Ernst Mahler, "a pioneer in developing research into the technical problems of the industry."

On September 23, 1931, almost eighty years after Kimberly entered Lawrence University, the Institute of Paper Chemistry, a graduate school devoted exclusively to the industry to which Kimberly had dedicated his life, formally opened the doors of its first building. It was fitting that Mahler chose that particular occasion to announce a special gift, the largest received by the Institute thus far: $100,000 from James C. Kimberly, J.A. Kimberly's son and president of Neenah Paper Company, to construct a memorial to his father. The resulting building, hailed by Henry Wriston as "an illustration of the great moral impulse which has made American philanthropy the wonder of the world." would represent the first structure named in honor of a Lawrence alumnus.

Construction of the new library, which was designed by Chicago architect Chester A. Walcott, began in the spring of 1932. On June 23, 1932, members of the Kimberly family joined the IPC and Lawrence communities, as well as more than two hundred industry executives, in a ceremony celebrating the laying of the building's cornerstone. Placed in the cornerstone box were the IPC dedication booklet, several copies of the IPC Bulletin, J.C. Kimberly's letter confirming the $100,000 gift, a program from Lawrence College's 1932 commencement exercises, and IPC course catalogues from 1930 and 1931. Kimberly himself laid the cornerstone, stating that, "it is the purpose of the Institute, through scientific methods and research, to raise the standard of the paper and pulp and allied industries to a higher level; the education of the student is a necessary means to this end. Without efficient manpower no industry can progress."

The J.A. Kimberly Memorial Library was dedicated on September 21, 1932, representing, as Wriston declared in his matriculation day speech, "the scientific progress of a great industry toward the development of which he [J.A. Kimberly] made great contribution by the application of his energy, his intelligence, and his appreciation of scientific work."

The Institute's First Semester Course Catalog

COURSE 1:
INORGANIC TECHNICAL ANALYSIS
Professor Youtz
DESCRIPTION: Methods of analysis and interpretation of the data obtained by the experimentation of important raw and intermediate materials used in the pulp and paper industry.
HOURS: 2 hours lecture a week, 2 afternoons laboratory a week.
REQUIRED TEXTS:
- *The Manufacture of Pulp and Paper* Volumes III, IV, and V
- *Chemische Betriebskontrolle* by Schwalbe-Sieber

COURSE 2:
CHEMISTRY OF CELLULOSE AND ALLIED PRODUCTS
Dr. Darling
DESCRIPTION: The introductory course covers a discussion of the chemistry of carbohydrates, their structure, and reactions. This is followed by the chemistry of cellulose from the standpoint of its known chemical reactions and a similar study is included of lignin.
HOURS: 2 hours lecture a week, 1 afternoon laboratory a week.
REQUIRED TEXTS:
- *Textbook of Cellulose Chemistry* by Emil Heuser
- *The Chemistry of Wood* by Hawley and Wise
- Standard Methods of Testing Used by the Forest Products Laboratory at Madison, Wisconsin

COURSE 3:
STRUCTURE AND PHYSICAL PROPERTIES OF WOOD AND PLANTS
Professor Rogers
DESCRIPTION: The source, structure, and important properties of the raw, fibrous materials used in pulp making are discussed. Wood identification from a practical standpoint and suitability of the various woods for pulp purposes are included.
HOURS: 3 hours lecture a week.

COURSE 4:
MICROSCOPY OF PAPER FIBERS
Dr. Otto Kress
DESCRIPTION: The staining and identification of the various fibers used in papermaking and the analysis of fibre content of different kinds of paper are explained and practiced.
HOURS: 2 hours lecture a week.
REQUIRED TEXTS:
- *TAPPI Paper Testing Methods*

COURSE 5:
PAPER DYING
Dr. Otto Kress
DESCRIPTION: The dyestuffs and pigments classified according to the method used in the industry are discussed from the standpoint of suitability, strength, fastness, etc.. Dyeings will be tested from a strength and money value.
HOURS: 1 hour lecture a week, 2 afternoons laboratory a week.
REQUIRED TEXTS:
- *The Manufacture of Pulp and Paper* Volume IV

COURSE 6:
PAPER TESTING
Dr. Otto Kress
DESCRIPTION: The chemical and physical methods used in paper testing are discussed and practiced.
HOURS: 2 hours lecture a week
REQUIRED TEXTS:
- *The Manufacture of Pulp and Paper* Volume V
- *TAPPI Paper Testing Methods*

COURSE 7:
PULPING PROCESSES
Dr. Otto Kress
DESCRIPTION: The mechanical, sulphite, soda, and sulphate processes, as well as the newer processes such as the Semi-Chemical and Keora Processes, are discussed. Visits will be made to the mills adjacent to Appleton where these processes can been seen and studied in operation.
HOURS: 4 hours per week.
REQUIRED TEXTS:
- *The Manufacture of Pulp and Paper* Volume III

COURSE 8:
TECHNICAL GERMAN
Professor Cast
DESCRIPTION: Advanced technical German to train the student so that he can use to advantage the technical German literature.
HOURS: 3 hours lecture a week.

COURSE 9:
ABSTRACTS AND BIBLIOGRAPHIES
Miss Roseth
DESCRIPTION: The methods and purposes
of abstracting technical articles, the filing
of abstracts, the methods of constructing
technical bibliographies, and their use.
HOURS: 1 hour lecture a week.

In addition to the classes listed above, each
student will be required to participate in a
series of Outside Lectures during which experts
on various subjects from the mills as well as
representatives from manufacturers selling
supplies and equipment to the industry will
give talks on their special subjects.

*When you get out of there
with a doctor's degree it
carries, shall we say, a lot
of authority with it. When
you get out and about in
a mill and they find out you've got a
doctor's degree in papermaking, what
you've got to say is very definitely listened to.*

— **Kenneth Hay,** entering class 1937

Clarence J. West

Clarence J. West born in Brighton, Michigan, in
1886. After earning a teaching degree from Michigan
State Normal College in Ypsilanti, Michigan in 1908,
West received his doctorate in physiological organic
chemistry at the University of Michigan in 1912 under
one of the world's leading organic chemists, Dr. Moses
Gomberg.

West became interested in paper industry while
working at Arthur D. Little, Inc., in Boston. He went to
Washington, D.C. in 1921 to work as the director of the
Research Information Service and editor of publications
at the National Research Council, a position he held
until he came to Appleton in July of 1936 as the editor
of the Institute of Paper Chemistry.

West maintained his editorial position at the Institute
until his death in 1952. His accomplishments and
honors during that sixteen-year span are numerous. He was held in the highest
regard by his students and colleagues alike. Dr. Louis Wise, an Institute research
associate and professor, once said of West: "He was a man of strong opinions,
and he would not tolerate sloth or shoddiness. He drove himself without mercy
and he was admittedly an idealist." West's publications list at the time of his
death numbered more than seven hundred books, articles, translations, and book
reviews in the eld of pulp and paper technology. He was very involved in TAPPI,
serving for more than thirty years as the chairman of the Committee on Abstracts
and Bibliography. TAPPI recognized West's contributions to the organization and
to the industry by honoring him with their Gold Medal in 1937. His acceptance
speech aptly sums up his career at the Institute:

"Since I have been at he Institute of Paper Chemistry, I have learned
that, as far as I am personally concerned, I have been building, during
the past fteen years, a reserve on information which enables me to
answer, with a minimum of time and eort, the questions thrown at me
by the sta of the Institute. And knowing those men, I feel sure that you
will acknowledge that they are ace high as pitchers when it comes to
throwing questions."

*I had good rapport with the library personnel, including Dr. West. He was a stamp
collector and shared with Berwyn Thomas and me. I recall how grateful I was to
have him give me an early U.S. stamp titled "Cattle in a Snowstorm." I cannot
recall the denomination but it was black and dated 1898.*

— Bob Miller, entering class 1936

Outside the
Classroom

One Saturday, Johnny Bard and I took a canoe trip up the Fox River, putting in behind Sage Hall. Up river we made portage over the dam and onto Lake Winnebago. After paddling a considerable distance down the lake, some weather set in with an adverse wind and rain. The waves came up and we were not in the safest circumstances. We beat a hasty retreat back to the dam. It was an extremely grueling task fighting both wind and waves with some bailing to boot. We were rather shot when we reached the river again. I do not believe I have ever worked so hard in my life.

— **Bob Miller,** entering class 1936

We could fit in with anything that was going on at Lawrence because we had student passes. We had typical college fun. Of course, we dated the Lawrence girls. They were usually very anxious to date us, the older guys. We went to football games and went skating.

— **Kenneth Hay,** entering class 1937

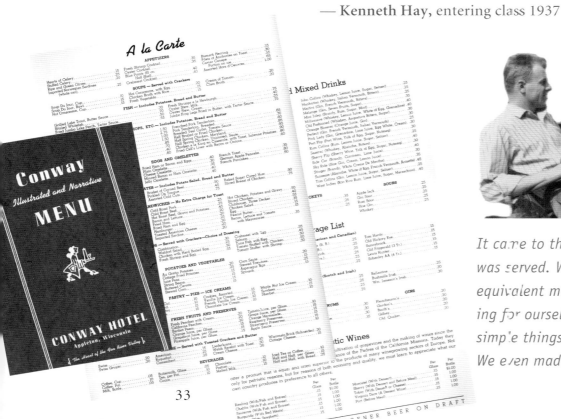

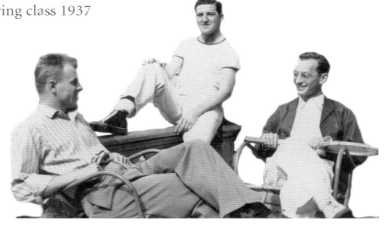

It came to the point that we didn't like the food that was served. We convinced Harry Lewis to give us the equivalent money to buy our own food and started cooking for ourselves. We had a hot plate and would make simple things like Campbell's beans and Campbell's soup. We even made toast on the hot plate.

— **George Ingle,** entering class 1938

33

In East House, where we lived with three other couples, we got into a long-range bridge contest with another couple. The boys against the girls — if the girls won, we would have to take them out to dinner. If the boys won, we were gonna have a big dinner cooked by our wives. I don't know how many months we played this bridge game — we just kept adding to the scores. After several months, we decided to try and figure out who won. We added all the scorecards and I think the girls won. What was amazing was that after all the hundreds of thousands of points, the difference was like one hundred and eighty or something like that. We still laugh about it.

— **John McEwen,** entering class 1939

We would have stag parties where we would all dress in tuxedoes or suits and go to restaurants in town. Everybody would always say, "who are all those guys all dressed up?" But we just did it to have a little fun dressing up.

— **Daniel Adams,** entering class 1939

We used to go to the basketball and football games as a big group. We played a lot of handball at the gym across the street. We sometimes played three-handed with three people. That was a lot of fun and a lot of exercise.

— **Edwin Loutzenheiser,** entering class 1939

The Bush Trip
in the 1930s

ONE OF THE quintessential Institute experiences is the Bush Trip. Though it has evolved significantly over the years – from that first one-day hike into Wisconsin's North Woods in 1930 to the one-month course in wood technology taught by Dr. Isenberg at Trees for Tomorrow to the trips of today sporting more modern conveniences – the primary goal of the Bush Trip has not changed. It was, is, and hopefully always will be an opportunity for students to get to know the men – and, increasingly, the women – with whom they will be sharing all the ups and downs of their Institute experience.

We went north to some logging camp. It was pretty much directed toward pulp wood sticks and was quite complete in operation. For some reason, toward the end of the day, I became separated from the group and they left without me. Guess there was no head count. The logging camp treated me to a sumptuous dinner while waiting for a car to return to pick me up. That was my introduction to the Institute of Paper Chemistry.

— **Bob Miller**, entering class 1936

I have wonderful memories of that trip. Professor Isenberg was with us – he was a wood specialist. We visited a logging camp, we visited a paper mill, and we visited a seeding plant. As a class, we became well acquainted.

— **Al Schenck**, entering class 1938

We had a bus and Irv Isenberg, who we called coach - a very responsible guy, a very cheerful guy, and very informative - he was a leader. I forgot the name of the bus driver but he was a jolly soul. Isenberg made the trip very useful. It was a lot of fun and we learned a lot. One funny thing - I was the only one who brought swimming trunks. There was Golden Lake there so we decided to go for a swim. So I said anybody who wants to borrow my trunks can, but I go first. I hate to put on cold, wet trunks. So I went first. It was cold, miserably cold. I didn't stay in long. Then Ken Arnold borrowed my trunks and jumped in, then jumped out immediately. He couldn't take it. That was a fun experience. We got to know each other - a lot of sociability.

— **George Ingle**, entering class 1938

The experience stood me in good stead. The Institute has certainly made a lasting contribution to the industry and can be proud of its record. I have no regrets.

— **Bob Miller**, entering class 1936

We would get up every morning and go in and have breakfast. There was a table full of makings of sandwiches for the day and then we go out and work with the lumberjacks. At first I saw these guys carrying these big bags and I thought 'I don't need a big bag of food' but after the second day I was carrying a great big bag. You'd be out there early in the morning and you'd need lunch and snacks. We used to jump in the lake to clean up with soap. One thing we found out was the lumberjacks did not like snakes. So you could have fun by capturing a few snakes and putting them in your shirt or around your waist and if they were giving you too much trouble, then you took out the snake. It was a very good way to become acquainted with the fifteen guys you were going be living with and studying with for four years.

— **Edwin Loutzenheiser**, entering class 1939

CHAPTER 2

1940-
1949

It was devastating. We came home for lunch and there was a bridge game going. We were all watching the game. Then the radio came on and said Pearl Harbor had been attacked.

— **Daniel Adams**, entering class 1939

On that fateful date - it was a Sunday - a bunch of the first year group had just returned from lunch at one of the restaurants along College Avenue and were together in one of the bed-rooms at South House, where we lived the first year. We were listening to the radio and heard President Roosevelt broadcast that this was a day that will "live in infamy!" We all thought, at that point, that we would not be students attending the IPC very long but would be in one of the military services serving our country.

— **Ben Haug**, entering class 1941

The Institute had closed out its first decade with a bang. Paper companies representing all four corners of the United States were applying for membership at a rapid pace, cutting-edge equipment was being brought in daily, and some of the country's most brilliant scientific minds had come to teach at the Institute. More than three hundred applications were coming in each new school year, each begging one of the coveted fifteen spots open each fall. The future certainly looked bright. In spite of the upbeat outlook on life in Appleton at the end of the 1930s, the Institute kept a wary eye on events unfolding across the Atlantic. American involvement in the war would be devastating to an institution built around young men of draft age…

The effects of World War II on life at the Institute of Paper Chemistry can hardly be underestimated. Rations and shortages caused by events in Europe and Asia strained the Institute's resources tremendously, and educational activities virtually ceased for more than a year as the vast majority of students left their studies behind to join a branch of the armed services. Research work at the Institute shifted gears as scientists offered their services to the United States government; by 1942, the Institute was carrying more than thirty projects directly related to national defense.

WORLD WAR II continued to impact the Institute even after the cessation of hostilities. Most students returned to their studies older, wiser, more world-weary – and in many cases married, forcing the Institute to revise its policy on married students. As Walt Bublitz, entering class 1941, explained, "The first couple of years after the war were a mess. You had fellows who came trickling in over different classes and years. Trying to fit all the students together and get classes for everyone caused many headaches."

The Institute's second decade of existence began smoothly enough. The budget grew from a mere $30,000 in 1930 to more than $330,000 by 1940 as more than fifty paper companies became members of the Institute. Much of the extra money was used for student scholarships; by 1940, the Institute was offering yearly scholarships of $650 for first-year students, $700 for second-year students, $900 for third-year students, and $925 for fourth-year students. The staff, numbering just three in 1930, had grown to ninety-five in 1940 and the equipment used by Institute staff and students was worth more than $1.2 million – impressive when compared with the $50 worth of equipment used by the first entering class.

Irving Isenberg

Dr. Irving Isenberg was born in 1909 in Buffalo, New York. He attended Buffalo Technical High School and the College of Forestry at Syracuse University, where he received a bachelor of science degree in 1931 and a master of science degree in 1932. His PhD in forestry came in 1936 from the University of California-Berkeley. Isenberg joined the IPC staff in 1937 as a research associate and instructor in fiber microscopy.

In 1940, the Institute created the Wood Technology Group and named Isenberg its Group Leader. In addition to teaching courses in forestry, wood and fiber chemistry, and microscopy and running the fiber identification laboratory, Isenberg was also responsible for the tree plantation that was cultivated in the valley behind the Institute.

Isenberg spent his entire professional career as a member of the Institute's faculty. He was the author of numerous publications, including two books, *Pulp and Paper Microscopy* and *Pulpwoods of the United States and Canada*, that are still used today. Isenberg retired from the Institute in July of 1973 and was named Professor Emeritus, a title which he held until his death in 2001.

Who plants the trees and measures their span?
Who is this weighty, solid man?
Both chemist he, and botanist
Compiler and microscopist.
Teacher and forester in one –
Woods he explores, by grain – or ton.

— *The Insti-Tooter*, September 1952

I still feel that they [Institute people] are some of the best people I have ever known.

— Victor Burstein, entering class 1940

The Institute's course offerings changed as well; a necessity, thought the school's administrators, in order to keep pace with a rapidly changing industry. A Wood Technology Section was created under the direction of Dr. Irving Isenberg and, in connection with this group, a tree plantation was cultivated in the valley behind the Institute's main buildings. A new course for second-year and fourth-year students was added – speech coaching, taught by Lawrence's Ed Schoenberger, who later became the IPC Dean of Students. This class was initiated in conjunction with a new requirement that all PhD candidates must present a talk on their research work before the entire faculty. Schoenberger instructed IPC students in the art of speaking distinctly, forcefully, and with absolute poise. "The ability to think on their feet," Schoenberger wrote in an Institute newsletter detailing the new course offering, "will stand the boys in good stead after they leave the Institute." The course proved very successful; by 1941, it had expanded into a four-year program.

The early 1940s saw a flurry of construction and the arrival of cutting-edge equipment. In June of 1941, the Institute received its first electron microscope. The microscope – only the second one of its kind made by the RCA Manufacturing Company – was capable of magnifications up to 30,000 diameters and through further photographic enlargements, up to 100,000 diameters, allowing its users to view particles as small as 1/100 millionths of an inch.

In December of 1941, work began on a three-story addition to one of the wings of the Institute's present structures. The addition, completed in the summer of 1942, housed Dr. John Graff and his fiber microscope as well as the rest of the analytical and microanalytical, fiber microscopy, and wood technology sections, on the top floor; a semi-commercial lab, with storage space for supplies on the second floor; and new offices and labs for the engineering and physics sections, a room for the electron microscope, calibration facilities for the brightness tester, a first aid room, a dark room, a humidity room, two laboratory cubicles, and the spectroscopy lab on the ground floor.

Emil Heuser

In January of 1938, the subject of cellulose chemistry was forever changed at the Institute of Paper Chemistry with the appointment of Dr. Emil Heuser to the Cellulose Group. Bringing to the job, according to Westbrook Steele, an "unusual combination of theoretical and practical knowledge, both of cellulose chemistry and pulp and paper making, as well as rayon and its manufacture, gained from years of study and teaching and also from actual contact with these industries in Germany and Canada," Heuser proved an invaluable member of the Institute's staff during his ten-year stint as Group Leader.

Born in Stralsund, Germany, in 1882 Heuser studied at the Technical Universities of Munich and Karlsruhe under such famed chemists as Bunte, Engler, Haber, and Le Blanc. After completing his thesis at Austria's University of Graz, Heuser returned to Karlsruhe to obtain his doctoral degree. His dissertation, an experimental study of certain complex organic compounds supervised by the legendary Dr. Friedric Shcholl, was very well received in the field.

Upon graduation from Karlsruhe Heuser spent three years gaining practical experience in various mills throughout Germany and Austria. In 1912, he became the chair of cellulose chemistry at the Technical University of Darmstadt, a position made vacant by Professor C.G. Schwalbe, then the leading exponent of cellulose chemistry in Germany. During his tenure at Darmstadt, Heuser's lectures on organic chemistry, chemistry of cellulose, and the chemical technology of pulp, paper, dyes, and textiles were often supplemented by his many original investigations on both theoretical and practical sides of cellulose, lignin, and non cellulose carbohydrates, as well as pulping, bleaching, and other issues pertaining to the manufacture of paper. In 1916, Heuser took a short leave of absence from Darmstadt to engage in a study of the industrial utilization of cellulose and other waste products. He returned to Darmstadt as a full professor in 1918 and remained there until 1923, when he resigned to take a position as the Director of Research at the Vereignigte Glanzsto-Fabriken, manufacturers of rayon and photographic films. In 1926, as the manufacture of rayon pulp became a pressing problem in North America, Heuser accepted a position as Director of Research of the Canadian International Paper Company in Hawkesbury, Ontario, Canada. Heuser held this position until his appointment to the staff of the Institute of Paper Chemistry in 1938.

Heuser is perhaps best remembered in the academic world for his lengthy bibliography of scholarly books and articles. HLisehrbuch der Cellulose-Chemiewent through three separate printings in German, with the second edition being translated into both English and Russian. He edited six volumes of the Technik und Praxis der Papierfabrikation, as well as Cellulosechemie, which combined with Der Papier-Fabrikartin 1937. Heuser's most famous work, The Chemistry of Cellulose, six-hundred-page tome still considered a classic in the field of cellulose chemistry, was published in 1944.

As a professor, Heuser was noted for his meticulous habits and old-school style of teaching. It was common knowledge among Institute men that should you happen upon Dr. Heuser's office before class you would inevitably catch him practicing the day's lecture, for his exacting nature demanded that each lecture be precisely fifty-five minutes long. George Martin, entering class 1941, remembers Heuser's reputation as a ladies' man. "He would come to all the dances and things in white tie and tails," Martin recollects. "You'd be dancing with your date and you'd see her smile and he'd be bowing to her. Next thing you'd know, he'd be tapping you on the shoulder to see if he could dance with your date. He was quite a guy."

Heuser was a fixture at the Institute until 1947, when health issues forced him into a lifestyle much more relaxed than the rigorous one offered by academia. During Heuser's farewell reception, Westbrook Steele aptly summed up the German scientist's career:

When Dr. Heuser came to us, it was his intention and his hope that he would find with us the opportunity to round out his career. Often he told me that in the Institute, he found the ideal opportunity for the utilization of his talents.

CHEMICAL AND ENGINEERING NEWS

Receives TAPPI Medal for Contributions to Cellulose Chemistry (Page 675)

EMIL HEUSER

By August of 1941, the United States had, according to historian James M. Burns, "crossed the threshold from peace to war… as the war widened in Europe, the Atlantic lifeline came under attack, the British sought more aid, and public opinion changed to favor more intervention." Concern over the possibility of active involvement in the war led the Selective Service System to begin assigning classifications to all men of draft age. At IPC, all students in good standing who were not Reserve Officers were placed under Class II-A, the general action for satisfactory students of graduate technical schools. An investigation of the Institute's academic program and activities in May of 1943 led the Selective Service System to determine that the classification could continue, as, according to a letter sent to the school from the Field Service of

National Headquarters, "the courses of study offered are preparing students for activities essential to the support of the war effort; that serious consideration should be given to the occupational classification of those students in preparation or training for whom you are willing to certify may be reasonably expected to successfully complete the courses of instruction in which they are engaged."

The months following the attack on Pearl Harbor saw a drastic alteration of the Institute's academic program. Citing the urgent need for accelerating the school's coursework, third-year IPC students remained in Appleton engaging in PhD research rather than leaving for the traditional summer job in the paper industry. This policy, which resulted in the graduating classes of 1943, 1944,

and 1945 only spending two summers in industry, was to remain in effect through the duration of the war. Despite such hardships, the Institute maintained a positive outlook for the future. As Westbrook Steele told the assembled industry fellows at the 1942 Executives' Conference, "The Institute started in a critical period; it has grown through a critical period in the belief that it would be available for the crises that lay ahead and that its performance would justify its continued growth through the results it achieved for those who maintain it."

Dr. Al Howells

After I graduated from the Institute and worked for Camp Manufacturing Company, later Union Camp Corporation, I usually attended the annual TAPPI meeting in New York City and went to the IPC alumni dinner. About 150 alumni attended. Harry Lewis would introduce each of the alumni telling where they worked, what their job was, and some news about the family of the alumnus. His performance reinforced the feeling that the Institute and its alumni were all one family.

— **Keith Bradway,** entering class 1948

The Institute's First International Student

The Institute's contributions to the war effort were enormous. As Harry Lewis wrote in the July 1942 newsletter, "suffice it to say that when peace is declared, we will have made our contributions." Within six months of the United States' entrance into the war, the Institute was involved in more then thirty national defense projects. Among these were the development of new antiseptics for use in the paper industry and other fields; continuation of the wetstrength gum investigation; discovery of new substitute materials for those no longer available; camouflage of paper, textiles and other materials; and the development of a new source of tricresyl phosphate and paracresol, which proved of great interested to the United States Navy. Two former Institute students were involved in the technical development of synthetic rubber, while another was instrumental in the creation of a high active gas Dr. Al Howels, chief of the Institute's Plastics Section, worked closely with the Vidal Research Corporation on the use of nonphenolic resins for paper-based plastics, while Dr. Boris Berkan supervised research work on the utilization of milkweed by-products.

The most famous of the wartime undertakings was, of course, the Paper House Project, developed by Institute scientists under contract with the Office of Production Research and Development of the War Production Board. Erected in August of 1944 and made entirely from waste paper pressed into panels, the Paper House was designed to meet a need for temporary housing for people left homeless in war areas – "a low-cost structure able to resist tropical heat or arctic snow, rain or wind."

When the IPC Board of Trustees met in October of 1929, contemplating requirements for admission, they decided unanimously that only American citizens would be considered. Dr. Kress, in a 1932 speech to a group of paper mill superintendents, said the decision was based on the sheer folly – "ridiculousness" Kress called it – of spending money supplied by the American pulp and paper industry to educate foreign men who would very likely return to their home countries and support their own pulp and paper industries whose "competition is absolutely ruinous to the paper industry in our own country." So, despite the dozens of applications received from interested students from Japan, China and India, the Institute stuck firmly to its policy and admitted only American citizens.

Just as World War II changed so many of the Institute's original policies, it also changed the status of international applicants. In August of 1947, the Institute's first international student, Biswanath Sen – dubbed "Ben Sen" by his classmates - made the trip from his home in Calcutta to begin classes. Sen's five-year stint at the Institute, culminating in a PhD in 1952, was quite successful; after his first full year at IPC, he was honored with the Paper and Twine Associated award for outstanding performance.

Keith Bradway, entering class 1948, recalls one amusing encounter with Sen during the 1948 Bush Trip:

I found some of the features [of wood technology] fascinating. I would sometimes exclaim at what I saw with expressions like "Wow!" or "Holy Cow!" Ben Sen, who was from India, sat at the table with me and after a few days told me with great mock sincerity, "Keith, I don't say things like "Jesus Christ!" I don't think you should say "Holy Cow!"

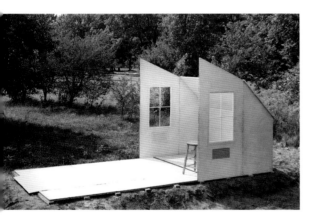

decker bunks to show how shelter could be provided for a family of four. They even fashioned some paper furnishings, including cellulose windows and a paper window shade.

The Paper House stood on the IPC grounds until 1952, when it was dismantled. During its eight-year existence, the structure withstood hot weather, extended periods of rain and mist, winds reaching speeds of more than sixty miles per hour, and several blizzards. Unfortunately, the house was never called into military service. The British government showed strong interest in the structures in late 1944, but their request for 250,000 of them proved too great for the chipboard scarcity brought about by the war.

The Paper House came in a bundle of materials that weighed 1,029 pounds and could be assembled in about an hour. The paper panels, which were treated to be weather and fire resistant, were strong enough to withstand a load of more than 6,000 pounds. The house needed no framing or studding; rather the panels were joined by a system of metal connectors that did not show from either side of the panels.

The Paper House was designed to accommodate four people. The structure's designers, led by Dr. Johannes Van den Akker, furnished the house with double-

By May of 1943, seven IPC students had asked for a leave of absence and volunteered for service, while six others, already reserve officers, were immediately called to duty. That left only seventeen students to make up the second-, third-, and fourth-year classes. Many staff members requested leaves as well, while others abandoned their regular research work in order to focus on new and vital paper developments for the war effort.

The last wartime degrees were conferred in May of 1944. The 1944-45 school year saw no new students matriculating; the May 1945 graduation ceremonies represented the first time that Lawrence College had awarded no IPC degrees since 1931. Five students entered for the 1945-46 school year. Two left for the armed services within one term and two more were unable to keep up with their coursework and did not return for a second term, leaving just one regular student in the class. The 1945 Executives' Conference was cancelled due to wartime travel restrictions; it was the first year since 1936 that no conference was held.

Friedrich "Fritz" Brauns

A native of Germany, Brauns pursued his education at several prestigious universities, finally settling at the University of Berlin, where he studied under the Nobel Prize-winning organic chemist Emil Fischer. After earning his PhD in 1914, Brauns continued to gild his own organic chemistry resume with work at the University of Munich, Waldhof Cellulose Works, and then at the Department of Cellulose and Industrial Chemistry at McGill University in Montreal.

Brauns was appointed to the staff of the Institute of Paper Chemistry in 1935 as a research associate and instructor in organic chemistry. It was here that he put his well-deserved reputation in the field to the test. To date, no one had been able to isolate lignin without the use of strong reagents, which altered wood from its natural state and as a result, destroyed its use in papermaking. To isolate lignin would provide the industry with an important source of income from what had traditionally been a waste product.

It took Brauns some time, but he eventually succeeded where no one else had, forever leaving his mark on organic chemistry and the pulp and paper industry.

Brauns, known as "Mr. Ligneen" to his students, retired from the Institute in 1955. As Professor Emeritus, Brauns continued as a consulting chemist for several years. In 1960, he published a supplement to his 1952 magnum opus *The Chemistry of Lignin*, noting advancements in the field from 1949-1958.

Dr. Brauns I remember as a character with a heavy accent. During one preparation in an open hood in his lab, I recall smoking a cigar as an early warning of the evolution of a noxious gas – the cigar would take on a foul taste in its presence.
— Bob Miller, entering class 1936

Fritz Brauns - he was a real German immigrant type and very gruff and hard to get to know, but beneath it all he was a lignin chemist.
— Walt Bublitz, entering class 1941

Fritz Brauns - he had flown airplanes for the German airforce in WWI. He was a meticulous character and he insisted that we had good laboratory procedure habits.
— George Martin, entering class 1941

Fritz Brauns and Buck Buchanan gave an oral test as a final for the lignin course. I did not do well on oral exams, growing flustered and feeling it necessary to give a quick answer. One question put to me was, "What color is given by phloroglucinol by angiosperm lignin?" That should be one of the simplest and most basic questions about lignin. But one of the students had been experimenting with a bright green color developed when spruce wood was contacted with fuming hydrochloric acid. Flustered, I said green. Fritz turned to Buck and said, "I thought that if I demonstrated the red color of the phloroglucinol test in class they would be sure to remember it. But I was wrong!" In spite of that I passed the course.
— Keith Bradway, entering class 1948

George R. Sears

A physicist with an extensive background in chemistry, Dr. Sears was at home in all phases of our academic and research activities. His intellectual curiosity was unlimited, and over the years he gained an understanding of the technology of this industry that very few have ever rivaled. A teacher by instinct, he encouraged and stimulated both students and staff.

— John Strange, 1965 Executives' Conference

George Sears was born in Beaver Dam, Wisconsin, in 1904. After a short stint at Ripon College, he transferred to the University of Wisconsin, where he received both his B.A. and M.A. degrees. He spent four years as a chemist at the Du Pont Experimental Station in Wilmington, Delaware, before returning to the University of Wisconsin to complete his PhD in 1936.

Sears came to the Institute in late 1936 as a research assistant and a professor of physics. He was promoted to research associate in 1941 and transferred into the physical chemistry section in 1948, where he was named Group Leader. His final assignment, which he held until his death in April of 1965, came in 1953 when he was designated Chief of the newly formed Graphic Arts Section.

A short vignette published in the December 1949 issue of the *Institute Reporter* serves as an apt illustration of the character of Dr. Sears:

When paper men are in distress   He's here, and there, and everywhere.
Their troubles come to G.R.S.   With all his friendliness, I'd hate
Who with his active, loyal crew   To meet George in a hot debate.
Will see each "physchem" problem through   His arguments have wider scope
George has no time to mope or nap   Than an electron microscope.
With all those headaches in his lap.   His thrusts are keen, but I should mention
They tell me though that he's a menace   They just produce surface tension.
When on the courts playing tennis   No words of his give rise to tears
Despite his silvery, thinning hair   He may be sharp – but never Sears.

I relish one exchange I had with George Sears who taught a course in electricity. He used the term bias, meaning a voltage deliberately applied in a vacuum tube. I asked him what it meant. George asked, "Do you do any sewing?"

I knew the use of the term bias in sewing and I had done some, but I didn't want to admit it so I said no.

George said, "Well, if you don't do any sewing, why don't you do some reading?"

That joke at a student's expense was totally unlike George, but his analysis of my study habits was right on the money.

— Keith Bradway, entering class 1948

The cessation of hostilities in Europe and Japan were cause for celebration throughout the world. As the shouts of jubilation faded, millions of weary war veterans returned to civilian life. Many, anxious to reap the benefits of the GI Bill, chose to continue the education the war forced them to abandon. Others made the decision to pursue higher education for the first time. In the years immediately following World War II, enrollment at the nation's colleges and universities doubled, and university officials were faced with the seemingly endless task of finding classroom space and living quarters to accommodate the wave of new and returning students.

In order to avoid using capital funds for dormitories, the Institute had, in the past, rented space for student housing from Lawrence College. The post-war enrollment boom, however, ended this arrangement. Lawrence, facing its own housing crisis in 1946, reclaimed North House for its own use, leading to the Institute's purchase of a residence at 933 East College Avenue known as Mory House, intending to use it as a single student dormitory. In 1948, in celebration of Otto Kress's contributions to the creation and growth of the Institute, Mory House was renamed in his honor and was thereafter known as Kress House.

With the Institute's single student housing issues resolved, Institute administrators next turned to the problem

*It has had a strong impact. I was never sorry I went there.
It was a great career. The paper industry was a fine industry
to work in. We were able to raise a family and get them all
through college and grad school on my paycheck. It was an
interesting time leading an interesting life*

— George Martin, entering class 1941

of accommodations for the married members of the student body. This had never
been an issue, for until World War II, only unmarried students were allowed to
matriculate. By 1943, it was obvious that the Institute was going to have to revise
this policy; in his August 1943 newsletter, Lewis reiterated a comment made by
Ted Danziger, entering class 1943: "By the time we all get back to the Institute we
are going to have to worry about what to do with our children in addition to Dr.
Van den Akker's mechanics course."

Some married couples made their homes in East House. The Alton Street residence
could accommodate four married couples in two-room apartments with a
common kitchen area and a study area set up in the basement. Other couples
lived in West House (formerly called the A.B. Fisher House), which was designed
in a manner similar to East House and housed six married couples. Finally, in

Sidney D. Wells

Sidney D. Wells was born in Boston in 1885. He
graduated from New Hampshire's famous Phillips Exeter
Academy in 1903 and received his Bachelor of Science
degree from the Massachusetts Institute of Technology
in 1907. After a few years as a chemical engineer for the
Mead Pulp and Paper Company, Wells joined the staff of
the United State Forest Products Laboratory at Madison
as an engineer in 1910. He remained there until 1925,
working on a variety of research projects, including the
preparation of *Bulletin 1485*, a summary of pulping and
grinding characteristics of a large variety of American
wood for the United States Department of Agriculture,
and a series of studies on the value of flax, straw, and
cotton linters as papermaking materials.

Wells left the Forest Products Laboratory in 1925 to
become the director of the Paper Mills Laboratories,
Inc., in Illinois. In 1930, he went to work as the
technical director of the Nekoosa-Edwards Paper
Company, where he developed a successful multi-
bleaching technique for kraft pulp. In 1932, Wells
became the technical adviser for the Combined Locks
Paper Company, perfecting a method of de-inking
groundwood paper, working particularly with old
telephone directories. He joined the consulting firm
of Paulson and Wells in Appleton in 1935, where he
remained until he came to the Institute as a research
associate and an instructor in pulp and paper technology
in 1933.

Wells' fifteen-year career in academia was as
distinguished as his experience in research and in the
paper industry. He published more than thirty papers
on a wide variety of subjects ranging from the effects
of adhesives on fiberboard
manufacture, the use of sodium
sulfite in alkaline digestions,
the utilization of spent liquors,
and low sulfidity kraft pulping to
the cooking of bagasse, straw,
cornstalks, and cottonwood.

Wells retired from the Institute in August of 1953 and
was given the title of Research Associate Emeritus. At
Wells' retirement celebration, his friend and colleague
Dr. Louis Wise honored him with the following tribute:
"His achievements, and they were many, depended on
thought and on quiet, painstaking effort."

1946, the Institute acquired eight Quonset Huts, which were immediately shipped to Appleton from Tacoma, Washington. These prefabricated, semi-cylindrical steel structures – "tin cans," as they were commonly called by soldiers and students alike – had been designed at the Naval Air Station at Quonset Point, Rhode Island, and proved an interesting solution to the housing shortages on college and university campuses across the country. The Institute's Quonsets were set up in a colony called West Court, where they provided fifteen apartments with a common laundry room. Under the original Lanham Act, which relinquished the units formerly owned by the federal government to private institutions, the Quonsets were

to be removed by July 25, 1949; however, a new law passed in 1948 extended the date indefinitely. These unique living arrangements certainly changed life at the Institute; as Lewis pointed out in his April 1947 newsletter, "the general flavor of the Institute body has changed with the importation of all those wives and children."

Dr. Otto Kress

By the fall of 1946, life had begun to return to normal at the Institute of Paper Chemistry. The first "post-war" class arrived in Appleton on August 26, 1946, for their orientation, while many other returning veterans attempted to pick up their graduate studies where they left off in the early 1940s. Plans were made

for refresher training programs to help reorient the GIs to academic life. Each veteran represented a unique situation; Lewis and his administrators were forced to handle each circumstance individually.

Several important curriculum changes coincided with the return of the students who had left their studies behind to join the armed services. The Institute pared down "tool" courses, along with moving all the physics courses to the first year. Dr. Rowland introduced a new colloid chemistry class that dealt with the physical properties of the high molecular compounds; he called it "colloid chemistry modernized." Additionally, the infamous third-year problems were introduced into the third-year program as a means of teaching how research is organized and determining whether the students had the capacity for planning and carrying on research.

It provided me with an opportunity, which, as time goes on, I appreciate more… it gave me an opportunity to do something that was difficult and it tested you – God knows it did. It taught you discipline. In my case, it taught me how to write and how to report and how to manage a project. I put it down as one of the truly significant parts of my life and my career. You never know what would have happened if I hadn't gone to the Institute but I think it gave me a status… having a doctorate and being in the paper business… and having gone an institute that's run and managed and paid for by the paper business… you got recognition that you wouldn't get otherwise.

— Bill Haselton, entering class 1949

The 1940s ended with a bang, although perhaps one of a little less magnitude than the one that began the decade. Otto Kress, the Institute's first full-time staff member, announced his retirement in February of 1948, closing what many view as the first chapter in the Institute's history. At the same time, the Institute began a more intense recruiting program to bolster flagging interest in graduate education, a trend seen in graduate schools throughout the country. Lewis opined that many World War II veterans felt that they were too old to continue their educations once they had completed four years of undergraduate training.

By the end of 1949, the Institute boasted more than two hundred staff members and a $2 million research center. The one hundred and seven member companies represented seventy percent of all pulp and paper production in the United States, while the Institute's library had grown to more than thirteen thousand volumes, making it one of the largest and most complete collections in the world. As John Strange pointed out at the decade's end, "the steady and virile growth of the Institute through the Depression and war years is an abundant verification of the soundness of the framework which was originally laid down by the charter members."

The Westbrook Steel Medal

In 1941, Westbrook Steele, one of the key figures in the development of the Institute of Paper Chemistry, established an award in his name to be presented to a graduating PhD student. The Westbrook Steele Medal was to be awarded to a student who, through his or her dissertation, possessed an understanding of the relationship of the subject of investigation to the broader problems of pulp and papermaking; who demonstrated originality and soundness of approach to the subject; who showed ingenuity and thoroughness in his or her techniques; and who exemplified craftsmanship in preparation and presentation of the dissertation.

Westbrook Steele Medal Winners

1941..........Robert A. Stillings	1962..........Edwin W. Arnold	
1942..........William H. Lane	1963..........Frederick J. Vermillion, Jr.	
1943..........Daniel O. Adams	1964..........Carl A. Jentzen	
1944..........Charles M. Sigvardt	1965..........Philip H. Emery, Jr.	
1947..........Arthur J. Haug	1966..........Harold L. Hintz	
1948..........John S. Barton	1967..........Robert J. Morgan	
1949..........Joseph C. Brown, Jr.	1968..........Charles E. Dunning	
1950..........Ellsworth H. Shriver II	1969..........R. Paul Kibblewhite	
1951..........William L. Irgmanson	1970..........Kari I. Ebeling	
1952..........Thomas G. Zentner		
1953..........William R. Haselton		
1954..........Samuel M. Rollinson		
1955..........Robert W. Hisey		
1956..........Arthur C. Dreshfield, Jr.		
1957..........John R. Parkinson		
1958..........William H. Wiseman		
1959..........Charles W. Carroll		
1960..........Richard H. Cornell		
1961..........Ronald B. Estridge		

Life in a Quonset Hut

THE POST-WORLD WAR II ERA brought into effect several changes in Institute policy and procedure. Among the more notable was the end of a rule that had been in effect since the Institute's inception – that a student must remain single in order to maintain his scholarship. Naturally, students found ways around this policy. Jean Hess, wife of Cecil Hess, entering

class 1946, recalls the story of one student who had been repeatedly warned of his "fraternization" with a female during his time at the Institute. "After he received his diploma and was assured that it was signed," Mrs. Hess remembers, "the young man introduced his wife to the dean!"

The Institute was forced to review and revise this policy when the World War II classes returned to resume their studies. In addition to military experience, many of these young men also acquired brides during their time in the service. Desperate for housing for these married couples, the Institute acquired eight Quonset huts that were placed in two rows in a field along West Court Street.

What follows is a collection of recollections and remembrances of the experiences of several Institute students who lived in the Quonset Village. "During the bad times when the icebox water ran all over the floor – when we were cold because the oil had run out - when someone had not followed the wash hut schedule and we had diapers

to wash or dry – when a cloudburst or blizzard had impeded our husbands' trek to the Institute labs – when new babies cried all night – when budgets were running low," laughs Mrs. Hess. "We would look at each other and say, 'I suppose some day we will look back on all this and laugh!' And now, we do."

They weren't the most luxurious of accommodations. I can remember how cold they were in the Appleton winters. You had a space heater in there, an oil-fired space heater, and you had an electric fan up in the dome to blow some of the warm air back down again… and we had honest-to-goodness iceboxes. An ice man came around with a cake of ice that you bought and put in there. You had to remember to put a pan under there for when the melted ice water dripped and you had to remember to empty that. After once forgetting to empty the pan, I came home from the lab with a drill and a funnel and made modification number one. I drilled a hole underneath the icebox and put the funnel in it and therefore never had to worry about emptying the thing again. Pretty soon, every other Quonset hut had adopted my procedure.

— George Martin, entering class 1941

It was interesting… they were split in half and there was a married couple in each end. They consisted of three rooms and a bath and a shower. There was a living room/kitchen, and then one bedroom, and then another small bedroom/study, heated by a central oil-burning stove, very little insulation either in the walls, ceiling, or floor. It was cold. But it was survivable.

— Bill Haselton, entering class 1949

In the wintertime when it got really cold, the internal layer was held to the exterior metal layer by metal rivets and in the mornings they'd have ice on them… we shared our Quonset with a guy named Jim Schoettler and his wife. The way they were set up was that there was a fire escape that was a door about a foot tall and two feet wide between the two bedrooms in the back of each of the halves. We got to know the Schoettlers really well by visiting back and forth through that little door.

— George Mead entering class 1950

We had a freshly painted one-half Quonset at 16 West Court. The paint job was a horrible pink. First order of business was to repaint. The color we selected – a pleasing brown - was viewed as extreme by the Institute's painter but it was popular at the time.

— John Parkinson entering class 1951

Living in a Quonset hut was comfortable enough except for the ice on the ceiling in the winter. You got to be so close to the person next to you… you got to know each other pretty well.

— Richard Barker, entering class 1958

The thing that both Mary Anne and I remember the most is living in the Quonset Huts. They were cold and they smelled… thank God we didn't have any kids back then!

— Joseph Koleske, entering class 1958

You could stand in one place and you could be in every room at one time. You could always tell how cold it was by how much frost was on the nails in the Quonset. Then in the winter, the rabbits would come underneath the Quonset huts. There was aluminum foil for insulation and you could hear them scrambling around down there.

— Carl Jentzen, entering class 1959

Outside the Classroom

My home was in Neenah and I would go home on weekends fairly often and I recall on Thanksgiving, my mother would ask me to bring the fellows home. My mother was quite delighted to see her turkey disappear.

— **Victor Burstein**, entering class 1940

The $650 scholarship provided South House boarding for 9 months. I did my laundry in the basement. It provided for three quarters of tuition, books, and lab fees. It provided three meals a day in Appleton restaurants for nine months. I ate three meals a day for $1.00 a day. We got a break buying meal tickets - $5.50 worth for $5.00. We ate breakfast and lunch at Hairless Herb's Horrible Hash House- the Checkerboard restaurant on College Avenue on Lawrence Campus.

— **Ben Haug**, entering class 1941

We liked to play volleyball quite a bit. We also like to play ping-pong and going to the football games.

— **Bob Boehm**, entering class 1948

Incidentally, in our group there were five of us that each pitched in $7 and for $35 we bought a 1926 Essex Super Six. We managed to keep that car going. One of the funniest things was when we went out to the Executives' Conference at the country club and all the executives were driving up in their fancy automobiles and they had valet parking. The five of us drive up in our Essex Super Six and we made quite a sensation. It lasted a long time.

— **George Martin**, entering class 1941

We had parties, usually in the dorm. This was when the Kress House was down the end of College Avenue. It was a big house that someone had given to the Institute. Bob McKee was on the faculty on the Institute for many years and he lived behind us and every time we had a party you could set your clock by it - at midnight, the police would be there at the door. We would wake him up every time!

— **Otto Kroeschell**, entering class 1949

We did a lot of partying… our class was inclined to party.

— **Dan Kane**, entering class 1948

A highlight of the year at Kress House was a homecoming party on the weekend of the Lawrence College Homecoming. As a part of the party a skit was given. In my second year I worked with Otto Kroeschell and Bill Hoge to produce a skit. We used mostly music from "South Pacific." The skit was called "South River" after the street location of the Institute. The song "There is Nothing Like a Dame" was converted to "There is Nothing Like a Brain." The song "Bloody Mary" became "Bloody Harry," a jab at Harry Lewis.

— **Keith Bradway**, entering class 1948

The Bush Trip in the 1940s

THE BUSH TRIP – the traditional sojourn into the Northern woods that begins a student's IPC experience – received a makeover by the end of the 1940s. Since the trip's inception in September of 1930, the Institute had taken first-year students to the University of Michigan's forestry camp at Golden Lake. These trips ranged from one day to two weeks in the woods. In 1948, however, the trip was moved from Golden Lake to the Trees for Tomorrow camp at Eagle River and became a month-long course in wood technology taught by Dr. Irving Isenberg. At Trees for Tomorrow, the students were able to cover the subject by both precept and practice. In addition to classroom-style lectures, students visited the forest experiment station, forest rangers' station, the Hugo Sauer nursery, Rhinelander Paper Company, and the Goodman Lumber Company.

The first thing we did - we went to a lumber camp in northern Wisconsin. We were there for three or four days and learned to identify trees. I remember waking up hungry for breakfast and having pancakes that were very, very good.

— **Victor Burstein**, entering class 1940

It was two weeks in upper Michigan, along the shores of Lake Superior. It was an introduction to forestry, forest management, and ultimately pulp and paper. We stayed in the University of Michigan forestry camp. We went around to the different forestry operations up there, saw logging and hauling of logs into the mills. They had steam engines in those days that carried the logs in. To me it was absolutely fabulous because I had never been in the North Woods before. We had a great time getting to know each other. It was marvelous.

— **Walt Bublitz**, entering class 1941

It was fun; it was new to all of us because we were green.

— **Richard Brown,** entering class 1946

We visited several nearby paper mills and a sawmill, but Irv Isenberg found it hard to find modern woodcutting operations for us to watch. One day he was directed to a site where a lone worker was cutting down an aspen tree with a large bow saw. He was not working however, but sitting on a stump. One of the students asked Irv to see why he wasn't working. Irv dutifully approached the man and came back, saying, "He's just resting. He's tired from all that sawing."

— **Keith Bradway,** entering class 1948

That was a very cold summer up in Eagle River. We were up there a couple of weeks. It was interesting… we went to a sawmill, and a couple of paper mills… we went with the forest rangers out to look at the deer and the deer damage. It was to give you a sense of the forestry side of things because you didn't do much of that later. Later on it was more of the academic, scientific, chemistry, physics, and all the rest.

— **Bill Haselton,** entering class 1949

It was quite wonderful. We met in Appleton - 14 guys from all over the country. We were transported in a special Appleton bus. The bus driver was Andy Kangus. He was awfully nice. We went to upper Michigan. It was held at the University of Michigan forestry camp at Golden Lake, Michigan. We had a wonderful two weeks and got acquainted with one another and nobody shaved for two weeks. We looked motley by the end of the two-week period. We would play touch football games. It was getting acquainted with one another and soaking up tree knowledge. We went into Iron Mountain, Michigan, on Saturday night and we found a few places to relax and have fun. We had a good Saturday evening. By the time the two weeks were over, we were very well acquainted. We were all men at that time - no women students yet.

— **George Martin,** entering class 1941

I remember clearly being in a laboratory and looking at pieces of wood and trying to identify them. It was late at night and we went on field trips in the daytime and we had to identify wood by looking at it under a microscope. We did that at night after we got back from the field trips. We'd chat and holler at each other.

— **Otto Kroeschell,** entering class 1949

CHAPTER 3

1950-1959

The 1950s – which many historians agree actually began in 1946 with the end of World War II and the return of hundreds of thousands of veterans to civilian life – was a decade symbolized by beginnings. Emerging from economic depression and shortages resulting from the war, Americans were eager to embrace the prosperity that seemed inevitable. The "baby boom" that followed the war increased the population of the country several times over; by 1954, annual births topped four million for the first time in history, a trend that would continue until 1965. A direct result of his population explosion was the birth of the American Dream, the desire of young American to live in relative comfort and stability in the suburbs sprouting up around major cities.

The Institute was not immune to these trends. By the early 1950s, more than half of the student body was married, and many had children. When the Quonset huts that had served as married student housing since the war's end became increasingly harder to maintain, the Institute was forced to reconsider its housing options. What followed was the Institute's version of the American Dream – its own suburbia in the form of West Court...

Γhe 1950s was a decade of "booms." The baby boom, the industry boom, the building boom – the United States was alive and well and wanted the world to know it. The Institute of Paper Chemistry was no exception.

J. Edward Todd

ON THE OCCASION of the Institute's Silver Anniversary in 1954. Dean Harry Lewis remarked that it was a wonder students could hear the lectures of their professors over the noise of the construction that was taking place. Indeed, construction was a key theme characterizing the Institute of the 1950s.

In 1929, the Institute's founders agreed to set aside $410,000 to build a complete modern semi-plant to be used for research and training. At the same time, however, The Royal Technical Institute of Stockholm announced its plans to create a similar plant. The Institute's founders agreed to delay their own project until the Swedish venture could be evaluated. When finally put into operation in 1949, it was deemed too costly for the Institute to maintain and operate to justify its use as a research and demonstration tool.

With the plans for the semi-plant cast aside. it became obvious that the Institute still required additional laboratory equipment and devices, which, in turn, called for additional space and facilities. The project was costly, as the designs called for heavy and expensive per-square-foot loads. A better option, it was decided at the 1951 Executives' Conference, would be to erect a new building of lighter, less costly construction, move some of the Institute's existing activities there, and then adapt the vacated space where floor load, electrical, and plumbing facilities were already available.

The Institute's building boom kicked off in the fall of 1951 with the renovation of the old semi-commercial lab. When the building was first erected more than twenty years before, several clips were left in the wall to potentially accommodate another story. By December of 1951, a beautiful mezzanine floor lay across the

Dr. J. Edward Todd – "Ed" to his friends and colleagues, Dr. Todd to his students – was born in Vermillion, South Dakota, in 1897. After obtaining his A.B. degree from the University of Kansas in 1918, Todd enlisted in the Air Service, volunteering for Near East Relief to help with reconstruction following the First World War. After spending a year in Constantinople, where he was responsible for the transportation of relief supplies to the interior stations of the Caucasus area, Todd spent several years in academia, first at the University of Vermont, then as the business officer of Cornell College in Iowa. He returned to school and completed his M.A. in 1934 and his PhD in 1940, both from the Teachers' College of Columbia University.

Todd came to Appleton in 1942 to serve as the Institute's Assistant Dean. His main interests lying in the fields of higher education administration, psychology, and philosophy, Todd was best known to students for his administration of a series of aptitude exams during the first days of the bush trip.

Todd spent a total of twenty-four years at the Institute. He was appointed Dean of Admissions in 1950, a position he held until his semi-retirement in 1962. Todd served the Institute in a consultant capacity for five additional years before officially retiring in 1967. He passed away in 1973.

Dean Todd was a character, but he was really on the side of the students.
— Arthur Dreshfield, entering class 1951

beams, creating a new space for Dr. Roy Whitney's chemical engineering laboratory and a home for equipment that had previously been scattered all over the Institute. A special explosion-proof room was added in the building's southeast corner to house the wood extraction unit and its related equipment as well as a stainless steel reaction vessel for alkaline fusions. A new humidity room and machine shop completed the facilities.

Construction on the new General Activities Building, first discussed at the 1951 Executives' Conference, began in the summer of 1952. Designed to match the present main building in size and appearance, the new building contained all administrative offices, business and education offices, classrooms, an auditorium designed to seat two hundred people, and a museum – twenty-one thousand square feet spread over two stories, a basement, and a sub-basement.

The General Activities Building was completed in the late spring of 1953 at a cost of $347,500. During the June 4 cornerstone ceremony – held indoors due to a heavy thunderstorm – the Chairman of the Institute's Board of Trustees, Ernst Mahler, dedicated the building "to the abiding faith we share in the future."

The General Activities Building contributed to the growth of the Institute in a variety of ways. The new laboratory and office space led to the expansion of the research staff, which led to the expansion of the research program. Moreover, the additional space allowed more students to attend the Institute. Before the expansion, the Institute could support a maximum entering class of fifteen and student body of fifty-five. With the new facilities, an entering class of twenty and a student body of seventy-five could be accommodated.

The enlarged student body – and the wives and children that accompanied many of them – resulted in the Institute's next building frenzy. In November of 1954, the Institute announced plans to construct five new apartment buildings for married students. Each building – two two-story units and three one-story units – was designed to provide housing for four married couples with a living room, a dining alcove, a kitchen, a bedroom, a study/ nursery, and a bathroom.

The five apartment buildings were completed in July of 1955 at a cost of $275,000. A sixth building – another one-story unit - was completed the following September. A seventh unit was built in January of 1957 and an eighth in the spring of 1958. The Institute's own little suburb was named West Court; more often, however, it was simply referred to as "Fertility Row!"

 The Institute has been very important in my life and I'm glad I had the opportunity to go there. You could do anything you wanted to do with an Institute education.

— **Vincent Russo**, entering class 1952

 It was an awesome place.

— **Frederick Vermillion**, entering class 1958

 *I think the Institute gave you a well-rounded technical background and also taught you a way to think.*

— **Carl Lentzen**, entering class 1959

The building boom continued throughout the 1950s. At the 1956 Executives' Conference, a $735,000 expansion program was announced, promising to add close to thirty-seven thousand square feet to the Institute's present quarters. Construction on the new spaces – an addition to the Container Building, a new building to house pilot plant equipment, and the enclosure of the court around the present buildings – began in May of 1957.

The addition to the Container Building was completed in January of 1958. The basement was renovated to house the Container Division, while the main floor was expanded to meet the increasing requirements in paper evaluation and graphic arts. Two new humidity rooms – one large and one small - were added, as well as a large chemical laboratory for graphic arts and five new offices for the staff of the groups occupying the building.

Shortly afterward, another building – South Laboratory – was completed at the rear of the campus, adding sixteen thousand square feet of laboratory space. The first floor was leased to the Sulphite Pulp Manufacturers' Research League, who had designed it to meet their needs for research and pilot plant facilities and for office space and conference rooms.

Finally, in July of 1958, the final stage of the proposed expansion program – the Court Addition – was completed. Designed to join the west rear of the General Activities Building with the southwest wing of the Institute's main research lab, the addition formed an enclosed inner court that was to be maintained as a beautiful green space. Lewis called the space a memorial to the Institute's former librarian, Edith Stroschneider, who passed away in July of 1956, for "her tulip bulbs still grow and bloom under the windows of the library…where she spent her rare periods of rest and recreation."

Dr. Philip N. Joranson

The Court Addition added twenty-three thousand square feet of lab and office space. Students loved the two new air-conditioned classrooms, while the space vacated by the moves allowed for more lab room for student thesis research as well as for expansion by the analytical chemistry, chemical engineering, and biology sections.

The completion of the expansion program – which ended up costing the Institute some $950,000 – did not end the 1950s building boom, however. In November of 1958, the Institute received a $50,000 grant from the Louis Calder Foundation for a new lab to be known as the Lou Calder Plant Biochemistry Laboratory. The funds, donated by Louis Calder, the President and Director of the Perkins-Goodwin Company in New York City, allowed the purchase of ultracentrifuge and electrophoresis equipment as well as complete and modern facilities for freeze-drying biological and biochemical preparations. One year later, the Calder Foundation contributed another

I enjoyed it from the time I got there until the time I left. A lot of the guys didn't - they couldn't wait to finish up and get out…they had other things to do. But I really enjoyed doing it; it was one of the most fun things I've ever done. It provided a solid foundation for a career in the paper business. Going to the Institute was one of the smartest things I ever did.

— **John Schulz**, entering class 1955

The technical aspect wasn't as important as the discipline it took. That was discipline that I needed. I learned to think of things in an entirely different way.

— **John Vaughan**, entering class 1958

$30,000 gift to establish an updated electron microscopy and diffraction laboratory that would permit diffraction studies not possible with the Institute's twenty-year old electron microscope.

The Institute's new research facilities spawned a flurry of research activity throughout the 1950s. One project that proved of supreme importance to the field of medicine was research done on vanillin, which ultimately resulted in a cure for histoplasmosis – otherwise known as "Valley Fever," a uniformly fatal disease in children. Institute researchers worked for several years with vanillin, a compound derived from spent sulphite liquor, finally discovering a way to turn it into vanillic acid. From there, ethyl vanillate was created and proved to be an effective weapon against fungi, the cause of histoplasmosis. In 1952, the Institute turned its findings over to a research team at Vanderbilt University – and then offered to finance the clinical trials. "So far as we know," Westbrook Steele told the 1952 Executives' Conference, "this is the first time that one educational institution on its own account and from its own research reserves had financed research at another institution of higher learning."

Shu Tang "S.T." Han

Originally from Hangchow, China, S.T. Han joined the Institute staff in 1949 as a research associate and professor in the Chemical Engineering Department. He left for a brief period in the mid-1950s for a position at Beloit Iron Works, returning in August of 1958 to continue his academic and research responsibilities in the chemical engineering lab.

In 1964, Han left the Engineering and Technology Section to serve as a research associate in the Dean's office, where his responsibilities included the formulation and implementation of programs resulting from both internal and external examination of scientific trends and movements engaging the interest of the Institute. In 1966, Han was named chair of the Engineering and Technology Section, succeeding the late Bill Irgmanson. He held this position until his retirement in 1977, at which time he was awarded Emeritus status.

S.T. Han was a very brilliant chemical engineer and professor, yet his love was cowboy movies. He wanted guys with white hats and black hats, the good guys and the bad guys. When S.T. would go to the movies, it had to be a cowboy movie or he wouldn't stay.

— Vincent Russo, entering class 1952

S.T. was brilliant and always helpful. The recollection we all have of him is standing in the auditorium writing these long equations on the blackboard with his right hand and dragging an eraser across behind him with his left hand so that you could hardly find time to get it all down in your notes before it was erased.

— Robert Jones, entering class 1957

The professor that made an impression on everybody in my day was S.T. Han, who taught chemical engineering. He was enthusiastic and took great pleasure in challenging the students. Everybody who took his courses felt challenged but really enjoyed them.

— Jim Burke, entering class 1961

S.T. was a heavy smoker. One day he was up there in the front of the classroom, drawing equations on the board and solving a problem. He had a cigarette in one hand and he had the chalk in his other hand, and when he was done, he put the chalk in his mouth! But nobody laughed, because S.T. was a pretty strict, sensitive guy, and if you laughed you might've flunked the course!

— Al Jones, entering class 1962

S.T. Han would walk around the room and then suddenly stop and ask you a question. No one ever wanted to answer the questions, but he wouldn't leave until you answered correctly.

— Robert Morgan, entering class 1962

George W. Mead

George W. Mead was born in Milwaukee, Wisconsin, on October 11, 1927. After completing his secondary schooling in Connecticut, Mead attended Yale University, where he earned his Bachelor of Science degree in chemistry in 1950.

"Really, I went through my senior year with loose ends, wondering what I was going to do with myself," said Mead. "I think there was sort of an understanding that I would come back here to Wisconsin Rapids and work for our company, at that time called Consolidated Water Power and Paper Company, but I had no credentials, really, other than a degree in chemistry and that didn't seem to me like it was going to carry me very far."

It was around this time that Mead saw a bulletin board posting advertising the Institute. The notion of a school devoted to the study of pulp and paper technology intrigued him and he sent his application a few days later. The answer from the Institute was positive; Mead was accepted into the entering class of 1950 with a full scholarship. "It was," remembers Mead, "quite a thrill."

Mead's Institute experience began with a bush trip. "We got acclimated to forestry practices in a very limited but hands-on way. We visited a whole bunch of various wood consumers, a lumber mill, and several pulp and paper mills throughout the area. That whole trip was very worthwhile. Besides that, it gave us a chance to get together, the fifteen of us, and get to know each other and that was a really important factor too," Mead recalls.

Upon returning from his bush trip adventure, Mead, along with his wife and child, settled into his half of the Quonset hut he shared with classmate Jim Schoettler. "They were...spartan," said Mead, "and, frankly, that might even be too generous a word! It was snug in the physical sense. It was not snug in the warm sense."

Mead quickly became acclimated to the Institute course work and routine. He fondly recalls professors and administrators such as Johannes Van den Akker, Irv Isenberg, John Green, Roy Whitney, and Harry Lewis. "There's a story kicking around out there about me trying to dry out a solvent solution in one of John's (Green) ovens and blowing the oven up, which is true. I did it," admits Mead. He also recalls the toughness of Van den Akker's classes: "He was the filter. As you got halfway through his course he threw a tough test at you and you found out who were the sheep and who were the goats right off the bat. As far as I could tell, that test was the one key element that sorted the class out as to who was going to stay and who wasn't."

In May of 1954, the Institute began a new research program in Forest Tree Genetics. The program, led by Dr. Philip N. Joranson and financed by Rhinelander Paper Company and Marathon Corporation, sought to determine how and to what degree genetic make-up influenced both qualitative and quantitative aspects of the growth of trees. The program's eventual goal was to breed a new, improved species of tree that would yield more tons of paper per acre of forest.

By May of 1955, Joranson's research into the genetic make-up of trees uncovered a variety of species with more than the normal two sets of chromosomes. Such

trees, it was discovered, grew faster and contained several other characteristics that made them desirable as pulpwood. By the summer of 1955, the Institute had more than five thousand seedlings and grafts with more than the normal number of chromosomes, received from Mexico, Holland, Czechoslovakia, Italy, Korea, Canada, and Sweden. With these experimental plants, Joranson set out to determine if chromosome number could be altered by various influences such as chemicals, heat, and various types of irradiation. As he told his audience at the 1955 Executives; Conference: "We wonder...if it is within the power of man to guide the evolution of certain trees toward

properties and characteristics which will be even more useful that those nature has already provided."

The research, academic, and administrative groups at the Institute also underwent substantial changes during the 1950s. At the 1950 Executives' Conference, the Institute's Board of Trustees was completely realigned to bring it to the level of other large educational institutions. Westbrook Steele, previously the Institute's Executive Director, became President, John Strange, previously Secretary/Treasurer, was elected Vice-President, and C.B.

Mead graduated from the Institute in 1952 with his Masters' degree. He immediately went to work at Consolidated as a chemical engineer. "Had I come right out of college, I don't think I'd have felt very prepared," he said. "But having those two years at the Institute gave me a tremendous leg up in terms of credentials and some knowledge about the industry I wouldn't have had otherwise."

Mead continues his relationship with the Institute even today. "I've enjoyed my relationship with the Institute tremendously. I'm proud of it and I hope to see it continue to thrive in its own way. It's been a huge contributor to the industry and a huge contributor to my own success and, as such, I feel obligated to continue my support."

Mead then went on to express his feelings about the Institute in relation to the industry that supports it "Our industry was pretty technologically inept when the Institute was first formed. While I don't think the Institute or its graduates can take the credit for having

created the technological upsurge that has taken place since 1928 or so, the fact is that it couldn't have taken place without the Institute graduates out there to implement it, to help put it into place. The Institute's influence on the industry is probably as great as any institution could have possibly had. Our industry is struggling and it had been for many years. It is comparable to many other basic industries in that respect.

The industry would have been a heck of a lot worse off if it hadn't been for the Institute. I think that's clear. The other institutions overseas and those schools that had at least some paper influence wouldn't have been able to fill that gap. To me, the Institute created the atmosphere of technological aggressiveness which it's been under for a long time now. We haven't solved all the problems by a long shot. We still have a very inefficient papermaking process. There's way too much water, way too much energy and our pulp mills still stink. The process in general is ten times more efficient than it was when the Institute first formed, but it's still got a long way to go. We've come a long way."

Sitterson, previously Assistant Secretary, was elected secretary. Ernst Mahler, who had been the President of the Board of Trustees since the Institute's inception, was given the title of Chairman of the board, while D.C. Everest and John L. Riegel became the Vice-Chairmen.

The 1950s saw the formation of several new academic groups that served to enhance the education of the future leaders of the pulp and paper industry. In 1951, the Carbohydrate Group was formed under the direction of Dr. E.V. "Jack" White, an expert in the hemicellulose and plant gum field. In 1953, the Graphic Arts Section was created with Dr. George Sears as its chief. Sears'

repositioning led to the appointment of John Swanson as the leader of the Physical Chemistry Group, which was renamed the Colloidal Chemistry Group shortly thereafter. Finally, in 1955, Dr. A. Neil McLeod, who received his PhD from Cornell University, joined the staff as an economist, a position designed to help the students and staff on matters relating to the fields of economics and marketing.

These new staff appointments and new academic groups led to yet another revision of the Institute's curriculum. First-year students continued their strong emphasis on the theoretical foundation of the sciences. Second-year students continued these basic

studies, but added the processes of the pulp and paper industry to their coursework. In 1955, a new course titled "Wood as a Raw Material," focusing on the biological, physical, and chemical properties of wood, was added to the second-year curriculum, along with a new requirement that second-year students take on a field of special study as a preliminary to the doctoral program. The third-year program consisted of three sets of technical problems of a broad and diversified nature designed to give students an opportunity to demonstrate their ability to analyze situations known to exist in industry. The fourth-year program was devoted to the student's original research.

Mr. W. Irving Osborne, Jr.

Dr. David L. Luke

Dr. A. Neil McLeod

Dr. Ernst Mahler

Dr. Harry F. Lewis

Dr. Douglas M. Knight

Dr. Roy Whitney

Mr. John Strange

If Otto Kress's 1948 retirement constituted the closing of the first chapter of the Institute's history, then the period from 1954 to 1957 might well be considered the closing of the second. In February of 1954, Dr. Douglas Maitland Knight, formerly a professor of English Literature at Yale University, was installed as the eleventh president of Lawrence College, succeeding Dr. Nathan Pusey, who was chosen to serve as president of Harvard.

In 1955, Westbrook Steele announced his retirement as the Institute's President. Chosen as his successor was John G. Strange, who had served the Institute in a variety of capacities since the early 1930s. Six months later, in March of 1956, Dr. Harry Lewis announced his retirement as the Institute's Dean. Dr. Roy Whitney was chosen to succeed Lewis.

Concluding the wave of retirements was that of Ernst Mahler as the Chairman of the Institute's Board of Trustees in 1957. He was succeeded by W. Irving Osborne Jr., President of Cornell Paperboard Products Company in Milwaukee. David L. Luke, President of the West Virginia Pulp and Paper Company, was named Vice-Chairman.

The Institute truly experienced a "Coming of Age" – as the theme of the 1950 Executives' Conference predicted – in the 1950s. By the end of the decade, the Institute was supported by one hundred and twenty-eight member companies paying more than $720,000 a year in dues. Two hundred and sixty-three staff members worked in offices and laboratories valued at more than $3

An Institute education doesn't guarantee anything – nothing ever does - but it does open doors.

— Thomas Czepiel, entering class 1954

I think it gave me a good foundation for going out and accomplishing something and contributing something to the companies I worked for. I appreciated that. I had knowledge of the industry and the chemistry that was involved in the process. I wasn't too self-assured when I finished college, but after going to the Institute, I felt I knew what I was doing. All the relationships that were built there were lasting.

— Austin Anthis, entering class 1950

Mr. Westbrook Steele

Dr. Nathan M. Pusey

Irwin A. Pearl

A native of Seattle, Irwin Pearl received his bachelor's, master's, and doctoral degrees in chemistry from the University of Washington. He completed some post-doctoral work in lignin with Dr. H. K. Benson at the university before coming to the Institute in 1941 as a research associate.

As a researcher at the Institute, Pearl worked extensively in the fields of stream pollution and by-product utilization. In 1955, he succeeded Dr. Fritz Brauns as the leader of the Lignin Group. He retired from the Institute in 1976 as a senior research associate in the division of natural materials and systems and a professor of chemistry.

George G. Jernegan

George Jernegan received a Bachelor of Arts degree from Beloit College in 1943 and a Master of Arts degree from the University of Iowa in 1947. He joined the Institute staff in September of 1954 as a staff associate in the Dean's office, coming from Beloit College, where he was an assistant professor of Education and Psychology. Jernegan familiarized himself with the paper industry early in his career and was a major contributor to a publication entitled *A Guide to Career Opportunities in the Paper Industry*.

As a member of the Dean's office, Jernegan was responsible for a variety of extracurricular academic programs such as industry seminars and the summer Fiber Microscopy course. He advanced to the position of director of Continuing Education in 1958. In 1960, Jernegan succeeded Edwin Schoenberger as the Dean of Students, a position he held until his death in 1963. Jernegan was awarded Emeritus status posthumously.

Said John Strange during a memorial service held for Jernegan: "He will long remain among us through memories of his companionship, through his contributions to our program, and through the continuing work of students whose lives he touched so frequently and so positively."

million. The Institute's library held more than twenty-one thousand bound volumes and subscribed to four hundred periodicals in seventeen languages.

The 1950s also saw the Institute's alumni beginning to seek greater involvement. In 1953, a new recruiting program allowed alumni to speak at colleges and universities on the Institute's behalf. In 1958, the Institute's administrative offices were delighted to hear of the organization of an alumni association by the alumni themselves. The alumni association, still active today, served as an important vehicle of communication between alumni and the Institute as well as providing a mechanism for the nomination of alumni trustees.

Yet through it all, the primary focus of the Institute remained true to its vision: attracting promising students, guiding them, educating them, and placing them in the industry. "If we succeed in that," Mahler promised, "we shall succeed in all."

Those were great days and those were great people. The teachers were a great influence on all of us. I've enjoyed my relationship with the Institute tremendously. I'm proud of it and I hope to see it continue to thrive in its own way. It's been a huge contributor to the industry and a huge contributor to my own success.

— **George Mead,** entering class 1950

Johannes Van den Akker

Johannes Archibald Van den Akker was born in Los Angeles, California, on December 5, 1904. He received his bachelor of science degree in physics with an engineering minor from the California Institute of Technology in Pasadena in 1926; he was awarded his PhD from that same institution in 1931 for his work in determining the correctness of quantum theory in the domain of heavy metals and energetic photoelectrons. He continued this research first as a postdoctoral student at Caltech, then as a researcher and instructor in physics at Washington University in St. Louis.

In 1935, "Van," as he was affectionately called by his students and colleagues, joined the staff of the Institute as the chair of the Physics Section, a position he held until his retirement in 1970. In addition to those responsibilities, Van also served as chair of the Mathematics Section during his last fourteen years at IPC.

Van's research interests were wide and varied. Considered one of the country's – and indeed, the world's – top physicists, his areas of expertise were in the fields of optics and thermodynamics. His research in super calendering, mechanical properties of individual pulp fibers, mechanical properties of paper webs, and the optical properties of paper proved vitally important to the United States paper industry.

Van officially retired from the Institute in 1970 and was honored with the title of Professor Emeritus. From 1971 to 1982, he was a research and development consultant for the American Can Company in Neenah; he also served as a consultant for the James River Corporation from 1982 to 1985.

Van's career was filled with numerous honors. He spent 1961 and 1962 in England as a Fulbright Scholar at the University of Manchester Institute of Science and Technology. TAPPI, an organization to which Van was extremely devoted, awarded the physicist the 1967 Research and Development Award as well as the 1968 Gold Medal. He co-authored ten books, contributed to the first and second editions of the *Encyclopedia of Physics*, and penned more than one hundred articles for various scientific and technical journals.

Van den Akker...he was certainly one of my favorites. He was brilliant...very congenial and an excellent instructor. His courses were difficult. You had to study very hard, but he made them interesting. He was one of the favorites.
— Joe Atchinson, entering class 1938

Van had a lot of fun in him – he was a good party man. He was always invited to the student parties. I also played a lot of four-wall handball with Van. I had the great embarrassment one day to hit him with the ball. Hard driven, in the back of the neck – I knocked him out cold. I picked him up and he woke up and said something like, "don't worry – I'm not going to flunk you for this."
— George Ingle, entering class 1938

Van den Akker was one of the great physicists of the world in my mind.
— Daniel Adams, entering class 1939

He was a great one. He was a great personal friend to me later on. I had left a fraternity pin on a cute blonde at Rice and, after seven months, I got a Dear John letter and I was so broken up that I lost interest in the work. Van den Akker took me aside and talked to me like a Dutch uncle and said we all had to hit some bumps in life and we had to pick up and keep going. He was a friend through life and I remember sending him a card on his ninetieth birthday. He lived to a ripe old age. He was outstanding.
— George Martin, entering class 1941

Dr. Van Dan Akker was the most rigorous professor... he gave very good courses but they were tough.
— Richard Brown, entering class 1946

Van was just a tremendously intelligent and demanding guy. He was the filter. As you got halfway through his course he threw a tough test at you and you found out who were the sheep and who were the goats right off the

bat. As far as I could tell, that was the one key element that sorted the class out as to who was going to stay and who wasn't.
— George Mead, entering class 1950

I remember Van's TV antenna. In those days, there were no television stations up in the Fox River valley area. The nearest stations were in Milwaukee, about 100 miles away. So you had to put up a high tower to put up an antenna to receive the TV, which probably only came in about 3 hours a night anyway. So Van designed one himself – a steel structure – he basically enlisted a few of us to help him stand it up erect and get it set up. So it worked for six months or a year, perhaps, and then we had a really heavy windstorm come through and the thing blew down. When we talked about how it was too bad the tower blew down, he said, "You know, Art, you can't trust the weather bureau." I said, "What do you mean, Van? A big storm came up." He said, "No! I designed that tower to withstand seventy-five mile an hour winds. They said the maximum gusts were sixty-seven, but I know they were wrong, because the tower would still be up if we hadn't had gusts over sixty-seven miles an hour." I thought to myself, wow, he's confident in his computations.
— Arthur Dreshfield, entering class 1951

I thought he was a wonderful person and a wonderful teacher. As a thesis advisor, he was first-class because he left me pretty much alone, and I appreciated that. If I needed help, though, he was always available.
— John Schulz, entering class 1955

There was something about the way he challenged you with problems, problems that made you want to go the extra mile and try to understand and delve into the problems he gave to you. I found him particularly valuable and enjoyable.
— David Fary, entering class 1960

I learned so much from him. I learned how to write from him and I learned how to research from him. He is such a classical individual. He was a very tough teacher, almost severe. I heard before I came to the Institute that if you can make it through Van den Akker's class, then you can make it through the Institute. I thought he was very delightful.
— Harry Spiegelberg, entering class 1961

Van den Akker was very interesting and dynamic person. He always made tests that made you think a lot because he didn't ask questions that he talked about in classes.

He always came up with different things that made you test the limits of what you had been taught and how to put things together.

— Arne Ahlen, entering class 1963

He was the best teacher I ever had – ever, anywhere. He was able to describe relatively complex things, and sometimes very complex things, so clearly. When explaining a theory, he was always able to bring it down to practice. He was so open, although in a way he was kind of a formal guy...he always made you feel that he was open to you at any time....he was so knowledgeable and a world-wide expert....one of the guys that seemed to literally have it all, seemed to have no weakness.

— Jim Farrand, entering class 1964

My favorite was Van den Akker - he was absolutely terrific. He was a fundamentalist all the way – "think through your problems from the base up and work it out."

— David Dumbleton, entering class 1966

You would walk out of Van's class knowing that you really learned something that was very important and you could actually use what you'd learned.

— Jim Ferris, entering class 1967

Van den Akker - he was a super gentleman, a very knowledgeable person and a very good teacher. I really owe a lot to him.

— A. Nurhan Becidyan, entering class 1969

Kyle Ward, Jr.

Originally from Beaumont, Texas, Kyle Ward, Jr., received his Bachelor of Science degree from the University of Texas in 1923, his Master of Science degree from George Washington University in 1926, and his PhD from the Friedrich Wilhelm University in Berlin in 1932, where he studied under Professor Pringsheim, one of the world's eminent sugar chemists. Upon his graduation, Ward worked as a research chemist for Hercules Power Company in Wilmington, Delaware, for several years before joining the staff of the Southern Regional Research Laboratory in New Orleans as the head of the Cotton Fibers Division in 1939. He held this position until he came to the Institute in 1951 as Dr. Emil Heuser's successor in the Cellulose Group.

Most of Ward's research was conducted in the fields of cellulose and textiles, especially cotton. He is credited with synthesizing the first member of the nitrogen mustard group, chemical agents now used to treat certain types of cancer. He also conducted pioneer research on naval stores such as turpentines, gums, and resins.

Ward's career was filled with awards and honors. In 1945, he received a certificate of appreciation for services with the Technical Industrial Intelligence Committee of the Joint Chiefs of Staff during World War II, and he was named one of the top ten cellulose chemists in the United States by the Chicago Section of the American Chemical Society in 1947. He was named a TAPPI Fellow in December of 1973 and was awarded the Anselme Payen Award of the Cellulose Paper and Textile Division of the American Chemical Society in 1977. Ward also authored numerous scientific papers and published and contributed to several books in area of cellulose chemistry.

In 1966, Ward succeed Dr. Bertie Browning as the chairman of the Organic Chemistry Section. He held this position until late 1967, when he turned it over to Dr. John Green. Ward continued to serve the Institute in a variety of staff interests and activities until his official retirement in October of 1968. Ward was honored with Emeritus status, which he maintained until his death in 1997.

Kyle Ward - he was a cellulose chemist, an author and just about everything else. He was a wonderful man.

— Richard Barker, entering class 1958

The IPC:
An Epic in the Honor of Its 25th Birthday

In '29, housed in the Gym,
Our space and manpower were quite slim.
But now in 1954
We house 200 souls or more.
And tho' we've really grown, I'd say
Please let us not forget the day
When we were insecure and small,
Or brag too much because we're tall.
Since ones from tiny seedlings grew
It's well to prize those seedlings too.

And now I trust my withered Muse
Won't bore you, but will you amuse.
With lyre, cymbal, drum, and lute
She'll first salute the Institute
By calling for three rousing cheers
For our few early pioneers.

Her first verse might be aimed I guess
At that stout warrior OTTO KRESS
Whose forthright personality
Oft served to boost the I.P.C
He'd undertake most any chore,

And then find time for many more,
(Provided he'd be found at home
Because quite often Doc would roam.
And even now, his itching foot
In Florida can ne'er stay put.)

When restive Kress moved o'er the map
Dean HARRY LEWIS took the rap
As mate, out in our storm-tossed boat,
Helping to keep the "kraft" afloat
So – a salaam to H.F.L.
Who helped to man that bark so well.

An accolade to WESTBROOK STEELE
Whose energy and tireless zeal
Kept everything on even keel;
Whose words, we know, had wide appeal
To those who in the industry
Sponsored out youthful I.P.C.

Our prexy flew o'er dale and hill
To gain another member mill.
His batting average proved sky high

For seldom did a mill slip by.

More often staying within range
Was our kind Veep – I mean JOHN
STRANGE
Who serves as treasurer as well,
Which from our point-of-view is swell
Because with Strange up near our head
We'll never fear the taint of Red.

Our secretary is C.B.
Tho' ne'er a Navy man was he.
Perhaps you'd think he'd be at sea
When projects flood the I.P.C.
Yes - problems come in by the score
And, when they're solved he garners more.
(With all those items on the beach,
One wonders who finds time to teach.)

Yet – graduate work here is unique
With three fine DEANS up at the peak.
The teacher's rank is somewhat lesser,
For you'll find nary a professor.

The title which the teachers rate
Is termed RESEARCH ASSOCIATE.
(And yet kind friends – what's in a name?
We seem to get there just the same.)

Who worries about heat and light,
And whether things are going right?
Who guards the portals of the till?
Who keeps fool-items off the bill?
Quietly sitting in his den
THOMAS B. WADSWORTH –
known as Ben.
Problems increasing with our pace
He meets with dignity and grace,
A nice bouquet should go to thee –
Hardworking, gentle Thomas B.

A mighty floral horseshoe should
Be handed to the pulping brood
MACLAURIN – JOHNNY PECKHAM –
STONE –
HELLEUR – e'en tho' we often moan
When eating lunch – and get their smell
Arising from that lower well.

We'd like to mention everyone,
But that would hardly prove much fun.
And it would be a scurvy trick
To let this issue get too thick.

Our students all deserve great praise
For working nights as well as days,

Making their work a source of pride
While raising families on the side.

Alumni, too, in high repute
Strengthen the Paper Institute.

So orchids to our colleagues all
Whether they're short or rather tall.
Whether they're stout or somewhat lean,
Whether they're slow or rather keen,
Whether they're young or old,
Whether they're modest or too bold,
Whether their hair be black or red,
Or if but a few hairs grace their head.

The chemists and the analysts,
The physicists, biologists,
Cambium layers, geneticists,
Graphic artists, economists.
(Now isn't that a motley crew?
I'm sure my Muse has skipped a few.)

The maintenance crews, the electricians,
The painters, amateur musicians,
The messengers, the stock-room boys,
The janitors – those men of Roy's,
Howell's plasticians, Bob's containers
(And all their various retainers.)

The editors, photographer
And every bibliographer,
The secretaries (Delia's ladies

Who would consign our scrawls to Hades)
Fliers and Coders daren't be missed,
Nor our patient receptionist.
Our business group, librarians –
(Yes, even those barbarians
Who smoke under NO SMOKING signs.
Orchids to them? I mean big fines.)

My Muse would mention those few bores
Who throw waste paper on the floors,
Or leave the lights on (which I turn off)
(But now the party's getting rough.)
Even those sinners are nice folks
Who litter rooms while drinking cokes.

These carping lines may leave a pall
We'd best hand orchids to THEM ALL!
Then let's join hands in unity
And further this the I.P.C.

- By "Sapiens"
May 1954
The Insti-Tooter

We were blessed with people who were very good at what they do. They were really inspirational to the students.

— William Trice,
entering class 1958

Outside the Classroom

In the spring and the fall, I played outside - baseball, football, things like that. I loved to sail. A guy named Jerry had a sailboat on Lake Winnebago. We often sailed in Neenah Harbor. We gave the boat the nickname "dry lab." When someone asked me where I was going in the afternoon, I would just say that I was going to the lab!

— **Arthur Dreshfield,** entering class 1951

We played ball - I was the shortstop on the softball team. A friend and I bought a raft for $40 and we had many memorable trips on the river in it. We did that whenever we could get away.

— **Richard Barker,** entering class 1958

We had a pretty heavy work schedule, but there was always time for something, particularly when I stayed in Kress House. I'd say most every weekend, except maybe when exams were pretty heavy, we'd have a party of some sort.

— **John Schulz,** entering class 1955

I was married, so my social life was based around the married students. We went on fishing trips and I learned how to play golf. There was a golf course right behind our apartment. We also played lots of bridge. We were a very close-knit group of students in the married housing. We didn't have money to do much in town. Most of our activities were limited to the campus.

— **Robert Guide,** entering class 1954

We didn't do a lot of stopping in the bars, though I do remember one memorable occasion. I guess it must have been the end of my first year that Leo McDonnell and I decided to go to every bar on College Avenue - up one side and down the other - and have a beer in each one of them.

— **Vincent Russo,** entering class 1952

The student body would organize dances and parties - the single guys in Press House would have parties and we would go over there. We were much more active in that area than former student bodies had been. A couple of the guys took some of the apples from the old apple orchard and ran them through the refiner and made hard cider.

— **William Trice,** entering class 1958

There were four of us from the South that had an interesting time with the weather up there. We learned to ice skate a bit - threw snowballs and made snowmen. In the wintertime, Lawrence College had an enclosed swimming pool, so we could go swimming. One time I didn't dry my hair and it was sub-zero weather and the water on my hair just froze. That was an interesting experience.

— **Austin Anthis,** entering class 1950

We had an active social life without any money. We went fishing to put meat on the table. Several of us became avid fisherman and we often borrowed the biology department's net to smelt. We all ended up with enough smelt sometimes to last the winter season. Everyone that wanted to had a garden patch and we raised our own vegetables. The most interesting thing was that we made about two hundred gallons of hard cider using the pulp laboratory. Student housing was in the midst of apple orchard and the apples weren't good to eat. One year we gathered about two hundred pounds of apples, then went to the lab and used refining gear to get many gallons of juice. We set up a fermentation house in the basement of Kress House and produced enough to fuel a New Year's Eve party.

— **John Vaughan,** entering class 1958

We did play cards sometimes and the married couples would get together. We did a lot of fishing after we finished working on our theses. I would go to the lake with my friend and study and fish at the same time.

— **Joseph Koleske,** entering class 1958

I remember making apple cider – hard apple cider – out of apples from the apple trees over at West Court and using laboratory equipment to make it. We would throw a big party for ourselves and the faculty over at Kress House with the things we produced. We had a pretty good time. I remember having a pretty good New Year's Eve party the second year we were there. I was married by that time. We had it down at Aston Hill House. We decided we were going to burn the Christmas tree. Well, the thing got away from us and fortunately our wives were smarter than we were and threw baking soda on it. We would have burnt the house down, trying to shove it into the fireplace.

— **Robert Jones,** entering class 1957

The Bush Trip in the 1950s

I remember a number of mills we visited. They would usually treat us very well because they were trying to leave a good impression with some of the students because some of them might want to work there later on.

— **Austin Anthis,** entering class 1950

We got our families settled in Appleton and then we headed up north. We stayed at the Trees for Tomorrow camp in Eagle River. Isenberg taught a course in wood identification. We also got acclimated to forestry practices in a very limited but hands-on way. We visited a whole bunch of various wood consumers, a lumber mill, and several pulp and paper mills throughout the area. That whole trip was very worthwhile. Besides that, it gave us a chance to get together, the fifteen of us, and get to know each other and that was a really important factor too.

— **George Mead,** entering class 1950

The bush trip was certainly a neat introduction. It was so different from anything we'd had in undergraduate school. The subject matter was interesting, but going up to a beautiful part of northern Wisconsin was just great. Being allowed to see first hand what a forest was like, not just studying it academically – how the hardwoods and the softwoods all fit together – was a plus.

— **Arthur Dreshfield,** entering class 1951

One of the class mottos was developed in the Trees for Tomorrow. When in doubt, sack out - forget it and take a nap. There are certain things you can do and certain things you can't do - sometimes you quit trying and take a nap. When you wake up, you take a new perspective.

— **John Parkinson,** entering class 1951

It was a fine education. I was really happy with the career I had as a result - the work was interesting and challenging.

— **Arthur Dreshfield,** entering class 1951

It was a unique type of education that prepared me to move ahead in the industry. It taught us how to think for ourselves, how to attack problems and how to go after them and deliver them. We weren't going out to be scientists; we were going out to be technical managers. It was a tough grind, but I think they were some of the best years of my life. I have very positive memories from it even though it was very hard work.

— Robert Jones, entering class 1957

We got to visit a number of mills and get a sense of what the industry was like. It was a camp-like setting, so we played a little softball in the afternoons, which was fun. I remember my glasses getting broken. I broke my glasses the first day out and we had to find a place in Eagle River that could piece them together.

— Vincent Russo, entering class 1952

I went there knowing nothing about the Institute or about the paper industry. Many of the other guys there were very familiar with it. Some of them had worked in paper mills or had come from paper families. I had a lot of adjusting to do. It was a good learning experience and a chance to get to know the classmates.

— John Schulz, entering class 1955

The togetherness - we got know each other really well.

— Richard Barker, entering class 1958

We bonded pretty well. After touring the forestry land and the water resources, we went fishing. When the sun went down, we got the bus driver to take us to some bars around town. He would pick us up at midnight and we would start all over again the next day. One night we fried all the fish we saved and had a beer bash.

— William Trice, entering class 1958

I thought it was one of the best things we could have done. There were twenty-five of us in the class and it was nice to start classes knowing one another. About half of the class had been out from undergrad for a few years. About half were married. The week helped bond us into a cohesive group.

— John Vaughan, entering class 1958

CHAPTER 4

1960-1969

We stand today on the edge of a new frontier . . . a frontier of unknown opportunities and perils, a frontier of unfulfilled hopes and threats. The new frontier of which I speak is not a set of promises—it is a set of challenges.

— **John F. Kennedy,** Los Angeles, California, July 15, 1960

Some call it the best of times, others the worst of times, but one thing is certain – the 1960s changed America forever. Radical activism swept the country, bringing with it a restructuring of American society, politics, and culture. The 1960s also saw a revitalization of political and cultural conservatism that paved the way for our modern political arrangement. Above all, it was the age of youth, with seventy million children of the post-World War II baby boom com ing of age and desiring change – whatever the direction.

The Institute of Paper Chemistry – at times, seemingly a world unto itself – was also standing, as President Kennedy so eloquently stated, "on the edge of a new frontier." No longer a child in the worrisome Depression years, no longer an awkward teenager during the wartime years, no longer a cocky young adult during the 1950s – the Institute was now fully grown and entering its heyday. Despite the string of retirements that characterized the end of the previous decade, the In stitute's staff still boasted some of the most prominent scientific minds in the country. Those minds were presented the challenge of not only educating the "best and the brightest" who came to Appleton to study pulp and paper technology but also to conduct research that would lead the American pulp and paper industry to the edge of a new frontier as well…

John W. Green

The Institute of Paper Chemistry entered the 1960s with the same attitudes of hope and optimism that permeated the rest of the country. A fresh, young president dared the nation to face the challenges posed by the arrival of the new decade with courage and dignity – to "ask not what your country can do for you - ask what you can do for your country." In Appleton, Institute President John Strange issued a similar challenge to faculty and staff during his speech to the 1960 Executives' Conference: "to continue and strengthen our research efforts…to equip ourselves with the latest in scientific tools…to reach a state of intellectual readiness for the more difficult questions and challenges which are not so very far down the road."

THE BUILDING BOOM of the 1950s did not abate with the dawning of the new decade. In late 1961, plans were announced for a new education and activities center to be built on West Avenue. The new building was made possible by a $325,000 grant from the Louis Calder Foundation, which had also donated funds for the Louis Calder Plant Biochemistry Lab, an electron microscope and auxiliary equipment, and the Lou Calder Scholarship Fund.

Construction on the Lou Calder Student Center began in March of 1962. The building was comprised of two wings. The first was an assembly hall capable of seating two hundred people for seminars and conferences or one hundred for dining. The second wing consisted of a two-story housing unit containing twenty-four single rooms, a small kitchen, and a dining room. The housing wing provided residence for the Institute's single students as well as guest rooms for visiting scientists and lecturers. A communal lounge and lobby

Dr. John Green received his undergraduate degree from Princeton University and his Master of Science degree from the University of Pennsylvania. He then returned to Princeton to complete his PhD in organic chemistry. He joined the staff of the Institute of Paper Chemistry in 1938 as a member of Dr. Emil Heuser's Cellulose Group.

During World War II, Green, along with the majority of his IPC colleagues, focused his attention on research projects directly relating to wartime activities. After the war, he began to explore what would become his lifelong research interest – simple sugars. Throughout the 1950s and 1960s, Green's research centered on the not-so-simple acids formed from sugars in alkaline pulp liquors.

Green was named a Senior Research Associate in 1966. In 1967, he was chosen to succeed Dr. Kyle Ward as the Chairman of the Institute's Organic Chemistry Section, a position he maintained until his retirement in 1977.

John Green was a great guy. I got to know him fairly well when I was taking his analytical chemistry class. There's a story kicking around out there about me trying to dry out a solvent solution in one of John's ovens and blowing the oven up, which is true. I did it.

— George Mead, entering class 1950

John Green was always interested in students' ideas and was always happy to sit down and talk about something - not only technical things but things about life in general. He was always available.

— John Schulz, entering class 1955

He was a very personable guy. He got along well with the students. We were chemical engineers and he was teaching us organic - he was very helpful in working us through that. There was a great rapport between John Green and his students.

— Robert Jones, entering class 1957

area joined the two wings. The building, completed in the fall of 1962, was designed to be a harmonious part of West Court Village, which was once again enlarged by the construction of the tenth student apartment building during that same year.

In May of 1967, the Institute's trustees approved a $5,000,000 development program designed to increase graduate student enrollment by one-third, improve the quality of the graduate education program, improve, extend, and accelerate research activity, improve and greatly expand activities relating to the collection, storage, retrieval and dissemination of

scientific and technological information, place the continuing education program on a year-round schedule, and, ultimately, to carry forward more vigorously the long-range programs of education and research which the Institute had undertaken on behalf of a group of growing industries.

The program commenced in the summer of 1967 when the Inland Container Corporation made a gift of $1,000,000, the largest single gift in the Institute's history. The money was to be applied toward the cost of building and equipping a $1.5 million graduate research center to be used for research and research training of students admitted to doctoral candidacy. The thirty-two thousand square-foot

building, named the Krannert Graduate Research Center in honor of Herman C. Krannert, who founded Inland Container in 1925, also featured an auditorium with a seating capacity of three hundred and sixty. The building was dedicated during the 1969 Executives' Conference.

The new auditorium allowed the Institute to move forward in another phase of the development program, which involved transforming the old auditorium in the General Activities Building into a computer center. The center, featuring a "third generation" IBM System 360-Model 44 and complementary equipment, was completed in December of 1968 at a cost of $600,000. The new computer system was a vast

That was a really good time in my life.

— Harry Spiegelberg, entering class 1961

improvement over the IBM 1640 that had previously been used by the Institute, and the new computer center greatly expanded and enhanced the processing, retrieval, and utilization of scientific information.

The final stage of the development program was the construction of a new nineteen thousand square-foot continuing education center, which began in July of 1969. Designed to put the continuing education program on a year-round schedule, the new building was outfitted with a large seminar room two small seminar rooms, a lounge area, a kitchen, dining facilities, and twenty-eight dormitory rooms.

Herman C. Krannert

For me, it was a big benefit because it forced me to think in terms of systems that were very broad. Also, getting through it gave you a sense of confidence that there wasn't any technical area that you couldn't deal with. It kept me from being intimidated by new subjects

— David Fary, entering class 1960

The array of construction projects throughout the 1960s were necessary to create the space needed for the numerous research projects undertaken during the decade. On April 1, 1960, a $600,000 pioneering research program underwritten by the pulp and paper industry and led by the Institute of Paper Chemistry commenced. The program, which quickly gained international recognition, awarded grants to scientific researchers in various

parts of the world for long-range and pioneering research studies that held potential for importance to the pulp and paper industry.

The resulting research placed a strong emphasis on high polymers. Studies were grouped into four categories. The first contained three studies on biological, biochemical, and biophysical concepts and theories as applied to natural high polymers that took place at the Institute, at Lawrence College, and at Yale University. The second category consisted of seven studies focused on the organic chemistry of certain natural polymers, particularly the polysaccharides. Two of the studies took place at the Institute; the other five took place at the University of British Columbia,

Ohio State University, the University of Edinburgh, the Royal Institute of Technology at Stockholm, and Purdue University.

The third category contained two studies in the physical chemistry of both natural and synthetic polymers, one at the Pulp and Paper Research Institute of Canada and one at Rensselaer Polytechnic Institute. Finally, the fourth category was made up of three studies in basic engineering and technology conducted at New York University, the Massachusetts Institute of Technology, and the Finnish Pulp and Paper Research Institute at Helsinki.

The Institute embarked on many more important research projects throughout the 1960s. In 1960, a joint project with the Nebraska Agricultural Research Fund Committee was announced. A series of three separate projects aimed at

It couldn't have been better - it was the way a university education ought to be. It was a great opportunity to mix with an intellectual community.

— **David Dumbleton**, entering class 1966

preserving agriculture's present starch market in the paper industry took place over the course of a year under the direction of Dr. John Swanson, the head of the Institute's Physical Chemistry Section.

In May of 1963, a project that had been initiated in 1949 under the direction of Dr. Roy Whitney, Dr. Johannes Van den Akker, and Dr. Leonard Dearth but given classified status by the United State government, gained national recognition. IPC 1478 filter paper - small piece of felt-like paper that enables scientists to measure and predict "fallout" from nuclear explosions – was researched, developed, and hand-produced by Institute researchers at the request of the federal government as part of a program of sampling the atmosphere for radioactive debris from nuclear explosions. The paper, which could filter radioactive particles about one micron (forty millionths of a inch) from the atmosphere, was tested during "Project Ashcan," a series of test runs performed by the Defense Atomic Support Agency. The tests involved sampling runs U-2 aircraft up to seventy thousand feet, balloon runs up to one hundred and twenty thousand feet, and a space probe run up to two hundred and fifty thousand feet.

Mr. Dean Einspahr

It was a multi-disciplined education. We were focused toward the industry, sure, but we were not focused toward a single discipline. We took physics, chemistry, forestry, mechanics – you name it.

— Bob Moran, entering class 1966

Edgar E. Dickey

Originally from Cleveland, Ohio, Ed Dickey received his Bachelor of Science degree from Ohio Wesleyan in 1934 and his Master of Science degree in chemistry from Ohio State University in 1941. He completed his PhD in carbohydrate chemistry while on the Ohio State staff as a member of the university's Research Foundation. Dickey joined the Institute staff in 1949 to work in what was at that time considered the brand-new field of chromatography.

By the mid-1950s, Dickey was considered an expert in radiochemistry - the tagging of various compounds with radioisotopes and following the resultant radio-activity in reactions. Citing his impressive teaching record at the Institute, membership on students' special studies and doctoral thesis committees, and various academic committees as well as his familiarity with the industry, the Institute's Board of Trustees named Dickey Dean of Students in 1963. He maintained this position until 1966, when he was succeeded by John Farker. Dickey returned to his previous position as a Senior Research Associate in the Organic Chemistry Section. He retired in October of 1976 and was honored with Emeritus status.

You say "the isolation's tricky?"
Just hand it in to E.E. Dickey!
In lecture room or seminar,
Ed's output is far above "par"
His background's wide in chemistry,
In humor, and humanity.
Often on Ed students depend,
Because he is their selfless friend
For colleagues he sees problems through
Which lesser men could never do
We're lucky to have E.E.D
Upon our happy faculty.
— The Insti-Tooter, March 1952

There was a couple - Mr. and Mrs. Dickey. He was the Dean of Students. They were such a warm couple, very inviting and friendly and open.
— Richard Erickson, entering class 1965

Ed Dickey was just a wonderful person and really a character. He was certainly one of the high points at the Institute.
— Dick Ottman, entering class 1956

Roy Whitney

Originally from Milo, Maine, Dr. Roy Whitney earned his Bachelor of Science degree from MIT in 1935, then his Master of Science degree from the same institution in 1937. Upon graduation, he joined the staff of the Bangor Station School of Chemical Engineering Practice, where he was first the assistant director, then the director, in charge of a program of plant development work and its relation to the plant operations. It was during this time that Whitney developed a special interest in pulp and paper manufacture.

In 1942, Whitney joined the MIT faculty as an assistant professor of chemical engineering, a position he held until 1945, the same year he completed his doctorate in chemical engineering. After World War II, Whitney became a professor of chemical engineering at the University of Maine at Orono. He was with the university until 1947, when he joined that staff of the Institute as a research associate and head of the chemical engineering program.

In 1956, Whitney succeeded Dr. Harry Lewis as the Dean of the Institute. In 1958, he was elected to the Institute's Board of Trustee as the Vice President of Academic Affairs, a position created in recognition of the growth of the Institute and the importance of its academic program. His progressive educational philosophy - "disciplined intellectual curiosity and the opportunity to exercise it," as he told the 1956 Executives' Conference – was a large contributor to the worldwide recognition the Institute gained throughout the 1950s and 1960s and the high regard with which it was viewed.

Whitney's professional honors were legion. In 1948, he received national recognition for contributions to the profession of chemical engineering by the American Institute of Chemical Engineers. He was named an Outstanding Educator of America for 1974, and he was the recipient of the 1980 TAPPI Gold Medal.

Whitney served as the Institute's Vice President of Academic Affairs until 1977. He then served two years as the assistant to the President before his official retirement in 1979, at which time he was named Professor Emeritus of chemical engineering. During a ceremony honoring his contributions to the Institute's research and academic programs, Whitney spoke to the assembled crowd: "I have thoroughly enjoyed every moment while working here and I will always be interested in the Institute, its people, and its progress."

Roy Whitney was a great engineer. He was a super guy and a wonderful teacher.
— George Mead, entering class 1950

Because of his impact on the students, Roy Whitney was as impressive a mentor as anyone ever had. He brought to the students enthusiasm for the industry.
— Vincent Russo, entering class 1952

Roy was an outstanding chemical engineer and an impressive person academically. He was very fair, but demanding. I used the things he taught throughout my life and career.
— Robert Guide, entering class 1954

Dean Whitney was the kind of guy who really looked out for all of us. He was a stern disciplinarian, but he was an excellent teacher, too. He was really an outstanding dean and made the difference for a lot of us in getting through school.
— Robert Jones, entering class 1957

The Forest Tree Genetics program was begun in 1954 under the direction of Dr. Philip Joranson. Financed by Rhinelander Paper Company and Marathon Corporation, the program sought to determine how and to what degree genetic make-up influenced both qualitative and quantitative aspects of the growth of trees. Its goal was to breed a new, improved species of tree that would yield more tons of paper per acre of forest. A series of crossbreeding experiments led to the development of a Bigtooth Hybrid Aspen in the late 1950s.

Dr. Lawson Winton

Dr. George Jernegan

It was a very good maturing process for a guy – an excellent growth experience. It was always a good, comfortable place where you felt secure and you felt part of the group. When you look at the whole society and how impersonal everything's become, you can see that it was one of those last bastions of fellowship, where you developed together and supported each other. The stretch of five years I was there was probably the greatest time of my life…so many neat things happening - my kids were starting to grow up and all the things happening there.

— Jim Farrand, entering class 1964

In May of 1963, the Institute leased from the state of Wisconsin sixty acres of woodlands in the Black River Falls Forest near Millston to be used as a test site for growth of new types of trees developed in Joranson's program, now under the direction of Dr. Dean Einspahr. The test plot was chosen to see how well particular hybrids do in sandy, dry soil; other test sites at Eagle River, Cornucopia, and Marenisco offered other types of soils and environments.

In June of 1963, another test plot was developed in Clintonville. The ten-acre site, selected, like the Millston site, for its sandy soil, was planted with Larch, Bigtooth Aspen, Quaking Aspen, and Bigtooth Aspen crossed with Poplar. Thirty-six trees were planted nine feet apart on the test plots. The Institute set as its goal favorable results within twenty to twenty-five years.

The greatest success of the Institute's Forest Genetics program came in April of 1969 when Dr. Lawson Winton, a member of Einspahr's team, culminated six years of research with the announcement of the world's first "test-tube tree" – the first time a complete tree had been produced by the tissue culture process.

Research on the "super tree" began at the Institute in 1962. Eventually a method to eliminate the need for sexual propagation was discovered, making possible the growing and reproducing cells outside the natural body of an organism.

Institute scientists chose a type of Quaking Aspen tree called the triploid Aspen for their project because of its rapid growth characteristics and its ability to develop new shoots after harvesting. Of the five trees were developed over the course of one year, three survived; two of the three had reached three feet in height by the time

the project was announced to the public. It was, according to Arnold Grummer, the Institute's Editor of General Publications and responsible for the Institute's communications with the public, "just wonderful…simply unbelievable."

Despite a long series of successful research efforts throughout the decade, several issues concerned the Institute during the

Dr. Arild Miller

Dr. J. Edward Todd

Dr. Douglas Knight

Dr. Curtis Tarr

Dr. Edgar Dickey

Dr. John Parker

1960s. In May of 1960, the Institute's Board of Trustees learned of a $125,000 deficit from the previous year's $2.1 million operating budget, caused by a growing disparity between membership dues and outlay for educational purposes as well as a transitory lag in cooperative services revenue. Needing a solution to the fiscal crisis, the Board decided to raise membership dues and maximum contracts by twenty-five percent, representing the first general increase in membership dues since Institute was founded.

During that same Executives' Conference, the Institute's Dean, Dr. Roy Whitney, revealed to the Board the difficulties the Institute was having in finding quality students to fill the school's classrooms. The number of students in chemical engineering was declining and the "classical physics" – mechanics, heat, light, and sound – were rapidly disappearing from the academic scene as the "glamour fields" of mathematics and physics were taking over. By 1962, student enrollment had dropped to fifty-four and the Instititue was forced to reverse a policy that had been in place since the school's inception – that all students admitted to the Institute were expected to complete the PhD program. The new policy allowed admittance of students who only planned to get a Masters degree.

There were also several staff and administration changes throughout the 1960s. George Jernegan replaced Dr. Edwin Schoenberger as the Dean of Students in 1960, while Dr. Arild J. Miller took over the position of Director of Admissions from Dr. J. Edward Todd, who announced his retirement in 1961. In November of 1962, Dr. Douglas M. Knight, Lawrence's president, was elected president of Duke

I thought the Institute did a good job of preparing people for running an industry that has some growth to it.

— Jim Burke,
entering class 1961

It was certainly a positive experience. I made a lot of good friends there.

— Arne Ahlen,
entering class 1963

I am proud to be an Institute graduate. The Institute is famous for producing generalists, not specialists. My life story is about being a generalist and being an inquisitive person. That is why I am in the position that I am in right now. I was taught to think out of the box.

— A. Nurhan Becidyan,
entering class 1969

University, thus demonstrating once again that Lawrence served as somewhat of a "proving ground" for major university presidents (Dr. Henry Wriston left Lawrence to assume the presidency of Brown University, while Dr. Nathan Pusey left Lawrence to be the president of Harvard). Knight's replacement, Dr. Curtis W. Tarr, previously Assistant Dean of Humanities and Sciences at Stanford University, was chosen in May of 1963.

In the spring of 1963, Dr. Edgar Dickey replaced Jernegan as Dean of Students. He maintained this position until the summer of 1966, when he resigned to focus more on teaching and his research in organic chemistry. He was succeeded by John M. Parker, who served as the Dean of Students until the Institute's move to Atlanta in 1989

The decade ended with a massive reorganization of the Institute's one hundred and seventy-member staff. Four new research divisions were created, including a division of industrial and environmental systems, a division of materials engineering and processes, a division of natural materials and systems, and a division of informational services. The new system, which allowed research problems to be looked at with a broader view and in relation to other fields of concern in the same division, allowed research to transcend artificial divisions created by the academic disciplines and bring

several areas of researchers into the study of one specific field. John Strange explained the new system to the 1969 Executives' Conference: "When a problem cuts across several fields or groups of people - and most of them do nowadays - structuring can be vital to sensible progress."

In addition to the internal issues that the Institute faced throughout the turbulent 1960s, several external factors also gave life in Appleton a little "shake-up." In the wake of the twelve harrowing days of the Cuban Missile Crisis in the fall of 1962, the Institute became one of seventeen private buildings and schools in Outagamie County licensed as public fallout shelters due to its status as a building with a protection factor of one hundred or better, meaning the relation between the amount of radiation from fallout that would be received by a protected person within a shelter compared to an unprotected person outside. The basement areas of the General Activities Building, the Central Research Building, and the South Research Building were stocked with supplies for six hundred and sixty-five people.

The Vietnam War also began to play a role in Institute life in the mid-1960s. By February of 1968, ten of the first-year students – about eighty percent of the class – became eligible for the draft

following a new rule that wiped out blanket draft deferments. The deferred status of some three hundred thousand students throughout the country came to an end. Many of these students chose to enlist and get their military service out of the way before starting graduate school. This trend played a significant role in the Institute's recruiting efforts through the duration of the war.

"As most graduate schools turn more and more to the federal government for support and guidance," Dr. Roy Whitney stated, "our devotion to the pulp and paper industry becomes increasingly a mark of distinction and a point of pride... we need students that will bring not only specific knowledge but an ability to look beyond the manifestation to the underlying principles and to utilize these principles in orderly and logical development."

Louis E. Wise

My main interest is in teaching – in helping in the development of young men – not only intellectually, but ethically as well. My relationship with students has usually been quite informal. The men feel free to consult me whenever need arises. They have access to my personal library and to my laboratory and to my time as well.

— Dr. Louis E. Wise, 1947

Louis Elsberg Wise was born in New York City in 1888. After obtaining his Bachelor of Arts degree in 1907, he entered Columbia University, where he earned his PhD in organic chemistry in 1911. He spent the next three years in instructional positions at Columbia and at the University of Missouri before joining the United States Department of Agriculture as a biochemist. After World War I, Wise joined the staff of the New York State College of Forestry at Syracuse as a professor of forest chemistry. He remained at Syracuse until 1932, when ill health forced him to take a leave of absence from teaching. He spent nine years in Florida writing and abstracting.

Wise joined the staff of the Institute in the spring of 1942 as a research associate and instructor in wood chemistry. His research interests were varied; he was particularly interested in cellulose and hemicelluloses with special reference to the isolation and properties of arabogalactan from Larchwood. Wise authored more than one hundred publications in the fields of pure organic chemistry, essential and fatty oils, soil chemistry, biochemistry, wood chemistry, and pulp and paper. With L.F. Hawley of the Forest Products Laboratory, he published one of the definitive volumes in his field, *The Chemistry of Wood*, in 1926.

Wise earned numerous honors throughout the course of his career. In 1944, he was named one of the "American Men in Science" in the field of wood chemistry. He received the TAPPI Gold Medal in 1960, and was the recipient of the first Anselme Payen Award given by the Cellulose, Wood, and Fiber Chemistry Division of the American Chemical Society in 1962. Upon his retirement in 1966, he was awarded a Master of Science *ad eundem* from Lawrence College as well as the honor of being named one of the youngest Emeritus Professors in the history of the Institute. He passed away in 1980 at the age of 92.

Conscience (Study in Grey)
By Louis E. Wise

How lonely are those children's playgrounds;
  Their swings deserted;
  Slides encrusted with grey snow
Melting to form dark puddles at their base.

These bring to mind our own dark consciences;
  Not white like the newly fallen snow,
  Not yet graphitic black – but grey.
  These serve for most of us.

  Few consciences are white,
  And, perhaps more are ebony black.
White ones belong to men like Bunche,
  Pauling, Luther King, Luthuli.
  And a few friends who all love peace.

  These white ones hold no fears,
  Nor do they compromise with Truth.
  Their owners feel compassion,
And seek to understand what motivates
Those men of bitterness and violence.
Whose dark activities defile the days
And plastic bombs tear through the night.

Deep Purple
By Louis E. Wise

  A girl once lay on a purple couch
  Her eye held a violet gleam;
And she wrote a wee note on a lavender card
  By the light of an amethyst beam.

  Can I ever forget that lavender card,
  With its weird impassioned caress.
Or the violet gleam, or the amethyst beam,
  Or the girl in the Tyrian dress?

Well, all this happened six decades ago,
  And of course I can laugh at it now,
But the violet gleam and the lavender card
THEN – brought beads of sweat to my brow.

Louis Wise was an introspective person, very quiet. Very intelligent.

— Bob Boehm, entering class 1948

Dr. Wise could occasionally throw parties for students – always lots of fun.

— John Parkinson, entering class 1951

Louis Wise came out of a tough situation in Europe, so he still did his abstracting by taking old envelopes and opening them and using them as paper to write on. I mean, there we were, surrounded by all kinds of paper and Louis Wise was still being very frugal about the use of paper based on his own experiences.

— Vincent Russo, entering class 1952

I had a fortunate experience in being Dr. Wise's last student. He was the finest gentleman I have ever known as a person, scientist, and humanitarian. He was my mentor. We hit it off personally and professionally. He and his family became friends. Our children saw them as grandparents. We spent time together socially. Dr. Wise was not only a scientist, but also a published poet. He taught me to write. He would read two copies of my quarterly reports - one from a technical standpoint and one from a literary standpoint. That was the better of the two educations I got - writing. He didn't do that for anyone else. It was part of our personal repertoire. It was his gift to me.

— John Vaughan, entering class 1958

Women at the Institute

IN SEPTEMBER of 1967 the Institute experienced yet another watershed moment: the acceptance of the first female student in the school's thirty-seven year history.

Mrs. Anna Schmierer broke the Institute's longstanding "men only" tradition. Originally from Medford, Massachusetts, Schmierer earned her undergraduate degree in biochemistry from Bates College in 1963. After a stint at Smith, Kline, and French Pharmaceuticals, Schmierer – often described as a "pioneering spirit" by friends and colleagues alike – became the first research chemist at the S.D. Warren Company in Westbrook, Maine.

Schmierer's introduction to the Institute came in the form of a casual conversation with John Swanson. She sent in her application and received her acceptance letter just days after her husband, an optometrist, was drafted into the armed services. He went to Vietnam; she came to Appleton.

Schmierer spent one year at the Institute, ultimately deciding to pursue another course of study elsewhere. In an article in the January 21, 1968, issue of the *Appleton Post-Crescent*, Schmierer described her Institute experience: "The students and faculty have always treated me well. They tend to be protective and really concerned that I like it here and do well."

Here, two female students from the 1970s detail their experiences in what had for so long been a man's world.

I didn't realize it at the time, but we were really breaking ground. There were three women in my class – we pretty much doubled the number of women who had ever attended the Institute. We were a watershed year – there were female students every year after that. It was never that big a deal. The guys were used to having women in their undergraduate classes. It was always like one big family – we did everything together.

— **Paula Stoppler,** entering class 1975

I never noticed being treated differently or being made to feel like I shouldn't be there. I was always treated with a great deal of respect. For that time, that was saying something – so many fields were still predominantly male and you had to fight to get anywhere. I never felt that way at the Institute.

— **Gail Carels,** entering class 1977

Outside the
Classroom

We lived in a little village for the married students. There was a lot of socialization and camaraderie there. We had parties quite often. We shared baby-sitters and we were all great friends. Many of those friendships still exist for Bonnie and I today.

— **Harry Spiegelberg,** entering class 1961

Appleton was the ideal community for us to settle in. It was just a nice environment and a neat town.

— **Richard Erickson,** entering class 1965

We frequently got together at Kress House, especially on the week-ends. A lot of the guys were hunters and they would get several deer during deer season. I can remember going over to Kress House where they would have a deer fry. We'd have steaks and shish kabobs and all kinds of things.

— **Jim Farrand,** entering class 1964

Lawrence was a source of social interaction, but Kress House was the place to party. Not a lot, though - we were a nerdy, technical group, always occupied with our work!

— **Richard Peterson,** entering class 1964

We would often go to the married couples' houses for dinner - they were really nice about inviting the bachelors. We also spent a lot of time at the Red Carpet Inn in the basement of the Calder Center. We had several graduation parties down there.

— **A. Nurhan Becidyan,** entering class 1969

The married students would socialize a lot. One of the big things was Green Bay Packers games. Anytime they would play a televised game, we had a party at someone's house. We also played a lot of bridge. We would organize bridge tournaments or play with other couples.

— **Robert Morgan,** entering class 1962

There was always something going on as far as social engagements. You couldn't go more than two or three days before there was a get-together of some sort. It was a very close-knit group.

— **Jim Ferris,** entering class 1967

We had access to the Lawrence gymnasium and we played a lot of handball there. We also played volleyball and I was on an Institute recreational softball team for several years. And there were picnics and parties and those kinds of typical college things.

— **Al Jones,** entering class 1962

I spent a lot of time in bars. For those of us who came to Wisconsin from the outside, that's the thing that always amazed us. There were a lot of taverns there.

— **Jim Burke,** entering class 1961

The Bush Trip
in the 1960s

I was – and still am - a city boy. I had never spent the night in the forest before. It was primitive, but fun. I had a great time.
— **A. Nurhan Becidyan,** entering class 1969

It was a great opportunity to see what the Wisconsin industry was like.

— **Jim Ferris,** entering class 1967

We went out in the woods a couple times and saw some logging operations. There were trees that the ranger had marked that the logger could take. The logger would go up and fell the tree, then drop the tree so that the butt of the tree was downhill. Then he would go up and knock the big branches off with his axe or chainsaw. After that, he would hitch his horse to the tree and signal the horse. The horse would walk towards the road, dragging the tree down the hill. In the meantime, the logger would go cut down one or two more trees and start knocking the branches off. When he saw the horse was down to the road, he'd go and unhitch it, then bring it back up and hitch it to the next tree. It was so labor intensive – it's absolutely inconceivable today.

— **Al Jones,** entering class 1962

We went up to Eagle River. We played a lot of volleyball when we had free time. Mostly we went around to look at the forestry operations of some of the different companies located there.

— **Jim Burke,** entering class 1961

I enjoyed the opportunity to bond with the other students and learn something in the process.

— **Harry Spiegelberg,** entering class 1961

*It was definitely one of the highlights of
the Institute. It was an outstanding thing
they did because it was the time that really
brought us all together. It was a time of real
bonding and developing camaraderie.*

— Jim Farrand, entering class 1964

*We went up to Trees for Tomorrow camp
with Irv Isenberg. I really enjoyed it. I
learned a lot on that trip. It was really good
for me to get into the botany of the business
and to learn about all those trees and the
commercial side of forestry. It was absolutely
a great way to begin.*

— David Dumbleton, entering class 1966

*The Institute gave me
the combination of a
technical and a business
background to go directly
out of school into an
industrial environment
and make fairly
significant contributions
to the industry.*

— Richard Peterson,
entering class 1964

*When I left the Institute, graduates were highly regarded and very
much in demand throughout the industry. Institute graduates
went into pretty responsible positions in a short period of time. It
was a wonderful opportunity to get an education and then to be
appreciated for what you knew.*

*I enjoyed my time in Appleton and it certainly led me through a
career that I thought was really interesting. I had the chance to do,
and learn, and contribute throughout my career. I'm sure I would've
done those things in some other industry, but the Institute certainly
provided a ready opportunity for that.*

— Al Jones, entering class 1962

CHAPTER 5 1970- 1979

The 1970s saw a continuation of the social activism that so definitely characterized the previous decade. Women's rights, gay rights, environmentalism – everyone had a cause.

Many of these causes played out on the campus of the Institute of Paper Chemistry as well as on the national stage. The 1970s saw the Institute's first female graduate and then the presence of women in each entering class. Environmentalism took center stage for the Institute's scientists, who spent staggering amounts of time on research projects designed to boost environmental awareness in the United States pulp and paper industry…

The 1970s saw a perceptible shift away from the social activism of the 1960s and into social activities designed to heighten one's own pleasure. Indeed, this shift inspired American novelist Tom Wolfe to christen the 1970s "The Me Decade."

ONE ELEMENT OF SOCIAL ACTIVISM that survived this shift, however, was environmentalism. Publications such as Rachel Carson's *Silent Spring* and a series of environmental disasters such as the Cuyahoga River fire and the Love Canal crisis inspired increasing awareness of human threats to the natural world as early as 1962. By the mid-1970s, the majority of Americans were well aware of the damage that industry was doing to air, water, and the earth itself, leading to the creation of governmental agencies such at the Environmental Protection Agency as well as a series of campaigns – such as Earth Day - designed to promote global environmental awareness.

Following the worldwide trend, environmentalism became a key component of the Institute's research program. In 1970, a new division was created for research and development in industrial and environmental systems that proved a significant force in the battle against pollution. A central laboratory for environmental studies was developed to provide an organized systems research approach to industry-wide problems of environmental quality, alternatives in pollution abatement measures, and an organization designed to undertake research for federal and state agencies through contracts, grants, or cost-sharing arrangements.

The Institute's most labor-intensive environmental project of the decade began in 1971 when Institute researchers were asked by five hundred and

The Institute's First Female Graduate

Originally from Maine, Marilyn Hobart Kinsey attended the University of Connecticut's School of Engineering for a brief period before settling into the pulp and paper program at the University of Manchester in England. As she told the *Post-Crescent* in a June 1970 interview, "I felt that the bias against women would be less of a factor in the pulp and paper industry." She earned her B.Sc degree in paper science in 1967.

In 1968, after researching several European pulp and paper graduate programs, including the program at the Norwegian Pulp and Paper Research Institute in Trondheim, Norway, Kinsey made the decision to return to the United States for her graduate education. "I had become so acclimated to living in Europe," she said in a 2006 interview, "that I thought that if I didn't come back to the States at that point in my life, I probably never would." She applied to the Institute of Paper Chemistry and was accepted as a member of the 1968 entering class. Kinsey was the third woman admitted to the Institute in its twenty-nine year history.

Kinsey remembers her time in Appleton fondly. "It was a fun community," she recalled. "I never felt like I was being given special treatment or that I was being discriminated against. We were all there to learn and we were all on the same basis. We all had nice housing, good facilities, and good professors. It has certainly been good for me to have had a broad education and I'm glad the Institute gave me the opportunity. I also think it was good for the Institute to begin to accept and welcome women students."

forty separate outfalls of ninety-one pulp and paper mills throughout the country to perform more than thirty thousand tests on approximately twenty-two hundred samples of paper industry effluent – all within a ten-month span. Three specific events led to the paper industry's panic and the demands upon the Institute. The first was the discovery of mercury contamination in the spring of 1970, the second was the federal government's reaction to Refuse Act 1899 in early 1971, and the third was the discovery of polychlorinated biphenyl (PCB) in foodstuffs beginning in 1971.

In early 1971, Institute researchers began a series of tests on the mercury levels in bodies of water upon which paper mills were located, in order to inform the public, the federal government, and the industrial consumers of paper, namely the food packaging industry.

The industry's demands became more frenzied a few months later as the Refuse Act gained national recognition. Two specific aspects of the Refuse Act were of particular significance to the paper industry; first, that a permit from the US Army Corps of Engineers was required before any industrial plant could dump refuse into waters, and second, that "waters" were defined as any "navigable waters or tributary thereof." This essentially included almost every running

or still body of water in the country, with the possible exception of a small farmer's pond or a seasonal streamlet. The paper industry, which utilized close to one hundred tons of water for every ton of paper produced, became extremely concerned when executives realized that the permits required by the Refuse Act demanded a list of chemicals and various physical matter, including specific amounts, contained in effluent from every outfall of every plant. For Institute researchers, this translated into every sample requiring tests for up to fifty different parameters.

The Institute prepared by acquiring new and more sophisticated testing equipment, such as the Atomic Absorption Spectrometer, designed to detect mercury at levels of parts per billion. The Institute's staff was also realigned to deal with the testing and recording of results. Dr.

Irwin Pearl was named coordinator of the program, while the majority of the testing was done under Dr. Dwight Easty's analytical chemistry group.

The original deadline for obtaining the necessary permits was July 1, 1971, which quickly proved impossible for Institute researchers. As Dr. Pearl commented in June 1971, "there isn't enough testing capacity in the country to take care of the situation." The testing process was complicated for a variety of reasons. Some of the samples required additives to ensure that they remained stable until testing time. Other samples were contaminated by extraneous material often found in the waters around pulp and paper mills, such as the noncellulose components of trees. Since test parameters assumed that chemicals were being checked in essentially clear water, such extraneous material often rendered the results invalid.

I think it was incredibly beneficial to take a field like chemistry and make it into something practical.

— Jerry Sajbel, entering class 1977

The family atmosphere…the warm association you have with the guys you went to school with and the professors at the school…the genuineness of it…cold winters, everybody's freezing, nobody had much money - but pulling together to make it a great experience. To me, that's what it was all about.

— Gene Millard, entering class 1970

The federal government permitted the deadline to be extended to October 1, 1971, for a portion of the test results. Members from other Institute research groups came to work in Dr. Easty's analytical group and staff members were put on three around-the-clock shifts seven day a week until the testing was completed. Not a single Institute client failed to meet the application deadline and receive the necessary permits.

The rising interest in environmental projects did nothing to detract attention from the Institute's other research projects, however. In 1970, the Institute nurseries were expanded to handle the production of improved hybrid aspens as part of the "Super Tree" program begun at the Institute in the 1960s. By 1972 more than one hundred and fifty thousand hybrids had been planted. Those planted at the program's inception now reaching an average height of forty feet and five inches in diameter. One thousand of these hybrids had survived at an altitude of two miles in Colorado in a climate ranging from forty degrees below zero to seventy degrees above.

In April of 1972, one of four test tube trees – the first to be produced by tissue culture – was planted in the National Arboretum in Washington D.C. in commemoration of the one hundredth anniversary of Arbor

Harry A. Posner, Jr.

Harry A. Posner, Jr., received his Bachelor of Science degree from the University of Southern California in 1958 and immediately began his career with Bell Telephone Laboratories as a member of the technical staff of Bell's White Sands Laboratory in New Mexico. At the same time, he began work on his Master of Science degree in electrical engineering at New Mexico State University.

In 1963, Posner was transferred to Bell's headquarters in New Jersey as supervisor of the Advanced Systems Design Group, where he was in charge of operation details and control systems for the Nike Zeus and Nike-X antiballistic missile programs. Posner remained in New Jersey until 1966 when he returned to New Mexico as director of the Physical Sciences Laboratory of New Mexico State University.

In 1968, Posner joined Stanford Research Institute as director of systems research and head of its Huntsville, Alabama, plant. He spent the next six years in a variety of positions within Stanford Research Institute, including assistant executive director of the engineering systems division in Menlo Park, California, and director of the Institute's Washington office where he was primarily responsible for relations with various government agencies. Prior to joining the IPC staff, Posner served Stanford Research Institute as the director of Omaha Riverfront Development Project, where he was responsible for the management of a six-county urban and rural planning and redevelopment program in the Omaha-Council Bluffs area.

In 1974, Posner was chosen to succeed John Strange as the Institute's fourth president. Posner led the Institute through its final Appleton era, turning the presidency over to Dr. Richard Matula in 1986. Posner was named President Emeritus and awarded an honorary Doctor of Science degree from Lawrence University.

Arnold E. Grummer

Originally from Latimer, Iowa, Arnold Grummer earned his bachelor of arts degree in English from the Iowa State Teacher's College at the University of Northern Iowa and his master of arts degree from Iowa State University in Speech and Creative Writing. He joined the staff of the Aid Association for Lutherans in 1957 as a member of the advertising department, a position he held until coming to the Institute in 1961.

At the Institute, Grummer held the title of Editor of General Publications. His responsibilities included the preparation and editing of non-technical institutional and academic publications as well as the preparation of news releases and other general public communications. In an interview with the Post-Crescent, Grummer once described his job as "basically that of communicating between a scientist and a non-scientist." In addition to his responsibilities as Editor, Grummer was also a faculty member in the General Studies department, where he worked with Institute students on both oral and written communications.

In 1957 Grummer began assisting the Institute's former dean, Dr. Harry Lewis, in his duties as the Curator of the Dard Hunter Paper Museum. After Lewis's death in 1969, Grummer was named Curator, a position he held until his retirement from the Institute in 1975.

When asked about the general atmosphere of the Institute throughout the 1960s and 1970s in a 2004 interview, Grummer replied, "It was a complete intellectual environment. It was a think-tank rivaling anything existing anywhere on any subject."

Arild Miller

Dr. Arild J. Miller earned his Bachelor of Arts degree from Carleton College and his PhD in physical chemistry from Purdue University. After a stint with the Manhattan Project as a research chemist at Oak Ridge, Tennessee, during World War II, Miller joined the faculty of Carleton College's Chemistry Department.

Miller remained at Carleton College until 1960, spending his last several years there as the department head. In April of 1960, he joined the staff of the Institute as a member of the dean's office administrative group holding the title of associate director of admissions. He was named director of admissions in 1962 and was appointed assistant dean in 1964 in recognition of his numerous contributions to the Institute's academic program. He retired from the Institute in 1982 as the school's associate dean and was named Emeritus Professor of Chemistry.

I'll always remember Arild Miller as my introduction to the Institute.

— Al Jones, entering class 1962

I remember being very impressed with Arild Miller and the way he interviewed – he just presented himself really well, like he was in a class of his own.

— David Graves, entering class 1975

Day and in honor of J. Sterling Morton, who founded Arbor Day. Two more of the trees were planted on the Institute grounds, while the fourth was planted at the Wisconsin State Capitol Building in Madison.

The economic recession that ravaged the United States in the early 1970s had a profound impact on the Institute. By 1972, due to soaring inflation and a wave of mergers and consolidations, more than sixty member companies had disappeared from the Institute's ranks, leaving a huge dues deficit and eventually contributing to the fiscal crisis of 1974.

The crisis, blamed on the rapid acceleration of inflation and the lack of price increase recourse from educational institutions, was solved by the immediate contribution of hundreds of thousands of dollars from the Institute's member companies and, ultimately, the raising of member dues by twenty-five percent.

These events, as well as a series of sweeping administrative changes throughout the early 1970s, led to a radical restructuring of the Institute's administrative and academic policies. The research program underwent a shift from a program of individual and group contract research projects to a program of fewer but larger

I wouldn't trade it for anything. Getting my PhD opened up doors that would not have been there otherwise.

— Rick Hartman, entering class 1977

The Institute was a great way to start my adult life. It allowed me to have a great deal of fun while I was learning, then go out and have a great career. I feel I lucked into it.

— Paula Stoppler, entering class 1975

The whole concept of being a scientific generalist has been very useful to me. One of the things I really took away from it was the ability to think about things in a different kind of way, not just the straight and narrow.

— Gail Carels, entering class 1977

coordinated projects, reflecting the technological priorities of the pulp and paper
industry. This shift was a result of the work of the Research Advisory Committee
(RAC), a nine-member group created in 1971 to serve in a consultative capacity
to the Institute's research, information, and service programs. By 1974, the RAC
had discovered that the major areas of interest to the industry were research aimed
at raw materials, reducing energy requirements, reducing capital intensiveness,
board and paper properties, and specifications that are most economically related
to end uses. Such findings led to the development of five major areas under which
Institute research projects would fall: Raw Materials Research, Energy Research,
Environmental Research, Capital Conservation Research, and Paper and Board
Performance Properties Measurement. By 1976, the Institute was carrying sixteen
major research projects that fell within one of the five categories.

The findings of the RAC and the subsequent shift in the Institute's research
program in turn played a role in the restructuring of academic programs. An
increase in student enrollment was a top priority during the first half of the 1970s,
as the Institute, like so many other academic institutions, was still feeling the effect
of the Vietnam War draft. Enrollment had climbed back up to its pre-war level of
about seventy students by the beginning of the 1973-1974 academic year, but this
still fell short of the Institute's goal of one hundred students, which would bring
enrollment to capacity with the Institute's present facilities.

By 1979, the Institute's academic committee was forced to introduce a variety
of curriculum changes designed to keep pace with the rapidly changing research
interests of the industry. Among the changes were shifting the course in the
physical chemistry of high polymers from an elective to a required course in

Hardev S. "Doug" Dugal

Originally from Dehra Dun, India, Dr. Hardev Dugal – known to Institutors as "Doug" – received his B.S. from Agra University, his A.H.B.I.T in Chemical Technology from the Harcourt Butler Technological Institute in Kampur, India, and his PhD from the Technishe Hochschule at Darmstadt, Germany.

Dugal's affiliation with the Institute began in November of 1964, when he received an appointment as a post-doctoral fellow in the physical chemistry section. He held this position until 1966, when he returned to India to conduct research.

Dugal returned to the Institute in 1969 and was appointed to the polymer chemistry group of the physical chemistry section. In 1975, based on his activism in both national and international environmental fields, Dugal was chosen to direct the Institute's new Environmental Sciences Division, a position he held for seven years. In 1982, Dugal was named director of the Information Services Division and head of the Institute's Department of Special Studies, where he remained until his retirement from the Institute in 1989.

John Strange

Born in Neenah, Wisconsin, in 1911, John Strange spent his entire professional career in a variety of positions at the Institute of Paper Chemistry. His first position, following his 1932 graduation from Lawrence College, was as administrative assistant in charge of paper codes. His administrative talents soon caught the attention of the Institute's top officers; indeed, Dr. Henry Wriston, president of Lawrence and the director of the Institute of Paper Chemistry, once said of him, "John Strange has become a skillful and an admirable administrative officer." Strange was selected as the Institute's secretary in 1936.

With the advent of World War II, Strange turned his attention to wartime duties. He played a key role in the creation of the War Products Development Section, Pulp and Paper Division, of the War Production Board, where, as the section's chief, he oversaw the development of some forty special paper products designed to meet wartime requirements. He resigned his position with the War Production Board in 1943 to return to his duties as the Institute's secretary. Following the resignation of Ralph Watts in late 1943, Strange combined his role as secretary with that of treasurer. In 1950, Strange's role at the Institute evolved into that of vice president and treasurer and, in 1955, following the retirement of Westbrook Steele, he was named the Institute's third President.

Strange's contributions to the Institute can hardly be underestimated. As the Institute's dean, Dr. Harry Lewis, once stated, "He [Strange] has a very real and constructive understanding of the purposes and objectives of the Institute and an unusual knowledge of the industry it serves." Strange's tenure as the Institute's president saw vast changes in both graduate education and in the United States paper industry. Strange handled these changes with his usual cool demeanor; under his leadership, the Institute thrived both academically and financially.

Strange retired from the Institute in 1974, turning the Institute's presidency over to Harry Posner. He was subsequently named President Emeritus and remained active in Institute affairs until his death in 1992.

Now that he is no longer with us, and it will not embarrass him to tears, I simply wish to say that I hold no man in the respect that I hold John G. Strange. His intellect, his erudition, and his person — I consider it an immense privilege to have had the opportunity to work with him. I consider him to have been the completion of my education.

— Arnold Grummer, IPC Editor of General Publications, 1960-1975

the interdisciplinary core as well as the introduction of a new course designed to present a broad overview of the technical, political, social, and economic implications of environmental protection. Special emphasis was placed on the problems and consequences of such protection for the pulp and paper industry.

The 1970s marked yet another "changing of the guard" in the Institute's record books. In 1974, Harry Posner, Jr., formerly of the Stanford Research Institute, was chosen to succeed John Strange as the Institute's fourth President. Two years later, Dr. Harry Cullinan, the former chair of the chemical engineering department at the State University of New York at Buffalo, succeeded Dr. Roy Whitney as the Institute's Dean.

As the Institute's fiftieth anniversary approached and plans for the "IPC-50" celebration began to take shape, Bruce Smart, chairman of the academic policy committee, reminded industry executives that "our future needs for educated people, dedicated to paper, are as great or greater than they have ever been," thus setting the stage for the Institute's next fifty years.

Mr. Harry Posner

It was a really interesting experience to be plowing along there, hoping that you can figure it all out - hoping that you can come up with an understanding, and a thesis, and data, something that people who have a range of views of the world will find compelling.

— **Alan Button,** entering class 1973

Mr. John Strange

What was really unique about the Institute was that it was a relatively a small group of people all studying a similar curriculum related to a particular industry. It was exciting because you knew that when you got out there were companies that were really interested in hiring you.

— **David Graves,** entering class 1975

Dr. Harry Cullinan

I really feel that the most valuable thing that I learned was how to solve problems. It's important to understand chemistry and science, but it's more important to know how to apply those things to problem solving. I discovered that once you got out into the real world of work that solving problems was really what it was all about. Teamwork was important there, just as it is important in the real world. I learned how to work well with others and how to engage people in a wide spectrum of activities.

— **Peter Balousek,** entering class 1974

Dr. Roy Whitney

The Institute's
Night Before Christmas

'TWAS THE NIGHT before Christmas and in the IPC halls,

Not a creature was stirring no one was washing the wall.

Beakers were hung in the racks with great care,

In hopes that the Nobel would soon be there.

The students were nestled all snug in their beds,

While visions of fellowships danced through their heads.

And Chuck in his last Opel and I in my cap,

Had just settled down for a long winter's nap.

When on top of the lab there arose such a clatter,

I sprang from my desk to see what was the matter.

Away to the stairwell I flew like a flash.

Tore open the door and fell on my…

The moon on the breast of the new fallen snow,

Gave a luster of midday to the objects below.

When what to my wondering eyes should appear,

But a new Buick Century and eight tiny reindeer.

With a tall, tanned driver so lively and quick,

I knew in a moment it couldn't be St. Nick!

More rapid than eagles, his coursers they came.

And he whistled and shouted and called them by name.

Now Wendall, now Doug, now Arild and Harry!

On Roy, on Earl, on John and Terry…

To the head of the Board, to a paper mill's call,

Dash away, dash away, dash away all!

As dry leaves before the wild hurricane fly,

When met with an obstacle mount to the sky,

So off to the airport the coursers they flew,

With cases of research and a proposal or two.

And then in a twinkling I heard in the halls,

The moans and groans an A-200 problem recalls.

As I drew in my head and was turning around,

My problem advisor came in with a bound.

He was dressed in lab white from his head to his foot,

And his clothes were all tarnished with precipitator soot.

A bundle of problems he had flung on his back,

And he looked like a peddler just opening his pack.

His eyes how they twinkled! His dimples how merry!

His cheeks were like roses, his nose like a cherry!

His droll little mouth was drawn up in a bow,

But the light in his eyes was cold as the snow.

He was chubby and cerebral, a right jolly old elf.

And I laughed when I saw him in spite of myself.

A wink of his eye and a twist of his head,

Soon gave me to know I had plenty to dread.

He spoke not a word but went straight to his work,

And passed out the problems, then turned with a jerk.

And laying a test tube aside of his nose,

And giving a nod, up the fume hood he rose.

He sprang to his desk, to his student gave a whistle,

And away they all flew like the down of a thistle.

But I heard him exclaim as they all ran in fright,

"Happy Christmas to all and to all a Good Night!"

The Institute Reporter
December 12, 1979

John Swanson

Born and raised in Sioux City, Iowa, John Swanson received his Bachelor of Science degree from Morningside College in 1940. After some graduate studies at Iowa State, Swanson joined the Institute staff in 1941 as a member of the physical chemistry group under Dr. George Sears. Much of Swanson's early research was focused on better adhesives and he was soon known for his expertise on the uses of materials such as guar and locust bean gum.

In 1953, the physical chemistry group was renamed the colloid chemistry group with Swanson as its group leader. He was later named director of the Institute's division of natural materials and systems, a position he held until his retirement in 1982.

Swanson's career was filled with numerous awards and honors. In 1972, he was chosen as an Outstanding Educator of America as part of a program honoring distinguished men and women for their exceptional service, achievements, and leadership in the field of education. He was presented with an honorary Doctor of Science degree from Morningside College in 1972 and an honorary Master of Science degree from Lawrence University in 1982. Considered an expert on paper surfaces, Swanson lectured at universities and research institutes throughout the United States, South America, and Europe.

John Swanson – he was absolutely the best. He was an outstanding professor.

—Robert Jones, entering class 1957

John Swanson was a very knowledgeable person. I think he was the most practical of the professors we had. He spent a lot of his time out working for member companies who had problems. Because of that, he could offer a great deal more practical knowledge about how things happened in paper mills.

—Carl Jentzen, entering class 1959

Swanson was one of my favorite professors, probably because even though he taught a lot of theory, he also tended to put things in a practical context.

—David Fary, entering class 1960

John Swanson was outstanding in the classroom.

—Jim Burke, entering class 1961

Swanson was a very effective lecturer.

—Harry Spiegelberg, entering class 1961

The thing I remember most about Swanson's class was his demonstration of the marangoni effect, which is when surface tension causes the alcohol in a martini glass to rise. We sat and watched martini glasses for a long time, waiting for the alcohol to go up and down.

—Arne Ahlen, entering class 1963

Even though he did not have a PhD, I would not exchange him for the knowledge of ten PhDs. He was a very good scientist and a very thorough scientist. He was a good teacher who conveyed the message extremely well to the students. What you learned from John were things you could apply later on in life while working in the industry. He wasn't theoretical - he was very practical. That was what we needed

—A. Nurhan Becidyan, entering class 1969

The courses I took with John Swanson taught me how to be a scientist. I remember this one time that he asked me a question in class. I got it right and he asked me how I knew it was the right answer. I told him it was a gut reaction. I'll never forget what he told me – 'Gut reactions are not just guesses - they are learned reactions. You are actually bringing together all of your learning. It is not just a guess - finally your entire education is working for you.'

—Gerry Ring, entering class 1974

Outside the
Classroom

Everyone was in the same boat - not a lot of money - so we did a lot of just getting together on Friday nights down at the Red Carpet Inn and making our own fun. Sometimes we'd have an official party, like for Halloween or Christmas, but most of the time it was just getting together to play cards or ping-pong and listen to records.

— **Gene Millard,** *entering class 1970*

We often spent a bunch of time unwinding in the Red Carpet Inn.

— **Paula Stoppler,** *entering class 1975*

We did a lot of fun things. I remember sledding – we took trays from the cafeteria and went sledding down the hill at Lawrence onto the river. We used to go cross-country skiing and snow-shoeing – a lot of winter sports. We often went to the movies and to bars - all the normal things.

— **Gail Carels,** *entering class 1977*

It was a great social scene. We always had a lot of fun.
— Alan Button, *entering class 1973*

We all lived in the student housing, so it was like our own little neighborhood.
— Peter Balousek, *entering class 1974*

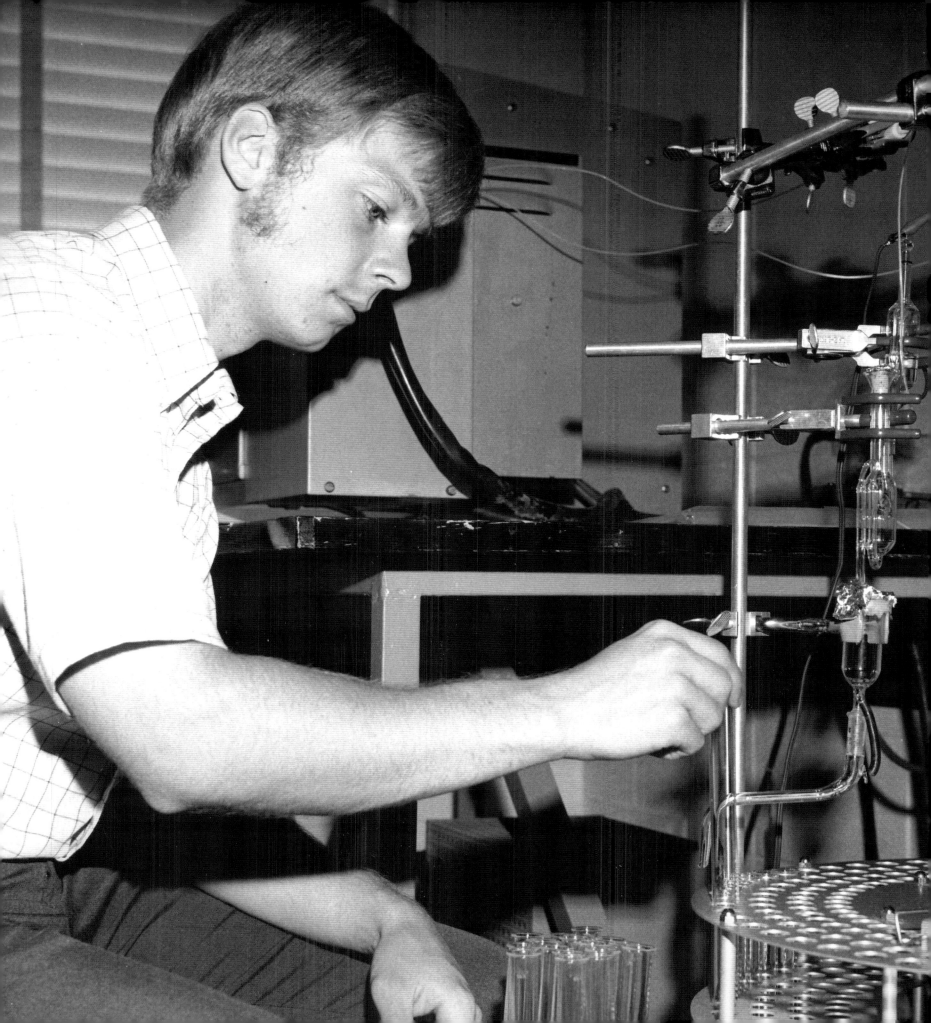

CHAPTER 6

1980-1989

The 1980s played host to the shift between the industrial era that had characterized the United States since the Gilded Age and the new information age that would become the country's future. Silicon Valley emerged as the technology capital of the world as numerous and rapid advancements were made in sectors of technology ranging from medicine to electronics. Personal computers, video game systems, and even mobile phones targeted the modern consumer.

Like the rest of the country, the Institute of Paper Chemistry strove to keep pace with the rapid technological changes....

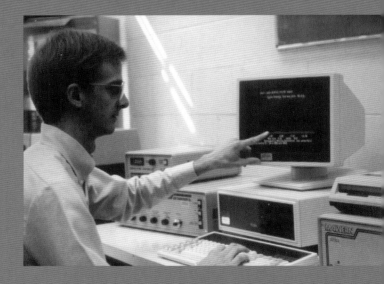

Energy was a hot topic in the United States throughout the 1970s and 1980s. Rising inflation. thriving commodity prices, the dominance of OPEC, the war between Iran and Iraq – all led to energy appearing, as Kenneth L. Fisher stated in an article in Forbes magazine, "unstoppable."

John M. Parker

THE INSTITUTE OF PAPER CHEMISTRY followed suit. At the May 1980 Executives' Conference, Dr. Douglas Wahren, vice president of research, announced that the Institute's research program would be placing a much greater emphasis on energy via a three-year energy project subsidized by the United States Department of Energy. The project focused on four areas: a study designed to identify where energy goes in a paper mill to determine if energy flows could be altered or redesigned for greater process control and efficient utilization; the development of a means of energy accounting that would assign a value to energy in its various forms according to its ability to do work; a workable definition of energy leverage points; and the identification of specific projects to reduce energy consumption in the paper industry

The early 1980s also saw the Institute striving to keep pace with the latest designs in computer technology. In 1980, a Burroughs B-6930 computer was ordered with funds from a $2.5 million fundraising drive begun in December of 1979. The new

computer. replacing the IBM computer used for the past twelve years, was delivered in 1981. It was more than ten times faster than the IBM, as well as having a vastly increased memory capacity. Designed to handle most of the Institute's scientific and administrative needs, the Burroughs B-6930 was able to

Originally from Fairfield, Connecticut, John Parker received his Bachelor of Science degree from Central Connecticut State College and his Master of Education degree from Boston University. After staff positions at Deerfield Academy, Boston University, and Union College, Parker was named dean of student personnel services at Onondaga Community College in Syracuse, New York.

Parker came to Appleton in 1966 to succeed Edgar E. Dickey as the Institute's dean of students. He held this position until the Institute's move to Atlanta in 1989. Parker was named Emeritus Dean of Students upon his retirement.

When we were on the bush trip, John Parker made us introduce ourselves every time we stopped somewhere. It was a painful experience for me because I was so shy in those days, but, looking back, I guess it was one of the things that helped me get over my shyness.
— Gerry Ring, entering class 1974

John Parker always made sure to really welcome new students to the Institute. He wanted everyone to become familiar with the campus and with Appleton and everything.
— Chris Leuttgen, entering class 1985

What I remember the most about my introduction to the Institute was that John Parker, the dean of students, made it a point to pick me up from the airport himself. It really made me feel valued like I was more than just a number to them.
— Jill Wallin, entering class 1988

communicate electronically with other data storage systems and computers in distant locations. Initially, the new computer was accessed through one of ten terminals scattered throughout the Institute; several more terminals were added by the end of the year.

By the mid-1980s, the Institute could no longer ignore the fact that the pulp and paper industry was in the midst of significant change. Foreign competition, the development of a world market, and a wave of mergers and consolidations all transformed the industry in numerous ways. These changes, in turn, affected the Institute, which depended on the industry for its survival. Static budgets, personnel reductions, and a need for major refurbishing of equipment beleaguered the administration and the board of trustees.

In February of 1986, Dr. Richard A. Matula, former Dean of Louisiana State University's College of Engineering, was named the fifth President of the Institute of Paper Chemistry, succeeding Harry A. Posner, who had held the title since 1974. Matula's first task was to initiate a strategic plan to set the stage for the future of the Institute by examining its needs and goals. By the summer of 1986, he had visited more than seventy pulp and paper industry executives to gather their thoughts and views on the direction of the industry and, subsequently, of the Institute. Utilizing Matula's findings as well as his own observations, a consultant was brought in to develop the strategic plan.

A task force was created in the spring of 1987, and by the following fall, was ready to present its conclusions to the Institute's board of trustees. A world-class pulp and paper institute that was capable of producing technologically excellent graduates who could also be team builders based upon cross-disciplinary knowledge was necessary, the task force concluded, in order for the United States pulp and paper industry to be competitive into the twenty-first century. Access to a large research university, the task force further advised, would be the key step in facilitating the plan.

The task force had already looked into several possible locations. The Institute wanted, according to an interview with Dr. Matula in 1989, "to be close to a university known for its accomplishments in technological research and to be close to a major city that could offer Institute employees a high quality of life." Further

It was a lot of fun – a good time in my life. The camaraderie among the students was excellent. It was a great education and it served you really well once you were out in the industry.

— **Steve Jones,** entering class 1984

criteria included proximity to other research centers and to an international airport with regular and reliable air service to different parts of the world. The Georgia Institute of Technology in Atlanta met – and exceeded – the criteria. Georgia Tech and the State of Georgia were eager to cooperate with the Institute. The state offered more than $12 million in relocation funds, while the Georgia Board of Regents donated almost five acres of land for the construction of a new building and Georgia Tech offered to build a new parking lot adjacent to the new building. In addition, the Institute's member companies, noting that the new location was a hub of the pulp and paper industry with the potential to become an international pulp and paper center, agreed to pay double the amount of their annual dues for a period of two and a half years a sum of more than $18 million.

On December 11, 1987, the Institute's Board of Trustees approved the plan to create an alliance with the Georgia Institute of Technology and relocate the Institute to Atlanta, stating that with the move, the Institute would be "establishing a close

Thomas M. Grace

Originally from Beaver Dam, Wisconsin, Thomas M. Grace received his Bachelor of Science degree in chemical engineering from the University of Wisconsin-Madison in 1960 and his PhD, also in chemical engineering, from the University of Minnesota in 1963. After receiving his doctorate, Grace spent two years as an aerospace technologist conducting experimental and analytical studies at NASA's Lewis Research Center in Cleveland, Ohio.

Grace joined the staff of the Institute of Paper Chemistry in December of 1965 as a member of the technology section. He was named chairman of the Institute's Department of Engineering in 1970, a position he held until 1974. Grace then served as a professor and a senior research associate until the Institute's move to Atlanta in 1989. He held an adjunct professorship at the Institute from 1989 to 1994, then a part-time position from 1995 to 1997. Upon his retirement, Grace was named Professor Emeritus.

Grace's research interests lay in the field of chemical recovery. In 1971, he began what proved to be groundbreaking research in the field by applying basic chemistry and heat transfer principles to the problem of black liquor fouling. The results of his research became the basis for improved design and operation of black liquor evaporators over next three decades.

Grace's career was filled with numerous awards and honors. While a professor at the Institute, he advised eleven doctoral candidates, all of whom received their PhD degrees. He taught five different academic courses in areas ranging from thermodynamics to the recovery of pulping chemicals. He received the AIChE Forest Products Division Award in 1984 and was named a TAPPI Fellow in 1987. In 2001, he was honored with the Gunnar Nicholson Gold Medal.

I had the good fortune to join Tom's research group at the Institute in 1976. I count the four years I spent there with Tom as the most important in shaping my career. Tom was a great mentor and a great teacher.

— Dr. William James Frederick, Jr., Director
Institute of Paper Science and Technology at Georgia Tech
2003 - present

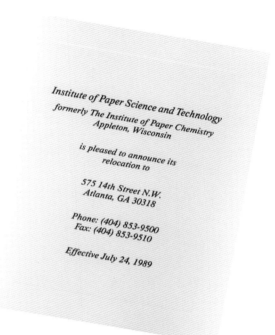

Institute of Paper Science and Technology
formerly The Institute of Paper Chemistry
Appleton, Wisconsin

is pleased to announce its
relocation to

575 14th Street N.W.
Atlanta, GA 30318

Phone: (404) 853-9500
Fax: (404) 853-9510

Effective July 24, 1989

alliance with a major research university that has significant strengths in engineering and science, offering [Institute] students and professors access to computers and laboratory facilities that it could not afford in Appleton."

By the following spring, the decision was made to relocate the Institute in the summer of 1989. Each member of the Institute's two hundred and twenty-five member staff was invited to move with the Institute. Throughout the summer and

fall of 1988, the Institute financed several short trips to Atlanta, allowing Institute employees and their families to see the area for themselves. Ultimately, more than one-third of the staff – the majority of them senior staff members – decided to relocate with the Institute, while the others opted for retirement or moving on to other jobs.

By the spring of 1989, the Institute had leased from the Georgia Tech Foundation a building on the corner of 14th Street and Hemphill Street to be used as a temporary

facility until a permanent home could be constructed on the land donated by the Georgia Board of Regents at the corner of 10th Street and Hemphill Street on the western edge of the Georgia Tech campus. Renovation began in mid-April to ready the building for occupancy the following July.

In June, shortly after the Institute graduated its 1,302nd – and final – student from its Appleton campus, the school's accreditation was transferred from the North-Central Association of Colleges and Schools to the Southern Association of Colleges and Schools. June 30, 1989,

They trained me, they educated me, and they made me challenge myself. It was a very positive experience and I enjoyed it immensely. I would definitely say that I am the man I am today because I went there.

— **Russell Ross**, entering class 1988

It was a really positive experience for me – excellent preparation for my later training in chemical engineering.

— **Peter Ryan**, entering class 1983

Gwen Redding

Gwen Redding received her Bachelor of Science degree from Kansas State University and her Master of Science degree from Louisiana State University. From 1972 to 1975, she held two governor-appointed jobs in the Louisiana state government, first as the director of the Louisiana Bureau of Women and later as the deputy director of the Louisiana Division of Human Services. In 1975, Redding joined the staff of Louisiana State University as the director of Equal Opportunities Programs. In 1978, she transferred to the university's College of Engineering, where she served as the director of Engineering Services, assistant to the dean for administrative activities, and the director of Minority Programs.

Redding came to the Institute in 1987 as a consultant. A year later, she was named vice president of administration and corporate secretary. As the Institute's chief administrative and financial officer, Redding was largely responsible for organizing the Institute's 1989 move to Atlanta, working closely with the moving company to facilitate the process. In Atlanta, Redding played a significant role in the interior design of the Paper Tricentennial Building, which was completed in 1993.

Redding's administrative duties at the Institute include direct supervision of the graphics and publications department, the library, the museum, building maintenance, and the abstractors. She left the Institute in 1996 to return to the private sector.

Harry T. Cullinan, Jr.

Dr. Harry T. Cullinan, Jr., received his Bachelor of Science degree in chemical engineering from the University of Detroit in 1961 and his Master of Science and PhD degrees from the Carnegie Institute of Technology in 1963 and 1965, respectively. Before entering academia, Cullinan worked as a research engineer at Avon Cosmetics and Westinghouse Research and as a consultant to the Nuclear Materials and Equipment Company and the Western New York Nuclear Research Center in Buffalo.

In 1964, Cullinan joined the faculty of the State University of New York at Buffalo. He was named chair of the chemical engineering department in 1969, a position he held until his appointment to the Institute's staff.

In the spring of 1976, Cullinan was chosen to succeed Dr. Roy Whitney as the Institute's dean. In 1977, he was given the additional title of Vice President of Academic Affairs. Cullinan also served the Institute as a senior research associate, focusing much of his research on brownstock washing, stock refining, and recycled fiber. Cullinan left the Institute in 1987.

Earl W. Malcolm

After receiving his Bachelor of Science degree from Western Michigan University, Earl Malcolm entered the Institute of Paper Chemistry as a first-year student in 1959. He received his Master of Science degree in 1961 and his PhD in 1964.

Malcolm spent two years as a research chemist for Dow Chemical's James River Division and eleven years as a project manager in the product development department at Connecticut's C.H. Dexter and Sons before returning to the Institute as a senior research associate and director of the Institute's delignification division in 1976.

Malcolm advised more than fifty doctoral students during his twenty-four year tenure at the Institute. He held five patents and authored and coauthored numerous books and papers. In 1988, Malcolm received the Joseph K. Perkins Leadership and Service Award for TAPPI's Pulp Manufacture Division. He was named the Institute's associate Vice President of Research in 1999, a position he held until his retirement in 2000.

Dr. Malcolm had a wealth of knowledge and a great sense of humor.

— Brian Boyer, entering class 199

marked the last day of work for Institute employees not relocating to Atlanta, and on July 7, the first employees reported for work at the Industrial Research Facility to unpack the approximately one hundred truckloads of Institute furniture, equipment, and materials that made the nine hundred-mile trip from Appleton to Atlanta.

On August 1, 1989, the formal agreement between the Institute of Paper Science and Technology and the Georgia Institute of Technology was signed by IPST president Dr. Richard Matula and Georgia Tech president Dr. John Patrick Crecine. As Dr. Matula stated in an interview printed in the TAPPI Journal shortly after the signing, "With our new facilities and association with Georgia Tech, we will produce graduates who will help the industry be competitive into the twenty-first century." On September 20, the students of the Institute of Paper Science and Technology, sixteen of them first-years, began their first full day of classes in Atlanta.

The Institute was a family environment that prided itself on producing the best possible future leaders of the pulp and paper industry.

— Mick Beck, entering class 1985

It was a sad and memorable time, wandering around the empty, silent buildings at the end of the first era of the 'Tute. There were laboratories, meeting rooms. and offices, which, once upon a time, were full of activity and excitement with experiments, lectures, PAC meetings, and seminars. It was a ghost structure, reminiscent of past glory and proud history. The laboratories were the places where many of the great inventions related to pulping and papermaking were made, the working environments of the brightest and most skillful people dedicated to our industry. The classrooms were places where the masters in paper chemistry, pulping, lignin, cellulose, hemicellulose, wood chemistry, paper physics, papermaking, and recovery taught. What a privilege to be their pupils!

— Nick Triantafillopoulos,
entering class 1984

Richard Matula

Originally from Chicago, Richard Matula received his Bachelor of Science, Master of Science, and PhD degrees, all in mechanical engineering, from Purdue University. After completing his doctorate in 1964, Matula began his career in academia, teaching in a variety of undergraduate, graduate, and post-doctoral settings at the University of Michigan, the University of California, and Purdue University.

Matula's experience in academic administration began at Drexel University, where he served as the chairman of the mechanical engineering and mechanics department, director of the Environmental Studies Institute, and chairman of the thermal and fluid science group. He joined the faculty of Louisiana State University as the Dean of the College of Engineering in 1976.

Matula was chosen by the Institute's Board of Trustee to serve as President of the Institute of Paper Chemistry in late 1985 and assumed his duties in February of 1986. He left the Institute in 1995.

Dr. Matula was a visionary person with not only the perception but also the management ability to put necessary things in motion for accomplishing the vision. He often worked twelve and sixteen hour days and weekends in order to plan and outline the work necessary to attain change in institutions. Throughout his career, he was known as an administrator who could 'turn things around.'
— Gwen E. Redding, Vice President of Administration, Institute of Paper Science and Technology, 1987-1996

Dr. Matula was always smiling. I really enjoyed working with him.
— Connie Ford Adams, Administrative Assistant to the President, Institute of Paper Science and Technology, 1989 - present

Donald R. Dimmel

Donald R. Dimmel received his Bachelor of Science degree from the University of Minnesota in 1962 and his PhD degree in organic chemistry from Purdue University in 1966. After a post-doctoral position at New York's Cornell University, Dimmel spent four years as a senior research chemist at Hercules, Inc., in Wilmington, Delaware. He was a member of the faculty at Marquette University when he accepted a position as a research associate and a professor of chemistry at the Institute of Paper Chemistry in 1978.

Dimmel's research interests lay in the area of wood chemistry. He is considered an expert in the fundamental organic chemistry associated with pulping and bleaching reactions, including lignin and carbohydrate degradation reactions. While on the Institute's faculty, Dimmel served as an advisor to ten doctoral candidates and was honored with the Teacher of the Year Award twice. He authored or coauthored more than one hundred publications, including the book Lignins and Lignans, which was published in 2006. He retired from the Institute in 2002 as a professor, a senior fellow, and the leader of the process chemistry unit.

Dr. Dimmel was a character. I really enjoyed his sense of humor. He was an excellent pool player, too. I remember quite a few students being humbled by his skills at the pool table at the Red Carpet Inn.
— Tom Merchant, entering class 1987

Don Dimmel was a great organic chemist.
— Brian Boyer, entering class 1991

I use to play racquetball with Dr. Dimmel at SAC. The problem was that I was 5'5" and Dr. Dimmel was over six feet tall. I was afraid that he was going to hit me when he was swinging his racquet with his long arms, so I would be way up against the wall of the court. Then he would make a nice shot to the opposite side of the court. I could never react fast enough to recover and he would most often win the point. It really was a lot of fun, even though I lost a lot!
— Karen Turnboom, entering class 1991

Outside the Classroom

Friday afternoons were always a great time at the Institute. The RCI usually stocked inexpensive beers, but on Friday afternoons, we would always buy a few cases of more expensive beer. It was a great chance to socialize with the other students and even some of the faculty members.

— **Chris Luettgen,** entering class 1985

Wisconsin was a great place. We were really a part of the town – you'd be surprised at how many Institute students married Appleton girls. We always had a great time in the local bars, especially Cleo's, which was my favorite.

— **Pete Westervelt,** entering class 1980

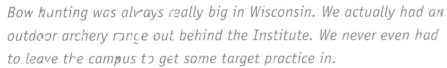

Bow hunting was always really big in Wisconsin. We actually had an outdoor archery range out behind the Institute. We never even had to leave the campus to get some target practice in.

— **Mick Beck,** entering class 1935

We spent a lot of time at the Red Carpet Inn, our own little bar and pool room in the basement of the resident hall. It was great place to relax and have a few beers after class.

— **Andrew Jones,** entering class 1985

Lots of athletics activities – we'd play racquetball, basketball, golf, football. I remember one particular football game – it was the middle of winter and there was about two feet of snow on the ground. We played a really physical game of tackle football in the snow.

— **Steve Jones,** entering class 1984

The Bush Trip
in the 1980s

I remember my time at the Institute as one of the few times in my life that I was solely focused on learning and not on worrying about what I was going to do afterwards. It was an outstanding experience and I wouldn't trade it for anything.

— **Pete Westervelt,** entering class 1980

My favorite memory of the bush trip is a discus-throwing competition that we had late one night. We used tree slices in lieu of an actual discus!

— **Andrew Jones,** entering class 1985

It was a great social occasion – a chance for us to get to know one another. Wisconsin is a fun place and we ended up going out a lot, which led to one really funny incident. One night, we stayed at this bar longer than anyone else. We were completely lost; we had no idea where Trees for Tomorrow was. We were wandering around the town trying to figure out how to get back when we came across the only building that still had its lights on – the police station. We went in and asked for directions. This one cop was kind enough to give us a ride back to the camp. I'm sure that made a great impression on our classmates and professors – us coming back in a police car!

— **Pete Westervelt,** entering class 1980

Since I had grown up in northern Wisconsin, I had been to most of those place a million times. But it was still an incredible start to the Institute experience. Of course, it was even more incredible for me because I met my future wife on that trip!

— **Russell Ross,** entering class 1988

It was a lot of tedious work, but it was also a lot of fun. I remember playing volleyball at the Eagle River camp and going into the town to see "A Fish Called Wanda," which had just come out.

— **Jill Wallin,** entering class 1988

I feel very fortunate to have had the opportunity to attend the Institute and learn everything that they were teaching there. Wherever it is located, I still feel the need to be a strong supporter of it, to give back to it in return for all it has given me.

— **Chris Luettgen,** entering class 1985

CHAPTER 7

1990-1999

If *the key theme of the 1980s* was rapid technological change, then the theme of the 1990s was the improvement and mainstreaming of those technolgies. The popularization of personal computers during the 1980s led to what is commonly know as the "dot-com boom" and the creation of the World Wide Web during the 1990s; an increased interest in the mysteries of outer space led to greater space exploration and a revolution in astronomy with the launching of the Hubble Telescope in 1990.

The Institute, too, faced what was perhaps the most significant change in its sixty-year history during the 1980s – a complete relocation. After settling in Atlanta during the summer of 1989, the Institute was faced with the challenge of making the most of its new facilities and educational program...

Students, faculty, and staff quickly settled into the routine of life at the new Institute of Paper Science and Technology. Classes were held and research was conducted – indeed, the pace was quite similar to that of the Appleton campus.

IN OCTOBER OF 1989, Charles E. "Chuck" Miller successfully defended his dissertation on the effects of polymer partitioning on fines retention, marking the first successful defense in the Institute of Paper Science and Technology's brief history. Five months later, on March 25, 1990, the Institute held its first commencement exercises in the Georgia Pacific Auditorium on Peachtree Street, awarding sixteen Master of Science degrees and six PhD degrees. A short six months after that, in September of 1990, a full class of thirty students began their coursework at the Institute.

James L. Ferris

Dr. James L. Ferris received his Bachelor of Science degree in chemical engineering from the University of Washington in 1966. After a stint at the Weyerhaeuser Company as a project engineer in the Everett Kraft Mill, he applied to graduate school at the Institute of Paper Chemistry and was accepted as a member of the entering class of 1967.

Ferris fondly remembers the familial atmosphere that was such a part of Institute life. "When you first arrived at the Institute," he recalls, "you were immediately welcomed into this huge, sprawling family. As soon as you got your keys from the dean and got settled, they would take you around and introduce you to everybody. Then they'd take your picture. As soon as they could, they'd distribute your picture to every professor, administrator, and secretary and they would all memorize your face and your name. So you'd be walking down the street or down the hall and people would call out 'Hey, Jim! How're you doing? All moved in? How do you like it so far?' It was simply amazing."

Ferris received his Master of Science degree from the Institute in 1969 and his PhD in 1974, spending the years 1970 to 1972 at the Naval Officer Candidate School in Newport, Rhode Island, and serving as a line officer on destroyers in the Western Pacific. He returned to Weyerhaeuser in 1974 as a bleaching scientist in the company's research division. A few years later, he became a global technical service manager, traveling around the world introducing new products and troubleshooting problems with existing products. Ferris spent the next fifteen years moving between a variety of positions in the company's research and business divisions. He was named vice president of research and development in 1988, a position he officially held until December 31, 1995.

In June of 1995, Ferris was asked to serve a temporary six-month term as the vice president of research at the Institute of Paper Science and Technology. He accepted the position and was instrumental in shaping the Institute's short-term strategic plan. Impressed with Ferris's experience and leadership skills, the Institute's Board of Trustees asked Ferris to become a candidate in the search for a new president. Initially hesitant, Ferris eventually entered his name. He was selected in late 1995.

Ferris's responsibilities as the sixth president of the Institute of Paper Science and Technology began on January 1, 1996. Working with Dr. Ronald Estridge, another Institute alum who had served as the Institute's interim president from June 1995 to December 1995, Ferris set as one of his immediate goals the re-creation of the familial atmosphere that he was so familiar with from his own time in Appleton. "I wanted to get the Institute back to some of its basic principles," he said. "When the students showed up to begin their graduate studies, I wanted everyone to know their names and faces, just like everyone at the Institute in Appleton had known mine."

Ferris retired from his position as the Institute's president in June of 2003. At the 2003 PIMA Annual International Management Conference, he was presented with the Lifetime Achievement Award in recognition for his years of dedicated service to the international pulp and paper industry.

I have nothing but the highest regard for Jim Ferris. He did an outstanding job managing things through a very difficult period and he was able to keep the Institute focused on both its educational responsibilities and its responsibilities to the industry.

— Paul Saueracker, Trustee,
Institute of Paper Science and Technology,
1997 – 2003

Dr. Ferris was a great president who always had a plan. And had it not been for him, I would have never read the book Who Moved My Cheese? *!*
— Connie Ford Adams
Administrative Assistant to the President,
Institute of Paper Science and Technology,
1989 - present

It quickly became apparent that the facilities at the Industrial Research Facility were ill-equipped for the number of students and faculty conducting research there. A new, much larger building was critical to the Institute's success.

Drawings and bid documents for the planned facility at the corner of 10th Street and Hemphill Street were finalized in February of 1990. A groundbreaking ceremony was held on May 10.

The Paper Tricentennial Building was completed in September of 1992. The

161,000-square-foot, five-story structure, built at a cost of $28.7 million, contained sixty-four laboratories, three classrooms, one hundred and seven private offices, six conference rooms, an executive conference room, a boardroom, a library, a large auditorium, a seminar room, and space for a museum.

The months of April and May of 1993 were a time of dedications and celebrations. On April 6, 1993, the library was dedicated in the name of Dr. William R. Haselton, who had made a significant gift for its development. Haselton, an Institute alumnus who had recently retired from a successful career in the pulp and paper industry, was honored with a plaque reading "This library is dedicated to William R. Haselton in recognition of his long association with the Institute of

Paper Science and Technology as student, alumnus, trustee, and donor; and for his many professional and managerial achievements during the course of a distinguished career in the pulp and paper industry."

Two days later, the Institute held an enormous celebration in honor of the dedication of the Paper Tricentennial Building (PTB). Governor Zell Miller, former governor Joe Frank Harris, and Dr. H. Dean Propst, the chancellor of the Board of Regents of the University System of Georgia, attended the festivities. Finally, on May 6, 1993, a reception was held celebrating the completion of the American Museum of Papermaking.

The new state-of-the-art facilities in the PTB led to a massive reorganization of the Institute's research divisions. The Research Services Division was created to provide focus for research service activities within IPST and to enhance technical support for industry. Dr. Barry Crouse was named director of the division, which included the Institute's chemical analysis, microscopy and fiber analysis, optical properties, and paper analysis groups.

The Chemical and Biological Sciences Division was reorganized with Dr. Earl

The people I met while I was a student at the Institute left a very profound impression on me. My classmates, my professors – I received what I feel is a world-class education.

— **Coray Harper,** entering class 1993

Malcolm as its director to focus its efforts on improving raw materials and their conversion into pulp for papermaking and other applications. Chemical recovery, corrosion and materials engineering, forest biology, pulping and bleaching, and wood chemistry were all a part of the division. Finally, the Engineering and Paper Materials Division was created to focus on the manufacture, characterization, and performance of paper and related materials. Dr. Richard Ellis was named division director, supervising the container research, paper physics, papermaking, process simulation and control, and surface science groups.

Sweeping administrative changes were part of life at the Institute during the mid-1990s. In early 1995, Dr. Richard Matula, who had been the Institute's President since 1986, resigned from the position to return to the private sector. Shortly thereafter, Dr. Ronald Estridge, an Institute alum who had recently retired from a long and very successful career at the James River Corporation, was asked to serve as interim president for a six-month period until a new president could be chosen.

Estridge's time as the Institute's President, however brief, was the beginning of a new era at the Institute. As Dr. Robert Moran,

David Orloff

Originally from Philadelphia, Dr. David Orloff received his Bachelor of Science and Master of Science degrees, both in mechanical engineering, from Drexel University. He received his PhD degree in Applied Mechanics, also from Drexel, in 1974. His thesis research, supported by funding from the U.S. Air Force, involved elucidating the chemical kinetics of fluorocarbon and oxygen flames.

From 1974 through 1983, Orloff was a faculty member at the University of South Carolina, where he taught courses in thermodynamics, statistical thermodynamics, fluid mechanics, heat transfer, mass transfer, combustion, material science, and process design in the school's mechanical engineering department. In 1983, he joined the staff of the Kendall Company, first as the section head of the web forming and thermal bonding research section and later as the program manager of the non-wovens research section.

In 1988, Orloff became a faculty member at the Institute of Paper Science and Technology, teaching courses in thermodynamics, heat transfer, mass transfer, and papermaking processes. In 1992, he was named director of the engineering and paper materials division, a position he held until 1997.

Since 1988, Orloff has led the Institute's research efforts on the development of impulse drying technology, focusing on mathematical analysis and experimental investigation of the de-watering of paper via new pressing and drying concepts. His research resulted in eight United States patents and numerous associated foreign patents, as well as a series of pilot paper machine trials at the Beloit Corporation.

In 1999, Orloff was named the Institute's assistant vice president of research and technology transfer. Shortly thereafter, he became dean of research and technology transfer, responsible for the management of internally and externally funded research programs, interfacing with the member companies through the research advisory committee, working with federal agencies to identify new funding opportunities, and assuring the rapid transfer of technology to member companies.

Since the Institute's merger with Georgia Tech in 2003, Orloff has served as a professor of engineering in the George W. Woodruff School of Mechanical Engineering. His current research involves development of an understanding of pore expansion during flash evaporation in moist paper webs, which holds the potential to enhance the benefits of impulse drying.

Dr. Richard Matula

Dr. Ronald Estridge

Dr. James L. Ferris

entering class 1966 and past chairman of the Institute's alumni association, pointed out, "his [Estridge's] brief tenure was invaluable in bringing about a new and sharper focus on spending, research direction, and most importantly, a customer-focused approach to IPST's activities."

Estridge served as the Institute's President until January 1, 1996, when Dr. James L. Ferris, another Institute alum, took the reins. Ferris, who had worked for Weyerhaeuser in a variety of positions since 1974, most recently as Vice President of Research and Development, had come to the Institute during the summer of 1995 to serve a six-month term as the vice president of research. During the fall of 1995, Ferris was asked by the search committee to become a candidate for IPST president. He agreed, and was selected by the committee in late 1995.

Ferris went on to continue many of the programs initiated by Estridge, including the restructuring of senior faculty and research and technical staff and the revitalization of the Institute's employee council. Also important on Ferris's agenda was the creation of two vice presidential positions. Woody Rice, who had been with the Institute as a consultant since 1993, was chosen for Vice President of Development, while Dr. Gary Baum, a former Institute faculty member who had most recently served as the chairman of the Department of Wood and Paper Science at North Carolina State University, was named Vice President of Research and Academic Affairs. Gwen Redding, who had been with the Institute since 1988 as Vice President of Administration, left the Institute in 1996.

Within two years of Ferris's appointment as the Institute's President, the Institute had gained fifty-five new faculty and staff. His goal, which was attained in 1998, was a staff of two hundred and fifty.

The Institute's academic program experienced several major transitions in 1999. In August, Georgia Tech underwent what was commonly known as the "Semester Conversion," a program legislated by the Georgia Board of Regents to effectively end the quarter system. In order to maintain an identical academic calendar with Georgia Tech, IPST made the conversion as well. The Master's program, which had been a six-quarter program since 1992, was now four semesters. This led to a reorganization of some of the Institute's traditional courses, with several being merged to accommodate the longer semesters.

It was also during the fall of 1999 that the Management Sciences Certificate Program, which was begun in 1998, began to gain recognition. A joint program with Georgia Tech's Dupree College of Management, the certificate required two courses in Business Skills for Technology Managers and Leadership and Technology Management, both taught by IPST faculty, as well as a third course chosen from the Dupree College's elective menu on a subject such as negotiation and conflict resolution, international business environments, managing resources in the technology firm, or processes of technological innovation.

Gary A. Baum

Dr. Gary A. Baum received his Bachelor of Science degree in math and physics from Wisconsin State University and his Master of Science and PhD degrees in physics from Oklahoma State University. He joined the staff of the Institute of Paper Chemistry in 1969 as a research associate and an associate professor of physics. He was named group leader of the physical chemistry group in 1974 and was appointed director of the paper materials division in 1987.

Baum left the Institute in 1988 to join the James River Corporation as the director of Corporate R&D. In 1994, he left James River to become the chairman of the department of wood and paper science at North Carolina State University, a position he held until returning to the Institute as Vice President of Research and Academic Affairs in May of 1996.

Possessing excellent personal and technical reputations within the industry and academia, Baum succeeded in providing strong intellectual, technical, and administrative leadership in planning, coordinating, and maintaining the Institute's academic program and its research divisions. He retired from the Institute in June of 2002 to start his own company, Paper-Future Technologies LCC, which is devoted to applications of new techniques and uses for paper.

Gary Baum was a tough guy, but fair, very fair. He expected the best out of the students, and he usually got it.

— Rick Hartman, entering class 1977

Dr. Baum always amazed me with his high levels of professionalism and depth of knowledge. He was a fountain of information.

— Jerry Sajbel, entering class 1977

William R. Haselton

Originally from Glen Falls, New York, Dr. William R. Haselton became interested in engineering at an early age. After three years in the Navy, eight months of which he spent in the Philippines, he enrolled at Rensselaer Polytechnic Institute and received his Bachelor of Science degree in chemical engineering in the spring of 1949. He entered the Institute of Paper Chemistry the following fall.

Haselton remembers the challenges of being a student at the Institute. "The professors were very professional, very stern. Most had been teaching since before World War II, which took them back into a definite, distinct era in academia. They taught you well, but there wasn't any room for diversion."

Haselton still prides himself on the discipline he was generally able to maintain while he was a student at the Institute. "I was married, I had a child, I was living in a Quonset hut, and I had only a minimal income, so there was a lot of motivation there for me to finish up and get a real job," he recalls. Haselton's discipline ultimately paid off, for his tenure as an Institute student was filled with awards and honors. In 1950, he was the winner of the annual student award given by the Paper and Twine Association, selected by the Institute for exceptional accomplishment. In 1953, he was awarded the Westbrook Steele gold medal for outstanding thesis work for his research on gas absorption of wood and gas absorption techniques in studying paper pulp structure.

After graduating from the Institute in 1953, Haselton joined the staff of Rhinelander Paper Company as technical director. When Rhinelander was acquired by St. Regis Paper Company in 1956, Haselton went on to assume a variety of positions in the new company, including

vice president and general manager of the forest products division and senior vice president for timberlands and forest products. In 1958, he was named executive vice president of operation, responsible for all operations of the Rhinelander plant with the exception of sales and corporate financial matters.

Haselton was elected Director of St. Regis Paper Company in 1972 and President in 1973. In 1979, he was elected Chief Executive Officer, and he was named Chairman of the Board in 1981. When St. Regis merged with Champion International Corporation in 1984, Haselton became Vice Chairman and a member of the board of board of directors.

Haselton's contributions to the United States pulp and paper industry have been numerous. He was named Papermaker of the Year in 1982 and Packaging Man of the Year in 1989. He served as president and chairman of the board of the National Forest Products Association and was a member of the executive committee of the American Paper Institute. Haselton was also a member of the IPST board of trustees from 1979 through 1988, serving on the executive committee and as chairman of the finance committee.

In 1992, Haselton contributed a substantial monetary gift to the Institute, stating that "several years ago I reached a decision that the Institute had made a major difference in my business career and my life in general. And for this reason, I became interested in showing my appreciation in some appropriate and tangible way." The William R. Haselton Library was dedicated on April 6, 1993.

Over the years, there's never been a doubt in my mind that choosing the opportunity for graduate study at the Institute was an extremely key element in what turned out to be an interesting and rather successful lifetime involvement with the forest products industry. I have to say it was one of the most stimulating and most rewarding and most interesting experiences of my life.

— Dr. William R. Haselton, April 3, 1993

Bill's ongoing generosity and commitment to IPST's future growth as the international center of technical excellence in the field of pulp and paper in one more milestone in the development of the Institute and a shining example of the ongoing support if IPST's alumni.

— Dr. James Ferris, President
Institute of Paper Science and Technology
1996-2003

Barry Crouse

Dr. Barry Crouse received his Bachelor of Science degree from Rutgers University in 1967, his Master of Science degree from the University of Maine in 1968, and his PhD from Duke University in 1972. He spent twenty-two years in the paper technology development division of Eastman Kodak, leaving in 1989 to join the staff of the Institute of Paper Science and Technology as a professor of chemistry and the director of the research services division.

Crouse left the Institute in late 1993 to establish his own consulting firm, but returned in July of 1995 to take the position of director of academic affairs. "I really wanted to be part of the team to help guide the Institute through this transition period," he said in 1995, referring to the sweeping administrative changes that were occurring at the time.

As the Institute's dean, Crouse focused on increasing the number of incoming students each year and on helping those students find positions in the industry following graduation. He was primarily responsible for the creation of a dual degree program with Georgia Tech and played a large role in integrating the Institute's academic program into Tech's. Dr. Crouse passed away in 2003.

Barry was the best sort of teacher, the kind who helped you set foot on the path of discovery to find out who you might be and what you might become. He would be uncomfortable to see you scarring your knees and scraping your knuckles, but he would not interfere with the growing process, beyond a few gentle but pointed words.

— Giselle Ow Yang, entering class 1994

Barry Crouse was one of my favorites. I always appreciated his guidance.

— Georgia Caruthers Malinsky, entering class 2000

Ronald Estridge

Originally from High Point, North Carolina, Dr. Ronald B. Estridge received his Bachelor of Science degree in chemical engineering from North Carolina State University in 1956 and his Master of Science and PhD degrees from the Institute of Paper Chemistry in 1959 and 1961, respectively. While at the Institute, Estridge was honored with the NPTA Award for Outstanding First Year Student and the Westbrook Steele Gold Medal for his thesis: "The Initial Retention of Fibers by Wire Grids."

After a stint in the United States Army stationed at Valley Station, Kentucky, Estridge joined the Albemarle Paper Manufacturing Company in Richmond, Virginia, as a senior development engineer. In 1974, he joined James River as the vice president of corporate development and executive vice president of the company's Massachusetts subsidiary. After serving the company in a variety of capacities, including group vice president of industrial specialties, executive vice president responsible for specialty and communications paper, and vice president and group executive of specialty paper, Estridge retired from James River as the senior vice president of technology in October of 1994.

In the spring of 1995, Estridge was chosen by the Institute's Board of Trustees to serve as the Institute's interim president following the resignation of Dr. Richard Matula, making him the first president who was also an Institute alumnus. Estridge was succeeded by another Institute alum, Dr. Jim Ferris, in January of 1996.

Everything I did was a true labor of love.
— Dr. Ronald B. Estridge, Appleton, Wisconsin, August 1996

Dr. Estridge was always extremely kind and thoughtful. I remember we had a United Way drawing and the prize was a roundtrip ticket anywhere in the continental United States. Dr. Estridge won the drawing! As he received his prize, we all heard someone in the back of the room shout 'give it to your secretary.' And he did! I couldn't believe it! I used the ticket to visit my parents in Arizona.
— Connie Ford Adams, Administrative Assistant to the President, Institute of Paper Science and Technology, 1989 - present

Richard L. Ellis

Dr. Richard Ellis received his Bachelor of Science and Master of Science degrees from Marshall University and completed his PhD at the University of Cincinnati in 1972. After fifteen years with Union Camp Corporation in a variety of technical positions, Ellis joined the staff of the Institute of Paper Science and Technology in September of 1989 as the director of the engineering and paper materials division, which focuses on the manufacture, characterization, and performance of paper and related materials. In addition to his duties as the division's director, Ellis was also a professor of engineering, with his research focused on paper physics, the dynamics of paper webs, and fluid mechanics.

In 1993, Ellis was named the Institute's vice president of research and academic affairs, making him IPST's chief scientific and academic officer. He left the Institute in 1995.

Dick Ellis was a very gregarious man, a very fun-loving guy. He had great rapport with the students.

— Brian Boyer, entering class 1991

Thomas J. McDonough

Dr. Thomas J. McDonough received his B.A. Sc., his M.A. Sc., and his PhD degrees from the University of Toronto, finishing in 1972. After several years in the paper and allied industries, he joined the staff of the Institute of Paper Chemistry in 1978 as a research associate and a professor of engineering.

McDonough was one of approximately eighty-five Institute faculty and staff members who relocated to Atlanta in 1989. Throughout his tenure, McDonough served as a professor, chairman of academic council, faculty chairman, associate vice president of research and academic affairs, and associate director of academic affairs. He directed numerous research projects in the science and technology of pulp manufacture, with emphasis on the technology, chemistry, kinetics, and environmental implications of pulp manufacture. McDonough served as advisor to sixteen doctoral candidates and published more than forty journal articles and book chapters throughout his career. He was named a TAPPI Fellow in 1995.

In 2000, based on his technical and academic experience, McDonough was named Center Director for the Center for Paper Business and Industry Studies (CPBIS). He retired from the Institute in 2002, although he continues to serve as the part-time Director Emeritus of CPBIS.

Tom McDonough likes to tell a story about how when people came to interview for faculty positions at the Institute, the hiring committees would always put them out in front of the Friday afternoon seminar crowd. Most of the graduate students were there. Tom says he vividly remembers me going after him about some of the ways he was presenting his information and analyzing all his answers!

— Alan Button, entering class 1973

Dr. McDonough was a fantastic teacher. He was really funny and he was easy to trust. He looked out for the students.

— William Allcock, entering class 1994

Tom McDonough had just joined the faculty as I was finishing up. He saw me through the last year or so of my thesis research. He was great – I had a lot of respect for him.

— Peter Balousek, entering class 1974

Dr. McDonough was usually pretty laid-back, but he was really intelligent and was good at explaining things. I always had lots of questions since I had never done any pulping before, but he made it really easy to learn.

— Sean Taylor, entering class 2000

Outside the Classroom

I spent a lot of time with the other students. We did a lot of whitewater rafting up in Tennessee and North Georgia and we'd go to Oktoberfest in Helen every year.

— **Brian Boyer,** entering class 1991

I spent more than twelve hours a day with other students. We went to classes together, studied together, worked on projects together, ate supper together, and studied some more. It wasn't all work, though – we played volleyball, softball and other intramural sports together as well.

— **Karen Turnboom,** entering class 1991

Most of the students formed study groups right away and that really built the camaraderie. We often took advantage of the things that Georgia Tech offered like bowling, the music room, and the gym.

— **Coray Harper,** entering class 1993

It wasn't all work. We usually spent our lunch hour playing cards. We played intramural soccer at Georgia Tech and hung out across the street at Billy Bob's a lot in the evenings. We used to go to this bar called Dirty Al's on Tuesday nights to play trivia. Usually we would win just enough to pay our bar tab.

— **William Allcock,** entering class 1994

The Bush Trip
in the 1990s

We went down to the Florida panhandle and went around to several different pulp mills. We saw all kinds of large machinery, but since I was so new to the program, I couldn't distinguish one kind of machinery from another. It was a great chance to see what the industry was all about, though.

The bush trip was also a great time to establish good ties and strong bonds between the people that we would be studying with and working with for the next few years. It wasn't all just visiting pulp mills; we spent a lot of time just hanging out on the beach and hitting the beach bars at night.

— **Brian Boyer,** entering class 1991

It was a very rewarding experience. I truly feel that I wouldn't be in the position I am today had I not gone to the Institute. I learned a lot about the paper industry and its people. It helped me become confident in my abilities.

— **Karen Turnboom,** entering class 1991

The Institute was really good at teaching basic problem-solving - taking what you know, thinking your way through the problem, and asking the right kind of questions. It's the one thing I've used consistently throughout my life.

— **William Allcock**, entering class 1994

It was a great experience once you got used to the mosquitoes! It was sort of an initiation to the Institute, I guess – a good chance to meet your classmates and get to know people.

— **Coray Harper**, entering class 1993

The mills and the woodlands that we visited were interesting and a good introduction to the paper industry, but what I remember the most was body surfing in Pensacola!

— **William Allcock**, entering class 1994

I remember trips to several pulp and paper mills and visiting a forestry plantation where we learned how they geminated trees from seeds, grow them, and thin the crop. It was a great opportunity to learn more about the paper industry in the southern part of the country.

— **Karen Turnboom**, entering class 1991

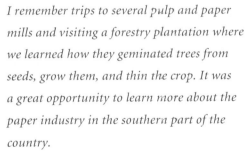

CHAPTER 8

2000-present

The new millennium has seen an escalation of the numerous social issues that had plagued the latter half of the previous decade, especially the rise of terrorism and the brisk expansion of economic globalization. The widespread use of constantly improving communication devices such as mobile phones and the Internet have made the once-abstract concept of a global marketplace a reality.

Naturally, the creation of this global marketplace has had a profound impact on American industry, and the paper industry is no exception. Mergers, consolidations, and weak domestic and global economic conditions have led to a series of challenges unlike anything the American pulp and paper industry has ever faced before.

These challenges faced by the industry have, in turn, affected the Institute in numerous ways. After the Institute had lost nineteen of its fifty-three member companies to mergers and consolidations, it became more and more apparent that in order to survive, the Institute needed to consider an alliance of its own…

During the opening ceremony of the 2000 Executives' Conference, the theme of which was "Delivering Value to a Changing World," Institute president Dr. Jim Ferris spoke of the enormous changes that were transforming the structure of American industry. "The world is changing around us, and we must change as individuals, as companies, and as an industry faster than any of us would like," he told audience members. "And to make it more interesting, we really don't know how this transition will end up or how it will affect us as individuals, as companies, or as an industry."

THE INSTITUTE WAS NO STRANGER to change. Numerous developments in the paper industry, in education, and, indeed, in society in general throughout the previous seventy years had certainly given

William J. Frederick, Jr.

Originally from Bangor, Maine, Dr. William J. Frederick, Jr., received his Bachelor of Science, Master of Science, and PhD degrees, all in chemical engineering, from the University of Maine. After a series of non-academic research positions at General Motors, Battelle Memorial Institute, and United States Department of Agriculture's Forest Products Laboratory in Madison, Wisconsin, Frederick joined the faculty of the Institute of Paper Chemistry as a research associate in the materials engineering and processes division in the spring of 1976. Frederick stated that he took the position, one of several offered, because it was the most interesting and involved "the opportunity to co industrial research as well as teaching and working with graduate students."

In 1980, Frederick left the Institute to take a position as the group leader of the recovery technology applications division of the Weyerhaeuser Company in Tacoma, Washington. He left Weyerhaeuser in 1983 to rejoin academia as an associate professor of chemical engineering at Oregon State University. He became the department head in 1991.

In 1996, Frederick, who, in addition to his responsibilities at Oregon State had served in adjunct positions at both the bo Akademi University in Turku, Finland, and at the Institute of Paper Science and Technology, was approached by IPST President Dr. James Ferris about rejoining the Institute as a professor of chemical recovery engineering. "At that point," Frederick said, "I had basically rebuilt the entire chemical engineering department at Oregon State – I had hired half of the people in it. Things were going really well there and I wanted the opportunity for a new challenge. I went back to IPST because I

thought that I'd have the opportunity to make a difference again." Frederick was named director of the Institute's chemical recovery and corrosion division in 1997, working in areas of chemical engineering, chemical reaction engineering, heat transfer, and electrolyte thermodynamics.

In August of 2001, Frederick was named the CEI Professor of Green Chemistry at Chalmers University of Technology in Gothenburg Sweden, where he remained until his appointment as the director of the Institute of Paper Science of Technology at Georgia Tech in September of 2003. "He [Frederick] brings an impressive set of credentials to the job of director. He's been a leading researcher and administrator, and he has strong ties to the Institute," said Dr. Ron Rousseau, the chair of Georgia Tech's School of Chemical and Biomolecular Engineering, upon Frederick's appointment. "Also important is that he is well-connected to the pulp and paper industry. He knows the strengths of IPST and he knows the opportunities for strengthening the delivery of research output to member companies."

In addition to his duties as the Institute's director, Frederick also holds the position of professor in the schools of Chemical and Biomolecular Engineering and Materials Science and Engineering at Georgia Tech. His favorite part of his job is, without a doubt, working with the students. "I got into the education business and I stayed in the education business because I got such enjoyment out of working with young people and young minds," he says. "I enjoy watching those minds develop and be put to work. Students are usually so open to new ideas."

Jim Frederick and I played basketball together. We also liked to goof around when we were doing thesis work – that was generally how it was between Institute professors and students.
— Rick Hartman, entering class 1977

Dr. Frederick is a great person, very fair and super to work with. I say 'work with' because he makes you feel like you work with him, not for him. And what a great family man!
— Connie Ford Adams, Administrative Assistant to the President, Institute of Paper Science and Technology, 1989 - present

the school its share of transformations. The transformation that loomed on the Institute's horizon, however, was bigger and more disconcerting than any faced previously.

The Institute entered the new millennium still flying high from the honors and triumphs of the latter half of the previous decade. In May of 2000, the Institute was recognized as the fifth most innovative institution in the nation based on a survey from the Research Foundation of the State University of New York. With rankings based on the number of patents produced within an institution and the number of faculty at the institution, the Institute's fifth-place ranking came from its record of twenty-nine patents per one hundred

faculty members for the 1998 research year. More than two hundred and fifty of the top research institutions in the country were included in the survey; the Institute placed ahead of MIT, Georgia Tech, Stanford, and Princeton.

The following fall, the Institute announced what was considered one of its highest achievements to date. On October 3, 2000, the Alfred P. Sloan Foundation declared that its board of trustees had approved the funding of its newest Center for Industry Studies. Named the Center for Paper Business and Industry Studies (CPBIS) and residing at the Institute and Georgia Tech, the new center set as its focus the business fundamentals impacting the global paper market with the purpose of generating research and producing experts for the paper industry. Five specific areas deemed of interest to the paper industry were chosen: globalization, commercialization, community interactions, workplace transformation, and enterprise effectiveness.

CPBIS was the sixteenth of the Sloan Foundation's Centers for Industry Studies, joining other centers at places such as

Harvard, MIT, Stanford, Wharton, and Columbia that are designed to create an academic community that understands industries and to encourage a direct approach to the companies and people of each industry for data collection and observation. The Sloan Foundation, a non-profit, philanthropic organization established in 1934 by Alfred P. Sloan, Jr., a longtime president and chairman of General Motors, granted CPBIS $2.04 million, which was then supplemented by $1 million in direct industry-based funding.

More than eighty-five Institute and Georgia Tech faculty members participated in the Sloan Foundation proposal. Dr. James McNutt, former president and CEO of Jaako Poyry Consulting, was named the Center's executive director, while Dr. Tom McDonough, a senior IPST faculty member, was named director. Dr. Gus Giebelhaus and Dr. Steve Vallas, both professors in Georgia Tech's School of History, Technology, and Society, and Dr. Vinod Singhal, a professor of operations management in Georgia Tech's Dupree College of Management, were named associate directors.

The development of the Center for Paper Business and Industry Studies represented a bond between the Institute of Paper Science and Technology and Georgia Tech

Sujit Banerjee

Dr. Sujit Banerjee received his B.Sc. degree in chemistry from the Indian Institute of Technology at Kharagpur in 1969 and his PhD in physical-organic chemistry from Montreal's Concordia University in 1974. After conducting postdoctoral research in physical-organic chemistry at McMaster University, Banerjee joined the staff of Syracuse Research Corporation in 1977 as a senior scientist. In 1983, he was named group leader of the Department of Nuclear Energy at the Brookhaven National Laboratory, a position he held until 1989.

An expert in environmental science with emphasis on the fate and transport of xenobiotics and aquatic technology, Banerjee joined the Institute staff in 1989 as the leader of the chemical analysis group. He holds several United States patents and has authored and co-authored numerous books, book chapters, and articles. In 1995, Banerjee, along with Dr. Terrance Conners of Mississippi State University, edited the groundbreaking Surface Analysis of Paper, which examines surface analysis techniques from a paper industry perspective and places heavy emphasis on applications. Banerjee was chosen by Institute students as the 2006 IPST Teacher of the Year.

In 2003, Banerjee joined the faculty of the School of Chemical and Biomolecular Engineering at Georgia Tech. His current research focuses on issues in the forest products industry with a strong emphasis on developing the fundamentals and taking them to commercial implementation. Banerjee's research group has set as its present goal the development of new techniques and novel materials for application in the pulp and paper industry.

– a bond that was growing steadily as Institute faculty and students became more and more involved with, as IPST president Jim Ferris called them, "their Georgia Tech counterparts."

As the first year of the new millennium waned, it was obvious that the paper industry was going through a change unlike any it had ever experienced – and it was taking the Institute with it. Rapid consolidations and mergers within the industry resulted in IPST's loss of nineteen of its fifty-three member companies over a three-year period. With rumors of even more merger activity on the horizon, the Institute began to suffer the damaging effects of an enormous loss of revenue.

In the fall of 2001, the Institute's Board of Trustees asked the Institute to define what became known as "the Georgia Tech alternative" – that is, to examine the possibilities of an alliance between the two institutions. A team, sanctioned by the Chancellor of the University System of Georgia and working closely with the Institute's Alumni Association Executive Committee, was created to look into the possible benefits of an alliance, which, in addition to the financial benefits, included access to the broad array of new technology centers at Georgia Tech.

On September 24, 2002, after examining the prospects of alliance with several different colleges and universities, the Institute announced its decision to pursue a strategic alliance between IPST and Georgia Tech, effective July 1, 2003. Renamed the Institute of Paper Science and Technology at Georgia Tech, the Institute would become one of Georgia Tech's four large interdisciplinary research institutes, continuing to offer graduate degrees in paper science and engineering.

Dr. James McNutt

Dr. Tom McDunough

Dr. Jim Ferris

The following December, Dr. Jim Ferris, who had been the Institute's President since 1996, announced his retirement effective June 30, 2003. An international search began immediately for someone to fill the position of Director of the new IPST at Georgia Tech.

In the spring of 2003, Dr. Ronald W. Rousseau, chairman of Georgia Tech's School of Chemical Engineering, was named the Institute's interim director, responsible for shaping the new organization during its transition period. Woody Rice, who had served as the Institute's Vice President of Development

since 1993, was elected President of the Institute of Paper Science and Technology in July of 2003, responsible for overseeing the smooth operation and transfer of various properties and assets from the Institute to Georgia Tech.

On July 17, 2003, it was announced that Dr. William "Jim" Frederick, Jr., the CEI Professor of Green Chemistry and Chemical Engineering at Chalmers University of Technology in Gothenburg, Sweden, had accepted appointment as the new Director of the Institute of Paper Science and Technology at Georgia Tech. He began his duties which, in addition to his responsibilities as the Institute's director, included a faculty position in Georgia Tech's School of Chemical and Biomolecular Engineering, on September 1.

The transition took approximately eighteen months. On December 14, 2004, Dr. Wayne Clough, Georgia Tech's President, and Woody Rice signed the final agreements integrating IPST into Georgia Tech. The integration was declared complete on December 31, 2004, and the Institute of Paper Science and Technology at Georgia Tech was left in the capable hands of Dr. Jim Frederick.

Georgia Tech is an outstanding school, and merging the research and academic operations of IPST with them is a very positive outcome in our search for a merger partner. A key element in our final decision was our desire to position the Institute where it can access the broadest set of advanced engineering skills needed by this industry to increase its global competitiveness. Georgia Tech has an outstanding science, computing, and engineering skill base that we can draw upon. The paper industry desperately needs innovative technologies, and we look forward to supporting their development through the new IPST at Georgia Tech.

— **A.D. "Pete" Correll,** Past Chairman, IPST Board of Trustees

The merger with Georgia Tech is a logical extension of our already close relationship that has developed since we moved to this campus in 1989. In becoming part of Georgia Tech, we simply take the final step to unite these two institutions. Our faculty and students are already heavily involved in activities with their Georgia Tech counterparts, and removing the organizational barrier will benefit us all as we continue to pursue our academic and research missions to serve our customers.

— **Dr. James Ferris,** President, Institute of Paper Science and Technology, 1996-2003

Elwood J. "Woody" Rice

Originally from Cornwall, Ontario, Canada, Woody Rice began his long career in the paper industry at a young age, working summers at Howard Smith Paper Mills. After attending Royal Military College of Canada at Kingston, Rice spent four years studying electrical engineering at Montreal's McGill University. He then went to work for Hercules Inc., a large chemical company based in Wilmington, Delaware. Rice spent most of his career in field and home office management in the paper technology group, which supplied paper chemicals to companies around the world. By the time Rice retired from Hercules in 1992, he had been promoted to group vice president of the paper technology group, responsible for its worldwide growth and operation.

Following his retirement, Rice was approached by IPST President Dr. Richard Matula and asked to aid the Institute in the development of some strategic marketing for the Institute membership. He soon became a fulltime consultant and, in 1993, was elected the Institute's new Vice President of Development, a position he held until the Institute's decision to merge with Georgia Tech in 2003. As the Vice President of Development, Rice was responsible for the development and maintenance of industry support, long-range government funding, and member company relations, all of which his long career and experience in the worldwide paper industry had prepared him for.

In July of 2003, Rice was elected President of the Institute of Paper Science and Technology, succeeding Dr. James Ferris. His role as President was to oversee the smooth operation and the transfer of various properties and assets from the Institute to Georgia Tech. In January of 2005, he handed the reins to Dr. Jim Frederick, who was chosen as the Director of the Institute of Paper Science and Technology at Georgia Tech.

Woody has many fond memories of his thirteen-year tenure at the Institute, including the privileging of awarding an honorary doctoral degree to George Mead II during the Institute's 74th Commencement exercises in 2004, which he calls one of the highlights of his career. He has been an avid supporter and life member of the American Museum of Papermaking, serving on the museum's Board of Trustees. Rice is also an active member of TAPPI and PIMA and has served on the boards of pulp and paper foundations at the University of Maine and North Carolina State University, as well as on the boards of various United States and foreign corporations.

David E. White

Dr. David E. White received his Bachelor of Science, Master of Science, and PhD degrees, all in chemical engineering, from the University of Pennsylvania. After completing his dissertation, "Diffusion-Limited Heterogeneous Catalytic Reactions on a Rotating Disk," in 1972, White spent four years as a research engineer at E.I. DuPont De Nemours and Company, where he was responsible for process development and scale-up.

White joined the staff of Union Camp Corporation as a research scientist in 1976. He spent the next twenty-three years with Union Camp in a variety of positions, conducting engineering research and design in papermaking, separations, reactor design, start-ups, and mill modelling for environmental compliance.

In 1999, White came to the Institute of Paper Science and Technology as the project leader for Project ROCIT (Redefining Our Core Industry Technologies), a venture designed to identify new technologies with potential to make a significant change in the cost competitiveness of the United States pulp and paper industry. In 2001, he was named director of technology transfer, where he was responsible for working with principle investigators to assure that research conducted at the Institute focused on the customer's needs.

White, whose areas of expertise include multi-phase pilot evaluation, computer modeling, papermaking, pulp bleaching, chemical and pulp/paper separations, and recycling, holds six United States patents and has been the recipient of several prestigious awards, including the American Chemical Society's Hero of Chemistry award in 1997. He was chosen as the Institute's Associate Director of Research in 2005. White's current research focuses on modified filler commercialization, future needs for digital printing, wood property effects on pulp yield, and forest products industry energy benchmarking.

Cyrus Aidun

Dr. Cyrus Aidun received his Bachelor of Science and Master of Science degrees from Rensselaer Polytechnic Institute in 1978 and 1980, respectively. He earned his PhD in mechanical engineering from Clarkson University in Potsdam, New York, in 1985.

Shortly after completing his doctoral research, Aidun was appointed a postdoctoral research associate in the chemical engineering department and a research fellow at the Mathematical Sciences Institute at Cornell University. He was then appointed a senior research consultant in computational fluid dynamics at the university's National Science Foundation's Supercomputer Center.

Aidun left Cornell in 1987, spending a year at Battelle Research Laboratories before joining the faculty of the Institute of Paper Science and Technology in 1988. As a professor of engineering, he taught courses in fluid mechanics, applied mathematics, fundamentals of liquid coating, thermodynamics, and heat transfer.

In 1992, Aidun was the recipient of the prestigious National Science Foundation Young Investigator Award, a highly competitive honor sought after by top faculty in major research universities. In 2000, he was responsible for the invention of a technology that essentially redesigned the flow mechanism in the fiber network-forming process. The result was a stronger paper made with less fiber and energy that, according to Woody Rice, the Institute's vice president of development, "will rank among the top advances in the papermaking industry over the last twenty-five years and should continue to be cutting-edge well into the twenty-first century."

In 2001, Aidun was chosen as the director of the Particulate and Multiphase Processes program at the National Science Foundation, where he managed the national funding of the program's research. Aidun was then named professor of fluid mechanics, paper science and engineering, and biotransport at Georgia Tech's George W. Woodruff School of Mechanical Engineering in 2003, where he had been an adjunct faculty member since 1989. His current projects continue his research in multiphase flow and have expanded into new multidisciplinary areas in biomedical research and nanoscale suspension flow with applications to value-added paper for cell culture in medical and pharmaceutical industries.

Cyrus Aidun was a very good teacher and an amazingly intelligent man.

— William Allcock, entering class 1994

Howard L. "Jeff" Empie, Jr.

Dr. Howard L. "Jeff" Empie received his Bachelor of Science degree from Syracuse University in 1964, his Master of Science degree from the Massachusetts Institute of Technology in 1965, and his PhD degree from the University of Minnesota in 1969. He worked in process research and development at the corporate research center of Hercules, Inc., from 1969 to 1978. In 1979, Empie joined International Paper as a senior research engineer in kraft chemical recovery at the company's corporate center.

Empie left International Paper in 1989 to join the staff of the Institute of Paper Science and Technology as a professor of engineering, teaching courses in reaction engineering, advanced chemical recovery, chemical engineering kinetics, mass and energy balances, and unit operations. Empie, who has advised numerous Masters' and PhD candidates during his tenure at the Institute, was chosen by Institute students for the 1994 Teacher of the Year award.

Empie joined the School of Chemical and Biomolecular Engineering at Georgia Tech in 2003 as a professor of chemical engineering. His current research focuses on reduction of white liquor deadload and purging chloride from the kraft liquor cycle, which involves using electrodialysis in a unique way that, in addition to solving a mill's chloride purge problem, should actually help mills show a profit.

Arthur J. Ragauskas

Born in Sudbury, Ontario, Canada, Dr. Arthur J. Ragauskas received his Honors B.Sc. degree in 1980 and his PhD in 1985, both in chemistry, from the University of Western Ontario. He spent two years as a National Science and Engineering Research Council of Canada (NSERC) Postdoctoral Fellow, studying carbohydrate chemistry at the University of Alberta, then another year in postdoctoral research at Colorado State University. In 1987, Ragauskas was named a National Research Council research associate, working in the field of immunochemistry and concentrating on the synthesis of salmonella trisaccharide epitopes.

Ragauskas joined the Institute staff in 1989 as a professor of wood chemistry, conducting research on the fundamental principles involved in the photoyellowing of mechanical pulp.

Ragauskas has supervised eighteen PhD students, sixteen Masters' students, and seventeen postdoctoral research fellows throughout his tenure at the Institute, several of whom have received national and international awards. He has published more than seventy journal articles and presented his research at numerous national and international conferences. In 1999, Ragauskas was chosen by Institute students to receive the Teacher of the Year Award, and in 2004, he was honored with the prestigious TAPPI Fellow Award, given in recognition of meritorious service to TAPPI and to the pulp and paper industry.

In 2003, Ragauskas became a member of the faculty of Georgia Tech's School of Chemistry and Biochemistry. His current research is in the field of carbohydrate chemistry, with the primary objective to harness the possibilities inherent in the chemistry of cellulose, the most abundant of Earth's organic chemicals.

Dr. Ragauskas was quite a character. We always laughed a lot.

— Brian Boyer, entering class 1991

The professor I remember the most is Dr. Art Ragauskas. He was my advisor and he left a huge impression on me. He taught me how to schedule my classes, which was really helpful while I was in school. He also provided me with a perspective of the industry in terms of keeping your eyes a little bit ahead and keeping your ear to the ground, so to speak, in order to keep your career fresh – how important it was not to get stale.

— Corey Harper, entering class 1993

The Robert C. Williams
Paper Museum
at Georgia Tech

I think the American Museum of Papermaking is the soul of the Institute. We see the history of not only IPST, but the history of the paper industry reflected in the Museum. We see the beauty that paper can bring to the world. It is not just an attachment; it is a very important part of what we do. It's very important for those of us who spend most of our time in the science and engineering worlds — it brings the artistic world to us in a very nice way. I'm very glad we have the museum. I've often told people that I think that's the best part of the deal that Georgia Tech got when they agreed to take on IPST.

—Dr. William J. Frederick, Director,
Institute of Paper Science and
Technology at Georgia Tech,
2003 – present

The idea of a museum dedicated exclusively to paper and paper-related artifacts is almost as old as the Institute itself. A wasp's nest representing papermaking in nature was accepted as a donation by the Institute's Technical Director, Dr. Otto Kress, in 1934; two years later, Mr. Westbrook Steele, the Institute's Executive Secretary, accepted a donation of 1871 commercially made sulfite-pulp paper. More items, including microscopes, fibers, and testing equipment, were added to the collection over time and found a home in a glass display case near one of the Institute laboratories.

IN 1939, at the urging of Massachusetts Institute of Technology President Dr. Karl Taylor Compton, Dard Hunter, a world-renowned expert on the history of paper and papermaking, established a paper museum at MIT in Cambridge, Massachusetts. His goal, which remains part of the museum's mission statement to this day, was to "stimulate interest in the ancient craft of papermaking and promote understanding of present-day paper.." Artifacts representing papermaking activities in countries around the world were artfully arranged in glass display cases by Hunter himself.

By 1950, however, Hunter had become disillusioned with slow trickle of visitors the museum was receiving. The retirement of Dr. Compton, a long-time advocate of Hunter and his collection, did not help matters. By 1951, the collection had been moved to a much smaller facility in the school's Hayden Library and the Dard Hunter Paper Museum had become a seldom-used and somewhat obscure research center.

To collect, preserve,
increase and disseminate knowledge
about papermaking –
past, present and future.

I remember being able to go down to the basement and visit the museum while it was in Appleton. It was great there, but there is really no comparison to how wonderful it's become here in Atlanta. It's a fantastic resource for the Institute, for the public, and for the industry. Cindy [Bowden] has done a wonderful job of capitalizing on all of the museum's assets. She's turned the collection into what is now truly a global resource.

— Dr. James Ferris, President, Institute of Paper Science and Technology, 1996-2003

As far as I am concerned, the Institute advanced a long way in the building up of its national and international stature through the acquisition of the Dard Hunter Museum. Here it occupies an area of approximately four thousand square feet in quarters largely designed for it. This collection is the world's finest...it should draw many people to the Institute.

— Dr. Harry F. Lewis, Dean, Institute of Paper Chemistry, 1930-1956

It wasn't long before the Institute learned of the floundering situation at MIT. Institute Vice President and Treasurer John Strange began correspondence with Dard Hunter shortly thereafter and, by 1954, the Institute had offered to reestablish the Dard Hunter Paper Museum in Appleton. The arrangement was finalized on July 30, 1954, with Hunter himself named curator of the collection which was displayed in a bomb-proof room in the basement of the General Activities Building. The museum officially opened to the public in early 1955. Hunter was quite pleased with the arrangements in Appleton; as he told a Peruvian acquaintance, Victor von Hagen, in a letter dated February 17, 1960, "the paper museum is now serving a more useful purpose than at MIT, as in Appleton it is seen by many more interested people than formerly."

Dard Hunter was the museum's curator until his death in 1966, at which time the Institute's former Dean of Students, Dr. Harry Lewis, who had retired from his position in 1956 and had been assisting Hunter with the collection for more than ten years, took over for a two-year period.

The museum grew by leaps and bounds over the next twenty years as the collection was increasingly enlarged by donations of various paper and paper-related artifacts. As Doug Stone, a museum advisory board member who also assisted with the first major attempt to catalogue the collection in 1980, pointed out, "gradually, others in the local paper community became more aware of who Dard Hunter was and the extensiveness of his work. This inspired them to look at their own collections and periodically donate artifacts, paper specimens and books."

When the Institute made its nine hundred-mile move to Atlanta in 1989, the Dard Hunter Collection was packed away as well – a major undertaking that required the services of a variety of museum and preservation specialists. Once in Atlanta, the facilities of the newly renamed Institute of Paper Science and Technology proved too limited to accommodate the collection. It remained in boxes until construction of the Paper Tricentennial Building, the Institute's

Dard Hunter was very well known and respected throughout the papermaking community, much of which was centered in Wisconsin's Fox River Valley. Hunter was an artist of paper history, someone they learned a lot from, who traveled widely and understood the history of different papermaking cultures. Needless to say, everyone in Appleton and the surrounding areas were thrilled to learn that the Institute was to acquire Dard's collection!

— Doug Stone, Advisory Board Member, 1995 - present

Dard Hunter

Originally from Steubanville, Ohio, William Joseph "Dard" Hunter was absorbed into a world of paper and printmaking at a young age as he routinely assisted his father in the family's newspaper business. After a short period as a staff artist for his father's Chillicothe, Ohio, paper, Hunter set out to see the country as an assistant to his brother, Philip, an accomplished magician. It was during one of these tours that Hunter became fascinated with the American Arts and Crafts Movement.

In the early summer of 1904, Hunter applied for a summer internship with Elbert Hubbard's Roycrofters in East Aurora, New York. Hubbard, a leading proponent of the Arts and Crafts Movement, at first denied Hunter's application, but Hunter, ever persistent, simply traveled to East Aurora anyway and was eventually hired and began to develop his artistic talents in a variety of media, including graphic design, stained glass, and metalwork.

Hunter became captivated by early European papermaking and printing during a 1911 trip to London and was overcome by a desire to learn more about the centuries-old art of hand papermaking. Upon his return to America, Hunter and his wife, Edith, moved to Marlborough, New York, to build a paper mill on Jew's Creek with the goal of producing handmade paper for American artists and printers who had, until then, relied upon European papermakers to fulfill their handmade paper needs. Relying exclusively upon seventeenth century hand papermaking techniques, such as depending entirely upon a water wheel to power the mill, Hunter continued to practice the creed he had learned at the hands of Elbert Hubbard and the Roycrofters - that a hand-crafted object was inherently more desirable, beautiful, serviceable, and worthy of human endeavor than anything made by a machine.

In 1919, Hunter returned to Chillicothe, where he purchased the Mountain House, which was built in the early 1850s. He immediately reconstructed one of the wings to form a letterpress printing studio, which he named Mountain House Press.

Dard Hunter devoted the rest of his life to researching, collecting, writing, and publishing the world's history of hand papermaking and printing, crisscrossing the globe dozens of times to some of the most remote places on earth to study the world's various papermaking cultures. He eventually authored twenty books on paper and papermaking, eight of which were printed by hand. The artifacts and paper samples he collected on his journeys form the bulk of the Dard Hunter Collection, originally housed at the Massachusetts Institute of Technology and now featured in the Robert C. Williams Paper Museum at Georgia Tech in Atlanta.

of its cofounder Robert C. Williams, who had retired as the company's chairman, president, and CEO in 1995. The endowment played a large role in the expansion of the museum's new traveling exhibition program, which was met with remarkable accolades.

permanent home, was completed in late 1992. A reception celebrating the official grand opening of the American Museum of Papermaking was held on May 6, 1993.

In the spring of 1996, the museum, which

was receiving more than ten thousand visitors annually, was officially renamed the Robert C. Williams American Museum of Papermaking, the result of a significant endowment gift from the James River Corporation in recognition

The many rare artifacts that traveled from Appleton are now part of a permanent collection in Atlanta tracing the fascinating history of papermaking from its earliest antecedents to the advanced technology

of today – from ancient Summerian cuneiform tablets and Egyptian papyrus scrolls to the exquisite chiaroscuro watermarked papers still made in Fabriano, a well-known papermaking center in the Marches region of Italy. In 2005, the George W. Mead Education Center, created with generous funds from the Mead-Witter Foundation, doubled public space capacity, which has enabled the museum to increase educational and public programming while also allowing greater public access to artifacts from the permanent collection as well as to the museum's impressive rare book collection.

The museum's critically acclaimed changing exhibition gallery showcases various interpretations and uses of paper as a viable and diverse medium by hosting exhibitions by contemporary artists working in the allied fields of paper, printmaking, and book arts.

Through the offerings of the gallery, museum visitors are not only able to view artistic applications of many of the processes described by the interpretive display of the expressive uses of paper, but also to connect to paper as a living art, not just an ancient craft transformed through technology to purely utilitarian uses. Recent exhibitions have included brilliant cast pulp paintings, an outstanding selection of the finest work in handmade paper created by art students

The Dard Hunter Paper Museum shows the antiquity and the universality of paper. By a sweep of the eye, a visitor may scan centuries and in several steps he can cross whole continents engaged in this ancient craft. The museum tells us more than the story of paper and its evolution. Paper has been a part of man's culture. To know the story of paper is to see man keeping records, engaging in commerce, creating literature, responding to beauty and worshipping a deity.

— Dr. Edwin W. Schoenberger, Dean, Institute of Paper Chemistry, 1956-1960

from throughout the United States in the museum's tri-annual collegiate handmade paper art show, an exhibition of exquisite sculptural book forms, a display of richly embellished collages and assemblages incorporating handmade paper and found objects, marvelous colored pulp paintings with environmental images and themes, handmade paper quilts, and a selection of fine handmade books and book designs created by educators throughout the Southeast. The gallery also features scholarly exhibits, which illustrate various cultural traditions of papermaking and an examination of papermaking from a historical perspective. A variety of artist-led workshops and lectures accompany each

exhibition. In hosting these exhibitions, the museum provides the public with a broader experience while giving artists the opportunity to display their art in a space that connects their work historically, physically, and conceptually.

Outreach is a vital part of the museum's mission. In addition to the thousands of schoolchildren that visit the museum for guided tours each year, more than one million visitors have experienced the world of paper and papermaking through the museum's two traveling interactive exhibitions. In the first interactive exhibit, called PaperQuest, children are able to crawl through five sections of a paper machine, play computer games in a paper mill control room, play games about where paper can be found in the home, and see artifacts in the global history area. They are given the opportunity to make a piece of paper from recycled blue jean material at the papermaking station. The second interactive exhibit, A Child's View of Papermaking, allows children to climb down from the top floor of the two-story exhibit through the drying cylinders of a paper machine while learning about the different professions in papermaking.

Another traveling exhibition, The World of Paper, was seen by more than eleven million visitors during its eighteen-month display at Atlanta's Hartsfield-Jackson

International Airport. Featuring artifacts from the museum's permanent collection as well as a series of handmade paper artwork, the exhibition then traveled to the Museo de Bellas Artes in Santiago, Chile, where it was met with the largest opening reception in the history of the museum. An upcoming exhibition partners the Robert C. Williams Paper Museum at Georgia Tech with the Museo Della Carta e Filligrana Italy with the intention of creating an international virtual exhibition to focus on the little understood but significant contributions of paper to the evolution of the European Renaissance. The new exhibit will explore a nearly unexamined view of paper's arrival in Italy and its spread through Europe during a time when scholarship flourished and books, the printed word, and literacy extended their influence.

The Robert C. Williams Paper Museum at Georgia Tech fulfills a vital role as a communicator and a vehicle for the preservation and study of paper-making's important past and continuing contribution to our culture. By allowing visitors to examine paper from its origins to its contemporary interpretations, the museum is a monument to the rich history, the global present, and the very bright future of a product to which we are all connected.

156

STEPHEN M. MILLER'S

BIBLE

SNAPSHOTS

STEPHEN M. MILLER'S

BIBLE
SNAPSHOTS

LAVISHLY ILLUSTRATED BIBLE GUIDE WITH
EVERYTHING BUT THE PREACHING

BARBOUR
PUBLISHING

The author is represented by The Steve Laube Agency LLC, Phoenix, Arizona.

ISBN 978-1-60260-689-0

Member of the
Evangelical Christian
Publishers Association

Printed in the United States of America.

CONTENTS

10 TOUGH QUESTIONS ATHEISTS ASK

From abortion to zealots

INTRODUCTION

THINK OF THIS AS A GIFT certificate from Starbucks. That's where the story begins. It'l end at Pizza Hut, far as I can tell.

Starbucks sits in the corner of the grocery store closest to our home. My wife, Linda, stopped by there a few weeks ago to get a free cup of coffee for her birthday. Think "one-stop sip and shop." Linda does.

It's Friday, almost a week after Valentine's Day.

Up to the counter walks a boy of middle-school age, around 12. He asks the lone Starbucks employee, Carol, if he can use his Walmart gift certificate at the grocery store.

Carol says she's sorry, but he'll need to use it at Walmart—the closest one is across town.

The boy walks away. Head down. He lingers by the flowers.

"Something's wrong," Carol says to my wife, handing her the coffee. "I may go and buy that certificate from him."

Carol excuses herself and goes over to the boy. A few moments later, she's reaching for the wrapping paper that customers use to bundle up flowers.

Linda knows she has five dollars in her purse, so she starts walking over there. Discovering she has eight dollars, she slips it to Carol and asks her to use it to help the boy.

Linda wheels her cart off to shop.

A few minutes later, a voice over the store intercom calls Linda back to Starbucks.

The boy is standing there, cradling a dozen yellow roses. He wants to talk to Linda.

"My parents are celebrating Valentine's Day today," he tells her. "They couldn't afford to do it on Valentine's Day. I wanted to buy them some flowers."

He asks, "Do I need to pay you for these?"

"No," Linda says. "Just tell your mom you love her."

Before Linda leaves, Carol slips her a Starbucks gift certificate with a note penciled on it: "God bless."

The next day, Linda's driving home from visiting her mom in a neighboring town. She calls me on the hands-free phone system she has in the car. We agree to order pizza at one of our favorite shops. I'll call it in, and she'll pick it up on her way home. That's the plan. Oddly, the pizza shop's phone line is busy. I've never had that happen there before. The line stays busy for several attempted calls over several minutes. I phone Linda back. We agree to Pizza Hut, another favorite. They have a super special: two medium pizzas for $10. I place the order online.

They never get it.

Maybe I sent it to the wrong store. Who knows?

Linda ends up waiting in the lobby while they quickly cook up our pizzas.

While she's standing there, in walks the Starbucks boy and his mom.

"She's the lady who helped me," Linda hears the boy whisper.

"Are you Carol?" the mother asks my wife.

"No," Linda answers. "Carol is the one who works at Starbucks."

"She's the other lady who helped me," the boy says.

The mom thanks Linda and offers to pay her back.

"No," Linda says. "You've got a special boy. I did that for him."

. . . .

I don't know if this was a series of coincidences— or Jesus conducting an orchestra.

But if Jesus made music, that's the kind of song I'd expect to hear.

. . . .

When I write books about the Bible—books like this one—I'm trying to make a little music, too. What's surprising to some folks is who I'm writing this music for.

It's not for Christians. There are lots of books out there for them.

I'm writing for people who have one thing in common with the Starbucks boy.

They're searching.

Maybe they're just curious, pure and simple. They want to know more about the Bible and Christianity—and they don't need a sermon in the process.

Maybe they're feeling a bit bummed in spirit, and they're looking for a little insight that might somehow help them.

Maybe they feel beyond help, and they're walking with their heads hung down.

I'm not sure this book will do for a reader what my wife's eight dollars helped do for that boy.

But I can hope.

. . . .

In the pages that follow, you'll see a few snapshots of what the Bible teaches and what Christians try to practice.

But if you've got that Starbucks story down, you're well on the way.

In the meantime, to quote a Starbucks gift certificate, "God bless."

Steph M. Muller

STEPHEN M. MILLER
StephenMillerBooks.com

P.S.: Everybody reads a P.S., so here's where I'll say thanks to all the pros who helped bring this book to life. To name a few who invested a hunk of time: Paul K. Muckley, editor; Steve Laube, agent; Faceout Studio, designers; Donna Maltese, copy editor and fact checker; along with the Barbour publishing team of Annie Tipton, Ashley Casteel, and Ashley Schrock.

BIBLE: FAST PASS

BIBLE LIBRARY: 66 BOOKS

HISTORY OF BEGINNINGS

GENESIS
Beginning of universe, humanity, Jewish race

LAWS

EXODUS
Moses frees Jews from Egyptian slavery
LEVITICUS
Jews organize as a nation
NUMBERS
Jews spend 40 years in the badlands
DEUTERONOMY
Moses reviews Jewish laws and dies

HISTORY OF JEWS

JOSHUA
Jews invade and retake homeland

JUDGES
Heroes rescue Jews from oppressors
RUTH
Arab woman becomes mother of
King David's family
1, 2 SAMUEL
Saul becomes Israel's first king, followed by David
1, 2 KINGS
Israel splits in two; both nations fall within 400 years
1, 2 CHRONICLES
Jewish history, tailored to show God at work
EZRA
Jews return home from exile in Iraq
NEHEMIAH
Jews rebuild Jerusalem's walls
ESTHER
Jew becomes Iranian queen, saves Jews from genocide

POETRY

JOB
Loses his wealth, health, children; blames God
PSALMS
Jewish songs of worship
PROVERBS
Practical advice for young men
ECCLESIASTES
One man's search for the meaning of life

SONG OF SONGS

Intimate, erotic love song

ISAIAH

Warns Jews to stop sinning

JEREMIAH

Lives to see predictions come true: Jewish nation falls

LAMENTATIONS

Eyewitness to Jerusalem's fall describes the horrors

EZEKIEL

Predicts end of Jewish nation, followed by its rebirth

DANIEL

Exiled Jew advises Babylonians (Iraq) and Persians (Iran)

HOSEA

Marries a hooker to illustrate Jewish nation's unfaithfulness

JOEL

Warns of a locust-like invasion of warriors

AMOS

Defends the poor and accuses exploitive, rich Jews

OBADIAH

Condemns nation of Edom for murdering Jewish refugees

JONAH

Reluctant prophet convinces people of Nineveh (in Iraq) to repent

MICAH

Predicts the Messiah will come from Bethlehem

NAHUM

Predicts the end of the Iraqi-based Assyrian Empire

HABAKKUK

Vows to trust God no matter what

ZEPHANIAH

Predicts the end of humanity

HAGGAI

Convinces Jews to rebuild their Temple

ZECHARIAH

Predicts the coming of a savior

MALACHI

Accuses rehab Jews suffering a spiritual relapse

GOSPELS ABOUT JESUS

MATTHEW

Jesus' story, emphasizing prophecies he fulfills

MARK

Most action-packed account of Jesus' life

LUKE

A doctor's take on Jesus' life and ministry

JOHN

Jesus' story, emphasizing his teachings

HISTORY: BIRTH OF THE CHURCH

ACTS

Jesus' disciples jumpstart the Christian movement

PAUL'S LETTERS TO CHURCHES

ROMANS
What Christians believe about Jesus and eternal life

1, 2 CORINTHIANS
Paul tries to solve problems in the Corinthian church

GALATIANS
Christianity is about a bunch of grace, not a bunch of rules

EPHESIANS
Tips for how to live the Christian life

PHILIPPIANS
Paul's thank-you letter to a generous congregation

COLOSSIANS
Dealing with heretics in the church

1, 2 THESSALONIANS
Jesus is coming back, but in the meantime don't get lazy

PAUL'S LETTERS TO INDIVIDUALS

1, 2 TIMOTHY
Advice about how to pastor a church

TITUS
Advice about how to pastor a tough congregation

PHILEMON
Letter of recommendation for a runaway slave turning himself in

LETTERS TO THE CHURCH AT LARGE

HEBREWS
Essay arguing that Jesus made the Jewish religion obsolete

JAMES
Christian do's and don'ts

1, 2 PETER
Advice for persecuted Christians

1, 2, 3 JOHN
Warning against "antichrists" who say Jesus only pretended to die

JUDE
Fighting the heresy that it's okay to sin because God forgives

PROPHECY ABOUT END TIMES

REVELATION
Visions of disaster on earth and of Jesus coming back for his followers

HOW DID WE GET THE BIBLE?

SHORT ANSWER: NO ONE KNOWS.

The process was gradual. Bible experts agree on that much.

To settle the Jewish Bible, which most Christians call the Old Testament, no committee of rabbis toed up to a table, debated weeks on end, and eventually reached a compromise on which Jewish books were kosher enough to get a stamp of approval: INSPIRED BY GOD. Ditto for the Christian add-on called the New Testament.

There were committees of Jewish and Christian scholars. But Bible historians generally agree that these scholars simply confirmed what the scattered community of faith had grown to believe over the previous centuries: that this collection of books had already become sacred.

OLD TESTAMENT: WHO WROTE IT AND PUT IT TOGETHER?

GOD. God is first on record to write anything reported in the Bible.

He etched the 10 Commandments onto stone tablets; "the words on them were written by God himself" (Exodus 32:16).

MOSES. Moses wrote, too. He's credited with writing the hundreds of laws God gave him—laws scattered throughout the books of Exodus, Leviticus, Numbers, and Deuteronomy. "Moses wrote this entire body of instruction in a book and gave it to the priests" (Deuteronomy 31:9). Ancient tradition also credits him with Genesis.

WORD OF MOUTH. Scholars guess that Jews passed along most of the oldest stories in the Bible by word of mouth from one generation to the next, since few could read or write.

PALACE OFFICIALS. Some scholars guess that, once Israel organized into a nation under King David, palace officials began writing down these stories to preserve the history of their nation.

PROPHETS, POETS, AND KINGS. There's no byline on most Bible books. But there are on some. "Jeremiah dictated all the prophecies that the LORD had given him, Baruch [a professional scribe] wrote them on a scroll" (Jeremiah 36:4). "David composed a funeral song for Saul and Jonathan" (2 Samuel 1:17). King David is also credited with writing or at least inspiring nearly half the psalms.

EXILED JEWS. Jews probably began pulling together all these writings, scholars speculate, after Babylonian invaders from what is now Iraq dismantled the Jewish nation and exiled Jewish survivors to Babylon. Without a temple, Jews gradually became "people of the book." They met in small groups that became known as synagogues. And there they read the writings of their people: laws, history, poetry, and prophecies.

Jewish scholars say that the first books their ancestors embraced as God-sent were the first five books of the Bible—known as the Law: Genesis through Deuteronomy. A summary of the laws, Deuteronomy may have been the lost "Book of the Law" (2 Kings 22:8) found in the temple in the 600s BC, a few decades before Babylonians destroyed the temple in 586 BC.

In time, Jews also embraced the books of the

prophets, and then finally the collection of other writings such as Psalms, Proverbs, and Job.

ROMAN JEWS. After Rome destroyed the last Jewish temple in AD 70, Jews once again found themselves without a worship center. No longer could they offer animal sacrifices—a main way they expressed their faith. As they had done when Babylonians leveled their temple 600 years earlier, the Jews again turned to their sacred writings.

Scholar councils met to debate whether or not some books belonged in their Bible—books like Esther and the Song of Songs, which don't even mention God. But by this time they couldn't do anything but argue. For Jews throughout the world had already embraced the Old Testament books that Jews and Christians alike still revere as holy.

NEW TESTAMENT: WHO WROTE IT AND PUT IT TOGETHER?

PAUL. Before anyone wrote the four Gospels about Jesus, a traveling missionary named Paul was writing letters to churches he had started. He also wrote a few to colleagues in ministry—church leaders Timothy, Titus, and Philemon.

Churches kept the letters, copied them, and passed them around for others to read. Almost from the beginning, many scholars say, Christians treated Paul's letters as authoritative. In time, these letters would make up nearly half the books of the New Testament: 13 of 27.

PETER. Leader of the original dozen disciples

STAMP OF APPROVAL. Church leaders in AD 397 gather in the North African coastal town of Carthage, in what is now Tunisia. There, they agree that the Christian Bible should include the Jewish Bible (Old Testament) along with the 27 New Testament books that most Christians today still consider sacred.

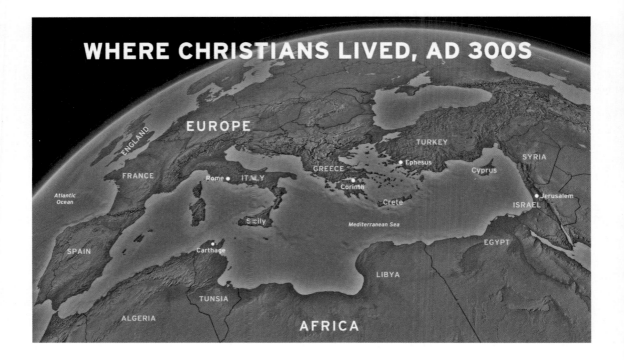

EUROPE

ENGLAND

FRANCE

Atlantic
Ocean

Rome • ITALY

SPAIN

Carthage

ALGERIA

TUNISIA

Sicily

TURKEY

GREECE

Corinth

Crete

Mediterranean Sea

LIBYA

AFRICA

• Ephesus

SYRIA

Cyprus

• Jerusalem

ISRAEL

EGYPT

of Jesus, he's credited with writing two letters named after him.

JAMES, BROTHER OF JESUS. Leader of the church in Jerusalem, he's usually the James credited with writing the short book named after him—a practical book about how to live the Christian life. Another contender: the apostle James.

APOSTLES AND COLLEAGUES. No one knows who wrote the stories of Jesus: Matthew, Mark, Luke, and John. The writers never identify themselves. But the books earned their names because of who the early church leaders in the AD 100s said wrote them: disciples of Jesus. Matthew and John, along with associates of the disciples, John Mark and a physician named Luke, both of whom traveled with Paul.

The apostle John is also credited with writing the three short letters named after him. Some credit him with Revelation, though many others say another John wrote this book of prophecy.

All of these Gospels and letters circulated, along with other Christian writings. Over the centuries that followed, individual church leaders argued over which writings were God-sent. But in time, the church at large seemed to decide. It decided by using the writings in worship. The list of 27 books that Christians revere shows up for the first time in an Easter letter that Bishop Athanasius wrote in AD 367 to churches he supervised.

These are the fountains of salvation, and they who thirst may be satisfied with the living words they contain.

Thirty years later, a council of church leaders agreed, and acknowledged that the 27 books were:
:: written by apostles or their close associate
:: widely recognized in local churches as messages from God
:: in line with traditional Christian teachings.

SHOPPING FOR THE PERFECT BIBLE

THINK ICE CREAM.

That's the best way to select a Bible. You gotta sample it.

Bible experts love dipping into the New American Standard Bible. The New Revised Standard Version, too. That's because scholars say those versions most accurately reflect the original text. Trouble is, they're tougher to read than most other Bibles. They sound like a scholar lecturing, while most folks prefer a Bible that sounds like a friend chatting.

That's why one popular tip for choosing a Bible is to go with a version that's easy to understand.

If you love Shakespeare, knock yourself out with the King James Version. Shakespeare was still writing plays when scholars translated that Bible.

As a general rule, the more recent the translation, the closer it is to the way we talk. That's because language flows like a river, always changing.

On the next page is a "Top 10" sampling of popular Bible translations—starting with the easiest to read. To compare other Bibles and more Bible verses, jump on the Internet and check out a free Bible comparison site, such as BibleGateway.com.

HOW TO MAKE A NEW BIBLE TRANSLATION:

Think sausage.

That's how one Bible translator described the process of creating modern translations of the Bible. His name: Daniel Taylor, a communications specialist for the New Living Translation.

Like sausage, he explained, it's a process no one wants to see.

Scholars meet around a table and grind out the words they think best reflect the ancient originals—or at least their understanding of the ancient originals.

Taylor says that word choices shot down by group consensus at nine in the morning sometimes rise from the dead late in the day, when scholars are tired and hungry.

This humanity-flawed process is one reason most Bible translations keep getting revised. Another reason: language, fluid like a stream, is constantly changing.

BIBLE TRANSLATORS AT WORK. Father Stephen J. Hartdegen, seated, and Jesuit Father Francis T. Gignac work on a revised edition of the New American Bible, an English translation for Catholics. Hartdegen coordinated the 1970 original and the 1986 revision of the New Testament. Gignac chaired the board of editors for the 1986 revision.

BIBLE VERSION	READING LEVEL	YEAR RELEASED
NEW INTERNATIONAL READER'S VERSION	Grade 2.9* (8-year-old child)	1998 revised edition
CONTEMPORARY ENGLISH VERSION	5.4 (10-year-old)	1995
NEW CENTURY VERSION	5.6 (11-year-old)	1991 revised
NEW LIVING TRANSLATION	6.3 (11-year-old)	2007 revised
ENGLISH STANDARD VERSION	7.4 (12-year-old)	2001
NEW INTERNATIONAL VERSION	7.8 (13-year-old)	2011 revised
NEW KING JAMES VERSION	8 (13-year-old)	1982
THE MESSAGE	Varies wildly—often grades 5-10; 2 Timothy 3 reads at grade 10 (15-year-old).	2002
KING JAMES VERSION	12 (17-year-old)	1611
TODAY'S NEW INTERNATIONAL VERSION	Not available; 2 Timothy 3 reads at grade 13 (18-year-old).	2005

2 TIMOTHY 3:16	PROVERBS 3:5–6
God has breathed life into all of Scripture. It is useful for teaching us what is true. It is useful for correcting our mistakes. It is useful for making our lives whole again and for doing what is right.	Trust in the LORD with all your heart. Do not depend on your own understanding. In all your ways remember him. Then he will make your paths smooth and straight.
Everything in the Scriptures is God's Word. All of it is useful for teaching and helping people and for correcting them and showing them how to live.	With all your heart you must trust the LORD and not your own judgment. Always let him lead you, and he will clear the road for you to follow.
All Scripture is inspired by God and is useful for teaching, for showing people what is wrong in their lives, for correcting faults, and for teaching how to live right.	Trust the LORD with all your heart, and don't depend on your own understanding. Remember the LORD in all you do, and he will give you success.
All Scripture is inspired by God and is useful to teach us what is true and to make us realize what is wrong in our lives. It corrects us when we are wrong and teaches us to do what is right.	Trust in the LORD with all your heart; do not depend on your own understanding. Seek his will in all you do, and he will show you which path to take.
All Scripture is breathed out by God and profitable for teaching, for reproof, for correction, and for training in righteousness.	Trust in the LORD with all your heart, and do not lean on your own understanding. In all your ways acknowledge him, and he will make straight your paths.
All Scripture is God-breathed and is useful for teaching, rebuking, correcting and training in righteousness.	Trust in the LORD with all your heart and lean not on your own understanding; in all your ways submit to him, and he will make your paths straight.
All Scripture is given by inspiration of God, and is profitable for doctrine, for reproof, for correction, for instruction in righteousness.	Trust in the LORD with all your heart, and lean not on your own understanding; in all your ways acknowledge Him, and He shall direct your paths.
Every part of Scripture is God-breathed and useful one way or another—showing us truth, exposing our rebellion, correcting our mistakes, training us to live God's way.	Trust GOD from the bottom of your heart; don't try to figure out everything on your own. Listen for GOD's voice in everything you do, everywhere you go; he's the one who will keep you on track.
All scripture *is* given by inspiration of God, and is profitable for doctrine, for reproof, for correction, for instruction in righteousness.	Trust in the LORD with all thine heart; and lean not unto thine own understanding. In all thy ways acknowledge him, and he shall direct thy paths.
All Scripture is God-breathed and is useful for teaching, rebuking, correcting and training in righteousness.	Trust in the LORD with all your heart and lean not on your own understanding; in all your ways submit to him, and he will make your paths straight.

*By comparison, many newspapers try to maintain reading levels of no higher than grade 8, meaning a 13-year-old eighth grader could understand it.

BIBLE: FAST PASS > 19

TWO GREAT WAYS TO STUDY THE BIBLE

WAY 1: Pick a book that snags your interest. Maybe it's the action-packed Gospel of Mark. Or maybe James, a short letter brimming with advice about how to live the Christian life.

WAY 2: Pick a topic on your mind. Money worries, perhaps. Or temptation.

NOT A WAY: If you're a Bible newbie, don't even think about starting at Genesis and expecting to plow through all 66 books of the Bible. Most readers bail by the time they hit the long census report in Numbers. And that's if they make it through the hundreds of obsolete laws in Leviticus.

Especially for Bible newcomers, many ministers say, it's best to start with a book or a topic that interests you.

BY THE BOOK

If you're interested in knowing more about Jesus, any one of the four Gospels would do: Matthew, Mark, Luke, or John. For folks new to the Bible, Mark might be a good choice because it's the shortest and fastest-paced Gospel. John is the most cerebral; it focuses on Jesus' teaching more than his travels and his miracles.

SUPER-SIZED BIBLE. A visitor to the Royal Ontario Museum studies an enlarged picture from one of the famous Dead Sea Scrolls. The ancient library of about 800 scrolls (mostly in fingernail-size pieces) was discovered near the Dead Sea in 1947–1956. They include books of the Old Testament written in Jesus' century and 200 years earlier. These scrolls are 1,000 years older than the copies used to translate the King James Version of the Bible.

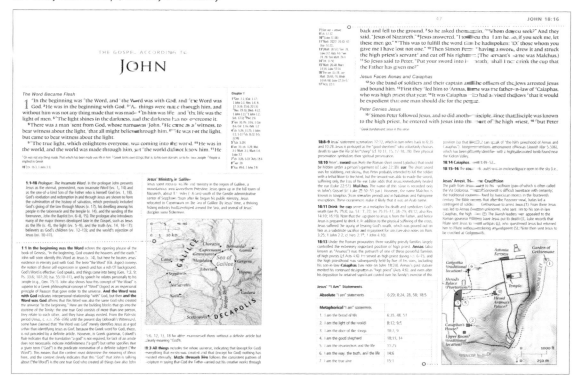

Someone eager to know how Christians should behave might read Paul's letter of advice to the church at Ephesus (see the book of Ephesians) or at Philippi (see the book of Philippians).

STUDY BIBLE. If you're going to study the Bible this way, one book at a time, consider getting a study Bible. These Bibles feature notes in the margin, along with maps, charts, and short articles. All these extras add insightful background. They also address some of the questions you'll be asking as you read through the Bible.

ONE-VOLUME BIBLE COMMENTARY. For more inquisitive readers, there are one-book commentaries on the Bible. These are a bit like beefed-up study Bibles, with just the notes. So you'll need to BYOB (bring your own Bible).

A SET OF BIBLE COMMENTARIES. For the brainiacs, there are books that offer detailed verse-by-verse comments about individual books of the Bible—an entire commentary book on just the Gospel of John, for example. Some of these are easy to read. Others should be prescribed as a sedative for normal human beings because they read like they're written from one scholar to another. So look before you leap to the checkout counter.

Other helpful study tools: a Bible dictionary, a Bible atlas, and a concordance that gives you every verse in the Bible where a particular word appears, such as *sacrifice*. Many Bible study software packages offer all of these, a library of resources in one digital package. Notables of the moment: Logos/Libronix, WORDSearch, PC Study Bible, BibleWorks, Glo.

Sometimes, you might want to know what the Bible says about one particular topic: abortion, homosexuality, divorce, drinking alcohol, or forgiveness.

That's why so much of *Bible Snapshots* points out those passages, in the section called "What the Bible Says About. . ."

Books that help us study topics like these are called topical concordances. *Bible Snapshots* contains just a condensed version, focusing only on some of the more popular topics, which are accompanied by some of the most crucial Bible passages dealing with those topics. Other concordances are exhaustive, covering every word in the Bible. We can even look up every verse that includes the word *the,* though it's hard to imagine why anyone would want to. Most Bible software allows us to do the same thing.

But a topical concordance includes Bible passages that wouldn't turn up in a word search. If we want to know what the Bible says about gambling, for example, we should probably look at the bet Samson made with his wedding guests in Judges 14. But the word *gamble* or *gambling* doesn't show up in that story. So a topical concordance does what a word search can't.

WARNING: There's one big problem with studying the Bible by topic. It's easy to take a statement out of context—to read one sentence and skip the rest of the passage.

It's even easier to warp the context if we already have our mind made up, and we're just looking for a verse to rubber-stamp our brain.

Let's say you're a deadbeat Christian who thinks you're saved by faith alone and that you don't need to lend a hand to anyone else. You'd love something Paul says:

DON'T READ POETRY LIKE IT'S ROCKET SCIENCE.

When trying to figure out what a writer is saying, consider the style of writing: the genre. That's what scholars recommend.

The Bible library of 66 books serves up a short stack of genres: Jewish laws, history, poetry, wisdom sayings, prophecy, eyewitness stories about Jesus, open letters to the church at large, and private letters to individuals.

If we're reading poetry, scholars say, we should read as though the writer is driving with a poetic license.

There's probably no astrophysics, many scholars say, in the story of Joshua ordering the sun and moon to "stand still" (Joshua 10:12). His prayer is a poem. He may simply have been asking God to let his men fight in the shade, since they were already weary from an all-night march up into the hills. "Stand still" can also mean "stop," as in "stop shining." If that's what Joshua was asking, he got his wish. A storm rolled in and hail killed more of the enemy than Joshua's army did.

DON'T TAKE PROPHECY LITERALLY.

Most prophecy is written as poetry, and many scholars say we should read it that way.

We can take the main point literally, they say, but often not the details.

In one vision, for example, Daniel sees bizarre animals fighting each other. The angel Gabriel says they aren't really animals. They represent the battling empires of Persia (Iran) and Greece (Daniel 8:20–21).

Without Gabriel's help, Daniel didn't have a clue how to interpret his own vision. Scholars say that should caution us to keep an open mind when we're reading passages written in the same genre—apocalyptic poetry, famous for its over-the-top symbolism. The genre also shows up in Revelation and Ezekiel.

WHY BOTHER READING A 2,000-YEAR-OLD BOOK?

Christians say it's one of the ways God talks to us. God once talked to his people through prophets, apostles, and his Son. Today God still talks through the words of ancients, preserved in the Bible. Some of what they had to say is merely history—which doesn't apply to life today. But some is considered great advice that works in any century: "Don't pick on people, jump on their failures, criticize their faults—unless, of course, you want the same treatment. That critical spirit has a way of boomeranging" (Matthew 7:1–2 MSG).

▲ **PAST TENSE.** Four-year-old Nathaniel, an Amish boy in Pennsylvania, pauses for a picture during his day of chores, which include hauling firewood. Amish folks seek the simple life—in a way that seems time-locked in a lost century. Yet the Amish see benefits in their link to the past, including stronger family bonds. In a similar way, Christians embrace the Bible as an ancient book with timeless insights.

We are not set right with God by rule-keeping but only through personal faith in Jesus Christ.
Galatians 2:16 MSG

But if you'd like to argue the opposite, here's a line that reads like a punch in the mouth:

Faith by itself isn't enough. Unless it produces good deeds, it is dead and useless.
James 2:17

Here's the trouble. When you look at the context—the verses surrounding those noted above—Paul and James agree with each other. These particular quotes simply address different problems. Paul is arguing against Jewish Christians who are trying to convince his non-Jewish converts that they need to obey all the ancient Jewish rules, such as circumcision and eating only kosher food. Paul says non-Jews don't need to do that. James, pastor of the Jerusalem church, faces a different problem. He's trying to motivate do-nothing Christians to do something—to act like Good Samaritans and help people in need.

Paul agreed with that: "Whenever we have the opportunity, we should do good to everyone" (Galatians 6:10).

Don't read just one sentence and think you understand it. Look for context clues.

ILLUSTRATED BIBLE HISTORY TIMELINE

BIBLE EVENTS

BEFORE 4,000 BC
: God creates world

BEFORE 2500 BC
: Noah and family survive Flood

START

4.5 BILLION BC
: Earth, solar system emerge

2500 BC
: Giza Pyramids built

WORLD EVENTS

BIBLE EVENTS

1000 BC
King David names
Jerusalem Jewish capital

930 BC
Israel splits: Israel in
north, Judah south

722 BC
Assyria (Iraq)
conquers Israel

1279 BC
Rameses the Great
rules Egypt

900 BC
Mayan culture
mysteriously
disappears

776 BC
First known
Olympic Games has
one event: footrace

WORLD EVENTS

BIBLE EVENTS

33 (OR 30)
Jesus dies

46
Paul starts churches
during mission trips

64
Romans execute
Peter, Paul

64
Most of Rome burns;
Nero blames Christians

WORLD EVENTS

2100 BC
Abraham moves
from Iraq to Israel

1440 (OR 1275) BC
Moses leads Jews out
of Egyptian slavery

2000 BC
Stonehenge
built in England

1279 BC
Rameses the Great
rules Egypt

(continued>>)

(continued>>)

586 BC
Babylon (Iraq) conquers
Judah, exiles Jews

6 BC
(BETWEEN 7-4)
Jesus is born

30 AD
(OR 28)
Jesus begins ministry

200 BC
Scribes start library
of Dead Sea Scrolls

26 AD
Pontius Pilate starts
10 years as governor
of Judea

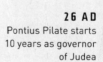

95
John records his
visions in Revelation

END

70
Romans crush
Jewish revolt,
destroy Jerusalem

90
Roman Emperor
Domitian goes by title
"Master and God"

CHRISTIANITY: FAST PASS

CHRISTIANITY, THE SPECS

MAJOR WORLD RELIGIONS

SLICING THE RELIGION PIE. There are about seven billion souls in the world today.

:: About one in three lays claim to the Christian faith—the world's largest religion.

:: Nearly one in four claims the Muslim religion.

:: Another near one-in-four line up with the two biggest Eastern religions: Hinduism and Buddhism.

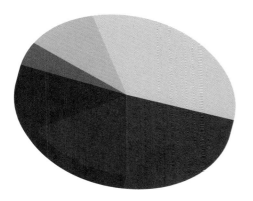

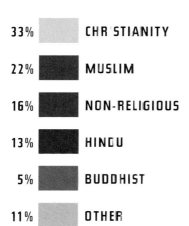

33%	CHRISTIANITY
22%	MUSLIM
16%	NON-RELIGIOUS
13%	HINDU
5%	BUDDHIST
11%	OTHER

CHRISTIAN HOLY DAYS

SUNDAY. Most Christians worship on Sunday, to commemorate the Sunday morning resurrection of Jesus. Some groups, such as the Seventh-day Adventists, worship on the Jewish Sabbath of Saturday—the day Jesus worshipped. To accommodate the busy schedules of people today, some churches offer worship services Friday through Sunday.

EASTER. Considered by many Christians the most important day of the year, Easter is the day they celebrate the resurrection of Jesus. Most Christians celebrate this springtime holy day on:
:: the first Sunday
:: after the first full moon
:: after the spring equinox (the first day of spring).

LENT. For the 40 days leading up to Easter, many Christians fast or give up something. Christians chose 40 days since that's how long Jesus fasted in the Judean badlands after his baptism, just before he started his ministry. In early church history, Christians during Lent ate just one meal a day—in the evening. Today, many give up soft drinks, chocolate, or some other pleasure.

CHRISTMAS. December 25 is the day most Christians commemorate the birthday of Jesus. No one knows when Jesus was born, or even in what season of the year. Many guess it wasn't winter, since the Bible says shepherds were outside at night, watching their sheep. Scholars speculate that early Christians chose December 25 as an alternative to pagan celebrations marking the winter solstice (first day of winter).

FOUR LARGEST CHRISTIAN GROUPS

EAST-WEST CHURCH
SPLIT 1054 AD

EARLY CHRISTIANITY

FRAGMENTS OF FAITH. Disagreements over belief, rituals, and the church's role in politics led Pope Leo IX to excommunicate the leader of the church in the East, Michael Cerularius, patriarch of Constantinople, in what is now Turkey. Cerularius retaliated, excommunicating the pope and launching what became the Eastern Orthodox Church. Corruption in the Roman Catholic Church about 500 years later churned up a reform movement that spawned the Protestant Church. At the same time England's King Henry VIII broke from the Catholic Church after the pope refused to annul the king's marriage. King Henry's Church of England became known as the Anglican Church.

ANGLICAN, 70 MILLION

EASTERN ORTHODOX, 225 MILLION

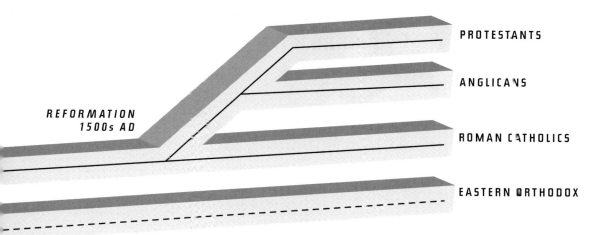

REFORMATION
1500s AD

PROTESTANTS

ANGLICANS

ROMAN CATHOLICS

EASTERN ORTHODOX

PROTESTANT, 600 MILLION

Baptist, 110 million

Methodist, 75 million

Presbyterian, 75 million

Lutheran, 66 million

ROMAN CATHOLIC, 1 BILLION

*estimates vary

	CHRISTIANITY	ISLAM
NUMBER OF FOLLOWERS	2.25 billion	1.5 billion
MAIN LOCATIONS	Europe, N/S America	Asia, Middle East, N. Africa
DATE FOUNDED	AD 33	AD 622
FOUNDER	Jesus (about 6 BC–AD 33)	Muhammad (about 570–632)
GOD	Eternal, all-powerful. One God revealed as three persons: Father, Son, and Holy Spirit.	There is "no God but Allah."
JESUS	Son of God the Father. Virgin-born. Sinless. Died for sins of humanity. Rose from dead. Ascended to heaven.	A prophet, much like Islam's founder, Muhammad. Not God's Son. Not crucified and risen from the dead.
SACRED WRITINGS	Bible: Old Testament (Jewish Bible), New Testament; some add the Apocrypha.	Qur'an, along with Hadith, the story and sayings of Muhammad. Bible is corrupted by changes.
WORSHIP PRACTICES	Prayer, reading Bible, worship at church on Sundays, baptism, communion (Mass).	Five Pillars of Islam: Daily confession of faith in God, pray five times a day facing Mecca, fast during month of Ramadan, donate to the poor, make a pilgrimage to Mecca.
SALVATION/ DELIVERANCE	All have sinned but can find forgiveness by repenting and believing that Jesus is God's Son who died to take the death-penalty punishment for sin.	Obey Five Pillars of faith (above). God will decide punishment and rewards based on what a person does in life.
AFTERLIFE	God will judge everyone. The righteous will live with him forever, the unrighteous will suffer eternally (hell).	Infidels suffer in hell. Faithful Muslims enjoy bliss in Paradise, with all the physical pleasures they had to abstain from on earth.

HINDUISM	BUDDHISM
900 million	360 million
India, UK, US	China, Japan, Korea
3000s BC	500s BC
Developed over many centuries.	Siddhartha Gautama, aka Buddha (about 563 BC–483 BC)
One supreme reality (Brahman) expressed as many gods, each subject to karma and other forces of the universe.	Some are atheists. Some worship Buddha and other divine "forces."
Some consider him enlightened, even a god. Other Hindus discredit him.	No reference to Jesus.
Many, accumulated over centuries—including *Vedas, Upanishads, Bhagavad Gita*.	*Lotus Sutra,* said to contain the teachings of Buddha.
Chanting, yoga, meditation, devotion to a god, offerings for the gods, monk-like self denial.	Chanting the Daimoko, a phrase that sums up the *Lotus Sutra*; meditation; pilgrimage to headquarters on Mount Fuji.
By following the spiritual disciplines (above), people can end the cycle of reincarnations.	Follow eight-fold path, especially right understanding, speech, effort, and thoughts to attain good health, happiness, and union with Buddha.
Unenlightened are reincarnated. Enlightened souls become one with universe, like a drop of water in the ocean.	Reincarnation, with the hope of eventually reaching union with Buddha and ceasing to exist as an individual.

There are about 14 million Jews in the world.

BIG EVENTS IN CHRISTIAN HISTORY

START

6 BC Jesus is born.

30 Jesus begins ministry.

33 Jesus crucified, resurrected; Christian movement starts.

Athanasius (293–373)

325 Council of church leaders in Nicea, Turkey, declares Jesus divine—opposing a movement saying he was human.

367 First known list of New Testament books appear in Bishop Athanasius's letter to churches.

392 Emperor adopts Christianity as religion of Roman Empire.

John Wycliffe (1330–1384)

1095 Pope Urban II launches First Crusade to take Holy Land from Muslims.

1273 Thomas Aquinas writes a summary of Christian beliefs, *Summary of Theology*, which theologians still use.

1380 John Wycliffe directs translation of Bible into English.

Henry VIII (1491–1547)

1517 Martin Luther lists 95 criticisms of Catholic Church, sparking the Protestant movement.

1534 Henry VIII declares himself head of England's church after pope refuses to annul his marriage; result is Anglican Church.

1536 John Calvin of France writes theology book saying God decides who is saved and who isn't, a teaching many Baptists and Presbyterians accept.

Dietrich Bonhoeffer (1906–1945)

1854 Missionary Hudson Taylor arrives in China.

1921 First Christian radio broadcast covers Pittsburgh, Pennsylvania.

1945 Nazis execute Christian pastor and scholar Dietrich Bonhoeffer.

Constantine
(about 280–337)

(continued>>)

46 Paul starts missionary trips.

70 Romans destroy Jerusalem Temple, ending the Jewish sacrificial system.

313 Roman Emperor Constantine legalizes Christianity.

Jerome
(about 340–420)

ROMAN CATHOLIC

(continued>>)

EASTERN ORTHODOX

405 Jerome translates Bible into Latin.

732 Battle of Tours, in France, where Christians defeat Muslim invaders

1054 Church splits: Roman Catholics and Eastern Orthodox

(continued>>)

1453 Johann Gutenberg creates first printed Bible.

1478 Spanish Inquisition forces Jews, Muslims, and others to convert to Christianity, or die.

1512 Michelangelo finishes Sistine Chapel ceiling.

John Wesley (1703–1791)

(continued>>)

1611 English scholars translate King James Version of the Bible.

1735 Sermons of Jonathan Edwards spark American revival: Great Awakening.

1738 John Wesley of England has spiritual experience; his preaching starts the Methodist church.

Billy Graham 1950s

END

1947 Billy Graham begins "crusades," preaching to thousands.

1948 Mother Teresa starts work among poor of Calcutta, India.

1963 Martin Luther King Jr. leads march on Washington, for civil rights.

WHAT IT TAKES TO BE A CHRISTIAN

EVEN CHRISTIANS DON'T AGREE on what it takes to qualify as a legit Christian—a serious follower of Jesus.

Part of the problem, many say, is the Bible. Some folks say it sends mixed signals—producing Christians of different stripes.

BOTTOM-LINE CHRISTIANS. Faith in Jesus is all it takes, many insist. Jesus said as much, several times. The most famous example comes in his conversation with an inquisitive Jewish scholar named Nicodemus:

:: *"God loved the world so much that he gave his one and only Son. Anyone who believes in him will not die but will have eternal life" (John 3:16 NIrV).*

BORN AGAIN CHRISTIANS. Many church groups say we need a conversion experience— a moment of repentance followed by a new and more godly lifestyle. These Christians take their cue from something else Jesus said to Nicodemus:

:: *"I tell you the truth, unless you are born again, you cannot see the Kingdom of God" (John 3:3).*

DIPPED CHRISTIANS. Many believers, especially some in Baptist churches, say we need to get baptized, pronto. They point to the example of the first Christians, who followed Peter's advice:

:: *"Each of you must repent of your sins and turn to God, and be baptized in the name of Jesus Christ for the forgiveness of your sins" (Acts 2:38).*

For first-generation Christians, baptism in the Bible often reads like it's tag-teamed with conversion. One example shows up in advice Ananias gave to Paul, newly converted and healed of blindness:

:: *"What are you waiting for? Get up and be baptized. Have your sins washed away by calling on the name of the Lord" (Acts 22:16).*

POPE-APPROVED CHRISTIANS. Roman Catholics teach that we're saved by obeying our church leaders, especially Christ's spokesman on earth, the pope. Many Catholics consider the pope a continuation of the religious dynasty Jesus started with Peter, whom Catholics say was the first pope:

:: *"You are Peter. On this rock I will build my church. . . . I will give you the keys of the kingdom of heaven; the things you don't allow on earth will be the things that God does not allow, and the things you allow on earth will be the things that God allows" (Matthew 16:18–19 NCV).*

Most Protestants say they understand that to mean Jesus gave Peter the responsibility of leading the initial phase of the Christian movement—which Peter did by preaching the first sermon after Jesus ascended to heaven. That sermon in Jerusalem produced about 3,000 converts (Acts 2:41).

PASTOR-APPROVED CHRISTIANS. Many churches have their own rules. They use them as a spiritual tale of the tape—to see if someone measures up to the requirements for church membership.

Rules like: Don't smoke, dance, or drink

BAPTIZING BABES. A priest baptizes a child in a ritual marking the child as one whose parents will raise her in a Christian home. The Catholic Church urges parents to have their babies baptized within a few weeks after birth, since in the ancient church entire families were baptized (Acts 16:33). Many other Christian groups refuse to baptize infants. These churches say that baptismal candidates should be old enough to understand what it means to confess faith in Jesus.

alcohol. But give 10 percent of your income to the church. For support of these minister-generated rules, some point to passages such as this:

:: *"Honor those who are your leaders in the Lord's work. They work hard among you and give you spiritual guidance. Show them great respect and wholehearted love because of their work"* (1 Thessalonians 5:12–13).

Many Christians say that some church rules have more to do with personal opinion (pet peeves) than with Bible teachings. They argue that Jews in Bible times danced and drank; Jesus' first miracle on record was to turn water into wine (see "Drugs and Alcohol," page 113). Tithing was a Jewish practice; Christians gave offerings (see "Tithing," page 226).

ACTIVIST CHRISTIANS. Faith alone isn't enough, some Christians argue. Real Christians don't keep their religion bottled up inside. They live it.

:: *"Faith by itself isn't enough. Unless it produces good deeds, it is dead and useless. Now someone may argue, 'Some people have faith; others have good deeds.' But I say, 'How can you show me your faith if you don't have good deeds? I will show you my faith by my good deeds' "* (James 2:17–18).

CREED-QUOTING CHRISTIANS. Early Christian leaders summed up what they considered key Christian beliefs. They put them in a creed that many churches today ask their people to recite in worship services from time to time. One of the most popular is the Apostle's Creed. The first reported copy dates to about AD 215.

:: *I believe in God, the Father Almighty, maker of heaven and earth. And in Jesus Christ, his only Son, our Lord, who was conceived by the Holy*

HIGHWAY TO HEAVEN

ROMAN ROAD TO SALVATION

Paul's letter to the church in Rome works a bit like a spiritual map, some Christians say, for it points the way to salvation.

We're all sinners. "Everyone has sinned; we all fall short of God's glorious standard" (Romans 3:23).

Sin is a capital offense. "When people sin, they earn what sin pays—death" (Romans 6:23 NCV).

Jesus took the death penalty for us. "While we were still sinners, Christ died for us" (Romans 5:8 NIrV).

Belief is the key to forgiveness. "People are made right with God when they believe that Jesus sacrificed his life, shedding his blood" (Romans 3:25).

Confession is good for the soul. "If you confess with your mouth that Jesus is Lord and believe in your heart that God raised him from the dead, you will be saved" (Romans 10:9).

Via Appia, ancient road to Rome

Spirit, and born of the Virgin Mary, suffered under Pontius Pilate, was crucified, died, and was buried. He descended to the dead. On the third day he rose again from the dead. He ascended into heaven and sits at the right hand of the Father. From there he will come to judge the living and the dead. I believe in the Holy Spirit, the Holy Christian Church, the communion of saints, the forgiveness of sins, the resurrection of the body, and the life everlasting

Most Christians seem to consider creeds helpful. They also seem to appreciate Bible passages about how a Christian should behave, along with the guidance they get from their pastors and their priests. But they think for themselves, too. They don't simply buy into the party line just because someone tells them to. They want to see the speaker's source of authority—clearly presented in the Bible.

For this reason, many Christians lean toward bottom-line Christianity, arguing that it's hard to trump Jesus who saw nothing more than faith and in response said, "Your sins are forgiven" (Matthew 9:2).

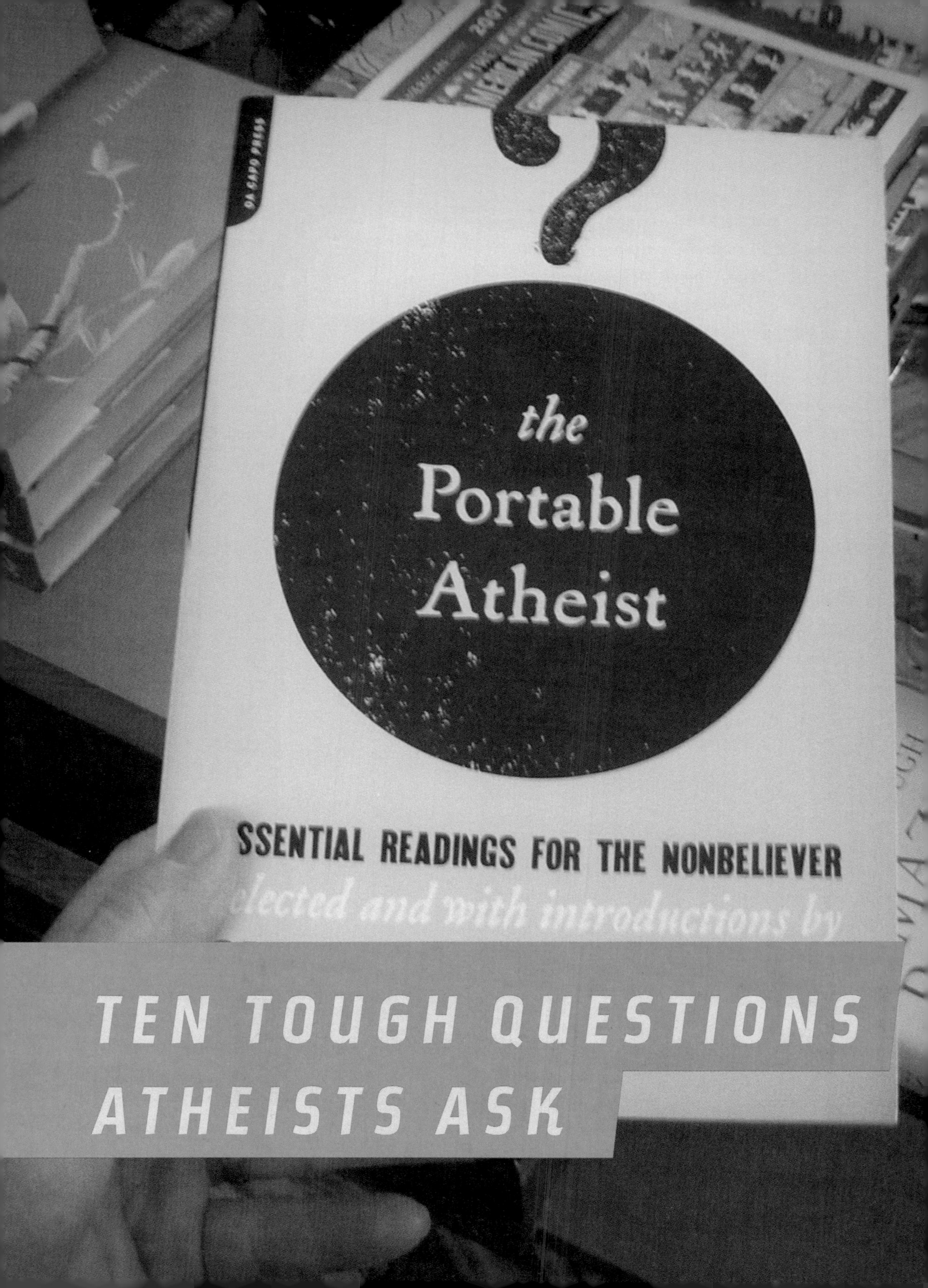

DA CAPO PRESS

the
Portable
Atheist

ESSENTIAL READINGS FOR THE NONBELIEVER

elected and with introductions by

TEN TOUGH QUESTIONS
ATHEISTS ASK

THESE AREN'T DEBATE TIPS to help Christians beat down non-believers in a Mouth Crusade of slashing tongues and spurting saliva.

Jesus had more respect for non-believers than that.

Without exception, as far as the Bible reports it, he treated them with dignity—and with far more kindness than he showed to strutting religious leaders whom he called "Frauds! You're like manicured grave plots, grass clipped and the flowers bright, but six feet down it's all rotting bones and worm-eaten flesh" (Matthew 23:27 MSG).

Serious questions of non-believers deserve honest answers, especially when the answers seem unconvincing.

1. IF THERE IS A GOD, WHY DOESN'T HE SHOW HIMSELF—OR AT LEAST SAY HELLO?

Most Christians would love it if God paid them a visit. They'd pummel him with questions.

And if God is omnipresent—as the Bible implies—why not show up? He could appear to all seven billion humans at once.

Why he doesn't do that is a confounding mystery. Christians, as well as non-Christians, would really love to replace faith with fact. They'd like some answers, too.

But even in Bible stories where God does show up, in one way or another, he's not big into answering questions—especially "why" questions.

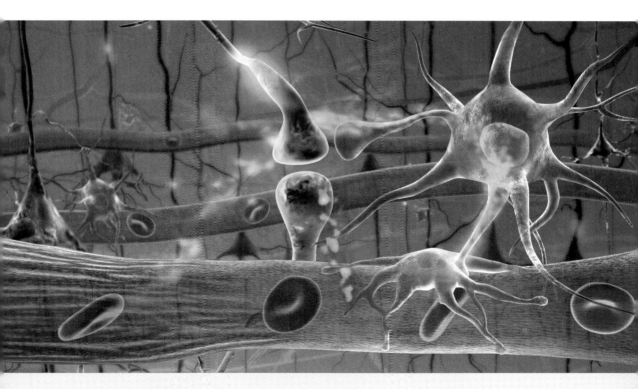

FAITH IN GOD—A NO-BRAINER? Star-shaped neurons flash signals to each other along a network of blood vessels and support cells in the brain. The Bible says there's no excuse for not believing in God, since creation is all around us—and you can't get something from nothing (unless you jump into quantum physics and redefine *nothing* as something, which could sound like arguing over what the definition of *is* is). Christians insist that something as wonderful as creation—from the tiniest cells to sprawling galaxies—must have come from Some Kind of Wonderful.

Of all the people in the Bible who deserved a "why" answer, Job is probably at the top of the list. He had done nothing wrong, but he lost his health, wealth, and family (see page 318).

Job asked God why. God showed up, as the Bible says he occasionally does—sometimes in physical manifestations, though more often in dreams and visions. But instead of answering Job's question, God himself asked a heaping helping of questions. Such as:

:: *Have you ever told the morning to wake up, roll out of bed, and hit the ground running?*
:: *Can you squeeze rain out of a cloud?*
:: *Were you the one who taught the lion how to hunt?*
                    Job 38:12, 34, 39 AUTHOR'S PARAPHRASE

Questions like those, some Christians say, suggest that God does reveal himself and talk to us—through his creation.

The apostle Paul explains:

The basic reality of God is plain enough. Open your eyes and there it is! By taking a long and thoughtful look at what God has created, people have always been able to see what their eyes as such can't see: eternal power, for instance, and the mystery of his divine being. So nobody has a good excuse.
                    Romans 1:19–20 MSG

"The God who made the world and everything in it. . .doesn't play hide-and-seek with us. He's not remote; he's near. We live and move in him, can't get away from him!"
                    Acts 17:24, 27–28 MSG

Beyond this, many Christians say God still reveals himself in personal ways, as he did in Bible times. Sometimes in mystical ways: visions and vivid dreams as dramatic as some in the Bible. Sometimes in miracles that confound even unbelievers. And often in "coincidences" so incredible that it would seem to take more faith to believe they happened by chance rather than by a higher power.

2. IF GOD IS SO GOOD, WHY DOESN'T HE DO ANYTHING WHEN WE'RE SUFFERING?

Christians swear at God sometimes. Industrial-strength swearing. Some lose their faith.

It's all because of wrenching stories that drive this question.

:: *Fire guts a New York City apartment. Sitting on the closet floor, huddled in the fetal position—the charred body of a lone little girl.*
:: *After his first day of kindergarten, an excited boy spots his mom across the street. He darts toward her. A Kansas City dump truck runs him over. His mother sees it all.*

Where the hell was God?

Even Christians ask it that way.

Personal story. As I was working on this section of the book, some folks in my circle of family and friends experienced a double tragedy.

First tragedy. A two-year-old girl, Anighya Payne, drowned in Walden Pond at what was supposed to be a wedding in the backyard of her grandparents; the wedding was cancelled. Anighya (uh-NIGH-yah), who would have been the flower girl, was a cousin of my daughter's roommate; both my daughter and her roommate are pediatric nurses.

While the family prepared the backyard for the wedding, the toddler wandered about 100 yards to the pond. When the family realized she

EPIDEMIC. Citizens of Mexico City, many wearing masks, gather to pray for an end to a flu epidemic that had already closed the schools, killed at least 16 people, and left nearly a thousand others sick.

was missing, they found her floating facedown in the water. The nurse and her boyfriend, a firefighter, jumped in and started CPR. It failed.

Second tragedy. The firefighter boyfriend lost a colleague in a fire later that day—the first firefighter in the history of this Kansas City suburb to lose his life in the line of work. He was searching for people inside a burning house. As it turned out, no one was there, in spite of worried reports to the contrary.

Firemen charge into burning buildings and don't come out alive. And mere human beings would risk their life to save a drowning child.

Yet an almighty God—supposedly the Ultimate Good Guy—won't lift a finger?

The night the toddler died, my prayer included something like this: "I understand how a family could get distracted and lose track of the little girl. What distracted you?"

There is no adequate answer to a question like this. Pressed, some Christians will admit that.

"His ways are higher than our ways." That's one clichéd response Christians sometimes offer.

It's not convincing. After hearing that, no one walks away thinking, *Oh, that makes sense now. I*

might be too dumb to get it, but I'm not too dumb to get that I don't get it.

Though the cliché might not sound convincing, it is the bottom line.

Christians don't get it. No one does. No one understands why a good God doesn't step into human history and put a stop to the misery. Yet Christians give God the benefit of the doubt. They figure that the creator of a universe so exquisitely designed—from subatomic particles to sprawling galaxies—must have a plan.

Jesus said as much. His disciples pointed out a man born blind. They assumed the man deserved his blindness. It was a common misconception among Jews in ancient times—that people in tough situations deserved what they got. So the disciples asked Jesus if the man was blind because of his own sins or if he was suffering from the sins of his parents.

"This happened so the power of God could be seen in him," Jesus answered. "I am the light of the world" (John 9:3, 5). Then he healed the man who had lived in darkness. Miracles like this eventually sparked the Christian movement by convincing people that Jesus and his disciples had God's backing.

So do we start trying to figure out God, pondering the possible reasons behind a misery, maybe even looking for the good side of genocide?

That's not only a waste of time, most sensible Christians would say. It's dangerous. We can reach warped conclusions that would seem to rationalize ungodly behavior in God's name: the Spanish Inquisition, the Salem witch hunts, or the Holocaust.

A better response, some say, is to consider the hypocrisy of criticizing God.

Much of the misery is of our own doing. And many of the cures are within our power.

We build cities on flood plains, fault lines, and tornado alleys—then we shake our fists at God when we discover the buildings can't handle floods, quakes, or tornadoes.

We grow crops with pesticides, sell them with preservatives, and then moan about acid reflux and diseases up the wazoo.

We watch from across the globe as a political demigod wipes out a rival race or people of a different religion—as though we humans are incapable of creating a league of nations united for peace and charged with the responsibility of stopping this kind of violence.

Since we can't figure God out, some activist Christians say, we should at least take advantage of the God-given power we do have to solve problems we accuse God of ignoring.

3. WHY IS GOD SUCH A JERK IN THE OLD TESTAMENT?

God's biographers portray him as a baby killer—on a scale with genocidal mass murderers.

Not in the New Testament. There, he's the proud Father of a pacifist rabbi who tells people "Do not resist an evil person!" (Matthew 5:39).

But in the Old Testament, God *is* the Evil Person. That's how he comes across to plenty of Bible readers.

Consider a few seemingly ungodly quotes that Old Testament writers attribute to God:

:: **KILL EVERYONE**. *"Leave nothing alive in the cities of the land the LORD your God is giving you. Completely destroy these people"* (Deuteronomy 20:16–17 NCV).

    —To Moses, ordering Jews invading what is now Israel to kill all Canaanites—men, women, children, and even animals

:: **I'M MAD ENOUGH TO KILL ALL THE JEWS**. *"I've seen how stubborn and rebellious they are. So don't try to stop me! I am going to wipe them out"* (Deuteronomy 9:13–14 CEV).

    —To Moses, after Jews worshipped a gold calf during the Exodus. (Moses talks God out of the slaughter.)

:: **TAKE YOUR PICK OF THREE WAYS TO DIE**. *"You may choose three years of famine, three months of destruction by the sword of your enemies, or three days of severe plague"* (1 Chronicles 21:12).

    —To King David, who somehow sinned by taking a census. David chose option three, and 70,000 Jews died in a plague.

Christians typically defend God in one of two ways. They'll try to justify his actions. Or they'll admit they don't understand what's going on. Some add a third option: Maybe God got misquoted.

Perhaps the toughest action to justify is the genocide of Canaan residents.

Moses offered this rationale: "If you allow them to live, they will persuade you to worship their disgusting gods" (Deuteronomy 20:18 CEV). Canaanite religion was disgusting because some of the worship involved infant sacrifice and sex rituals with pagan priestesses.

The warning Moses gave came true, as the Bible reports history. Rather than kill all the Canaanites, Jews learned to live with some of them as neighbors—and eventually adopted their religions.

God put up with the idolatry for about 400 years. All the while, he sent prophets to remind the Jews of the agreement their ancestors made with him, and to warn them about the penalty clause for continued idolatry: eviction from the

THE WORD OF THE LORD. I will cover you with garbage, treat you like trash, and rub you in the dirt" (Nahum 3:6 CEV). That's God giving nasty Assyrians (Iraq) what for, as quoted by the prophet Nahum. Some scholars say the harsh words prophets attributed to God are more likely their own attempt to convey God's general message—in this case, that Judgment Day was coming for Assyria and for other nations that terrorized the Jews.

land. "The LORD will scatter you among all the nations" (Deuteronomy 28:64).

Babylonian invaders from what is now Iraq defeated and exiled the Jews in 586 BC. The exile lasted about 50 years. Then God gave the Jews a second chance. They rebuilt their nation—without the idols.

Background like this can, for some people of faith, soften the impact of God's apparent callousness. In this case, God ordered the destruction of one generation to protect countless generations from adopting lethal worship practices.

That explanation isn't good enough for some Christians.

They wonder if Moses got his divine wires crossed, or if the Bible writer punched up the story with an extra dose of drama, making God out to be angrier and meaner than he was.

Other Bible experts wonder if the prophets may have gotten just the most basic direction from God, such as "Tell the people to turn from idols," and then added their own take on the how-to and on the consequences outlined in the ancient agreement between God and the Jews. Punishment for persistent sin included disease, drought, crop failure, invasion, and exile.

Perhaps these prophets tried to do what the Puritan preacher Jonathan Edwards (1703–1758) actually did. He terrified early Americans into a revival called the Great Awakening. His technique: preaching fire-and-brimstone sermons such as "Sinners in the Hands of an Angry God." Possibly, some scholars suggest, ancient prophets tried to do that, too. They took the Bible's warnings and ran with them, applying them to their day. As a result, they painted God with a club more often than with a carrot.

Many Christians, however, just scratch their head and wonder why the compassionate Jesus doesn't seem to look very much like his Father. But they decide to give God the benefit of the doubt, if for no other reason than because of something Jesus said: "Anyone who has seen me has seen the Father!" (John 14:9).

4. WHY TREAT THE BIBLE AS GOD'S MESSAGE WHEN NO ONE HAS A CLUE WHO WROTE MOST OF IT?

No one knows how many humans got ink on their fingers from writing the Bible. The most common guess is 40 or more. But it's just a guess.

There are 66 books in the Protestant

Bible—plus a dozen more in Catholic and Orthodox Bibles. Pitifully few books bother to name their author.

Some that do spark debates. Psalms, for example. David gets credit for writing about half of the songs. But scholars say his byline allows wiggle room: "of David" could mean it's by him, about him, for him, or inspired by him.

Regardless of who dipped into the ink, most Christians agree that Bible writers got their inspiration from God.

For two main reasons.

JESUS TREATED THE BIBLE AS GOD-INSPIRED. Jesus, Paul, and other stars of the New Testament spoke of their Jewish Bible as inspired. Jesus quoted it often, treating it as a source of guidance. Paul described it this way:

Everything in the Scriptures is God's Word. All of it is useful for teaching and helping people and for correcting them and showing them how to live. The Scriptures train God's servants to do all kinds of good deeds.

2 Timothy 3:16–17 CEV

THE MAIN TEACHINGS SOUND GOOD AND GODLY. Though there's plenty of horrible history reported in the Bible—stories not intended as model behavior—the main teachings ring true for Christians.

Love God, the creator of life.

Love others, treating them with the same kind of dignity you'd want from them.

Jesus said these two rules to live by are the most important commandments. "These two commands are pegs; everything in God's Law and the Prophets hangs from them" (Matthew 22:40 MSG).

A sampling of other rules that make sense to most Christians:

:: *"Settle your differences quickly."*

:: *"Don't pick on people, jump on their failures, criticize their faults—unless, of course, you want the same treatment."*

:: *"Faith by itself isn't enough. Unless it produces good deeds, it is dead and useless."*

Matthew 5:25; Matthew 7:1 MSG; James 2:17

5. IF THE BIBLE IS GOD'S WORD, WHY IS IT FULL OF BLATANT CONTRADICTIONS AND OBVIOUS MISTAKES?

If God had picked up a pen and had written the Bible in English, perhaps no one would have found any mistakes—except, of course, an English teacher; they have more rules than God knows makes sense. And I probably just broke one with that sentence.

The trouble is, many Christians explain, humans got involved.

Some Christians insist that the original copies of every sentence in the Bible were error-free—as though God's inspiration of the writer was so intense that God might as well have dictated the words. Other Christians argue that this sounds like Bible worship instead of God worship—with the Bible as a tree-pulp idol.

Besides, many Christians add, there's no point in debating the originals. We don't have them. What we have are copies of copies, from translations of translations. The question for today is: How reliable are the Bibles we hold in our hands?

Reliable enough, the vast majority of Christians agree.

The Bible is reliable enough to teach us everything we need to know about God, about how to live as God's people, and about how to find salvation through faith in Jesus.

Christians typically approach apparent contradictions and mistakes in the Bible one of two ways:

:: **ARGUE THAT THERE'S NO MISTAKE.** *Their bottom line: God can't make a mistake; the Bible is God's Word; so the Bible can't be mistaken.*

:: **ADMIT THE MISTAKE WITHOUT BLAMING GOD.** *Their bottom line: humans make mistakes, humans were involved in the process of producing the Bible, and the mistakes are minor and don't diminish the core message of the Bible.*

One apparent mistake: a census report that doesn't add up.

Jews exiled in what is now Iraq return home to Israel. Ezra and Nehemiah tell the story of the same wave of returning refugees. Both agree that 42,360 Jews came home (Ezra 2:64; Nehemiah 7:66). But neither hits that number in the breakdown of the various groups. If we add up Ezra's list of refugees, we get 29,818. Nehemiah's list tallies 31,089.

Christians of the error-free-Bible persuasion offer explanations such as this: the breakdowns don't add up to 42,360 because this grand tally includes all the people while the breakdown lists include only the men.

There's a second problem, though. One of several discrepancies between the two breakdown lists has Ezra saying there were 200 singing men and women, while Nehemiah says there were 245 (Ezra 2:65; Nehemiah 7:67). Error-free-Bible folks say that one census took place early in the trip while the other took place after the Jews arrived home. So if Nehemiah's census took place later, the choir recruited an extra 45 singers.

Many Bible scholars, perhaps most, say there were probably mistakes made in copying the lists

A scribe touches up a scroll.

from one worn-out scroll to a new scroll.

Some error-free-Bible folks reject that notion. They argue that God oversees the process of preserving his message, protecting it from mistakes. Other Christians seem relaxed in allowing for some humanity in the process, confident that there's not nearly enough of it to erode the divinity.

6. WHY WOULD ANY INTELLIGENT, RATIONAL PERSON BELIEVE BIBLE STORIES ABOUT A TALKING SNAKE, THE SUN STOPPING IN THE SKY, THE VIRGIN BIRTH, AND DEAD PEOPLE COMING BACK TO LIFE?

Not all Christians do.

Some don't believe in the talking snake of creation's story in Genesis. Or that Joshua literally stopped the sun in the sky. Some don't even believe in the Virgin Birth. Others doubt the resurrection of the dead—the resurrection of Jesus included.

Christians are that diverse in their beliefs.

Of course, some Christians will call other Christians heretics. A few medieval types might bonfires for the other hot dogs.

Many Christians, perhaps most, read the creation story as literal fact. Others treat it more like the marriage between a parable and a myth—as a fictional story with a factual message: the creator was God, not some deity from Babylon (Iraq) who starred in ancient Babylonian creation stories circulating in Bible times.

As for the battlefield report that "the sun stood still and the moon stayed in place until the nation of Israel had defeated its enemies" (Joshua 10:13), some Christians argue that anyone who can create the universe can certainly give the sun and moon the appearance of stopping in the sky.

Science-savvy Christians understand that it wouldn't be the sun and moon that stopped; it would be the earth that stopped spinning. It's this spinning, at about 1,000 mph (1,600 kph), that gives the illusion that the sun and moon move. If the spinning stopped, scientists theorize, the atmosphere would continue the momentum, sweeping the earth with a 1,000 mph wind.

A more likely explanation of the battlefield report, say these Christians, comes from the fact that it's a poem—and that we should give the writer some poetic license. Also, the Hebrew word that says the sun and moon "stood still" is *damam,* which can also mean "stopped shining." The Bible does report that thick storm clouds rolled in. "Hail killed more of the enemy than the Israelites killed with the sword" (Joshua 10:11).

EAT DIRT AND DIE. For luring Eve into breaking God's one and only law—eating forbidden fruit from the Tree of Life—God condemns the snake "to slink on your belly and eat dirt all your life" (Genesis 3:14 MSG).

even wish they could hang, gut, and burn the heretics like folks did in the good ol' days.

But if God allows human beings to think what they please, many Christians argue, perhaps God's people should do the same—and save

7. THE BIBLE SAYS THERE'S JUST ONE GOD, BUT JESUS SAYS HE'S DIVINE, TOO; HOW COULD ANYONE BELIEVE BOTH?

That's exactly why most Jews rejected Jesus 2,000 years ago, and still reject him today.

It doesn't matter if he can heal the sick, walk

on water, and raise the dead—himself included. He's no god. Not as far as the Jews are concerned.

To the devout Jew, there's no verse in their Bible more important than this: "The LORD is the one and only God" (Deuteronomy 6:4 NIRV).

The Lord is one. Not two. Certainly not three: Father, Son, and Holy Spirit.

Sadly, the Bible doesn't settle this conflict in a way that would make sense to many rational thinkers.

The closest it comes is the Gospel of John—the story of Jesus written with just one purpose: "so that you may believe that Jesus is the Christ, the Son of God" (John 20:31 NIRV). In John's Gospel, Jesus simply says, "I am in the Father and the Father is in me" (John 14:10).

Jesus doesn't even try to explain how this could possibly be—how two separate entities could be one. Perhaps, some Christians speculate, it's because humans limited to the physical dimension couldn't possibly understand this aspect of the spiritual dimension.

Even Jesus' disciples don't get it.

"Lord, show us the Father, and we will be satisfied," Philip tells him (John 14:8).

"Don't you believe?" Jesus asks, obviously frustrated. "At least believe because of the work you have seen me do" (John 14:10–11).

That's as far as the Bible writers go in addressing the matter of Jesus' divinity. They report creation-caliber miracles of Jesus: turning water into wine, calming storms, walking on water, and raising the dead. And they figure if that doesn't convince people that Jesus is who he says he is, nothing will.

Divine Trinity, in a painting from the Middle Ages

8. ISN'T IT POSSIBLE THAT THE REASON JESUS SEEMED TO FULFILL SO MANY PROPHECIES IS BECAUSE NEW TESTAMENT WRITERS MADE IT LOOK THAT WAY SINCE THEY WROTE ABOUT JESUS SEVERAL HUNDRED YEARS AFTER THE PROPHECIES?

Sure. The disciples of Jesus could have lied about him.

They could have said he:

:: was born in Bethlehem, to fulfill the prophecy in Micah 5:2
:: ministered in Galilee, to fulfill Isaiah 9:1–2
:: was introduced by an advance man, John the Baptist, to fulfill Malachi 3:1
:: rode a donkey on Palm Sunday, to fulfill Zechariah 9:9
:: was betrayed for 30 pieces of silver, to fulfill Zechariah 11:12.

The list goes on for dozens of prophecies.

The come-back question Christians ask is this: would the disciples have died to preserve these lies—the same disciples who hid like cowards after Jesus was arrested, to save themselves? Early Christian writers report that nearly all the disciples died a martyr's death. Roman writers help substantiate the claim; first-century historian Josephus, who was both a Roman citizen and a Jew, said Nero ordered the execution of Peter, leader of the disciples.

Most Christians find it hard to believe that a group of men could experience such a remarkable turnaround in character—from cowardly to lionhearted—had they not seen for themselves the resurrected Jesus and believed he was who he said he was.

9. WHY BELIEVE IN AN AFTERLIFE WHEN THERE'S NO RELIABLE RECORD OF ANY DEAD SOUL COMING BACK TO CONFIRM IT?

Christians today rely on a couple of sources that point to life after death: the Bible and medically documented near-death experiences.

BIBLE

The Bible reports several stories of resurrections and contact with the dead.

:: *King Saul channels the spirit of the prophet Samuel (1 Samuel 28:12).*

:: *Moses and Elijah appear on the Mount of Transfiguration with Jesus many centuries after they died (Matthew 17:3).*

:: *Jesus rises from the dead and is seen by more than 500 of his followers (1 Corinthians 15:6). First-century Roman historian Josephus reported the disciples' claim that Jesus came back to life.*

:: *Jesus appears to Paul as a voice speaking from within a blinding light (Acts 9:5).*

NEAR-DEATH EXPERIENCES

Physicians and other researchers over the past several decades have interviewed thousands of people who were clinically dead—no heartbeat, no breathing.

People often report an awareness of being dead, a sense of peace and unconditional love, and the appearance of intense light—all of which many physicians say can be explained by the physics of a human body shutting down.

Yet some reports seem to defy medical explanation.

Researchers say that some of the most mystifying reports are from people who say they had out-of-body experiences. Some of these people are said to have accurately described things they couldn't otherwise have seen: readings on monitors and surgical instruments used while the patient was under general anesthesia, along with medical procedures performed and which members of the medical team performed them.

It's a tad tough to explain these as the physics of a body turning its lights off.

Some Christians say the widespread emergence of near-death experiences is God at work using science to nudge skeptics toward faith. Many non-believers argue that near-death

HOUDINI, MAGICIAN AND MEDIUM BUSTER. Harry Houdini (1874–1926) exposed magicians passing themselves off as spiritualists by using their tricks to convince grieving families they could talk with the dead relatives. Houdini went to séances, accompanied by a reporter who published the stories and a police officer who arrested the magicians for fraud. Houdini promised his wife that if it was possible to communicate from the place of the dead, he would contact her in a séance with a code. She tried for 10 years before giving up.

experiences are more likely a passing fad, popular among people struggling with their mortality and grasping at something that looks like an eternal life preserver.

10. SINCE RELIGION HAS CAUSED SO MUCH WAR AND SUFFERING, OFTEN SPAWNED BY INTOLERANCE, WOULDN'T THE WORLD BE BETTER OFF WITHOUT IT?

First of all, it's not going to happen.

Religions have been around since the Neanderthals of 70,000 BC, some say, evidenced by corpses buried with food, red ochre (used to paint cave art), and other objects—suggesting Neanderthals believed in an afterlife. And it seems religion is here to stay, at least into the foreseeable future—courtesy of modern-day Neanderthals, some non-religious people might rag.

The tally of religious folks compared to non-religious varies widely from one country to the next. Only six out of ten Chinese say they're religious, according to the Association of Religion Data Archives. But a whopping nine out of ten Americans say they're religious. Worldwide, the average is more than eight out of ten.

Eliminating organized religion, it seems, would take a miracle of God.

Some might argue it would be in God's best interest to do just that, given what intolerant religious groups have done in his name.

:: **CRUSADES**. *Three centuries of Crusades, in which popes ordered European Christians to capture the Holy Land from Muslim locals, partly to protect Christian pilgrims who were being mistreated.*

:: **HOLY WAR**. *Jihad holy wars—in ancient times and modern—with the intent of jamming Islam down the throats of unwilling souls by all means necessary.*

:: **FORCED CONVERSION**. *Jews forcing non-Jews to convert in ancient times (that's how King Herod the Great's family became Jewish). And in modern times, Jews segregating non-Jews—Palestinian Muslims in particular—to live in what some describe as Apartheid-like camps and isolated communities.*

:: **SLAVERY**. *From Bible times through the 1800s, many Christians not only approved of slavery—considering Africans subhuman—they bought and sold slaves. John Newton bought and sold slaves long after writing the hymn "Amazing Grace." The Church of England owned slaves in the West Indies.*

There's a flip side to religion, though.

HOSPITALS. Religious groups started many hospitals. Even today, most hospitals in America are nonprofit, many of which are sponsored by a religious group.

HOMELESS MISSIONS. Churches and other religious groups usually operate these.

BOY SCOUTS AND GIRL SCOUTS. Religious groups are often the sponsors.

AA GROUPS. Many meet in worship centers.

RELIEF VOLUNTEERS. Religious groups sponsor many of the teams traveling to disaster areas, providing relief from hurricanes, tornadoes, tsunamis, earthquakes, and floods.

COLLEGES. Churches founded many colleges, including Harvard and Yale (Puritan), Princeton (Presbyterian), along with Oxford and Dartmouth. By 1860 there were 246 colleges in America—only 17 of them state-sponsored. Most of the rest were backed by churches and other religious groups.

ART. Some of the world's greatest masterpieces

are paintings and sculptures of religious scenes. Michelangelo's Sistine Chapel, for one.

ARCHITECTURE. From the pyramids of Egypt, to the cathedrals of Europe, to the mosques of the Middle East, religious buildings provide some of the world's most inspiring architecture.

LANGUAGE. Many written languages were invented for the sole purpose of giving the Bible to people who had only a spoken language. Translators are still working on many dialects.

When it comes to religion, the question is whether the good outweighs the bad. The problem is how to pile the good onto one side of the scale and the bad onto the other.

The exercise is hypothetical. Religion is here to stay, it seems. The challenge for people of faith is to weed out the bad religious practices and to nurture the good—sometimes with the help of nonreligious people. Many of the nonreligious are gifted in the art of pointing out flaws, like a quality-control inspector would do. Wise people of faith, some Christians suggest, treat those critiques as helpful, not as destructive—even if the critic may have intended them otherwise.

AN ANSWER TO PRAYER. Entertainer Danny Thomas (1912–1991) said he started what is now St. Jude Children's Research Hospital in Memphis after an answer to prayer. As a struggling actor, he desperately prayed for direction in his life, calling on Saint Jude, the Catholic patron saint of lost causes. In gratitude for his career success, Thomas founded what became one of the nation's leading centers for treating cancer in children.

BIBLE SURVIVAL GUIDE

WHEN LIFE GETS DICEY AND FAITH RUNS THIN: BIBLE ADVICE, ENCOURAGEMENT, AND HOPE

A disclaimer seems in order.

Bible verses in this section aren't spiritual prescriptions for everyone in the situations I'm mentioning. They're merely a collection of verses that have helped others, and may help you.

You make the call.

PEOPLE PROBLEMS

A FRIEND LET ME DOWN

ADMIT THE PAIN. "My enemies are not the ones who sneer and make fun. I could put up with that. . . . But it was my closest friend, the one I trusted most" (Psalm 55:12–13 CEV).

SEEING EYE TO EYE. *"If your friend does you wrong, confront him. If he has a change of heart and says he's sorry, forgive him"* (Luke 17:3 AUTHOR'S PARAPHRASE). That's advice Jesus gave his followers. Easier said than done, many followers today would argue.

BIBLE SNAPSHOTS OF FRIENDSHIP:

DAVID AND JONATHAN. Young David and crown prince Jonathan were best friends. But Jonathan's father, King Saul, became jealous of David's growing popularity after David killed Goliath. When Saul decided to have David assassinated, Jonathan risked his own life to warn his friend (1 Samuel 20).

PETER AND JESUS. Peter, along with brothers James and John, were Jesus' three closest disciples—his best friends. When Jews arrested Jesus, the disciples ran. Peter denied he even knew Jesus, probably to protect himself from arrest. Jesus forgave him, and several weeks later Peter boldly preached a sermon that launched the Christian movement in Jerusalem, the same town where he had betrayed Jesus.

OFFER KINDNESS INSTEAD OF RETALIATION. "Don't insist on getting even; that's not for you to do. 'I'll do the judging,' says God. . . . If you see your enemy hungry, go buy that person lunch, or if he's thirsty, get him a drink. Your generosity will surprise him with goodness. Don't let evil get the best of you; get the best of evil by doing good" (Romans 12:19–21 MSG).

DON'T GIVE UP ON FRIENDSHIP. "You are better off to have a friend than to be all alone. . . . If you fall, your friend can help you up. But if you fall without having a friend nearby, you are really in trouble" (Ecclesiastes 4:9–10 CEV).

TO FIND A FRIEND, BE A FRIEND. "A man who has friends must himself be friendly" (Proverbs 18:24 NKJV).

DON'T LET YOUR FRIENDS DOWN. "A friend is always loyal" (Proverbs 17:17).

WHEN ALL FRIENDS FAIL YOU, THERE'S ONE WHO WON'T. "Even if my father and mother abandon me, the Lord will hold me close" (Psalm 27:10).

THE PERSON I LOVE HAS CHEATED ON ME

ALTERNATIVE TO DIVORCE: FORGIVENESS. Jesus, talking with a woman caught in the act of adultery: " 'Where is everyone? Isn't there anyone left to accuse you?' 'No sir,' the woman answered. Then Jesus told her, 'I am not going to accuse you either. You may go now, but don't sin anymore'" (John 8:10-11 CEV).

This conversation took place after Jesus disbursed the crowd of accusers planning to stone her. He did it with one sentence: "If any of you have never sinned, then go ahead and throw the first stone at her!" (John 8:7 CEV).

GOD WON'T LEAVE YOU. "God will never walk away from his people" (Psalm 94:14 MSG).

I'M FACING A DIVORCE

GOD HATES THE PAIN IT CAUSES. "'I hate divorce,' says the Lord God of Israel. 'I hate it when people do anything that harms others'" (Malachi 2:16 NIrV).

DON'T LET ANGER CONSUME YOU. "Go ahead and be angry. You do well to be angry—but don't use your anger as fuel for revenge. And don't stay angry. . . . Don't give the Devil that kind of foothold in your life" (Ephesians 4:26-27 MSG).

DIVORCE IS THE LAST RESORT, WHEN PEOPLE WON'T REPENT OR FORGIVE. "Moses provided for divorce as a concession to your hardheartedness, but it is not part of God's original plan" (Matthew 19:8 MSG).

AS BEST YOU CAN, LET GO OF YOUR WORRIES. "Give all your worries and cares to God, for he cares about you" (1 Peter 5:7).

(See also "Divorce," page 110.)

MY EX TREATS ME LIKE DIRT

TREAT YOUR EX LIKE ROYALTY. "Love your enemies. Let them bring out the best in you, not the worst. When someone gives you a hard time, respond with the energies of prayer, for then you are working out of your true selves, your God-created selves" (Matthew 5:44–45 MSG).

TREAT YOUR EX LIKE YOU WANT TO BE TREATED. "Ask yourself what you want people to do for you, then grab the initiative and do it for them" (Matthew 7:12 MSG).

BURY THE BITTERNESS. "Do not be bitter or angry or mad. Never shout angrily or say things to hurt others. . . . Be kind and loving to each other, and forgive each other just as God forgave you in Christ" (Ephesians 4:31–32 NCV).

LET THE PRESSURE MAKE YOU STRONGER. "You know that under pressure, your faith-life is forced into the open and shows its true colors. . . . Let it do its work so you become mature" (James 1:3–4 MSG).

I'VE COMMITTED ADULTERY

THAT'S BUSTING ONE OF THE TOP-TEN RULES TO LIVE BY. "You must not commit adultery" (Exodus 20:14).

IT'S SELF-DESTRUCTIVE. "Adultery is a brainless act, soul-destroying, self-destructive" (Proverbs 6:32 MSG).

Avoid the lustful look.

PLAY WITH FIRE, GET BURNED. "What makes you think you can you build a fire in your pants and not get burned?" (Proverbs 6:27 AUTHOR'S PARAPHRASE).

IT'S NOT THE UNPARDONABLE SIN. "Give up your sin. Ask God to forgive you. He'll do it. He'll give you a fresh start, too" (Acts 3:19 AUTHOR'S PARAPHRASE).

GOD FORGIVES AND FORGETS. "I, yes I, am the one who takes care of your sins—that's what I do. I don't keep a list of your sins" (Isaiah 43:25 MSG).

AVOID THE LUSTFUL LOOK. "You know the commandment which says, 'Be faithful in marriage.' But I tell you that if you look at another woman and want her, you are already unfaithful in your thoughts" (Matthew 5:27–28 CEV).

MAKE A DEAL WITH YOUR EYES. "I made an agreement with my eyes. I promised not to look at another woman with sexual longing" (Job 31:1 NIRV).

MY KIDS DON'T RESPECT ME

THEY'RE HURTING THEMSELVES. "Don't be a fool and disobey your parents. Be smart! Accept correction" (Proverbs 15:5 CEV).

BIBLE SNAPSHOT OF DISRESPECT FOR PARENT:

DAVID AND HIS SON ABSALOM.

Absalom's sister was raped by their half-brother, crown prince Amnon. When David refused to punish Amnon, Absalom grew to hate both men. In time, Absalom murdered his rapist brother and launched a doomed coup against his father. Absalom died in the battle (2 Samuel 18:14).

RESPECT IS A TWO-WAY STREET. "Children, do what your parents tell you. This delights the Master no end. Parents, don't come down too hard on your children or you'll crush their spirits" (Colossians 3:20–21 MSG).

LET GO OF ANY ANGER OR BITTERNESS ABOUT IT. "Stop being bitter and angry and mad at others. Don't yell at one another . . . . Instead, be kind and merciful, and forgive others, just as God forgave you" (Ephesians 4:31–32 CEV).

MONEY WOES

I HATE LIVING FROM PAYCHECK TO PAYCHECK

THE TROUBLE WITH WEALTH. "It's terribly hard for rich people to get into the kingdom of heaven!" (Matthew 19:23 CEV).

MONEY DOESN'T DEFINE YOU. "Life is not defined by what you have" (Luke 12:15 MSG).

MONEY ISN'T THE SOURCE OF YOUR SECURITY. "The LORD is my shepherd. He gives me everything I need" (Psalm 23:1 NIRV).

MONEY ISN'T THE SOURCE OF YOUR HAPPINESS. "How meaningless to think that wealth brings true happiness! The more you have, the more people come to help you spend it. So what good is wealth—except perhaps to watch it slip through your fingers!" (Ecclesiastes 5:10–11).

CONSIDER THE LILIES OF THE FIELD. Red anemones cloak a field in Galilee, a farming area in northern Israel where Jesus once ministered. These springtime wildflowers may have been the "lilies of the field" Jesus pointed out in a sermon about money. "Solomon with all his wealth wasn't as well clothed as one of them. God gives such beauty to everything that grows in the fields . . . He will surely do even more for you! Why do you have such little faith?" (Matthew 6:29–30 CEV).

STORE UP TREASURE IN HEAVEN, WHERE IT'S SECURE. "Don't hoard treasure down here. . . . Stockpile treasure in heaven, where it's safe. . . . It's obvious, isn't it? The place where your treasure is, is the place you will most want to be" (Matthew 6:19–21 MSG).

RELAX; GOD'S GOT YOUR BACK. "What I'm trying to do here is to get you to relax. . . . You'll find all your everyday human concerns will be met. . . . And don't get worked up about what may or may not happen tomorrow. God will help you deal with whatever hard things come up when the time comes" (Matthew 6:31, 33–34 MSG).

I HAVE A GAMBLING PROBLEM

IT'S A KIND OF SLAVERY. "Some of you say, 'We can do anything we want to.' But I tell you that not everything is good for us. So I refuse to let anything have power over me" (1 Corinthians 6:12 CEV).

DON'T LET GREED DRIVE YOU. "Anyone who is greedy is serving a false god" (Ephesians 5:5 NCV).

EASY COME, EASY GO. "Money that comes easily disappears quickly, but money that is gathered little by little will grow" (Proverbs 13:11 NCV).

OUT OF LUCK. "What will happen to you for offering food and wine to the gods you call 'Good Luck' and 'Fate'? Your luck will end!" (Isaiah 65:11–12 CEV).

ALTERNATIVE TO GAMBLING: CONTENTMENT. "I have learned the secret of being content no matter what happens. I am content whether I am well fed or hungry. I am content whether I have more than enough or not enough. I can do everything by the power of Christ. He gives me strength" (Philippians 4:12–13 NIrv).

A FRIEND HAS ASKED ME TO COSIGN A LOAN

RUN, DON'T WALK. "My child, if you have put up security for a friend's debt or agreed to guarantee the debt of a stranger—if you have trapped yourself by your agreement and are caught by what you said—follow my advice and save yourself, for you have placed yourself at your friend's mercy. Now swallow your pride; go and beg to have your name erased. Don't put it off; do it now! Don't rest until you do. Save yourself like a gazelle escaping from a hunter, like a bird fleeing from a net" (Proverbs 6:1–5). This isn't the 11th commandment, scholars say. It's not a sin to cosign. But it's fiscally foolish, according to the writers of Proverbs—whom many scholars say was an assortment of elderly men offering practical advice to young men.

CAREER CONCERNS

I LOST MY JOB

YOU'VE GOT CONNECTIONS. "My God will meet all your needs. He will meet them in keeping with

UPWARDLY MOBILE. Waiting for a green light at the crosswalk, a young businessman gets a surprise portrait. In a survey conducted among 5,000 American households for a nonprofit management group called The Conference Board, 45 percent said they are satisfied with their jobs. That's down from 61 percent reported 20 years earlier. One reason for today's dissatisfaction, according to Francis Green, writing in the Princeton University Press book *Demanding Work*, is "the taste for reducing workers' control over their daily tasks. . . . The lesson is that, for the benefit of working people, there needs to be less intervention and control from above, and more discretion and self-determination from below."

his wonderful riches that come to you because you belong to Christ Jesus" (Philippians 4:19 NIrv).

DON'T LOSE SLEEP WORRYING. "Look at the birds, free and unfettered, not tied down to a job description, careless in the care of God. And you count far more to him than birds" (Matthew 6:26 MSG).

(See also "I hate living from paycheck to paycheck," page 56.)

I HATE MY JOB

CHANGE YOUR MIND OR CHANGE YOUR JOB. "The best that people can do is eat, drink, and enjoy their work. I saw that even this comes from God" (Ecclesiastes 2:24 NCV).

FIND WORK YOU ENJOY AND EXCEL AT IT. "Enjoy the work you do here on earth. Whatever work you do, do your best" (Ecclesiastes 9:9–10 NCV).

MAKE THE MOST OF YOUR TIME BY ENJOYING WORK. "Here's what I've decided is the best way to live: Take care of yourself, have a good time, and make the most of whatever job you have for as long as God gives you life. And that's about it" (Ecclesiastes 5:18 MSG).

MY BOSS IS EVERYONE YOU'D NEVER WANT TO WORK FOR, DUMPED INTO ONE BONE BAG

MAKE NO BONES ABOUT IT. "Do everything readily and cheerfully—no bickering, no second-guessing allowed! Go out into the world uncorrupted, a breath of fresh air in this squalid and polluted society. Provide people with a glimpse of good living and of the living God. Carry the light-giving Message into the night" (Philippians 2:14–15 MSG).

GRIN AND BEAR IT. "Work with a smile on your face, always keeping in mind that no matter who happens to be giving the orders, you're really serving God" (Ephesians 6:7 MSG).

EVEN SLAVE DRIVERS DESERVE RESPECT. "Whoever is a slave must make the best of it, giving respect to his master so that outsiders don't blame God and our teaching for his behavior" (1 Timothy 6:1 MSG).

HEALTH TROUBLES

I'M SICK

PRAY. When the prophet Isaiah told ailing King Hezekiah that he wouldn't get well, Hezekiah "turned his face to the wall and prayed to the LORD" (Isaiah 38:2). Theologians say something about that prayer must have changed Hezekiah,

because God changed his plans: "I have heard your prayer and seen your tears. I will add fifteen years to your life" (Isaiah 38:5).

ASK FOR PRAYER. "Are you sick? Call the church leaders together to pray and anoint you with oil. . . . Believing-prayer will heal you, and Jesus will put you on your feet" (James 5:14–15 MSG). This advice sounds like it will always work. It doesn't. The caveat appears in the prayer Jesus prayed shortly before his arrest. He asked God to spare him from the crucifixion, adding: "Yet I want your will to be done, not mine" (Luke 22:42).

I'M DYING

YOU'RE IN GOD'S HANDS. "The life of every creature and the breath of all people are in God's hand" (Job 12:10 NCV).

HIVES IN HIDING. Elle Moss, in a touched-up portrait that obscures the hives on her face. She has them all over her body as well. She said an allergist suggested she might be allergic to something in her mattress. So she bought a cover to zip over it along with organic sheets and pillow covers. The Bible, written long before modern medicine, offers few remedies for illness beyond prayer. But at least in Bible times, prayer didn't make things worse; many "remedies" did. Writing a series of Roman science books called *Natural History*, Pliny (AD 23–79) offered this prescription for quelling an itching rash: apply mud mixed with donkey urine. Applied to a baby's behind, that sounds like a prescription for diaper rash with a kick.

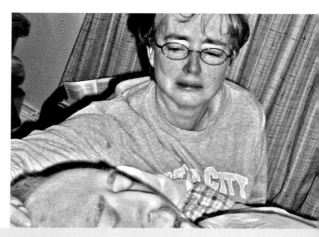

GOOD-BYE. The author's wife, Linda Miller, sits a moment with her father, Rev. Donald E. Burnes, age 80. He died a short time earlier while the family was gathered around him praying the Lord's Prayer.

DON'T BE AFRAID. "I may walk through valleys as dark as death, but I won't be afraid. You are with me" (Psalm 23:4 CEV).

MAKE OUT YOUR WILL. "This is what the LORD says: 'Set your affairs in order, for you are going to die. You will not recover from this illness' " (Isaiah 38:1). This is the prophet Isaiah talking to King Hezekiah.

RISING FROM THE DEAD. "The corpse that's planted is no beauty, but when it's raised, it's glorious. Put in the ground weak, it comes up powerful. The seed sown is natural; the seed grown is supernatural—same seed, same body, but what a difference from when it goes down in physical mortality to when it is raised up in spiritual immortality!" (1 Corinthians 15:43–44 MSG).

LIFE AFTER DEATH. "I saw Heaven. . . . I heard a voice thunder from the Throne: 'Look! Look! God has moved into the neighborhood, making his home with men and women! . . . He'll wipe every tear from their eyes. Death is gone for good—tears gone, crying gone, pain gone'" (Revelation 21:1, 3–4 MSG). (See also "Eternal Life," page 117.)

SPIRITUAL TROUBLES

THERE'S SOMEONE I CAN'T FORGIVE

GIVE THEM A BREAK; GOD GAVE YOU ONE.

"Put up with each other. Forgive the things you are holding against one another. Forgive, just as the Lord forgave you" (Colossians 3:13 NIrV).

DON'T GIVE UP TRYING TO FORGIVE. "If you forgive those who sin against you, your heavenly Father will forgive you. But if you refuse to forgive others, your Father will not forgive your sins" (Matthew 6:14–15). Many scholars say the point is that only a hypocrite would have the nerve to ask God for forgiveness, yet refuse to forgive others. Jesus knows that some of the things people do to us are hard to forgive, perhaps even impossible in our lifetime. But using a touch of exaggeration, many scholars say, Jesus urges people to work at forgiving others; hanging on to the bitterness is self-destructive and capable of crippling our spiritual life.

FORGIVENESS FOR REPEAT OFFENDERS. "Peter got up the nerve to ask, 'Master, how many times do I forgive a brother or sister who hurts me? Seven?' Jesus replied, 'Seven! Hardly. Try seventy times seven' " (Matthew 18:21–22 MSG).

I'VE DONE SOMETHING SO TERRIBLE THAT I CAN'T FORGIVE MYSELF

GOD FORGIVES EVEN THE COMBO SIN OF ADULTERY AND MURDER. "David confessed to Nathan, 'I have sinned against the LORD.' Nathan replied, 'Yes, but the LORD has forgiven you' " (2 Samuel 12:13). This, after David got Bathsheba pregnant and then arranged for her husband to die on the battlefield to cover up the adultery.

ADMIT THE SIN, AND ASK FOR FORGIVE-NESS. "If we admit that we have sinned, he will forgive us our sins. He will forgive every wrong thing we have done. He will make us pure" (1 John 1:9 NIrV).

GOD IS EAGER TO FORGIVE. "'Let's settle this,' says the LORD. 'Though your sins are like scarlet, I will make them as white as snow'" (Isaiah 1:18).

SINS BE GONE. "How far has the LORD taken our sins from us? Farther than the distance from east to west!" (Psalm 103:12 CEV).

OPEN YOUR EYES. "Ever since the world was created, people have seen the earth and sky. Through everything God made, they can clearly see his invisible qualities—his eternal power and divine nature. So they have no excuse for not knowing God" (Romans 1:20).

JOIN THE CROWD. "Long enough, God—you've ignored me long enough. I've looked at the back of your head long enough. Long enough I've carried this ton of trouble, lived with a stomach full of pain" (Psalm 13:1–2 MSG).

IT'S TEMPORARY. End of the same song just quoted: "I'm celebrating your rescue. I'm singing at the top of my lungs, I'm so full of answered prayers" (Psalm 13:5–6 MSG).

HE'S NOT ONLY LISTENING, HE'S WITH YOU. "When you're in over your head, I'll be there with you. When you're in rough waters, you will not go down. . . . So don't be afraid: I'm with you" (Isaiah 43:2, 5 MSG).

TRUST GOD EVEN WHEN THE WORLD FALLS APART. "Though the apples are worm-eaten and the wheat fields stunted, though the sheep pens are sheepless and the cattle barns empty, I'm singing joyful praise to God. . . . Counting on God's Rule to prevail" (Habakkuk 3:17–19 MSG).

I CAN'T BELIEVE THAT CHRISTIANITY IS THE ONE AND ONLY RELIGION THAT GETS IT RIGHT

WHO SAYS CHRISTIANS GET IT RIGHT? Jesus: "Here's what I propose: 'Don't hit back at all.' If someone strikes you, stand there and take it. If someone drags you into court and sues for the shirt off your back, giftwrap your best coat and make a present of it" (Matthew 5:39–40 MSG). That's a full-blooded pacifist talking. Many Christians, perhaps most, would strike back faster than a reflex. Christians struggle with many of the teachings of Jesus.

JESUS, THE ONLY WAY TO SALVATION? "I am the way, the truth, and the life. No one can come to the Father except through me" (John 14:6). Christians disagree about how to understand this. Theories:

:: Some say that given the context when John was writing this Gospel, decades after Jesus, that John wasn't talking about the host of other religions. He was talking about the Jewish faith. Christians were being persecuted. And John was quoting Jesus in an attempt to keep persecuted Jewish Christians from giving up on the faith and going back to the safe Jewish religion.

:: Another theory is that everyone will eventually acknowledge Jesus as Savior, in the next life if not this one.

:: Some Christians say everyone will be saved; they quote Colossians 1:20, "All the broken and dislocated pieces of the universe—people and things, animals and atoms—get properly fixed and fit together in vibrant harmonies, all because of his [Jesus'] death, his blood that poured down from the Cross" (MSG).

:: The "way" of Jesus is death and resurrection. We die to an old, sinful lifestyle. And we're reborn into a new way of thinking and living. This "way" is taught in many religions.

NOT YOUR TYPICAL SOLICITOR. "I stand at the door and knock" (Revelation 3:20). That's Jesus talking. Many students of the Bible say if we don't let him into our lives, we shouldn't expect him to let us into heaven.

:: The traditional Christian view, though, is that a person has to have faith in Jesus in this lifetime if he or she wants to live forever with him in the next. These Christians quote the apostle Peter: "Jesus is the only One who can save people. No one else in the world is able to save us" (Acts 4:12 NCV).

I FEEL EMPTY, SPIRITUALLY WEAK

AHEAD: WIND BENEATH YOUR WINGS. "Those who trust in the Lᴏʀᴅ will receive new strength. They will fly as high as eagles. They will run and not get tired. They will walk and not grow weak" (Isaiah 40:31 NIrv).

ALSO: RENEWAL, HEALING. "He renews our hopes and heals our bodies" (Psalm 147:3 CEV).

GOD'S LOVE WON'T LET YOU GO. "I am convinced that nothing can ever separate us from his love. Death can't, and life can't. The angels won't, and all the powers of hell itself cannot keep God's love away. Our fears for today, our worries about tomorrow, or where we are—high above the sky, or in the deepest ocean—nothing will ever be able to separate us from the love of God demonstrated by our Lord Jesus Christ when he

PUTTING KAYA DOWN. A tumor makes it hard for Kaya to breathe. One last walk through her favorite park. A trip to the vet. A needle. And good-bye. For many people, the loss of a pet is as wrenching as any pain on earth. Methodist founder and circuit-riding preacher John Wesley (1703–1791) said he expected to be reunited in heaven with the faithful horse he rode for 10 years.

died for us" (Romans 8:38–39 TLB). Even when we can't feel the love, it's there. So said the apostle Paul, assuring believers in Rome.

GOD'S HAND STEADIES YOU. "Don't panic. I'm with you. There's no need to fear for I'm your God. I'll give you strength. I'll help you. I'll hold you steady, keep a firm grip on you" (Isaiah 41:10 MSG).

IT'S ONE THING AFTER ANOTHER, AND I CAN'T TAKE IT ANYMORE

FOLLOWING IN THE FOOTSTEPS OF JESUS. "We've been surrounded and battered by troubles, but we're not demoralized; we're not sure what to do, but we know that God knows what to do; we've been spiritually terrorized, but God hasn't left our side; we've been thrown down, but we haven't broken. What they did to Jesus, they do to us—trial and torture" (2 Corinthians 4:8–10 MSG).

HIDE. "GOD is good, a hiding place in tough times. He recognizes and welcomes anyone looking for help, no matter how desperate the trouble" (Nahum 1:7–8 MSG).

THERE'S A RESCUE COMING. "LORD, even when I have trouble all around me, you will keep me alive. When my enemies are angry, you will reach down and save me by your power" (Psalm 138:7 NCV).

THERE'S NO POINT IN WORRYING. "Can you add even one hour to your life by worrying?" (Matthew 6:27 NIrV).

GIVE AWAY YOUR WORRIES. "Give all your worries to him, because he cares about you" (1 Peter 5:7 NCV).

ACCEPT GOD'S HELP AND PASS IT ON. "Father of all mercy! God of all healing counsel! He comes alongside us when we go through hard times, and before you know it, he brings us alongside someone else who is going through hard times so that we can be there for that person just as God was there for us" (2 Corinthians 1:3–4 MSG).

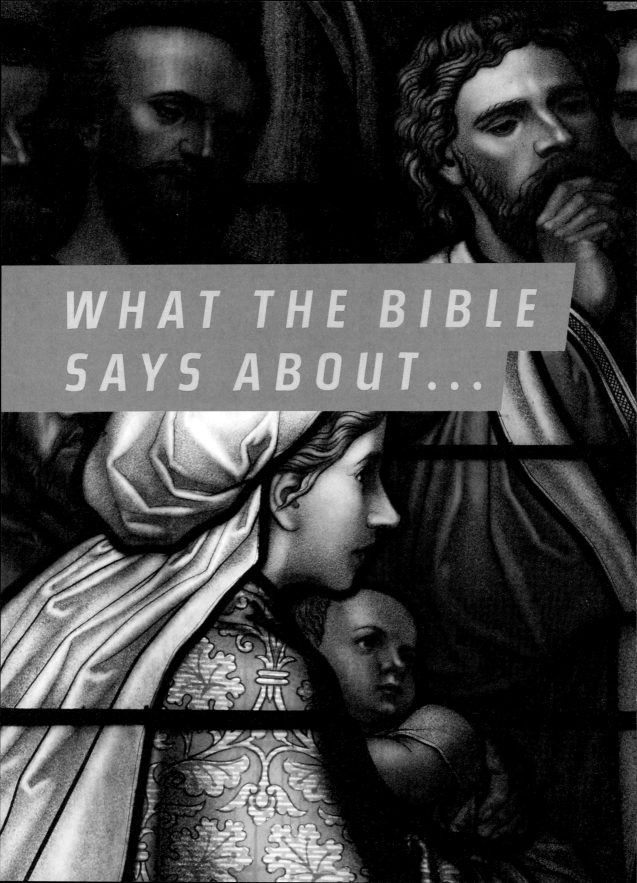

WHAT THE BIBLE SAYS ABOUT...

TOUCH OF GOD. Michelangelo's depiction of God creating Adam decorates the Sistine Chapel ceiling in Rome. Many Christians argue that since human life comes from God, we shouldn't presume it's okay for us to end it early with abortions. Other Christians argue that since the Bible never mentions abortion, we should defer to the wishes of the pregnant woman.

ABORTION

The Bible doesn't talk about abortion. Not directly. But many Christians say the Bible offers principles to guide us.

:: *"You created my body from a tiny drop. Then you tied my bones together with muscles and covered them with flesh and skin. You, the source of my life, showered me with kindness and watched over me"* (Job 10:10–12 CEV). Some Christians use this verse to insist that life begins at conception, "from a tiny drop." Others argue that Job wasn't talking science—he was asking for God's help by appealing to the fact that it was God who created him in the first place.

:: *"You are the one who put me together inside my mother's body"* (Psalm 139:13 CEV). Some Christians say this passage shows that a fetus is God-made, fully human, and for those reasons should not be aborted. Others say the words are the lyrics of a song—that a poet is thanking God for caring about him not only while he was growing inside the uterus, but "even before I was born" (Psalm 139:16 CEV).

:: *"Do not murder"* (Deuteronomy 5:17 CEV). Many Christians call abortion murder. Others say that every murder in the Bible refers to a breathing human, never to an unborn child.

:: *God breathed life into the man, and the man started breathing* (Genesis 2:7 CEV). Some say a fetus becomes human only when it takes its first breath. But the Bible never says when humanity begins, or when God places a spiritual soul within a physical body—if that's the process. Some argue from logic that if God knows everything, he knows which children will be aborted—and he won't place a soul within them. But that's just a guess; some would say a reckless guess.

:: *"He [John the Baptist] will be filled with the Holy Spirit, even before his birth"* (Luke 1:15). This suggests to some Christians that the fetus has a soul for the Holy Spirit to fill. But many Bible translations say the Spirit will fill John "from the time he is born" (NIrv), or some variation of that phrase. The original language seems to work either way because of its vague phrasing, "from his mother's womb" (KJV).

:: *Suppose a pregnant woman suffers a miscarriage as the result of an injury. . . . If she isn't badly hurt, the one who injured her must pay whatever fine her husband demands and the judges approve. But if she is seriously injured, the payment will be life for life* (Exodus 21:22–23 CEV). The penalty is death for accidentally killing a pregnant woman, but the penalty is just a fine for causing a miscarriage—as though the mother is more valuable than the fetus. This tracks with similar laws from Hammurabi's Code (sections 209–210, written in the 1700s BC, several centuries before the laws of Moses): execution for injury causing death, but only a fine of 10 silver coins for injury causing a miscarriage. Some Bible translations, how-

AFTER THE ABORTION

For those who regret their decision to abort and can't get over the guilt:

:: "Do not remember the sins and wrong things I did when I was young. But remember to love me always because you are good, LORD" (Psalm 25:7 NCV).

:: "If we admit that we have sinned, he will forgive us our sins. He will forgive every wrong thing we have done" (1 John 1:9 NIrv).

ABORTION STATS

1.2 million women got abortions in the US

407,000 women ages 20–24 got abortions*

200,000 women were under age 19

755,000 were pregnant for less than 9 weeks

508,000 were woman who didn't have children

age bracket with most abortions

Source: U.S. Census Bureau for 2006, most recent year on record

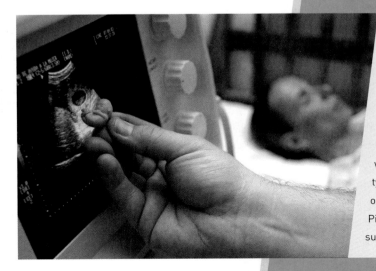

NINE WEEKS. Mayela Bolado, 31, undergoes an ultrasound when she's nine weeks pregnant. Six out of 10 abortions in the United States take place at nine weeks gestation or less. The cut-off for abortions varies from state to state, but abortions are rarely allowed after 24 weeks (six months). The most common type of medical abortion is performed by oral medication nicknamed the Abortion Pill. After nine weeks, abortion requires surgery.

THE ANCIENTS, ON ABORTION

"A woman is to bear children for the city from the age of 20 to the age of 40. . .[after age 40] they should be very careful not to let a single fetus see the light of day."

—*Plato*, Greek philosopher reporting in *Republic* the teachings of Socrates and others, about 427–347 BC

"Some women take medicines to destroy the germ of future life in their own bodies. They commit infanticide before they have given birth to the infant."

—*Minucius Felix*, Roman Christian, about AD 160–250

"You should not murder a child by abortion or destruction [killing a newborn, often by abandoning it to the elements— a common method of birth control]."

—*Didache*, first known Christian manual of behavior, AD 100s

"There is no difference between killing a life that has already been born or one that is in the process of birth."

—*Tertullian*, Christian scholar, about AD 160–225

"The poor abandon their newborn children [exposing them to weather and wild animals]. The rich kill the fruit of their own bodies in the womb so their inheritance isn't spread thin, destroying their own children in the womb with murderous poisons."

—*Saint Ambrose*, Italian bishop, about AD 339–397

BIRTH CONTROL.

"When couples have children in excess, let abortion be procured before sense and life have begun."

—*Aristotle*, Greek philosopher writing in *Politics*, about 384–322 BC

CHRISTIAN TEACHINGS TO CONSIDER

Christians live on both sides of the abortion debate.

Many lobby for compassion toward the unborn child, arguing that the reason most pregnant women abort is because their pregnancy comes at an inconvenient time.

Others lobby for compassion toward the woman in a crisis pregnancy—a crisis that might stem from rape, incest, health problems, or terrible timing that could devastate a career or crush a family with financial pressure.

The Holy Spirit is our guide. When the Bible falls silent on tough topics, some Christians say they expect God's Spirit to speak up with an inner voice, offering advice tailored to their situation. Their go-to verse is a promise Jesus gave his disciples: "I will ask the Father to send you the Holy Spirit who will help you and always be with you. The Spirit will show you what is true" (John 14:16–17 CEV).

Christians help the helpless. That's the point of Jesus' famous parable of the Good Samaritan (Luke 10:30–39). *Helpless* can apply to the unborn life and to the woman in a crisis pregnancy. Some believers says it's inconsistent with the teachings of Jesus to demand that a woman deliver an unwanted child, and then to abandon both the woman and her child.

Christians put others first. Jesus didn't chase comfort and convenience; he put the needs of others ahead of his own. Some say pregnant women should put the needs of their unborn child above their own. Others say Christians shouldn't be so judgmental toward women with unwanted pregnancies, but should consider their needs as well.

God created us. "Nothing was created except through him" (John 1:3). When we kill anything, we kill something God created. The implication, Christians agree, is that people shouldn't take the life of anyone or anything thoughtlessly.

ever, say the Bible calls for the death penalty if either the mother or the child dies. Scholars disagree over how to interpret these verses.

ABUSE

:: *"Treat others as you want them to treat you"* (Matthew 7:12 CEV). This is Jesus teaching what has become known as the Golden Rule.

:: *I hate it when people do anything that harms others* (Malachi 2:16 NIrV).

:: *A man's anger doesn't produce the kind of life God wants* (James 1:20 NIrV).

:: *When people curse us, we bless them. When they hurt us, we put up with it* (1 Corinthians 4:12 NCV). This is the apostle Paul describing his life as a persecuted traveling minister. It's not a recommendation for coping with abuse. Paul defended himself several times by legal means (Acts 16:37–38).

:: *"Look, my virgin daughter and his concubine are here. I'll bring them out for you. Abuse them if you must, but don't do anything so senselessly vile to this man"* (Judges 19:24 MSG). These are the words of a host protecting his male guest from gang rape by offering the mob of men his daughter and the guest's concubine, a woman who acts as a wife. Not a high point in the history of chivalry.

:: *The mouth of the wicked is a dark cave of abuse* (Proverbs 10:6 MSG).

COMFORT FOR VICTIMS

:: *GOD's a safe-house for the battered, a sanctuary during bad times* (Psalm 9:9 MSG).

:: *The LORD remains faithful forever. He stands up for those who are beaten down* (Psalm 146:6–7 NIrV).

:: He will save them from people who do mean things to them. Their lives are very special to him (Psalm 72:14 NIrv). A song praising Israel's national leader, the king.

(See also *Exploitation*.)

ADDICTIONS (BAD HABITS)

WHAT IT'S LIKE
:: I want to do what is right, but I can't. I want to do what is good, but I don't. I don't want to do what is wrong, but I do it anyway. . . . Who will free me from this life that is dominated by sin and death? Thank God! The answer is in Jesus Christ (Romans 7:18–19, 24–25).
:: They can't think straight anymore. Feeling no pain, they let themselves go . . . addicted to every sort of perversion. But that's no life for you. You learned Christ! . . . . Everything—and I do mean everything—connected with that old way of life has to go. It's rotten through and through. Get rid of it! And then take on an entirely new way of life. . .a life renewed from the inside (Ephesians 4:19–20, 22–24 MSG).
:: People are slaves of whatever controls them (2 Peter 2:19 CEV).

ADVICE FOR OVERCOMING
:: Bad friends will ruin good habits (1 Corinthians 15:33 NCV).
:: Not everything is good for you . . I must not become a slave to anything (1 Corinthians 6:12).
:: "Stay awake and pray for strength against temptation. The spirit wants to do what is right, but the body is weak" (Mark 14:38 NCV).
:: Don't think about how to satisfy what your sinful nature wants (Romans 13:14 NLT).

:: The temptations in your life are no different from what others experience. And God is faithful. He will not allow the temptation to be more than you can stand. When you are tempted, he will show you a way out (1 Corinthians 10:13).
:: God's saving grace has appeared to all people. It teaches us to say no to godless ways and sinful longings. We must control ourselves (Titus 2:11–12 NIrv).
:: Control yourselves and be careful! The devil, your enemy, goes around like a roaring lion looking for someone to eat. Refuse to give in to him (1 Peter 5:8–9 NCV).
:: Be careful. When you think you are standing firm, you might fall (1 Corinthians 10:12 NIrv).

(See also *Drugs and Alcohol; Pornography*.)

ADULTERY

:: Don't think you've preserved your virtue simply by staying out of bed. Your heart can be corrupted by lust even quicker than your body. Those leering looks you think nobody notices— they also corrupt (Matthew 5:28 MSG).

SEX ADVICE FROM WISE OLD MEN

Proverbs is a collection of snappy one-liners—wise sayings from old men, intended for young men who don't know any better.

From the college of Lessons Learned the Hard Way, here's a sampling of what the senior gents have to say to Junior about sex. (Each proverb is paraphrased by the author.)

A bull shouldn't visit a butcher shop. "Let's roll in the sack till the sun comes up. When the hubby's away, the Mrs. will play" (Proverbs 7:18–19). This is a woman's invitation to a young man. It's an invitation that the wise writer says is like inviting a bull to slaughter: "Many have been slaughtered because of women like her" (Proverbs 7:26).

Water your own garden. "Don't go around watering someone else's garden by having sex with another man's wife. Water your own garden and have fun doing it, like you did when you first got married" (Proverbs 5:16, 18).

Pants on fire. "What makes you think you can build a fire in your pants and not get burned?" (Proverbs 6:27).

Shortcut to the grave. "Sleep with another man's wife and you just might wake up dead" (Proverbs 6:26).

DON'T CALL HER HONEY. In fact, don't call her at all. "The lips of another man's wife may taste sweeter than a big bite of honeycomb. But where there's honey, there're bees. And they know how to sting you where it hurts" (Proverbs 5:3–4 AUTHOR'S PARAPHRASE).

:: *Save yourself for your wife and don't have sex with other women* (Proverbs 5:17 CEV).

:: *Sexual drives are strong, but marriage is strong enough to contain them and provide for a balanced and fulfilling sexual life in a world of sexual disorder* (1 Corinthians 7:2 MSG).

:: *Sexual sins are different from all others. In sexual sin we violate the sacredness of our own bodies. . . . Didn't you realize that your body is a sacred place, the place of the Holy Spirit?* (1 Corinthians 6:18–19 MSG).

ANGELS

Angels of the Bible are divine beings God uses to deliver messages, punish evil people, and protect good people from harm.

PROTECTION

:: *All the angels are spirits who serve God and are sent to help those who will receive salvation* (Hebrews 1:14 NCV).

- :: The angel of the Lord stands guard around those who have respect for him (Psalm 34:7 NIrV).
- :: "Don't think these little children are worth nothing. I tell you that they have angels in heaven who are always with my Father" (Matthew 18:10 NCV).
- :: "I could ask my Father for thousands of angels to protect us, and he would send them instantly" (Matthew 26:53). This is Jesus talking to his disciples as he's being arrested.
- :: The angel of God that usually traveled in front of Israel's army moved behind them. Also, the pillar of cloud moved. . .between the Egyptians and the Israelites (Exodus 14: 9–20 NCV). An angel protects the Israelite refugees from the advancing Egyptian chariots.

PUNISHMENT

- :: He [God] dispatched against them a band of destroying angels (Psalm 78:49). This is a song of praise for God delivering the Jews from slavery in Egypt.
- :: "I will send an angel before you to drive out the Canaanites" (Exodus 33:2). God's promise to Jews of the Exodus out of Egypt.
- :: God expelled them [Adam and Eve] from the Garden of Eden. . .and stationed angel-cherubim. . .guarding the path to the Tree-of-Life (Genesis 3:23–24 MSG).

DELIVERING MESSAGES

- :: The angel said, "I am Gabriel! I stand in the very presence of God. It was he who sent me to bring you this good news!" (Luke 1:19).
- :: A very large group of angels from heaven joined the first angel, praising God and saying: "Give glory to God in heaven, and on earth let there be peace among the people who please God" (Luke 2:13–14 NCV). Bethlehem shepherds wit-

"WARRIOR OF GOD." That's what this angel's belt buckle says. Some angels are fighters. Michael seemed to fight off a demon "spirit prince" (Daniel 10:13). He also crushed what sounds like a Satan-led revolt among angels in heaven (Revelation 12:7).

ness this on the night of Jesus' birth.

- :: An angel of the Lord appeared to Joseph in a dream. "Get up! Flee to Egypt with the child and his mother," the angel said. "Stay there until I tell you to return, because Herod is going to search for the child to kill him" (Matthew 2:13).

:: God's angel spoke to Philip: "At noon today I want you to walk over to that desolate road that goes from Jerusalem down to Gaza." He got up and went (Acts 8:26–27 MSG).

IN DISGUISE

:: Don't forget to show hospitality to strangers, for some who have done this have entertained angels without realizing it! (Hebrews 13:2).

ANGER

:: Bridle your anger. . .cool your pipes—it only makes things worse (Psalm 37:8 MSG).
:: Controlling your temper is better than being a hero who captures a city (Proverbs 16:32 CEV).
:: "Don't sin by letting anger control you." Don't let the sun go down while you are still angry (Ephesians 4:26). Some kinds of anger are reasonable, and they won't fade when the sun does. If a friend or family member deeply hurts you, you may still be angry in the morning. Perhaps with good reason.

WHAT GOT JESUS FIRED UP?

Jesus got angry. Several times.
Table-flipping angry. I'll-show-you angry.

FLIPPING TABLES

When Jesus arrived in Jerusalem the week before his crucifixion, he went into the Temple to worship. There, in the large courtyard, he saw vendors selling cattle, sheep, and doves. The critters were likely priest-approved sacrificial animals available at convenience-store prices. There were currency traders, too, who charged a fee to switch out foreign currency for coins accepted in Temple offerings.

What Jesus did. "Jesus put together a whip out of strips of leather and chased them out of the Temple, stampeding the sheep and cattle, upending the tables of the loan sharks, spilling coins left and right" (John 2:15 MSG).

Why he did it. "Stop turning my Father's house into a shopping mall!" (John 2:16 MSG). For one thing, the "money changers" were conducting noisy business in the courtyard where non-Jews worshipped; this was as close as they were allowed to get to the sanctuary. For another, some scholars say, the merchants were probably overcharging big-time.

"I'LL SHOW YOU"

One Sabbath, a group of Jewish scholars called Pharisees watched Jesus to see if he would heal someone. They taught that practicing the healing arts was work and that people shouldn't work on the day of rest and worship. Sure enough a man with a crippled hand showed up. When Jesus asked the group if it was okay to help the helpless on the Sabbath, the Pharisees didn't say a thing.

What Jesus did. Jesus was "furious at their hard-nosed religion. He said to the man, 'Hold out your hand.' He held it out—it was as good as new!" (Mark 3:5 MSG).

Why he did it. "People were not made for the good of the Sabbath. The Sabbath was made for the good of people" (Mark 2:27 CEV).

GRAVEYARD ANGER. When Jesus saw the sisters and friends of dead Lazarus sobbing, he wept, too—and "a deep anger welled up within him" (John 11:33). Bible experts say they're not sure why. Perhaps he was angry about their lack of faith in his ability to raise the dead, some say. Or maybe he was angry at the pain death causes.

But the point is to resolve—as quickly as possible—whatever problem caused the anger. And then move on with your life.

:: *A kind answer soothes angry feelings, but harsh words stir them up* (Proverbs 15:1 CEV).

:: *A wise person stays calm when insulted* (Proverbs 12:16).

:: *Do not become angry easily because anger will not help you live the right kind of life God wants* (James 1:19–20 NCV).

(See also *Grudges, Hate, Revenge.*)

ANTICHRIST

The Bible uses the word *antichrist* in only four short verses—none of which is in Revelation. Centuries after Bible times, sometime after AD 600, preachers started linking these four verses to other Bible descriptions of an evil ruler. That's how Christians came up with the idea that in the last days of human history an evil Antichrist will rule the world. The idea stuck. And the idea stinks—many Bible scholars add.

EVERY "ANTICHRIST" IN THE BIBLE

:: *You have heard that the Antichrist is coming, and already many such antichrists have appeared. From this we know that the last hour has come* (1 John 2:18).

:: *Anyone who denies the Father and the Son is an antichrist* (1 John 2:22).

:: *If someone claims to be a prophet and does not acknowledge the truth about Jesus, that person is not from God. Such a person has the spirit of the Antichrist, which you heard is coming into the world and indeed is already here* (1 John 4:3).

:: *Many deceivers have gone out into the world. They deny that Jesus Christ came in a real body. Such a person is a deceiver and an antichrist* (2 John 1:7).

SUPPOSED LINKS TO "ANTICHRIST"

:: *False messiahs and false prophets will rise up and perform great signs and wonders so as to deceive, if possible, even God's chosen ones* (Matthew 24:24). That's Jesus talking about the future. Some Bible experts say he was talking about the fall of Jerusalem; Romans destroyed the city and the Temple in AD 70, crushing a Jewish revolt. Jesus told his disciples it would happen during *"this generation"* (Matthew 24:34).

:: *That day [Jesus' return] will not come until there is a great rebellion against God and the man of lawlessness is revealed—the one who brings destruction. He will exalt himself and defy everything that people call god and every object of worship. He will even sit in the temple of God, claiming that he himself is God* (2 Thessalonians 2:3-4). Some scholars say this describes the Romans and their emperor who was worshipped as a god. Others say the "great rebellion" is yet to come.

:: *The beast was allowed to wage war against God's holy people and to conquer them. And he was given authority to rule over every tribe and people and language and nation. And all the people who belong to this world worshiped the beast* (Revelation 13:7-8). Some link the Antichrist to one of the two "beasts" mentioned in Revelation. Some scholars say the beasts of Revelation refer to the Roman Empire and the emperor, which controlled most of the civilized world in Bible times. Others say the beasts refer to nasty folks yet to come, or perhaps to people in the past as well as the future.

APOSTLES

Top-level church leaders personally commissioned by Jesus to spread his teachings. Apostles included traveling preacher Paul, along with Jesus' 11 surviving disciples (Judas committed suicide after betraying Jesus to Jewish leaders who orchestrated his arrest and execution).

:: *Here are the names of the twelve apostles: first, Simon (also called Peter), then Andrew (Peter's brother), James (son of Zebedee), John (James's brother), Philip, Bartholomew, Thomas, Matthew (the tax collector), James (son of Alphaeus), Thaddaeus, Simon (the zealot), Judas Iscariot (who later betrayed him)* (Matthew 10:2-4). In every list, Peter's name is first, suggesting he led the group after Jesus left.

:: *Now we must choose a replacement for Judas from among the men who were with us the entire time we were traveling with the Lord Jesus—from the time he was baptized by John until the day he was taken from us. Whoever is chosen will join us as a witness of Jesus' resurrection* (Acts 1:21-22). Some scholars say this is as close as the Bible comes to defining *apostle.* Paul, however, would have been an exception to this rule, since he first encountered Jesus only in a vision-like experience after Jesus returned to heaven (Acts 9:5).

:: *The Twelve called a meeting of all the believers. They said, "We apostles should spend our time teaching the word of God, not running a food program"* (Acts 6:2). As the Christian movement grew, the apostles found themselves spending more and more time serving the poor. So they arranged for associates to pick up that part of the ministry so the apostles could focus on spreading the teachings of Jesus.

:: *Am I not an apostle? Haven't I seen Jesus our Lord with my own eyes?* (1 Corinthians 9:1). Paul defended himself against critics who said he wasn't a legit apostle.

:: *You are the body of Christ. Each one of you is a part of it. First, God has appointed apostles in the church. Second, he has appointed prophets. Third, he has appointed teachers . . . . He also appointed those able to help others* (1 Corinthians 12:27-28 NIRV). Apostles get top billing in Paul's list of church leaders and their associates.

APPEARANCE

:: *Looks aren't everything. Don't be impressed with his looks and stature. . . . God judges persons differently than humans do. Men and women look at the face; God looks into the heart* (1 Samuel 16:7 MSG). This is what God told the prophet Samuel when Samuel was about to anoint David's older brother as Israel's future king.

:: *It is not fancy hair, gold jewelry, or fine clothes that should make you beautiful. No, your beauty should come from within you—the beauty of a gentle and quiet spirit that will never be destroyed and is very precious to God* (1 Peter 3:3-4 NCV).

:: *Beauty does not last* (Proverbs 31:30).

:: *I want women to get in there with the men in humility before God, not primping before a mirror or chasing the latest fashions but doing something beautiful for God and becoming beautiful doing it* (1 Timothy 2:9-10 MSG).

EXCEPTION TO THE RULE. The Bible says good looks don't last. But for some folks, a few decades don't hurt.

ARGUMENTS

AVOID THEM

:: *It makes you look good when you avoid a fight— only fools love to quarrel* (Proverbs 20:3 CEV).

:: *Excuse yourself from any conversation that turns into a foolish and uninformed debate because you know they only provoke fights . . .be gentle—no matter who you are dealing with* (2 Timothy 2:23-24 THE VOICE).

SETTLE THEM QUICKLY

:: *The start of a quarrel is like a leak in a dam, so stop it before it bursts* (Proverbs 17:14 MSG).

:: *Make the first move; make things right with him [your enemy]. After all, if you leave the*

GO AHEAD. PULL MY EAR. An African wild dog (Lycaon pictus) seems all ears—accessorized with teeth. Like most wild dogs of Bible times, the critter makes for one fine proverb: ""Interfering in someone else's argument is as foolish as yanking a dog's ears" (Proverbs 26:17).

first move to him, knowing his track record, you're likely to end up in court, maybe even jail (Matthew 5:25 MSG).

HOW TO STOP THEM

:: *A kind answer soothes angry feelings, but harsh words stir them up* (Proverbs 15:1 CEV).

:: *After a first and second warning, avoid someone who causes arguments* (Titus 3:10 NCV).

:: *Regarding life together and getting along with each other, you don't need me to tell you what to do. You're God-taught in these matters. Just love one another!* (1 Thessalonians 4:9 MSG). We usually know how to end an argument. Often, the trick is to give ourselves the time and space to calm down, and then to swallow our pride and say the tough words: "I'm sorry."

WHEN IT'S GOOD TO ARGUE

:: *When Peter came to Antioch, I told him to his face that I was against what he was doing. He was clearly wrong* (Galatians 2:11 NIrV). Paul publicly criticized Peter for a public injustice. Peter had stopped eating with non-Jewish Christians right after a group of Jewish Christians arrived in town. These Jews said it was wrong to mingle with non-Jews, even if those non-Jews were Christians. Paul stood up for what he believed was right.

Israel's holiest relic, it was a gold-covered wooden chest that contained the 10 Commandments that Moses got at Mount Sinai. Jews kept it in the most sacred room of the Jerusalem Temple. Most scholars speculate that invaders confiscated it—perhaps the Babylonians from what is now Iraq—when they leveled the city and the Temple in 586 BC.

:: *"Have the people make an Ark of acacia wood— a sacred chest 45 inches long, 27 inches wide, and 27 inches high [115 x 69 x 69 cm]. Overlay it inside and outside with pure gold. . . . Place inside the Ark the stone tablets inscribed with the terms of the covenant, which I will give to you"* (Exodus 25:10–11, 21).

:: *They marched . . . with the Ark of the LORD's Covenant moving ahead of them to show them where to stop and rest* (Numbers 10:33). The Ark, carried by priests, led Jews on their exodus away from Egypt.

:: *Joshua said to the priests, "Lift up the Ark of the Covenant and lead the people across the river". . . . As soon as the feet of the priests who were carrying the Ark touched the water at the river's edge, the water above that point began backing up . . .until the riverbed was dry. Then all the people crossed over near the town of Jericho* (Joshua 3:6, 15–16).

:: *"Israel has been defeated by the Philistines,"* the messenger replied. *"The people have been slaughtered. . . . And the Ark of God has been captured"* (1 Samuel 4:17). Philistines kept the Ark for several months, until they realized it seemed cursed to them. Skin sores that sound like the bubonic plague erupted on Philistines wherever they took the Ark, showing it off as war trophy. Before a year was up, Philistines returned the Ark to the Jews.

:: *Priests carried the Ark of the LORD's Covenant into the inner sanctuary of the Temple—the Most Holy Place* (1 Kings 8:6). After King Solomon built the Jerusalem Temple, this inner room became the Ark's permanent home.

RAIDERS OF THE LOST ARK. Actors John Rhys-Davies, left, and Harrison Ford lift a Hollywood replica of the Ark of the Covenant.

A location, supposedly in Israel, where some Bible experts say the forces of God will defeat the forces of Satan once and for all in an end-time battle. Many others say the prophecy is just a symbol of God's judgment—a colorful way of assuring persecuted Christians in Bible times that though evil seemed to be winning at the moment, it would lose the war.

:: *Evil spirits. . .went to every king on earth, to bring them together for a war against God All-Powerful. . . . Those armies came together in a place that in Hebrew is called Armagedon* (Revelation 16:14, 16 CEV). There's apparently no such place. Not in the Bible or in known history. *Armageddon* is the English version of the word. The Hebrew version sounds more like Harmageddon. Many Bible experts speculate the place is a reference to *Har Megiddo,* meaning "hill of Megiddo." That's an ancient hilltop fortress overlooking the Jezreel Valley in northern Israel. Napoleon called this valley the "perfect battlefield." Many armies have clashed there—from Egyptians fighting Canaanites in the 1400s BC to modern-day Israelis fighting off a Syrian artillery attack on Ramat David Airbase in the valley in 1973.

The return of Jesus to heaven after his crucifixion and resurrection.

:: *"You will be my witnesses from one end of the earth to the other." After Jesus said this, he was taken up to heaven. They [the disciples] watched until a cloud hid him from their sight* (Acts 1:8–9 NIrv).

Wise men who followed the star of Bethlehem at the birth of Jesus were probably astrologers who

Jezreel Valley, from Carmel Mountains

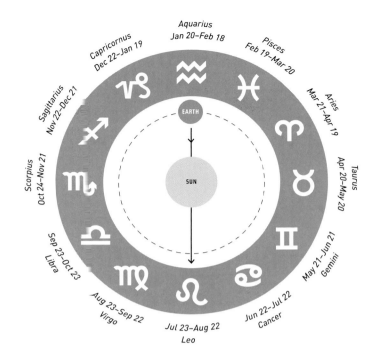

Aquarius
Jan 20–Feb 18

Capricornus
Dec 22–Jan 19

Pisces
Feb 19–Mar 20

Sagittarius
Nov 22–Dec 21

Aries
Mar 21–Apr 19

Scorpius
Oct 24–Nov 21

Taurus
Apr 20–May 20

EARTH

SUN

Gemini
May 21–Jun 21

Libra
Sep 23–Oct 23

Cancer
Jun 22–Jul 22

Virgo
Aug 23–Sep 22

Leo
Jul 23–Aug 22

ZODIAC. Our astrological sign is determined by an imaginary line. It's drawn from the earth through the sun on the date of our birth. The constellation it points to becomes our sign. For people born July 23–August 22, the line points to Leo. The Bible says it's foolish to use stars to predict the future. Light years away, some of them burned out centuries before we were born.

tried to predict the future by studying the stars. But the Bible says astrology is fake.

:: *Do not act like the other nations, who try to read their future in the stars. Do not be afraid of their predictions, even though other nations are terrified by them. Their ways are futile and foolish* (Jeremiah 10:2–3).

:: *You have advisors by the ton—your astrologers and stargazers, who try to tell you what the future holds. But they are as useless as dried grass burning in the fire* (Isaiah 47:13–14 TLB).

(See also *Occult.*)

ATHEIST, AGNOSTIC

Atheists say they don't believe in God. Agnostics say they don't know if God exists—that maybe there is a God, and maybe there isn't.

:: *Ever since the world was created, people have seen the earth and sky. Through everything God made, they can clearly see his invisible qualities—his eternal power and divine nature. So they have no excuse for not knowing God* (Romans 1:20).

:: *The heavens declare the glory of God, and the skies announce what his hands have made* (Psalm 19:1 NCV).

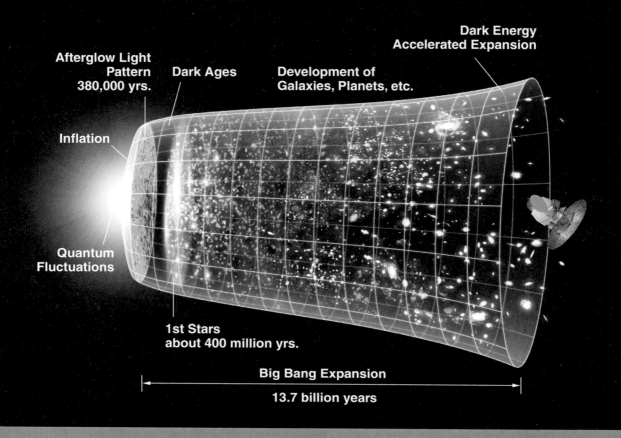

Afterglow Light
Pattern
380,000 yrs.

Dark Ages

Development of
Galaxies, Planets, etc.

Dark Energy
Accelerated Expansion

Inflation

Quantum
Fluctuations

1st Stars
about 400 million yrs.

Big Bang Expansion

13.7 billion years

BANG. A NASA illustration shows what astrophysicists speculate is the nearly 14-billion-year history of our still-expanding universe, beginning with a Big Bang.

BIG BANG QUERY: WHO PULLED THE TRIGGER?

Some Christians say they don't have enough faith not to believe in God.

They can't even work up the faith to believe that their computer snapped itself together. So how on earth could they supersize the scale, mustering up the faith to believe that's what happened to the universe?

Creation itself defies the laws of physics, they argue. In traditional physics, you can't create something from nothing. For that, you have to venture into the zone of quantum physics, and creatively redefine nothing as something—a vacuum, for example.

Yet many Christians say the answer to the mystery behind creation lies outside physics, in a spiritual dimension. Many argue that even if the universe began with a Big Bang, someone had to pull the trigger.

Physicist Albert Einstein lobbied for the peaceful coexistence of science and religion. He said he felt "utter humility toward the unattainable secrets of the harmony of the cosmos." Atheists, he complained, can't hear the "music of the spheres." He was talking about the spheres of science and religion. He explained that "science without religion is lame. Religion without science is blind."

:: *"God who made the world and everything in it. . . makes the creatures; the creatures don't make him. Starting from scratch, he made the entire human race and made the earth hospitable, with plenty of time and space for living so we could seek after God, and not just grope around in the dark but actually find him. He doesn't play hide-and-seek with us. He's not remote; he's near. We live and move in him, can't get away from him!"* (Acts 17:24–28 MSG).

:: *Only a fool would say, "There is no God!"* (Psalm 14:1 CEV).

:: *The wicked are too proud to seek God. They seem to think that God is dead.* (Psalm 10:4) These could include agnostics, who say they don't know if God exists. So they don't commit themselves either way and end up ignoring him.

(See also "If there's a God, why doesn't he show himself—or at least say hello?" page 39)

ATONEMENT

An easy way to remember what this means is to break up the word: "at-one-ment." It means we're "at one" with God because he has forgiven us. Jews in Old Testament times found atonement through animal sacrifices. Christians claim that their atonement is based on the sacrifice of Jesus.

:: *The life of each creature is in its blood. So I have given you the blood of animals to pay for your sin on the altar. Blood is life. That is why blood pays for your sin* (Leviticus 17:11 NIrV). In God's eyes, sin is a capital offense. The Bible says it has been from the time of Adam and Eve. That's when God warned the first couple

that if they broke his one and only rule by eating the forbidden fruit, "you are sure to die" (Genesis 2:17). Some say death entered the world when they ate the fruit, and that if Adam and Eve hadn't eaten it, they might have lived forever.

:: *Jesus Christ. . .is the sacrifice that atones for our sins—and not only our sins but the sins of all the world* (1 John 2:1–2).

:: *Christ died once for our sins. . . . Christ did this to bring you to God* (1 Peter 3:18 CEV).

ATTITUDE

:: *A relaxed attitude lengthens a man's life* (Proverbs 14:30 TLB). But don't count on it. At least not as a promise from God. Proverbs is a collection of advice from elderly men—general observations they've made over the years. In general, they've noticed that easy-going people keep going longer.

:: *Have the same attitude that Christ Jesus had. Though he was God. . .he gave up his divine privileges; he took the humble position of a slave and was born as a human being* (Philippians 2:5–7).

:: *"You're blessed when you're content with just who you are—no more, no less. That's the moment you find yourselves proud owners of everything that can't be bought"* (Matthew 5:5 MSG). These are the words of Jesus, as he starts his famous Sermon on the Mount with a prescription for spiritual happiness: the Beatitudes. Or as some have described them, the Be Happy Attitudes.

:: *May God. . .help you to live in complete harmony with each other—each with the attitude of Christ toward the other* (Romans 15:5 TLB).

:: *Since Jesus went through everything you're going through and more, learn to think like him. Think of your sufferings as a weaning from that old sinful habit of always expecting to get your own way. Then you'll be able to live out your days free to pursue what God wants instead of being tyrannized by what you want* (1 Peter 4:1–2 MSG).

BACKSLIDING

A person of faith rejects God and turns to a sinful lifestyle. Some Christians—including many Baptists—say that once you're saved, there's nothing you can do to lose your salvation. Other Christians disagree. Here are some key verses that Christians on both sides of the debate turn to for support.

ONCE SAVED, ALWAYS SAVED

:: *"My sheep listen to my voice; I know them, and they follow me. I give them eternal life, and they will never perish. No one can snatch them away from me, for my Father has given them to me, and he is more powerful than anyone else. No one can snatch them from the Father's hand"* (John 10:27–29) That's Jesus talking about his followers. Christians who don't believe in "once saved, always saved" argue that to keep from being "snatched away," we have to continue listening to Jesus and following him. If we don't, we can end up like a sheep that nibbles its way into a lion's den.

:: *He [God] has given us new birth. . . . It is a gift that can never be destroyed. It can never spoil or even fade away. It is kept in heaven for you. Through faith you are kept safe by God's power. Your salvation is going to be completed* (1 Peter 1:4–5 NIrV). Christians who say it's possible to lose salvation say our spiritual security comes "through faith." It's based on the condition that we continue trusting in God.

BELIEVERS CAN LOSE THEIR SALVATION

:: *We must listen very carefully to the truth we have heard, or we may drift away from it. . . . It is impossible to bring back to repentance those who were once enlightened—those who have experienced the good things of heaven and shared in the Holy Spirit, who have tasted the goodness of the word of God and the power of the age to come—and who then turn away from God* (Hebrews 2:1; 6:4–6). Some Christians who teach "once saved, always saved" say the writer is talking about people who never fully believed—they "tasted" spiritual truth but never fully digested it. Others acknowledge that the people were true believers, but insist that they didn't lose their salvation. Instead, they just lost their ability to become "mature" believers, who are referred to at the beginning of chapter 6. Some say the writer is exaggerating. The point of the book, many Bible experts say, is to stop Jewish Christians from going back to their old, safer religion of Judaism. To these believers, the Hebrews writer seems to be saying, "If you leave the church, you won't be coming back."

:: *Some people have left the faith, because they wanted to get more money, but they have caused themselves much sorrow* (1 Timothy 6:10 NCV). Christians favoring "once saved, always saved" acknowledge that we can leave the faith, but the faith won't leave us—we are saved regardless of what we do.

:: *Do not let those evil people lead you away by the wrong they do. Be careful so you will not* fall from your strong faith. (2 Peter 3:17 NCV). But if you do fall, say the "once saved, always saved" folks, you'll fall into the arms of a loving Jesus who will carry you to heaven.

:: *Christ brought you over to God's side and put your lives together, whole and holy in his presence. You don't walk away from a gift like that!* (Colossians 1:22–23 MSG). "Once saved, always saved" believers say that no matter where we walk, the gift of salvation—Jesus our Savior—walks with us.

:: *"Many will turn away from me"* (Matthew 24:10). That's Jesus, predicting persecution so intense that it will drive some Christians away from the faith. But many today teach that even if we reject Jesus, he won't reject us.

(See also *Eternal Security, Predestination, Sin.*)

BAPTISM

In this worship ritual, a Christian is dipped into water—or sometimes sprinkled. This symbolizes that God has washed away our sins and given us new life.

:: *Going under the water was a burial of your old life; coming up out of it was a resurrection, God raising you from the dead as he did Christ* (Colossians 2:12 MSG). Christians rise from the baptismal water in a dramatic and public statement: I have become a new person—a Christian, washed clean of my sins.

HOLY WATER. Emotion runs high for many Christian pilgrims getting baptized in the same river in which Jesus was baptized: the Jordan.

:: *John was baptizing people in the desert and preaching a baptism of changed hearts and lives for the forgiveness of sins. All the people from Judea and Jerusalem were going out to him. They confessed their sins and were baptized by him in the Jordan River* (Mark 1:4–5 NCV). John started the ritual that became Christian baptism. He may have adapted it from a Jewish cleaning ritual that involved taking a bath before worshipping God.

:: *Jesus was baptized. And as soon as he came out of the water. . .a voice from heaven said, "This is my own dear Son, and I am pleased with him"* (Matthew 3:16–17 CEV). Though Jesus had committed no sins, he insisted on being baptized—perhaps as an example for others to follow.

:: *Go and preach the good news to everyone in the world. Anyone who believes me and is baptized will be saved* (Mark 16:15–16 CEV). Words like this, from Jesus, have led some Christians to conclude that we have to be baptized to make it into heaven. Most Christians, however, say baptism is simply a helpful ritual to observe—not a requirement. Elsewhere, many explain, Jesus and the apostle Paul both made it clear that we are saved by faith in God, not by any rituals we perform (John 3:16; Ephesians 2:8–9).

:: *On that day about three thousand believed his [Peter's] message and were baptized* (Acts 2:41 CEV). The church was born when Peter preached in Jerusalem several weeks after the Crucifixion. People who joined what became the Christian movement took a public stand by getting baptized.

:: *The jailer took Paul and Silas and washed their wounds. Right away he and his whole family were baptized* (Acts 16:33 NIrV). This is from a story about Paul and Silas converting their jailer. Converts to the new Christian movement not only got baptized, they often had their entire family baptized as well. That's one reason some churches baptize infants.

BAPTISM WITH THE HOLY SPIRIT

Jesus promised his disciples that after he left they would be "baptized with the Holy Spirit" (Acts 1:5) in a spiritual experience that would give them the courage and wisdom to spread his teachings around the world (Acts 1:8). Some Pentecostal Christians teach that this baptism allows believers to speak in heavenly languages. Some churches that embrace the Bible teachings of British theo-

PENTECOSTAL PRAYER. Members of the Imperial Valley Pentecostal Church in El Centro, California, lift their hands in prayer. Many Pentecostal Christians say that baptism with the Holy Spirit enables them to pray in the language of heaven.

logian John Wesley (1703–91) say this baptism cleanses believers of original sin, or the tendency to sin. Some call this "entire sanctification," and explain it as a maturing experience that usually takes place after conversion. Other Christians teach that God's Spirit lives in all believers, guiding them in their walk of faith.

:: *"In just a few days you will be baptized with the Holy Spirit. . . . You will receive power when the Holy Spirit comes upon you. And you will be my witnesses, telling people about me everywhere. . .to the ends of the earth"* (Acts 1:5, 8). That's Jesus talking to his disciples shortly before his ascension into the sky.

:: *When the Feast of Pentecost came, they were all together in one place. Without warning there was a sound like a strong wind, gale force—no one could tell where it came from. It filled the whole building. Then, like a wildfire, the Holy Spirit spread through their ranks, and they started speaking in a number of different languages as the Spirit prompted them* (Acts

2:1-4 MSG). Jewish pilgrims from throughout the Roman world who had come to Jerusalem to celebrate the festival were surprised to hear the followers of Jesus speaking in the very languages the pilgrims spoke.

:: *"Each of you must repent of your sins and turn to God, and be baptized in the name of Jesus Christ for the forgiveness for your sins. Then you will receive the gift of the Holy Spirit"* (Acts 2:38). Peter tells the Jerusalem crowd that though God once gave the Holy Spirit to select leaders, like kings and prophets, now he makes his Spirit available to everyone who turns to God.

:: *God has given us the Holy Spirit, who fills our hearts with his love* (Romans 5:5 CEV).

:: *We have all been baptized into one body [the body of Christ] by one Spirit, and we all share the same Spirit* (1 Corinthians 12:13).

(See also *Holiness; Holy Spirit; Tongues, Speaking in.*)

BEATITUDES

A collection of sayings at the beginning of Jesus' famous Sermon on the Mount. Some of these sayings are intended to encourage people who are suffering. Others describe the kind of people God wants us to become. *Beatitude* means happy or blessed. The sayings appear in Matthew 5:3–12, with a condensed version in Luke 6:20–23.

:: *"You're blessed when you're at the end of your rope. With less of you there is more of God"* (Matthew 5:3 MSG).

:: *"Blessed are those who suffer for doing what is right. The kingdom of heaven belongs to them"* (Matthew 5:10 NIrV).

BELIEF

When it comes to spiritual matters, beliefs are often based on faith, not on scientific fact. Perhaps the most important Christian beliefs are these: Jesus is the divine Son of God who died for the sins of humanity and then rose from the dead. For more key beliefs, see the "Apostles Creed," page 36.

:: *"God loved the world so much that he gave his one and only Son, so that everyone who believes in him will not perish but have eternal life"* (John 3:16). Founder of the Protestant movement Martin Luther (1483–1546) said this one sentence sums up all the Bible teachings about Jesus.

:: *"I have always believed you are the Messiah, the Son of God, the one who has come into the world from God"* (John 11:27). This is Martha talking to Jesus just before he raises her brother, Lazarus, from the dead.

:: *I wrote this book for one reason: to convince you that Jesus is the Messiah the prophets said was coming to save us, and that he is the Son of God. If you believe this about Jesus, you will live forever* (John 20:31 AUTHOR'S PARAPHRASE). John's book is a collection of carefully chosen evidence to support his argument, especially Jesus' godlike miracles and his inspired teachings.

:: *Face it—if there's no resurrection for Christ, everything we've told you is smoke and mirrors, and everything you've staked your life on is smoke and mirrors* (1 Corinthians 15:14 MSG). Paul, writing about the importance of Jesus' resurrection. If Jesus wasn't raised from the dead, Christians are dead wrong— and should send out a search party looking for God.

:: The Scriptures tell us, "Abraham believed God, and God counted him as righteous because of his faith" (Romans 4:3).

(See also *Faith*.)

BIBLE

The Bible is the sacred book of Jews and Christians. The Jewish Bible is what Christians call the Old Testament, though arranged in a different order. The Christian Bible adds at least the 27 books of the New Testament, though Catholics, Orthodox Christians, and some other Christian groups add more books—up to more than a dozen—written between the time of the Old and New Testaments. The collection is called the *Apocrypha*, a Greek word meaning "hidden."

:: There's nothing like the written Word of God for showing you the way to salvation through faith in Christ Jesus. Every part of Scripture is God-breathed and useful one way or another— showing us truth, exposing our rebellion, correcting our mistakes, training us to live God's way. Through the Word we are put together and shaped up for the tasks God has for us (2 Timothy 3:15–17 MSG). Paul wrote this, referring to his Bible—the Old Testament. Within a few decades, Christians were calling the letters of Paul scripture, too.

:: The Scriptures give us hope and encouragement as we wait patiently for God's promises to be fulfilled (Romans 15:4).

:: The sacred writings contain preliminary reports by the prophets on God's Son (Romans 1:2–3 MSG). Paul is talking about prophecies in the Old Testament that Christians say Jesus fulfilled.

:: "You have your heads in your Bibles constantly because you think you'll find eternal life there. But you miss the forest for the trees. These Scriptures are all about me! And here I am, standing right before you, and you aren't willing to receive from me the life you say you want" (John 5:39–40 MSG). Jesus talking to Jewish scholars.

:: "People do not live by bread alone, but by every word that comes from the mouth of God" (Matthew 4:4). This is Jesus talking as he fasts and prays in the Judean badlands before launching his ministry. He's quoting from the Jewish Bible, Deuteronomy 8:3, to fight off Satan's temptation to break his fast and eat some food.

:: The Bereans were eager to hear what Paul and Silas said and studied the Scriptures every day to find out if these things were true (Acts 17:11 NCV). "Scriptures" here mean the Jewish Bible.

(See also "How did we get the Bible?" page 14; "If the Bible is God's Word, why is it full of blatant contradictions and obvious mistakes?" page 44.)

BLASPHEMY

Blasphemy in the Bible often means slandering God with lies and mean-spirited attacks.

:: They blaspheme your name [God] and stand in arrogance against you (Psalm 139:20 TLB).

:: Jesus replied. . . . "You will see the Son of Man seated in the place of power at God's right hand and coming on the clouds of heaven." Then the high priest tore his clothing to show his horror and said, "Blasphemy! Why do we need other witnesses? You have all heard his blasphemy. What is your verdict?" "Guilty!" they shouted. "He deserves to die!" (Matthew 26:64–66). Bible experts say the blasphemy here is that Jesus claimed to be the Messiah, at the very least. At most, he implied he was divine. His line about "coming on the clouds of heaven" draws from a prophecy in Daniel 7:13–14, which seems to refer to a godlike ruler with celestial authority.

:: *Every sin and blasphemy can be forgiven— except blasphemy against the Holy Spirit, which will never be forgiven* (Matthew 12:31).

(See also "The unforgivable sin" page 213.)

BLESSING

In the Bible, *blessing* can have several meanings. It can mean praise. It can be words or actions that make someone else happy. Or it can be an upbeat declaration about someone, wishing—or sometimes promising—good things for him or her in the future, such as a big family and prosperity.

:: *God created human beings. . . . God blessed them: "Prosper! Reproduce! Fill Earth! Take charge! Be responsible for fish in the sea and birds in the air, for every living thing that moves on the face of Earth"* (Genesis 1:27–28 MSG). God puts Adam and Eve in charge of his creation.

:: *God made a promise to Abraham. . . . "I will surely bless you and give you many descendants"* (Hebrews 6:13–14 NCV).

:: *Isaac. . .blessed his son. . . . "May many nations become your servants, and may they bow down to you. May you be the master over your brothers, and may your mother's sons bow down to you. All who curse you will be cursed, and all who bless you will be blessed"* (Genesis 27:27, 29). Old Isaac, fearing he's about to die,

offered this deathbed blessing for his oldest son, Esau—a tradition in ancient times. Unfortunately, Isaac only thought he was blessing Esau. Instead, Jacob, the younger son, tricked the nearly blind Isaac by pretending to be Esau. Blessings like this weren't considered a mere wish or a prayer. People treated the spoken words of a blessing as though they unleashed a power to make things happen— and the power couldn't be retracted.

:: *Bless the LORD, O my soul, and all that is within me, bless his holy name!* (Psalm 103:1 ESV).

BODY PIERCING

The Bible doesn't talk about the kind of body piercing popular in recent years, such as pierced ears—or the less-common and more painful

HOLY. Body piercing—anything from head to toe—has become a fashion statement in recent years. To some, the statement is art. To others, it's "ouch."

piercing of tongues, belly buttons, or genitals. But some see implied cautions in the Bible's portrayal of the human body as God's masterpiece.

:: *God created human beings in his own image. . . . Then God looked over all he had made, and he saw that it was very good!* (Genesis 1:27, 31). Of everything God created, humans got the highest praise: "excellent." All others are described as "good."
:: *You [God] formed me in my mother's womb. . . . Body and soul, I am marvelously made!* (Psalm 139:13–14 msg).
:: *"Publicly pierce his ear"* (Exodus 21:6). This permanently marked a person as a slave for life.

(See also *Tattoos*.)

BORN AGAIN

:: *"No one can see God's kingdom without being born again"* (John 3:3 nirv). Some Bible versions translated "born again" as "born from above." Many say it simply means to become a Christian. For some people, the change in lifestyle is so dramatic that it seems appropriate to describe the conversion experience as a spiritual rebirth.
:: *"No one can enter the Kingdom of God without being born of water and the Spirit"* (John 3:5). This is Jesus' explanation of what it means to be "born again." But many wonder what he meant by "born of water and the Spirit." Some guess it's a reference to the spiritual awakening that prophets predicted would happen once the Messiah came: "I will sprinkle clean water on you, and you will be clean. . . . I will put my Spirit inside

you and help you live by my rules" (Ezekiel 36:25, 27 ncv).

CAPITAL PUNISHMENT

God ordered Jews to execute people for certain crimes, including murder and adultery. But many Christians say Jesus launched a new way of life that excludes killing killers—or anyone else.

CAPITAL OFFENSES (THE SHORT LIST)

:: *"If someone plans and murders another person on purpose, put him to death"* (Exodus 21:14 ncv). God, however, spared two famous murderers: Cain, who killed his brother, and King David, who committed adultery with Bathsheba and then arranged the death of her husband.
:: *"If a man is discovered committing adultery, both he and the woman must die"* (Deuteronomy 22:22).
:: *"Anyone who hits his father or his mother must be put to death"* (Exodus 21:15 ncv).
:: *"Anyone who kidnaps someone. . .must be put to death"* (Exodus 21:16 ncv).

NEW COMMANDMENTS

:: *"You know that you have been taught, 'An eye for an eye and a tooth for a tooth.' But I tell you not to try to get even with a person who has done something to you"* (Matthew 5:38–39 cev). With this single statement, Jesus is declaring that the old Jewish law of retaliation is now obsolete (Exodus 21:24).
:: *"Does no one condemn you? . . . . Neither do I"* (John 8:10–11 msg). The words of Jesus to a woman caught in adultery. Jesus talked religious leaders out of stoning her to death, even

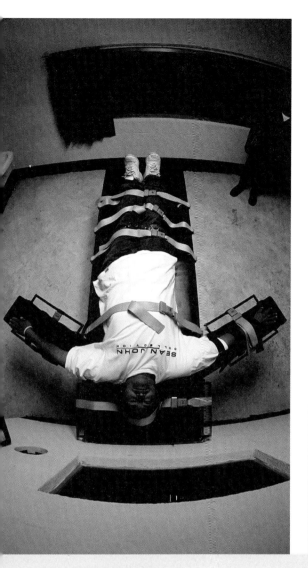

A NEW CROSS FOR CRIMINALS The execution table in a Guatemalan jail, viewed from a ceiling camera, looks a bit like the crosses Romans once used. This inmate isn't about to die. He's 42-year-old Walter Rivera of Salvador, serving 50 years for kidnapping and plagiarism. He's helping prison officials demonstrate lethal injection.

though by Jewish law, adultery was a capital offense. Instead of punishing the woman, Jesus forgave her.

:: *"Love your enemies. Let them bring out the best in you, not the worst"* (Matthew 5:44 MSG).

CELIBACY

Big families were considered blessed in Bible times. However, the apostle Paul, a single man, promoted the single lifestyle. He said single people can devote more time to ministry than they could if they had to take care of a family, too.

:: *The LORD God said, "It is not good for the man to be alone. I will make a helper who is just right for him." . . . Then the LORD God made a woman. . .and he brought her to the man* (Genesis 2:18, 22). Marriage is the default setting for humans. At least that's how many interpret this passage.

:: *I wish everyone were single like me—a simpler life in many ways! But celibacy is not for everyone any more than marriage is. God gives the gift of the single life to some, the gift of the married life to others* (1 Corinthians 7:7 MSG). Paul was writing this letter to new Christians in what is now Corinth, Greece.

:: *I want you to live as free of complications as possible. When you're unmarried, you're free to concentrate on simply pleasing the Master. Marriage involves you in all the nuts and bolts of domestic life and in wanting to please your spouse, leading to so many more demands on your attention. The time and energy that married people spend on caring for and nurturing each other, the unmarried can spend in becoming whole and holy instruments of God* (1 Corinthians 7:32–34 MSG).

CHEATING (DISHONESTY)

Cheating is a liar's way of getting ahead at the expense of others, according to Bible writers. Honesty is the Bible's policy.

:: *If you're honest in small things, you'll be honest in big things; If you're a crook in small things, you'll be a crook in big things* (Luke 16:10 MSG).

:: *"Don't cheat"* (Mark 10:19 MSG).

:: *Better to be poor and honest than a rich person no one can trust* (Proverbs 19:1 MSG).

:: *GOD cares about honesty in the workplace; your business is his business* (Proverbs 16:11 MSG).

:: *GOD hates cheating in the marketplace; he loves it when business is aboveboard* (Proverbs 11:1 MSG).

(See also *Honesty, Lying.*)

CHRISTIANITY

The world's leading religion is based on the teachings of Jesus.

:: *It was at Antioch [a city in Syria] that the believers were first called Christians* (Acts 11:26). Before then, converts to the teachings of Jesus called themselves "followers of the Way" (Acts 9:2). It wasn't until several years after the movement began that people started calling them "Christians," from the Greek word *Christos* (Messiah) and the Latin ending *ianus.* The combo word meant "belonging to Christ." Originally, this may have been a degrading name. Perhaps a bit like calling followers of Sung Myung Moon "Moonies," when they prefer being identified as members of the Unification Church. In time, follow-ers of Jesus grew to love the title "Christian" because it connected them to Christ.

:: *If someone asks about your Christian hope, always be ready to explain it. But do this in a gentle and respectful way* (1 Peter 3:15–16).

:: *It is no shame to suffer for being a Christian. Praise God for the privilege of being called by his name! . . . These trials make you partners with Christ in his suffering* (1 Peter 4:16, 13).

:: *Anyone who belongs to Christ has become a new person. The old life is gone; a new life has begun!* (2 Corinthians 5:17).

:: *"I am the way, the truth, and the life. No one can come to the Father except through me"* (John 14:6). Because of passages like this, most Christians insist that people have to accept Jesus as Savior to make it into heaven. Others speculate that we may be able to accept him after we die, though most Christians consider this heresy that has no support in the Bible. For many, a troubling question is what God will do with the billions of people throughout history who never heard enough about Jesus to consider Christianity. "In God we trust," others answer. Put another way, Christians trust in a God who perfectly blends fairness, justice, and love. They're counting on him to do the right thing.

(See also "What it takes to be a Christian," page 34.)

CHURCH

The church is a community of people who follow the teachings of Jesus. It can refer to a meeting place, but it's not just that. Christians didn't start building churches until the AD 300s, after Rome legalized Christianity and adopted it as the

CHURCH IN JERUSALEM. A Greek Orthodox priest stands outside one of the oldest churches in the world: Jerusalem's Church of the Holy Sepulchre. It was built in the AD 300s, shortly after the Roman Empire legalized Christianity. Most Bible experts agree it was probably built over both the tomb of Jesus as well as the nearby site of his execution. Today, the church is one of Jerusalem's most popular tourist attractions.

empire's official religion. Before that, members of this outlawed faith met in small groups—often in homes.

COME TO CHURCH

:: *You should not stay away from the church meetings, as some are doing, but you should meet together and encourage each other* (Hebrews 10:25 NCV).

:: *"Where two or three gather together as my followers, I am there among them"* (Matthew 18:20). That's Jesus talking.

THE CHURCH'S JOB

:: *"Go everywhere in the world, and tell the Good News to everyone"* (Mark 16:15 NCV). These are the last words of Jesus to his disciples—a mission statement known as the Great Commission. He didn't say, "Go talk among yourselves." The church of the Bible wasn't a holy club reserved for saints. It was an assorted group of folks meeting to learn about Jesus and to share what they learned with others.

:: *"You need to know that I have other sheep in addition to those in this pen. I need to gather and bring them, too. They'll also recognize my voice. Then it will be one flock, one Shepherd"* (John 10:16 MSG).

:: *Let us aim for harmony in the church and try to build each other up* (Romans 14:19).

:: *Just as our bodies have many parts and each part has a special function, so it is with Christ's body. . . . God has given us different gifts. . . . If your gift is serving others, serve them well. If you are a teacher, teach well. If your gift is to encourage others, be encouraging. If it is giving, give generously. If God has given you leadership ability, take the responsibility seriously* (Romans 12:4–8).

:: *Together you are the body of Christ. Each o[ne] of you is part of his body. First, God chose so[me] people to be apostles and prophets and teac[h]ers for the church. But he also chose some [to] work miracles or heal the sick or help oth[ers] or be leaders or speak different kinds of l[an]guages* (1 Corinthians 12:27–28 CEV).

:: *I am told that a man in your church is livin[g in] sin with his stepmother. . . . It isn't my respo[nsi]bility to judge outsiders, but it certainly is y[our] responsibility to judge those inside the church who are sinning* (1 Corinthians 5:1, 12).

LEADERS

:: *When it comes to the church, he [Jesus] organizes and holds it together* (Colossians 1:17 MSG).

:: *A leader must be well-thought-of, committed to his wife, cool and collected, accessible, and hospitable. He must know what he's talking about, not be overfond of wine, not pushy but gentle, not thin-skinned, not money-hungry. He must handle his own affairs well, attentive to his own children and having their respect. . . . He must not be a new believer, lest the position go to his head and the Devil trip him up. Outsiders must think well of him* (1 Timothy 3:2–4, 6–7 MSG).

:: *"I say to you that you are Peter (which means 'rock'), and upon this rock I will build my church, and all the powers of hell will not conquer it"* (Matthew 16:18). These are the words of Jesus to his leading disciple. Roman Catholics say this is when Jesus appointed Peter to become what amounts to the first in a long line of popes. Protestants say Jesus was referring to the leadership Peter would give to the Christian movement, beginning with a sermon that would produce 3,000 converts in Jerusalem (Acts 2).

:: *If you are sick, ask the church leaders to come and pray for you* (James 5:14 CEV)

(See also *Worship*.)

COMMUNION (EUCHARIST, LORD'S SUPPER, MASS)

Many Christians consider this the most important worship ritual, one that Jesus established. Christians eat a piece of bread and drink a sip of wine or grape juice to commemorate Jesus' death on the cross. The torn bread represents his broken

BODY OF CHRIST IN BAGHDAD. Conducting Holy Communion, a priest gives a wafer to an Iraqi Christian at the Virgin Mary church in Baghdad. Some Christians say that during the communion service, the bread and wine become the actual body and blood of Jesus. Most Protestants disagree, saying it's just a symbol of his crucifixion suffering.

body. The juice represents his blood. Some Christians teach that the bread and juice become his actual body and blood.

:: *He [Jesus] broke the bread and handed it to his apostles. Then he said, "This is my body, which is given for you. Eat this as a way of remembering me!" After the meal he took another cup of wine in his hands. Then he said, "This is my blood. It is poured out for you"* (Luke 22:19–20 CEV).

:: *On the first day of the week, we gathered with the local believers to share in the Lord's Supper* (Acts 20:7). Jews considered Sunday the first day of the week.

:: *Examine your motives, test your heart, come to this meal in holy awe* (1 Corinthians 11:28 MSG).

:: *When you meet together, you are not really interested in the Lord's Supper. For some of you hurry to eat your own meal without sharing with others. As a result, some go hungry while others get drunk* (1 Corinthians 11:20–21). The apostle Paul criticizes Christians at Corinth for what sounds like turning the communion ritual into a Sunday potluck. He tells them to eat their meal at home.

COMPASSION

:: *"A despised Samaritan came along, and when he saw the man [injured by robbers], he felt compassion for him. Going over to him, the Samaritan soothed his wounds with olive oil and wine and bandaged them. Then he put the man on his own donkey and took him to an inn, where he took care of him"* (Luke 10:33–34). In this famous Parable of the Good Samaritan, Jesus teaches the importance of compassion. He links it to what he calls one of the most important commandments of all: loving our neighbor. The Samaritan represents who our neighbors are: any person we can help.

:: *"Then the people will ask, 'Lord, when did we fail to help you. . .?' The king will say to them, 'Whenever you failed to help any of my people, no matter how unimportant they seemed, you failed to do it for me' "* (Matthew 25:44–45 CEV). Jesus says that when we help others, it's the same as helping him.

:: *"I don't find you guilty either," Jesus said. "Go now and leave your life of sin"* (John 8:11 NIrV). Instead of punishing a woman caught in adultery, as Jewish law allowed, Jesus forgave her.

COMPLAINING

:: *It's better out in the desert than at home with a nagging, complaining wife* (Proverbs 21:19 CEV). Or husband. The book of Proverbs was written for young men, offering advice from older men. But we can probably count on this: given a chance the older women of Bible times would have warned younger women about crabby husbands.

:: *Do everything without complaining and arguing, so that no one can criticize you* (Philippians 2:14–15).

:: *Let everything you say be good and helpful, so that your words will be an encouragement to those who hear them* (Ephesians 4:29).

:: *"What have I done to deserve this? You've made me responsible for all these people . . . . They keep whining. . . . If this is the way you're going to treat me, just kill me now and end my miserable life!"* (Numbers 11:11, 13, 15 CEV). Constant complaining of the Exodus Jews frustrates Moses so much that he

asks God to put him out of his misery. God later offers to kill the Jews instead—an offer Moses rejects.

:: *"I can't stand my life—I hate it! I'm putting it all out on the table, all the bitterness of my life—I'm holding back nothing"* (Job 10:1 MSG). Job complains to God about losing his health, wealth, and family.

:: *I will wait to learn how God will answer my complaint* (Habakkuk 2:1 NCV). A prophet complains to God about what seems to be God's unfair treatment of the Jews. God graciously listens and responds.

(See also *Arguments, Criticism.*)

CONFESSION

The Bible says we should admit our sins not only to God, but to the people we hurt as well.

CONFESS TO GOD

:: *When I kept it all inside. . . The pressure never let up. . . . Then I let it all out; I said, "I'll make a clean breast of my failures to GOD." Suddenly the pressure was gone—my guilt dissolved, my sin disappeared* (Psalm 32:3–5 MSG).

:: *God is faithful and fair. If we admit that we have sinned, he will forgive us our sins. He will forgive every wrong thing we have done* (1 John 1:9 NIrV). After we confess, God removes all traces of our guilt. There may be consequences we have to face from others, but Judge God strikes his gavel on the desk and declares us "not guilty."

:: *Purify me from my sins, and I will be clean; wash me, and I will be whiter than snow. Oh, give me back my joy again* (Psalm 51:7–8).

:: *David prayed, "I am your servant. But what I did*

WHY CATHOLICS CONFESS TO A PRIEST.

Christians don't need to confess their sins to a Catholic priest, Protestants insist.

As the apostle Paul explained to his associate Timothy, "There is only one go-between for God and human beings. He is the man Christ Jesus" (1 Timothy 2:5 NIrV). Protestants say all we need to do is confess our sins to Jesus or to God the Father.

Not true, say most Catholics. Jesus is the go-between, or reconciler, because he died to pay the penalty for humanity's sins. But he also set up the system for reconciliation. Catholics say forgiveness comes through the church, headed by the pope—and that Jesus appointed Peter the first pope.

For Bible support, they quote Jesus

"You are Peter. On this rock I will build my church. . . . I will give you the keys of the kingdom of heaven; the things you don't allow on earth will be the things that God does not allow, and the things you allow on earth will be the things that God allows."

—JESUS TO PETER, MATTHEW 16:18–19 NCV

"If you forgive anyone's sins, they are forgiven."

—JESUS TO HIS DISCIPLES, JOHN 20:23

Protestants say those verses are a far cry from justifying the Catholic system of confessing sins to a priest. Instead, those verses show Jesus merely putting Peter in charge of the Christian movement and then reminding the disciples and all followers to forgive others.

PRIEST ON HOLD. A Catholic priest in Palermo, Sicily, waits in a confessional booth to hear the sins of his parishioners. He'll grant them absolution—forgiveness—if they complete the penance he assigns them, which often includes reciting prayers.

was stupid and terribly wrong. Please forgive me" (1 Chronicles 21:8 CEV). The Bible portrays King David as a man who was quick to confess after being confronted with his sin.

CONFESS TO EACH OTHER

:: *Make this your common practice: Confess your sins to each other and pray for each other so that you can live together whole and healed* (James 5:16 MSG). This doesn't mean we should tell everyone how bad we've been. Everyone has their spiritual struggles. But it does mean we should try to work things out with the people we've hurt.

CONVERSION

This is the change God makes in people once they decide to leave their sinful lifestyle and become followers of Jesus.

:: *Give up your old way of life with all its bad habits. Let the Spirit change your way of thinking and make you into a new person. You were created to be like God, and so you must please him and be truly holy* (Ephesians 4:22–24 CEV).

:: *Create in me a clean heart, O God. Renew a loyal spirit within me. . . . Restore to me the joy of your salvation, and make me willing to obey you* (Psalm 51:10, 12). A sinner's prayer.

:: *"Now it's time to change your ways! Turn to face God so he can wipe away your sins, pour out showers of blessing to refresh you"* (Acts 3:19–20 MSG).

:: *Everyone is talking about how you. . .turned away from idols to serve the true and living God* (1 Thessalonians 1:9 CEV).

(See also *Born Again*, *Repentance*.)

COURAGE

:: *"Be strong. Take courage. Don't be intimidated . . .because GOD, your God, is striding ahead of you. He's right there with you. He won't let you down; he won't leave you"* (Deuteronomy 31:6 MSG). In his last address to the Jewish nation, Moses inspires courage as the people prepare to cross the Jordan River and invade what is now Israel.

:: *My dear children, you belong to God. . .God's Spirit, who is in you, is greater than the devil, who is in the world* (1 John 4:4 NCV).

:: *God's Spirit doesn't make cowards out of us. The Spirit gives us power, love, and self-control* (2 Timothy 1:7 CEV).

:: *"Having hope will give you courage. You will be protected and will rest in safety. You will lie down unafraid"* (Job 11:18–19).

:: *Be strong and courageous, all you who put your hope in the LORD!* (Psalm 31:24).

CREATION

:: *In the beginning God created the heavens and the earth* (Genesis 1:1).

:: *GOD formed Man out of dirt from the ground and blew into his nostrils the breath of life. The Man came alive—a living soul!* (Genesis 2:7 MSG).

:: *Christ is the visible image of the invisible God. . . . Through him God created everything in the heavenly realms and on earth. He made the things we can see and the things we can't see. . . . He holds all creation together* (Colossians 1:15–17).

(See also "If there's a God, why doesn't he show himself—or at least say hello?" page 39.)

A STAR IS BORN. Lots of stars, actually. NASA's Hubble Space Telescope captures Carina Nebula towering three light years high. Stars inside stir the pillars of gas and dust, whipping up newborn stars, scientists say. Carina Nebula churns its stars some 7,500 light years from Earth. Light travels at 186,000 miles (300,000 km) a second, putting the moon 1.5 seconds away at light speed, Mars four minutes, and Saturn one hour.

As far as the Bible is concerned, criticism is something best kept between friends—in a spirit of loving concern, without anger or hypocrisy.

WHEN TO KEEP QUIET

:: *Every time you criticize someone, you condemn yourself. It takes one to know one. Judgmental criticism of others is a well-known way of escaping detection in your own crimes* (Romans 2:1 MSG).

:: *"Why do you notice the little piece of dust in your friend's eye, but you don't notice the big piece of wood in your own eye?"* (Luke 6:41 NCV). Or put another way, people in glass houses shouldn't take pot shots at their neighbor with a BB gun.

:: *Welcome all the Lord's followers, even those whose faith is weak. Don't criticize them for having beliefs that are different from yours . . . . Only their Lord can decide if they are doing right, and the Lord will make sure that they do right* (Romans 14:1, 4 CEV).

:: *Don't waste your constructive criticism on arrogant jerks. They'll only hate you for it. Save the sincere critique for people who care. They'll love you for it* (Proverbs 9:8 AUTHOR'S PARAPHRASE).

LISTEN TO CONSTRUCTIVE CRITICISM

:: *To one who listens, valid criticism is like a gold earring or other gold jewelry* (Proverbs 25:12).

:: *If you listen to constructive criticism, you will be at home among the wise* (Proverbs 15:31).

:: *Better to be criticized by a wise person than to be praised by a fool* (Ecclesiastes 7:5).

:: *If you ignore criticism, you will end in poverty and disgrace; if you accept correction, you will be honored* (Proverbs 13:18).

HOW TO DISARM YOUR CRITICS

:: *Keep a clear conscience before God so that when people throw mud at you, none of it will stick. They'll end up realizing that they're the ones who need a bath* (1 Peter 3:16 MSG).

(See also *Complaining, Insults, Judging Others.*)

CRUCIFIXION

The Roman Empire executed the worst criminals—murderers, traitors, rebels—by hanging them on a cross where they died a slow and torturous death. Some victims took days to die.

:: *Pilate. . .ordered his soldiers to beat Jesus with a whip and nail him to a cross* (Matthew 27:26 CEV).

:: *"If I am lifted up from the earth, I will draw all people toward me." Jesus said this to show*

Artist's depiction of Jesus wearing a crown of thorns, part of the torture leading up to the Crucifixion.

how he would die (John 12 32–33 NCV). Jesus' death and resurrection is what finally convinced his followers that he was God's Son, and that his promises of eternal life were true. The Christian movement started, and today is the world's largest religion.

:: *If we shared in Jesus' death by being baptized, we will be raised to life with him. We know that the persons we used to be were nailed to the cross with Jesus. . . . Think of yourselves as dead to the power of sin. But Christ Jesus has given life to you, and you live for God* (Romans 6:5–6, 11 CEV). The apostle Paul used Christian baptism as a symbol of burial, linking it to Jesus' death on the cross. His point is that baptism illustrates that our sinful life is dead. And when we came up out of the water, it was a symbol of our resurrection into a new life no longer controlled by sin.

CURSES (PROFANITY)

Some Christians say it's okay to use profane words in anger, as long as we don't use God's name that way. Others argue just the opposite. They see nothing wrong with the complaint: "Oh, God!" But they would never say, "Oh, [fill in the blank with a hammer-hits-thumb cuss word]." Actually, the Bible has a different take on profanity and cursing than most folks do today. In the Bible, a curse is a prayer that something bad will happen to someone. *Profane* means to treat something that's sacred as though it's not—like God's name. The Bible says Christians aren't supposed to curse others or abuse God's name. They're also to drop nasty words from their vocabulary.

:: *No using the name of GOD, your God, in curses or silly banter; GOD won't put up with the irreverent use of his name* (Exodus 20:7 MSG). This is number three of the 10 Commandments. If God ranks swear words, the abuse of his name is probably the worst offense since it's important enough to make it on his top 10 list of don'ts.

:: *Don't use foul or abusive language* (Ephesians 4:29).

:: *Make sure it's all gone for good: bad temper, irritability, meanness, profanity, dirty talk* (Colossians 3:8 MSG).

:: *Don't yell at one another or curse each other* (Ephesians 4:31 CEV).

:: *Your words show what is in your hearts. Good people bring good things out of their hearts, but evil people bring evil things out of their hearts* (Matthew 12:34–35 CEV).

DEATH

Plenty of people have quit the faith after watching loved ones die. It's common for the folks left behind to wonder why God didn't step into human history and save the person. But the Bible's message is that God did just that. He sent his Son, Jesus, to save us. Death is not the end of the road. The Bible teaches that for believers, death is the doorway into a spiritual dimension that never ends.

:: *Adam sinned, and that sin brought death into the world. Now everyone has sinned, and so everyone must die* (Romans 5:12 CEV). Some Christians speculate that the perfect world God created didn't include death—not until sin changed everything, perhaps a bit like a toxin introduced into creation.

:: *Even when walking through the dark valley of death I will not be afraid, for you are close beside me, guarding, guiding all the way* (Psalm 23:4 TLB). This chapter in the Bible is read to comfort the dying perhaps more than any other words ever written.

:: *Our days may come to seventy years, or eighty, if our strength endures. . .they quickly pass, and we fly away* (Psalm 90:10 TNIV).

:: *Christians who have died will rise from their graves* (1 Thessalonians 4:16).

:: *Our earthly bodies, the ones we have now that can die, must be transformed into heavenly bodies that cannot perish but will live forever* (1 Corinthians 15:53 TLB). Many speculate that our transformed "heavenly bodies" will be like the one Jesus had after his resurrection. He was able to eat, touch, be recognized, disappear, walk through walls, and levitate.

:: *When these bodies of ours are taken down like tents and folded away, they will be replaced by resurrection bodies in heaven* (2 Corinthians 5:1 MSG).

:: *Each person is destined to die once and after that comes judgment* (Hebrews 9:27). Many Christians use this verse to refute the idea of reincarnation.

:: *"He [God] will wipe every tear from their eyes, and there will be no more death or sorrow or crying or pain"* (Revelation 21:4).

:: *They cried all day long and would not eat anything. Everyone was sad because Saul, his son Jonathan, and many of the LORD's people had been killed in the battle* (2 Samuel 1:12 CEV). Philistines overran Saul's army. Mourning is a natural response to the death of someone we love.

DECISION-MAKING

:: *Plans fail without good advice. But they succeed when there are many advisers* (Proverbs 15:22 NIrV).

:: *If you don't have all the wisdom needed for this journey, then all you have to do is as God for it, and God, who is never stingy when it comes to wisdom, will grant all that you need* (James 1:5 THE VOICE).

:: *"Keep on asking. You'll get your answer. Keep on looking. You'll find what you're looking for"* (Matthew 7:7 AUTHOR'S PARAPHRASE). That's Jesus' advice.

TRYING TO AVOID GOD'S SECOND BEST.

Many Christians say it's tough to make decisions when they can't figure out what God wants them to do. When they ask and don't get. When they seek and don't find.

It seems rare these days for God to plainly tell someone what to do—as dramatically as he did in Bible times, with burning bushes, armed angels, and daytime visions. Most of the time, it seems, he lets people make the best choice they can, based on the Spirit-guided wisdom he has already given them. Some might call it common sense.

Whatever choice people make, the Bible teaches that God is flexible enough to make good things come of it. Wherever we go—anywhere from Abilene to Zimbabwe—God goes with us.

Christians want God's best. Many worry that if they don't make the right choice, they'll have to settle for God's second best.

But others ask, if God is with us wherever we go and in whatever we do, how can that be second best?

:: *I praise you, LORD, for being my guide. Even in the darkest night, your teachings fill my mind* (Psalm 16:7 CEV).

:: *Jesus went up on a mountain to pray, and he prayed to God all night. At daybreak he called together all of his disciples and chose twelve of them to be apostles* (Luke 6:12–13). Before Jesus decided which disciples to select from among his many followers, he spent the night in prayer.

:: *One day as they were worshiping God—they were also fasting as they waited for guidance—the Holy Spirit spoke: "Take Barnabas and Saul and commission them for the work I have called them to do"* (Acts 13:2 MSG). The Bible doesn't say how the Spirit communicated. But apparently the group felt assured that Barnabas and Saul (better known today by his Greek name: Paul) needed to begin missionary work. Maybe the men had been discussing it and were seeking God's direction in prayer.

:: *Paul and his friends went through Phrygia and Galatia [in what is now central Turkey], but the Holy Spirit would not let them preach in Asia [western Turkey]* (Acts 16 6 CEV). Somehow—again in a way the Bible doesn't describe—the Holy Spirit communicated to Paul. Perhaps the Spirit spoke as a quiet, inner voice. Or maybe it was more dramatic.

(See also *Prayer*.)

DEMONS

Evil spirits who oppose God The Bible portrays them as real entities, though no match for Jesus. Gospel writers say he exorcized demons from many people.

INHUMAN. "We are not fighting against humans. We are fighting against forces and authorities and against rulers of darkness and powers in the spiritual world" (Ephesians 6:12 CEV).

:: *I am convinced that nothing can ever separate us from God's love. Neither death nor life, neither angels nor demons* (Romans 8:38).

:: *In the later times some people will stop believing the faith. They will follow spirits that lie and teachings of demons* (1 Timothy 4:1 NCV).

:: *"Away with you, you cursed ones, into the eternal fire prepared for the devil and his demons"* (Matthew 25:41). That's Jesus, wrapping up a parable. He's saying that people who don't help the helpless can go to hell. Some Christians take the parable literally. Others say it's one of Jesus' many exaggerations—a technique he used to shock people into rethinking their preconceived notions.

WAS IT REALLY DEMON POSSESSION?

Some demon possessions in the Bible might sound like a physical problem.

"Whenever the demon attacks my son, it throws him to the ground and makes him foam at the mouth and grit his teeth in pain. Then he becomes stiff."

MARK 9:18 CEV

A doc today might diagnose that as epilepsy. Jesus didn't.

He called it a demon. He ordered it to come out of the boy, which made the demon scream. In other exorcisms, demons did more than scream. They had words with Jesus.

One demon, it seems, actually tried to exorcize Jesus away: "I adjure you by God, do not torment me" (Mark 5:7 NRSV). That's ancient magical spell lingo—similar to phrasing that shows up in surviving incantations.

It shows up in an ancient book of spells from the AD 300s—the Paris Magical Papyrus. One incantation even invokes the names of God, Jesus, and several others: "I adjure you by the God of the Hebrews, Jesus, Jaba, Jae, Abraoth. . . ."

Though demon possession seems absurd to many today—and unheard of in most civilized societies— many people of faith who have worked in developing nations insist that demons are alive and well and possessing people.

(See also *Satan.*)

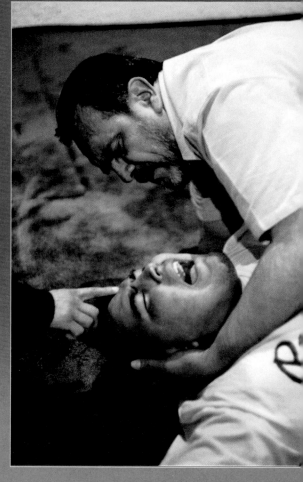

EXORCISM. Ministers perform an exorcism at the Cathedral of the Divine Savior in Mexico City.

JESUS THE EXORCIST

:: *That evening many demon-possessed people were brought to Jesus. He cast out the evil spirits with a simple command* (Matthew 8:16).

:: *When Jesus arrived on the other side of the lake, in the region of the Gadarenes, two men who were possessed by demons met him. . . . The demons begged, "If you cast us out, send us into that herd of pigs." "All right, go!" Jesus commanded them. So the demons came out of the men and entered the pigs, and the whole herd plunged down the steep hillside into the lake and drowned in the water* (Matthew 8:28, 31–32). Luke's version of the story says the demons go by the name Legion (Luke 8:30).

:: *Jesus called his twelve disciples together and*

gave them authority to cast out evil spirits and to heal every kind of disease (Matthew 10:1).

DEPRESSION

It's normal to get depressed from time to time. In some cases the problem is a matter of attitude, so the Bible offers spiritual encouragement—reminding us that God is in control. Other times the problem is a physical one, caused by chemical imbalances that warp our perspective, making our troubles seem worse than they are. Many Christians say God gave us doctors and medications to help with that.

DEPRESSED BIBLE HEROES

:: *"I would rather choke to death. That would be better than living in this body of mine. I hate my life"* (Job 7:15-16 NIrV). A not-so-patient Job gives God a piece of his mind after losing his vast herds to bandits, his health to an oozing skin disease, and his children to a windstorm that blows down a house and crushes them all.

:: *The Spirit of God left Saul and in its place a black mood sent by God settled on him. He was terrified. Saul's advisors said, "This awful tormenting depression from God is making your life miserable. O Master, let us help. Let us look for someone who can play the harp. When the black mood from God moves in, he'll play his music and you'll feel better"* (1 Samuel 16:14-16 MSG). Music therapy for treating depression is nothing new. The help it gave King Saul, however, was only temporary.

:: *Elijah was afraid. So he ran for his life. . . . He came to a small tree. He sat down under it. He prayed that he would die. "Lord, I've had enough"* (1 Kings 19:3-4 NIrV). God's treatment for Elijah's depression: carryout food (an angel delivered it), along with rest and a fresh challenge that offered hope.

:: *I am deeply troubled, and I don't know what to say. But I must not ask my Father to keep me from this time of suffering. In fact, I came into the world to suffer* (John 12:27 CEV). This is Jesus confiding in his disciples, shortly before his crucifixion.

:: *I had battles on the outside and fears on the inside. But God comforts those who are sad. He comforted me when Titus came. . . . He [Titus] told me about your deep sadness and concern for me. That made my joy greater than ever* (2 Corinthians 7:5-7 NIrV). Misery loves company because a shared load of trouble is easier to carry. The apostle Paul is discouraged by problems he faces until a friend arrives with news that others care.

HOPE FOR THE DEPRESSED

:: *My spirit, why are you so sad? Why are you so upset deep down inside me? Put your hope in God* (Psalm 42:11 NIrV).

:: *"Come to me, all of you who are weary and carry heavy burdens, and I will give you rest"* (Matthew 11:28). The words of Jesus.

:: *If your heart is broken, you'll find God right there; if you're kicked in the gut, he'll help you catch your breath* (Psalm 34:18 MSG).

:: *Give all your worries and cares to God, for he cares about you* (1 Peter 5:7).

:: *Darkness and despair will not go on forever . . . . The people who walk in darkness will see a great light* (Isaiah 9:1-2). This prophecy points to the coming of Jesus. "Wonderful Counselor. . .Prince of Peace" (verse 6).

:: *"In this godless world you will continue to experience difficulties. But take heart! I've*

DEPRESSED PROPHET. On the run from Queen Jezebel, who threatened to execute him, the prophet Elijah collapses at day's end, exhausted and praying for God to end his life. Instead, God sends an angel to give him warm bread and water. That's still part of the prescription for folks in crisis: food and rest, along with the time it takes to catch a fresh perspective on the problem.

conquered the world" (John 16:33 MSG). The words of Jesus to his followers.

:: *Though the fig trees are all destroyed. . .though the olive crops all fail, and the fields lie barren; even if the flocks die in the fields and the cattle barns are empty, yet I will rejoice in the LORD; I will be happy in the God of my salvation. The LORD God is my Strength, and he will give me the speed of a deer and bring me safely over the mountains* (Habakkuk 3:17–19 TLB). This is one of the Bible's most powerful statements of faith—offered by a man whose nation is about to get wiped off the map. On the brink of an invasion, the Jewish prophet vows to trust in God no matter what.

Private devotions are times people of faith set aside to read the Bible, think about it, and talk with God. When Christians do that, they're imitating Jesus, who knew the Scriptures well and who prayed often—sometimes "all night" (Luke 6:12).

:: *How can a young person live a clean life? By carefully reading the map of your Word. . . . I've banked your promises in the vault of my heart so I won't sin myself bankrupt. . . . I ponder every morsel of wisdom from you* (Psalm 119:9, 11, 15 MSG).

:: *Everything in the Scriptures is God's Word. All of it is useful for teaching and helping people and for correcting them and showing them how to live. The Scriptures train God's servants to do all kinds of good deeds* (2 Timothy 3:16–17 CEV). At this point in history, "Scripture" means the Jewish Bible, which Christians call the Old Testament. In time Christians add the New Testament to their library of sacred books.

:: *The Scriptures give us hope and encouragement as we wait patiently for God's promises to be fulfilled* (Romans 15:4).

:: *Study to shew thyself approved unto God, a workman that needeth not to be ashamed, rightly dividing the word of truth* (2 Timothy 2:15 KJV). Pardon the Shakespearian English from the 1600s, but the more recent versions take out the word "study." Paul is advising his friend, Pastor Timothy, to understand the Bible well enough to explain it and live it. And that takes study.

:: *The Bereans were eager to hear what Paul and Silas said and studied the Scriptures every day to find out if these things were true* (Acts 17:11 NCV).

:: *By your words I can see where I'm going; they throw a beam of light on my dark path* (Psalm 119:105 MSG).

:: *Listen to my voice in the morning, LORD. Each morning I bring my requests to you and wait expectantly* (Psalm 5:3). This writer was apparently a morning person. Others in the Bible had their devotions midday or in the evening. The prophet Daniel "prayed three times a day" (Daniel 6:10).

:: *You have accepted Christ Jesus as your Lord. Now keep on following him. Plant your roots in Christ and let him be the foundation for your life. Be strong in your faith, just as you were taught.* (Colossians 2:6–7 CEV). To grow in our relationship with Christ, we need to spend time with him.

:: *Nothing you do for the Lord is ever useless* (1 Corinthians 15:58).

:: *Don't envy sinners, but always continue to fear the LORD. You will be rewarded for this; your hope will not be disappointed* (Proverbs 23:17–18).

:: *We can rejoice, too, when we run into problems and trials, for we know that they help us develop endurance. And endurance develops strength of character, and character strengthens our confident hope of salvation. And this hope will not lead to disappointment* (Romans 5:3–5).

(See also *Depression*.)

:: *I am the* Lord, *and I consider all people the same, whether they are Israelites or foreigners* (Numbers 15:15 cev).

:: *Everything we know about God's Word is summed up in a single sentence: Love others as you love yourself. That's an act of true freedom* (Galatians 5:14 msg).

:: *How do you work up the nerve to call yourself a Christian if you treat one kind of person better than another? Take rich people, for example. Suppose a well-dressed man pays a visit to your church. Then along comes a homeless guy in shabby, stinky clothes. If you give Mr. Richie Rich a front-row seat and tell Mr. Stinky Cheese to sit way in the back, isn't discrimination like that downright mean and self-serving—take an offering why don't you?* (James 2:1–4 Author Paraphrase).

:: *In Christ's family there can be no division into Jew and non-Jew, slave and free, male and female. . . . You are all equal* (Galatians 3:28 msg).

:: *"Do not cheat or hurt a foreigner. . . . Do not cheat a widow or an orphan. If you do. . .I will be very angry"* (Exodus 22:21–24 ncv). Throughout the Bible, God is especially concerned about one group of people: the powerless. In Bible times, these included immigrants, orphans, and widows.

(See also *Prejudice*.)

Bible verses about divorce aren't quite what you'd call consistent. They veer off in more directions than arguments in a custody fight. But there's a reason for it. Each passage seems to address a different situation. Jesus, in one sermon, forbids divorce—without making any exceptions (Luke 16:18). But other times he allows divorce in cases involving sexual immorality (Matthew 19:9). Paul goes further. He allows divorce when a non-Christian spouse abandons a Christian spouse. The Bible is clear on this much about divorce: It's not kosher. It's caused by sin. And God hates it because it hurts people. Yet, even after divorce, there is forgiveness and healing.

GOD'S PLAN DIDN'T INCLUDE DIVORCE

:: *"I hate divorce," says the* God *of Israel. . . . "I hate the violent dismembering of the 'one flesh' of marriage." So watch yourselves. Don't let your guard down. Don't cheat* (Malachi 2:16 msg).

:: *God has joined the two together, so no one should separate them* (Matthew 19:6 ncv).

WHEN IT'S ALLOWED

:: *If a man marries a woman and then it happens that he no longer likes her because he has found something wrong with her, he may give her divorce papers, put them in her hand, and send her off* (Deuteronomy 24:1 msg). Jews in Jesus' day argued over what grounds for divorce. Some said the "something wrong with her" that Moses referred to was limited to adultery. Many Jews, however, seemed more modern in their thinking. "Something wrong" could include the little lady's cooking, her attitude, or even her aging chassis. Time for a trade-in.

IRRECONCILABLE DIFFERENCES. The Bible doesn't offer a list of acceptable reasons for getting a divorce. In theory, Jesus allowed for divorce in cases of adultery. But in practice, when asked to pass judgment on a woman caught in adultery, he forgave her and said, "Go now and leave your life of sin" (John 8:11 NIrV).

:: *"Moses wrote this command [allowing divorce] only as a concession to your hardhearted ways. In the original creation, God made male and female to be together"* (Mark 10:5–6 MSG). Jesus argues with Jewish scholars that even though the laws God gave through Moses permitted divorce (Deuteronomy 24:1), God intended marriage to last a lifetime.

:: *You have broken God's Law by marrying foreign women. . . . Divorce your foreign wives* (Ezra 10:10–11 CEV). The Jews had only recently regained their homeland. They had lost it to invaders—God's punishment for marrying non-Jews and worshipping the gods of their spouses. Afraid of losing their homeland again for the same sin, they agree to divorce their foreign wives, at the urging of a priest named Ezra. Some Bible experts say this was harsh and unnecessary—not a principle worth following then or now. Intermarriage wasn't the problem. Idolatry was.

:: "Whoever divorces his wife and marries someone else commits adultery—unless his wife has been unfaithful" (Matthew 19:9). Jesus allows "unfaithfulness" as a justifiable reason for divorcing. But scholars debate what "unfaithfulness" means. There are three popular options: adultery, premarital sex, and illegal marriages such as a man marrying his sister or his aunt. But even in cases of adultery, Jesus may well have urged forgiveness—given his refusal to condemn a woman caught in an affair (John 8:11).

:: If the husband or wife who isn't a believer insists on leaving, let them go. In such cases the Christian husband or wife is no longer bound to the other (1 Corinthians 7:15). Paul is dealing with a problem Jesus didn't address: believers married to non-believers. Offering his opinion, and admitting, "I do not have a direct command from the Lord" (verse 12), Paul advises Christians to let the non-Christians go if they want out of the marriage. Paul considers the agreement between God and his people more important than any marriage agreement. Christians aren't to surrender their faith to save their marriage.

WHEN IT'S NOT ALLOWED

:: If a Christian man has a wife who is not a believer and she is willing to continue living with him, he must not leave her. And if a Christian woman has a husband who is not a believer and he is willing to continue living with her, she must not leave him (1 Corinthians 7:12–13). Paul explains that by staying, the Christian might be able to convert the spouse and raise Christian children.

(See also *Marriage*.)

ABUSE: GROUNDS FOR DIVORCE?

Jesus said there's only one reason to get a divorce: adultery.

As a result, some churches refuse to ordain ministers divorced for any reason other than adultery.

Yet many scholars argue that when Jesus taught about divorce, he wasn't trying to produce a legal document outlining the only grounds for dissolving a marriage. Paul figured that out, they argue, when he added abandonment as another legit reason to end a marriage. When Jesus talked about divorce, he was working a debate—lobbying against quick-and-easy divorces advocated by a group of Jewish scholars. So Jesus served them up the counterpoint.

The compassionate Jesus, most scholars seem to agree, wouldn't expect folks to endure an abusive, loveless marriage for the rest of their lives.

Paul put it this way when he added abandonment to the biblical grounds for divorce: "God wants us to live in peace" (1 Corinthians 7:15 NIrV).

There's nothing peaceful about a torturous marriage.

DOUBT

:: Be helpful to all who may have doubts [about the faith] (Jude 1:22 CEV). Trust GOD from the bottom of your heart; don't try to figure out everything on your own. Listen for GOD's voice in everything you do, everywhere you go; he's the one who will keep you on track. Don't assume that you know it all (Proverbs 3:5–7 MSG).

:: People who doubt are like waves of the sea. The wind blows and tosses them around. A man like that shouldn't expect to receive anything from the Lord. He can't make up his mind. He can never decide what to do (James 1:6–8 NIrV).

:: *"Is anything too hard for the LORD?"* (Genesis 18:14). This is God's response to 90-year-old Sarah, whose doubt seems to make perfect sense. When she hears the news that she'll give birth to a son within the year, she laughs out loud. *No way,* she's thinking.

:: *"Unless I see the nail holes in his hands, put my finger in the nail holes, and stick my hand in his side, I won't believe it"* (John 20:25 MSG). That's Doubting Thomas telling the other disciples he won't believe Jesus has come back from the dead until he sees it for himself. When Jesus shows up a week later, Thomas says he now believes. Jesus replies, "Blessed are those who believe without seeing me" (John 20:29). Zinger.

(See also *Faith.*)

DRUGS AND ALCOHOL

Actually, the title's redundant. Alcohol is a drug, absorbed into the bloodstream and carried to organs throughout the body. But not everyone makes that connection.

TROUBLE IT CAUSES

:: *Wine makes you mean, beer makes you quarrelsome—a staggering drunk is not much fun* (Proverbs 20:1 MSG).

:: *Who are the people who are always crying the blues? Who do you know who reeks of self-pity? . . . Whose eyes are bleary and bloodshot? It's those who spend the night with a bottle, for whom drinking is serious business* (Proverbs 23:29–30 MSG).

:: *Don't judge wine by its label, or its bouquet,*

or its full-bodied flavor. Judge it rather by the hangover it leaves you with—the splitting headache, the queasy stomach. Do you really prefer seeing double, with your speech all slurred, reeling and seasick, drunk as a sailor? (Proverbs 23:31–34 MSG).

:: *Don't drink wine excessively. The drunken path is a reckless path. It leads nowhere* (Ephesians 5:18 THE VOICE).

:: *Kings and leaders should not get drunk. . . . Drinking makes you forget your responsibilities* (Proverbs 31:4–5 CEV).

DON'T PARTY TOO HEARTY

:: *You have spent enough time in the past doing what ungodly people choose to do. You lived a wild life. . . . You got drunk. You went to wild parties. . . . The Lord hates that* (1 Peter 4:3 NIrV).

:: *We should not have wild parties or get drunk* (Romans 13:13 NCV).

:: *It is better not to. . .drink wine or do anything else if it might cause another believer to stumble. You may believe there's nothing wrong with what you are doing, but keep it between yourself and God* (Romans 14:21–22). This doesn't mean Christians should abstain from alcohol just because others feel it's wrong. But a sensitive Christian wouldn't knowingly drink in front of a person who feels uncomfortable with drinking—and certainly not in front of a recovering alcoholic.

BIBLE DRINKERS AND NONDRINKERS

:: *Noah planted a vineyard and made some wine. He got drunk and passed out, naked in his tent* (Genesis 9:20–21 AUTHOR'S PARAPHRASE). Not one of Noah's shining moments.

:: *Go ahead and drink a little wine. . .it's good for your digestion, good medicine for what ails you*

(1 Timothy 5:23 MSG). Paul's advice to Pastor Timothy, who was having stomach problems.

:: *If any of you, man or woman, wants to make a special Nazirite vow, consecrating yourself totally to GOD, you must not drink any wine or beer, no intoxicating drink of any kind"* (Numbers 6:2–3 MSG). Strongman Samson and the prophet Samuel were both lifetime Nazirites.

Others, such as the apostle Paul, took the Nazirite vow for a short time—much like many Christians today who give up something for Lent as a way of remembering the sacrifices Jesus made for us.

:: *They gave Jesus some wine mixed with a drug to ease the pain. But when Jesus tasted what it was, he refused to drink it* (Matthew 27:34 CEV). Jesus apparently wanted a clear head while

SWALLOW THE ADVERTISING. Beer is a family drink. Healthy, friendly, downright patriotic. So brags a beer ad in 1879. Wise men who wrote the sayings in Proverbs, however, aren't so keen on the brew. Other Bible writers add their warnings about alcohol, too, though they stop short of declaring Prohibition.

WHY SOME CHRISTIANS DRINK, AND SOME DON'T.

It's tough to argue from the Bible that Christians shouldn't drink alcohol, many insist.

After all, Jesus' first miracle on record was to whip up enough wine to get a thousand people too drunk to drive a donkey cart—at least by today's measure of blood alcohol. He turned no less than 120 gallons (454 liters) of water into wine at a wedding celebration in the village of Cana (John 2).

Some argue it was grape juice. They should visit Israel in August and September, when grapes are harvested. It's hot. Grapes start to ferment right away.

JESUS DRANK

:: "The Son of Man appeared—He didn't fast, as John [the Baptist] had, but ate with sinners and drank wine. And the people said, 'This man is a glutton! He's a drunk!'" (Matthew 11:19 The Voice).

:: "He [Jesus] took a cup of wine and gave thanks to God for it" (Mark 14:23). This was at the Last Supper, in the springtime—six months or more after the grape harvest.

PAUL TOLD TIMOTHY TO DRINK

:: "Don't drink only water. You ought to drink a little wine for the sake of your stomach because you are sick so often" (1 Timothy 5:23).

KIDS DRANK WINE

Wine was the preferred drink during Roman times, served at nearly every meal. Even children drank at least a watered-down version. Wine, many speculate, was safer than some of the water. Alcohol killed bacteria and parasites in the water.

WHY SOME CHRISTIANS TODAY DON'T DRINK

In some local churches, all it takes is a strong-willed preacher telling members of his flock that if they drink, they'll burn in hell. Some would call that brainwashing by intimidation.

But many Christians have what they consider solid, well-reasoned arguments against drinking.

Family addicts. Some Christians avoid alcohol because they have alcoholics in their family, they've seen the damage it caused, and they fear they might have a genetic predisposition toward alcoholism.

Health risks. There are health risks to drinking wine, perhaps outweighing the benefits, some researchers say.

Benefits of a glass of red wine every day or two: lowers bad cholesterol, prevents heart damage, and reduces risk of blood clots and strokes.

Risks: high blood pressure, diseased livers, and injury caused by drowsiness.

The Mayo Clinic reports that grape juice produces the same effects as wine, without the risks. For those who choose wine, Mayo recommends no more than one glass a day for women and two for men.

Drunk drivers. Most people who drink and drive drunk genuinely believe they're driving safely. Christians don't want to be counted among those believers.

HERE'S TO LOWER CHOLESTEROL. Red wine lowers bad cholesterol, medical studies report. So does grape juice—without the buzz.

he died on the cross. So he refused a pain-killer sometimes given to victims of this lingering method of execution.

(See also *Addictions*.)

EDUCATION

Even in an ancient culture where few people could read or write, the Bible was already promoting the value of a good education.

:: *There is gold. There are plenty of rubies. But lips that speak knowledge are a priceless jewel* (Proverbs 20:15 NIrV).

:: *"My people are destroyed from lack of knowledge"* (Hosea 4:6 TNIV).

:: *The teaching of wise people is like a fountain that gives life. It turns those who listen to it away from the jaws of death* (Proverbs 13:14 NIrV).

:: *The commandments I give you today must be in your hearts. Make sure your children learn them. Talk about them when you are at home. Talk about them when you walk along the road. Speak about them when you go to bed. And speak about them when you get up* (Deuteronomy 6:6–7 NIrV).

:: *He [Apollos] refuted the Jews with powerful arguments in public debate. Using the Scriptures, he explained to them that Jesus was the Messiah* (Acts 18:28).

:: *When Jesus saw the crowds, he went up on a hill and sat down. His followers came to him, and he began to teach them* (Matthew 5:1–2 NCV). What follows is the most famous lecture in history: the Sermon on the Mount. Teaching was a big part of Jesus' ministry.

ENVIRONMENT

The Bible doesn't give us all the answers to the question, "Why are we here?" But it gives us one, many scholars agree. We're caretakers of God's creation.

:: *Then God said, "Let us make man in our likeness. Let them rule over the fish in the waters and the birds of the air. Let them rule over the livestock and over the whole earth. Let them rule over all of the creatures that move along the ground"* (Genesis 1:26 NIrV).

:: *The LORD God put the man in the Garden of Eden to take care of it and to look after it* (Genesis 2:15 CEV).

CARBON FOOTPRINT. Oceangoing trash washes ashore on the wind-blown (eastern) side of Niihau, the smallest of Hawaii's inhabited islands. The Bible's story of creation says God entrusted humans with looking after his world.

:: *A heart at peace gives life to the body, but envy rots the bones* (Proverbs 14:30 —NIV).

:: *Don't. . .wish you could succeed like the wicked. In no time they'll shrivel like grass clippings and wilt like cut flowers in the sun* (Psalm 37:1–2 MSG).

:: *I observed that most people are motivated to success because they envy their neighbors. But this, too, is meaningless—like chasing the wind* (Ecclesiastes 4:4).

(See also *Jealousy*.)

ETERNAL LIFE

Our bodies aren't built to last forever, but the Bible says our spirits inside those bodies certainly are. The Bible promises that those who die with faith in Jesus will inherit resurrection bodies— perhaps like the body of Jesus after his resurrection. He could walk, talk, and eat; touch and get touched. But he could also suddenly appear and disappear, and even levitate.

RESURRECTION BODIES

:: *Our earthly bodies are planted in the ground when we die, but they will be raised to live forever* (1 Corinthians 15:42).

:: *Jesus himself was suddenly standing there among them [the disciples after Jesus' resurrection]. "Peace be with you," he said. But the whole group was startled and frightened, thinking they were seeing a ghost! "Why are you frightened?" he asked. . . . "It's really me. Touch me and make sure that I am not a ghost . . . ." Then he asked them, "Do you have anything here to eat?" They gave him a piece of broiled fish, and he ate it* (Luke 24:36–39, 41–43).

GRAVESIDE SERVICE. A young couple mourns the death of a loved one. The apostle Paul said he didn't want Christians to grieve "like people who have no hope. . . . Christians who have died will rise from their graves" (1 Thessalonians 4:13, 16).

WHO WILL LIVE FOREVER?

:: *Everyone who hears my message and has faith in the one who sent me has eternal life and will never be condemned. They have already gone from death to life* (John 5:24 CEV). For believers, eternal life has already started.

:: *"God loved the world so much that he gave his one and only Son, so that everyone who believes in him will not perish but have eternal life"* (John 3:16).

:: *Work hard for sin your whole life and your pension is death. But God's gift is real life, eternal life, delivered by Jesus, our Master* (Romans 6:23 MSG).

:: *"Many of those whose bodies lie dead and buried will rise up, some to everlasting life and some to shame and everlasting disgrace"* (Daniel 12:2). Written just a few hundred years before Jesus, this is one of the few references in the Old Testament to a resurrection and eternal life. Most people in earlier days apparently didn't realize that their souls were built to last forever. But the Bible says the archangel Gabriel revealed this insight to the prophet Daniel.

ETERNAL SECURITY

Some Christians teach that God picks who will be saved—and that nothing can ever cause any of those people to lose their salvation. Many Baptists, Presbyterians, and Lutherans set up camp around this teaching. Others teach that a Christian's security depends on the kind of life that person lives—that salvation is a gift from God that he or she can reject. Methodists, Nazarenes, and Wesleyans pitch their tents around this interpretation of the Bible.

ONCE SAVED, ALWAYS SAVED

:: *"My sheep listen to my voice; I know them, and they follow me. I give them eternal life, and they will never perish. No one can snatch them away from me"* (Jesus, in John 10:27–28).

:: *He has given us new birth. . . . It is a gift that can never be destroyed. It can never spoil or even fade away. It is kept in heaven for you. Through faith you are kept safe by God's power. Your salvation is going to be completed* (1 Peter 1:4–5 NIrV).

SALVATION IS A LOCK. "Eternal life is foreordained for some, eternal damnation for others," wrote John Calvin (1509–1564), French scholar and theological father of several church groups, including many Baptists. Others say God lets people make their own choice because "he wants everyone to turn from sin and no one to be lost" (2 Peter 3:9 CEV).

:: *These people left our churches, but they never really belonged with us; otherwise they would have stayed with us. When they left, it proved that they did not belong with us* (1 John 2:19). As the argument goes, people who "backslide" into sin were never really saved in the first place. They were fake Christians.

COUNTERPOINT: HOW TO LOSE THE GIFT OF SALVATION

:: *You must remain faithful to what you have been taught from the beginning. If you do, you will remain in fellowship with the Son and with the Father. And in this fellowship we enjoy the eternal life he promised us* (1 John 2:24–25).

:: *If someone among you wanders away from the truth and is brought back, you can be sure that whoever brings the sinner back will save that person from death* (James 5:19–20).

:: *It is impossible to bring back to repentance those who were once enlightened—those who have experienced the good things of heaven and shared in the Holy Spirit, who have tasted the goodness of the word of God and the power of the age to come—and who then turn away from God* (Hebrews 6:4–6). Some say the writer was exaggerating to make a point. The setting, scholars say, is that many persecuted Jewish Christians were leaving the church and returning to the safer Jewish religion; Romans didn't persecute Jews. The writer wanted potential deserters to know that if they left the church but later decided to come back, they shouldn't expect to see a welcome mat.

(See also *Backsliding, Predestination.*)

EUTHANASIA (MERCY KILLING)

Bible writers have nothing against "youth in Asia," as one person I know misunderstood the similar-sounding term *euthanasia*. Nor does the Bible talk about mercy killing—ending the suffering of a dying person in a way similar to what veterinarians do for animals. Some Christians oppose it, arguing that God is the creator and sustainer of life, and that we're not supposed to murder. Others argue that in some cases, when a person is dying in torment, mercy killing is the most compassionate response.

FOR IT, AS A COMPASSIONATE OPTION

:: *Saul groaned to his armor bearer, "Take your sword and kill me before these pagan Philistines come to run me through and taunt and torture me." But his armor bearer was afraid and would not do it. So Saul took his own sword and fell on it* (1 Samuel 31:4).

:: *Don't be afraid of people. They can kill you, but they cannot harm your soul* (Matthew 10:28 CEV).

:: *Is anyone crying for help? GOD is listening, ready to rescue you* (Psalm 34:17 MSG). Just as physicians can be the hands of God healing a sick person, some Christians say, physicians can be the hands of God ending the torture of a terminal patient, if the law permits it.

:: *"I [Jesus] am the resurrection and the life. Anyone who believes in me will live, even if he dies"* (John 11:25 NIrV).

AGAINST IT, AS MURDER

:: *Don't you realize that your body is the temple of the Holy Spirit, who lives in you and was given to you by God? You do not belong to yourself, for God bought you with a high price. So you must honor God with your body* (1 Corinthians 6:19–20).

:: "You must not murder" (Exodus 20:13).

:: "If anyone takes a human life, that person's life will also be taken by human hands. For God made human beings in his own image" (Genesis 9:6).

:: My life is in your [God's] hands (Psalm 31:15 CEV).

EVOLUTION

The Bible says God created everything that exists. It doesn't say how. It answers only the question of who, many scholars insist. Genesis says God created the universe in six days. Some Christians take that literally, as six 24-hour days. Others take it figuratively, arguing that it wasn't until day four that God created the sun and moon—heavenly bodies essential for measuring a 24-hour day. For many Christians, *day* simply means some span of time, which could stretch for eons.

VERSES USED TO SUPPORT IT

:: A day is like a thousand years to the Lord, and a thousand years is like a day (2 Peter 3:8).

:: Then God said, "Let the land sprout with vegetation—every sort of seed-bearing plant." . . . And that is what happened. The land produced vegetation (Genesis 1:11–12). It was the land that produced vegetation, not God—at least not directly, as some Christians read the

story. It's also the ocean that produced sea life and the land that produced animals (Genesis 1:20, 24). God may have been conducting this concert of creation, some Christians would argue, but that doesn't mean he had to fiddle every note himself.

:: *Test everything that is said* (1 Thessalonians 5:21). A literal read of the seven-day creation story fails the scientific test, many Christians insist. So does the creationist theory that the earth is just a few thousand years old. Many Christians, especially those in the scientific fields of geology and astronomy, say there's too much solid evidence for an eons-old universe. They say they see God behind creation, but not as taught by the seven-day creationists.

VERSES USED TO OPPOSE IT

:: *In the last days scoffers will come, mocking the truth. . . . They deliberately forget that God made the heavens by the word of his command, and he brought the earth out from the water and surrounded it with water* (2 Peter 3:3, 5).

:: *Make sure no one captures you. They will try to capture you by using false reasoning that has no meaning. Their ideas depend on human teachings. They also depend on the basic things the people of this world believe. They don't depend on Christ* (Colossians 2:8 NIrv). The

SHAKING THE FAMILY TREE. Many Christians say they have a huge problem with the theory of evolution linking them to chimps. Yet most scientists studying the origins of humanity say if we shake our ancestral tree long enough, monkeys will fall out. Christians who embrace that scientific theory say they believe God created life, perhaps through evolution. ◄

theory of evolution is just that—a theory. But it's one that's widely accepted among scientists, almost universally accepted even among Christian scientists. Many Christians are repulsed by the idea that they evolved from primordial slime—as opposed to coming from the "dust of the ground" (Genesis 2:7). Others say they see no serious problem with evolution, arguing that at some point in human development God "breathed into his nostrils the breath of life; and man became a living soul" (Genesis 2:7 KJV).

:: *In the beginning God created the heavens and the earth* (Genesis 1:1).

:: *Everything was created by him [Jesus] and for him. Before anything was created, he was already there. He holds everything together* (Colossians 1:16–17 NIrv).

:: *The LORD God formed the man from the dust of the ground* (Genesis 2:7).

:: *God created human beings in his own image* (Genesis 1:27). And God wasn't monkeying around.

EXPLOITATION

:: *And a final word to you arrogant rich. . . . Your greedy luxuries are a cancer in your gut. . . . You thought you were piling up wealth. What you've piled up is judgment. All the workers you've exploited and cheated cry out for judgment* (James 5:1, 3–4 MSG).

:: *How dare you crush my people, grinding the faces of the poor into the dust?* (Isaiah 3:15).

:: *"Don't take advantage of widows, orphans, visitors, and the poor"* (Zechariah 7:10 MSG). "Visitors" are immigrants and other foreign newcomers to the land.

:: *"Do not cheat or hurt a foreigner. . . Do not cheat a widow or an orphan. If you do, and they cry out to me for help, I certainly will hear their cry. And I will be very angry"* (Exodus 22:21–24 NCV).

:: *Don't rob the poor just because you can, or exploit the needy in court* (Proverbs 22:22).

(See also *Abuse.*)

FAITH

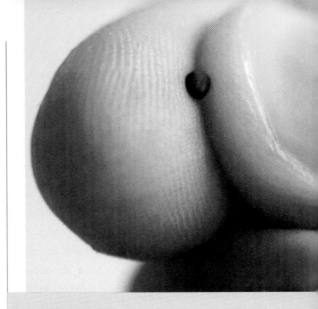

Faith is another word for trust. In the Bible it usually refers to trusting God. Trust in God, as the Bible teaches it, grows a bit like the trust we develop with our closest friends. Over time, our friends prove they are worthy of our trust. God does the same, Bible writers assure us.

A pinch of faith. Faith the size of one tiny mustard seed is all Jesus said people need. If they have it, great things can happen. Black mustard (*Brassica nigra*) grows in northern Israel, where Jesus ministered. Its seed reaches only about two millimeters across, about a sixteenth of an inch.

THE BIBLE'S DEFINITION

:: *Faith is the confidence that what we hope for will actually happen; it gives us assurance about things we cannot see* (Hebrews 11:1). The Bible's classic definition of faith.

PUTTING FAITH TO WORK

:: *It isn't enough just to have faith. . . . Faith that doesn't show itself by good works is no faith at all—it is dead and useless* (James 2:17 TLB). People who have faith in God show it by their actions—by doing what God says, such as helping the poor and living honorable lives.

:: *"If you had faith even as small as a mustard seed, you could say to this mountain, 'Move from here to there,' and it would move. Nothing would be impossible"* (Matthew 17:20). Bible experts say Jesus is probably using exaggeration to stress how important it is to have faith in God's power. He's not talk-

ing about mind over matter, arguing that we can get anything we want if we supercharge our faith. If that were true, we'd be the ones moving the mountains. But the Bible says it's God who does the work. We simply make the request—with the confidence that God has the power to do what we ask. Yet we also ask for his will, not ours. Jesus did the same thing on the night of his arrest, asking for both: "My Father! If it is possible, let this cup of suffering be taken away from me. Yet I want your will to be done, not mine" (Matthew 26:39).

:: *"I do believe! Help me to believe more!"* (Mark 9:24 NCV). That's a father's plea to Jesus. The man had asked Jesus to heal his son, "If you can." Jesus said there's no "if," and that all things are possible for those who believe.

FAITH MAKES MIRACLES HAPPEN.

Jesus said the greatest faith he ever saw in all of Israel was from a foreigner—a Roman soldier.

The soldier, a centurion, asked Jesus to heal his young servant. When Jesus agreed to go to the soldier's house, the man replied, "Just say the word from where you are, and my servant will be healed" (Matthew 8:8). Jesus healed the servant right then—long-distance.

Faith played a key role in many of the miracles Jesus performed. One woman worked her way through a crowd and touched Jesus' robe, hoping the touch would heal her from excessive menstrual bleeding she had suffered for a dozen years. Jesus turned to her and said, "Your faith has made you well" (Matthew 9:22).

Sometimes, lack of faith limited what Jesus chose to do. When he went back to his hometown of Nazareth, most people saw only the grown-up son of a carpenter. They couldn't accept him as the Messiah. "So he did only a few miracles there because of their unbelief" (Matthew 13:58).

FAITH LEADS TO SALVATION

:: *Without faith no one can please God. Anyone who comes to God must believe that he is real and that he rewards those who truly want to find him* (Hebrews 11:6 NCV).

:: *God's grace has saved you because of your faith in Christ. Your salvation doesn't come from anything you do. It is God's gift* (Ephesians 2:8 NIrV). We don't earn our way into heaven by doing good deeds for others. Salvation is God's gift for trusting in him. Abraham, father of the Jews, didn't do anything to earn God's favor. There weren't even any 10 Commandments to obey at that point, several centuries before Moses. Abraham simply trusted God. And because he did, "the LORD counted him as righteous because of his faith" (Genesis 15:6).

:: *The people of Israel, who tried so hard to get right with God. . .never succeeded. Why not? Because they were trying to get right with God by keeping the law instead of by trusting in him* (Romans 9:31–32).

:: *Every child of God can defeat the world, and our faith is what gives us this victory. No one can defeat the world without having faith in Jesus as the Son of God* (1 John 5:4–5 CEV).

FAMILY

The Bible says surprisingly little about how to raise a family. In fact most families that the Bible describes in detail are ones we'd file under "dysfunctional." Some "criminal." They had problems ranging from petty rivalries to incest, rape, and murder.

HONOR, OBEY YOUR PARENTS

:: *Respect your father and your mother* (Exodus 20:12 CEV). It's one of the 10 Commandments—Israel's 10 most bedrock rules, on which all its other laws are built.

:: *Children, always obey your parents, for this pleases the Lord* (Colossians 3:20). "Always" presumes the parents aren't telling their child to do something wrong.

:: *Jesus went with them to Nazareth and was obedient to them* (Luke 2:51 NCV). This is a note about 12-year-old Jesus and his parents, returning to their hometown after celebrating a religious holiday in Jerusalem.

EARN THE RESPECT OF YOUR CHILDREN

:: *Parents, don't be hard on your children. If you are, they might give up* (Colossians 3:21 CEV). When you realize you can't please someone no matter how hard you try, you stop trying.

:: *Church officials must be in control of their own families, and they must see that their children are obedient and always respectful. If they don't know how to control their own families, how can they look after God's people?* (1 Timothy

ROOM WITH A VIEW. After his siesta, King David takes a stroll on the palace roof, which served a bit like balconies do today. There, he sees Bathsheba, the wife of one of his soldiers. She's taking a bath, perhaps in her walled courtyard. David likes what he sees. And it's about to complicate his family life.

DAVID: NOT A MODEL FAMILY MAN.

King David may have been a wonderful king—Jewish history certainly paints that picture of him. But he was one rotten husband. And a lousy dad. At least as the Bible tells it.

ROTTEN HUSBAND

David already had at least seven wives when he decided to commit adultery with Bathsheba.

He got her pregnant.

To cover it up he arranged for her husband, a soldier, to get killed in a battle. David married Bathsheba.

LOUSY DAD

Son number one—Amnon, the crown prince who expected to inherit David's throne—raped his own half-sister. She was Tamar, full sister of Absalom.

David got angry. But he did nothing to punish Amnon.

If Absalom was nothing else, he was a vengeful brother. He had Amnon murdered. Then he fled the country.

David missed both of his sons. After three years he invited Absalom to come home. But he refused to see him for two more years. By then, Absalom hated his dad so much that he cooked up a coup. Father and son went to war against each other. Father won. Son died.

Sadly, David's story offers other examples of what not to do as a husband and a father.

But he did have one redeeming quality. It's one that would come in handy for someone in any family, whether criminally dysfunctional or not. Confronted with his sin, David was quick to repent. When the prophet Nathan accused him of stealing another man's wife, David said, "I have sinned against the LORD" (2 Samuel 12:13).

3:4–5 CEV). Spoken like a single guy who knows squat about kids, some argue. Unmarried Paul wrote this advice to Pastor Timothy, without adding qualifiers that many parents would like to see. Most parents agree that they shouldn't let their young children walk all over them, and over others. But there's a limit to how much control parents can exert over their children—especially during the teen and young adult years. Parents can't always be held responsible for the dumb decisions their kids make. After all, we adults don't hold our spiritual Father responsible for the dumb decisions we make. Yet in Bible times, families were more stay-at-home than families today are—and more connected because of it. So the children were more a reflection of their parents than kids are today.

DON'T CAUSE TROUBLE FOR YOUR FAMILY

:: *Those who bring trouble on their families inherit the wind* (Proverbs 11:29). As a general rule, if we make life miserable for our family, we shouldn't expect anything from them when the fertilizer hits the fan. Except perhaps a little extra distance.

TAKE CARE OF EACH OTHER

:: *If you have needy family members but don't lift a finger to help them, don't bother calling yourself a Christian. Atheists would have more compassion than you have* (1 Timothy 5:8 AUTHOR'S PARAPHRASE). In Bible times, there was no Social Security, Medicare, or private insurance policies covering assisted living for the elderly. Families looked out for each other.

(See also *Parents*.)

In the Bible, people sometimes went without food for spiritual reasons—often to express sorrow for sin. Jesus fasted "forty days" (Matthew 4:2; perhaps meaning "many days") before launching his ministry. Jewish law required only one day of fasting each year: the day of nationwide repentance known in the Bible as the Day of Atonement. Today Jews call it *Yom Kippur* (yome [rhymes with *home*] keep POOR). Pharisees fasted twice a week (Luke 18:12). But for some Jews, this was a ritual for little more than showing off how religious they were.

FAMOUS FASTERS OF THE BIBLE

:: *Moses remained there on the mountain with the LORD forty days and forty nights. In all that time he ate no bread and drank no water* (Exodus 34:28).

:: *Jesus was taken into the wild by the Spirit for the Test. The Devil was ready to give it. Jesus prepared for the Test by fasting forty days and forty nights* (Matthew 4:1–2 MSG).

:: *He [Paul] remained there [in Damascus] blind for three days and did not eat or drink* (Acts 9:9). This was after his vision of Jesus, which led to his conversion.

NON-FASTERS

:: *John's disciples came. They said to Jesus, "We and the Pharisees go without eating. Why don't your disciples go without eating?" Jesus answered, "How can the guests of the groom be sad while he is with them? The time will come when the groom will be taken away from them. Then they will fast"* (Matthew 9:14–15 NIrV).

HOW AND WHY TO FAST

:: *"When you fast, don't make it obvious, as the hypocrites do, for they try to look miserable and disheveled so people will admire them for their fasting. I tell you the truth, that is the only reward they will ever get"* (Matthew 6:16).

:: *Paul and Barnabas handpicked leaders in each church. After praying—their prayers intensified by fasting—they presented these new leaders to the Master to whom they had entrusted their lives* (Acts 14:23 MSG).

:: *All the Israelites went up to Bethel and wept in the presence of the LORD and fasted until evening* (Judges 20:26). They were expressing sorrow for men lost in a battle.

:: *They buried the bones under a small tree in Jabesh, and for seven days, they went without eating to show their sorrow* (1 Samuel 31:13 CEV). The Jews of the village of Jabesh, whom Saul had once rescued, bury Saul and his sons after they died in battle against the Philistines.

FEAR

:: *When I am afraid, I will put my trust in you [God]. . . . So why should I be afraid? What can mere mortals do to me?* (Psalm 56:3–4).

:: *Don't be afraid of people. They can kill you, but they cannot harm your soul* (Matthew 10:28 CEV).

:: *God's Spirit doesn't make cowards out of us. The Spirit gives us power, love, and self-control* (2 Timothy 1:7 CEV).

:: *There is no room in love for fear. Well-formed love banishes fear. Since fear is crippling, a fearful life—fear of death, fear of judgment—is one not yet fully formed in love* (1 John 4:18 MSG).

:: *"Don't be afraid, because the LORD your God will be with you everywhere you go"* (Joshua 1:9 NCV).

:: *God is our protection and our strength. He always helps in times of trouble. So we will not be afraid even if the earth shakes, or the mountains fall into the sea.* (Psalm 46:1–2 NCV).

:: *Being afraid of people can get you into trouble, but if you trust the LORD, you will be safe* (Proverbs 29:25 NCV).

FORGIVENESS

Forgiveness works two ways in the Bible. God forgives us, but we're supposed to forgive each other, too.

FORGIVENESS FROM GOD

:: *No matter how deep the stain of your sins, I can take it out and make you as clean as freshly fallen snow. Even if you are stained as red as crimson, I can make you white as wool!* (Isaiah 1:18 TLB).

:: *If we confess our sins to God, he can always be trusted to forgive us and take our sins away* (1 John 1:9 CEV).

:: *He has taken our sins away from us as far as the east is from west* (Psalm 103:12 NCV).

:: *"Our Father in heaven. . . . Forgive us our sins, as we have forgiven those who sin against us"* (Matthew 6:9, 12). From the Lord's Prayer, which Jesus taught the crowds in the famous Sermon on the Mount.

FORGIVING EACH OTHER

:: *"If you forgive those who sin against you, your heavenly Father will forgive you. But if you refuse to forgive others, your Father will not forgive your sins"* (Matthew 6:14–15). It's unthinkable, Jesus says, that his followers would have the nerve to ask God for forgiveness but would not forgive people who sinned against them. That's hypocrisy. Certainly, Jesus understands that some sins are harder to forgive than others. But forgiving is the goal. It's self-destructive to hang on to bitter feelings.

:: *Peter came to Jesus. He asked, "Lord, how many times should I forgive my brother when he sins against me? Up to seven times?" Jesus answered, "I tell you, not seven times, but 77 times"* (Matthew 18:21–22 NIrV). This is a metaphor, scholars say. Jesus' point: Our supply of forgiveness toward others should be as unlimited as God's supply of forgiveness toward us. We keep forgiving, even after sin 77.

:: *Make allowance for each other's faults, and forgive anyone who offends you. Remember, the Lord forgave you, so you must forgive others* (Colossians 3:13).

(See also *Justification, Salvation*.)

FRIENDSHIP

:: *A friend loves you no matter what* (Proverbs 17:17 AUTHOR'S PARAPHRASE).

:: *Friends come and friends go, but a true friend sticks by you like family* (Proverbs 18:24 MSG).

:: *Wounds from a sincere friend are better than many kisses from an enemy* (Proverbs 27:6). True friends tell us the truth, even when it hurts—them and us. But people who don't care much about us say whatever they think we want to hear, especially if it benefits them.

:: *I choose as my friends everyone who worships you and follows your teachings* (Psalm 119:63 CEV).

WHEN IT RAINS. Our best friends, the Bible says, are the people who stay with us in the tough times—after everyone else leaves. They're also the ones who can hurt us most when they let us down.

:: *Jonathan thought as much of David as he did of himself, so he asked David to promise once more that he would be a loyal friend* (1 Samuel 20:17 CEV). In words and actions, David and Jonathan are a great example of what it means to be best friends. Prince Jonathan even protected David from Jonathan's father, King Saul. And after Jonathan died, David looked after his friend's son, Mephibosheth (2 Samuel 9).

:: *My enemies are not the ones who sneer and make fun. I could put up with that. . . .But it was my closest friend, the one I trusted most* (Psalm 55:12–13 CEV).

(See also "A friend let me down," page 53.)

:: *Before you know it, a sense of God's wholeness, everything coming together for good, will come and settle you down. It's wonderful what happens when Christ displaces worry at the center of your life* (Philippians 4:7 MSG).

:: *"In this godless world you will continue to experience difficulties. But take heart! I've conquered the world"* (John 16:33 MSG).

:: *My dear children, you come from God and belong to God. . . . The Spirit in you is far stronger than anything in the world* (1 John 4:4 MSG).

:: *"I am leaving you with a gift—peace of mind and heart. And the peace I give is a gift the world cannot give. So don't be troubled or afraid"* (John 14:27).

GAMBLING

Many Christians oppose gambling because they don't like what they've seen it do to people. It can become addictive. It tends to exploit the poor who desperately want to break out of their poverty. And it prods people toward greed. Others say they consider it a relaxing form of entertainment, as long as they set a spending budget and stick with it.

BIBLE GAMBLERS

:: *"Let's make a bet: I'll tell you a riddle, and if you can tell me the right answer before the party is over, I'll give each one of you a shirt and a full change of clothing"* (Judges 14:12 CEV). That's Samson betting the Philistine guests at his wedding that they can't solve his riddle. They threatened Samson's bride into nagging the answer out of him, and then revealing it

to them. Samson got so angry that he left his wife and then killed Philistines in a neighboring city to steal their clothes so he could pay off his gambling debt.

:: *"We will gamble to see who gets it"* (John 19:24 CEV). Roman soldiers gambled to see who would get the robe of their crucifixion victim, Jesus.

BIBLE PRINCIPLES CAUTIONING GAMBLERS

:: *Lust for money brings trouble and nothing but trouble. Going down that path, some lose their footing in the faith completely and live to regret it bitterly ever after* (1 Timothy 6:10 MSG).

GO FISH. Belgian artist Georges Croegaert puts the *card* in cardinals with his painting, *The Winning Hand*. The Bible doesn't condemn gambling, but in those rare instances when gambling shows up, the scene turns violent.

:: *Don't love money; be satisfied with what you have. For God has said, "I will never fail you. I will never abandon you"* (Hebrews 13:5).

:: *Wealth from get-rich-quick schemes quickly disappears* (Proverbs 13:11). The Bible's prescription for getting ahead in the world is to work hard. Or as one sage put it: "Take a lesson from the ants, you lazybones" (Proverbs 6:6).

:: *Do not want anything that belongs to someone else* (Exodus 20:17 CEV). This is one of the 10 Commandments.

(See also *Addictions*.)

GOD THE FATHER

Creator of the universe and first person the Bible identifies in the Godhead, which Bible experts have come to call the Trinity: Father, Son, and Holy Spirit.

WHAT GOD IS LIKE

:: *In the beginning God created the heavens and the earth* (Genesis 1:1).

:: *God's eternal power and character cannot be seen. But from the beginning of creation, God has shown what these are like by all he has made* (Romans 1:20 CEV).

:: *The LORD is the everlasting God* (Isaiah 40:28).

:: *I am everywhere—both near and far, in heaven and on earth* (Jeremiah 23:23–24 CEV).

:: *I am the eternal God. . . . Tell them that the LORD, whose name is "I Am," has sent you* (Exodus 3:14–15 CEV). God's reply when Moses asked for God's name so the Jews enslaved in Egypt would know who sent him to free them.

HOW CAN THREE GODS BE ONE GOD?

The Bible does strange math.

It says there's just one God: "GOD the one and only!" (Deuteronomy 6:4 MSG). Then along comes his Son, Jesus Christ, who says "The Father and I are one" (John 10:30).

One plus one equals one.

When Jesus leaves, the Holy Spirit arrives. Now, one plus one plus one still equals one.

How's that possible?

Even Jesus didn't try to explain it. Perhaps he figured that we physics-bound humans couldn't possibly understand—that we have no frame of reference when it comes to picturing life in a spiritual dimension.

But Christians have certainly tried to figure it out. For centuries Bible scholars debated the relationship between God the Father, Son, and Holy Spirit. Some said there was just one God, and that Jesus was God on earth and the Holy Spirit is God at work in the world.

Yet Jesus prayed to his Father. Jesus also spoke of the Father and the Spirit as though they're distinct—for he told his disciples to baptize converts "in the name of the Father and the Son and the Holy Spirit" (Matthew 28:19).

Scholars, for the most part, gave up trying to figure out the Trinity in the AD 400s. That's when an African theologian named Augustine summed up the scholarly consensus: "The Father is God, the Son is God, the Holy Spirit is God. . .yet we do not say that there are three gods, but one God, the most exalted Trinity."

Experts couldn't explain it. But they decided to believe it anyway because it's in the Bible.

(See also *Trinity*, page 230; "The Bible says there's just one God, but Jesus says he's divine, too; how could anyone believe both?" page 46).

:: *You, Lord, are the only true and living God. You will rule for all time* (Jeremiah 10:10 CEV).

:: *God is love* (1 John 4:8).

:: *He doesn't do anything wrong. He is honest and fair* (Deuteronomy 32:4 NIrV).

:: *Nothing and no one is holy like God* (1 Samuel 2:2 MSG).

:: *"Anyone who has seen me has seen the Father!"* (John 14:9). That's Jesus talking to a disciple, Philip.

:: *"Is anything too hard for the Lord?"* (Genesis 18:14). That's what God said after Sarah laughed when she heard God announce that she and Abraham would soon have a son.

Sarah was 90 years old at the time. Abraham was almost 100.

WHAT GOD WANTS FROM US

:: *What do you think God expects from you? Just this: Live in his presence in holy reverence, follow the road he sets out for you, love him, serve God, your God, with everything you have in you* (Deuteronomy 10:12 MSG).

:: *I demand your complete loyalty—you must not worship any other god!* (Exodus 34:14 CEV). This is the first of the 10 Commandments. As first, it's considered the most important.

:: *"Don't desecrate my holy name. I insist on*

FAMILY PORTRAIT. God the Son rests on the lap of God the Father, while the Holy Spirit hovers—depicted as a dove because New Testament writers said that at Jesus' baptism, the Spirit descended on him "like a dove" (Matthew 3:16).

being treated with holy reverence" (Leviticus 22:32 MSG).

:: *Learn to do good. Seek justice. Help the oppressed* (Isaiah 1:17).

:: *"Judge fairly, and show mercy and kindness to one another. Do not oppress widows, orphans, foreigners, and the poor"* (Zechariah 7:9–10).

(See also *Holy Spirit, Jesus Christ.*)

GOLDEN RULE

:: *Treat others the way you'd want them to treat you* (Matthew 7:12 AUTHOR'S PARAPHRASE). This teaching of Jesus puts a positive spin on similar, older teachings often phrased in the negative: "Never impose on others what you would not choose for yourself," Confucius (about 551–479 BC).

GOSSIP

COVER YOUR MOUTH. Like a sneeze, gossip sprays trouble all over the place. Bible writers say don't—and don't trust any blabbermouth who does.

Gossip is a favorite pastime for many people—even folks who call themselves Christians. But the Bible has nothing good to say about it.

:: *Gossips can't keep secrets, so never confide in blabbermouths* (Proverbs 20:19 MSG).

:: *Listening to gossip is like eating junk food. You gobble it up. It hardens your heart* (Proverbs 18:8 AUTHOR'S PARAPHRASE).

:: *Though some tongues just love the taste of gossip, those who follow Jesus have better uses for language than that* (Ephesians 5:4 MSG).

:: *Evil people relish malicious conversation; the ears of liars itch for dirty gossip* (Proverbs 17:4 MSG).

:: *They. . .get into the habit of going from house to house. Next, they will start gossiping and become busybodies, talking about things that are none of their business* (1 Timothy 5:13 CEV). Apostle Paul warns Timothy, pastor of a church, about how people who have nothing to do often tend to fill their idle time with gossip.

:: *Don't spread harmful rumors* (Exodus 23:1 CEV).

:: *Gossip separates the best of friends* (Proverbs 16:28).

:: *Remind the believers. . .to speak no evil about anyone* (Titus 3:1–2 NCV).

GOVERNMENT

Jesus and writers of the New Testament lived at a time when their homeland was occupied by foreigners from what is now Italy. The Roman Empire had controlled what is now Israel for about a century. They also controlled most of the land surrounding the Mediterranean Sea. Yet Jesus and his disciples advised treating the invaders with respect.

:: *Remind the people to respect the government and be law-abiding, always ready to lend a helping hand* (Titus 3:1 MSG). This is Paul's advice to a church leader, Titus, ministering on the island of Crete.

:: *Obey the rulers who have authority over you. Only God can give authority to anyone, and he puts these rulers in their places of power. People who oppose the authorities are opposing what God has done* (Romans 13:1–2 CEV). Paul wrote this to Roman Christians living in the Roman Empire's capital city, Rome. Some Christians today wonder if Paul intended this for only those readers, or perhaps for just his generation. They wonder what he would say about modern dictators conducting genocide or wide-scale purges of opposition. In cases like these, there are Bible passages calling on God's people to help the helpless: "Speak up for the poor and helpless, and see that they get justice" (Proverbs 31:9).

:: *"Give to Caesar what belongs to Caesar, and give to God what belongs to God"* (Mark 12:17). That's Jesus answering a trick question. Jewish leaders opposed to him asked if Jews should pay taxes to their Roman occupiers. If he said yes, the Jewish people might turn against him. If he said no, he could get in trouble with the Romans.

GRACE

Grace is kindness or mercy that's undeserved. In the Bible it usually refers to God's mercy toward sinful people. Grace is God loving us where we are, but not being willing to leave us there. He loves us even while we're enslaved by sin, but he's working to set us free. The Bible teaches that the salvation people experience is because of God's grace.

:: *God saved you by his grace when you believed. And you can't take credit for this; it is a gift from God* (Ephesians 2:8).

:: *Sin will not be your master. . . . God's grace has set you free* (Romans 6:14 NIrV).

:: *I will be kind and treat you with mercy* (Isaiah 60:10 CEV).

:: *"My grace is all you need. My power works best in weakness"* (2 Corinthians 12:9). This is a promise Jesus gave to the apostle Paul, when Paul was struggling with an undisclosed, humiliating personal problem he called "a thorn in my flesh" (2 Corinthians 12:7).

:: *May God our Father and the Lord Jesus Christ give you grace and peace* (Romans 1:7). This was a common prayerful greeting among early Christians.

GREAT COMMISSION

This is the mission statement Jesus gives his disciples.

:: *Go to the people of all nations and make them my disciples. Baptize them in the name of the Father, the Son, and the Holy Spirit, and teach them to do everything I have told you* (Matthew 28:19–20 CEV).

:: *"You will be my witnesses, telling people about me everywhere—in Jerusalem, throughout Judea [now southern Israel], in Samaria*

GREAT EVANGELIST. Billy Graham, photographed in 1966, is considered by many Christians as the most effective evangelist in modern history. His ministry association estimates he preached to more than 200 million people in live audiences during his 55 years of ministry. In worship services where he preached, more than two million people reportedly stepped forward to accept Jesus as Savior.

[northern Israel], and to the ends of the earth" (Acts 1:8). These are the last words of Jesus, spoken to his disciples immediately before he ascended into the sky.

GREED

A go-to word among many rich folks who know how to get money and keep it, *greed* is a good-for-nothing word in the Bible. Bankrupt.

:: *Some people are always greedy for more, but the godly love to give!* (Proverbs 21:26).

:: *"Guard against every kind of greed. Life is not measured by how much you own"* (Luke 12:15). The advice of Jesus. His point is that though some people measure their worth in cash value, God doesn't. To him, cash is chump change.

:: *Your greedy luxuries are a cancer in your gut, destroying your life from within. You thought you were piling up wealth. What you've piled up is judgment. All the workers you've exploited and cheated cry out for judgment. The groans of the workers you used and abused are a roar in the ears of the Master Avenger. You've looted the earth and lived it up. But all you'll have to show for it is a fatter than usual corpse* (James 5:3–5 MSG).

:: *"The only thing on your mind is to get rich by cheating others"* (Jeremiah 22:17 NIrV). That's the prophet Jeremiah telling off the Jewish King Jehoiakim.

GRUDGES

:: *Stop being bitter and angry and mad at others* (Ephesians 4:31 CEV).

:: *"Forget about the wrong things people do to*

you, and do not try to get even. Love your neighbor as you love yourself" (Leviticus 19:18 NCV).

:: *"When you are praying, first forgive anyone you are holding a grudge against, so that your Father in heaven will forgive your sins, too"* (Mark 11:25). Advice of Jesus.

(See also *Anger, Revenge*.)

GUILT

:: *Clean the slate, God. . . . Then I can start this day sun-washed, scrubbed clean of the grime of sin* (Psalm 19:13 MSG).

:: *If we confess our sins, he will forgive our sins, because we can trust God to do what is right. He will cleanse us from all the wrongs we have done* (1 John 1:9 NCV).

:: *Purify me from my sins, and I will be clean; wash me, and I will be whiter than snow. . . . Remove the stain of my guilt. Create in me a clean heart, O God* (Psalm 51:7, 9–10).

:: *How happy you must be—you get a fresh start, your slate's wiped clean. . . . When I kept it [my sins] all inside. . . The pressure never let up . . . . Then I let it all out; I said, "I'll make a clean breast of my failures to GOD." Suddenly the pressure was gone—my guilt dissolved, my sin disappeared* (Psalm 32:1, 3–5 MSG).

(See also *Confession, Forgiveness*.)

HAPPINESS

:: *Give me happiness, O Lord, for I give myself to you* (Psalm 86:4).

:: *Those who want to do right more than anything*

else are happy, because God will fully satisfy them (Matthew 5:6 NCV). This is Jesus in his Sermon on the Mount, teaching the Beatitudes—sometimes called the Be Happy Attitudes.

:: *If we please God, he will make us wise, understanding, and happy. But if we sin, God will make us struggle for a living, then he will give all we own to someone who pleases him* (Ecclesiastes 2:26 CEV). At least that's the writer's observation, from his personal experience.

:: *Children with good sense make their parents happy, but foolish children make them sad* (Proverbs 10:1 CEV).

(See also *Joy*.)

HATE

:: *A bowl of boiled broccoli shared with someone you love beats barbecued sirloin eaten with someone who hates your guts* (Proverbs 15:17 AUTHOR'S PARAPHRASE).

:: *"You're familiar with the old written law, 'Love your friend,' and its unwritten companion, 'Hate your enemy.' I'm challenging that. I'm telling you to love your enemies. Let them bring out the best in you, not the worst"* (Matthew 5:43–44 MSG). Jesus was referring to Leviticus 19:18, "Love your neighbor as yourself."

:: *Those who hate you may try to fool you with their words. . . . But don't believe them, because their minds are full of evil thoughts. Lies can hide hate, but the evil will be plain to everyone* (Proverbs 26:24–26 NCV).

:: *If someone says, "I love God," but hates a Christian brother or sister, that person is a liar* (1 John 4:20).

(See also *Anger*.)

HEALING

What's the point of healing, some wonder, when everyone who gets healed ends up dead sooner or later? Because later is better than sooner, as far as most folks are concerned. In one story, God adds 15 years to the life of sick King Hezekiah (Isaiah 38:5). The Bible teaches that God is the source of healing. Jesus healed not only out of compassion, but to convince skeptics that his power came from God (John 9:3). The early church got its start partly—if not mainly—because of the healing miracles that the disciples of Jesus performed.

:: *Are you sick? Call the church leaders together to pray and anoint you with oil in the name of the Master. Believing-prayer will heal you, and Jesus will put you on your feet* (James 5:14-15 MSG). The Bible doesn't present this as a magic formula for healing. It's a prescription.

"YOUR FAITH HAS HEALED YOU." That's what Jesus tells a woman who touched his robe, believing that in this touch she would be healed. She suffered what sounds like a menstrual disorder, described as excessive bleeding (Mark 5:25–34).

Take your request to the Lord, with the faith to believe he has the power to heal. He may not choose to heal your illness. But one way or another, as the Bible tells it, he'll put you back on your feet—here on the planet or in heaven, healed temporarily or permanently.

:: *I will praise the LORD. . . . He forgives all my sins. He heals all my sicknesses. He saves my life from going down into the grave* (Psalm 103:2–4 NIrv).

:: *Jesus went along Lake Galilee. . . . Large crowds came and brought many people who were crippled or blind or lame or unable to talk. . . . And he healed them all. Everyone was amazed* (Matthew 15:29–31 CEV).

(See also *Miracles, Sickness.*)

HEAVEN

It's the eternal home of God, his angels, and the souls of God-loving humans. John described heaven, after seeing it in a vision reported in the last book of the Bible: Revelation. He said it had pearl gates, golden streets, and jasper walls (Revelation 21:17–21). But most scholars say these are just symbols—that John was using the most precious objects on earth to describe the indescribable majesty of an eternal, spiritual dimension that shatters the boundaries of understanding for folks confined in this physical world.

:: *"There is plenty of room for you in my Father's home. If that weren't so, would I have told you that I'm on my way to get a room ready for you? And if I'm on my way to get your room ready, I'll come back and get you so you can live where I live"* (John 14:2–3 MSG). Hours before Jesus is arrested, he comforts his disciples by

RUSSIAN ORTHODOX HEAVEN. Russian artist Viktor Vasnetsov (1848–1926) gives heaven a familiar look. Familiar to him, at least. Heaven's architecture takes its cue from the Russian Orthodox Church, framing angels and saintly souls.

PURGATORY, HEAVEN'S MUD ROOM.

It's where you knock the mud of sin off your boots before stepping foot into heaven.

That's one way of looking at purgatory—a place Protestants say doesn't exist.

Catholics teach that purgatory—a word meaning "purge" or "cleanse"—is a place Christians go to get purified for heaven after they die.

From there, believers who died with only minor unconfessed sins are ushered into heaven. Christians who committed more serious sins may have to undergo more intense punishment as penance. The most serious unconfessed sins—murder, for example—lead to hell.

Catholics base their teaching partly on the idea that God is "pure and cannot stand the sight of evil" (Habakkuk 1:13). But it's also based on a story written between the time of the Old Testament and New Testament—a story in their Bible but not in the Protestant Bible.

In this story a Jewish rebel leader, Judah, prayed for some of his dead soldiers who had sinned by taking idols with them into battle. After Judah prayed for the men, he took up an offering and sent it to priests at the Jerusalem Temple. By doing this, "he made atonement for the dead, so that they might be delivered from their sin" (2 Maccabees 12:45 NRSV).

Centuries later, church leaders started to take offerings for the dead. They said, essentially, that these contributions, which they called "indulgences," were fast-pass tickets out of purgatory for a person's dead loved ones. Saint Peter's huge church in Rome, where the pope addresses crowds today, was built with money raised from selling indulgences.

Reformer monk Martin Luther (1483–1546) said selling indulgences was nothing more than exploitive nonsense. The controversy he fired up started the Protestant movement, led by Catholics protesting abuses within the church.

EPISCOPALIANS BEWARE. One woman seems bent on saving Protestant souls, as she stands outside the Episcopalian Trinity Church on the corner of Wall Street and Broadway in New York City. According to Catholic teaching, if a Christian dies before confessing even minor sins to a Catholic priest, the person's soul has to endure purification in purgatory before moving on to heaven. Protestants say there's no such place as purgatory. Many devout Catholics say Protestants will never get the chance to see for themselves; since they never confessed their sins to a priest, Protestants go straight to hell.

promising that they will live forever with him in what sounds like heaven.

:: *"Today you will be with me in paradise"* (Luke 23:43). The words of crucified Jesus to a dying man hanging on a cross beside him.

:: *We are looking forward to the new heavens and new earth he has promised, a world filled with God's righteousness* (2 Peter 3:13). Whether speaking symbolically or literally, Peter says that on the day God judges everyone, "the heavens will be destroyed by fire, and everything else will melt in the heat" (2 Peter 3:12 CEV). Which would put creation in line for Universe 2.0. Or for something better— heaven, for example.

:: *I saw a new heaven and a new earth. . . . I saw New Jerusalem, that holy city, coming down from God in heaven. . . . I heard a loud voice shout. . .God's home is now with his people . . . . He will wipe all tears from their eyes, and there will be no more death, suffering, crying, or pain. These things of the past are gone forever* (Revelation 21:1–4 CEV). Many scholars say New Jerusalem is another way of referring to "heaven." Wherever heaven is, or whatever it's like, heartache and death don't exist there. But God does.

:: *The City shimmered like a precious gem, light-filled, pulsing light. . . . The twelve gates were twelve pearls, each gate a single pearl. The main street of the City was pure gold, translucent as glass. . . . The City doesn't need sun or moon for light. God's Glory is its light, the Lamb its lamp! . . . Nothing dirty or defiled will get into the City, and no one who defiles or deceives. Only those whose names are written in the Lamb's Book of Life will get in* (Revelation 21:12, 20, 23, 27 MSG). That's an excerpt from John's description of heaven.

:: *"Look down from your holy dwelling place in heaven and bless your people"* (Deuteronomy 26:15). From the beginning of Jewish history, people believed that God lived somewhere in the heavens. Yet some Christians say that the Bible's description of heaven suggests it doesn't have a galactic address, but that it exists in a spiritual dimension beyond the limits of physics.

HELL

Christians don't agree on how literally to take the Bible's teaching about hell. (See "Hell," page 497.)

:: *"In hell. . .the fire is never put out. Every person will be salted with fire"* (Mark 9:48–49 NCV). Jesus seems to be warning people that hell is a real place. Yet some wonder if he's speaking figuratively, talking about the reality of punishment and not offering a literal description of it.

HELL IS THE PITS. Literally, according to some Christians, since the Bible talks about "the dark pits of hell" (2 Peter 2:4 CEV). Others say it blazes with the light of "eternal fire" (Matthew 25:41). Still others wonder if the Bible's descriptions are more symbolic than literal, describing a place no one on earth would want to go.

Hell has an address. We can actually send mail there.

Good news: the temp is relatively mild, compared to a lake of burning sulfur.

Hell is the English translation of Gehenna [gah-HEN-uh]—a valley outside the walled city of Jerusalem, on the south side. For some reason, this valley became a symbol of God's judgment—and no one is sure why. Perhaps it's because this is where the Bible says Jews sacrificed their children to idols—a sin God eventually punished by deporting the Jews from their homeland. Or maybe the Jews used the valley as a dump, to burn their ever-smoldering garbage. But somewhere along history's time-line, this valley became a symbol of God's judgment—a bit like September 11 came to symbolize terrorism because of the attack on the World Trade Center in New York City.

A FEW THEORIES

Bible experts have many theories about hell. The reason for so many is partly because of the mysterious symbolism behind the word *hell*. And it's partly because of the confusing descriptions of this place—sometimes called "dark" and other times called a place brightened by "fire."

Physical fire. It's a real place where souls suffer for-ever in fire.

Separation from God. God wouldn't torture someone forever. When he punishes someone in the Bible, it's with the good intention of helping people—even if he strikes someone dead as an object lesson to show others that sin leads to death. Eternal torture, however, seems to serve no redemptive purpose. For this reason, some say, hell is more likely a place where sinners are separated from God. In life, they had wanted nothing to do with him. In death, they get their wish.

Eternal death. Fires of hell refer to annihilation. It's not the torture that lasts forever, it's the punishment. Since fire destroys what it touches, this is a symbolic way of saying God destroys sinners.

Everyone will be saved. God keeps reaching out to sinners, even in the next life. He keeps them alive, not to punish them but to reconcile with them. "Through him [Jesus] God reconciled everything to himself. He made peace with everything in heaven and on earth by means of Christ's blood on the cross" (Colossians 1:20). Reconciliation with everyone can't happen, some say, if there are people in hell. Many Christians, however, call this heresy. They say the Bible teaches that our eternal destiny is determined in this life.

HORSEBACK RIDING IN HELL. Saddled up, a man takes a ride in a valley park on Jerusalem's south side. Locals call this valley Hinnom. But it's also known by its ancient name *Gehenna*, or by its English name *hell*. Almost every time hell shows up in the English Bible, the original word points to this valley where Jerusalem Jews today enjoy picnics.

:: *"Don't be afraid of people, who can kill the body but cannot kill the soul. The only one you should fear is the one who can destroy the soul and the body in hell"* (Matthew 10:28 NCV). A "destroyed soul" suggests to some that *hell* means annihilation—eternal death, not eternal torture.

:: *"Go away from me into the fire that burns forever. It has been prepared for the devil and his angels"* (Matthew 25:41 NIrv). In a parable about a king separating goats from sheep, Jesus says hell is the destiny of people who refuse to help the poor. God will cut them from the herd that's headed for heaven.

HOME FOR FALLEN ANGELS

:: *God did not have pity on the angels that sinned. He had them tied up and thrown into the dark pits of hell until the time of judgment* (2 Peter 2:4 CEV).

:: *Then the devil. . .was thrown into the fiery lake of burning sulfur, joining the beast and the false prophet. There they will be tormented day and night forever and ever* (Revelation 20:10).

HOLINESS

Some Christians say believers can mature to a point where they don't sin anymore—at least they don't commit intentional sins. For them, *holiness* often means moral perfection, consistently resisting temptation. But for most Christians, moral perfection is a goal they say they'll never reach in this lifetime. For them, holiness is simply devotion to God. Objects used in ancient worship services, for example, such as lampstands, were made holy through rituals devoting them for sacred use. In the same way, people who

HOLY HUMANS?

"You must dedicate yourselves to me and be holy, just as I am holy" (Leviticus 11:44 CEV).

God said that to the Jews.

Jesus said much the same thing to his followers: "Be perfect, even as your Father in heaven is perfect" (Matthew 5:48).

Scholars are still trying to figure out what that means. The problem is that like the rest of us, they know we humans tend to be perfectly behaved only when we're unconscious.

One theory is that perfection is the goal of a lifetime—that we should try to follow the example of Jesus, especially in matters of loving others since that's the context of Jesus' statement. It's as though Jesus is saying: "You know right from wrong; now act like it. I know it takes time to learn how to love your neighbor and especially your enemy. But practice makes perfect."

Another theory is that God and Jesus weren't talking mainly about perfect behavior, but about complete devotion to God. When a Temple utensil, such as a bowl, was dedicated for use only in service to God, it was no longer considered common. It was separate and distinct from other bowls—devoted completely to God. We, too, become holy in God's eyes when we dedicate ourselves to him.

devoted themselves to God were considered holy and "set apart" from others. "Anything specially set apart for the LORD—whether a person, an animal, or family property. . .has been set apart as holy, and it belongs to the LORD" (Leviticus 27:28).

:: *God called us to be holy and does not want us to live in sin* (1 Thessalonians 4:7 NCV).

:: *May he [God] make you holy through and through. May your whole spirit, soul and body be kept free from blame. May you be without blame from now until our Lord Jesus Christ comes. The One who has chosen you is faith-*

"BE PERFECT." Orders like this—from the mouth of Jesus, no less—are enough to depress a monk. Sequestered in a monastery, even those churchmen devoted to meditation and prayer can't always get along with each other. Some Bible experts say Jesus was simply pointing his followers in the general direction of good behavior. Others say he wasn't talking about behavior at all, but about a Christian's status in life: he or she is reserved for God's use.

ful. He will do all these things (1 Thessalonians 5:23–24 NIrv). Drawing from passages like this, some churches teach that after we are saved we can experience a deeper work of God. In that second work, God defeats sin's power over us and changes our spiritual programming—getting rid of our tendency to sin. Some call this "entire sanctification" and say it opens the door to a sin-free life. Others say we can't be perfectly sin-free in this lifetime.

:: *You were taught to be made new in your hearts, to become a new person. That new person is made to be like God—made to be truly good and*

holy. So you must stop telling lies. . . . Those who are stealing must stop stealing and start working. . . . Never do anything evil. Be kind and loving to each other, and forgive each other just as God forgave you in Christ (Ephesians 4:23–25, 28, 31–32 NCV).

:: *"Make them holy by your truth"* (John 17:17). Jesus' prayer for his disciples.

:: *Now you are free from the power of sin and have become slaves of God. Now you do those things that lead to holiness and result in eternal life* (Romans 6:22).

:: *You are citizens along with all of God's holy people. You are members of God's family* (Ephesians 2:19). Paul, writing to non-Jewish believers.

(See also *Sin*.)

HOLY SPIRIT

The Holy Spirit is the third person of the Trinity, along with God the Father and Jesus. In the Old Testament, it's hard to tell the difference between God the Father and God the Holy Spirit. Their names usually seem woven together: "Spirit of God." Back then, the Holy Spirit seemed sent to empower only key spiritual leaders, such as kings like David: "The Spirit of the LORD came powerfully upon David from that day on" (1 Samuel 16:13). But the prophets quoted God as promising that one day "I will pour out my Spirit upon all people" (Joel 2:28). The New Testament teaches that this time came a few weeks after the resurrection of Jesus.

:: *"I will ask the Father, and he will give you another Helper to be with you forever—the Spirit of truth. The world cannot accept him,* because it does not see him or know him. But you know him, because he lives with you and he will be in you" (John 14:16–17 NCV).

:: You are not ruled by your sinful selves. You are ruled by the Spirit, if that Spirit of God really lives in you. . . . If you use your lives to do the wrong things your sinful selves want, you will die spiritually. But if you use the Spirit's help to stop doing the wrong things you do with your body, you will have true life (Romans 8:9, 13 NCV).

:: "The Holy Spirit comes and fills you with power from heaven" (Luke 24:49).

:: God's Spirit makes us loving, happy, peaceful, patient, kind, good, faithful, gentle, and self-controlled. (Galatians 5:22–23 CEV).

:: There are different kinds of spiritual gifts, but they all come from the same Spirit (1 Corinthians 12:4 CEV).

(See also *Baptism with the Holy Spirit, God the Father, Jesus Christ.*)

HOMOSEXUALITY

There's one word that describes what the Bible teaches about homosexual sex, most Christians would agree. It's the same word the Bible uses to offer advice about heterosexual sex before marriage: *Don't.*

:: " 'Do not have sex with a man as you would have sex with a woman. I hate that' " (Leviticus 18:22 NIrV). This is Moses quoting God's list of rules about sex.

:: God let them go. They were filled with shameful longings. Their women committed sexual acts that were not natural. In the same way, the men turned away from their natural love for women. They burned with sexual longing for

CHRISTIANS ON BOTH SIDES OF THE GAY DEBATE.

Only about half a dozen short Bible passages refer to homosexual behavior. All of them call it sin.

The Bible doesn't come right out and say what's wrong with the gay lifestyle. But it does describe homosexuality with words that give us a clue: *unnatural* and *perversion*.

This implies homosexuality is wrong because it's the opposite of what God intended for human sexuality. The creation story says God designed us as heterosexuals. It's this design that keeps our species alive.

Not all Christians agree that homosexuality is wrong. That's why some churches ordain gay ministers and conduct same-sex marriages.

Here are three key arguments pro-gay Christians make, along with the counterpoint by other Christians.

IT'S IN THE GENES

:: Genetic factors contribute to homosexuality, and it would be unfair of God the Creator to condemn people for doing what he programmed them to do.

Counterpoint: Unmarried heterosexuals face the same challenge. So do alcoholics, who have a genetic predisposition to alcohol addiction. The only Christian response is abstinence. Jesus and Paul each abstained from sex.

GAY IS NATURAL FOR SOME FOLKS

:: Paul wasn't condemning homosexuality, but heterosexuals experimenting with it. That's what he meant by saying they "committed sexual acts that were not natural" (Romans 1:26 NIrV).

Counterpoint: Paul was pointing back to the creation story and to all of the Jewish scriptures that condemn homosexual behavior and that say God intended sex to be shared between a man and a woman.

THE LAWS ARE OBSOLETE

:: Just as old Jewish laws about kosher food and circumcision became obsolete when Jesus arrived with his message of God's love and mercy, so did legalistic rules about sex. That's why Jesus never condemned the gay lifestyle.

Counterpoint: New Testament writers, Paul among them, declare that the moral laws of the Old Testament—laws such as those about murder, stealing, and sexual sins—are still in force.

Though most Christians insist that practicing homosexuality is wrong, they stop short of saying it's sinful to have homosexual desires. Sexual sin comes to life when sex is performed outside the boundaries God set up: marriage with a partner of the opposite sex.

Should homosexuals be allowed to join churches and even serve as church leaders?

Many Christians think of it this way: They substitute the tag "homosexuals" with categories such as "greedy people," "liars," or another kind of sin—because they say the Bible describes homosexual behavior as just one of many sins. It doesn't rate sin on a scale of 1 to 10, with homosexuality as a 10 and cheating on a test as a 1.

Based on this kind of reasoning, many Christians answer yes—let gay people join the church and even work as leaders. The caveat for many Christians, however, is that the homosexuals have to make the same pledge as other sinners in the church—a pledge to allow the teachings of Jesus to mold them into new creatures, which in their case would involve living a disciplined life of abstinence. If they can do that, then they should be welcomed into the church. There, they can sing with the rest of the church an old Charles Wesley hymn about a God who "breaks the power of cancelled sin; He sets the prisoner free."

That doesn't mean every Christian homosexual will be "cured" of the homosexual desire any more than the rest of us are cured of our harmful desires. But it does mean that they don't have to be enslaved by their sin and that they can devote each day to living for God.

There are many Christians, too, who wouldn't require this pledge because they don't consider homosexuality sinful.

Homosexuality is a divisive topic that has already split entire denominations and may continue to do so.

each other. Men did shameful things with other men. They suffered in their bodies for all the twisted things they did (Romans 1:26–27 NIrV).

:: Those who indulge in sexual sin. . .or commit adultery, or are male prostitutes, or practice homosexuality. . .none of these will inherit the Kingdom of God (1 Corinthians 6:9–10).

:: God created humans to be like himself; he made men and women. God gave them his blessing and said: Have a lot of children! (Genesis 1:27–28 CEV). God designed men and women as heterosexuals, according to the creation story.

HONESTY

:: An honest answer is a sign of true friendship (Proverbs 24:26 CEV).

:: What joy for those whose record the LORD has cleared of guilt, whose lives are lived in complete honesty! (Psalm 32:2).

:: "A person must do what is right. He must be honest and tell the truth. He must not get rich by cheating others" (Isaiah 33:15 NIrV).

:: We don't want anyone suspecting us of taking one penny of this money for ourselves. We're being as careful in our reputation with the public as in our reputation with God (2 Corinthians 8:20–21 MSG). Paul is talking about an offering he is collecting for the poor in Jerusalem.

:: Corrupt tax collectors came to be baptized and asked, "Teacher, what should we do?" He replied. "Collect no more taxes than the government requires" (Luke 3:12–13). That's Jesus talking, telling them to keep it honest.

(See also *Cheating*.)

HOPE

:: "His name [Jesus] will be the hope of all the world" (Matthew 12:21).

:: Why am I discouraged? Why is my heart so sad? I will put my hope in God! (Psalm 42:5).

:: "Blessed are those who trust in the LORD and have made the LORD their hope and confidence" (Jeremiah 17:7).

:: I pray that God, who gives hope, will bless you with complete happiness and peace because of your faith. And may the power of the Holy Spirit fill you with hope (Romans 15:13 CEV).

FROM SUFFERING TO HOPE. "Suffering gives us the strength to go on. The strength to go on produces character. Character produces hope. And hope will never let us down" (Romans 5:3–5 NIrV).

:: Even when there was no reason for hope, Abraham kept hoping—believing that he would become the father of many nations. . . . Abraham never wavered in believing God's promise. In fact, his faith grew stronger (Romans 4:18, 20).

:: If we see what we are waiting for, that is not really hope. People do not hope for something they already have. But we are hoping for something we do not have yet, and we are waiting for it patiently (Romans 8:24–25 NCV).

:: I find rest in God; only he gives me hope. He is my rock and my salvation. He is my defender; I will not be defeated (Psalm 62:5–6 NCV).

:: You are the God who saves me. All day long I put my hope in you (Psalm 25:5).

:: We do not want you to. . .grieve like the rest, who have no hope. We believe that Jesus died and rose again. . . . The Lord himself will come down from heaven. . . . After that, we who are still alive. . .will be caught up together with them in the clouds to meet the Lord in the air. And so we will be with the Lord forever (1 Thessalonians 4:13–14, 16–17 TNIV).

(See also *Faith*.)

HUMILITY

This is a character trait the Bible encourages. It's the opposite of self-absorbed pride.

:: Don't try to impress others. Be humble, thinking of others as better than yourselves (Philippians 2:3).

:: Think the same way that Christ Jesus thought . . . . He became like one of us. Christ was humble (Philippians 2:5–8 CEV).

:: "Anyone who becomes as humble as this little child is the greatest in the Kingdom of Heaven" (Matthew 18:4). That's Jesus talking.

:: During the meal Jesus stood up and took off his outer clothing. Taking a towel, he wrapped it around his waist. Then he poured water into a bowl and began to wash the followers' feet. . . . When he had finished washing their feet, he put on his clothes and sat down again. He asked, "Do you understand what I have just done for you? . . . I did this as an example so that you should do as I have done for you" (John 13:4–5, 12, 15 NCV). Jesus was practicing what he preached—a rabbi master acting like a servant.

:: "Look, your King is coming to you. He is humble, riding on a donkey" (Matthew 21:5).

:: When you are invited to a wedding feast, don't sit in the best place. . . . Go and sit in the worst place. Then the one who invited you may come and say, "My friend, take a better seat!" You will then be honored in front of all the other guests. If you put yourself above others, you will be put down. But if you humble yourself, you will be honored (Luke 14:8, 10–11 CEV). Jesus takes advantage of dinner guests jostling for position to teach an object lesson about spiritual etiquette.

(See also *Pride*.)

HYPOCRISY

One of the sins that fired the anger of Jesus most of all was hypocrisy—especially in people who claimed to serve God but who were serving only themselves.

:: "I can't stand your religious meetings. I'm fed up with your conferences and conventions . . .your religion projects, your pretentious slogans and goals. . .your fund-raising schemes, your public relations and image making. I've had all I can take of your noisy ego-music. When was the last time you sang to me? Do you know what I want? I want justice—oceans of it. I want fairness—rivers of it. That's what I want. That's all I want" (Amos 5:21–24 MSG). Worship is nothing but interactive theater if we don't take it with us.

:: "You're hopeless, you religion scholars. . . ! Frauds! You're like manicured grave plots, grass clipped and the flowers bright, but six feet down it's all rotting bones and worm-eaten flesh" (Matthew 23:27 MSG). That's Jesus talking to self-absorbed Jewish scholars.

:: "Frauds! Isaiah's prophecy of you hit the bull's-eye: These people make a big show of saying the right thing, but their heart isn't in it. They act like they're worshiping me, but they don't mean it" (Matthew 15:7–9 MSG). Jesus is criticizing religion scholars. He calls them frauds many times during his frequent clashes with them.

:: "How can you think of saying, 'Friend, let me help you get rid of that speck in your eye,' when you can't see past the log in your own eye? Hypocrite!" (Luke 6:42). Jesus, warning his audience not to judge others.

:: "When you give to someone in need, don't do as the hypocrites do—blowing trumpets in the synagogues and streets to call attention to their acts of charity! I tell you the truth, they have received all the reward they will ever get" (Matthew 6:2). This is Jesus preaching in the famous Sermon on the Mount.

:: "When you pray, don't be like the hypocrites who love to pray publicly. . .where everyone can see them" (Matthew 6:5).

IMMANUEL

Immanuel (em-MAN-u-el) is a Hebrew name. It means "God is with us." The prophet Isaiah predicted the birth of a child named Immanuel. Matthew's Gospel said Jesus fulfilled the prophecy.

:: "The virgin will conceive a child! She will give birth to a son and will call him Immanuel" (Isaiah 7:14).

:: The angel said [to Joseph in a dream], "Do not be afraid to take Mary as your wife. For the child within her was conceived by the Holy Spirit. And she will have a son, and you are to name him Jesus. . . ." All of this occurred to fulfill the Lord's message through his prophet: "Look! The virgin will conceive a child! She will give birth to a son, and they will call him Immanuel, which means 'God is with us' " (Matthew 1:20–23).

INCARNATION

God becomes human.

:: The Word [Jesus] became a human being. He made his home with us. We have seen his glory. It is the glory of the one and only Son. He came from the Father. And he was full of grace and truth (John 1:14 NIrV).

:: The good news is about God's Son. As a human being, the Son of God belonged to King David's family line. By the power of the Holy Spirit,

MOTHER OF GOD. Christians teach that God stepped into human history in the form of Jesus, becoming completely human while remaining completely God. Scholars admit they can't explain it. But they say Christians believe it because the Bible says it's so.

he was appointed to be the mighty Son of God because he rose from the dead. He is Jesus Christ our Lord (Romans 1:3–4 NIrV).

:: *Christ is the visible image of the invisible God. . . . God in all his fullness was pleased to live in Christ* (Colossians 1:15, 19).

:: *Christ was truly God. . . . He gave up everything and became a slave, when he became like one of us* (Philippians 2:6–7 CEV).

:: *God was in Christ, offering peace and forgiveness to the people of this world* (2 Corinthians 5:19 CEV).

(For background on Jesus as "the Word" see *Jesus Christ*.)

INCEST

:: *"You must never have sexual relations with a close relative"* (Leviticus 18:6). Jewish law clarifies what a "close relative" is: parent, stepparent, brother or sister, stepbrother or stepsister, aunt, uncle, daughter-in-law, son-in-law, or the child or grandchild of someone with whom the person has had sex (Leviticus 18:6–17). Marriage between cousins was allowed.

:: *I can hardly believe the report about the sexual immorality going on among you—something that even pagans don't do. I am told that a man in your church is living in sin with his stepmother. . . . You should remove this man from your fellowship* (1 Corinthians 5:1–2).

ABRAHAM MARRIES HIS HALF-SISTER.

Oddly enough, the father and mother of the Jewish race were brother and sister. Abraham married his half-sister Sarah. They had the same father, but different mothers (Genesis 20:12).

Under Jewish law—which didn't come until almost 1,000 years later—such marriages were forbidden, considered incest. And yet this marriage started the Jewish race, God's Chosen People.

Why would God allow such a marriage for Abraham, and then forbid it later?

The Bible doesn't say.

Perhaps for this pivotal marriage in Jewish history, Sarah's spirit was more important than her genetics. The vast majority of people in Abraham's hometown of Ur, in what is now southern Iraq, worshiped idols.

:: *"It is against God's law for you to marry your brother's wife"* (Mark 6:18). Quoting Jewish law, that's what John the Baptist told Herod Antipas, ruler of Galilee. Herod had married his brother's ex-wife after she divorced Herod's brother. John got decapitated for that remark. Herod's new wife insisted on it.

INFERTILITY

Today, as in Bible times, infertility is a heartbreaker for many couples. Especially for the women.

THE PAIN

:: *When Rachel saw that she wasn't having any children for Jacob, she became jealous of her sister. She pleaded with Jacob, "Give me children, or I'll die!" Then Jacob became furious with Rachel. "Am I God?" he asked. "He's the one who has kept you from having children!"* (Genesis 30:1–2). Rachel later has two sons, Joseph and then Benjamin, though she dies delivering Benjamin.

:: *Elkanah had two wives, Hannah and Peninnah. Peninnah had children, but Hannah did not. . . . So Peninnah would taunt Hannah and make fun of her because the LORD had kept her from having children. . . . Hannah would be reduced to tears and would not even eat. "Why are you crying, Hannah?" Elkanah would ask. "Why aren't you eating? Why be downhearted just because you have no children? You have me—isn't that better than having ten sons?"* (1 Samuel 1:2, 6–8). Apparently not. But Hannah eventually gives birth to Samuel, who grows up to become a prophet.

INCOMPLETE. Job One for a woman in Bible times was to produce children to help with the work. When she didn't, she not only felt empty—she felt ashamed. Others tended to think God was punishing her.

THE COMFORT

:: *Pile your troubles on GOD's shoulders—he'll carry your load, he'll help you out* (Psalm 55:22 MSG).

:: *"Nothing is impossible with God"* (Luke 1:37). That doesn't mean he'll cure the infertility, many scholars would say. But at the very least, he'll give the couple strength to cope and help them find peace.

:: *The LORD is my strength and shield. I trust him with all my heart. He helps me, and my heart is filled with joy* (Psalm 28:7).

INSULTS

The Bible points people away from this nastiness—toward patience and kindness.

DON'T

:: *"Do not insult the deaf"* (Leviticus 19:14).

:: *Don't bad-mouth each other, friends. It's God's Word, his Message, his Royal Rule, that takes a beating in that kind of talk. You're supposed to be honoring the Message* (James 4:11 MSG).

IT HURTS

:: *It was not an enemy insulting me. I could stand that. . . . But it is you. . .my companion and good friend* (Psalm 55:12–13 NCV).

HOW TO REACT

:: *Losing your temper is foolish; ignoring an insult is smart* (Proverbs 12:16 CEV).

:: *I don't let it bother me when people give me a hard time for being a Christian. Religious profiling. Insults. Bullying. I know I'm weak. But Jesus is strong. So I delegate the problem to him. He can handle it* (2 Corinthians 12:10 AUTHOR'S PARAPHRASE).

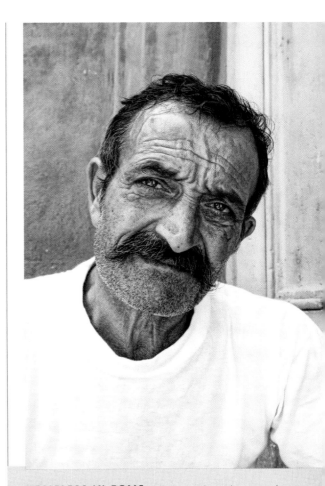

HOMELESS IN ROME. Like most homeless people, Vespucci endures the occasional insult—that he's lazy, not lost. One ancient song seems an apt response: "Their insults have broken my heart, and I am in despair. If only one person would show some pity; if only one would turn and comfort me" (Psalm 69:20). Vespucci says his dream is to find his son.

:: *He [Jesus] did not retaliate when he was insulted, nor threaten revenge when he suffered. He left his case in the hands of God* (1 Peter 2:23).

(See also *Criticism*.)

HAZARDOUS TO YOUR HEALTH

:: *An angry person is dangerous, but a jealous person is even worse* (Proverbs 27:4 CEV).

:: *Jealousy detonates rage in a cheated husband; wild for revenge, he won't make allowances. Nothing you say or pay will make it all right; neither bribes nor reason will satisfy him* (Proverbs 6:34–35 MSG).

SOURCE OF THE FIRST MURDER

:: *The LORD accepted Abel and his gift, but he did not accept Cain and his gift. This made Cain very angry, and he looked dejected. . . . Cain attacked his brother, Abel, and killed him* (Genesis 4:4–5, 8). Jealousy provided the motive for the world's first murder. The Bible never says why God rejected Cain's offering, but the implication is that Cain had one rotten attitude.

DON'T MEASURE YOURSELF BY OTHERS

:: *Do your own work well, and then you will have something to be proud of. But don't compare yourself with others* (Galatians 6:4 CEV).

GOD'S JEALOUSY

:: *"You must worship no other gods, for the LORD, whose very name is Jealous, is a God who is jealous about his relationship with you"* (Exodus 34:14).

(See also *Envy.*)

"Jesus Christ" isn't his name. It's his name and his title—a bit like "Jesus, PhD." Only in this case it's "Jesus, Messiah." The title means "Anointed One," and it refers to people chosen by God for special service, such as a king or a priest. The Bible calls King David an anointed one. But Jesus is more than just another king. The Bible portrays him as the King of kings. Even more, it describes him as the Son of God, and as God in the flesh.

JESUS AT CREATION

:: *In the beginning, the Word [Jesus] was already there. The Word was with God, and the Word was God. He was with God in the beginning. All things were made through him. Nothing that has been made was made without him* (John 1:1–3 NIRV). *Word* is from the Greek term *Logos* (low-GOES). Greek philosophers used that word to describe the mysterious power behind the universe. Jews taught that God used his word to speak creation into existence: "God said, 'Let there be light,' and there was light' " (Genesis 1:3). So this term, *Word*, communicated to people in both the Jewish culture and in the rest of the Mediterranean world that Jesus is divine.

SON OF GOD

:: *"You will have a son. His name will be Jesus. He will be great and will be called the Son of God Most High. The Lord God will make him king, as his ancestor David was. . . . And his kingdom will never end"* (Luke 1:31–33 CEV). The angel Gabriel to Mary.

:: *Mary asked the angel, "But how can this happen? I am a virgin." The angel replied, "The Holy Spirit will come upon you, and the power of the Most High will overshadow you"* (Luke 1:34–35).

:: *The Word [Jesus] became flesh and blood, and moved into the neighborhood. We saw the glory*

with our own eyes, the one-of-a-kind glory, like Father, like Son* (John 1:14 MSG).

:: *This Son perfectly mirrors God, and is stamped with God's nature. He holds everything together by what he says—powerful words!* (Hebrews 1:3 MSG).

TEACHER AND HEALER

:: *Jesus was about thirty years old when he began his public ministry. Jesus was known as the son of Joseph* (Luke 3:23).

:: *Jesus went all over Galilee. There he taught in the synagogues. He preached the good news of God's kingdom. He healed every illness and sickness the people had* (Matthew 4:23 NIrv).

:: *God's Spirit is on me; he's chosen me to preach the Message of good news to the poor, sent me to announce pardon to prisoners and recovery of sight to the blind, to set the burdened and battered free, to announce, "This is God's year to act!"* (Luke 4:18-19 MSG). Jesus quotes a prophecy from Isaiah, claiming it as part of his mission statement.

:: *Jesus said, "Love the Lord your God with all your passion and prayer and intelligence. . . . Love others as well as you love yourself"* (Matthew 22:37, 39 MSG). Jesus said these two laws were the most important in the Bible—the bedrock foundation on which all other laws rest.

SAVIOR

:: *"God loved the world so much that he gave his one and only Son. Anyone who believes in him will not die but will have eternal life. God did not send his Son into the world to judge the world. He sent his Son to save the world"* (John 3:16-17 NIrv).

:: *"I am the good shepherd. The good shepherd sacrifices his life for the sheep"* (John 10:11).

:: *The servant was pierced because we had sinned. He was crushed because we had done what was evil. He was punished to make us whole again. His wounds have healed us. . . . And the LORD has placed on his servant the sins of all of us* (Isaiah 53:5-6 NIrv). A prophecy written 700 years before Jesus, but which New Testament writers said pointed to Jesus. Many Jewish scholars say this suffering servant refers to the Jewish people, suffering through the Babylonian invasion that wiped the Jewish nation off the political map in 586 BC. Babylonians came from what is now Iraq.

:: *"You are looking for Jesus of Nazareth, who was crucified. He isn't here! He is risen from the dead!"* (Mark 16:6). An angel, talking to women who have come to Jesus' grave to finish preparing his body for burial.

COMING AGAIN

:: *"I am going there to prepare a place for each of you. After I have done this, I will come back and take you with me. Then we will be together"* (John 14:2-3 CEV). After telling his disciples that he will die, Jesus comforts them with assurances that he will return.

:: *"In the future you will see the Son of Man seated in the place of power at God's right hand and coming on the clouds of heaven"* (Matthew 26:64). Jesus, speaking at his trial.

(See also *God the Father, Holy Spirit, Messiah.*)

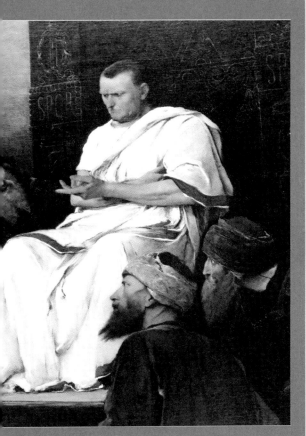

Pontius Pilate, governor of Judea from about AD 26–37.

JESUS IN A ROMAN HISTORY BOOK.

The Bible isn't the only book from Jesus' century that talks about him.

A Roman historian—Josephus (about AD 37–100)—had this to say about him:

"There was a wise man who was called Jesus, and his conduct was good. . . . Pilate condemned him to be crucified and to die. And those who had become his disciples did not abandon their loyalty to him. They reported that he had appeared to them three days after his crucifixion, and that he was alive."

ANTIQUITIES OF THE JEWS

JOKES, DIRTY

:: *Obscene stories, foolish talk, and coarse jokes—these are not for you* (Ephesians 5:4).
:: *Let nothing foul or dirty come out of your mouth* (Ephesians 4:29 MSG).
:: *Now is the time to get rid of anger, rage, malicious behavior, slander, and dirty language* (Colossians 3:8).

JOY

:: *Always be joyful because you belong to the Lord. I will say it again. Be joyful* (Philippians 4:4 NIrv).
:: *Shout to the LORD with joy, everyone on earth. Worship the LORD with gladness. Come to him with songs of joy. I want you to realize that the LORD is God. He made us, and we belong to him. We are his people. We are the sheep belonging to his flock* (Psalm 100:1–3 NIrv).
:: *Fruit the Holy Spirit produces is love, joy and peace* (Galatians 5:22 NIrv).

IN TOUGH TIMES

:: *Paul and Silas. . .stripped and beaten with wooden rods. . .were thrown into prison. . . . Around midnight Paul and Silas were praying and singing hymns to God, and the other prisoners were listening* (Acts 16:22, 23, 25).
:: *Churches in Macedonia. . .are being tested by many troubles, and they are very poor. But they are also filled with abundant joy, which has overflowed in rich generosity* (2 Corinthians 8:1–2).

(See also *Happiness*.)

There's a time to judge others. And there's a time to mind our own business, leaving the judgment to God. The Bible talks about both situations. Christians have a right—even an obligation—to judge sin among their congregation and to impose discipline. But only God has the right to judge a person's motives and spiritual condition.

TIME TO JUDGE

:: *I can hardly believe the report. . . . I am told that a man in your church is living in sin with his stepmother. . . . You should remove this man from your fellowship* (1 Corinthians 5:1–2). Paul says that confronting the man and expelling him from church might get him to come to his spiritual senses, repent, and change his lifestyle. That's the intent—restoration, not punishment.

:: *"If a Christian friend in your church hurts you by doing something seriously wrong, gently tell your friend about it. If you can work it out, you've saved your friendship. If your attempt fails, try again—this time with one or two witnesses. If that fails, too, take the matter to the church leaders. If your friend refuses to listen to the church, treat that person as a sinful outsider—not as a Christian friend"* (Matthew 18:15–17 AUTHOR'S PARAPHRASE).

:: *Don't listen to any charge against a church leader, unless at least two or three people bring the same charges. But if any of the leaders should keep on sinning, they must be corrected in front of the whole group, as a warning to everyone else* (1 Timothy 5:19–20 CEV).

:: *When one of you has a dispute with another believer, how dare you file a lawsuit and ask a secular court to decide the matter instead of taking it to other believers! . . . Isn't there anyone in all the church who is wise enough to decide these issues? But instead, one believer sues another—right in front of unbelievers!* (1 Corinthians 6:1, 5–6). Paul pleads with Christians in the same congregation to work out their differences.

TIME TO MIND OUR OWN BUSINESS

:: *"Don't pick on people, jump on their failures, criticize their faults—unless, of course, you want the same treatment. That critical spirit has a way of boomeranging"* (Matthew 7:1–2 MSG). In his famous Sermon on the Mount, Jesus warns that if we're harsh in our judgments of others, people will tend to judge us harshly, too. And he adds in later verses that we've got faults of our own.

:: *Every time you criticize someone, you condemn yourself. It takes one to know one. Judgmental criticism of others is a well-known way of escaping detection in your own crimes* (Romans 2:1 MSG).

:: *"All right, hurl the stones at her until she dies. But only he who never sinned may throw the first!"* (John 8:7 TLB). Jesus is talking to a group of Jews asking his permission to stone a woman to death. She was caught having sex with a man other than her husband. The men eventually drop their stones and walk away.

:: *Welcome with open arms fellow believers who don't see things the way you do. And don't jump all over them every time they do or say something you don't agree with—even when it seems that they are strong on opinions but weak in the faith department* (Romans 14:1 MSG). Paul is telling Christians not to condemn each other over debatable subjects, such as whether or not to eat kosher meat.

The Bible talks about a Last Judgment, when God will separate good people from evil ones, rewarding the good and punishing the bad. Scholars debate how literally to take any of the Bible's descriptions of reward and punishment.

:: *Each person is destined to die once and after that comes judgment* (Hebrews 9:27).

:: *"On judgment day, people will have to account for every careless word they have spoken"* (Matthew 12:36 NIrv).

:: *We must all stand before Christ to be judged. We will each receive whatever we deserve for the good or evil we have done in this earthly body* (2 Corinthians 5:10).

:: *I saw the dead, both great and small, standing before God's throne. . . . And all were judged according to their deeds. . . . And anyone whose name was not found recorded in the Book of Life was thrown into the lake of fire* (Revelation 20:12–13, 15). "Lake of fire," many Bible experts say, is another way of referring to hell.

As the Bible reports it, God is perfectly just. And he wants to see us practicing justice more than he wants to see worship rituals, such as the animal sacrifices of Old Testament times.

OF GOD

:: *The Lord reigns forever. . . . He will judge the world with justice. . . . The Lord is known for his justice* (Psalm 9:7–8, 16).

:: *The righteous Lord loves justice* (Psalm 11:7).

OF GOD'S PEOPLE

:: *"I hate all your show and pretense—the hypocrisy of your religious festivals. . . . I will not accept your burnt offerings. . . . Away with your noisy hymns. . . . Instead, I want to see a mighty flood of justice, an endless river of righteous living"* (Amos 5:21–24).

:: *Turn your courts into true halls of justice* (Amos 5:15).

:: *"In a lawsuit, you must not deny justice to the poor"* (Exodus 23:6).

NOT GUILTY. High-priced lawyer Robert Shapiro, left, directs a legal dream team that manages to get former football star O. J. Simpson, right, acquitted of the murder of Simpson's ex-wife and one of her friends. Many saw this acquittal in 1994 as proof that if you have the money to hire the best lawyers, you can gut justice. Jurors in a civil trial three years later found Simpson liable in the wrongful death of both victims. Bible writers plead for a fair and balanced justice system.

JUSTIFICATION

A Bible scholar's term, it refers to people getting right with God. But God's the one making it happen, by offering forgiveness. Some Christians explain it this way: *Justify* means "just as if I had never sinned."

:: *God has shown us how to become right with him. . . . We are made right with God by putting our faith in Jesus Christ. That happens to all who believe* (Romans 3:21–22 NIrV).

:: *You can't make things right between you and God. A lifetime of good deeds won't do it. Good news: God already did it—2,000 years ago when he sent his Son to take the punishment for your sins. All you have to do is believe it* (Romans 4:5 AUTHOR'S PARAPHRASE).

:: *We have been made right with God because of our faith. Now we have peace with him because of our Lord Jesus Christ* (Romans 5:1 NIrV).

(See also *Forgiveness, Salvation.*)

KINDNESS

:: *Kind words are like honey—sweet to the soul and healthy for the body* (Proverbs 16:24).

:: *Be kind to each other, tenderhearted, forgiving one another, just as God through Christ has forgiven you* (Ephesians 4:32).

:: *The LORD is righteous in everything he does; he is filled with kindness* (Psalm 145:17).

KINGDOM OF GOD (OF HEAVEN)

The kingdom of God and the kingdom of heaven mean the same thing. Surprisingly, most scholars say, they don't mean heaven. Both phrases refer to everyone devoted to God—willing subjects of God, in heaven and on earth. People who refuse to obey God are not citizens of his kingdom. Jesus invited people to become citizens of God's kingdom.

:: *"The Kingdom of God can't be detected by visible signs. You won't be able to say, 'Here it is!' or 'It's over there!' For the Kingdom of God is already among you"* (Luke 17:20–21). That's Jesus talking.

BIG HEARTS IN THE BIG APPLE. Near Central Park in New York City, a couple notices a man laboring to get to the bus stop. He has to rest after every few steps. When the couple offers to lend a hand, he gratefully accepts, as a passerby smiles her approval. ▼

:: "God's kingdom is here. Change your life and believe the Message" (Mark 1:15 MSG).

:: "How can I describe the Kingdom of God? What story should I use to illustrate it? It is like a mustard seed planted in the ground. It is the smallest of all seeds, but it becomes the largest of all garden plants" (Mark 4:30–32). Jesus used parables to help people understand what God's kingdom is like and how God's people should live as citizens of God's kingdom.

:: "The Kingdom of Heaven is like a merchant on the lookout for choice pearls. When he discovered a pearl of great value, he sold everything he owned and bought it!" (Matthew 13:45–46).

:: Unjust people who don't care about God will not be joining in his kingdom. Those who use and abuse each other, use and abuse sex, use and abuse the earth and everything in it, don't qualify as citizens in God's kingdom (1 Corinthians 6:9–10 MSG).

:: "God blesses those who are poor and realize their need for him, for the Kingdom of Heaven is theirs" (Matthew 5:3). Jesus begins his famous Sermon on the Mount with this statement, part of a short section in the sermon called the Beatitudes. These Beatitudes describe some of the ideal characteristics of a citizen in God's kingdom. A sampling: they are humble and merciful, they are pure-hearted, and they work for peace.

LAMB OF GOD

Some Bible writers called Jesus the Lamb of God because he became like a sacrificial lamb, dying to atone for the sins of humans. Jewish law said that sacrificial lambs couldn't have any defects.

:: John [the Baptist] saw Jesus coming toward him and said, "Look! The Lamb of God who takes away the sin of the world!" (John 1:29).

:: God paid a ransom to save you. . . . And the ransom he paid was not mere gold or silver. It was the precious blood of Christ, the sinless, spotless Lamb of God (1 Peter 1:18–19).

LAST DAYS (END TIMES)

In the Bible, "last days" or "end times" doesn't always refer to the final months or years of human life on earth. Scholars say it sometimes refers to the end of the Jewish nation, wiped off the political map in 586 BC by Babylonian invaders from what is now Iran. It can also refer to the fall of Jerusalem in AD 70, when Romans destroyed the city and its Temple—ending the Jewish sacrificial system of worship.

THEORY 1: THEY STARTED 2,000 YEARS AGO

:: Dear children, we are living in the last days (1 John 2:18 NIRV). John wrote that roughly 700,000 days ago—about 1,900 years. Many scholars say that by "last days" John was talking about the final stage in God's plan to save humanity from the self-destructive effects of sin. The "last days" begins with Jesus' first coming as the ultimate sacrifice for sins. And it ends when he comes again to take his followers to their eternal reward.

:: " 'In the last days,' God says, 'I will pour out my Spirit upon all people' " (Acts 2:17). The apostle Peter, quoting a prophecy in Joel, declared that God had fulfilled this prediction on that very day, with the arrival of the Holy Spirit.

:: God chose him [Jesus] as your ransom long before the world began, but he has now revealed him to you in these last days (1 Peter 1:20).

BIG BANG, THE SEQUEL. A nuke gets tested on a French Polynesian atoll in 1970. Some students of the Bible read about the last days and say they see links to a nuclear holocaust. Yet the Bible says the "last days" began during the time of Jesus. And many Bible experts say the "end times" the Bible talks about usually refers to the end of Jerusalem in AD 70, when a Roman invasion force leveled the city and its Jewish Temple. The Jewish religion never recovered. The main worship practice—which involved offering animal sacrifices at the Temple—came to an end.

THEORY 2: THEY'LL END WHEN JESUS RETURNS

:: *[Jesus' disciples ask him], "What sign will signal your return and the end of the world?" Jesus told them. . ."The Good News about the Kingdom will be preached throughout the whole world, so that all nations will hear it; and then the end will come. . . . And they will see the Son of Man coming on the clouds of heaven with power and great glory"* (Matthew 24:3–4, 14, 30). Jesus offers a long list of signs,

many of which scholars say were fulfilled when Romans destroyed Jerusalem in AD 70. Some early believers apparently saw the link because as the Roman army approached, many Christians saved themselves by taking Jesus' advice: "Those in Judea must flee to the hills" (Matthew 24:16). Other signs Jesus talked about, however, seem to point to a day yet to come. The speech is laced in symbolism, scholars say. So it's hard to know what to take literally.

:: *As my vision continued that night, I saw someone like a son of man coming with the clouds of heaven. . . . He was given authority, honor, and sovereignty over all the nations. . . . His rule is eternal* (Daniel 7:13–14). New Testament writers and Jesus himself seemed to understand Daniel's vision as a prediction of Jesus' Second Coming.

LAST SUPPER

The last meal Jesus ate with his disciples, hours before his arrest. Jews tried him overnight. The next morning, they convinced the Roman governor, Pilate, to crucify him. Christians commemorate the meal and Jesus' sacrificial death with a ritual called by various names: communion, the Lord's Supper, Mass, the Eucharist.

:: *Jesus took some bread and blessed it. Then he broke it in pieces and gave it to the disciples, saying, "Take it, for this is my body." And he took a cup of wine. . . . And he said to them, "This is my blood. . . . It is poured out as a sacrifice for many"* (Mark 14:22–24).

(See also *Communion.*)

JESUS' LAST MEAL, A few hours before his arrest, Jesus has one final meal with his 12 disciples. He gives them bread and wine, saying it is his body and blood. He asks that in the days to come, whenever they eat the bread and drink the wine, they remember him. This began what is perhaps Christianity's most revered ritual: Holy Communion.

LAUGHTER

:: *I'm thanking you, GOD, from a full heart, I'm writing the book on your wonders. I'm whistling, laughing, and jumping for joy* (Psalm 9:1-2 MSG).

:: *There is a time to cry. And there's a time to laugh. There is a time to be sad. And there's a time to dance* (Ecclesiastes 3:4 NIrV).

:: *Don't laugh when your enemy falls; don't crow over his collapse* (Proverbs 24:17 MSG).

LAW

Law in the Bible usually refers to the laws God gave the Jewish people, delivered by Moses at Mount Sinai. These laws aren't just the 10 Commandments. They include the hundreds of other laws about how to live and worship. They're preserved in the books of Exodus, Leviticus, Numbers, and Deuteronomy. Moses said he got these laws from God during the year that he and the other Jews camped at the foot of Mount Sinai, after their escape from slavery in Egypt.

:: *These are the laws, decrees, and regulations that Moses gave to the people of Israel when they left Egypt* (Deuteronomy 4:45).

:: *"You must diligently obey the commands of the Lord your God—all the laws and decrees he has given you. Do what is right and good in the Lord's sight, so all will go well with you"* (Deuteronomy 6:17–18).

:: *"The day is coming," says the Lord, "when I will make a new covenant with the people of Israel and Judah. This covenant will not be like the one I made with their ancestors when I took them by the hand and brought them out of the land of Egypt. They broke that covenant. . . . But this is the new covenant I will make with the people of Israel on that day," says the Lord. "I will put my instructions deep within them, and I will write them on their hearts"* (Jeremiah 31:31–33).

:: *When God speaks of a "new" covenant, it means he has made the first one obsolete. It is now out of date and will soon disappear* (Hebrews 8:13). New Testament writers taught that the arrival of the Holy Spirit marked the beginning of God's new agreement with people. They no longer had to follow Old Testament laws. Instead, they would follow their hearts, guided by God's Spirit.

(See also *10 Commandments*.)

LAZINESS

There were apparently a lot of lazy people in Bible times, because there are plenty of verses addressing laziness—about 20 in Proverbs alone. Every Bible verse about laziness condemns it. Here are a few of the more interesting:

CLEAN AND JERK. Ants can lift anywhere from 10 to 50 times their own weight, depending on the ant. Their skeleton on the outside gives their muscles extra leverage. And they seem forever using that leverage, constantly working. That may be why Bible writers pointed them out as a great example to follow: "You lazy fool, look at an ant. Watch it closely; let it teach you a thing or two" (Proverbs 6:6 MSG).

:: *Just as a door turns on its hinges, so a lazy-bones turns back over in bed* (Proverbs 26:14 MSG).

:: *Keep away from every believer who doesn't want to work. . . . When we were with you, we gave you a rule. We said, "Anyone who will not work will not eat"* (2 Thessalonians 3:6, 10 NIrV). Paul wasn't opposing social welfare, which offers help for people who can't work. He was against what scholars guess was a group of Christians who thought Jesus was coming back at any moment. So they quit working and lived off the generosity of others.

:: *Hiring a lazy person is like eating leftovers from a trash can. Eventually, it'll make you want to puke* (Proverbs 10:26 AUTHOR'S PARAPHRASE).

:: *Lazy people come up with crazy excuses for not working. "I can't cut the grass today. There's a cougar on the loose!"* (Proverbs 22:13 AUTHOR'S PARAPHRASE).

:: *Lazy people want all they can get. They get what they deserve: a big pile of nothing. It's the hard workers who get what they want, and deserve what they get* (Proverbs 13:4 AUTHOR'S PARAPHRASE).

:: *Do not be lazy but work hard, serving the Lord with all your heart* (Romans 12:11 NCV).

LEADERSHIP

:: *"Whoever wants to be a leader among you must be your servant. . . . For even the Son of Man came not to be served but to serve"* (Matthew 20:26, 28).

:: *It's important that a church leader, responsible for the affairs in God's house, be looked up to—not pushy, not short-tempered, not a drunk, not a bully, not money-hungry. He must welcome people, be helpful, wise, fair, reverent, have a good grip on himself, and have a good grip on the Message, knowing how to use the truth to either spur people on in knowledge or stop them in their tracks if they oppose it* (Titus 1:7-9 MSG). This was Paul's advice to Titus, who was starting churches and selecting church leaders on the island of Crete.

LEGALISM

Some groups of Jews in Bible times—especially scholars called Pharisees—taught that people could earn God's favor by keeping a long list of religious rules, not only the laws in the Bible, but laws promoted by leading rabbis throughout the centuries. These rules were a bit like the rules in some church manuals today: don't drink alcohol, don't smoke, and don't gamble. Many Jews considered these man-made rules every bit as important as the 10 Commandments. Jesus disagreed.

RULE MAKER. Pharisees, the Jewish scholars of Jesus' day, observed a bunch of religious rules not in the Bible. And they expected others to follow those rules, too. Some rule-bent preachers today do the same kind of thing, many Christians say. They come up with their own rules, and try to guilt people into following them. That approach didn't work on Jesus.

:: "You're hopeless, you religion scholars and Pharisees! Frauds! You keep meticulous account books, tithing on every nickel and dime you get, but on the meat of God's Law, things like fairness and compassion and commitment—the absolute basics!—you carelessly take it or leave it" (Matthew 23:23 MSG).

:: No one can ever be made right with God by doing what the law commands. The law simply shows us how sinful we are (Romans 3:20).

:: Even though the Gentiles were not trying to follow God's standards, they were made right with God. And it was by faith that this took place. But the people of Israel, who tried so hard to get right with God by keeping the law, never succeeded. Why not? Because they were trying to get right with God by keeping the law instead of by trusting in him (Romans 9:30–32).

:: God saved you by his grace when you believed. And you can't take credit for this; it is a gift from God. Salvation is not a reward for the good things we have done (Ephesians 2:8–9).

:: I was a member of the Pharisees, who demand the strictest obedience to the Jewish law. . . . I once thought these things were valuable, but now I consider them worthless because of what Christ has done. . . . I no longer count on my own righteousness through obeying the law; rather, I become righteous through faith in Christ (Philippians 3:5, 7, 9). This is the apostle Paul talking.

:: Christ has already accomplished the purpose for which the law was given. As a result, all who believe in him are made right with God (Romans 10:4). The law was given to point people to God. As the New Testament writers tell it, the life and teachings of Jesus did that better than any list of laws ever could.

(See also *Law*.)

LONELINESS

:: "You can be sure that I am always with you, to the very end" (Matthew 28:20 NIrV). That's Jesus talking to his followers.

:: God has said, "I will never leave you. I will never desert you" (Hebrews 13:5 NIrV).

:: "Don't be afraid, for I am with you. Don't be discouraged, for I am your God" (Isaiah 41:10).

:: I'm absolutely convinced that nothing—nothing living or dead, angelic or demonic, today or tomorrow, high or low, thinkable or unthinkable—absolutely nothing can get between us and God's love because of the way that Jesus our Master has embraced us (Romans 8:38–39 MSG).

:: God gives the lonely a home (Psalm 68:6 NCV).

ALONE IN A CROWD. Surrounded by hundreds of souls in New York City's Grand Central Station, one woman waits alone. ▶

LORD

It doesn't mean "God," though it can refer to him. A title of respect, *lord* can mean "ruler," "master," or even "sir."

GOD THE FATHER

:: "I am the LORD your God, who rescued you from the land of Egypt, the place of your slavery" (Exodus 20:2).

JESUS

:: At the name of Jesus every knee should bow . . .and every tongue confess that Jesus Christ is Lord (Philippians 2:10–11).

HUMANS

:: *"Listen, my lord, you are an honored prince among us"* (Genesis 23:6). Hittite elders, addressing Abraham, father of the Jews.

LOVE

Love isn't just a feeling. It's a decision to act in the best interest of someone else because we want that person to be happy.

THE GREATEST LOVE OF ALL

:: *"This is the very best way to love. Put your life on the line for your friends"* (John 15:13 MSG). Fortunately, most of us never have to do this. But many have—often on the battlefield or in other moments of extreme danger.

:: *This is how we've come to understand and experience love: Christ sacrificed his life for us. This is why we ought to live sacrificially for our fellow believers, and not just be out for ourselves* (1 John 3:16 MSG). Using Jesus as the ultimate example of selflessness, John urges Christians to follow Christ's example of putting others first.

ROMANTIC LOVE

:: *A bowl of vegetables with someone you love is better than steak with someone you hate* (Proverbs 15:17).

:: *Kiss me and kiss me again, for your love is sweeter than wine* (Song of Solomon 1:2).

:: *My lover is mine, and I am his* (Song of Solomon 2:16).

:: *The passion of love bursting into flame is more powerful than death, stronger than the grave. Love cannot be drowned by oceans or floods;*

LOVE FOR THE LONG HAUL. With a peck in the park, an elderly gentleman lets it be known: when it comes to the love of his life, there's still life to the love.

it cannot be bought, no matter what is offered (Song of Solomon 8:6–7 CEV).

THE IMPORTANCE OF LOVE

:: " 'Love the LORD your God with all your heart, all your soul, and all your mind.' This is the first and greatest commandment. A second is equally important: 'Love your neighbor as yourself' " (Matthew 22:37–39). This is the answer Jesus gives to a scholar asking which of the hundreds of commandments in the Bible is the most important.

:: The three most important things to have are faith, hope and love. But the greatest of them is love (1 Corinthians 13:13 NIrV). In an entire chapter praising the value of love, Paul says there's no trait better.

GOD'S LOVE FOR US

:: God loved the people of this world so much that he gave his only Son, so that everyone who has faith in him will have eternal life and never really die (John 3:16 CEV). This is what some Christian scholars have said is the Bible's message summed up in one sentence.

:: Nothing in all creation will ever be able to separate us from the love of God that is revealed in Christ Jesus our Lord (Romans 8:39).

:: His faithful love endures forever (Psalm 106:1). Repeated dozens of times throughout the Old Testament, this is one of the Bible's most popular ways of describing God—which may be why a New Testament writer concluded: "God is love" (1 John 4:8).

LOVE OTHERS

:: "Here is my command. Love each other, just as I have loved you" (John 15:12 NIrV). A quote from Jesus.

WHEN WE ONLY THINK IT'S LOVE

Sometimes it's hard to tell the difference between love and lust.

At first, they may feel a lot alike. Whether we're in love or in lust, we want to be with the person we desire.

But love and lust approach that goal in radically different ways.

Love is selfless and will actually let go—if that's what the other person wants. When we love another, we put that person's wishes ahead of our own.

Lust is selfish. It tries to figure out ways to manipulate the target. And that's what the person is to us, a target.

In the Bible, a prince named Amnon fell in lust with his half-sister—though he called it love. Pretending to be sick, he arranged for her to come to his bedroom and feed him. He raped her. Afterward, "He hated her even more than he had loved her" (2 Samuel 13:15).

For those wondering if it's love or lust, here's a clue. It's from the Bible's famous essay on the nature of love:

Love cares more for others than for self. Love doesn't want what it doesn't have. . . . Doesn't force itself on others, isn't always "me first."

1 CORINTHIANS 13:4–5 MSG

:: *"Your love for one another will prove to the world that you are my disciples"* (John 13:35).

:: *Don't just pretend that you love others. . . . Love each other with genuine affection, and take delight in honoring each other* (Romans 12:9–10).

:: *"Love your enemies! Do good to those who hate you"* (Luke 6:27).

:: *Put up with each other, and forgive anyone who does you wrong, just as Christ has forgiven you. Love is more important than anything else. It is what ties everything completely together* (Colossians 3:13–14 CEV).

:: *Most important of all, continue to show deep love for each other, for love covers a multitude of sins* (1 Peter 4:8). We sometimes make big mistakes that hurt others. But if the people know we love them, they'll overlook a lot.

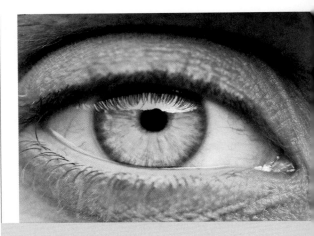

EYE OF THE BEHOLDER. Seen through the eyes of love, another person is our master—someone we want only to please. Seen through the eyes of lust, another person is our servant—someone we want only to please us.

LUST

:: *"Don't think you can get by with 'Look but don't touch.' The leering, longing look of lust can get you into trouble, too. Think 'deer in the headlights' "* (Matthew 5:28 AUTHOR'S PARAPHRASE). Jesus teaches that sin begins in the mind and works its way out to behavior. But even before we act on a lustful thought, merely dwelling on it is dangerous and harmful. For a deer caught in the headlights, that humming sound in the darkened distance isn't the mating moan of Bambi's daddy. It's a diesel truck.

:: *"I warned my eyeballs. If they stare at a pretty woman as though they're undressing her, I'll make them go cross-eyed"* (Job 31:1 AUTHOR'S PARAPHRASE).

:: *Run from anything that stimulates youthful lust* (2 Timothy 2:22).

:: *Keep your minds on whatever is true, pure, right,* holy, friendly, and proper (Philippians 4:8 CEV).

:: *If they can't control themselves, they should go ahead and marry. It's better to marry than to burn with lust* (1 Corinthians 7:9). That's Paul's advice to unmarried people.

:: *Have nothing to do with sexual immorality, impurity, lust, and evil desires* (Colossians 3:5).

(See also *Love, Sex.*)

LYING

:: *Riffraff and rascals talk out of both sides of their mouths* (Proverbs 6:12 MSG).

:: *Telling lies about others is as harmful as hitting them with an ax, wounding them with a sword, or shooting them with a sharp arrow* (Proverbs 25:18).

:: *Do not tell lies about others* (Exodus 20:16 CEV). This is one of the 10 Commandments.

(See also *Cheating.*)

GOD'S PLAN FOR MARRIAGE

:: *A man leaves his father and mother and is joined to his wife, and the two are united into one* (Genesis 2:24).

:: *"They are no longer two people, but one. And no one should separate a couple that God has joined together"* (Mark 10:8–9 CEV).

HOW TO KEEP THE MARRIAGE HEALTHY

:: *A truly good wife is the most precious treasure a man can find. . . . Show her respect—praise her in public* (Proverbs 31:10, 31 CEV).

:: *Submit to one another out of reverence for Christ. For wives, this means submit to your husbands as to the Lord. . . . For husbands, this means love your wives, just as Christ loved the church. He gave up his life for her* (Ephesians 5:21–22, 25). Old-school preachers emphasized verse 22, telling wives to submit to their husbands. But the entire section starts in verse 21, with mutual submission—each putting the other first.

:: *Honor marriage, and guard the sacredness of sexual intimacy between wife and husband* (Hebrews 13:4 MSG).

LOOKING FOR MRS. GOOD CZAR. Eighteen-year-old Russian Czar Alexis (1629–76), future father of Peter the Great, gets his pick of a bride. All six are finalists from a nationwide beauty hunt organized by the czar's guardian—who just happened to be looking for a wife himself. He chose the sister of the woman Alexis married.

:: *The marriage bed must be a place of mutuality—the husband seeking to satisfy his wife, the wife seeking to satisfy her husband. Marriage is not a place to "stand up for your rights." Marriage is a decision to serve the other, whether in bed or out* (1 Corinthians 7:3–4 MSG).

CHRISTIANS MARRIED TO NON-CHRISTIANS

:: *If you are a man with a wife who is not a believer but who still wants to live with you, hold on to her. If you are a woman with a husband who is not a believer but he wants to live with you, hold on to him. . . . You never know, wife: The way you handle this might bring your husband not only back to you but to God. You never know, husband: The way you handle this might bring your wife not only back to you but to God* (1 Corinthians 7:12–13, 16 MSG).

SURPRISING FACTS

:: *"A newly married man must not be drafted into the army or given any other official responsibilities. He must be free to spend one year at home, bringing happiness to the wife he has married"* (Deuteronomy 24:5).

:: *"People in this world get married. . . . But it will not be like that when the dead rise. Those who are considered worthy to take part in what happens at that time won't get married. . . . They are like the angels. They are God's children. They will be given a new form of life"* (Luke 20:34–36 NIrV). Answering a question about who in heaven will be the husband of a widow who remarried, Jesus says in heaven we'll all be single, like the angels.

(See also *Sex.*)

Considered a spiritual practice—often associated with prayer—meditation is thinking about God and about things of God, such as how to live like citizens of his kingdom.

:: *"Don't for a minute let this Book of The Revelation be out of mind. Ponder and meditate on it day and night, making sure you practice everything written in it"* (Joshua 1:8 MSG). The "Book" was the laws God had given Moses to deliver to the Jews. It was the only Bible they had at the moment.

:: *Happy are those who. . .love the LORD's teachings, and they think about those teachings day and night* (Psalm 1:1–2 NCV).

:: *Let my words and my thoughts be pleasing to you, LORD* (Psalm 19:14 CEV).

(See also *Prayer.*)

MORNING DEVOTIONS. A Russian monk starts the day by turning his thoughts to God, in prayer and Bible reading.

It's helping people who can't help themselves. And, sometimes, it's showing kindness to someone who doesn't come anywhere close to deserving it. The Bible says that's what God does for humans when he offers them forgiveness even before they ask for it.

:: *"Have mercy on others. God had mercy on you"* (Luke 6:36 AUTHOR'S PARAPHRASE).

:: *"God blesses those who are merciful, for they will be shown mercy"* (Matthew 5:7). Jesus, delivering one of his Beatitudes during his Sermon on the Mount.

:: *If you refuse to act kindly, you can hardly expect to be treated kindly. Kind mercy wins over harsh judgment every time* (James 2:13 MSG).

:: *God has chosen you and made you his holy people. He loves you. So you should always clothe yourselves with mercy, kindness, humility, gentleness, and patience* (Colossians 3:12 NCV).

(See also *Grace.*)

MESSIAH

It's a Hebrew word. But in Greek, the international language of Jesus' day, *messiah* translates into "christ." In English, *messiah* and *christ* both mean the same thing. It's a title: "the anointed one." Jews often referred to their kings as God's "anointed one." As part of the coronation ceremony, a priest would anoint the king's head with olive oil. When Romans occupied the Jewish homeland, many Jews expected God to send a warrior king messiah to save them from this oppression. Instead, the New Testament says God sent a pacifist rabbi Messiah to save them from themselves.

TO ANOINT A KING. This golden flask held the sacred olive oil used to anoint England's King Charles 1 (1600–49). Messiah means "the anointed one," and in Bible times the term commonly referred to the king. In Jesus' day, the Jews were expecting a unique Messiah who would restore the lost glory of Israel.

:: *Samuel took the flask of olive oil he had brought and anointed David with the oil. And the Spirit of the LORD came powerfully upon David from that day on* (1 Samuel 16:13).

:: *"The Anointed One will be killed, appearing to have accomplished nothing, and a ruler will arise whose armies will destroy the city and the Temple"* (Daniel 9:26). Some Bible students say this prophecy, dated to several centuries before Jesus, sounds like it's talking about his crucifixion and about what happened to Jerusalem some 40 years after his ministry. Roman armies led by Titus leveled Jerusalem, destroying the only Jewish Temple in existence. It has never been rebuilt. A

1,300-year-old Muslim shrine now sits on the spot: the shimmering, gold-crested Dome of the Rock—Jerusalem's defining landmark.

:: *Herod brought together the chief priests. . .and asked them, "Where will the Messiah be born?" They told him, "He will be born in Bethlehem, just as the prophet wrote, 'Bethlehem. . . . From your town will come a leader, who will be like a shepherd for my people Israel' "* (Matthew 2:4–6 CEV). King Herod was reacting to news that wise men had come to worship the newborn king of the Jews. Herod presumed the long-awaited messiah had finally arrived, since he didn't have a newborn son. Intent on preserving his dynasty, Herod reportedly ordered the execution of baby boys in Bethlehem.

:: *The woman said [to Jesus], "I know the Messiah is coming—the one who is called Christ. When he comes, he will explain everything to us." Then Jesus told her, "I AM the Messiah!"* (John 4:25–26).

:: *Andrew went to find his brother, Simon [Peter], and told him, "We have found the Messiah"* (John 1:41). Andrew was talking about Jesus.

:: *The kingdom of the world is now the Kingdom of our God and his Messiah! He will rule forever and ever!* (Revelation 11:15 MSG).

MIRACLES

In the Bible, miracles are God using his power in a way that seems to defy a rational, scientific explanation. Sometimes God works on his own, like when he appears before Moses in the burning bush. Sometimes God works through individuals such as prophets or Jesus' disciples. People believed Jesus and later his disciples, the Bible says, mainly because their miracles provided jaw-dropping evidence that they got their power

EXODUS BADLANDS. Moses led two to three million Jews through these south Sinai badlands, according to a literal reading of the Bible story. Some Christians say the numbers of Israelites were probably much lower, given the harsh conditions of the land.

DANGER: MIRACLE BUSTERS AHEAD

Try offering a reasonable explanation for a miracle in the Bible—any miracle—and see what you get. It doesn't take a prophet to call this one.

You'll irritate the devil out of some Christians.

:: **Moses leads two to three million souls— the population of Chicago—through the desolate Sinai badlands.** For 40 years. He actually led about 600,000 men, according to Exodus 12:37. But the numbers mushroom into millions when we add women and children. Some scholars say those numbers are symbolic and that Moses probably led only about 20,000 souls. (See "Two to three million refugees," page 258.)

:: **God stops the Jordan River so the Jews can cross into the Promised Land** (Joshua 3:16). The river sits on a fault line. Quakes have shaken loose steep cliffs upstream, which have dammed up the river many times, as in 1927 at the same site mentioned in the Bible: the riverside village of Adam north of Jericho. (See page 278.)

:: **God drops Jericho's walls a short time later** (Joshua 6:20). Aftershocks might have caused it, some speculate. (See page 278.)

Scholars who pitch ideas like these are diminishing God, some Christians insist. They're dissing the supernatural side of God's miracles. And they're ignoring the obvious, literal read that the writer intended—that God performed a supernatural miracle.

But some scholars argue that offering ideas about how God did what he did doesn't diminish the fact that it was still God doing the doing. However he did it.

Most Bible scholars agree there are miracles in the Bible that defy scientific explanation. But the experts are quick to add that some miracles track quite nicely with science. And the scholars say it shouldn't bother us when God works within the laws of physics, since he created them.

from God. Miracles—not the least of which was Jesus rising from the dead—jump-started the Christian movement.

:: *"What if they won't believe me or listen to me? What if they say, 'The Lord never appeared to you'?"* (Exodus 4:1). That's Moses telling God the Jews in Egypt might not believe God sent him to free them. God shows Moses several miracles he'll perform to convince the Jews.

:: *"You have seen the Lord perform all these mighty deeds with your own eyes!"* (Deuteronomy 11:7). Moses is reminding the Jews during their exodus out of Egypt about the many miracles God used to free them: plagues that convinced Pharaoh to free them; parting the water for an escape route when Pharaoh changed his mind and sent his army to bring them back; food and water in the desolate badlands.

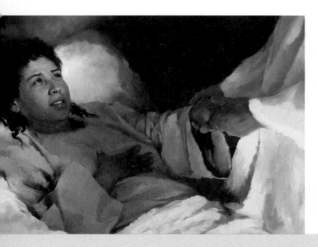

RAISING THE DEAD. Jesus overhears messengers telling Jairus, synagogue leader in the fishing village of Capernaum, that his sick daughter has died. Jesus goes home with him and abruptly stops the weeping crowd by raising the girl from the dead—one of several people the Bible says he resurrected.

:: *Jesus traveled throughout the region of Galilee, teaching in the synagogues. . . . People soon began bringing to him all who were sick. And whatever their sickness or disease, or if they were demon possessed or epileptic or paralyzed—he healed them all* (Matthew 4:23–24).

:: *Because of the miraculous signs Jesus did in Jerusalem at the Passover celebration, many began to trust in him* (John 2:23). These miracles are what convinced many skeptics that Jesus was the genuine, God-endorsed article—the Messiah that the prophets had said was coming to save Israel.

:: *Jesus provided far more God-revealing signs [miracles] than are written down in this book. These are written down so you will believe that Jesus is the Messiah, the Son of God, and in the act of believing, have real and eternal life* (John 20:30–31 MSG).

:: *"It is not this man's sin or his parents' sin that made him blind. This man was born blind so that God's power could be shown in him"* (John 9:3 NCV). Jesus explains the reason for the blind man's disease moments before healing him.

(See also *Healing*.)

MODESTY

:: *Ladies, dress modestly. Wear decent clothes that don't accessorize your curves or showcase your other body parts that tempt men. You really shouldn't be drawing attention to yourself in this way, crowning yourself like a beauty queen with a fancy hairdo and draping your body with the sleek designer clothes and*

LOOKER. Church leaders Peter and Paul both asked women to dress modestly. Paul, a bachelor, asked the ladies to please cover their tempting curves, perhaps because female curves attract male eyeballs like steelies to a magnet.

lavish jewelry you'd expect to see on runway models. Model Christianity instead. Don't work on looking beautiful. Work on being beautiful (1 Timothy 2:9–10 AUTHOR'S PARAPHRASE). This is Paul's advice, which he wants Pastor Timothy to pass along to the congregation in Ephesus, on what is now Turkey's west coast. For the record, Paul was single.

:: *Don't depend on things like fancy hairdos or gold jewelry or expensive clothes to make you look beautiful. Be beautiful in your heart by being gentle and quiet. This kind of beauty will last, and God considers it very special* (1 Peter 3:3–4 CEV).

(See also *Temptation*.)

MONEY

We're fond of money. Most of us want as much as we can get. But the Bible plants danger signs all around money.

DANGERS

:: *Those who love money will never have enough. How meaningless to think that wealth brings true happiness! The more you have, the more people come to help you spend it. So what good is wealth—except perhaps to watch it slip through your fingers!* (Ecclesiastes 5:10–11).

:: *"Don't store treasures for yourselves here on earth where moths and rust will destroy them and thieves can break in and steal them. But store your treasures in heaven . . . . Your heart will be where your treasure is"* (Matthew 6:19–21 NCV).

:: *Keep your lives free from the love of money, and be satisfied with what you have* (Hebrews 13:5 NCV).

:: *"It is easier for a camel to go through the eye of a needle than for a rich person to enter the Kingdom of God!"* (Mark 10:25). Most Bible experts say Jesus was exaggerating a bit to make his point that money often lures people into building their own kingdom instead of working hard at being a good citizen in God's kingdom.

:: *"No servant can serve two masters at the same time. He will hate one of them and love the other. . . . You can't serve God and Money at the same time"* (Luke 16:13 NIrV).

:: *The love of money causes all kinds of trouble. Some people want money so much that they have given up their faith and caused themselves a lot of pain* (1 Timothy 6:10 CEV).

BE GENEROUS

:: *Remind the rich to be generous and share what they have* (1 Timothy 6:17–19 CEV).

:: *"I have demonstrated to you how necessary it is to work on behalf of the weak and not exploit them. You'll not likely go wrong here if you keep remembering that our Master said, 'You're far happier giving than getting' "* (Acts 20:35 MSG). That's Paul saying a last good-bye to believers from Ephesus, whom he says he never expects to see again. He's arrested in Jerusalem later.

:: *"Give and you'll receive far more than you ever gave. Give a box lightly packed. Get back a box tightly packed: filled, shaken to settle the contents, and filled some more. The bigger box you give, the bigger box you get. Life works that way in God's kingdom"* (Luke 6:38 AUTHOR'S PARAPHRASE).

:: *If someone has enough money to live well and sees a brother or sister in need but shows no compassion—how can God's love be in that person?* (1 John 3:17).

Music was important to worshippers in Bible times. Psalms is actually a collection of song lyrics once set to music. If the words are any clue, the music covered a wide range of styles—from whining blues sung by complaining souls to be-bopping jigs suitable for dancing.

LET THE MUSIC BEGIN

:: *I'm ready, God. . .ready from head to toe, ready to sing, ready to raise a tune: "Wake up, soul! Wake up, harp! Wake up, lute!"* (Psalm 57:7–8 MSG).

:: *Sing joyfully to God! . . . Let the music begin. Play the tambourines. Play sweet music on harps and lyres* (Psalm 81:1–2 NIrV).

:: *Come, everyone! Clap your hands! Shout to God with joyful praise! For the LORD Most High is awesome* (Psalm 47:1–2).

MUSIC MAKERS

:: *Miriam. . .led the other women out to play their tambourines and to dance. Then she sang to them: "Sing praises to the LORD for his*

MUSIC THERAPY. With the soothing strum of a harp, young David calms King Saul—who's suffering from chronic depression. Royal advisors came up with the idea. "Let us find a good musician to play the harp whenever the tormenting spirit troubles you. He will play soothing music, and you will soon be well again" (1 Samuel 16:16).

great victory! He has thrown the horses and their riders into the sea" (Exodus 15:20–21 CEV). This was a victory song after God parted the water for the Jews to escape from Egypt, and then the water collapsed onto the Egyptian army, drowning the soldiers as they chased the Jews.

:: *Saul's advisors said, "This awful tormenting depression from God is making your life miserable. O master, let us help. Let us look for someone who can play the harp. When the black mood from God moves in, he'll play his music and you'll feel better"* (1 Samuel 16:15–16 MSG). Before the shepherd boy David became a giant killer, he worked as King Saul's music therapist, playing a harp to calm him.

:: *About midnight Paul and Silas were praying and singing praises to God, while the other prisoners listened* (Acts 16:25 CEV).

:: *David chose some people to be in charge of the music in the house of the LORD* (1 Chronicles 6:31 NCV). After King David set up a tent worship center in Jerusalem, he assigned singers and instrumentalists—nearly 300—to help lead worship there. His son Solomon later built the Temple there.

OBESITY (OVEREATING)

Obesity wasn't nearly the problem in Bible times that it is in many developed nations today. That's because most people back then had to sweat through hard physical labor to survive. They burned off the calories, and they didn't have nearly as much rich food to eat.

:: *All they want is easy street. . . . Those who live there make their bellies their gods; belches are their praise; all they can think*

of is their appetites (Philippians 3:18–19 MSG). The apostle Paul is talking about people who worship the pleasures of life instead of worshipping God.

:: *Your body is a sacred place, the place of the Holy Spirit. . . . Don't you see that you can't live however you please, squandering what God paid such a high price for? The physical part of*

CIRCUS FAT, CIRCA 1941. A generation ago, a man weighing in at about 300 pounds (136 kg) could land a gig on the "Fattest Man" sideshow at the Vermont State Fair. Today, with one in three Americans obese, he'd be just another vender selling corndogs. A person is diagnosed as obese if they have a body mass index (BMI) of 30 or higher; it's a ratio of height to weight. The Centers for Disease Control website has a BMI calculator. Type in your height and weight. Example: if you're 5 foot 10 inches (177 cm) and 210 pounds (95 kg), don't time-travel to your grandpa's Vermont. Your BMI is 30.1.

you is not some piece of property belonging to the spiritual part of you. God owns the whole works. So let people see God in and through your body (1 Corinthians 6:19–20 MSG).

:: *Here's what I want you to do, God helping you: Take your everyday, ordinary life—your sleeping, eating, going-to-work, and walking-around life—and place it before God as an offering* (Romans 12:1 MSG).

:: *"I will destroy those who are fat and power-ful. I will feed them, yes—feed them justice!"* (Ezekiel 34:16). Most people described in the Bible as overweight—as in this case—are rich people who got that way by exploiting the poor. Many developing nations of the world today complain that this is exactly what wealthier nations are doing to them—getting rich and fat off of the products they produce at slave wages.

:: *You women of Samaria are fat cows! You mistreat and abuse the poor and needy, then you say to your husbands, "Bring us more drinks!"* (Amos 4:1 CEV).

OCCULT

Bible writers say it's wrong to consult fortune-tellers or psychics who try to conjure up the dead or predict the future. But as is often the case, the Bible doesn't bother to explain why. One guess: there are good and bad spirits out there—the Bible says so—and the only way we can be sure we're getting advice from a good spirit is to consult God. We don't need a psychic for that.

:: *"I will be against anyone who goes to mediums and fortune-tellers for advice, because that person is being unfaithful to me"* (Leviticus 20:6 NCV). This is one of the laws Moses said God asked him to pass along to the Jews.

:: *Don't let anyone use magic or witchcraft, or try to explain the meaning of signs. Don't let anyone try to control others with magic, and don't let them be mediums or try to talk with the spirits of dead people. The LORD hates anyone who does these things* (Deuteronomy 18:10–12 NCV).

:: *"There's a woman at Endor who can talk to*

spirits of the dead" (1 Samuel 28:7 CEV). The night before his last battle, King Saul asked a psychic to call up the spirit of the dead prophet Samuel to find out how the battle

PSYCHIC CATS OF SANTA MONICA. One brown and white cat spins the fortune-telling wheel on the table. The black cat paws a tiny fortune scroll out of a bowl. The cat in the red jacket takes the money. If we follow the Bible's advice, we don't pull up a chair.

would end. To the psychic's horror, Samuel appeared, and then he correctly predicted that when the battle was over, Saul and his sons would be dead.

:: *"I will put an end to all witchcraft, and there will be no more fortune-tellers"* (Micah 5:12). The prophet Micah predicts that God will punish the Jews for their serial sinning, including sins involving the occult.

:: *We are not fighting against humans. We are fighting against forces and authorities and against rulers of darkness and powers in the spiritual world* (Ephesians 6:12 cev). Though these forces aren't part of the physical dimension, the Bible says they're as real as we are—and they can affect us for better or worse.

(See also *Astrology*.)

ORIGINAL SIN (SINFUL NATURE)

Original sin isn't just the first sin committed by Adam and Eve: eating the forbidden fruit.

It's a sin that affects everyone now, according to many Bible experts. As the theory goes, this sin somehow contaminated God's perfect world, as though it released a spiritual toxin that poisons everyone. Because of this, everyone is born sinful by nature—inclined to do wrong even when they want to do right. Some scholars put it this way: everyone sinned in Adam, humanity's first representative (a tough idea to grasp), and everyone has sinned since Adam (a phrase most folks admit they understand all too well).

HOW IT GOT HERE

:: *When Adam sinned, sin entered the world. Adam's sin brought death, so death spread to everyone, for everyone sinned* (Romans 5:12).

HOW IT AFFECTS US

:: *There is nothing good in my sinful nature. I want to do what is good, but I can't. I don't do the good things I want to do. I keep on doing the evil things I don't want to do* (Romans 7:18–20 nirv).

THE FIRST SIN. As the Bible tells it, God gave the first human couple one rule to obey: don't eat fruit from a particular tree because it's a killer. Adam and Eve ate it anyhow. In that moment, many scholars say, the very nature of human beings changed. Not for the better.

:: *I love God's law with all my heart. But there is another power within me that is at war with my mind. This power makes me a slave to the sin that is still within me* (Romans 7:22–23).

WHAT TO DO ABOUT IT

:: *Who will free me from this life that is dominated by sin and death? Thank God! The answer is in Jesus Christ our Lord* (Romans 7:24–25).

:: *The Holy Spirit will give you life that comes from Christ Jesus and will set you free from sin and death* (Romans 8:2 CEV).

:: *You must not give sin a vote in the way you conduct your lives. Don't give it the time of day. Don't even run little errands that are connected with that old way of life. Throw yourselves wholeheartedly and full-time. . .into God's way of doing things. Sin can't tell you how to live. After all, you're not living under that old tyranny any longer. . . . All your lives you've let sin tell you what to do. But thank God you've started listening to a new master* (Romans 6:12–14, 16–17 MSG).

:: *Don't think about how to satisfy what your sinful nature wants* (Romans 13:14 NIrV). In the Greek language the apostle Paul used when he wrote, "sinful nature" is *sarx* (rhymes with "sharks"). It literally means "flesh," as in, "The spirit is willing, but the flesh is weak" (Matthew 26:41 NIV). Paul teaches that though our spirit isn't strong enough to manhandle sin, God's Spirit is. Paul adds that believers have access to that divine power because "God's Spirit lives in you" (1 Corinthians 3:16 NCV).

(See also *Sin*.)

PARABLES

Like a fable, it's a fictional story offering a lesson to live by. Jesus used parables a lot when he taught. The word pictures they created helped people see how to apply spiritual ideas to their lives. The famous parable of the Good Samaritan, for example, is the story of a non-Jewish man helping a Jewish stranger, even though most Jews seemed to hate Samaritans as much as some Israelis today hate Palestinians. Yet this story helped people understand that when the Bible says we're to love our neighbor, *neighbor* means anyone in our vicinity who needs help. Whether the neighbor likes us or not.

:: *Jesus always used stories and illustrations like these when speaking to the crowds. In fact, he never spoke to them without using such parables. This fulfilled what God had spoken through the prophet: "I will speak to you in parables. I will explain things hidden since the creation of the world"* (Matthew 13:34–35).

:: *The disciples came up and asked [Jesus], "Why do you tell stories?" He replied, "You've been given insight into God's kingdom. . . . Not everybody has this gift. . . . That's why I tell stories: to create readiness, to nudge the people toward receptive insight. . . . I don't want Isaiah's forecast repeated all over again: Your ears are open but you don't hear a thing"* (Matthew 13:10–11, 13–14 MSG).

:: *"The kingdom of heaven is like treasure that was hidden in a field. When a man found it. . .he went and sold everything he had. And he bought that field"* (Matthew 13:44 NIrV). Jesus used parables like this to help people understand how important it is to become citizens of God's kingdom. In other parables, he gave them a glimpse at how God's people should behave.

Paradise is apparently another word for heaven, as Bible writers use the term. It comes from a word that means "garden," and may point back to the Garden of Eden.

:: *"I assure you, today you will be with me in paradise"* (Luke 23:43). Jesus, hanging on the cross. He was talking to another crucifixion victim hanging beside him.

:: *I do know that I was caught up to paradise and heard things so astounding that they cannot be expressed in words, things no human is allowed to tell* (2 Corinthians 12:3–4). Paul was writing about a mystical experience.

:: *"To everyone who is victorious I will give fruit from the tree of life in the paradise of God"* (Revelation 2:7).

There are 10 basic laws in the Bible, the 10 Commandments. All other laws in the Bible are based on these 10. The first four laws deal with our relationship to God. The last six deal with our relationship to others. The first of the final six—the top law for dealing with others—is to respect our parents.

RESPECT YOUR PARENTS

:: *Respect your father and your mother* (Exodus 20:12 CEV). Number six of the 10 Commandments.

:: *Children, do what your parents tell you. This is only right. "Honor your father and mother" is the first commandment that has a promise attached to it, namely, "so you will live well and have a long life"* (Ephesians 6:1–3 MSG).

BEFORE ASSISTED LIVING. Three generations living under one roof wasn't uncommon in Bible times. There was no other alternative for the elderly, who were no longer able to do all the hard work needed to keep food on the table.

TEACH YOUR CHILDREN WELL

:: *Teach your children right from wrong, and when they are grown they will still do right* (Proverbs 22:6 CEV).

:: *Don't exasperate your children by coming down hard on them. Take them by the hand and lead them in the way of the Master* (Ephesians 6:4 MSG).

:: *My child, obey the teachings of your parents, and wear their teachings as you would a lovely hat or a pretty necklace* (Proverbs 1:8–9 CEV).

DISCIPLINE THEM WHEN NEEDED

:: *If you love your children, you will correct them; if you don't love them, you won't correct them* (Proverbs 13:24 CEV).

:: *Correct your children, and they will be wise; children out of control disgrace their mothers* (Proverbs 29:15 CEV). And their fathers. And their grandparents. Maybe everyone else in their family, too.

:: *Don't be a fool and disobey your parents. Be smart! Accept correction* (Proverbs 15:5 CEV).

(See also *Family*.)

PASSOVER

A 3,000–year-old Jewish holiday. Jews gather for a meal rich in symbolism, to help them remember the release of their ancestors from Egyptian slavery during the time of Moses. God convinced the Egyptians to free the Jews by passing through Egypt and killing the oldest child in each family. But God passed over the Jewish families.

:: *"On that night I will pass through the land of Egypt and strike down every firstborn son. . . .*

But the blood on your doorposts will serve as a sign, marking the houses where you are staying. When I see the blood, I will pass over you" (Exodus 12:12–13).

:: *"This is a day to remember. Each year, from generation to generation, you must celebrate it as a special festival to the LORD"* (Exodus 12:14).

:: *"Passover begins in two days, and the Son of Man will be handed over to be crucified"* (Matthew 26:2). Jesus warns his disciples that the time has come for him to die.

PATIENCE

The Bible teaches that God is patient with us, and that he expects us to be patient with others. But like any other character trait, patience has to be cultivated. We've got to work at it.

GOD'S PATIENCE WITH US

:: *Don't you see how wonderfully kind, tolerant, and patient God is with you? . . . Can't you see that his kindness is intended to turn you from your sin?* (Romans 2:4).

WAIT PATIENTLY ON GOD'S TIMING

:: *Be patient. Wait for the LORD to act. Don't be upset when other people succeed. Don't be upset when they carry out their evil plans* (Psalm 37:7 NIrV).

CULTIVATE PATIENCE

:: *Be patient with each other, making allowance for each other's faults* (Ephesians 4:2).

:: *Better to be patient than powerful* (Proverbs 16:32).

:: *Patience is better than pride* (Ecclesiastes 7:8).

:: *Don't lose a minute in building on what you've been given, complementing your basic faith* with good character, spiritual understanding, alert discipline, passionate patience. . . . With these qualities active and growing in your lives . . . no day will pass without its reward as you mature in your experience of our Master Jesus (2 Peter 1:5–8 MSG).

:: Be patient with each person, attentive to individual needs. And be careful that when you get on each other's nerves you don't snap at each other (1 Thessalonians 5:14–15 MSG).

:: A servant of the Lord must not quarrel but must be kind to everyone. . .and be patient with difficult people (2 Timothy 2:24).

:: Be patient in trouble, and keep on praying (Romans 12:12).

THE VALUE OF PATIENCE

:: If you want to get your point across, use patience and gentle words. Together, they can break down the strongest defenses (Proverbs 25:15 AUTHOR'S PARAPHRASE).

:: God blesses those who patiently endure testing and temptation. Afterward they will receive the crown of life that God has promised to those who love him (James 1:12).

PEACE

Peace isn't the opposite of tough times. The Bible presents it as an attitude that God's people can experience in good times and bad. Inner peace comes from trusting that God's in control and that he's going to take care of us, in this life and in the next.

:: Don't worry about anything; instead, pray about everything. Tell God what you need, and thank him for all he has done. Then you will experience God's peace, which exceeds anything we

RESTING IN PEACE. A Jewish student in a Jerusalem rabbinical school catches a few z's. He could argue that it's the biblical thing to do: "In peace I will lie down and sleep, for you alone, O Lord, will keep me safe" (Psalm 4:8).

can understand. His peace will guard your hearts and minds as you live in Christ Jesus (Philippians 4:6–7).

:: I give you peace, the kind of peace that only I can give. It isn't like the peace that this world can give. So don't be worried or afraid (John 14:27 CEV). That's Jesus on the night of his arrest, assuring his disciples that they have nothing to fear.

:: "You can have peace because of me. In this world you will have trouble. But cheer up! I have won the battle over the world" (John 16:33 NIrV).

:: We have been made right with God because of our faith. Now we have peace with him because of our Lord Jesus Christ (Romans 5:1 NIrV).

:: Letting the Spirit control your mind leads to life and peace (Romans 8:6).

:: *Become wise by walking with the wise; hang out with fools and watch your life fall to pieces* (Proverbs 13:20 MSG).

:: *Don't be like the people of this world, but let God change the way you think. Then you will know how to do everything that is good and pleasing to him* (Romans 12:2 CEV).

:: *God blesses those people who refuse evil advice and won't follow sinners* (Psalm 1:1 CEV).

:: *"Don't live like the people of Egypt where you used to live, and don't live like the people of Canaan where I'm bringing you. Don't do what they do. Obey my laws and live by my decrees. I am your GOD"* (Leviticus 18:3–4 MSG). God's instruction to Jews Moses led out of slavery in Egypt and toward what is now Israel.

:: *They quit following the LORD. . . . They began to worship the gods of the people who lived around them, and that made the LORD angry* (Judges 2:12 NCV).

PENANCE

Some Christians express their sorrow for sins by performing an act of remorse. Roman Catholics and some Orthodox Christians confess their sins to a priest, who tells them what to do to express their regret. Often, it's repeating a prayer. Some Christians punish themselves by depriving themselves of something, such as food, water, or comfort—such as a warm blanket on a cold night. Protestants don't practice penance. They teach that when we confess our sins to God, we're forgiven because Jesus paid the penalty for our sins by dying on the cross.

STYLIN'. Kicking back with Brazilian hot chocolate in an Austin café, a young woman settles in for a comfy sip. Paul advised Christians against getting too settled in the ways of the world. "Don't become so well-adjusted to your culture that you fit into it without even thinking" (Romans 12:2 MSG).

HARDCORE PENANCE. Draped in his own blood, a Roman Catholic in San Pedro Cutud, Pampanga, in the Philippines, observes Good Friday by beating himself with bamboo rods laced to a whip—to express sorrow for his sins. Many Bible experts, however, say Paul took a stand against church leaders who prodded Christians toward painful practices he called "pious self-denial, and severe bodily discipline" (Colossians 2:23).

PROTESTANT VIEW

:: *God is faithful and fair. If we admit that we have sinned, he will forgive us our sins. He will forgive every wrong thing we have done. He will make us pure* (1 John 1:9 NIrV). No priest or penance needed.

CATHOLIC, ORTHODOX VIEW

:: *He [Jesus] breathed on them and said, "Receive the Holy Spirit. If you forgive anyone's sins, they are forgiven. If you do not forgive them, they are not forgiven"* (John 20:22–23). After his resurrection Jesus seems to give his disciples—future leaders of the church—authority to forgive sins. Most Protestants say that only God can forgive sins. So what Jesus was saying, they argue, is that the disciples—and all believers to come—are to tell people that God's forgiveness is available. Anyone who believes this message will be forgiven. Those who don't will not be forgiven. This verse is hotly debated.

HARVEST OFFERINGS. Jewish women at an Israeli *kibbutz* (kib-BOOTS), a collective agricultural community, reenact an ancient Jewish custom for Pentecost—a springtime harvest festival. In Bible times, Jews brought to the Jerusalem Temple offerings from the year's early harvest.

PENTECOST

Pentecost is a sacred day for Jews and Christians, for two different reasons. Jews celebrated Pentecost as a way to thank God for the first of their harvest. For Christians, Pentecost is the day the Holy Spirit arrived, shortly after Jesus ascended to heaven.

JEWISH PENTECOST

:: *"Count off seven weeks from when you first begin to cut the grain at the time of harvest. Then celebrate the Festival of Harvest to honor the LORD your God"* (Deuteronomy 16:9–10). Jews also called this the Festival of Weeks (named after seven weeks). Later, after Greek was the international language of the day, Jews began calling it the Festival of Pentecost (Greek for "50"), since it came 50 days after Passover. Jews today call it *Shavuot* (shah-voo-OUGHT), Hebrew for Weeks.

CHRISTIAN PENTECOST

:: *On the day of Pentecost all the believers were meeting together in one place. Suddenly, there was a sound from heaven like the roaring of a mighty windstorm, and it filled the house where they were sitting. . . . And everyone present was filled with the Holy Spirit and began speaking in other languages, as the Holy Spirit gave them this ability* (Acts 2:1–2, 4). The Holy Spirit not only gave the disciples miraculous power, but also the courage to preach about Jesus in Jerusalem—the very city that had crucified him just seven weeks earlier.

PERFECTION

:: *"Be perfect, just as your Father in heaven is perfect"* (Matthew 5:48 NIrV). Some Bible experts say Jesus wasn't talking about perfect behavior. Instead, he was urging people to devote themselves completely to God, since the Bible teaches that people or objects devoted to God are considered sacred, or holy. (See "Holy humans?" page 140.)

:: *We should stay away from everything that keeps our bodies and spirits from being clean. We should honor God and try to be completely like him* (2 Corinthians 7:1 CEV).

:: *Jesus told him, "If you want to be perfect, go and sell all your possessions and give the money to the poor, and you will have treasure in heaven. Then come, follow me." But when the young man heard this, he went away very sad, for he had many possessions* (Matthew 19:21–22). Jesus may have been trying to show the man that he was more devoted to building his own kingdom than he was to building God's kingdom.

:: *Why are you now trying to become perfect by your own human effort?* (Galatians 3:3). Paul tells Christians they can't earn their way into God's good favor by obeying a bunch of man-made rules. Instead, they follow the leading of God's Spirit living inside them. That's the kind of devotion God wants.

:: *"He is the Rock; his deeds are perfect. Everything he does is just and fair. He is a faithful God who does no wrong"* (Deuteronomy 32:4).

(See also *Holiness*.)

PERSECUTION

:: *"If the world hates you, remember that it hated me first"* (John 15:18).

:: *Let us keep looking to Jesus. . . . He put up with attacks from sinners. So think about him. Then you won't get tired. You won't lose hope* (Hebrews 12:2–3 NIrV).

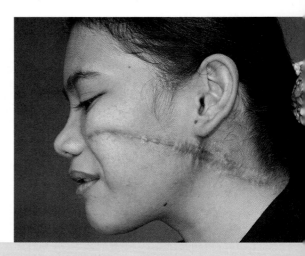

SOLE SURVIVOR. Muslims with machetes attacked four teenage girls walking to their Christian high school in Indonesia—decapitating three. Only Noviana Malewa, 14, survived—falling down a ravine and running away. A scar reminds her of how close she came to dying. Attackers tossed one girl's head in front of a nearby church with a note: "We will murder 100 more Christian teenagers and their heads will be presented as presents." Three attackers were caught, convicted of terrorism, and imprisoned—two for 14 years, one for 20. Indonesia has over 200 million Muslims, more than any other country.

:: *"Count yourself blessed every time someone cuts you down or throws you out, every time someone smears or blackens your name to discredit me. What it means is that the truth is too close for comfort and that that person is uncomfortable. You can be glad when that happens—skip like a lamb, if you like!—for even though they don't like it, I do. . .and all heaven applauds. And know that you are in good company; my preachers and witnesses have always been treated like this"* (Luke 6:22–23 MSG). That's Jesus talking.

:: *Troubles produce patience. And patience produces character* (Romans 5:3–4 NCV).

:: *Consider it a sheer gift, friends, when tests and challenges come at you from all sides. You know that under pressure, your faith-life is forced into the open and shows its true colors. So don't try to get out of anything prematurely. Let it do its work so you become mature and well-developed, not deficient in any way* (James 1:2–4 MSG).

PHARISEE

Jewish religion in Jesus' day, like today, had different groups—just as the church today has different denominations. Pharisees are portrayed in the Bible as rule-obsessed scholars who taught that anyone who wanted to please God not only had to obey the laws Moses gave, they also had to obey hundreds of unwritten laws passed down by Jewish scholars over the centuries. Jesus said many of the Pharisees were hypocrites—religious showoffs who ignored some of the most basic laws of God: compassion, justice, and humility. All the quotes below are from Jesus.

:: *"Pharisees! Frauds! You're like manicured grave plots, grass clipped and the flowers*

Pharisee: Jewish religion scholar

bright, but six feet down it's all rotting bones and worm-eaten flesh. People look at you and think you're saints, but beneath the skin you're total frauds" (Matthew 23:27–28 MSG).

:: *"Pharisees know the Law of Moses inside and out. So go ahead and respect their teachings about those laws. Just don't follow their example. They don't practice what they preach. They load you up with a bunch of extra laws not in the Bible—laws even they can't keep. But they never bother to tell you that. They just leave you feeling inadequate, guilty, and inferior to them"* (Matthew 23:2–5 AUTHOR'S PARAPHRASE).

:: *You Pharisees and teachers are show-offs, and you're in for trouble! You give God a tenth of the spices from your garden, such as mint, dill, and cumin. Yet you neglect the more important matters of the Law, such as justice, mercy, and faithfulness* (Matthew 23:23 CEV).

:: *"There's trouble ahead when you live only for the approval of others, saying what flatters them, doing what indulges them. Popularity contests are not truth contests. . . . Your task is to be true, not popular"* (Luke 6:26 MSG). This is Jesus preaching to a crowd.

:: *The disciples began to argue about which one of them would be the most important person. Jesus knew what they were thinking. So he took a little child and had the child stand beside him. Then he spoke to them. . . . "The least important person among all of you is the most important"* (Luke 9:46–48 NIrV).

:: *It's better to live humbly among the poor than to live it up among the rich and famous* (Proverbs 16:19 MSG).

:: *People are like grass. All of their glory is like the flowers in the field. The grass dries up. The flowers fall to the ground. But the word of the Lord stands forever* (1 Peter 1:24–25 NIrV).

:: *Don't be impressed with those who get rich and pile up fame and fortune. They can't take it with them; fame and fortune all get left behind. Just when they think they've arrived and folks praise them because they've made good, they enter the family burial plot where they'll never see sunshine again. We aren't immortal. We don't last long. Like our dogs, we age and weaken. And die* (Psalm 49:16–20 MSG).

:: *"What good would it do to get everything you want and lose you, the real you?"* (Luke 9:25 MSG).

PORNOGRAPHY

Sketchy drawings of sex acts existed in Bible times, but nothing close to the photos and films we have today. Very few people had access to those early, cartoonish-looking sketches. So the Bible doesn't talk about pornography as we know it. But it does condemn the lust and addiction that pornography feeds on—as well as the immodesty and the sexual immorality it glamorizes. Many charge that pornography creates unrealistic images of what people should look like, spurring dangerous body sculpting and destroying the marriages of couples who think their sex life doesn't measure up.

:: *"She fell in love with pictures that were painted on a wall—pictures of Babylonian military officers. . . . When she saw these paintings, she longed to give herself to them, so she sent messengers to Babylonia to invite them to come to her. So they came and committed adultery with her"* (Ezekiel 23:14, 16–17). Even in ancient times, pictures stimulated destructive sexual behavior. Though this story is symbolic, it draws from that fact. "She" represents the Jews. The point is that the Jews abandoned God by putting their trust in the world's superpower, Babylon.

:: *If you look at another woman and want her, you are already unfaithful in your thoughts* (Matthew 5:28 CEV).

:: *"I made a solemn pact with myself never to undress a girl with my eyes"* (Job 31:1 MSG).

:: *Get rid of your sexual sins and unclean acts. Don't let your feelings get out of control* (Colossians 3:5 NIrV).

:: *I want women to be modest in their appearance. They should wear decent and appropriate clothing and not draw attention to themselves* (1 Timothy 2:9). This is Paul's advice to Timothy, pastor of a church.

:: *Late one afternoon, David got up from a nap and was walking around on the flat roof of his palace. A beautiful young woman was down below in her courtyard, bathing* (2 Samuel 11:2 CEV). This story of King David and Bathsheba isn't about pornography. But there are similarities. David sees a naked woman and lusts for her. She's married, but he has sex with her anyhow. She ends up pregnant. Her husband, Uriah, is away at war—fighting for king and country. Yet to cover up the affair, David arranges for Uriah to die in battle. David marries Bathsheba. The child dies.

(See also *Addictions*.)

POVERTY

Many Jews in Bible times seemed to think that poor people deserved their fate—that God was punishing them for something. Yet Bible writers say it's just the opposite—that God has a special fondness for the poor, and that he wants his people to take care of them.

:: *Speak up for the poor and helpless, and see that they get justice* (Proverbs 31:9).

:: *"Work for justice. Help the down-and-out. Stand up for the homeless. Go to bat for the defenseless"* (Isaiah 1:17 MSG).

:: *Anyone who is kind to poor people lends to the LORD. God will reward him for what he has done* (Proverbs 19:17 NIrV).

:: *All the believers were united in heart and mind. And they felt that what they owned was not their own, so they shared everything they had. . . . There were no needy people among them, because those who owned land or houses would sell them and bring the money to the apostles to give to those in need* (Acts 4:32, 34–35).

BEGGING IN INDIA. Photographer Rohit Markande snaps this picture of a man asking for alms at a red light, on his way to dinner in New Delhi. Markande says he gave the man some money for "not pestering me vociferously like many others do, but instead standing with dignity and showing his genuine need for empathy."

PRAYER

Prayer isn't a chat with a do-nothing God. Not as the Bible tells it. Prayer has the power to change reality just as effectively as a child's sincere request to Mom or Dad can change things.

HOW TO PRAY

:: *"When you come before God, don't turn that into a theatrical production either. All these people making a regular show out of their prayers, hoping for stardom! Do you think God sits in a box seat?"* (Matthew 6:5 MSG). Jesus is criticizing religious leaders who use public prayer to draw attention to themselves.

:: *"Our Father in heaven, reveal who you are. Set the world right; do what's best—as above, so below. Keep us alive with three square meals. Keep us forgiven with you and forgiving others. Keep us safe from ourselves and the Devil. You're in charge! You can do anything you want! You're ablaze in beauty! Yes. Yes. Yes"* (Matthew 6:9–13 MSG). This is the Lord's Prayer. Jesus taught it to his disciples to show them how to keep their prayers short and simple.

:: *Pray every way you know how, for everyone you know. Pray especially for rulers and their governments to rule well* (1 Timothy 2:1–2 MSG).

:: *Jesus went off to a mountain to pray, and he spent the whole night there* (Luke 6:12 CEV). This was on the night before he chose his disciples.

PRAYER CHANGES THINGS

:: *"If you believe, you will get anything you ask for in prayer"* (Matthew 21:22 NCV). Scholars say Jesus is assuming we will do what he did on the night of his arrest and ask according to God's will. Jesus didn't want to be tortured on the cross, and he told God so. But he also said he was willing to die if necessary. Apparently it was.

:: *There is one thing we can be sure of when we come to God in prayer. If we ask anything in keeping with what he wants, he hears us* (1 John 5:14 NIrV).

:: *Hezekiah got sick and was almost dead. Isaiah the prophet went in and told him, "The LORD says you won't ever get well. You are going to die, so you had better start doing what needs to be done." Hezekiah turned toward the wall and prayed* (2 Kings 20:1–2 CEV). God's reply:

"I heard you pray, and I saw you cry. . . . I will let you live fifteen years more" (2 Kings 20:5–6 CEV). It's probably not that Hezekiah's request changed God's mind, scholars say. After all, how could someone who knows everything change his mind? It's more likely that the request somehow changed Hezekiah, and so God changed his plans to match the changes in the king.

:: *Moses begged the LORD his God and said, "LORD, don't let your anger destroy your people . . . ." So the LORD changed his mind and did not destroy the people as he had said he might* (Exodus 32:11, 14 NCV).

:: *"Don't be afraid, Daniel. Since the first day you began to pray for understanding and to humble yourself before your God, your request has been heard in heaven. I have come in answer to your prayer"* (Daniel 10:12). The words of an angel.

WHEN GOD'S ANSWER IS NO

:: *"Father, if it is possible, don't let this happen to me! Father, you can do anything. Don't make me suffer by having me drink from this cup. But do what you want, and not what I want"* (Mark 14:36 CEV). A few hours after Jesus prayed this prayer, he was hanging on the cross.

:: *So I wouldn't get a big head, I was given the gift of a handicap to keep me in constant touch with my limitations. . . . At first I didn't think of it as a gift, and begged God to remove it. Three times I did that, and then he told me, "My grace is enough; it's all you need"* (2 Corinthians 12:7–9 MSG).

:: *Never stop praying. Whatever happens, keep thanking God because of Jesus Christ. This is what God wants you to do* (1 Thessalonians 5:17–18 CEV).

APPEALING TO MARY. A Russian Orthodox Christian prays in front of an icon of the Virgin Mary. Catholic and Orthodox Christians sometimes direct their requests to Mary and departed saints, asking them to intercede on their behalf. It's a bit like recruiting a celestial lobbyist who has direct access to God. Most Protestants say we can skip the intermediaries and take our requests "boldly to the throne of our gracious God" (Hebrews 4:16).

:: *I waited patiently for the Lord to help me, and he turned to me and heard my cry* (Psalm 40:1). The songwriter implies that sometimes God's answer isn't an immediate yes or no, but wait.

:: *God has no use for the prayers of the people who won't listen to him* (Proverbs 28:9 MSG).

Some Christians say God decides ahead of time who will be saved and who won't. These include many Baptists and Presbyterians, along with other groups that embrace the Bible teachings of French scholar John Calvin (1509–1564). Many of these Christians argue that because we're sinful, we would choose sin over God. So God has to choose for us. Others say God offers salvation to everyone. We choose to accept or reject it. These churches include Methodists, the Salvation Army, Wesleyans, and others who take their theological cues from British scholar John Wesley (1703–1791) and Dutch theologian Jacobus Arminius (1560–1609).

OPTION 1: GOD CHOOSES WHO WILL BE SAVED

:: *Those God foreknew he also predestined to be conformed to the image of his Son* (Romans 8:29 TNIV).

:: *God said to Moses, "I will show mercy to anyone I choose, and I will show compassion to anyone I choose." So it is God who decides to show mercy. We can neither choose it nor work for it* (Romans 9:15–16).

:: *"No one can come to me unless the Father who sent me draws them to me"* (John 6:44).

:: *They stumble because they do not obey God's word, and so they meet the fate that was planned for them* (1 Peter 2:8).

:: *"I have chosen Saul for an important work. He must tell about me to those who are not Jews, to kings, and to the people of Israel"* (Acts 9:15 NCV). Saul, better known as the apostle Paul, was a Jewish persecutor of Christians. But Jesus appeared to Saul in a vision that converted him to the Christian faith. Still, some argue, Saul could have rejected Jesus.

◀ **GOD DOESN'T DECIDE FOR US.** That's the position of British minister John Wesley (1703–1791), founder of the Methodists and an opponent of the idea that God predestines some people to eternal reward and others to punishment. Wesley said God knows which direction we'll choose, but that the choice is ours: "What he knows, whether faith or unbelief, is in no wise caused by his knowledge. Men are as free in believing or not believing as if he did not know it at all."

:: *Even before I was born, God chose me and called me by his marvelous grace. Then it pleased him to reveal his Son to me so that I would proclaim the Good News about Jesus to the Gentiles* (Galatians 1:15–16). That's Paul talking. Some Christians say God's grace extends to everyone, because God wants everyone saved.

OPTION 2: GOD CHOOSES EVERYONE, WE ACCEPT OR REJECT

:: *He [God] wants not only us but everyone saved, you know, everyone to get to know the truth we've learned* (1 Timothy 2:4 MSG).
:: *God is patient, because he wants everyone to turn from sin and no one to be lost* (2 Peter 3:9 CEV).
:: *"God loved the world so much that he gave his one and only Son, so that everyone who believes in him will not perish but have eternal life"* (John 3:16).
:: *We are made right with God by placing our faith in Jesus Christ. And this is true for everyone who believes, no matter who we are* (Romans 3:22).
:: *We have been made holy through the sacrifice of the body of Jesus Christ once for all* (Hebrews 10:10 TNIV).

(See also *Eternal Security*.)

:: *Words like Jewish and non-Jewish, religious and irreligious, insider and outsider, uncivilized and uncouth, slave and free, mean nothing. From now on everyone is defined by Christ, everyone is included in Christ* (Colossians 3:11 MSG).
:: *In Christ's family there can be no division into Jew and non-Jew, slave and free, male and female. Among us you are all equal. That is, we are all in a common relationship with Jesus Christ* (Galatians 3:28 MSG).
:: *There is no difference between those who are Jews and those who are not. The same Lord is Lord of all* (Romans 10:12 NIrV).
:: *He [God] has no favorites* (Ephesians 6:9).

(See also *Discrimination*.)

ARAB ON THE BORDER. A Palestinian man sits by the Israeli border fence at Rafah, a city in the Palestinian-controlled Gaza Strip. Hatred runs generations deep between many Israelis and Palestinians. But if the apostle Paul is right, in God's eyes, "words like Jewish and non-Jewish. . .mean nothing."

:: *GOD can't stomach arrogance or pretense; believe me, he'll put those upstarts in their place* (Proverbs 16:5 MSG).

:: *Pride lands you flat on your face; humility prepares you for honors* (Proverbs 29:23 MSG).

:: *Pride leads only to shame; it is wise to be humble* (Proverbs 11:2 NCV).

:: *Pride only leads to arguments* (Proverbs 13:10 NCV).

:: *Pride leads to destruction; a proud attitude leads to ruin. It is better to be humble and be with those who suffer* (Proverbs 16:18–19 NCV).

:: *Though the LORD is great, he cares for the humble, but he keeps his distance from the proud* (Psalm 138:6).

(See also *Humility*.)

RAPE

:: *When a man comes upon a virgin who has never been engaged and grabs and rapes her and they are found out, the man who raped her has to give her father fifty pieces of silver. He has to marry her because he took advantage of her. And he can never divorce her* (Deuteronomy 22:28–29 MSG). Less than female-friendly, this law sounds like the perfect solution for a wife hunter—the guy who won't take no for an answer. Yet in this ancient culture, a raped woman was considered damaged goods, no longer marriage material. Even King David's beautiful daughter Tamar, once raped, never seemed to find a husband. She "lived as a desolate woman in her brother Absalom's house" (2 Samuel 13:20). This law made sure the victim would have a family, even in this age where men ruled and women were too often treated as property—which husbands could divorce on a whim.

:: *If an engaged woman is raped out in the country, only the man will be put to death. Do not punish the woman at all; she has done nothing wrong. . . . This crime is like murder, because the woman was alone out in the country when the man attacked her. She screamed, but there was no one to help her* (Deuteronomy 22:25–27 CEV).

:: *If a man comes upon a virgin in town, a girl who is engaged to another man, and sleeps with her, take both of them to the town gate and stone them until they die—the girl because she didn't yell out for help in the town and the man because he raped her, violating the fiancée of his neighbor. You must purge the evil from among you* (Deuteronomy 22:23–24 MSG).

:: *Amnon wouldn't listen to her [Tamar], and since he was stronger than she was, he raped her. Then suddenly Amnon's love turned to hate, and he hated her even more than he had loved her* (2 Samuel 13:14–15). This was King David's son raping his own half-sister because she refused to have sex with him. David didn't punish Amnon, but Tamar's full brother, Absalom, did. Absalom had the rapist assassinated.

:: *"He came into my room to rape me, but I screamed"* (Genesis 39:14). This was a lie that an Egyptian official's wife told about her household slave, Joseph, who had refused her demand to have sex with her. The official put Joseph in prison—a relatively mild punishment that suggests the official didn't believe his wife but wanted to protect her reputation.

Some Christians say that when Jesus returns, all believers—living and dead—will be snatched away. They call this event the *Rapture*. Oddly, the original Greek version of this word, *harpaz,* seems to have given us the English word for harpoon.

UP. Impressionist artist Salvador Dali said his painting of Christ's ascension was inspired by a colorful dream in which he saw the nucleus of an atom. Many Christians say they expect to ascend, too, when Christ returns to take them to heaven.

The Greek word means "caught up."

:: *The Lord himself will come down from heaven. We will hear a loud command. We will hear the voice of the leader of the angels. We will hear a blast from God's trumpet. Many who believe in Christ will have died already. They will rise first. After that, we who are still alive and are left will be caught up together with them. We will be taken up in the clouds. We will meet the Lord in the air. And we will be with him forever* (1 Thessalonians 4:16–17 NIrv). The apostle Paul writes this to new Christians in what is now northern Greece. They were worried about what would happen to believers who died before Jesus returned.

:: *We will not all die, but we will all be transformed! It will happen in a moment, in the blink of an eye, when the last trumpet is blown. For when the trumpet sounds, those who have died will be raised to live forever* (1 Corinthians 15:51–52).

(See also *Second Coming.*)

REGRET

:: *Distress that drives us to God. . .turns us around. It gets us back in the way of salvation. We never regret that kind of pain. But those who let distress drive them away from God are full of regrets, end up on a deathbed of regrets. And now, isn't it wonderful all the ways in which this distress has goaded you closer to God? You're more alive, more concerned, more sensitive, more reverent, more human, more passionate, more responsible* (2 Corinthians 7:10–11 MSG).

:: *God is faithful and fair. If we admit that we have sinned, he will forgive us our sins. He will*

forgive every wrong thing we have done. He will make us pure (1 John 1:9 NIrv).

:: *I focus on this one thing: Forgetting the past and looking forward to what lies ahead, I press on to reach the end of the race and receive the heavenly prize for which God, through Christ Jesus, is calling us* (Philippians 3:13–14).

(See also *Forgiveness, Repentance.*)

REPENTANCE

People who repent express sorrow for their sins. Beyond being sorry, they do something about it. They ask for God's forgiveness and for his help to stop living the kind of life that they know hurts themselves and others.

:: *"If my people. . .are sorry for what they have done, if they pray and obey me and stop their evil ways, I will hear them from heaven. I will forgive their sin"* (2 Chronicles 7:14 NCV).

:: *"Each of you must repent of your sins and turn to God, and be baptized in the name of Jesus Christ for the forgiveness for your sins. Then you will receive the gift of the Holy Spirit"* (Acts 2:38). This is Peter talking. It's his first known sermon after the resurrection of Jesus—the sermon that launched the Christian movement by convincing about 3,000 people in Jerusalem to repent.

:: *Turn to God! Give up your sins, and you will be forgiven. Then that time will come when the Lord will give you fresh strength* (Acts 3:19–20 CEV).

:: *God sometimes uses sorrow in our lives to help us turn away from sin and seek eternal life* (2 Corinthians 7:10 TLB).

(See also *Conversion, Forgiveness, Regret.*)

Saying "sorry" wasn't enough in the time of Moses. The Bible says that under God's direction, Moses set up a legal system to govern the emerging Jewish nation. Some of the laws required restitution—payback for damages caused in accidents and crimes.

KEEPING IT FAIR

:: *"The punishment must match the injury: a life for a life, an eye for an eye, a tooth for a tooth, a hand for a hand, a foot for a foot, a burn for a burn, a wound for a wound, a bruise for a bruise"* (Exodus 21:23–25). Some Bible experts say this law was to make sure the victim's family members didn't go overboard with the payback.

FOR STEALING

:: *"If someone steals an ox or sheep and then kills or sells it, the thief must pay back five oxen for each ox stolen, and four sheep for each sheep stolen. . . . If someone steals an ox or a donkey or a sheep and it is found in the thief's possession, then the thief must pay double the value of the stolen animal"* (Exodus 22:1, 4).

FOR MURDER

:: *"I will require the blood of anyone who takes another person's life. . . . Anyone who murders a fellow human must die"* (Genesis 9:5). See also *Capital Punishment.*

FOR ACCIDENTS

:: *"When there's a fight and in the fight a pregnant woman is hit so that she miscarries but is not otherwise hurt, the one responsible has to pay whatever the husband demands in compensation"*

OX PULL. A team of oxen pulls a plow through a field in Turkey, below the Taurus Mountains where the apostle Paul grew up. Jewish law said if you stole a man's ox and killed it or sold it, payback was five oxen (Exodus 22:1).

(Exodus 21:22 MSG). A set of Babylonian laws called Hammurabi's Code, from several centuries before Moses, ordered anyone causing a miscarriage to pay the woman's husband a fine of 10 silver coins.

:: *"Suppose two men quarrel, and one hits the other with a stone or fist, and the injured person does not die but is confined to bed. If he is later able to walk outside again, even with a crutch, the assailant will not be punished but must compensate his victim for lost wages and provide for his full recovery"* (Exodus 21:18–19).

:: *"Suppose a bull kills a man or woman with its horns. Then you must kill the bull. . . . The owner of the bull will not be held accountable. But suppose the bull has had the habit of attacking people. And suppose the owner has been warned but has not kept it fenced in. Then if it kills a man or woman, you must kill it. . . . The owner must also be put to death. But suppose payment is required of him instead. Then he can save his life by paying what is required"* (Exodus 21:28–30 NIrV).

RESURRECTION

New Testament writers said Jesus rose from the dead—and that everyone who puts their faith in Jesus will rise, too.

OF JESUS

:: *If Christ wasn't raised to life, our message is worthless, and so is your faith* (1 Corinthians 15:14 CEV). This is the apostle Paul, writing to a church in what is now Greece.

:: *The angel spoke to the women. . . . "I know you are looking for Jesus, who was crucified. He isn't here! He is risen from the dead, just as he said would happen. Come, see where his body was lying"* (Matthew 28:5–6).

:: *Jesus appeared to them [his disciples] and said, "Peace be with you." They thought they were seeing a ghost and were scared half to death. He continued. . . . "Touch me. Look me over from head to toe. A ghost doesn't have*

CHRISTIANITY'S TALLEST TALE. Jesus rises from the dead on Sunday morning after his Friday crucifixion. For Christians, everything depends on Jesus' resurrection. If the Bible writers got that wrong—and Jesus stayed dead—Christians "should be pitied more than anyone else in the world" (1 Corinthians 15:19 NCV). So said the apostle Paul.

RESURRECTED JESUS IN ROMAN HISTORY

There was a wise man who was called Jesus. . . . Pilate condemned him to be crucified. . . . His disciples didn't abandon their loyalty to him. They reported that he appeared to them three days after his crucifixion, and that he was alive.

JOSEPHUS (ABOUT AD 37–100),
A JEWISH HISTORIAN AND ROMAN CITIZEN,
ANTIQUITIES OF THE JEWS

muscle and bone like this" (Luke 24:36–39 MSG).

:: *"I am the living one. I died, but look—I am alive forever and ever!"* (Revelation 1:18).

OF ALL GODLY SOULS

:: *As to whether the dead will be raised—haven't you ever read. . .the story of the burning bush? Long after Abraham, Isaac, and Jacob had died, God said to Moses, "I am the God of Abraham. . . ."* So he is the God of the living, not the dead* (Mark 12:26–27). This is Jesus talking to religion scholars.

:: *Just as God raised Jesus, he will also raise us to life* (2 Corinthians 4:14 CEV).

:: *We believe that Jesus died and was raised to life. We also believe that when God brings Jesus back again, he will bring with him all who had faith in Jesus before they died* (1 Thessalonians 4:14 CEV).

:: *"My Father wants all who look to the Son and believe in him to have eternal life. I [Jesus] will raise them up on the last day"* (John 6:40 NIrV).

REVENGE

:: *"If someone takes unfair advantage of you, use the occasion to practice the servant life. No more tit-for-tat stuff. Live generously"* (Matthew 5:41–42 MSG).

:: *Don't pay back evil with evil. Don't pay back unkind words with unkind words. Instead, pay them back with kind words. That's what you have been chosen to do. You can receive a blessing by doing it* (1 Peter 3:9 NIrV).

:: *Dear friends, never take revenge. Leave that to the righteous anger of God. For the Scriptures say, "I will take revenge; I will pay them back," says the LORD* (Romans 12:19).

:: *"I only did to them what they did to me"* (Judges 15:11). Samson defending himself after his fellow Jewish neighbors complained that his attacks sparked a Philistine invasion into the Jewish homeland.
(See also *Grudges*.)

RITUAL

In worship services, a *ritual* is a ceremony—like baptism or communion—in which people perform certain actions to symbolize their faith or to commemorate an important event from their religion's history. Many Christians consider communion the most important worship ritual, one that Jesus established. They eat bread and drink wine or grape juice to remember his crucifixion. The torn pieces of bread help them recall his injured body, and the juice his shed blood. Jews atoned for their sins by ritually sacrificing animals.

COMMUNION

:: *Taking bread, he [Jesus] blessed it, broke it,*

and gave it to them, saying, *"This is my body, given for you. Eat it in my memory"* (Luke 22:19 MSG). Most Catholics and some other Christians teach that the bread and juice become Jesus' actual body and blood. Others say these are just symbols that help us remember how he suffered for us.

BAPTISM

:: *Going under the water was a burial of your old life; coming up out of it was a resurrection, God raising you from the dead as he did Christ* (Colossians 2:12 MSG). Christians rise from the baptismal water in a dramatic and public statement: I have become a new person—a Christian, washed clean of my sins.

JEWISH PASSOVER

:: *"Eat the meal with urgency, for this is the LORD's Passover. . . . This is a day to remember. Each year, from generation to generation, you must celebrate it as a special festival to the LORD. This is a law for all time"* (Exodus 12:11, 14). Jews have celebrated the springtime Passover festival for more than 3,000 years, since the time of Moses. It's to commemorate God delivering their ancestors from slavery in Egypt.

A RITUAL TO REMEMBER. Jews in Amsterdam, like observant Jews throughout the world, celebrate the springtime holiday of Passover (*Pesach*, in Hebrew). The meal is rich in symbolism—rituals intended to remind Jews of a miracle more than 3,000 years ago: the exodus, when God helped Moses lead their ancestors out of slavery in Egypt. Jews call this meal the *Seder* (SAY-dur), Hebrew for "order," since the meal follows a scripted order of worship. ▶

ANIMAL SACRIFICES

:: *"The animal you present as a burnt offering . . .must be a male with no defects. Bring it to the entrance of the Tabernacle [tent worship center] so you may be accepted by the L*ORD*. Lay your hand on the animal's head, and the L*ORD *will accept its death in your place to purify you, making you right with him"* (Leviticus 1:3–4).

(See also *Baptism, Communion, Passover, Sacrifices.*)

RULES

Jesus respected the basic rules God gave the Jews: the 10 Commandments. Those rules are intended to help people. They work like warning signs about danger ahead. But Jesus didn't think much of rules that religious leaders invented to manipulate people—especially rules that hurt more than helped.

RULES THAT HELP

:: *"The Sabbath was made to serve us; we weren't made to serve the Sabbath"* (Mark 2:27 MSG). Some Jewish scholars said it's wrong to treat sick people on the Sabbath. They said it's work—and the Bible orders Jews not to work on the Sabbath. But the Bible doesn't say that treating the sick was work. Jewish scholars jumped to that conclusion and made it law. When they criticized Jesus for breaking their law by healing the sick on the Sabbath, Jesus shot them down with this blunt reply.

:: *"Here is a simple, rule-of-thumb guide for behavior: Ask yourself what you want people to do for you, then grab the initiative and do it for them"* (Matthew 7:12 MSG). Known as the Golden Rule, this teaching of Jesus sums up

many Bible rules about how to behave.

:: *Follow the Lord's rules for doing his work, just as an athlete either follows the rules or is disqualified and wins no prize* (2 Timothy 2:5 TLB).

RULES THAT HURT

:: *"You write laws to give yourself loopholes— bypasses around some of God's most important rules. Like the 10 Commandments. God said honor your father and mother. But you tell people they can refuse to financially help their parents by saying the magic words: My money belongs to God"* (Mark 7:9–11 AUTHOR'S PARAPHRASE). As if heaven were running low on shekels. By declaring their assets devoted to God, they didn't have to give it away.

:: *He [Jesus] repealed the law code that had become so clogged with fine print and footnotes that it hindered more than it helped. Then he started over. Instead of continuing with two groups of people [Jews and non-Jews] separated by centuries of animosity and suspicion, he created a new kind of human being, a fresh start for everybody* (Ephesians 2:15 MSG). The old Jewish laws about circumcision, kosher foods, and other rules that distinguished God's people from others are now obsolete, according to New Testament writers. Those rules served their purpose of guiding people, but now the Holy Spirit picks up that assignment.

SABBATH

The Jewish day of rest and worship stretches from sunset on Friday through sunset on Saturday. Christians later switched their sacred day to Sunday, in honor of the day Jesus rose from the dead.

:: *God blessed the seventh day and declared it holy, because it was the day when he rested from all his work of creation* (Genesis 2:3).

:: *"Remember to keep the Sabbath day holy. Do all of your work in six days. But the seventh day is a Sabbath in honor of the Lord your God. Do not do any work on that day. . . . In six days I made the heavens and the earth. I made the oceans and everything in them. But I rested on the seventh day. So I blessed the Sabbath day and made it holy"* (Exodus 20:8–11 NIrV). This is one of the 10 Commandments that the Bible says God gave to Moses to pass on to the Jews.

:: *"You must not even light a fire in any of your homes on the Sabbath"* (Exodus 35:3). This is why observant Jews today don't even cook on the Sabbath; they prepare their meals ahead of time. The most tradition-minded Orthodox Jews today don't drive because cars run on burning fuel; turning the car on lights a fire.

:: *"The Sabbath was made to serve us; we weren't made to serve the Sabbath"* (Mark 2:27 MSG). Jewish scholars called Pharisees said it's wrong to treat sick people on the Sabbath. They said it's work—and the Bible orders Jews not to work on the Sabbath. Actually, the Bible doesn't say that treating the sick is work. But Jewish

SABBATH BLESSING. An Israeli father, mother, and grandmother bless the children as they begin Sabbath worship with the ceremonial lighting of candles—one candle for each person. The woman of the house usually lights the candles shortly before sunset. Traditions about the exact time of lighting vary. It's often at a particular minute, anywhere from 18 to 75 minutes before sunset. After the candles are lit, no work is allowed—not even putting out the match that lit the candles. The lighter may, however, drop the match on a metal plate to let it burn out on its own.

NOT ALLOWED ON THE SABBATH

Jews can't do the strangest things on the Sabbath—like talk on a cell phone or turn on a light switch. At least that's the case for the most tradition-minded, Orthodox Jews.

It all started with one simple rule in Bible times. One of the 10 Commandments: Don't work on the Sabbath. It was for their own good, to make sure they didn't work themselves to death.

But what qualifies as work? The Bible doesn't say much about it.

In time, Jewish scholars and rabbis started offering their personal opinions about how to apply this teaching to life—a bit like many preachers do today.

By the time Jesus began his ministry, a group of Jewish scholars called Pharisees had piled up generations of unwritten laws about what Jews could and couldn't do on the day of rest.

PROHIBITED	WHY
USING ANYTHING ELECTRICAL	It's sparked by fire, prohibited in Exodus 35:3.
DRIVING A CAR	Ditto above.
RIDING A BIKE	The chain could fall off. Tire could go flat. Fixing it is like making it new, which Jewish scholars say is an act of creation. God worked on creation six days, but rested on the Sabbath. Jews should rest, too.
CARRYING ANYTHING, EVEN HOUSE KEYS	"The LORD says, 'Make sure you do not carry a load on the Sabbath day. . . . Do not bring a load out of your houses on the Sabbath'" (Jeremiah 17:21–22 NIrV).
COOKING	"Tomorrow is a day of rest, a holy Sabbath to God. Whatever you plan to bake, bake today" (Exodus 16:23 MSG).
EATING OUT	Jews shouldn't make others work: "Do not do any work on that day. . . . It also applies to any outsiders who live in your cities" (Exodus 20:10 NIrV).

PARK IT. Russian immigrants pioneering a new settlement in Samaria, on the West Bank, are probably not on their way to the synagogue. Jews aren't allowed to ride bikes on the Sabbath.

scholars said it was better to be safe than sorry, in case God considered it work. So they made it an unwritten law—no treating sick people on the Sabbath unless it was a matter of life or death. When they criticized Jesus for breaking their law by healing the sick on the Sabbath, Jesus gave them this reply.

SACRED

As the Bible reports it, God considers anything or anyone devoted to him as holy.

:: *"You must be able to tell the difference between what is holy and what is not"* (Leviticus 10:10 NIrV).

:: *"You will be my kingdom of priests, my holy nation"* (Exodus 19:6). Since the Jews agreed to devote themselves to God by obeying him, God considered them holy.

:: *"Have the people make an Ark of acacia wood—a sacred chest 45 inches long, 27 inches wide, and 27 inches high [115 x 69 x 69 cm]. . . . When the Ark is finished, place inside it the stone tablets inscribed with the terms of the covenant, which I will give to you"* (Exodus 25:10, 16). The Ark of the Covenant was Israel's most sacred object.

:: *"Have the people of Israel build me a holy sanctuary so I can live among them"* (Exodus 25:8). Jews during the exodus out of Egypt made a tent worship center where they offered sacrifices to God. Centuries later, King Solomon

built the first permanent worship center: the Jerusalem Temple.

SACRIFICES

Jews brought animals and crops to the Jerusalem Temple as worship offerings. Some were simply offerings of gratitude. Others came with requests for forgiveness. New Testament writers said the sacrifice of Jesus ended the need for any more sacrifices. About 40 years after Jesus' death, Romans ended the Jewish sacrificial system by destroying the Jerusalem Temple—the only place Jewish law said Jews could offer sacrifices. The Temple has never been rebuilt.

:: *"I have given you the blood of animals to pay for your sin on the altar. Blood is life. That is why blood pays for your sin"* (Leviticus 17:11 NIrV). In God's eyes, sin is a capital offense. If there is sin, there will be blood—at least if the person wants forgiveness.

:: *"The man must place his hand on the head of the burnt offering. Then the LORD will accept it in place of him. It will pay for his sin. The*

BULLISH ON BLOOD. Two Roman priests lead a bull to the sacrificial altar while a flute player fills the air with a tune—possibly one snippet of a grand spectacle honoring the emperor. Animal sacrifice was common throughout the Mediterranean world in Bible times. Jews, however, offered sacrifices honoring only God.

young bull must be killed there in the sight of the LORD" (Leviticus 1:4-5 NIrV).

:: Jesus Christ. . .is the sacrifice that atones for our sins—and not only our sins but the sins of all the world (1 John 2:1-2).

(See more about Jewish sacrifices, pages 263–264.)

SAINTS

Some Bible translators use *saint* to describe anyone devoted to God. Many Christians, including Catholics and Eastern Orthodox, also use the term for people of extraordinary faith throughout history. Some were martyrs. Some reportedly performed miracles.

:: Love GOD, all you saints; GOD takes care of all who stay close to him (Psalm 31:23 MSG).

:: To all who are in Rome, beloved of God, called to be saints: Grace to you and peace from God our Father and the Lord Jesus Christ (Romans 1:7 NKJV). Paul addresses all Christians in Rome as saints.

SALVATION

:: God loved the people of this world so much that he gave his only Son, so that everyone who has faith in him will have eternal life and never really die (John 3:16 CEV). Condensed to a single verse, this is the message of the New Testament.

:: If you confess with your mouth that Jesus is Lord and believe in your heart that God raised him from the dead, you will be saved (Romans 10:9).

:: Everyone who calls on the name of the LORD will be saved (Romans 10:13).

:: Saving is all his [God's] idea, and all his work. All we do is trust him enough to let him do it. It's God's gift from start to finish! (Ephesians 2:8 MSG).

(See also *Justification, Faith, Grace,* "What it takes to be a Christian," page 34.)

SAINTS AMONG US. Sergius of Radonezh (about 1314–1392), one of the Russian Orthodox Church's most revered saints, offers a blessing. An ascetic monk, he lived alone in a hut in the woods, but was later joined by other monks in a community of faith that grew and built a monastery.

It's the process of becoming holy—which doesn't mean perfect in behavior. In the Bible, sanctification can refer to a person or object purified through cleansing rituals, such as a bath or a period of isolation. It can also refer to folks devoted to God—people who consider themselves God's people and who try to prove it by the way they live.

ANOINTING OIL. A vial of sacred olive oil rests in a church, awaiting an opportunity to anoint someone for healing, for baptism, or for some other act of worship. Jews in Bible times also consecrated worship objects and utensils, such as the altar and the Menorah lampstands. Anything or anyone anointed in this manner was considered sanctified, holy, devoted to God.

ENTIRE SANCTIFICATION.

Some church groups emphasize holiness and teach that Christians can become "entirely sanctified" in this life. Sin-free, or nearly so. Even holiness Christians such as Nazarenes, Wesleyans, and the Salvation Army debate which.

Some say sanctification is a two-step process.

First step: initial sanctification. That's when a person gets saved.

Second step: entire sanctification. This usually comes later, when a mature Christian decides to become fully devoted to God. Some Christians who call themselves sanctified say they had been fighting a tug-of-war with the sinful nature inside them—and losing the battles far too often. They say they wanted the war to end and the sinful nature defeated.

Many say this happens in a single moment of complete abandonment to God's will.

Others say sanctification is a lifelong process, and is never really entire until we reach heaven.

(See also *Baptism with the Holy Spirit, Original Sin.*)

SANCTIFYING RITUALS

:: *"Cleanse the altar by purifying it; make it holy by anointing it with oil. Purify the altar, and consecrate it every day for seven days. After that, the altar will be absolutely holy, and whatever touches it will become holy"* (Exodus 29:36–37).

SANCTIFIED PEOPLE

:: *God chose you. . .to be saved through the sanctifying work of the Spirit and through belief in the truth. . .the teachings we passed on to you* (2 Thessalonians 2:13, 15 NIV).

:: *God wants you to live a pure life. . . . God hasn't invited us into a disorderly, unkempt life but into something holy and beautiful—as beautiful on the inside as the outside* (1 Thessalonians 4:3, 7 MSG).

:: *Christ made us right with God; he made us pure and holy, and he freed us from sin* (1 Corinthians 1:30).

:: *Some dishes are made of gold or silver, while others are made of wood or clay. Some of these are special, and others are not. That's also how it is with people. The ones who stop doing evil and make themselves pure will become special. Their lives will be holy and pleasing to their Master, and they will be able to do all kinds of good deeds* (2 Timothy 2:20–21 CEV).

(See also *Holiness*.)

SATAN (DEVIL, LUCIFER)

The Bible portrays him as an all-too-real evil spirit, leader of an army of evil spirits.

:: *The Spirit who lives in you is greater than the spirit who lives in the world* (1 John 4:4). Jesus sometimes describes Satan as "the ruler of this world" (John 12:31).

:: *Resist the devil, and he will flee from you* (James 4:7).

:: *"I saw Satan fall from heaven like lightning! Look, I have given you authority over all the power of the enemy. . . . Nothing will injure you. But don't rejoice because evil spirits obey you; rejoice because your names are registered in heaven"* (Luke 10:18–20). The words of Jesus, to his followers.

LIAR. That's how Jesus describes Satan. "He is a liar and the father of lies" (John 8:44).

LOSER. Satan tumbles from power when Jesus rises from the dead. That's what some scholars say the Bible implies: "The Son. . .became flesh and blood. For only as a human being could he die, and only by dying could he break the power of the devil, who had the power of death" (Hebrews 2:14). ▲

SATAN, A FALLEN ANGEL?

It's not all that clear, some Bible experts say, that Satan was once an angel who led a revolt in heaven, lost, and got booted down to Planet Earth.

That's in spite of what the Bible reports:

:: "I saw Satan fall from heaven like lightning!" (Luke 10:18). So said Jesus.

:: "War broke out in heaven; Michael and his angels fought against. . . . Satan, the deceiver of the whole world—he was thrown down to the earth, and his angels were thrown down with him" (Revelation 12:7, 9 NRSV).

These Bible excerpts are open to interpretation, many scholars insist.

Jesus' quote, some say, could be nothing more than a graphic word picture. It might simply describe Satan's defeat when Jesus completes his mission on the cross and rises from the dead. As in, "I saw Satan fall like lightning from heaven" (TNIV)—emphasis on the fall, not the location.

Revelation's reference to a war in heaven is written in the highly symbolic style of apocalyptic literature. Many scholars say we shouldn't take it any more literally than poetry. This passage, too, some scholars say, could be a reference to Jesus' defeat of Satan at the cross.

THE MYSTERIOUS SATAN.

If we want to piece together a profile of Satan, the Bible isn't much help.

It does give us the heads-up that he's the big boy of the bad boys. But it takes its good ol' sweet time doing it, waiting until the century Jesus shows up. Even then, the Bible never clearly reveals who Satan is or where he came from.

Satan surfaces only three times in the Old Testament. Four, if we count the snake in the Garden of Eden. But the Genesis story simply IDs the critter as a talking snake. We have to wait until the last book of the Bible to find out that the creepy critter was Reptilian Satan: "The ancient serpent called the devil, or Satan" (Revelation 12:9).

All three other times, Old Testament writers simply call him the Accuser. *Satan* is the Hebrew word for "accuser." In the famous story of Job, Satan is the spirit being who goes to heaven and accuses Job of being a fraud. Satan insists that Job served God for only what he could get out of it: riches and good health. He convinces God to let him test Job's loyalty.

Satan shows up first as an evil spiritual entity when he tempts Jesus to serve him instead of God.

What the Bible does clearly reveal about Satan:

:: He's evil (John 8:44).
:: He leads demons (Matthew 25:41).
:: He can influence people (Luke 22:3).
:: He can't force people to obey him (James 4:7).
:: His knowledge and power are limited (Matthew 4:1–11; he failed to lure Jesus to the dark side).
:: Jesus defeated him by completing his mission of dying on the cross and rising from the dead (Hebrews 2:14).
:: He's doomed (Revelation 20:10).

:: *"Get out of here, Satan," Jesus told him. "For the Scriptures say, 'You must worship the LORD your God and serve only him'"* (Matthew 4:10). This is what Jesus said when Satan offered to let him rule the world in exchange for worshipping Satan.

:: *Let the Lord make you strong. Depend on his mighty power. Put on all of God's armor. Then you can stand firm against the devil's evil plans. Our fight is not against human beings. It is against the rulers, the authorities and the powers of this dark world. It is against the spiritual forces of evil in the heavenly world* (Ephesians 6:10–12 NIrV).

:: *Then the devil. . .was thrown into the fiery lake of burning sulfur, joining the beast and the false prophet. There they will be tormented day and night forever and ever* (Revelation 20:10).

(See also *Demons.*)

SECOND COMING

Before Jesus ascended to heaven, he assured his followers that he would come back for them.

:: *When the Master comes again to get us, those of us who are still alive will not get a jump on the dead and leave them behind. . . . The dead in Christ will rise—they'll go first. Then the rest of us who are still alive at the time will be caught up with them into the clouds to meet the Master. Oh, we'll be walking on air!* (1 Thessalonians 4:15–17 MSG).

:: *"After I go and prepare a place for you, I will come back and take you to be with me so that you may be where I am"* (John 14:3 NCV).

:: *"No one knows the day or hour when these things will happen, not even the angels in* heaven or the Son himself. Only the Father knows" (Matthew 24:36). But this hasn't stopped people from guessing—or from getting rich by writing books filled with their guesses.

:: *The day of the Lord's return will come unexpectedly, like a thief in the night* (1 Thessalonians 5:2).

:: *"Why are you men from Galilee [Jesus' disciples] standing here and looking up into the sky? Jesus has been taken to heaven. But he will come back in the same way that you have seen him go"* (Acts 1:11 CEV).

:: *Look, Jesus is coming with the clouds, and everyone will see him, even those who stabbed him. . . . Yes, this will happen!* (Revelation 1:7 NCV).

(See also *Rapture*.)

LOOKING UP. Some Christians today seem obsessed with the return of Jesus. Some insist the signs point to his imminent return. During Christian Generation One, some believers were so confident Jesus was coming back any day that they quit their jobs. The apostle Paul chewed them out. He told them to get back to work. That's pretty much what an angel told Jesus' 11 surviving disciples, after Jesus ascended into the sky: "Why are you standing here staring into heaven?" (Acts 1:11). The angel's implication: The last word out of Jesus' mouth wasn't *wait*. It was *witness*. "Tell everyone about me. . .everywhere in the world" (Acts 1:8 CEV).

The Bible devotes an entire book to love and sex—the Song of Songs, an intimate and sometimes erotic conversation between a man and a woman in love. Sex in the Bible is considered a good thing—as long as it's within marriage, within the species, and with the opposite sex.

WHEN TO SAY NO

:: *Potiphar's wife grabbed hold of his [Joseph's] coat and said, "Make love to me!" Joseph ran out of the house, leaving her hanging onto his coat* (Genesis 39:12 CEV).

:: *Those who indulge in sexual sin. . .or commit adultery, or are male prostitutes, or practice homosexuality. . .none of these will inherit the Kingdom of God* (1 Corinthians 6:9–10).

:: *"Do not have sex with an animal"* (Leviticus 18:23 NIrV).

:: *God wants you to be holy and to stay away from sexual sins. He wants each of you to learn to control your own body in a way that is holy and honorable. Don't use your body for sexual sin like the people who do not know God* (1 Thessalonians 4:3–5 NCV).

WHEN TO SAY YES

:: *A husband should satisfy his wife's sexual needs. And a wife should satisfy her husband's sexual needs. The wife's body does not belong only to her. It also belongs to her husband. In the same way, the husband's body does not belong only to him. It also belongs to his wife. You shouldn't stop giving yourselves to each other except when you both agree to do so. . . . Then you should come together again. In that way, Satan will not tempt you when you can't control yourselves* (1 Corinthians

PUBLIC SHOW OF AFFECTION. A drama queen in love, by the looks of her body language, a woman portrayed in Roman times doesn't seem shy about expressing her feelings. Neither does the love-drunk star of the Bible's only erotic book, the Song of Songs.

7:3–5 NIrV).

:: *Your wife is a fountain of fine wine—your own private stock. Drink. Enjoy. Satisfy yourself with the sweet intoxication that her body provides. Why would you even consider drinking up the slobber from another man's fountain? Yuck!* (Proverbs 5:18–20 AUTHOR'S PARAPHRASE).

:: *You are tall and supple, like the palm tree, and your full breasts are like sweet clusters of dates. I say, "I'm going to climb that palm tree! I'm going to caress its fruit!"* (Song of Songs 7:7–8 MSG). Unapologetically sensual, the Song of Songs reports the love talk of a young couple praising each other's physical features and expressing their shared desires about making love.

(See also *Adultery, Homosexuality, Marriage*.)

SHAME

:: *She [Eve] took some of the fruit and ate it. Then she gave some to her husband [Adam], who was with her, and he ate it, too. At that moment their eyes were opened, and they suddenly felt shame at their nakedness. So they sewed fig leaves together to cover themselves* (Genesis 3:6–7). From humanity's first reported sin, shame is what people get for doing something they know is wrong.

:: *He [Jesus] endured the shame of being nailed to a cross, because he knew that later on he would be glad he did* (Hebrews 12:2 CEV). Crucifixion was the most shameful form of execution in Roman times, reserved for the worst offenders. The Bible says Jesus died to pay the penalty for humanity's capital offense: sin against God. The shame humans deserved, he took upon himself.

:: *God is faithful and fair. If we admit that we have sinned, he will forgive us our sins. He will forgive every wrong thing we have done. He will make us pure* (1 John 1:9 NIrV). The Bible's cure for shame.

(See also *Forgiveness*.)

SICKNESS

:: *If you are sick, ask the church leaders to come and pray for you. Ask them to put olive oil on you in the name of the Lord. If you have faith when you pray for sick people, they will get well. The Lord will heal them, and if they have sinned, he will forgive them* (James 5:14–15 CEV). Bible experts aren't sure what to make of this. Some argue that subtle word meanings in the original Greek language could suggest James was talking about a spiritual healing. Others say it was physical healing. Some also point out that the faith James said is required comes from the people praying, not from the sick person. Also, miracles of healing were common at the beginning of the Christian movement, as the Bible reports it. So some students of the Bible wonder if the prescription and promise James offered were mainly for his generation. Even so, many Christians who become sick today ask their minister or priest to anoint and pray for their healing.

(See also *Healing*.)

SIN

Christians define *sin* different ways—two ways, mainly. Many Baptists, Presbyterians, and Lutherans say it's sin if we do something wrong in God's eyes—whether we realize it's wrong or not. So they say we sin every day. Jews offered sacrifices for those kinds of unintentional sins (Leviticus 4:2). Other Christians—including many Methodists, Nazarenes, and those in the Salvation Army—say we have to know it's wrong before it's sin. So they say we can go for stretches without sinning if we choose not to do what we know is wrong.

HOW TO KNOW IT'S SIN

:: *Remember, it is sin to know what you ought to do and then not do it* (James 4:17). That would suggest the flip side is true, as well: It's sin if you know it's wrong and you do it anyhow. James focused a lot of his criticism on do-nothing Christians, which may be why he phrased it the way he did.

EVERYONE HAS DONE IT

:: *Everyone has sinned and fallen short of God's glorious standard, and all need to be made right with God by his grace, which is a free gift* (Romans 3:23–24 NCV).

WHAT SIN DOES TO PEOPLE

:: *The payment for sin is death. But God gives us the free gift of life forever in Christ Jesus our Lord* (Romans 6:23 NCV).

:: *Your sins. . .have cut you off from God. Because of your sins, he has turned away and will not listen anymore* (Isaiah 59:2). Persistent sin builds a wall between us and God.

:: *If the power of sin within me keeps sabotaging my best intentions, I obviously need help! I realize that I don't have what it takes. . . . I decide to do good, but I don't really do it; I decide not to do bad, but then I do it anyway. . .*

THE UNFORGIVABLE SIN.

If you're worried that you committed the unforgivable sin—and many people are—you can stop.

Bible experts say that worrying is a sure sign you're not guilty.

The reason so many people worry about it is because of the way Jesus phrased what became a sound bite: "Every sin and blasphemy can be forgiven—except blasphemy against the Holy Spirit, which will never be forgiven" (Matthew 12:31).

Taken by itself, this sounds like we're doomed to toast if we swear at the Holy Spirit. One curse, doomed forever.

But Bible experts say it isn't so.

Jesus was talking to Jewish scholars who hated him so much that they insisted his miracles came from the devil. They looked at the miracle-working Son of God standing right in front of them, and they called him the son of Satan. They were hopeless; nothing could convince them to repent.

That's the unforgivable sin, many scholars say: refusal to repent. God won't forgive us if we don't repent.

BAD HAIRCUT, BAD BOY. John Dillinger (1903–1934)—one bold gangster in the roaring '20s—robbed two dozen banks, four police stations, and escaped from jail twice. A hooker immigrant in Chicago ratted him out to the FBI in exchange for the bureau's help in fighting her deportation. Dillinger resisted arrest by reaching for his gun and running. Agents shot him dead. By any Christian denominational definition, Dillinger was nasty. But as the Bible teaches it, not too nasty for God's forgiveness, had he been interested. ◀

I've tried everything and nothing helps. I'm at the end of my rope. Is there no one who can do anything for me? . . . The answer, thank God, is that Jesus Christ can and does (Romans 7:17-19, 24-25 MSG). This describes how the apostle Paul says sin can overpower our desire to do what's right. Alone, we're no match for sin. But with Christ, sin doesn't stand a chance. Christ rules, sin doesn't.

GOD'S SOLUTION TO SIN

:: *You know the story of how Adam landed us in the dilemma we're in—first sin, then death. . . . That sin disturbed relations with God in everything and everyone. . . . Here it is in a nutshell: Just as one person did it wrong and got us in all this trouble with sin and death, another person [Jesus] did it right and got us out of it* (Romans 5:12-13, 18 MSG).

:: *God gave Jesus to die for our sins, and he raised him to life, so that we would be made acceptable to God* (Romans 4:25 CEV).

:: *"Though your sins are bright red, they will be as white as snow. Even though they are deep red, they will be white like wool. But you have to be willing to change and obey me"* (Isaiah 1:18-19 NIrV).

:: *Christ showed up in order to get rid of sin. . . . No one who lives deeply in Christ makes a practice of sin. None of those who do practice sin have taken a good look at Christ* (1 John 3:5-6 MSG). Most Bible experts say John was warning against a sinful lifestyle, not the occasional sin that trips people up on their Christian journey. A person who persistently sins is following in the footsteps of someone other than Jesus.

(See also *Forgiveness, Salvation.*)

SMOKING

The Bible doesn't talk about smoking. Folks in the civilized world didn't pick up the habit until Christopher Columbus discovered it in the Americas during the 1400s. But the Bible encourages us to take good care of our bodies. And smoking seems the flip side of healthy—and perhaps a bit like sucking on the tailpipe of a Ford Fiesta while riding the back bumper during a demolition derby. Rare exceptions might include when

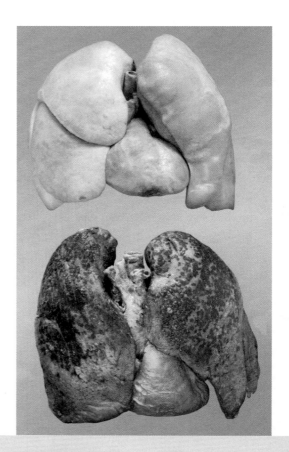

LIGHTLY TOASTED. Lungs diseased from smoking (bottom) have a crispy critter look about them. Smoking might not be a sin, as far as the Bible is concerned. But most physicians agree it's dumber than all get out.

smoking delivers helpful medication to someone who's sick. One caution that compassionate pastors sometimes offer Christians critical of smokers: smoking is one hard habit to break. With that in mind, some say it would be a good idea for Christians to cut smokers some slack: "Be patient with each other, making allowance for each other's faults" (Ephesians 4:2).

:: *Your body is a temple for the Holy Spirit who is in you. . . . So honor God with your bodies* (1 Corinthians 6:19–20 NCV).

:: *Give your bodies to God. Let them be a living sacrifice, holy—the kind he can accept. When you think of what he has done for you, is this too much to ask?* (Romans 12:1 TLB).

(See also *Drugs and Alcohol.*)

SON OF MAN

This was Jesus' favorite way of referring to himself. Some scholars say Jesus used it because it pointed both to his humanity and his divinity.

THE TITLE OF A HUMAN

:: *The LORD said, "Ezekiel, son of man, I want you to stand up and listen"* (Ezekiel 2:1 CEV). About 600 years earlier, God used this title for the prophet Ezekiel—apparently as a way of reminding the prophet that he was only human.

THE TITLE OF A DEITY

:: *I saw someone like a son of man coming with the clouds of heaven. . . . He was given authority, honor, and sovereignty over all the nations of the world, so that people of every race and nation and language would obey him. His rule*

is eternal—it will never end. His kingdom will never be destroyed (Daniel 7:13–14).

JESUS' FAVORITE TITLE FOR HIMSELF

:: *Jesus. . .asked his followers, "Who do people say the Son of Man is?" They answered, "Some say you are John the Baptist. Others say you are Elijah, and still others say you are Jeremiah or one of the prophets." Then Jesus asked them, "And who do you say I am?" Simon Peter answered, "You are the Christ, the Son of the living God"* (Matthew 16:13–16 NCV).

SOUL

The Bible uses the word *soul* in different ways. Sometimes it's just another word for a person. Other times it's the essence or spirit of the person that leaves the body at death.

PHYSICAL PERSON

:: *The LORD God formed man of the dust of the ground, and breathed into his nostrils the breath of life; and man became a living soul* (Genesis 2:7 KJV). Most modern Bibles translate the Hebrew word *nephesh* as "person" or "life" instead of "soul." The Bible uses that Hebrew word to describe both humans and animals, as though the word refers to the tangible, visible side of life.

:: *With my whole being, body and soul, I will shout joyfully to the living God* (Psalm 84:2).

SPIRITUAL PERSON

:: *For we know that when this earthly tent we live in is taken down (that is, when we die and leave this earthly body), we will have a house in heaven, an eternal body made for us by God*

BREATH OF LIFE. God himself blew the breath of life into the first human, the Bible says. In that moment, "The Man came alive—a living soul!" (Genesis 2:7 MSG). When the last breath leaves our body, the Bible says our soul goes, too. Bible writers compare our body to a tent—the temporary home of our soul living inside.

himself and not by human hands. . . . We will put on heavenly bodies; we will not be spirits without bodies (2 Corinthians 5:1, 3).

:: *May God himself. . .make you holy and whole, put you together—spirit, soul, and body—and keep you fit for the coming of our Master, Jesus Christ* (1 Thessalonians 5:23 MSG). Many Bible experts say it's unclear if there's any difference between "spirit" and "soul." Both may refer to the same thing: the essence of a person that lives on after the body dies. Greek philosophers taught that our souls existed before our bodies and would live on after our bodies die—as disembodied souls. New Testament writers disagree. They say that after our human bodies die, the souls of Christians will receive new "spiritual bodies" (1 Corinthians 15:44). Our souls won't hover around as ascended energy fields. Nor will they get absorbed into the oneness of the cosmos. Not as the Bible tells it. Our awareness and individualism will survive. (See "Eternal Life," page 117.)

:: *"What do you benefit if you gain the whole world but lose your own soul? Is anything worth more than your own soul?"* (Matthew 16:26).

:: *"Don't be afraid of those who want to kill your body; they cannot touch your soul. Fear only God, who can destroy both soul and body in hell"* (Matthew 10:28).

:: *Remember your Creator before you return to the dust you came from. That's when your spirit will go back to God who gave it* (Ecclesiastes 12:7 NIrV).

(See also *Spirit*.)

SPIRIT

Possibly another word for "soul," according to many Bible experts, *spirit* shows up in the Bible

as the invisible force within a person's body—the essence, character, and personality of that person. The word literally means "breath" or "blowing wind," which sounds a bit like the CPR procedure that breathes life back into a dying body. It also sounds like God's creation of Adam: "GOD formed Man out of dirt from the ground and blew into his nostrils the breath of life. The Man came alive—a living soul!" (Genesis 2:7 MSG). The Bible says our spirit lives on even after our body dies.

:: *"Father, I entrust my spirit into your hands!"* (Luke 23:46). The last words of Jesus while hanging on the cross.

:: *As they stoned him, Stephen prayed, "Lord Jesus, receive my spirit." He fell to his knees, shouting, "Lord, don't charge them with this sin!" And with that, he died* (Acts 7:59–60).

:: *All the people were crying and feeling sad because the girl was dead. . . . But Jesus took hold of her hand and called to her, "My child, stand up!" Her spirit came back into her, and she stood up at once* (Luke 8:52, 54–55 NCV).

(See also *Soul.*)

SPIRITUAL

Lots of folks say they're "spiritual, not religious"— meaning they believe in something. Perhaps it's a higher power. Maybe it's treating people kindly. But whatever it is, they generally keep it to themselves. No churchy rituals, rules, or creeds. One in five Americans said they fit the phrase, according to one recent study. But in the Bible, *spiritual* and *religious* often mean the same thing: devoted to God. Spiritual people are religious people. Spiritual gifts and spiritual needs all spin around religious beliefs and behavior.

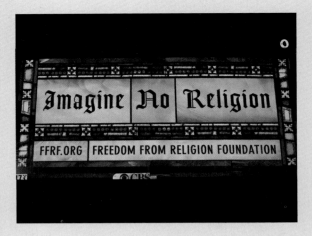

STAINED-GLASS BILLBOARD. Looking churchy, this billboard in downtown Harrisburg, Pennsylvania, plugs a website lobbying the interests of "atheists, agnostics, and skeptics." Their headline cause: "Defend the separation between government and religion." Surprisingly enough, some Christians say, Jesus may have agreed with that. At a time when Romans occupied Israel and the nation seemed ripe for Jewish political activism, Jesus didn't take the bait. Asked if Jews should pay the taxes Rome imposed on them, he simply said, "Give to Caesar what belongs to Caesar, and give to God what belongs to God" (Mark 12:17).

:: *There are different kinds of spiritual gifts, but the same Spirit is the source of them all. . . . To one person the Spirit gives the ability to give wise advice. . . . The same Spirit gives great faith to another, and to someone else the one Spirit gives the gift of healing* (1 Corinthians 12:4, 8–9).

:: *"Nineveh has more than 120,000 people living in spiritual darkness. . . . Shouldn't I feel sorry for such a great city?"* (Jonah 4:11). That's God talking to the prophet Jonah, who's pouting because God decided not to destroy the city after the people repented.

:: *"Humans can reproduce only human life, but the Holy Spirit gives birth to spiritual life"* (John 3:6).

:: *Don't let anyone capture you with empty philosophies and high-sounding nonsense that come from human thinking and from the spiritual powers of this world, rather than from Christ* (Colossians 2:8). The Bible says not all spirits are good. Even in the spiritual dimension, it seems, there's a battle between good and evil.

SPIRITUAL AND RELIGIOUS

:: *Honor those who are your leaders in the Lord's work. They work hard among you and give you spiritual guidance* (1 Thessalonians 5:12). Some see this as a link between spiritual and religious—private beliefs and public worship in a church setting.

:: *Obey your spiritual leaders, and do what they say. Their work is to watch over your souls, and they are accountable to God* (Hebrews 13:17).

:: *We are lying if we say we have fellowship with God but go on living in spiritual darkness; we are not practicing the truth. But if we are living in the light, as God is in the light, then we have fellowship with each other, and the blood of Jesus, his Son, cleanses us from all sin* (1 John 1:6–7).

(See also *Spiritual Gifts.*)

SPIRITUAL GIFTS

New Testament writers describe spiritual gifts as attitudes, abilities, and sometimes even people.

:: *What happens when we live God's way? He brings gifts into our lives, much the same way that fruit appears in an orchard—things like affection for others, exuberance about life, serenity* (Galatians 5:22 MSG).

:: *God has given us different gifts for doing certain things well. So if God has given you the ability to prophesy, speak out with as much faith as God has given you. If your gift is serving others, serve them well. If you are a teacher, teach well. If your gift is to encourage others, be encouraging. If it is giving, give generously. If God has given you leadership ability, take the responsibility seriously. And if you have a gift for showing kindness to others, do it gladly* (Romans 12:6–8).

:: *God has given each of you a gift from his great variety of spiritual gifts. Use them well to serve one another. Do you have the gift of speaking? Then speak as though God himself were speaking through you. Do you have the gift of helping others? Do it with all the strength and energy that God supplies* (1 Peter 4:10–11).

:: *These are the gifts Christ gave to the church: the apostles, the prophets, the evangelists, and the pastors and teachers. Their responsibility is to equip God's people to do his work and build up the church* (Ephesians 4:11–12).

(See also *Spiritual*.)

STEALING

:: *Do not steal* (Exodus 20:15 CEV). This is one of the 10 Commandments.

:: *"The thief's purpose is to steal. . . . My purpose is to give"* (John 10:10). These are the words of Jesus, the example Christians are to follow.

:: *Did you use to make ends meet by stealing? Well, no more! Get an honest job so that you can help others who can't work* (Ephesians 4:28 MSG).

:: *"Do you think you can rob. . .and then march into this Temple, set apart for my worship, and say, 'We're safe!' . . . . Do you think you can turn this Temple, set apart for my worship, into something like that? Well, think again"* (Jeremiah 7:9–11 MSG).

SUCCESS

Success for a Christian doesn't look anything like success in the business world—exactly the opposite, in fact. At least as the Bible tells it.

STOOPING FOR SUCCESS. In a painting from about 1300, Italian artist Duccio di Buoninsegna captures the object lesson Jesus gives Peter and the other disciples the day before his crucifixion. Real leaders don't live to be served. They live to serve.

:: *He [Jesus] began washing his disciples' feet. . . . Then he said: Do you understand what I have done. . . . I have set the example, and you should do for each other exactly what I have done for you. . . . God will bless you, if you do* (John 13:5, 12, 15, 17 CEV). True leaders in God's kingdom don't strut. They kneel.

:: *"You've observed how godless rulers throw their weight around, how quickly a little power goes to their heads. It's not going to be that way with you. Whoever wants to be great must become a servant. Whoever wants to be first among you must be your slave. That is what the Son of Man has done: He came to serve, not be served"* (Matthew 20:25–28 MSG).

:: *I realized that we work and do wonderful things just because we are jealous of others. This makes no more sense than chasing the wind* (Ecclesiastes 4:4 CEV). The reason this kind of success is meaningless: We die and our suc- cess dies with us. "We all come to the end of our lives as naked and empty-handed as on the day we were born" (Ecclesiastes 5:15).

:: *"You can't worship God and Money both"* (Matthew 6:24 MSG).

:: *Commit to the* LORD *everything you do. Then your plans will succeed* (Proverbs 16:3 NIrV).

SUFFERING

:: *Our physical body is becoming older and weaker, but our spirit inside us is made new every day. We have small troubles for a while now, but they are helping us gain an eternal glory that is much greater than the troubles. We set our eyes not on what we see but on what we cannot see. What we see will last only a short time, but what we cannot see will last forever* (2 Corinthians 4:16–18 NCV).

WHY DO WE HAVE TO SUFFER?

Suffering is one of the biggest reasons people reject Christianity. Many can't understand why a loving God would allow suffering.

Perhaps God asks the same about us, some scholars say—why we do little or nothing to help all the people suffering around us.

As for why God allows suffering, the Bible doesn't give us a full answer. He didn't even give old, suffering Job a clue, except to imply, "Trust me. I know what I'm doing." Job had lost his children, wealth, and health.

The Bible does show that God often uses suffering as a springboard for helping people, as he did with Joseph who got sold to slave-traders. God also sends suffering some- times as punishment, to get our attention and to point us toward holy living.

But much of our suffering—such as growing older and dying—may stem from what happened when sin entered God's perfect creation and somehow, mysteriously, changed it for the worse. Until then, death didn't seem on the agenda. That's what some Bible experts say.

Even so, the Bible says that our life on Earth is just a speck on the calendar. We will suffer some. But eternal joy is coming: "There will be no more death or sorrow or crying or pain. All these things are gone forever" (Revelation 21:4).

(See also "If God is so good, why doesn't he do anything when we're suffering?" page 40.)

:: *You're suffering now, but justice is on the way. When the Master Jesus appears out of heaven in a blaze of fire with his strong angels, he'll even up the score by settling accounts with those who gave you such a bad time* (2 Thessalonians 1:5–6 MSG).

:: *There's a lot of suffering to be entered into in this world—the kind of suffering Christ takes on. I welcome the chance to take my share in the church's part of that suffering* (Colossians 1:24 MSG). The apostle Paul writes this from jail, arrested for preaching about Jesus.

WHEN GOD USES SUFFERING FOR GOOD

:: *"Why was this man born blind? Was it because of his own sins or his parents' sins?"* (John 9:2). That's a question the disciples asked Jesus. His reply: "This happened so the power of God could be seen in him" (verse 3). Then Jesus healed the man.

:: *"You planned evil against me but God used those same plans for my good"* (Genesis 50:20 MSG). Joseph reassures his brothers that he won't kill them for selling him to slave-traders years earlier. Joseph said God used this event to elevate him to a high office in Egypt, which allowed him to save his extended family members by inviting them to come down and weather out a seven-year drought that was scorching Israel.

SUICIDE

Suicide doesn't appear to have been very common in Bible times. Though the Bible doesn't directly condemn suicide, many argue that scripture opposes it—at least in principle.

:: *"You must not murder"* (Exodus 20:13). That includes yourself. So said Bible experts even

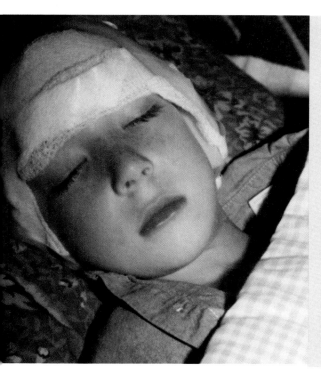

"JESUS DIDN'T MAKE ME RIGHT." Those are the words of five-year-old Brad Miller, the now-adult son of the author. Brad is shown here recovering at home from corrective ear surgery. His ears stuck out. Kids called him Dumbo Ears, after the Disney elephant. A self-insured denomination the author worked for refused to cover the elective surgery, even after an appeal with a letter of support from Brad's kindergarten teacher. The secular employer his wife worked for—a hospital—agreed to pay the tab.

from early Christian centuries—such as Augustine in the AD 400s.

:: *Why am I discouraged? Why is my heart so sad? I will put my hope in God!* (Psalm 42:5). Suicide suggests we've lost all hope—even our hope in God.

:: *When Judas. . .realized that Jesus had been condemned to die, he was filled with remorse. . .and went out and hanged himself* (Matthew 27:3, 5).

:: *When Ahithophel realized that his advice had not been followed, he saddled his donkey, went to his hometown, set his affairs in order, and*

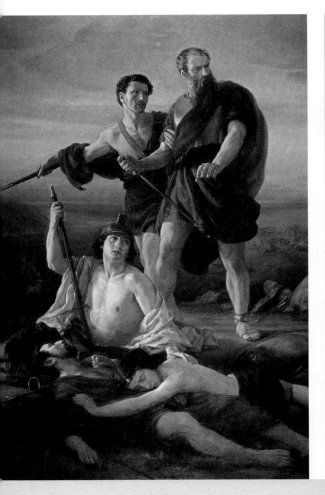

ALL IS LOST. His oldest sons dead and dying, King Saul watches as Philistines destroy his army at the Battle of Mount Gilboa. In one of the Bible's rare mentions of suicide, Saul falls on his sword after getting mortally wounded. He said if he didn't, his enemies would "taunt and torture me" (1 Samuel 31:4).

DOES SUICIDE LEAD TO HELL?

Some religious folks say that anyone who commits suicide is doomed to eternity in hell.

For support, the religious folks point to Bible verses like this:

Don't you know that you are God's temple and that God's Spirit lives in you? If anyone destroys God's temple, God will destroy that person.

1 CORINTHIANS 3:16–17 NCV

Yet suicide wasn't the topic of that letter. The writer, Paul, was pleading for unity in a fractured church. Most Bible experts say Paul was talking about people who tear a congregation of Christians apart with bickering, eventually destroying the community of faith. God will destroy the destroyers.

The Bible doesn't say what happens to a person who commits suicide. In fact, speaking from the realm of the dead, the prophet Samuel had this to say to King Saul, who would kill himself a few hours later: "Tomorrow . . .you and your sons will be here with me" (1 Samuel 28:19). Suicidal Saul would end up with saintly Samuel.

When it comes to judging the eternal destiny of suicide victims—or anyone else—most Christians say it's best to leave that to God. He knows people better than we do. Even we know that many of the people who take their own lives are physically ill and not thinking rationally.

God knows that, too.

hanged himself (2 Samuel 17:23). He backed the wrong man in a coup: Absalom, who revolted against his father, King David. Ahithophel may have figured he was doomed.

:: *The jailer woke up to see the prison doors wide open. He assumed the prisoners had escaped, so he drew his sword to kill himself. But Paul shouted to him, "Stop! Don't kill yourself! We are all here!"* (Acts 16:27-28). Romans tended to execute soldiers and jailers who let prisoners escape.

TATTOOS

Jews weren't supposed to scar or tattoo their bodies. Though early Christians rejected many Jewish rules as outdated, they agreed with Jews that the human body was God's masterpiece. Christians called it God's temple, the place where his Spirit lives in us. Because of this, some Christians today say that wearing a tattoo is a bit like spray-painting graffiti on the walls of a natural wonder—like the Grand Canyon—to improve the looks.

:: *"Do not mark your skin with tattoos. I am the Lord"* (Leviticus 19:28). This was an ancient Jewish law. Christians argue that they aren't bound by Jewish laws of the Old Testament. "When God speaks of a 'new' covenant, it means he has made the first one obsolete. It is now out of date" (Hebrews 8:13).

:: *I plead with you to give your bodies to God because of all he has done for you. Let them be a living and holy sacrifice—the kind he will find acceptable* (Romans 12:1).

:: *Don't you realize that your body is the temple of the Holy Spirit?* (1 Corinthians 6:19).

(See also *Body Piercing*.)

FASHION STATEMENT. People who get tattoos, some would say, are slaves to fashion—willing to shed their blood for a fleeting trend. In Bible times, people who got tattoos were often just slaves. Period. Greeks and Romans tattooed their slaves so they could be identified if they tried to escape.

TAX ADVICE FROM RABBIS.

Bible advice in two words: Pay up.

:: *Pay your taxes. . . . For government workers need to be paid. They are serving God in what they do* (Romans 13:6).

:: *"Give to Caesar what belongs to Caesar, and give to God what belongs to God"* (Matthew 22:21). That's Jesus answering a trick question intended to get him in trouble. The question: Should Jews pay taxes imposed by the Roman Empire, occupying what is now Israel. A "no" answer could get him arrested as a rebel. A "yes" answer would alienate followers of his who wanted him to lead a revolt that would boot Romans out of the country.

:: *"We don't want to upset these tax collectors. So go to the lake and fish. After you catch the first fish, open its mouth and you will find a coin. Take that coin and give it to the tax collectors for you and me"* (Matthew 17:27 NCV). This is Jesus telling Peter where he can find the money to pay the annual tax due for the upkeep of the Jewish Temple in Jerusalem.

:: *Submit to governing authorities. For all authority comes from God, and those in positions of authority have been placed there by God. . . . You must submit to them, not only to avoid punishment, but also to keep a clear conscience* (Romans 13:1, 5). The apostle Paul was saying this to Christians in Rome, capital city of an empire famous for its extreme taxation and extravagant spending.

Jews hated paying taxes to Rome, a foreign empire occupying their homeland.

What made it worse was that Rome often contracted with locals to collect the taxes. Locals knew their neighbors and had a clue about their assets. These homegrown taxmen earned a reputation for gouging. Rabbis advised Jews to evade these taxes and to treat anyone collecting them like the plague in a bone bag.

A sampling from ancient Jewish writings:

Lie. *"It's perfectly acceptable to tell murderers, robbers, or tax collectors that the money you have is for a temple offering, or that you're a member of the king's family and exempt from taxes."*

Mishnah, NEDARIM 3:4

Lock your doors. *"If a tax collector goes inside a house, everything in the house becomes ritually unclean and needs to go through purification rituals."*

Mishnah, TOHOROTH 7:6

Don't touch a taxman's money. *"Don't take change back from the wallet of a tax collector. And don't accept any charitable contributions from them, either."*

Talmud, BABA METZIA 10:1

GIVE IT TO CAESAR. Jewish scholars show Jesus a Roman coin like this one, bearing the picture and name of Caesar Tiberius Augustus (ruled AD 14–37). They ask him a loaded question: Should Jews pay Roman taxes? Pointing out the emperor's picture, Jesus says they should give to Caesar what belongs to him—and then do the same for God.

:: *It's smart to be patient, but it's stupid to lose your temper* (Proverbs 14:29 CEV).

:: *Let short-tempered people get what's coming to them. Don't try to put out the fires they start unless you want to make a career of it. If you do, invest in fire retardant knickers because you're going to get burned* (Proverbs 19:19 AUTHOR'S PARAPHRASE).

:: *Your old life is dead. . . . And that means killing off everything connected with that way of death. . . . So make sure it's all gone for good: bad temper, irritability, meanness, profanity* (Colossians 3:3, 5, 8 MSG).

:: *It is obvious what kind of life develops out of trying to get your own way all the time. . .a brutal temper; an impotence to love or be loved; divided homes and divided lives* (Galatians 5:19–20 MSG).

(See also *Anger*.)

TEMPTATION

:: *No test or temptation that comes your way is beyond the course of what others have had to face. All you need to remember is that God will never let you down; he'll never let you be pushed past your limit; he'll always be there to help you come through it* (1 Corinthians 10:13 MSG).

:: *Don't blame God when you are tempted! . . . We are tempted by our own desires that drag us off and trap us. Our desires make us sin, and when sin is finished with us, it leaves us dead* (James 1:13–15 CEV).

:: *The devil came to Jesus to tempt him, saying, "If you are the Son of God, tell these rocks to become bread." Jesus answered, "It is written in the Scriptures, 'A person lives not on bread alone, but by everything God says' "* (Matthew 4:3–4 NCV). When Jesus was tempted while praying and fasting in the desert, he fought off the temptations by quoting relevant Bible verses.

:: *Yell a loud no to the Devil and watch him scamper. Say a quiet yes to God and he'll be there in no time* (James 4:7–8 MSG).

:: *"Pray for strength against temptation. The spirit wants to do what is right, but the body is weak"* (Mark 14:38 NCV).

10 COMMANDMENTS

These are the first laws the Bible says God gave Moses at Mount Sinai. All other religious laws in the Bible are based on these 10.

:: *Do not worship any god except me.*
Do not make idols. . . .
Do not misuse my name. . . .
Remember that the Sabbath day belongs to me. . . .
Respect your father and mother. . . .
Do not murder.
Be faithful in marriage.
Do not steal.
Do not tell lies about others.
Do not want anything that belongs to someone else.
EXODUS 20:3–4, 7–8, 12–17 CEV

TITHING

Jews in Bible times gave a tenth of their income to the Jerusalem Temple. This paid for Temple upkeep, salaries of Temple workers, and it provided charitable support for the poor. There's no mention in the Bible of Christians tithing, though. But the Bible does say they gave offerings.

JEWISH TITHES

:: *"A tenth of the land's produce, whether grain from the ground or fruit from the trees, is GOD's"* (Leviticus 27:30 MSG). This applied to animals and other assets, too. Animals, crops, and currency were all presented as gifts to God at the worship center.

TEN PERCENT OFF THE TOP. Jewish law required God's people to give 10 percent of their harvest and other income to support the Jerusalem Temple and the priesthood. To do less was criticized as robbing God.

WHY CHRISTIANS DIDN'T TITHE.

Tithing 10 percent of your income is Jewish. Not Christian. That's what church historians say.

At least it wasn't Christian for almost 1,900 years—until some cash-strapped preachers in the late 1800s figured out it was a great way to raise money.

The first Christians refused to tithe because they considered it legalistic, and one of the many Jewish laws that didn't apply anymore. Christians didn't have to get circumcised. They didn't have to eat kosher food. And they didn't have to tithe.

All those rules were part of God's old covenant agreement with the Jews. Christians said Jesus' arrival marked the beginning of God's new plan. "God put the old plan on the shelf. And it stays there, gathering dust" (Hebrews 8:13 MSG).

Enter: American preachers with dust rags.

Churches had been funded by taxes—as many still are in some countries. Early Americans felt that religion was important enough to be supported by public dollars. But in 1833, states started rescinding the religious tax.

Suddenly, churches were scrambling to raise money, right at the time they were launching expensive missionary campaigns abroad. They took offerings. They collected pledges. They even rented pews—best seats in the front.

Preachers, desperately looking for ways to motivate their donors, turned to the Bible. There, they not only resurrected the old Jewish law about tithing—church historians say they warped it into a Christian requirement. They insisted that the law about tithing was as relevant and timeless as the laws in the 10 Commandments. The only difference is that instead of bringing money to the Jerusalem Temple, Christians should bring it to the local church.

Today, tithing remains the top source of income for most churches.

Some church historians have suggested a compromise. Present "10 percent giving" as a good guideline for Christians wanting to support the ministry of their local church. But don't sell it as a biblical requirement.

DIDN'T TITHE. John Wesley (1703–1791), founder of Methodists, may have said a flowery version of "Make all you can, save all you can, give all you can." And he may have died broke, because he gave his wealth away. But he didn't tithe. And he didn't preach tithing. Nor did John Calvin (1509–1564), theological father of many Baptists and Presbyterians. Nor Martin Luther (1483–1546), founder of the Protestant movement. Nor Augustine (about AD 354–430), considered one of the greatest minds in the Christian faith. Christian tithing wasn't invented until long after these church leaders: in the mid-1800s.

:: *"Bring your full tithe to the Temple treasury so there will be ample provisions in my Temple. Test me in this and see if I don't open up heaven itself to you and pour out blessings beyond your wildest dreams"* (Malachi 3:10 MSG).

:: *"Do honest people rob God? But you rob me day after day. You ask, 'How have we robbed you?' The tithe and the offering—that's how!"* (Malachi 3:8 MSG). Some Jews were skipping the tithes. Others were giving injured or diseased livestock instead of healthy animals as the law required.

:: *"Hypocrites! For you are careful to tithe even the tiniest income from your herb gardens, but you ignore the more important aspects of the law—justice, mercy, and faith"* (Matthew 23:23). That's Jesus talking to Jewish religion scholars.

CHRISTIAN OFFERINGS

:: *You must each decide in your heart how much to give. And don't give reluctantly or in response to pressure. "For God loves a person who gives cheerfully"* (2 Corinthians 9:7). This is part of Paul's fund-raising letter for an offering he was collecting for believers in Jerusalem.

:: *Regarding the relief offering for poor Christians that is being collected. . . Every Sunday each of you make an offering and put it in safe-keeping. Be as generous as you can. When I get there you'll have it ready, and I won't have to make a special appeal* (1 Corinthians 16:1–2 MSG). The apostle Paul collects an offering for poor Christians in Jerusalem.

:: *Churches in Macedonia province. . .though desperately poor. . .gave offerings of whatever they could—far more than they could afford!—pleading for the privilege of helping out in the relief of poor Christians. This was totally spontaneous, entirely their own idea, and caught us completely off guard* (2 Corinthians 8:1–5 MSG).

:: *Believers. . .felt that what they owned was not their own, so they shared everything they had . . . . There were no needy people among them, because those who owned land or houses would sell them and bring the money to the apostles to give to those in need* (Acts 4:32, 34–35).

:: *Tell those rich in this world's wealth. . .to be rich in helping others, to be extravagantly generous. If they do that, they'll build a treasury that will last* (1 Timothy 6:17–19 MSG).

TOLERANCE

OF OTHERS

:: *Be patient with each other, making allowance for each other's faults because of your love* (Ephesians 4:2).

:: *If someone asks about your Christian hope, always be ready to explain it. But do this in a gentle and respectful way* (1 Peter 3:15–16).

OF GOD

:: *Don't you see how wonderfully kind, tolerant, and patient God is with you? . . . Can't you see that his kindness is intended to turn you from your sin?* (Romans 2:4).

WHEN NOT TO TOLERATE

:: *You have such admirable tolerance for impostors who rob your freedom, rip you off, steal you blind, put you down—even slap your face! I shouldn't admit it to you, but our stomachs aren't strong enough to tolerate that kind of stuff* (2 Corinthians 11:20–21 MSG). Paul is warning Christians about false teachers intruding into the church and preaching heresy.

(See also *Patience*.)

Some churches, especially Pentecostal denominations, teach that speaking in "heavenly languages" is evidence that a Christian has received the Holy Spirit. To outsiders, the language sounds like gibberish. But often someone in the group claims to be able to translate the language. Bible writers report that early Christians spoke in heavenly languages. The book of Acts also says that when the Holy Spirit first arrived, the disciples were able to speak in earthly languages they hadn't learned.

EARTHLY LANGUAGES

:: *All of them [the disciples and other follow-ers of Jesus] were filled with the Holy Spirit. They began to speak in languages they had not known before. . . . Godly Jews from every country in the world were staying in Jerusalem. . . . They were bewildered because they each heard*

TONGUES OF FIRE. When the Holy Spirit descends on the disciples, as Jesus said would happen, the room fills with the sound of wind. And tongues of fire settle above the disciples' heads. These are perfect symbols of what comes next. The disciples go outside and empty their lungs with words of fire—boldly telling the story of Jesus in the very city that had crucified him a few weeks earlier. Miraculously, the Bible says the men could speak in languages they hadn't learned—which allowed Jewish pilgrims who had come from other countries for the Pentecost festival to hear the story of Jesus for themselves.

the believers speaking in their own language (Acts 2:4–6 NIrv).

HEAVENLY LANGUAGES

:: *If you have the ability to speak in tongues, you will be talking only to God, since people won't be able to understand you. You will be speaking by the power of the Spirit, but it will all be mysterious* (1 Corinthians 14:2).

:: *So what if I could speak a bunch of languages—including the language of angels in heaven. If there's no love inside me, I might as well suck a cork. Anything I'd say would come across as nothing but an irritating noise—like a car alarm that won't shut up* (1 Corinthians 13:1 AUTHOR'S PARAPHRASE).

:: *If unbelievers. . .come into your church meeting and hear everyone speaking in an unknown language, they will think you are crazy. . . . No more than two or three should speak in tongues. They must speak one at a time, and someone must interpret what they say. But if no one is present who can interpret, they must be silent in your church meeting and speak in tongues to God privately* (1 Corinthians 14:23, 27–28).

TRINITY

Christians teach that there is one God who expresses himself as three beings: God the Father, God the Son, and God the Holy Spirit. The word *trinity* isn't in the Bible. But most Christian scholars say the teaching is clearly there.

WHY MOST JEWS DON'T BELIEVE IT

:: *Listen, Israel! The LORD our God is the only true God!* (Deuteronomy 6:4 CEV). That's Moses talking to Jews during the Exodus, reviewing the laws God gave them. They're not to worship any other god, which, as far as most Jews are concerned, would include Jesus, who claims to be God's Son.

HOW JESUS EXPLAINED IT

:: *"I am in my Father and my Father is in me. If you can't believe that, believe what you see— these works"* (John 14:11 MSG). Jesus tells his disciples that even if they can't grasp the idea of there being a Father/Son deity, they should at least give him the benefit of the doubt because of the miracles they've seen him do—like raising the dead, calming storms, and walking on water.

:: *"I am going to the Father. The Father is greater than I am"* (John 14:28 NIrv).

JESUS, THE DEITY

:: *In the beginning the Word already existed. The Word was with God, and the Word was God* (John 1:1). *Word* refers to Jesus: "The Word became human. . . . And we have seen his glory, the glory of the Father's one and only Son" (John 1:14).

:: *"God sent his Son into the world not to judge the world, but to save the world"* (John 3:17).

MENTION OF THE THREE TOGETHER

:: *"Go and make disciples of all nations. Baptize them in the name of the Father and of the Son and of the Holy Spirit"* (Matthew 28:19 NIrv). This is Jesus' instruction to his disciples.

:: *After his baptism, as Jesus came up out of the water, the heavens were opened and he saw the Spirit of God descending like a dove and settling on him. And a voice from heaven said, "This is my dearly loved Son, who brings me great joy"* (Matthew 3:16–17).

(See also "The Bible says there's just one God, but Jesus says he's divine, too; how could anyone believe both?" page 46.)

UNPARDONABLE SIN

:: "Every sin and blasphemy can be forgiven—except blasphemy against the Holy Spirit, which will never be forgiven. . . . Anyone who speaks against the Holy Spirit will never be forgiven, either in this world or in the world to come" (Matthew 12:31–32).

(See "The unforgivable sin" page 213.)

VIRGIN BIRTH

Two of the four Gospels about Jesus tell the story of his birth: Matthew and Luke. Both say Mary, the mother of Jesus, miraculously became pregnant—while she was still a virgin. Jesus had no human, biological father. Joseph, however, was his legal father. Some Bible experts say this part of the story is an exaggeration, added late. This is partly because there's no mention of the virgin birth in the earliest New Testament writings, such as the letters Paul wrote in the AD 50s and 60s.

VIRGIN BIRTHS TODAY

Some Christians wonder why it's so hard for people to believe that with God's help Mary became pregnant—no sex required. After all, they argue, even humans can manage to pull that off. We call it in vitro fertilization. No sex required.

HAIL MARY. Both New Testament writers who tell the story of Jesus' birth say his mother, Mary, was a virgin when she conceived him, in a miracle performed by the Holy Spirit. In time, some Christians began praying to Mary as the mother of Jesus, asking her to intercede for them. After all, some argue, she once convinced Jesus to turn water into wine, in spite of his reluctance (John 2:1–5).

And it's also because Christians in the early few centuries put a lot of stock in virginity and the celibate lifestyle. Yet most Christians, especially Catholics, say they believe in the virgin birth.

:: *The angel said to her [Mary]. . . . "You will become pregnant and give birth to a son." . . . "How can this happen?" Mary asked the angel. "I am a virgin." The angel answered, "The Holy Spirit will come to you. The power of the Most High God will cover you. . . . Nothing is impossible with God"* (Luke 1:30–31, 34–35, 37 NIrv).

:: *This is how Jesus the Messiah was born. His mother, Mary, was engaged to be married to Joseph. But before the marriage took place, while she was still a virgin, she became pregnant through the power of the Holy Spirit* (Matthew 1:18).

:: *All of this occurred to fulfill the Lord's message through his prophet: "Look! The virgin will conceive a child! She will give birth to a son, and they will call him Immanuel, which means 'God is with us' "* (Matthew 1:22–23). Matthew quotes prophecies from Isaiah 7:14. There, however, the Hebrew word sometimes translated virgin can also mean "young woman." But New Testament authors wrote in Greek. There, the Greek word means a woman who has not had sexual relations with a man.

WAR

God led so many battles in Old Testament times that many people—some Jews included—thought of him as the god of war. Then along came Jesus with a new message about how to deal with enemies.

GOD AT WAR

:: *"Today you are going into battle against*

SHOULD WE KILL FOR JESUS?

We can die for Jesus, but we shouldn't kill for him.

That's how many Christians interpret the teachings of Jesus.

These Christians are pacifists, against fighting—in a war or in any other setting.

When a nation's leader issues a call to arms against "evildoers," as President George W. Bush once did, vowing to rid the world of terrorists, pacifist Christians reply with Jesus' call to disarm:

"But I say to you, Do not resist an evildoer."
MATTHEW 5:39 NRSV

Uncomfortable as it is to hear this, scholars say Jesus may have meant exactly what he said. He lived and died by these very words. Kidnapped for a secret trial, he didn't resist. And when Peter drew a sword to fight off the kidnappers, Jesus gave Peter the sword speech: If you live by the sword, you'll die by the sword.

Now obsolete are all the old Jewish laws about an eye for an eye, execution of criminals, and fighting wars to defend justice—that's what some Christians say.

Non-pacifist Christians, however, ask why God would bother giving us a survival instinct if he didn't intend for us to use it. But a counterpoint might be: Why would God give single people a sex drive and tell them not to use it? The answer to both questions: God knows; and in God we trust.

Non-pacifist Christians interpret the antiviolence teachings of Jesus in many ways. Here are two. Jesus' teaching is:

:: a snapshot of what heaven is like and what Christians should strive for on earth—an unreachable goal that we should try to reach, as best we can

:: advice for Jesus' first-generation disciples only, to help jump-start the church with M&M'S: miracles and meekness.

While we struggle to figure out how to do what Jesus said we should do, one practical solution scholars offer is this: When in doubt, don't kill.

your enemies. *Don't be scared. . . . The L*ORD *your God is going with you. He'll fight for you. He'll help you win the battle"* (Deuteronomy 20:3–4 NIrv). These are words of Moses shortly before the Jews invade what is now Israel.

:: *Whenever you capture towns in the land the L*ORD *your God is giving you, be sure to kill all the people. . . . If you allow them to live, they will persuade you to worship their disgusting gods, and you will be unfaithful to the L*ORD (Deuteronomy 20:16, 18 CEV). What Moses warned the Jews about is exactly what happened. Enemy survivors in Canaan would teach the Jews to worship idols.

JESUS CALLING FOR PEACE

:: *"Love your enemies! Pray for those who persecute you!"* (Matthew 5:44). This is what Jesus told his fellow Jews after nearly a century of occupation by Roman forces. Jewish freedom fighters rebelled against Rome about 35 years later and were crushed. Romans leveled Jerusalem and destroyed the Temple, which has never been rebuilt.

:: *"Blessed are the peacemakers, for they will be called children of God"* (Matthew 5:9 TNIV).

:: *"Put your sword away. Anyone who lives by fighting will die by fighting. Don't you know that I could ask my Father, and right away he would send me more than twelve armies of angels?"* (Matthew 26:52–53 CEV). Jesus is talking to Peter, who's trying to defend him from Temple police who have come to arrest him for trial and crucifixion.

SWORD OF THE LORD. Backed up by Jesus—at least by his picture on banners—a Crusader prepares for a pope-endorsed battle with Muslims. Arab Muslims had overrun about two-thirds of the Christian world by AD 1000, including what are now parts of Israel, Syria, Egypt, and Turkey. Crusaders enjoyed early victories. But the Christian-Muslim wars raged on for centuries. By the 1300s, Muslims had recaptured the land and were fighting their way into Europe, expanding what had become the Ottoman Empire. Based in Turkey, the empire endured until its collapse in 1922.

OUR WEAKNESS

:: *"My grace is all you need. My power works best in weakness"* (2 Corinthians 12:9). The apostle Paul quotes Jesus, and then adds: "When I am weak, then I am strong" (verse 10). For anyone doubting the power of weakness, consider how a loving husband responds when his wife cries.

:: *In certain ways we are weak, but the Spirit is here to help us. For example, when we don't know what to pray for, the Spirit prays for us in ways that cannot be put into words* (Romans 8:26 CEV).

:: *"Keep watch and pray, so that you will not give in to temptation. For the spirit is willing, but the body is weak!"* (Matthew 26:41). Jesus, advising some of his disciples on the night of his arrest.

WEAKNESS IN OTHERS

:: *Take tender care of those who are weak. Be patient with everyone* (1 Thessalonians 5:14).

:: *Accept other believers who are weak in faith, and don't argue with them about what they think is right or wrong. . . . They are responsible to the Lord, so let him judge whether they are right or wrong. And with the Lord's help, they will do what is right and will receive his approval* (Romans 14:1, 4).

:: *When I am with those who are weak, I share their weakness, for I want to bring the weak to Christ. Yes, I try to find common ground with everyone, doing everything I can to save some* (1 Corinthians 9:22). That's the apostle Paul, writing to Christians in what is now Corinth, Greece.

In Bible times, conventional wisdom said rich people were rich because God was rewarding them. Yet a persistent message in the Bible is that too often rich people are rich because they know how to exploit others and how to hoard their money when they should be using it to help the needy.

:: *A final word to you arrogant rich. . . . Your money is corrupt and your fine clothes stink. . . . You thought you were piling up wealth. What you've piled up is judgment. All the workers you've exploited and cheated cry out for judgment. The groans of the workers you used and abused are a roar in the ears of the Master Avenger* (James 5:1–4 MSG).

:: *Those who love money will never have enough. How meaningless to think that wealth brings true happiness! The more you have, the more people come to help you spend it. So what good is wealth—except perhaps to watch it slip through your fingers!* (Ecclesiastes 5:10–11).

:: *All our busy rushing ends in nothing. We heap up wealth, not knowing who will spend it. And so, Lord, where do I put my hope? My only hope is in you* (Psalm 39:6–7).

:: *Don't be dismayed when the wicked grow rich and their homes become ever more splendid. For when they die, they take nothing with them* (Psalm 49:16–17).

:: *Lust for money brings trouble and nothing but trouble. Going down that path, some lose their footing in the faith completely* (1 Timothy 6:10 MSG).

:: *"You can't worship two gods at once. Loving one god, you'll end up hating the other. Adoration of one feeds contempt for the other. You can't worship God and Money both"* (Matthew 6:24 MSG).

SHOPPING SPREE. A well-to-do Roman family shops for a work of art they can showcase in their home. Many Bible writers—especially prophets—portrayed the wealthy as selfish souls with the compassion and sensitivity of a leech at a blood drive.

:: *"Don't store up treasures here on earth...where thieves break in and steal. Store your treasures in heaven. . . . Wherever your treasure is, there the desires of your heart will also be"* (Matthew 6:19-21). This is part of Jesus' most famous sermon, the Sermon on the Mount.

:: *Choose a good reputation over great riches; being held in high esteem is better than silver or gold* (Proverbs 22:1).

:: *Honor the LORD with your wealth. . . . Then he will fill your barns with grain, and your vats will overflow with good wine* (Proverbs 3:9-10). Most Bible experts say this isn't a guarantee. It's a general observation of elderly sages, offering advice to young men.

(See also *Money*.)

WISDOM

:: If you need wisdom, ask our generous God, and he will give it to you (James 1:5).

:: Real wisdom, God's wisdom, begins with a holy life and is characterized by getting along with others. It is gentle and reasonable, overflowing with mercy (James 3:17 MSG).

:: Watch your step. Use your head. . . . Don't live carelessly, unthinkingly. Make sure you understand what the Master wants (Ephesians 5:15–17 MSG).

:: "Have respect for me [God]. That will prove you are wise" (Job 28:28 NIrV).

:: God gives out Wisdom free, is plainspoken in Knowledge and Understanding. He's a rich mine of Common Sense for those who live well (Proverbs 2:6–7 MSG).

:: Thinking about your [God's] teachings gives me better understanding than my teachers, and obeying your laws makes me wiser than those who have lived a long time (Psalm 119:99–100 CEV).

WITNESSING

:: "Go and make disciples of all the nations, baptizing them in the name of the Father and the Son and the Holy Spirit. Teach these new disciples to obey all the commands I have given you" (Matthew 28:19–20). Known as the Great Commission, these are the last words of Jesus to his disciples.

:: "You will be able to be my witnesses in Jerusalem, all over Judea and Samaria, even to the ends of the world" (Acts 1:8 MSG).

:: If someone asks about your Christian hope, always be ready to explain it. But do this in a gentle and respectful way (1 Peter 3:15–16).

:: Never be ashamed to tell others about our Lord (2 Timothy 1:8).

:: I am not ashamed of the good news. It is God's power. And it will save everyone who believes (Romans 1:16 NIrV).

:: You may say that there are still four months until harvest time. But I tell you to look, and you will see that the fields are ripe and ready to harvest (John 4:35 CEV). Jesus explains that he's talking about a harvest of souls: "gathering a harvest that brings eternal life" (verse 36).

:: I try to find common ground with everyone, doing everything I can to save some (1 Corinthians 9:22).

:: I always try to please others instead of myself, in the hope that many of them will be saved (1 Corinthians 10:33 CEV).

:: Paul went into the synagogue as he usually did. For three Sabbath days in a row he talked about the Scriptures with the Jews. He explained and proved that the Christ had to suffer and rise from the dead (Acts 17:2–3 NIrV).

WORK (JOB, CAREER)

:: Enjoy the work you do here on earth. Whatever work you do, do your best (Ecclesiastes 9:9–10 NCV).

:: There is nothing better for people than to be happy in their work. That is why we are here! (Ecclesiastes 3:22).

:: The best thing we can do is to enjoy eating, drinking, and working. I believe these are God's gifts to us (Ecclesiastes 2:24 CEV).

:: We gave you this command: "Those unwilling to work will not get to eat." Yet we hear that some of you are living idle lives, refusing to work and meddling in other people's business. We command such people and urge them in the

PALESTINIAN POTTER. Working from a wad of clay, a 1930s potter, in what is now Israel, spins a bowl on a foot-powered pottery wheel.

:: *Give all your worries and cares to God, for he cares about you* (1 Peter 5:7).

:: *The battle is not yours, but God's* (2 Chronicles 20:15). These are God's words to a Jewish king who's about to face an invasion force. But these words are repeated throughout the Bible, as though they apply to all of life's battles for those who serve God.

:: *Don't fret or worry. Instead of worrying, pray. Let petitions and praises shape your worries into prayers, letting God know your concerns. Before you know it, a sense of God's wholeness, everything coming together for good, will come and settle you down. It's wonderful what happens when Christ displaces worry at the center of your life* (Philippians 4:6–7 MSG).

:: *Don't worry about having something to eat or wear. . . . Can worry make you live longer? . . . Only people who don't know God are always worrying about such things. Your Father knows what you need. But put God's work first, and these things will be yours as well* (Luke 12:22, 25, 30–31 CEV). Even if we're cold and starving, destined to die, the Bible says God gives us what we need: life that never ends.

:: *I give you peace, the kind of peace that only I can give. It isn't like the peace that this world can give. So don't be worried or afraid* (John 14:27 CEV).

WORSHIP

Some people say they worship best when they're alone—during a walk outside, watching the stars in the sky, or even watching the stars on TV. Though the Bible tells of people worshipping

name of the Lord Jesus Christ to settle down and work to earn their own living (2 Thessalonians 3:10–12). The apostle Paul wasn't talking about people unable to work—people who would depend on government support today. He was talking about people unwilling but able.

:: *Lazy people want all they can get. They get what they deserve: a big pile of nothing. It's the hard workers who get what they want, and deserve what they get* (Proverbs 13:4 AUTHOR'S PARAPHRASE).

:: *"Those who work deserve their pay"* (Luke 10:7).

:: *Work the first six days of the week, but rest and relax on the seventh day* (Exodus 23:12 CEV). One of the 10 Commandments is to take a break from work one day a week.

:: *"Let us make human beings in our image . . .so they can be responsible for the fish in the sea, the birds in the air, the cattle, and, yes, Earth itself"* (Genesis 1:26 MSG). Humanity's job description, as it appears in the creation story.

God when they're alone, it also teaches that it's important to worship with other believers—that healthy spiritual relationships help us grow, and that we need each other.

CALL TO WORSHIP

:: *Let us not neglect our meeting together, as some people do* (Hebrews 10:25).

:: *"Where two or three gather together as my followers, I am there among them"* (Matthew 18:20).

:: *You have six days when you can do your work, but the seventh day of each week is holy. . . . Rest on the Sabbath and come together for worship* (Leviticus 23:3 CEV). Number four of the 10 Commandments. Jews worship from sunset Friday to sunset Saturday. In honor of Jesus' resurrection, Christians started worshipping on Sundays.

:: *Jesus went to Nazareth, where he had been brought up. On the Sabbath day he went into the synagogue as he usually did* (Luke 4:16 NIrV).

:: *Because of your great mercy, I come to your house, LORD, and I am filled with wonder as I bow down to worship* (Psalm 5:7 CEV).

HOW TO WORSHIP

:: *Worship the LORD with gladness. Come before him, singing with joy* (Psalm 100:2).

:: *What do you think GOD expects from you? Just this: . . .follow the road he sets out for you, love him, serve GOD, your God, with everything you have in you. . .live a good life* (Deuteronomy 10:12 MSG).

PRETEND WORSHIP

:: *You are nothing but show-offs! . . . "All of you praise me with your words, but you never really think about me. It is useless for you to worship*

me, when you teach rules made up by humans" (Mark 7:6–7 CEV).

:: *Do you think all GOD wants are. . .empty rituals just for show? He wants you to listen to him! Plain listening is the thing, not staging a lavish religious production* (1 Samuel 15:22 MSG).

RELIGION IN ROMANIA. A priest instructs young people in the basics of the faith. Location: Saint Emeric Catholic Church, Gelence, Romania—where Christians have worshipped for 800 years, since the time of the Crusades.

:: *No other gods, only me* (Exodus 20:3 MSG). That's the first and most important of the 10 Commandments.

YAHWEH

Pronounced YAH-way—not YAH-who, as the author once heard it pronounced by a Sunday school teacher—this is the personal name of God. Many Jews say it's a name too holy to say out loud. When they come to that Hebrew word in their Bible, they read it as "Lord." Most English Bibles follow that custom, using LORD in capital letters: "I am the LORD your God" (Exodus 20:2). *LORD,* in the original Hebrew language of the Old Testament, was written as *YHWH.* It's a shorthand technique, skipping vowels. Scholars today can only guess which vowels the Jews intended. Earlier Bibles translated the word *Jehovah.* But most scholars today say *Yahweh* is the more likely pronunciation.

:: *God said to Moses. . . . "I appeared to Abraham, to Isaac, and to Jacob as El-Shaddai [shad-EYE]—'God Almighty'—but I did not reveal my name, Yahweh"* (Exodus 6:2–3).

:: *"The LORD is a warrior; Yahweh is his name!"* (Exodus 15:3).

:: *God replied to Moses, "I AM WHO I AM. . . . Say this to the people of Israel: Yahweh, the God of your ancestors—the God of Abraham, the God of Isaac, and the God of Jacob—has sent me to you"* (Exodus 3:14–15).

ZEALOTS

These were Jewish insurrectionists. They considered themselves freedom fighters because they wanted to end Rome's century-long occupation of the Jewish homeland. One of Jesus' disciples is described as a zealot: Simon (not Simon Peter). Some Bible experts say Simon may have been simply a Jew zealous about his faith. But most say he was more likely a former rebel.

:: *Here are the names of the twelve apostles. . . Matthew (the tax collector). . .Simon (the zealot). . .* (Matthew 10:2–4). An odd combo. Matthew was a Jew who collaborated with the Roman occupiers by taxing his fellow Jews for the benefit of Rome and himself. Simon, if he was a former rebel in the Zealot movement, would have targeted Jews like Matthew for assassination. Jesus put them on the same team.

BIBLE SNAPSHOTS:

GENESIS TO REVELATION

GENESIS

PARADISE POLLUTED: THE SIN THAT POISONED THE PLANET

IN ONE SENTENCE

God creates paradise on earth, but humans contaminate his creation with sin, forcing him to launch a long-term plan to save people from the damage that sin causes.

SOUND BITE

"Let there be light."
—*God*
GENESIS 1:3

ON LOCATION

TIME. Creation of the universe through about 1800 BC, the time of Abraham's great-grandson, Joseph.

PLACE. The Middle East, mainly in countries of the river-fed Fertile Crescent where civilization began.

NEWSMAKERS

GOD, creator of the universe. He tops off creation by making humans and giving them freedom to make decisions.

ADAM AND EVE, the first humans. They break the only rule God gives them, which unleashes sin into the world and somehow contaminates it.

NOAH, flood survivor. He builds a huge barge, saving himself, his family, and pairs of animals from a flood that wipes out civilization.

ABRAHAM, father of the Jews. God promises to give Abraham's descendants the land of Canaan, roughly modern Israel.

JACOB, father of the 12 tribes of Israel. Descendants of his 12 sons produce the tribes that form the nation of Israel.

VEGETARIAN HEAVEN ON EARTH.
In a Netherlands forest, a lone doe steps out into the light. Today, during hunting season, it could be lights out. But hints in the Genesis creation story, according to some, suggest that animals and humans once lived in peace.

GOD CREATES A PERFECT WORLD. Out of the great nothing that once existed, God creates the universe. Some Bible experts see a springboard pattern in the story.

:: Day one: light. It becomes the source material for day four's creation: sun, moon, and stars.

:: Day two: sea and sky. They're habitats for inhumanity created on day five: fish, birds, and other swimming and flying critters.

:: Day three: earth, teeming with plants. Habitat for humanity, creation's grand finale on day six. *(Genesis 1)*

SIX DAYS? God does it all in six "days." Christians debate what a *day* is. Some say it's a day as we know it—24 hours. Others say that's unlikely because:

:: "With the Lord a day is like a thousand years. And a thousand years are like a day" (2 Peter 3:8 NIrV).

:: It wasn't until day four that God created the sun and moon, used to measure 24-hour days.

GOD CREATED HUMAN BEINGS IN HIS OWN IMAGE (Genesis 1:26). Theories about what it means:

:: We're God's representatives on earth, entrusted with God-like authority as earth's caretakers.

:: We're created with God-like characteristics: love, creativity, morality, reason, and a soul built to last an eternity.

CREATION WHEN? Most astrophysicists agree that the universe began with a burst of light: the Big Bang, an explosion of compressed matter that reassembled into stars, planets, and galaxies. Based on measurements of the still-expanding universe, scientists say the bang took place almost 14 billion years ago. Many Christians say if creation began with a bang, God pulled the trigger. Other Christians, tracking Bible genealogies back to Adam, say God created the world about 6,000 years ago.

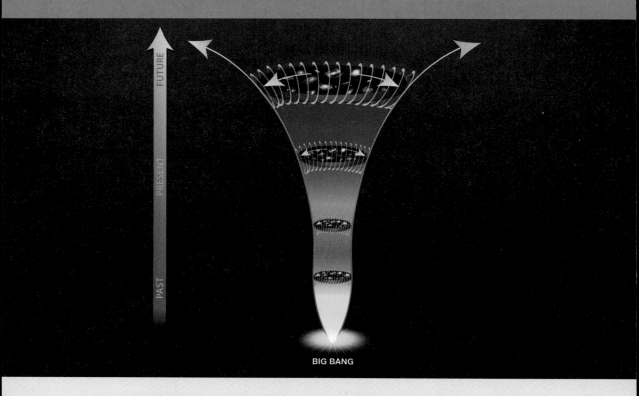

FUTURE

PRESENT

PAST

BIG BANG

LET THERE BE LIGHT. Time begins with a Big Bang, according to a popular scientific theory. The explosive thrust propels creation's substance, which gradually forms into our still-expanding universe. One theory says this momentum will eventually stop and the universe will fall back into place—the Big Crunch. But another says the expansion will continue until everything spreads so far apart that there's nothing left to see in the sky—the Big Blackout.

HUMANS TRASH THE WORLD WITH SIN. Living in paradise, Adam and Eve break God's one rule. They eat forbidden fruit from the tree of life. God warned if they did, they'd die. A snake, identified in the Bible's last book as "Satan" (Revelation 12:9), convinces Eve that God lied. Eve bites. So does Adam. Something about this sin corrupts creation. Incoming: more sin, sickness, pain, and death. (*Genesis 2–3*)

EVICTED. God banishes Adam and Eve from the Garden of Eden paradise after they eat fruit from a tree that God said would kill them. Somewhere east of Eden they die—Adam at age 930.

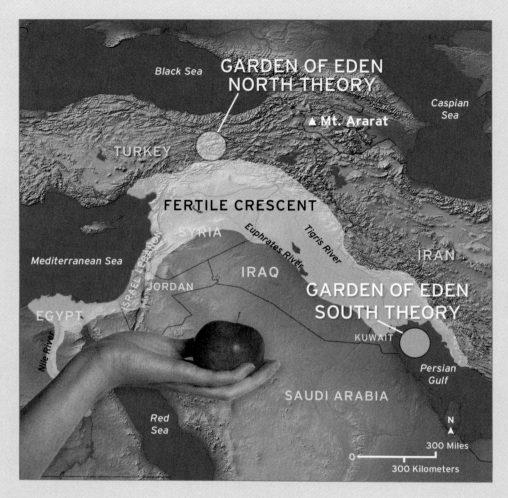

GARDEN OF EDEN. The Bible offers one clue about the location of this paradise: a river flows out of Eden and branches off into four rivers. One theory places Eden in the mountains of Turkey, the source of several rivers and streams. Another puts it in the Persian Gulf, a former river valley eventually flooded by the ocean.

HOW DID SIN CHANGE THE WORLD? After condemning Eve to painful childbearing, God sentences Adam to a lifetime of hard labor, growing crops in a never-ending fight for survival against "the ground. . . cursed because of you" (Genesis 3:17). Some speculate that before sin:

:: Adam and Eve were immortal

:: all creatures were vegetarians, living in peace

:: crops grew in the weedless wild.

DID PEOPLE REALLY LIVE FOR CENTURIES? Probably not, say many Christians. The high ages reported may have been a way to express respect. Sumerian writings from the first known civilization report that their kings lived for thousands of years. Some Christians, however, note that life spans dropped to normal after the flood. They wonder if the flood somehow released harmful toxins or changed the atmosphere in some harmful way, reducing humanity's life span. There's no science to back that up, though.

GOD WASHES THE WORLD WITH A FLOOD. Like an infectious plague, sin runs wild. Cain, the oldest son of Adam and Eve, murders his little brother. Within 10 generations, humans become so evil that God decides they need a fresh start—a new Adam. He chooses Noah, "the only blameless person living." At God's instruction, Noah builds a barge that saves his family and some animals from a flood that kills every breathing thing. *(Genesis 6–8)*

NOAH'S HOTEL, ROOMS AVAILABLE. Location: Hong Kong. It's a luxury hotel opened in 2009, showcasing a full-size replica of Noah's ark—complete with 67 paired sculptures of wild animals.

DID THE FLOOD COVER THE ENTIRE PLANET? No human could have confirmed it. Yet many Christians insist the flood did turn Earth into Waterworld. Using Bible genealogies, they say it happened about 4,000 years ago. Other Christians side with most geologists who say there's no physical evidence of a global flood. Many of these Christians say it's more likely the flood was regional, wiping out villages built in the Tigris and Euphrates river valleys of Iraq and Iran, where civilization started. Archaeologists found evidence of such a flood occurring about 5,000 years ago.

NOAH'S ARK. Longer than a football field and half as wide, Noah's floating warehouse was still only about half the size of a typical cruise ship. Length: 150 yards (137 meters). Width: 25 yards (23 meters). Height: 15 yards (14 meters). Gutted, before beams and floors were added, this ark had the storage capacity of about 370 railroad boxcars. It held Noah's family, pairs of animals, and the supplies they needed for the year they had to wait for the floodwater to subside.

TWO BY TWO. God tells Noah to load the boat with one pair of each land animal, male and female. Also, Noah must bring seven pairs of all birds and of all animals approved for sacrifice—such as sheep, goats, and cattle.

Fragment of the Epic of Gilgamesh,
copied about 600 BC

IRAQ'S VERSION OF NOAH. The man who built the ark and loaded it with his family and pairs of animals wasn't Noah. Not according to an ancient Iraqi story called the Epic of Gilgamesh. There, the ark builder was Utnapishtim, a name that sounds like a blessing after a sneeze. This man, like Noah, also released a dove after the flood to see if the water had receded enough for the bird to land somewhere. Iraqi Noah was just a bit player in this story about a Babylonian king, Gilgamesh, who scholars say may have lived about 2600 BC. That would place the story more than a thousand years before Moses, who, according to Jewish tradition, wrote Genesis.

GOD SENDS IRAQI ABRAHAM TO ISRAEL.

Abraham and his wife, Sarah, live in the busy riverside city of Ur, in what is now southern Iraq. His father, Terah, decides to move the extended family to Canaan, in what is now Israel. But following the Euphrates River toward the seacoast, they stop a little more than halfway, settling in Haran, Turkey. When Terah dies, God tells Abraham to continue on to Canaan, promising to give him the land and make him into a great nation there. *(Genesis 11–12)*

FLAMMABLE: SODOM AND GOMORRAH.

Abraham's nephew, Lot, moves to Canaan with him. When their herds grow too large to graze together, the men part. Abraham stays in Canaan's hilly heartland. Lot moves to the city of Sodom in the fertile Jordan River Valley. The Bible says the twin cities of Sodom and Gomorrah are obsessively evil. God decides to destroy them. He sends two angels to get Lot out of town shortly before fire incinerates both cities. *(Genesis 13, 19)*

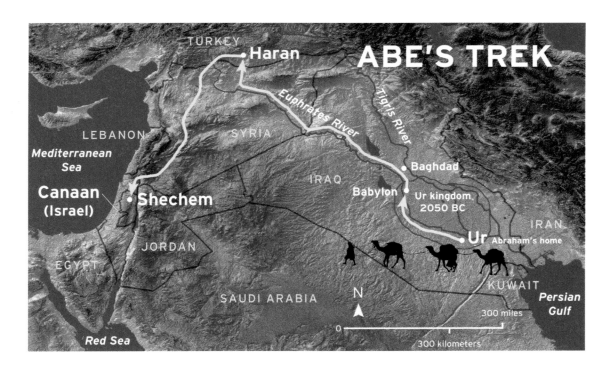

ABE'S TREK

CHILDLESS ABE AND SARAH. Abraham is 75 years old and his infertile wife, Sarah, is 66 when God promises to give them children and make their family into a great nation. Twenty-five years later, the Bible says, 90-year-old Sarah finally gets pregnant. She names her son Isaac. It means "laughter," as in, who's not going to get a laugh out of this kid growing up, saying, "They're not my great-grandparents."

WHAT DESTROYED THE CITIES? "Fire and burning sulfur from the sky" (Genesis 19:24). The region is rich in minerals, including sulfur and salt, and natural gas. One theory is that a tremor in this earthquake-prone area ripped a hole into a pocket of gas, which was ignited by lightning or a lamp in the city. Fire and mineral exploded into the sky and rained throughout the plain.

As Abraham raises his knife to sacrifice his only son, an angel suddenly appears and stops him.

ABRAHAM ALMOST MURDERS HIS SON. God will outlaw human sacrifice in a few centuries, during Moses' day. But for now, he tells Abraham to sacrifice his only son, Isaac. Ever obedient, Abraham takes Isaac on a three-day trip to "the land of Moriah." They climb a hill that Jewish tradition says is now the Jerusalem ridge. When Abraham raises his knife to kill Isaac, an angel stops him. The Bible calls this a test of faith. *(Genesis 22)*

WHY DID GOD HAVE TO TEST ABRAHAM? It's not that God was worried Abraham would fail, some Bible experts say. The near-sacrifice spotlights the extraordinary faith of Abraham. It also doubles as a prophecy in 3D, a foreshadowing of what God would do with his Son. What Abraham was willing to do, God did. Jesus died.

JACOB, A ROTTEN LITTLE BROTHER. Isaac marries Rebekah. They have twins. Daddy's boy: Esau, the first to see daylight. Momma's boy: Jacob, born clutching Esau's heel. The oldest son, by custom, gets a double dip of inheritance—and becomes leader of the extended family when the father dies. Jacob, it seems, steals both. He gets the first for a bowl of soup, in trade with hungry Esau. And he gets Isaac's deathbed blessing by pretending to be Esau. *(Genesis 25–27)*

Empty-handed from a hunt, and famished, Esau agrees to trade his inheritance for a bowl of his brother Jacob's red stew.

TWO SONS, TWO BLESSINGS. Nearly blind, Isaac can't tell he's giving Jacob the blessing he intended for Esau—a blessing the ancients apparently felt they couldn't retract. For Jacob: "May many nations become your servants. . . . May you be the master over your brothers." For Esau: "You will live by your sword, and you will serve your brother."

JACOB ON THE RUN. Livid at losing his legit blessing, Esau starts plotting to kill Jacob. Rebekah finds out and sends Jacob to her brother in Haran, in what is now Turkey. It's a long walk from their home in Beersheba—more than a month. About 700 miles (1,100 km).

JACOB WAKES UP WITH THE WRONG WIFE.
It's a honeymoon nightmare. When Jacob gets to Haran, he falls in love with his uncle Laban's youngest daughter, Rachel. She's gorgeous. Her sister, Leah, not so much. Jacob proposes. Laban says Jacob can marry Rachel only after working as his employee for seven years. At the wedding, however, Laban switches daughters. The next morning he tells a furious Jacob that it's custom to marry off the oldest daughter first. *(Genesis 29)*

JACOB'S DANGEROUS FAMILY REUNION.
Jacob spends 20 years in Haran. Fourteen paying off his wedding debts to the father of the brides. Six working for himself, building his herds and getting rich. Homesick, he packs up his family and heads south. Fearing that Esau might still be mad enough to kill him, Jacob sends gifts ahead, hoping to soothe him. No need. Esau, rich himself, welcomes Jacob with hugs and kisses and tears of joy. *(Genesis 31–33)*

BATTLE OF THE BABY MAKERS. Sister brides Rachel and Leah compete for Jacob's affection by trying to provide him with babies, especially sons. Each sister goes so far as to give Jacob their maid as a surrogate mother. The four ladies produce a dozen sons whose extended families will become the 12 tribes of Israel.

ONE WEEK, ONE MAN, TWO WEDDINGS.
Laban agrees to let Jacob marry Rachel, too. But first, Jacob has to spend a week celebrating the wife he didn't want. Then he has to work another seven years for his uncle. Many Bible readers, remembering how Jacob swindled his brother and blind father, say the wedding scam couldn't have happened to a more deserving person.

WRESTLING GOD. As Jacob's caravan crosses the Jordan River back into Canaan, he stays behind for the night, certainly terrified about Esau. A man comes along that Jacob somehow seems to associate with God, because Jacob grabs him and won't let go until the man blesses him. They wrestle all night. At daybreak, the man blesses him and renames him "Israel." Jacob names the camp "face of God" because he says he has seen God face-to-face, and lived. Some wonder if the story is a metaphor about Jacob's lifetime of struggles— first with Esau, then with Laban, but ultimately with God.

SELLING BROTHER JOE TO SLAVE TRADERS. Jacob has a favorite son: Joseph, first child of his favorite wife, Rachel. Joseph is son 11 of 12. His older brothers hate him because it's clear Jacob loves him best. At age 17, Joseph is spoiled. When slave traders bound for Egypt arrive, Joseph's older brothers sell him. They keep the expensive robe Jacob gave him. They rip it, dip it in blood, and let Jacob conclude a wild animal ate him. *(Genesis 37)*

JOSEPH, SENTENCED TO PRISON FOR ATTEMPTED RAPE. Sold in Egypt, Joseph ends up working as a household slave for Potiphar, captain of the palace guard. Suddenly reformed, Joseph becomes a model slave. Potiphar takes a liking to the hard worker and puts him in charge of his household. Mrs. Potiphar also takes a liking to the "handsome and well-built young man." Cougar alert. Joseph rejects her advances. She screams rape. Joseph goes to prison. *(Genesis 39)*

EIGHTY BUCKS FOR LITTLE BROTHER. Joseph sold for about eight ounces (228 grams) of silver. That's about $80 when silver sells for $10 an ounce. But in Old Testament times, that was the going rate for a teenage slave—and the salary of a shepherd for two years.

COUGAR ATTACK. The lady of the house, Potiphar's wife, decides to help herself to the teenage help—Joseph, the new household slave. Run, Joseph, run!

PRISON DREAMS. Pharaoh's baker and wine taster land in prison with Joseph. Both of these former palace servants have bizarre dreams that Joseph correctly interprets—predicting their future.

:: Wine taster. He dreams of a vine with three branches that produce grapes. He squeezes the grapes into a cup for the king. Interpretation: He'll be back at work in three days.

:: Baker. He dreams of three baskets of pastries stacked on his head for the pharaoh, but birds ate them. Interpretation: He'll be impaled on a pole in three days, birds picking his flesh.

JOSEPH'S DREAM JOB. When Pharaoh has two bizarre dreams, the palace wine taster remembers Joseph's ability to interpret them. The king sees seven scrawny cows eat seven fat cows, then sees seven withered heads of grain eat seven healthy ones. Joseph says this means Egypt will enjoy seven years of bumper crops followed by seven years of famine that will consume the stockpile. Impressed, Pharaoh puts Joseph in charge of preparing Egypt for the famine. Suddenly, a Jew is Egypt's number two. *(Genesis 40)*

Drought drives Jews to Egypt

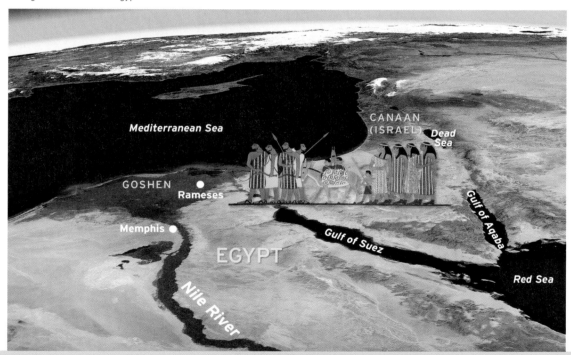

JEWS MIGRATE TO EGYPT. In a delicious twist of fate, Joseph's 10 brothers who sold him into slavery end up standing in front of him, hoping to buy grain during the famine. They don't recognize him, since he's 20 years older. But he recognizes them. He makes them sweat, accusing them of being spies. But when he learns of the regret they feel for what they did to him, he reveals who he is. With the king's approval, Joseph invites his entire extended family to weather out the famine in the drought-resistant Nile River Delta called Goshen—Egypt's premier grazing pastures. Jacob brings all 66 members of his family with him, kids and grandkids.

E X O D U S

JEWISH NATION ON A ROAD TRIP

IN ONE SENTENCE

After the Jews have spent 430 years in Egypt—a drought-driven migration that ended in slavery—Moses wins their freedom and begins leading them home to what is now Israel.

SOUND BITE

"Let my people go."
—*Moses, quoting God to Pharaoh*
EXODUS 5:1

ON LOCATION

TIME. About 1440 BC or 150 years later, 1290 BC; scholars debate which.

PLACE. Egypt.

EXODUS TO CANAAN WITHOUT A GPS

NEWSMAKERS

MOSES, leader of Jews. A Jew raised by a daughter of the Egyptian king, Moses later sides with his enslaved people and leads them to freedom.

AARON, older brother of Moses. He serves as a spokesman for his brother and later becomes Israel's first high priest.

PHARAOH, king of Egypt. He forces his people to suffer through 10 plagues before he agrees to free the Jews. *Pharaoh* is his title, not his name.

WELCOME GUESTS BECOME EXPLOITED SLAVES. A seven-year drought blisters what is now Israel. Pharaoh invites Jacob's family of about 70 to graze their flocks near the drought-resistant Nile River. The Jews stay long after the drought. Long enough to grow into a sizeable minority. The new pharaoh says they're a threat to national security. They might fight against the Egyptians. So in a preemptive strike, he rounds them up and turns them into a national asset: slave labor. *(Exodus 1)*

MOSES IN A BASKET. Tossing baby Jew boys in the Nile River becomes the patriotic thing to do in Egypt—at least it is when Moses is born. Population control. Pharaoh had tried thinning the Jewish population by working them to death, but that seemed only to juice up their libido. Moses' mother has a brainstorm. She complies with the order, but puts Moses in a waterproof basket. Near where the princess bathes. Who can resist a baby? The princess adopts him. *(Exodus 2:1–10)*

Handmade Egyptian mud bricks

MUD CITIES. Pharaoh forces the Jewish slaves to build entire cities, including the supply cities of Pithom and Rameses. The Jews make their own mud bricks, held together with straw, and dried in the sun. ▲

RUNAWAY PRINCE. The princess seems to know Moses is Jewish. Still, she raises him as a prince. Moses knows he's Jewish, too, at least by age 40. When he visits his enslaved people, he sees an Egyptian beating one of the workers. Moses kills the slave driver. When Pharaoh hears about it, he orders Moses executed. Moses runs for his life. He flees east across the Sinai Peninsula to Midian, on the border of what is now Jordan and Saudi Arabia. *(Exodus 2:11–15)* ▶

GOD WITH ROOTS. Moses stops running when he reaches the home of a shepherd who has seven daughters. Great odds for a bachelor. Moses marries Zipporah and settles into the life of a shepherd, working for his father-in-law. Forty years later God speaks to Moses from a burning bush and recruits him to go to Egypt and free the Jews. Moses refuses, saying he's not a good speaker. God replies, "Who do you think made the human mouth?" (Exodus 4:11 MSG). Moses goes.

TEN PLAGUES TO FREEDOM. "God who?" That's the question Pharaoh asks after Moses and Aaron tell him God wants the Jews freed. Pharaoh, considered a deity himself, must think the enslaved Jews have one sorry excuse of a god—no match for Egypt's gods. It takes 10 plagues to convince him otherwise. Some Bible experts say the plagues seem to target Egyptian gods with one natural disaster after another. *(Exodus 7–12)*

Frogs run amok fleeing the polluted Nile River—according to one theory that labels the 10 plagues of Egypt a string of natural disasters.

Rameses II

BEATEN. Pharaoh is considered the divine son of Egypt's greatest god, Re, the sun god in a sun-dominated desert nation. When the 10th plague takes the life of Pharaoh's oldest son, he admits defeat. He grants the request of Moses to free the Jews. Some scholars say Rameses II (1279–1213 BC) was the stubborn pharaoh Moses confronted. Others say Thutmose III (1479–1425 BC).

NATURAL DISASTERS, OR BATTLE OF THE GODS? Both, according to some scholars. They say the 10 plagues followed a fall-to-spring cycle of natural disasters intended to embarrass Egypt's gallery of gods.

PLAGUE	NATURAL DISASTER	GOD
Nile River turns red	Toxic bacteria from flooded swamps	Hapi, god of Nile
Frogs	Fleeing the poisoned river	Heqet, frog-headed god of birth
Gnats	Breeding in pools of receding water	Thoth, god of magic, can't help magicians
Flies	Laying eggs in decaying frogs	Ptah, creator god
Livestock disease	Anthrax from bad water	Hathor, shown with horns
Boils	Flies carrying diseases	Isis, health god
Hail	Common in Middle East	Shu, god of dry air
Locusts	Common	Min, god of crops
Three days of darkness	Spring sandstorm called "50 days"	Re, sun god
Death of oldest children	Firstborn get extra food, contaminated	Pharaoh (his son dies, too)

LAST SUPPER, FIRST PASSOVER. For the Jews, their last supper in captivity becomes an annual meal they'll celebrate every spring throughout history. The meal is called Passover because an angel passes over the Jewish houses to kill the firstborn children in each Egyptian family—the 10th and final plague. Jews prepare to flee by eating lamb or goat along with flatbread cooked in a rush. By meal's end, Pharaoh orders all Jews out of Egypt. *(Exodus 12)*

FLOUR AND WATER, HOLD THE YEAST. Looking and tasting more like a cracker than a loaf of bread, matzah (MAHTZ-uh) is the unleavened bread the Jews ate hours before their sudden release from slavery. They didn't have time to let bread dough rise. They had to eat and run.

TWO TO THREE MILLION REFUGEES? The Bible says Moses lead "603,550 men" (Exodus 38:26). Add one woman and a couple of kids for each man. That's over two million souls—in a land that looks like a Mars stand-in. (See photo pages 170–171.) Impossible, many say. One theory: The numbers are symbolic. In Hebrew, letters have numerical equivalents. If you tally the letters for "sons of Israel," a common way of referring to the Jews, you get 603,551. That's all the men in the census, plus Moses leading them.

A PATH THROUGH THE SEA. Moses leads the Jews south into the Sinai Peninsula badlands, avoiding Egyptian forts along the northern coastal route to Israel. Pharaoh decides it was foolish to free his slave laborers. He orders his chariot corps to herd them back. The Egyptians catch up with the refugees at a body of water experts say could be one of the area lakes or the Red Sea's Gulf of Suez. An all-night wind punches an escape route through the water. When Pharaoh's army follows, the water rushes in, drowning them all. *(Exodus 14)*

WATER FALL. Egyptian soldiers drown when the sea crashes in on them. Their mistake: trying to follow the Jews into a path that an overnight wind blew through the water.

Red Sea coral reef—underwater bridge

DID THE RED SEA REALLY PART? Separate scientific studies in 1992 and 2004 each concluded that an all-night wind could push back the beachfront water in the narrow Gulf of Suez, mimicking low tide. Jews may have crossed on a freshly exposed four-mile reef, one study speculates. When the wind stopped, water 10 feet (3 meters) deep would rush back within 30 minutes. In 1799, Napoleon almost drowned while riding horseback on a Red Sea beach as receding water rushed back to shore.

MANNA AND QUAIL: FAST FOOD TO GO. Starving, the Jews ask Moses why he brought them into the badlands to die when they had food in Egypt. God rains down sweet flakes called manna (*man-hu* in Hebrew, for "what is it?"). Manna covers the ground like morning frost. Jews use it to make sweet bread and cakes. God also sends in a massive flock of migrating quail, flying low and slow enough to catch by hand. *(Exodus 16, Numbers 10–11)*

Egyptians catching quail by hand (painting partly restored)

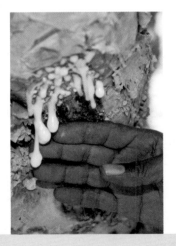

Collecting tree sap manna

MANNA. "It was white like coriander seeds. It tasted like wafers that were made with honey" (Exodus 16:31, NIrV). Some guess the sweet flakes may have been the dried secretions of a plant-sucking mealy bug, or tree sap. Herders today knock the dried sap off plants and use it as a sweetener. Some chefs have started cooking exotic dishes with it. Some varieties sell for over $20 an ounce (3 centigrams).

10 COMMANDMENTS. The Jews camp for about a year at the foot of Mount Sinai, where God had first appeared to Moses as a voice in a burning bush. God returns. He meets with Moses on the mountain and gives him hundreds of laws that will organize the Jews into a nation. The first 10 laws are the most important, and the basis for all the other laws:

:: No other gods
:: No idols
:: No irreverent use of God's name
:: Rest every Sabbath
:: Honor your father and mother
:: No murder
:: No adultery
:: No stealing
:: No lies about others
:: No craving what belongs to others. *(Exodus 20)*

TEMPLE IN A BACKPACK. Refugees on the road, the Jews have no place to worship. So God tells Moses to have them build one. They pool their resources and build a tent worship center, furnished with a portable altar, gold lampstands, and a linen wall of curtains to form a courtyard around the sacred space. Shaped like a boxcar, the tent sanctuary stretches 15 yards long and 5 yards wide and high (14 by 4.5 meters). *(Exodus 25–27)*

A FAMILY OF WORSHIP LEADERS. Moses doesn't get the job as Israel's worship leader. Though he delivers God's laws, which sets up Israel's sacrificial system of worship, his older brother, Aaron, gets the top job: high priest. Aaron's four sons serve as priests. They will manage the worship center and direct the people in offering their sacrifices to God. All Israel's

future priests are to come from Aaron's descendants. *(Exodus 28)*

LEVITES: WORSHIP ASSISTANTS. Aaron and Moses belonged to the tribe of Levi, descended from one of Jacob's 12 sons. God appoints the men of this tribe to serve as worship assistants. They will maintain the worship center, transport it, guard it, and help the priests with worship rituals such as slaughtering and cutting up sacrificial animals for burning on the altar. *(Exodus 28–29)*

High priest (in blue) with priest

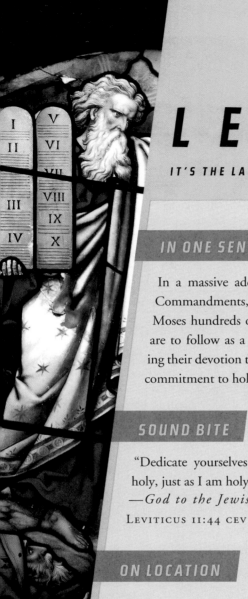

LEVITICUS

IT'S THE LAW

IN ONE SENTENCE

In a massive add-on to the 10 Commandments, God gives Moses hundreds of laws the Jews are to follow as a way of expressing their devotion to God and their commitment to holy living.

SOUND BITE

"Dedicate yourselves to me and be holy, just as I am holy."
—*God to the Jewish people*
LEVITICUS 11:44 CEV

ON LOCATION

TIME. About 1440 BC, according to some scholars, and about 1290 BC according to others.

PLACE. Camped about a year at the foot of Mount Sinai in Egypt's rugged Sinai Peninsula. It's uncertain which mountain that is. One tradition: *Jabal Musa* (Arabic: "mountain of Moses").

NEWSMAKERS

MOSES, leader of Jews during Exodus. He's the prophet God uses to deliver his laws to the people.

AARON, Israel's first high priest. Older brother of Moses, he's in charge of sacrifice rituals at the worship center.

The Great Escape
Possible Route to Mt. Sinai

Sacrifice in Solomon's Temple, high altar at left. Solomon built Israel's first temple several hundred years after the Exodus.

PEOPLE SIN, ANIMALS PAY THE PRICE. Sin is a capital offense in the eyes of a holy God. Any sin. But Moses says God will accept the death of animals as a substitute for people. Quoting God, Moses says it's actually the blood that atones for the sin because "life is in the blood" (Leviticus 17:11 CEV). Animals approved for sacrifices include cattle, sheep, and goats. The poor could offer less expensive animals: doves and pigeons. *(Leviticus 1, 17)*

BLOOD-RED WORSHIP—THE HOW-TO GUIDE. Sacrificed animals can't have any defects. A Jew takes a Grade-A animal to the worship center. He kills it in front of the priests, probably by cutting its throat. The priest splatters some of the animal's blood on the side of the altar. The worshipper then cuts the animal to pieces, washing its insides. The priest lays the animal in the fire on the altar. It produces "a pleasing aroma to the LORD." *(Leviticus 1)*

WHAT'S THE POINT OF THIS ANIMAL CRUELTY? Animal sacrifice is a graphic reminder to every Jew that sin is deadly serious, scholars explain. The worshipper lays his hand on the animal's head, perhaps a symbol of transferring his sin to the critter (Leviticus 1:4). What follows are sights, sounds, and smells that express the seriousness of sin:

:: the sight of a cut throat

:: the sound of a squeal

:: the smell of burnt meat.

FIVE SACRIFICES. Sin isn't the only reason Jews offer sacrifices to God. Sometimes, the Jews just want to say thanks. Other times, they need to show their remorse to people they hurt.

	WHAT'S OFFERED	WHAT HAPPENS
	Poor: pigeon, dove Rich: bull Others: sheep, goat	**BURNT OFFERING** Animal is cut up and burned on altar. **REASON:** Atones for sin.
	Baked goods, roasted kernels, flour	**GRAIN OFFERING** Priest burns some and keeps some as salary. **REASON:** Expresses thanks to God for the harvest.
	Goats, sheep, cattle, grain	**PEACE OFFERING** Priest burns some, keeps some as salary, gives some back for worshipper to eat. **REASON:** Expresses thanks for a special blessing, such as recovery from sickness.
	Priest: bull Others: goat, female sheep	**OFFERING FOR ACCIDENTAL SIN** Priest burns the fat, keeps the rest as salary. **REASON:** Purifies person who sinned without meaning to.
	Ram or value of ram	**RESTITUTION OFFERING** Priest burns some, keeps the rest. **REASON:** Expresses remorse to God or to someone harmed by wrongdoing.

GOD'S DAILY SIX-PACK OF BEER. God washed down barbecued sacrifices with a six-pack of beer every day, and twice on the Sabbath. Each day, when Jewish priests burned a pair of lambs in sacrifice to atone for sin, they had to throw in some beer. They pitched this drink-offering onto the altar fire with the meat: "a quart of strong beer with each lamb" (Numbers 28:7 MSG; see also Exodus 29:38). Two lambs. Two quarts (liters) of beer. Every day. Double that on the Sabbath. For humans drinking beer or wine, Bible writers urge moderation, though one sage prescribes it for anyone "dying" or "sad and troubled" (Proverbs 31:6 NIrV).

PLATE TO MOUTH, KEEPING IT KOSHER. God gives Moses a list of animals the Jews can and can't eat. The list makes no earthly sense, many scholars say. There's no health benefit to banning pork from the dinner table while serving up grasshoppers—chocolate-dipped or plain. God's point, according to many:

:: teach the Jews to obey him
:: help others see the Jews as an exemplary nation—one nation under God. *(Leviticus 11, 17)*

Prime rib is kosher, unless it's blood-pink.

FORBIDDEN DELIGHTS. Among the tasty food branded non-kosher—banned from the menu of observant Jews:

:: lobster, shrimp, oyster, crab, catfish, and any another sea critter that doesn't have scales and fins
:: pork, rabbit, and any other land animal that doesn't have split hooves and chew the cud (food in the stomach returned to the mouth for a second chewing, on purpose)
:: rare prime rib or any other meat pink with blood. Blood belongs to God, in sacrifices.

HAPPY NEW YEAR IN SEPTEMBER. Squealing its high-pitched shrill from the Judean highlands, a ram's horn "awakens the soul" to celebrate the autumn holiday of *Rosh Hashanah*, Jewish New Year. So said Jewish philosopher Maimonides (AD 1135–1204).

HAPPY HOLY HOLIDAYS. Moses tells the Jews to observe seven holy holidays each year, in addition to the weekly Sabbath day of rest from sundown Friday to sundown Saturday. All but one is joyful.

:: *Passover.* Early springtime meal to commemorate God freeing the Jews from Egyptian slavery; Hebrew: *Pesach.*
:: *Bread with no yeast.* A week to remember the Jews leaving Egypt in such a hurry they didn't have time to let bread dough rise for their last meal there.
:: *First Fruits.* Celebrating the barley harvest, around March.
:: *Pentecost.* Celebrating the continued harvest, 50 days after First Fruits; Hebrew: *Shavuot.*
:: *Trumpets.* Jewish New Year's Day in September or October; Hebrew: *Rosh Hashanah.*
:: *Day of Atonement.* National day of repentance; Hebrew: *Yom Kippur.*
:: *Shelters.* Week-long fall festival to commemorate the temporary homes of Exodus Jews living in the desert 40 years; Hebrew: *Sukkot.* *(Leviticus 23)*

NUMBERS

FORTY YEARS—ISRAEL'S SENTENCE

IN ONE SENTENCE

After the Jews refuse to invade the land God promised them, fearing reports of giants and heavily armed, walled cities, God condemns their sorry faith and sentences them to a generation in the badlands.

SOUND BITE

"All the people we saw were huge. We even saw giants. . . . Next to them we felt like grasshoppers."
—*Scouts just back from Canaan (Israel)*
NUMBERS 13:32–33

ON LOCATION

TIME. Span of 40 years starting around 1440 BC or 1290 BC, scholars debate which.

PLACE. From the Sinai Peninsula to the Kadesh oasis, ending east of the Jordan River in what is now Jordan.

NEWSMAKERS

MOSES, leader of the Jewish refugees. He leads them to the border of Canaan (Israel).

AARON, older brother of Moses. He leads the people in worship as their first high priest.

JOSHUA, warrior. He leads in battles and scouts the Promised Land.

Mount Sinai camp

Ever since the Jews fled Egypt, "The Lᴏʀᴅ went ahead of them. He guided them during the day with a pillar of cloud, and he provided light at night with a pillar of fire" (Exodus 13:21). Once, the pillar dropped back to provide a wall of fire, blocking the advance of Egypt's army (Exodus 14:19–20). During the year the Jews camped near Mount Sinai, the pillar rested above the tent worship center.

ON THE ROAD AGAIN. While the Jewish refugees camp for about a year at the foot of Mount Sinai, Moses organizes them into a 12-tribe nation— complete with hundreds of laws to govern them. Now it's time to move on toward the Promised Land. They know it because a pillar of light representing God's presence begins to move. This glowing beam led them out of Egypt and will lead them to the border of Canaan in what is now Israel. *(Numbers 1, 10)*

MILITARY CENSUS. Anticipating the battles ahead, Moses orders a census of "all the men twenty years old or older who are able to go to war" (Numbers 1:2–3). It's this census that gives Numbers its name. The tally is "603,550" (Numbers 1:46; Exodus 38:26). Many take this number literally. For one of several alternatives, see "Two to three million refugees?" page 258 .

INTEL REPORT: MISSION IMPOSSIBLE. That's the bad news from 10 of the dozen spies Moses sends to scout Canaan. The refugees have reached Canaan's southern border. But they refuse to go any farther. They're terrified by double-whammy news: They'll have to attack (1) walled cities (2) defended by giants. Spies Joshua and Caleb present the minority opinion, arguing that the land is good and God will certainly give it to them. *(Exodus 13–14)*

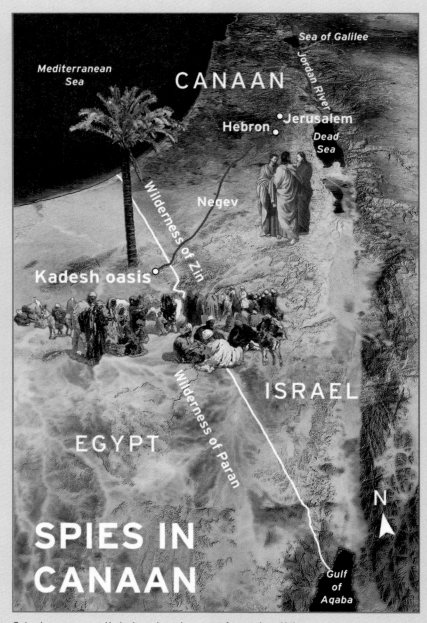

Spies leave camp at Kadesh oasis and scout as far north as Hebron.

GIANTS. Mummies and other burial remains suggest that Egyptian men often stood anywhere from 5 feet, 7 inches to 6 feet tall (170–182 cm). Not much different from men today. Jews were likely much the same, many say, though some evidence, such as the heights of ancient Jewish homes, puts them closer to the ground: about 5 feet (152 cm). The giants were apparently a Watusi-like people, genetically tuned to a higher altitude. The average Tutsi man stands 6 feet, 5 inches (196 cm) tall, with above-average men often stretching over 7 feet (213 cm). Quite the added fear factor in a club fest. David's famous enemy, Goliath, stood 7 feet tall to 10 feet (305 cm) by some ancient copies of the story.

REVOLT OF THE MOSES WANNABES. As the Jews settle into a lifetime of waiting, a man named Korah decides to challenge Moses and Aaron for the right to lead. Some 250 leaders join Korah's insurrection. Moses agrees to let God decide the matter. He tells them to bring incense burners to present to God—as though they're priests. God brings fire, too. Perhaps lightning. He incinerates the rebels. Except for Korah and a few others. They get swallowed up by an earthquake. *(Numbers 16)*

Rebels down under

Average height: 5 feet, 7 inches (170 cm)

ISRAEL'S SENTENCE—40 YEARS. Since this generation of Jews doesn't have the chutzpah to invade the Promised Land—in spite of all they've seen God do for them—they can sit out the rest of their lives in the barren badlands. God will wait for Generation Next. Of that first generation, the only two adults who will live long enough to step foot on Canaan will be the two spies who recommended trusting God: Joshua and Caleb. *(Numbers 14)*

GOD OVERRULED. Moses tells the Jews that God has now forbidden them from entering Canaan. But with a "we'll-show-God" abandon, they launch their own invasion into Canaan's hill country—without the support of Moses or God. The hills are alive with the sound of Canaanites. So the Jews run back to Moses *(Numbers 14)*.

Almond on the branch

AARON'S WALKING STICK GOES NUTS. To confirm Aaron's role as Israel's worship leader—the high priest—Moses collects the walking sticks of all 12 tribal leaders. Aaron represents the tribe of Levi. Each stick is engraved with the leader's name, and then placed overnight in the tent worship center beside the Ark of the Covenant, a chest that holds the 10 Commandments. By morning, Aaron's almond stick has *"sprouted, budded, blossomed, and produced ripe almonds!"* (Numbers 17:8). That not only seals Aaron's job, it earns a place for the stick inside the sacred chest.

KADESH OASIS. The Jews apparently served most of their 40-year sentence at this oasis. Some Bible experts place it about 90 miles (145 km) south of Jerusalem, on Egypt's side of the modern border with Israel. Today it's called Ein El-Qudeirat, Arabic for "Fountain of Unlimited Power"—a fine name for northern Sinai's largest oasis. Its daily flow of spring-fed water reaches about a quarter of a million gallons (nearly a million liters).

Horned viper, one of a half-dozen species of poisonous snakes in the area

SNAKES ON A PLAIN. After 40 years, the Jewish nation is on the move. Instead of pushing north, into armies that beat them in two out of three battles, they turn south. That puts them in a Martian landscape where they complain—even about God's cooking: "horrible manna!" God sends poisonous snakes. The Jews repent. God tells Moses to make a bronze snake. The snake-bit get healed when they look at it. *(Numbers 21)* ▲

A WELL-SPOKEN JACKASS. Arabs in Moab, modern Jordan, deploy their secret weapon: Balaam, a diviner famous for his inside track to the gods. Balaam's mission: stop the Jews by putting a hex on them. Ironically, Balaam's donkey sees what the seer can't: an armed angel blocking their path to the Jews. The donkey stops. Balaam beats it. The donkey complains, in words articulate for a jackass. Only then does the angel appear to Balaam, convincing him to bless the Jews. *(Numbers 22–24)* ▶

DEUTERONOMY

LAST WORDS OF MOSES: OBEY GOD

IN ONE SENTENCE

Knowing he'll soon die, 120-year-old Moses reviews for the grown-up kids of the Exodus all the laws God gave the Jews 40 years earlier, and he pleads with them not to make the same mistake as their parents who disobeyed God—and never lived to see the Promised Land because of it.

SOUND BITE

"The LORD is the one and only God. Love the LORD your God with all your heart."
—*Moses to the Jews*
DEUTERONOMY 6:4–5 NIrV

NEWSMAKERS

MOSES, liberator of the Jews from Egyptian slavery. He has led the refugees for the past 40 years.

JOSHUA, general of the Jewish militia. He becomes the successor to Moses.

ON LOCATION

TIME. 1400s BC or 1200s BC. Scholars debate which.

PLACE. Near what is today Israel's eastern border, across the Jordan River in what is now the Arab nation of Jordan.

HISTORY LESSON FROM THE MAN WHO LIVED IT. Nearly all the adults who left Egypt are dead. Many in this new generation never saw the miracles of God, like the parting of the sea. Or they were too young to remember them. So Moses traces not only the story of how they got here, on the brink of invading the Promised Land. He carefully reviews the laws God gave them—and he warns that disobedience cost their parents 40 years in the badlands. *(Deuteronomy 1–3)*

MOSES' AUDIENCE. Almost every adult who left Egypt when they were age 20 or older is dead. Only Moses is left, along with Joshua and Caleb, the two scouts who trusted God enough to recommend invading Canaan as God had ordered 40 years earlier—advice the crowd of Jews rejected. God said that except for Joshua and Caleb, "Not one of you from this wicked generation will live to see the good land I swore to give to your ancestors" (Deuteronomy 1:35).

DEUTERONOMY, THE NAME. It's Greek for "second law." The name stuck because this is the second time the laws show up in the Bible. To make sure the new generation knows about them, Moses repeats these laws from Exodus, Leviticus, and Numbers. He tells future Jews to do the same: "Repeat them again and again to your children" (Deuteronomy 6:7).

LOOKING UP TO THE LAW. On display in the Louvre Museum of Paris, the Code of Hammurabi is the oldest known set of laws, written at least 300 years before Moses. In about 1790 BC, craftsmen chiseled 281 laws onto this stone pillar that stands almost seven and a half feet high (2.25 meters).

DID MOSES BORROW SOME LAWS FROM IRAQ?
A few of the laws Moses quotes are similar to laws from Babylon's Code of Hammurabi, written several centuries before him in what is now Iraq. The "eye for an eye" of Exodus 21:24 sounds close to Hammurabi's law 196: "If a man put out the eye of another man, his eye shall be put out." But there are differences. Hammurabi gives nobles special treatment, like the option of paying a fine for the eye injury. And he sometimes punishes the innocent, like ordering a builder's child killed if a house the man built collapsed and killed another man's child.

THE MOST IMPORTANT JEWISH LAW. Jews don't have a formal statement of belief, like the Apostle's Creed, a document that sums up the key beliefs of many Christians. But if they did, it would include Deuteronomy 6:4–5. (See "Sound Bite," page 272.)

JEWISH BELIEFS 101. "I'm giving you the laws of the Lord today," Moses tells the crowd. "What other nation is great enough to have rules and laws that are as fair as these?" (Deuteronomy 4:8 NIrV). Then starting with the 10 Commandments—the laws on which all other Jewish laws are based—Moses goes over all the laws he says God expects the Jews to obey.

ONE BIG HAPPY FAMILY. A family tree grows four generations high, starring Mom and Dad: Frida and Shlomo Hameiri (top, center) of Safed, Israel. In the days of Moses, God promised that if the Jewish people obeyed his laws, they'd reap lots of everything good, kids included.

FINE PRINT IN GOD'S CONTRACT: PERKS, PENALTIES. There's a huge price to pay for disobeying God, Moses warns. But there are wonderful benefits for obeying him.

PERKS:

:: bumper crops

:: landscape of livestock

:: house full of kids

:: power over enemies.

PENALTIES:

:: crop failure

:: disease

:: invasion, and defeat

:: exile from the Promised Land.

(Deuteronomy 28–30)

NO PROMISED LAND FOR MOSES. In his last act as Israel's leader, Moses tells the people God won't let him cross the river into Canaan. Instead, Moses says, God has chosen Joshua to lead them during the invasion. Moses climbs Mount Nebo, where he's at least able to see the Promised Land. Then he dies. Some ancient copies of the story imply that "God buried him" (Deuteronomy 34:6 MSG). Others say "they" buried him, suggesting the Jews. The Jews mourn for a month. *(Deuteronomy 31–34)*

Moses taps water from a rock.

WHY GOD BANNED MOSES FROM CANAAN. Moses displeased God during a miracle. Moses was supposed to "speak to the rock. . .and it will pour out its water" (Numbers 20:8). But he hit it twice with his staff. And he seemed to take credit: "Must we bring you water from this rock?" It's unclear if either of these actions lies behind the vague reason God gave: "Because you did not trust me enough to demonstrate my holiness."

WHY JOSHUA? He is a seasoned warrior, leader of Israel's militia—experience that will come in handy during the next phase of the Exodus: the conquest of Canaan. More importantly, as the Bible tells it, he trusts God more than he trusts his common sense—essential for taking out double-walled cities like Jericho.

JOSHUA

JEWS ON THE WARPATH

IN ONE SENTENCE

With Moses dead, Joshua leads the Jews across the Jordan River where they defeat Canaanite armies and secure a foothold in the highlands of what are now Israel and the West Bank.

SOUND BITE

"The time has come for you to lead these people, the Israelites, across the Jordan River. . . . Wherever you set foot, you will be on land I have given you."
—*God to Joshua*
JOSHUA 1:2–3

NEWSMAKERS

JOSHUA, successor to Moses. God appoints Israel's general to lead the Israelites in a war to recapture their homeland.

RAHAB, a prostitute in Jericho. She helps Jewish spies who come to scout out the first target of the invasion force.

ON LOCATION

TIME. 1400s or 1200s BC. Scholars debate which.

PLACE. Joshua leads the Jews across the Jordan River, from what is now Jordan into the part of Canaan now called the West Bank and Israel.

TWO JEWS, ONE ARAB HOOKER. Camped at Acacia Grove in what is now Jordan, Joshua sends two spies on a half-day walk beyond the Jordan River. Their mission: scout the first target, Canaan's border town, Jericho. Lousy spies, they blow their cover and nearly get arrested while spending the night in the house of a prostitute, Rahab. She helps them escape after they promise that when the Jews attack, they'll spare her and her family. *(Joshua 1–2)*

JEW CROSSING. The invasion begins in springtime, when the Jordan River Valley is flooded. Not a problem. Priests carrying the sacred chest that holds the 10 Commandments lead the way. The moment they reach the river, the water stops. It dams up near the village of Adam, some 20 miles (32 km) upstream from Jericho. Red Sea crossing déjà vu. *(Joshua 3)*

JORDAN RIVER: STOP

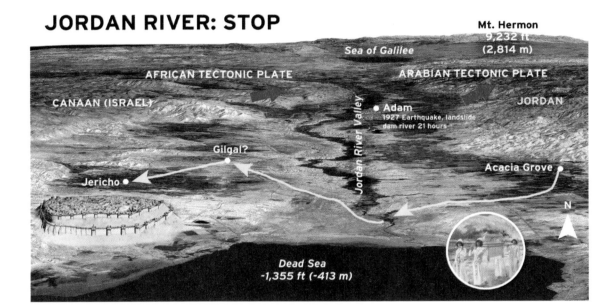

Mt. Hermon
9,232 ft
(2,814 m)

Sea of Galilee

AFRICAN TECTONIC PLATE

ARABIAN TECTONIC PLATE

CANAAN (ISRAEL)

JORDAN

Adam
1927 Earthquake, landslide
dam river 21 hours

Jordan River Valley

Gilgal?

Acacia Grove

Jericho

N

Dead Sea
-1,355 ft (-413 m)

JORDAN RIVER LANDSLIDES ON THE RECORD. The Jordan tracks along a quake-spawning fault line that has dammed the river many times—in 1927 near the very spot the Bible says the water piled up. The quake shook loose the 150-foot-high (46 meters) cliffs near Adam. A dirt wall dammed the river for 21 hours.

WHY DID THE SPIES GO TO A PROSTITUTE? Business or pleasure? The Bible's not saying. Some scholars imagine the worst. Others say a house of pleasure was the perfect place to gather intel. Locals stay away. Strangers come and go. ◀

JERICHO, JOSHUA'S SPEED BUMP. Six miles (9 km) west of the Jordan River, Jericho sits on a hilltop protected by double walls—one at the base of the hill, another at the top. The Jews march around the city once a day for six days. On day seven, they circle it seven times, priests blow ram horns, and militiamen scream till the walls drop. Jericho's only survivors: Rahab and her extended family. *(Joshua 6)*

Oasis town of Jericho, protected by double walls

FREEZE-FRAME: THE DAY THE SUN STOPPED. Villagers at Gibeon, a day's walk west of Jericho, make a peace treaty with the Jews. Neighboring Canaanites feel betrayed. They lay siege to Gibeon, which rushes a messenger to Joshua. The Jewish militia marches all night into the hills. Before the dawn attack, Joshua prays for the sun and moon to stop. The Bible says they did. Jews rout the Canaanites and hail finishes them off. *(Joshua 9–10)*

Hail caught in netting above a banana garden in Kibbutz Matzuva, Israel.

DID THE SUN STOP? Not likely, most scholars say. The Hebrew word for "stop" can mean "stop shining," perhaps a poetic way of asking for relief from the hot sun after a long march. Storm clouds roll in, pummeling the enemy with hail.

JOSHUA'S STRATEGY

MT. HERMON

Mediterranean Sea

Lake Huleh
• Hazor
◎ Merom

Madon • Sea of Galilee
• Achshaph
• Shimron

3 DESTROY NORTHERN FORCES

Jordan River

2 DESTROY SOUTHERN FORCES
Beth-Horon ◎   Bethel
Gezer •   • Ai
Aijalon •   ◎ Gibeon   Gilgal
      ◎ Jericho
Azekah •   • Jarmuth   • Jerusalem
     • Libnah
Lachish ◎   ◎ Makkedah   **1 INVASION STARTS**
      • Hebron   Dead Sea
   ◎ Eglon
    ◎ Debir

N

0   10   20 Miles
  20   30 Kilometers

• Army or city defeated
◎ Battle

OPERATION HIGH ROAD. Joshua's army takes the fight to Canaan's hill country, avoiding the plains. The hills are where his lightly armed militia has the best chance of running circles around heavily armored enemy soldiers backed up by chariot-charging archers. Joshua's Jews destroy half a dozen major cities in the southland. Then they turn north, wiping out coalition forces near the Sea of Galilee. With that victory, Jews control what is now central Israel. *(Joshua 10–11)* ▲

Profile of a prisoner in Egypt, possibly Canaanite (about 1200 BC)

PUTTING ISRAEL ON THE MAP. Apparently figuring the big battles are over, Joshua divides Canaan among Israel's 12 tribes. He orders each tribe to finish mopping up its territory. That's a mistake. In time, the Jews will learn to live alongside the remaining Canaanites. Moses had warned against this. He said if any Canaanites remained, the Jews would pick up their bad habits—like worshipping idols. Sadly, history would prove him right. *(Joshua 13–21)*

ISRAEL, THE NAME. The coalition of Jewish tribes takes the name God gave their forefather Jacob: "From now on you will be called Israel" (Genesis 32:28).

CITIES FOR JEWS ON THE RUN. Scattered throughout Israel are six "cities of refuge." People charged with crimes can flee to these cities for a trial rather than face the blood vengeance of a victim's family and friends.

ISRAEL'S BOUNDARIES. God tells Joshua he has given the Jews land from "the Negev wilderness in the south to the Lebanon mountains in the north, from the Euphrates River in the east to the Mediterranean Sea in the west" (Joshua 1:4). Solomon's kingdom stretched that far. But Joshua's tribes controlled mainly the hills in what is now central Israel. ▼

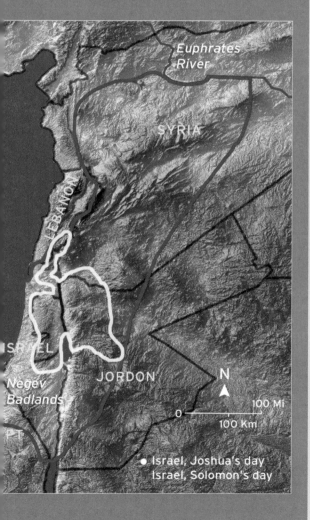

Euphrates River

SYRIA

LEBANON

ISRAEL

JORDON

N

Negev Badlands

100 Mi
0
100 Km

● Israel, Joshua's day
Israel, Solomon's day

GOOD-BYE, JOSH. Like Moses, elderly Joshua calls together Israel's leaders for one last meeting. At age 110, Joshua knows he'll die soon. "Be very careful to follow everything Moses wrote," he says, referring to the Jewish laws. Then urging the Jews to commit, Joshua says "Choose today whom you will serve. . . . But as for me and my family, we will serve the LORD." The elders agree. Joshua dies. *(Joshua 23–24)* ▲

JUDGES

HEROES TO THE RESCUE

IN ONE SENTENCE

When enemies terrorize the Jewish settlers, the Jews call on God, who sends heroes known as judges to defend the Jews.

SOUND BITE

"With the jawbone of a donkey, I've killed a thousand men!"
—*Samson*
JUDGES 15:16

ON LOCATION

TIME. After Joshua but before Israel's first king, from as early as 1375 BC to 1065 BC.

PLACE. Most stories take place in what are now Israel and Jordan.

NEWSMAKERS

SAMSON, a judge. A lover of Philistine women, Samson is no friend of Philistine men; he kills them by the thousands.

DELILAH, Samson's fatal attraction. Delilah betrays Samson for money.

GIDEON, a judge. Reluctant hero, Gideon has trouble believing God wants him to drive off invaders.

DEBORAH, a prophetess and judge. She leads a battle and wins, after the general refuses to go into battle without her.

Mount Tabor

MRS. GENERAL. Instead of driving out the Canaanites as Moses instructed, Jews treat them as neighbors—adopting bad habits such as idol worship. As punishment, God lets enemies terrorize them. When the Jews repent, God sends a leader like the prophetess Deborah. She gathers a militia on the slopes of Mount Tabor. An invasion army reinforced with 900 iron chariots prepares to engage the militia. Suddenly, a downpour floods the valley stream, trapping the chariots in mud. The invaders run for home. *(Judges 4)*

Jael's hammer

WHY DID A WOMAN PROPHET LEAD THE ARMY? The general wouldn't. Apparently he wasn't convinced that the Lord ordered this battle. So he insisted Deborah put her life on the line by going with them. She said that because of his doubt, a woman would get the glory.

DÉJÀ VU JEWS. Judges is a collection of stories, each following a predictable cycle. The Jews sin. God allows enemies to oppress them. The Jews repent and pray for help. God sends a savior. This happens 12 times, with God sending 12 judges.

WHAT WOMAN GOT THE GLORY FOR THE VICTORY? Deborah ordered the victorious attack when the rain began. Another woman, Jael, killed the enemy commander, Sisera. Running for his life, Sisera stopped to rest in Jael's tent. While he slept, she hammered a tent peg into the side of his head.

CAMEL CAVALRY. Gideon's story is the earliest known report of a camel cavalry used in attacks. Sprinting up to 40 miles per hour (64 km), camels could carry raiders into a harvest field faster than farmers could react. That's why Gideon, a farmer, worked in a pit to shake grain from cut stalks. From a distance, raiders couldn't see him.

GIDEON'S RANGERS. For seven years, camel-riding raiders from Midian (Saudi Arabia) plunder the Jewish harvest. God tells Gideon to raise an army; 32,000 Jews mass to fight 135,000 Arab invaders. God doesn't like those odds. Too many Jews. God wants Israel to see the victory as a miracle. So he has Gideon lead an elite strike force of 300, attacking at night by waving torches and blowing horns. In the darkness, many Midianites kill each other. Survivors of the chaos flee. *(Judges 6–7)*

DADDY HERO'S VOW DOOMS DAUGHTER. Some Jews settle in the land of Ammon (Jordan). That's because Ammonites had attacked the Exodus Jews, losing both the battle and their homeland. Years later the Ammonites rally to drive out the Jews. Jephthah (JEFF-thah), Jewish son of a prostitute, raises an army to crush the Ammo-nites. Pumped before battle, he vows to sacrifice the first thing that greets him when he gets home, victorious. His daughter welcomes him playing a tambourine. *(Judges 11)*

CHOPPED LADY STARTS CIVIL WAR. In an all-night gang rape, Jews from Benjamin's tribe kill a fellow Jew's wife. The widower chops her corpse, sending a piece to each of the 12 tribes—a grisly cry for justice. Benjamin's tribal leaders refuse to punish the rapists. The other 11 tribes attack and nearly annihilate Benjamin's tribe. Only 600 men survive. Regretting the overkill, coalition tribes give the survivors wives to repopulate Benjamin's territory. *(Judges 19–21)* ▲

SAMSON'S ANIMAL INSTINCTS. Sex is the motor driving Samson's story. Raised under a vow to never cut his hair, he grows up strong enough to defeat a thousand-man Philistine army with nothing but a donkey's jawbone. But he has a weakness: Philistine women. Philistine leaders offer his girlfriend, Delilah, a reward for the secret to his strength. A haircut follows. Samson becomes a slave, blinded. When his hair and strength return, he collapses a temple by pushing out the pillars. Samson dies with thousands of Philistines inside the building. *(Judges 13–16)* ▼

SAMSON'S WOMEN. Samson's story spins around three unsavory Philistine women and the trouble they caused him.

His wife. She tells wedding guests the answer to his riddle, causing him to lose an expensive bet. He storms off, eventually returning to find his bride remarried to the best man. Samson wages a one-man war against the Philistines, destroying their crops.

A hooker. Philistines wait to ambush Samson when they think he's weak, after sex. Instead, he's invigorated. Enough to rip the city gate off the wall and carry it 40 miles (64 km).

Delilah. She coaxes from him the secret of his haircut vow. Then she arranges a haircut for him while he's sleeping and turns him over to the authorities who gouge out his eyes.

RUTH

ARAB MOTHER OF ISRAEL'S GREATEST KINGS

IN ONE SENTENCE

An Arab widow from what is now Jordan moves to Bethlehem, marries a Jew, and becomes the mother of Israel's greatest dynasty of kings.

SOUND BITE

"Wherever you live, I will live. Your people will be my people, and your God will be my God."
—*Ruth to Naomi*
RUTH 1:16

ON LOCATION

TIME. About 1100 BC.

PLACE. The story takes place in two locations: (1) the country of Moab, in what is now Jordan, (2) the village of Bethlehem

NEWSMAKERS

RUTH, a widow woman from Moab. She gives birth to a son who will become the grandfather of King David.

NAOMI, Ruth's Jewish mother-in-law. When her husband and sons die in Moab, she decides to go home to Bethlehem.

BOAZ, a Jew who marries Ruth. A Bethlehem farmer, he admires the devotion Ruth shows to Naomi.

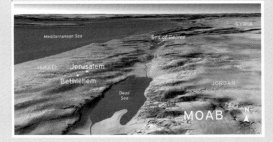

DAUGHTER-IN-LAW. A Bethlehem man moves his family to Moab to escape a drought. His two sons get married there, but the man and his sons all die. The man's wife, Naomi, decides to return home, hoping a relative will take her in. One daughter-in-law, Ruth, insists on going with her. The other returns to her Moabite family. *(Ruth 1)*

Farmers in the Bethlehem area gather wheat at the turn of the 1900s.

RUTH'S HARVEST PROPOSAL. Jewish law allows the poor to pick leftovers from the harvest. A rich farmer named Boaz admires the loyalty Ruth has shown his relative, Naomi. So he tells his workers to leave extra grain for her. Naomi becomes a matchmaker. She knows the law urging a dead man's closest relative to marry the widow. On Naomi's advice, Ruth sneaks under the covers of Boaz while he's sleeping in the field. When Boaz wakes, Ruth proposes. Delighted, Boaz accepts. The couple has a son: Obed, the father of Jesse, who's the father of David. *(Ruth 2–4)*

AND THE POINT IS? God loves everyone. Not just the Jews. Some Bible experts say Ruth's story works as argument against Ezra, a priest who orders Jews to divorce their non-Jewish wives (Ezra 10:10–11).

WHY MARRY YOUR RELATIVE'S WIDOW? It was an ancient form of welfare. Women had no rights and needed a husband, a son, or another relative to take care of them. In Ruth's case, Jewish law allowed her son to inherit the land that belonged to the family of Ruth's first husband. If Ruth had not remarried, someone else would have taken it from Naomi, possibly paying her for it but leaving her homeless.

1,2 SAMUEL

LIVESTOCK BOYS BECOME ISRAEL'S FIRST KINGS

IN ONE SENTENCE

A donkey herder and a shepherd—Saul and David—get the nod of God to become Israel's first two kings; there will be blood.

SOUND BITE

"How the mighty have fallen!"
—*David, after hearing of the death of Saul and his sons*
2 SAMUEL 1:25 NIV

ON LOCATION

TIME. During the 1000s BC.

PLACE. Most stories take place in Israel.

NEWSMAKERS

DAVID, Israel's second king. He's Israel's most famous and beloved ruler.

SAUL, Israel's first king. He becomes obsessed with killing young David, whose popularity soars after defeating the giant Goliath in combat.

SAMUEL, a prophet. Raised in the worship center by the priest Eli, Samuel grows up to lead Israel and then reluctantly appoint Saul as king.

BATHSHEBA, mother of King Solomon. A soldier's wife, she has an affair with King David, gets pregnant, and marries him after her husband dies in battle.

NATHAN, a prophet. He confronts David about the affair with Bathsheba.

SAMUEL: HANNAH'S MIRACLE BABY. Hannah is infertile. Many say it's God's doing—punishment for sin. Her husband's second wife, a baby dispenser, belittles Hannah. But the husband tries to console Hannah: "You have me." But hubby isn't enough. Sobbing at Israel's worship center, Hannah prays for a son, promising to let him serve God. The priest Eli doesn't hear her request, but sees pain pouring from her eyes. He asks God to grant her request. A son is born. *(1 Samuel 1)*

SAMUEL'S NIGHTMARE VISION. Hannah takes young Samuel to the worship center, where the priest Eli will teach him to serve God. One night in bed, Samuel hears God say Eli's family priesthood is doomed. Eli's two sons, both priests, commit adultery, steal sacrificial meat, and extort worshippers. God says they'll die young. Samuel doesn't want to tell Eli, but the old priest insists. Eli's reaction: God knows best. Philistines kill the two in battle. Eli dies when he gets the news. *(1 Samuel 2–4)*

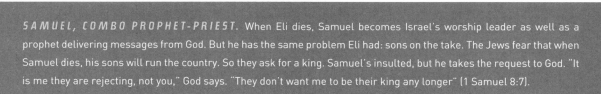

SAMUEL, COMBO PROPHET-PRIEST. When Eli dies, Samuel becomes Israel's worship leader as well as a prophet delivering messages from God. But he has the same problem Eli had: sons on the take. The Jews fear that when Samuel dies, his sons will run the country. So they ask for a king. Samuel's insulted, but he takes the request to God. "It is me they are rejecting, not you," God says. "They don't want me to be their king any longer" (1 Samuel 8:7).

DONKEY KING SAUL. Saul is rounding up stray donkeys for his dad when he meets Samuel. A day earlier, God had told Samuel that a man would show up about this time: Israel's future king. Trouble is, Saul doesn't want the job. Samuel anoints him anyhow, pouring olive oil on his head. When Samuel calls together Israel's elders to meet their king, Saul is hiding "among the baggage" and perhaps the pack animals that carry it—in his donkey comfort zone. *(1 Samuel 8–10)* ▲

Flasks for olive oil

SHEPHERD KING REPLACEMENT. Saul, a tall and handsome man, proves himself a charismatic leader and a skilled commander-in-chief. When enemies threaten, he rallies his militia of farmer-soldiers and leads them to victory. But he doesn't always obey God. He steals from defeated enemies when God tells him not to. And he performs a worship ritual reserved for priests. So God sends Samuel to Bethlehem to anoint the shepherd boy David as Israel's future king. *(1 Samuel 16)*

ANOINTING WITH OIL. Jews used olive oil, sometimes perfumed, to welcome guests—pouring it on their head or feet as a refreshing balm in a skin-dry desert land. Samuel introduced it as a royal ritual—a way of declaring someone as God's choice of king. One nickname for Israel's king: "God's anointed."

GOLIATH, BIG-HEADED. On the brink of a battle, with Philistine and Israelite armies camped on opposite sides of a valley, the Philistine champion steps forward. He shouts a challenge: Let's settle the war with mortal combat. He'll fight any Jew, winner take all. Goliath towers nearly seven feet (2 meters) tall, by oldest accounts. He bristles with state-of-the-art weaponry crafted from iron. His spear tip alone weighs as much as a 15-pound (7 kg) bowling ball. He goads the Jews for over a month, until shepherd boy David arrives with a care package for his brothers on the frontline—and a remnant of the Stone Age, for Goliath. *(1 Samuel 17)*

Slingshot ammo

David with Goliath's head and the slingshot stone that cut the giant down

REWARD FOR KILLING GOLIATH. King Saul tells his soldiers that anyone who defeats Goliath can live tax-free and marry the princess. Neither of which would be any good to a dead man, his soldiers apparently conclude. No sale.

DAVID'S CHUTZPAH. Still a teenager, David volunteers to fight Goliath. He figures the Philistine can't be any harder to kill than a lion or a bear. David says he killed both while protecting his flock. He may also figure he can outmaneuver Goliath, who's weighed down in armor—including a bronze coat of mail that may have outweighed David: 125 pounds (57 kg).

HOW TO DEFLATE A GIANT EGO. Philistines were fierce warriors, with Goliath their top-of-the-line model. When Goliath sees a Jewish boy walking toward him with a slingshot and a fistful of rocks, he doesn't laugh. It's hard to laugh at an insult.

MAN DOWN. Slingshots can propel a stone 100 yards (91 meters) a second. That's why some armies in the stone-rich Middle East fielded slingers. Apparently before Goliath gets close enough to heave his weighty spear, David flings a stone into his forehead. Goliath drops. David quickly decapitates him with the giant's own sword. Not surprisingly, the Philistines don't honor their deal to surrender if Goliath loses. They run home, chased by the suddenly courageous Jews.

SAUL GOES CRAZY JEALOUS. Suddenly number two on Israel's popularity charts, Saul slips into a funk. It starts with a song the dancing women sing as they cheer their soldiers home: "Saul has killed his thousands, and David his ten thousands!" Saul decides to go for a few thousand and one. He throws a spear at David. Three times. He sends David into battles, hoping he'll come back dead. Finally, he orders his men to murder him. David escapes, helped by his wife the princess. *(1 Samuel 18–19)* ▼

King Saul's son, Jonathan, prepares to fire an arrow—a signal to his friend David, in hiding, that Saul wants David dead.

MUSIC THERAPY FOR SAUL'S DEPRESSION.

Healthcare facilities today sometimes use music therapy to calm troubled spirits. That's what Saul's advisors recommend for his depression: soothing harp music. Unfortunately, the harpist they recruit is David—a bit like asking the Road Runner to massage the aching back of Wile E. Coyote.

SHEPHERD ON THE LAM. Overnight, David becomes a fugitive, sometimes hiding among Philistines. They respect him as the warrior who defeated their champion. Still the hero, David gathers a following of 600 men. Still the crazy, Saul directs his jealous obsession at hunting David down. One day he comes close—while using the bathroom in a cave. David sneaks up behind him and cuts off part of his robe to show Saul later that he could have killed him. Humiliated, Saul goes home. *(1 Samuel 21–27)* ▲

PRICE TAG FOR SAUL'S OBSESSION. Some Bible experts say the resources Saul used in trying to track down David should have been devoted to his real enemy, the Philistines. They were coming. And they would soon take control of the most strategic, fertile land in all of Israel: the Jezreel Valley, which some Bible students call the valley of Armageddon.

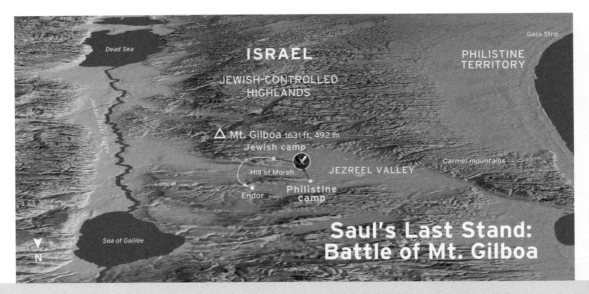

ISRAEL

JEWISH-CONTROLLED
HIGHLANDS

Dead Sea

Jordan River Valley

△ Mt. Gilboa 1631 ft, 492 m
Jewish camp

Hill of Moreh   JEZREEL VALLEY

Endor   Philistine
camp

Sea of Galilee

N

Gaza Strip

PHILISTINE
TERRITORY

Carmel mountains

Saul's Last Stand: Battle of Mt. Gilboa

PSYCHIC SIGHTING. Stunned at the size of the Philistine army, Saul wants to know what God says he should do. But Samuel, the prophet, is dead. Saul sneaks behind enemy lines to the village of Endor where he commits a Jewish capital offense: consulting a medium (Leviticus 20:27). Saul asks her to contact Samuel. To her horror—a reaction hinting she just might be a fraud—Samuel appears. Samuel says that by day's end tomorrow, Saul and his sons will be joining him.

SAUL'S SUICIDE. By the time Saul realizes that Philistines have invaded his Jezreel Valley, controlling the main coastal pass through the Carmel Mountains, it's too late. Saul can't muster a militia large enough to stop them. He tries. He dies. So do three of his sons. Wounded, with the battle lost, Saul falls on his sword to avoid capture and torture. One surviving son, Ishbosheth, becomes king. Timid and frightened, he lasts two years before two of his own soldiers assassinate him. *(1 Samuel 28–2 Samuel 4)* ▶

GIANT-KILLER KING. Jews rally around David and declare him king. Twice. After Saul dies, Jews in David's tribe of Judah appoint him king of their tribe—the largest of Israel's dozen tribes. Two years later, after the assassination of King Ishbosheth, the rest of the country adopts Judah's king. At age 30, the ex-fugitive is now king of all Israel. *(2 Samuel 1–5)*

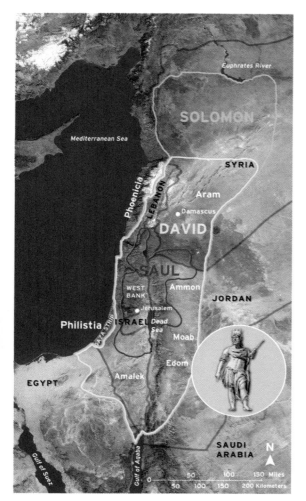

Israel's growth spurts

JEWISH CONQUEST 201. When Joshua and the Exodus Jews conquered Canaan, they controlled mainly the central hill country—an area smaller than modern Israel. Saul maintained status quo, defending those borders. David goes on the offense, attacking neighbor kingdoms and pushing Israel's border of influence into what are now Syria, Jordan, and Egypt. He even manages to pacify the Philistines, a powerful nation that had come close to assimilating the Jews into their culture. *(2 Samuel 8–10)* ◄

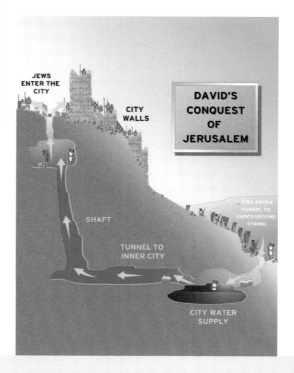

JERUSALEM, FROM ENEMY CITY TO CAPITAL. About seven years into his 40-year reign, King David decides that what Israel really needs is a new capital. He has been ruling in a city within his own tribe of Judah: Hebron, about a day's walk south of Jerusalem (17 miles, 28 km). Jerusalem is perfect for two reasons:

:: It's unconquered along a tribal border, so it won't suggest David favors one tribe

:: Built on a ridge, it'll be easy to defend. *(2 Samuel 5)* ▶

HOW DAVID CAPTURED JERUSALEM. So cocky were the Jebusites living inside the hilltop, walled city of Jerusalem that they taunted the Jewish army below. David's men found a secret way in: a 52-foot (16-meter) shaft that Jebusites used like a well, lowering their buckets into an underground spring. Soldiers apparently found a brush-covered tunnel into the spring then scaled the shaft and opened the city gates.

BATHSHEBA, WET AND NAKED. David already has a harem of at least seven wives when he catches sight of his neighbor Bathsheba taking a bath. She's the wife of a soldier who's about 60 miles (95 km) away, fighting David's battles. Alpha male, David helps himself to the lady, who gets pregnant. David calls home her husband, Uriah, hoping Uriah will sleep with his wife and think the baby is his. Uriah refuses the pleasure, saying he can't do this while his comrades are suffering. So David arranges for Uriah to die in battle. David marries the grieving widow. Their son dies. But Bathsheba will give birth again—to Israel's next king, Solomon. *(2 Samuel 11–12)*

WAS BATHSHEBA AN EXHIBITIONIST? Not likely. Not in that culture. Bathsheba may have been bathing in the walled courtyard of her home. Or possibly inside her house with a window open for ventilation in the afternoon heat. David was taking a stroll on the flat palace roof, which Jews used like we use a deck or a porch.

IT WASN'T JUST ANY BATH. This was a ritual cleansing. Bathsheba was following Jewish law, purifying herself one week after her monthly menstrual flow stopped (Leviticus 15:19). That means she wasn't just fragrant. She was fertile.

URIAH. Bathsheba's husband was one of the Thirty— David's elite strike force. Uriah's nickname, the Hittite, suggests he may have been a mercenary from what is now Syria or Turkey. Or maybe he was a Jew with some Hittite blood in him. Or he fought like a Hittite, people known for their battlefield prowess.

MY SON THE RAPIST. The Bible puffs David as a great king. But it cuts him off at the ankles when reporting on his family life. Unfaithful husband. No-show dad. And worst of all, David lets it slide when his oldest son, Amnon, crown prince, rapes his own half-sister, Tamar. David gets angry. Does nothing. He could execute Amnon or force him to marry Tamar. Jewish law allows either. Two years later, Tamar's full brother, Absalom, orchestrates Amnon's murder. *(2 Samuel 13)* ▲

FIRING FATHER. Absalom flees Israel, staying gone for three years. In a wisp of grace, David finally invites him home. In a stretch of stubbornness, David refuses to see him. For two years. By then Absalom is plotting a coup. He's next in line to become king. That may be why so many support him when he declares himself king and fires his aging, lame-duck dad. Absalom dies in the civil war that follows, though David had ordered his son spared. *(2 Samuel 14–19)* ▶

THREE DAGGERS FOR HAIRY. Absalom's thick hair weighs 5 pounds (about 2 kg). It kills him. Blowing in the wind as Absalom flees a lost battle, his hair gets stuck in a tree branch. Yanks him off his mule. David's general sees Absalom dangling like a bull's-eye and plants three daggers in his heart.

1,2 KINGS

ISRAEL: FROM GLORY TO GHOST TOWNS

IN ONE SENTENCE

Israel rises and shines during King Solomon's Golden Age, and then plummets through 400 years of mostly rotten kings who eventually manage to get the Jewish nation wiped off the map.

SOUND BITE

"He did what was evil in the LORD's sight."
—*Description of all but four Jewish kings in 350 years after Solomon*
1 KINGS 15:26

ON LOCATION

TIME. Spanning 400 years, from the mid-900s BC to the fall of the Jewish nation in 586 BC.

PLACE. Israel.

NEWSMAKERS

SOLOMON, king of Israel. David's son, he leads Israel during the country's most prosperous age.

ELIJAH, prophet. He challenges and defeats hundreds of pagan Canaanite prophets.

JEZEBEL, non-Jewish queen of Israel. Wife of King Ahab, she devotes herself to wiping out the Jewish religion.

SOLOMON'S REORGANIZATION
12 districts instead of tribes

SOLOMON IS KING, THANKS TO MOM. As old King David lies dying, his oldest son, Adonijah, throws a pre-coronation party for himself, the next king. The prophet Nathan and Solomon's mom, Bathsheba, form a tag team to get Solomon on the throne instead. They tell David about Adonijah's party and remind him that he promised Solomon the job—either being honest or exploiting his end-stage confusion. David immediately declares Solomon king. Party over. *(1 Kings 1–2)*

SOLOMON'S SPLIT DECISION. God promises to grant Solomon any wish. Solomon wishes for wisdom to rule. Done deal. The Bible's next story proves it. Two prostitutes share a room. Both sleep with their newborn sons. One mother rolls over her boy in her sleep, suffocating him. She swaps him for the live boy. The case goes to Solomon. He offers to settle the dispute by cutting the boy in half. The thieving mother agrees, which Solomon knows isn't motherly. Case solved. *(1 Kings 3)* ▼

SOLOMON, CUTTING TO THE FRONT OF THE LINE. Typically, a king's oldest son succeeded him. David had at least nine sons before Solomon. That's why some Bible experts suspect that Nathan and Bathsheba manipulated David to crown their choice of king. Solomon later executed his older brother Adonijah for appearing to lay the groundwork for a coup.

JERUSALEM'S FIRST TEMPLE. Jews had been worshipping God for almost 500 years at a tent worship center. With God's approval, Solomon begins the seven-year construction of the first Jewish Temple. He drafts nearly 200,000 workers. They import top-grade cedar from Lebanon. And they cut white limestone blocks from a Jerusalem-area quarry. The sanctuary building, which only priests can enter, measures 30 yards long, 10 yards wide, and 15 yards high (27 x 9 x 14 meters). Only the high priest is allowed in the back room, where Jews keep their most sacred relic: the Ark of the Covenant, a chest that holds the 10 Commandments. Most Jews worship God outside by sacrificing animals on the huge altar. Oversized basins hold water for washing the animals and cleaning away the blood. *(1 Kings 5–9)* ▲

Snow-laced cedars of Lebanon

TRADING LAND FOR LUMBER. Solomon gave away 20 towns in Galilee, northern Israel, in trade for cedar lumber from King Hiram of Tyre, in what is now Lebanon. Solomon apparently got a good deal, dirt cheap. When Hiram saw the land that extended his border, he renamed it: Cabul. It means "Worthless." ▲

SHEBA, SHOPPING QUEEN. The Queen of Sheba comes calling on Solomon, from a nation in what many Bible experts say is now Yemen some 1,500 miles (2,400 km) south of Jerusalem. The Bible says the queen wants to check out Solomon's wisdom. But what she may want even more, some scholars say, is to shop. She brings a loaded caravan of spices, jewels, and more than 9,000 pounds (4,000 kg) of gold. Solomon gives her whatever she asks for. Trade deals follow. *(1 Kings 10)*

SOLOMON'S STUPIDITY STARTS HERE. He gets married. A thousand times. It's custom among royalty to seal a peace treaty or a trade deal with a marriage. One king marries the princess daughter of another. The irony is that while Solomon may have done this for peace, that's not what you get when you put 1,000 high-maintenance queens in a single harem. Solomon's foreign wives wear him down spiritually, luring him into idol worship—the beginning of Israel's end. *(1 Kings 11)* ▼

Harem

SOLOMON, KING OF TRADE. Solomon ran a fleet of trade ships that sailed both the Red Sea and the Mediterranean, bringing back gold, gems, and exotic animals from Europe, Africa, and Arabia.

SHEBA ON AN INSCRIPTION? A newly discovered South Arabian inscription, dated to 300 years after Solomon, says the kingdom of Sabaea, possibly Sheba, once sent a trade expedition to Israel.

ISRAEL: ONE NATION, DIVISIBLE. As punishment for idolatry, God vows to leave Solomon's dynasty with just one tribe: Judah, in the south. Solomon's son, Rehoboam, brings the promise to life with a tough-guy act. Jews ask their new king for a break from Solomon's high taxes and from drafting workers. Rehoboam says if they think his dad was tough, wait till they see what he does. They don't. All the northern tribes secede from the union. They start their own country: Israel. *(1 Kings 12)*

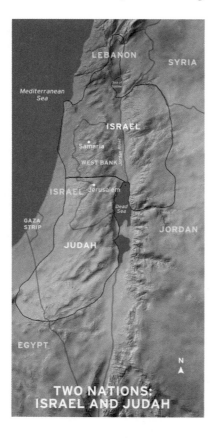

TWO NATIONS:
ISRAEL AND JUDAH

DRAFTED. Solomon drafted citizens to work on his building projects, just like some countries today draft soldiers for war. After a generation of this, the Jews wanted a break. Solomon's son refused to give up this source of free labor. His stubbornness cost him most of his country.

Baal with lightning spear.

MOUNT CARMEL BATTLE OF THE GODS. No Jew, Israel's Queen Jezebel hails from Lebanon. With King Ahab's support, she tries wiping out the Jewish religion. She starts killing God's prophets, replacing them with 850 devoted to her gods, Baal and Asherah. Jewish prophet Elijah challenges all 850 to a contest: call fire from the sky—seemingly easy for Baal, a rain god pictured with lightning. When God wins, the Jewish crowd mobs and executes the false prophets. Jezebel is ticked. *(1 Kings 17–20)*

ELIJAH RIDES THE WIND TO HEAVEN. Elijah knows it's his time to leave the planet, but he doesn't seem to know how it's going to happen. Directed by God, Elijah and his apprentice, Elisha, cross the Jordan River into what is now Jordan. "Suddenly a chariot of fire appeared, drawn by horses of fire. It drove between the two men, separating them, and Elijah was carried by a whirlwind into heaven" (2 Kings 2:11). ▲

JEZEBEL: ROYAL DOG FOOD. Elisha travels to Israel's eastern frontier and anoints a chariot corps commander, Jehu, to become Israel's next king. It's a green light to launch a coup against King Joram, Ahab's son. Jehu and his men race to Jezreel, site of the king's summer getaway palace. Jehu and his rebels kill King Joram. Then they convince the servants of Queen Mother Jezebel to pitch her out of a palace window. She splatters, and dogs devour her corpse. *(2 Kings 9–10)* ▶

JEZEBEL 2.0. One queen takes nastiness to new heights. And she may well have been Jezebel's daughter. The Bible says only that Athaliah (ath-uh-LIE-yah) was Ahab's daughter. Athaliah had been Queen Mother of the southern Jewish nation of Judah. But when her son the king died, she killed her grandchildren so she could rule as queen. She missed one grandson, Joash. Six years later, a priest who had been hiding the boy presented him as the rightful king. Like Jezebel, Grandma Athaliah died in the company of critters. Soldiers executed her at a gate where livestock enter the palace property (2 Kings 11:16).

Assyrians overrun Israel's capital city of Samaria

JEWISH NATION 1 OF 2 BITES THE DUST. Iraqi invaders wipe the northern Jewish nation of Israel off the map in 722 BC, about 200 years after the northern Jews declared their independence from Judah. The invaders are Assyrians, based in northern Iraq. But they control much of the Middle East, imposing taxes on weaker countries like Israel. Assyria invades after Israel's last king, Hoshea, decides to stop paying the tax. *(2 Kings 17)*

KID-KILLER RELIGION. Of Israel's original 12 tribes, only one remains: the southern Jewish nation of Judah. Israel in the north had survived about 200 years after declaring its independence from the south. Judah will last about another 150 years, only because it produces some godly kings; the north hadn't. But Judah eventually spawns the most vile king in Jewish history: Manasseh. He burns his son alive, sacrificing him to an idol. *(2 Kings 21)*

Assyrian from Iraq

GOOD SAMARITANS FROM IRAQ. Assyria's defeat of Israel produced Samaritans, a mixed race of Iraqi-Jews, one of whom stars in Jesus' parable of the Good Samaritan. Assyrians repopulated the Samaria region of Israel with their Iraqi settlers. Some married Jews in the area. Their children became known as Samaritans, a mixed race that many Jews in Jesus' day hated.

JERUSALEM'S LAST STAND. Babylonians based in southern Iraq crush Assyria's army and take control of the Middle East. Like Assyria, the new bullies force weaker nations to pay them taxes. Judah's last king makes the same mistake Israel's last king did some 150 years earlier. He refuses to pay his taxes. King Nebuchadnezzar comes to collect. He brings his army. They surround Jerusalem. Two and a half years later, in July of 586 BC, they break through the city wall. They take everything they want. Then they level Jerusalem. They execute many captives and take others to Iraq to keep an eye on them, so they don't reorganize. Iraqi Babylonians have erased the Jewish nation from the world map. *(2 Kings 25)*

KING NEBUCHADNEZZAR. He ruled Babylon at the height of the empire's glory (605–562 BC). He built the Hanging Gardens of Babylon, one of the Seven Wonders of the World. One ancient writer who said he had seen all seven called it the greatest wonder of all.

Siege tower/battering ram combo

BABYLONIAN BREAK-IN. When Babylonian armies surrounded a walled city, they usually weren't patient enough to simply wait, starving the defenders into surrender.

:: Catapults pummeled the wall and its defenders with boulders and sharp objects.

:: Archers climbed into rolling towers, to fight on the same level as wall-top defenders.

:: Battering rams tried to splinter the city's wooden gates.

:: Miners dug tunnels under the walls, and then collapsed the tunnels—hoping part of the wall would drop, too.

Leading Jerusalem's prisoners to Babylon

1,2 CHRONICLES

A SPIN DOC'S TAKE ON JEWISH HISTORY

IN ONE SENTENCE

As Jews return home from a 50-year exile in Iraq, wondering if they've lost the right to be called God's Chosen People, the Chronicler throws Jewish history into a positive spin with a reassuring message: God never gave up on them—and he never will.

SOUND BITE

"If my people, who are called by my name, will humble themselves, if they will pray and seek me and stop their evil ways, I will hear them from heaven. I will forgive their sin, and I will heal their land."
—*God's promise to King Solomon*
2 CHRONICLES 7:14 NIV

ON LOCATION

TIME. From Israel's first king in the 1000s BC until Jews return from exile in what is now Iraq, in the 500s BC.

PLACE. Most stories play out in Israel, with some scenes in Babylon, in what is now Iraq.

NEWSMAKERS

DAVID, Israel's second king. He secures Israel's borders and becomes the most revered king in Jewish history.

SOLOMON, David's son and successor. He becomes famous for wisdom, wealth, and a harem of 1,000 wives.

HEZEKIAH, Jewish king. Many Bible experts call him the godliest king in Jewish history.

Jews exiled in Babylon

GOD ISN'T FINISHED WITH THE JEWS. The anonymous Chronicler admits the Jews blew it. They broke their agreement with God. They lost their country. But there's hope. With what reads like a boring genealogy of some 2,000 names—from Adam all the way to the Chronicler's own time—he tracks God:

:: creating humans from dust

:: turning 100-year-old Abraham into the father of the Jews

:: empowering Joshua to sculpt a hostile land into a Jewish haven

:: providing the exiles with their leader Zerubbabel, a descendant of David—a source of kings for new Israel. *(1 Chronicles 1–9)*

TEMPLE MINISTERS. All ministry staff—from musicians to security guards—were Levites. They descended from the tribe of Jacob's son Levi. Priests had to descend from one family within Levi's tribe: Aaron, the brother of Moses and Israel's first high priest.

TEMPLE BLUEPRINT. King David is a man of war who secures the boundaries of Israel. But God doesn't want him building the Jerusalem Temple. That will wait for David's son Solomon. David does, however, stockpile supplies: limestone blocks, Lebanon cedar, 4,000 tons of gold, 40,000 tons of silver. He also organizes the Temple workforce: musicians, security guards, and 24 rotating ministry teams of priests and assistants, each serving two weeks a year. *(1 Chronicles 22–26)*

Cedar from Lebanon is floated down the sea to Israel.

Musician at Solomon's Temple

SOLOMON DEDICATES THE TEMPLE. It takes seven years for King Solomon's nearly 200,000 drafted workers to build the Temple. It takes 15 days for Solomon to dedicate it. He sacrifices 22,000 cattle and 120,000 sheep and goats, most of which the celebrating crowds probably ate. That's 16 animals a minute if the priests worked 10-hour days. God's glory—perhaps in a cloud of sacrificial smoke—glides into the Temple, temporarily driving out the priests. God declares this Temple as the only place he'll accept Jewish sacrifices. *(2 Chronicles 3–7)*

ISRAEL'S BLEAK BATTING AVERAGE. Jews are batting .666 for good kings. One strikeout: Saul. Two hits: David and Solomon. After that, the batting average plummets: four good kings in four centuries. Jews split into separate teams after Solomon. Israel in the north bats zero—not one good king out of 19. Southland Jews of Judah manage 4 of 20, batting .200. Both teams have to go. Israel first, falling to Assyrian invaders in 722 BC. *(2 Chronicles 10–36)*

GOD IN A CLOUD. God's "glory" fills the Temple. Many Bible experts compare this to
:: the "pillar of cloud" (Exodus 13:21) that earlier led the Jews out of Egypt
:: the "cloud of glory" (Ezekiel 10:4, 19) that a prophet saw later in a vision of God leaving the Temple because of Israel's persistent sins.

FOUR GOOD KINGS. The Bible tags most Jewish kings after Solomon as "evil." Four exceptions "did what was pleasing in the LORD's sight." They were Asa and his son Jehoshaphat, along with Hezekiah and Josiah.

GOOD-BYE, JERUSALEM. Four evil kings follow Josiah, Judah's last godly king. They make tragic decisions that transform Jerusalem into a rock pile. The last king, Zedekiah, surrounded by the Babylonian army laying siege to Jerusalem, remains stubborn, "refusing to turn to the LORD." Babylonians come to collect taxes, and the prophet Jeremiah advises Zedekiah to surrender. The invaders break through the walls, demolish the city, and exile most survivors to what is now Iraq. *(2 Chronicles 36)*

HELLO, NEW JERUSALEM. The Chronicler ends his tailored history on a positive note. Jerusalem lies in ruins, but there's reason to cheer. Babylon is dead and gone. King Cyrus of Persia, in what is now Iran, is the new master of the Middle East. And he has not only freed all of Babylon's political prisoners, including the Jews, he has an assignment for them. Rebuild the Jerusalem Temple: "Any of you who are the LORD's people may go there for this task" (2 Chronicles 36:22–23).

Zedekiah flees Jerusalem

ZEDEKIAH, KINGLY COWARD. When Babylonians broke through Jerusalem's wall, 32-year-old King Zedekiah abandoned his people. He and his guards made a run for it. Babylonians caught him near the Jordan River. They made him watch as they killed his sons. Then they gouged out his eyes and led him as a prisoner to Babylon.

EZRA

ISRAEL, STARTING OVER

IN ONE SENTENCE

After 50 years of exile in what is now Iraq, Jews are released to go home and start rebuilding Jerusalem, the Temple, and their nation—all of which lie in ruins.

SOUND BITE

"Divorce your foreign wives."
—*Ezra, to Jews in mixed marriages*
EZRA 10:11 CEV

ON LOCATION

TIME. Covers about 80 years (538 BC–458 BC), from when Cyrus frees the Jews until Ezra arrives in Jerusalem.

PLACE. Persian King Cyrus in what is now Iran frees Jews exiled mainly in Iraq. They return to what is now Israel.

NEWSMAKERS

EZRA, a Jewish priest. He teaches God's laws to Jews returning from exile.

CYRUS, king of Persia. He frees the Jews to go home and rebuild their nation.

PERSIAN EMPIRE

A FEW GIFTS FOR THE ROAD. Persians from what is now Iran defeat the Iraqi-based Babylonians and free Babylon's Jewish captives. Persian King Cyrus urges the Jews to go home and rebuild their Jerusalem Temple, which they do. Cyrus returns 5,400 sacred objects of gold and silver, which Babylonians had looted from the Temple, such as bowls and incense burners. Cyrus even pressures locals to send the Jews off with gifts of gold, silver, livestock, and travel supplies. *(Ezra 1–6)*

GETTING RID OF THE LITTLE LADY. Ezra, a priest, returns to Israel about 80 years later. A group of Jews greets him with a complaint: some Jewish men have married non-Jews. Moses warned that if Exodus Jews married outside their race they'd end up worshipping idols—and they'd lose their county, which is what happened. No Jew wants a repeat of that. Ezra convinces Jews in mixed marriages to divorce their wives and disown the children of those wives. *(Ezra 9–10)*

WAS GOD BEHIND EZRA'S DEMAND THAT JEWS DIVORCE THEIR NON-JEWISH SPOUSES? The Bible doesn't say. Some Bible experts, however, speculate that the story of Ruth from about 700 years earlier got preserved as a counterpoint to Ezra. Ruth was a non-Jew from what is now Jordan. She married a Bethlehem Jew. Their son grew up to become the grandfather of King David. Israel's greatest dynasty of kings owes its existence to an Arab mother.

NEHEMIAH

WINE GUY WITH A TASTE FOR CONSTRUCTION

Depressed at hearing that Jerusalem's walls are still busted a century after Jews returned from exile, a Jewish wine taster named Nehemiah, working in the Persian palace, gets his king's permission to repair the walls—a job he finishes in 52 days.

SOUND BITE

"The builders are pooped, the rubbish piles up; we're in over our heads, we can't build this wall."
—*Complaint of some Jews*
NEHEMIAH 4:10 MSG

ON LOCATION

TIME. Middle 400s BC.

PLACE. The story starts in Susa, capital of the Persian Empire in what is now Iran. It ends in Jerusalem.

NEWSMAKERS

NEHEMIAH, Jewish wine taster of the Persian king. He's granted a leave of absence to organize the rebuilding of Jerusalem's walls.

SANBALLAT, opponent of Nehemiah. He's a non-Jewish settler in the region who leads a group trying to stop Jews from rebuilding Jerusalem's walls.

EZRA, Jewish priest. He reads the laws of Moses aloud to the people.

IRAN BANKROLLS REPAIR OF JERUSALEM'S WALLS. Persian King Artaxerxes learns that Nehemiah is depressed because the walls of Jerusalem lie in heaps. When the king says he wants to help, Nehemiah asks for a leave of absence to repair the walls—and for free building supplies along with letters ordering regional governors to give him safe passage to Jerusalem some 1,000 miles (1,600 km) west. Nehemiah gets it all, plus a military escort. *(Nehemiah 1–2)*

ARMED BUILDERS AT WORK. Jerusalem-area Jews rally around Nehemiah's project. Non-Jews object. They fear the wall signals the rebirth of Israel. So they try to stop it by inviting Nehemiah to a meeting, where they plan to kill him. He refuses to go. Then they plot an attack on the workers. Nehemiah hears about it and turns half of his construction crew into armed guards. Workers rush through the repair work in just 52 days. *(Nehemiah 2–6)* ▼

MORE THAN A WINE TASTER. Wine stewards provided wine for the king and made sure it was safe to drink. They saw the king nearly every day, and sometimes developed into royal advisors. Assyrian King Sennacherib promoted his wine taster to "chief of administration" (Tobit 1:22 NRSV).

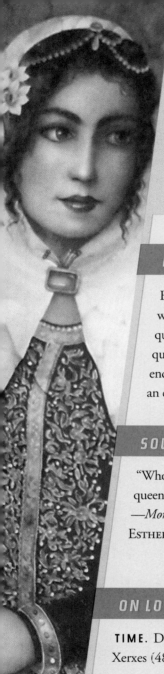

ESTHER

JEWISH QUEEN OF IRAN SAVES JEWS FROM HOLOCAUST

IN ONE SENTENCE

Esther, a young Jewish woman, wins a beauty contest to become queen of the Persian Empire, headquartered in what is now Iran, and ends up saving the Jewish race from an empire-wide holocaust.

SOUND BITE

"Who knows? Maybe you were made queen for just such a time as this."
—*Mordecai to Esther*
ESTHER 4:14 MSG

ON LOCATION

TIME. During the 21-year reign of King Xerxes (486–465 BC).

PLACE. Susa, capital of the Persian Empire that stretches from India to Ethiopia, south of Egypt.

NEWSMAKERS

ESTHER, new queen of Persia. A Jewish orphan raised by her cousin Mordecai, she wins a beauty contest and becomes queen of the Persian Empire.

XERXES (ZERK-zees), king of Persia. Wanting a wife upgrade, he agrees to judge an empire-wide beauty contest and marry the winner.

MORDECAI (MORE-duh-kigh), Esther's cousin. He may be a palace worker when the story starts.

HAMAN (HAY-mun), Persia's top appointed official. He plots the extermination of the Jewish race.

VASHTI (VASH-tee), dethroned queen. A trophy wife with an attitude, she refuses the king's request to let him show her off at his drunken bash. Xerxes demotes her to just another wife in the harem.

SHOWING THE QUEEN WHO'S BOSS. King Xerxes hosts a six-month celebration of his wealth and power. On the last day, after a week of heavy drinking with top soldiers and officials, Xerxes calls for Queen Vashti—to show off her good looks. She refuses; she's entertaining the officials' wives. Xerxes, embarrassed at looking henpecked, orders Vashti back to the chicken coop with all the other hens in his harem—never to see him again. *(Esther 1)*

JEWISH ORPHAN CROWNED QUEEN OF IRAN. With his queen demoted to harem wife, Xerxes agrees to a queen upgrade. His attendants search the empire and round up gorgeous virgins to stock his harem, Esther among them. The king's favorite virgin will become his queen. Esther gets pampered with a year of beauty treatments such as marinating in scented oil. She also gets the inside scoop from a harem eunuch on how to please the king. Winner. *(Esther 2)* ▼

PLANNING A HOLOCAUST. Prime Minister Haman hates that Mordecai refuses to bow to him. Haman plots insane revenge: kill Mordecai—and exterminate Mordecai's race. Haman convinces the king to let him wipe out a group of people "who do not obey the king's laws." Apparently not one for micromanaging, Xerxes seems to agree without asking who the people are. Neither Xerxes nor Haman realizes Esther is a Jew, which puts her in the bull's-eye. *(Esther 3)*

ESTHER'S KILLER PARTY. Haman sets the holocaust date for March 7, 474 BC. Esther's afraid to ask the king for help. It's because Persian law says the king can execute anyone who comes to him uninvited. But Esther's cousin Mordecai warns her that she'll die, too, in the racial purge. Esther fasts for three days, and then approaches the king. She invites him and Haman to a banquet, where she breaks the news: she's a Jew, doomed to die in Haman's plot. Xerxes executes Haman. *(Esther 5–7)*

ESTHER: A GODLESS BOOK. There's no mention of God in Esther. Some Bible experts say it's on purpose. They speculate that the writer wanted to draw in secular readers. Instead of preaching about how God looks after his people, the writer figured readers will reach that conclusion on their own. One hint of God: Mordecai tells Esther if she refuses to intercede for her people, deliverance would come "from some other place" (Esther 4:14).

"He's the one," Queen Esther says, pointing out Haman as the official plotting to exterminate her entire Jewish race.

Purim parade

PURIM: JEWISH MARDI GRAS. Jews celebrate the springtime festival of Purim (POOR-um) to commemorate Esther saving their race from genocide—a plot instigated in what is now Iran. In a party atmosphere, kids dress up in costumes, especially as characters in Esther's story, but anything goes: Batman, cowboys, and zombie clowns. Partiers exchange gifts and read aloud the story of Esther. Every time Haman's villainous name is spoken, listeners drown it out with screams and noisemakers.

J O B

NOT EVEN CLOSE TO PATIENT

When Job loses his kids, his herds, and his health, some friends show up and figure God must be punishing him for sin—and that if Job knows what's good for him, he'll repent, pronto.

SOUND BITE

"You, God, are the reason I am insulted and spit on."
—*Job to God*
JOB 17:6 CEV

ON LOCATION

TIME. Clues, such as a reference to Sabeans, point to Abraham's era, around 2000 BC.

PLACE. Uz, location unknown. One guess: Edom, along the Israeli-Jordan border.

NEWSMAKERS

JOB, a rich herder. He loses his herds, his children, and his health. Though he refuses to abandon his faith in God, he demands that God explain this mess.

JOB'S WIFE. While Job's suffering, she advises him to curse God so God will put him out of his misery.

JOB'S FRIENDS. Four guests arrive to comfort Job, but they end up accusing him of bringing these tragedies on himself by committing some terrible sin.

GOD. He enters the debate, defending Job's righteousness but accusing Job of not trusting him enough.

GOD'S DEAL WITH THE DEVIL. At a meeting in heaven, God brags to Satan about how great Job is: "a man of complete integrity." Satan says it's no wonder—since God is floating him through life in a blessed bubble: rich, healthy, and protected. Pop the bubble and see what happens. God tells Satan to pop away, but God imposes one restriction: "spare his life." *(Job 1–2)*

JOB'S WORSE-THAN-A-MONDAY. Satan targets Job's livestock assets, his children, and his health. In a single day:

:: Raiders rustle his 700 teams of oxen, 500 donkeys, and 3,000 camels, and kill his farmhands.

:: What sounds like a lightning fire burns to death his 7,000 sheep and his shepherds.

:: A windstorm collapses a house, crushing all 10 of his children.

Later, in a second test: boils erupt on Job's body. *(Job 1–2)* ▼

WAS IT REALLY SATAN? That's the Hebrew word for the being who tormented Job: *satan*. The word means "accuser." Some scholars say this particular accuser could have been an angel who patrolled Earth. If so, he was one devil of an angel.

IS THE STORY FACT OR FICTION? Some Bible experts say it really happened, and that some details track with life in Abraham's era. Others compare it to a parable. They say it's a fictional story with a message: bad things happen to good people through no fault of their own—so we should stop assuming they sinned.

FRIENDS WHO NEED TO TAKE "COMFORT 101." Several of Job's friends show up. For a week they comfort him with their silent presence. Then they open their mouths.

:: **ELIPHAZ**: "Those who plant trouble. . .harvest the same" (Job 4:8).

:: **BILDAD**: "Sinners are dragged from the safety of their tents to die a gruesome death" (Job 18:14 CEV).

:: **ZOPHAR**: "You haven't gotten half of what you deserve" (Job 11:6 MSG).

:: **ELIHU**: "You deserve the maximum penalty" (Job 34:36). ▲

JOB'S DEFENSE.

:: *I'm innocent:* "Stop assuming my guilt, for I have done no wrong" (Job 6:29).

:: *God's guilty:* "He [God] attacks me. . .without cause" (Job 9:17).

:: *Job's comforters are anything but:* "You're not doctors who came to treat me. You're quacks who came to irritate me with unintelligible duck sounds. Shut up and let me suffer in peace" (Job 13:4–5 AUTHOR'S PARAPHRASE).

Winter fog in Yosemite National Park, California

GOD'S DEFENSE: CREATION. After several long speeches—with Job's friends accusing him of sinning and Job questioning God's sense of justice—God arrives. His first words: "Why do you talk so much when you know so little?" (Job 38:2 CEV). God asks if they know how he set the stars in the sky or how he unrolls a blanket of fog. Job gets it. Trust God. No matter what. God restores Job's wealth and gives him 10 more children. *(Job 38–42)*

P S A L M S

CONCERT FOR AN AUDIENCE OF ONE: GOD

IN ONE SENTENCE

Jewish poets team up to put their prayers to music—targeting God with their raw emotion, everything from bitter complaints to high praise, from the blues to all that jazz.

SOUND BITE

"The LORD is my shepherd. He gives me everything I need. He lets me lie down in fields of green grass. He leads me beside quiet waters."
—*Songwriter to God*
PSALM 23:1–2 NIrV

ON LOCATION

TIME. The songs span nearly a thousand years, from Moses as early as the 1400s BC (some scholars say 1200s BC) to the time of the Jewish exile in Babylon (Iraq) in the 500s BC.

PLACE. Most songs are set in Israel.

NEWSMAKERS

GOD, The songs are intended for his ears.

DAVID, Israel's most famous king. Known to have played the harp and written songs, David is credited with either writing or inspiring almost half the psalms.

DAVID'S ISRAEL

SONGS SUNG BLUE. Jews call the book "Praises." That's *Tehillim* (tuh-hee-LEEM) in Hebrew. But nearly half the songs sound more like the blues:

:: **CRY FOR HELP**. "Hide me in the shadow of your wings. Protect me from wicked people who attack me" (Psalm 17:8–9).

:: **COMPLAINT ABOUT GOD'S SILENCE**. "How long will you forget me? Forever?" (Psalm 13:1).

:: **DOWN AND DIRTY ADVICE FOR GOD**. "Slap all my enemies in the face!" (Psalm 3:7). ▲

IN GOD WE TRUST. It's a persistent theme in Jewish songs. Even most writers down in the dumps

end their lyrics on this upbeat note of confidence in God. One writer, complaining that tears are his only food, eventually consoles himself: "Why is my heart so sad? I will put my hope in God! I will praise him again—my Savior and my God." *(Psalm 42)*

AUTHORS. Unknown. Seventy-three of the 150 psalms run this credit: "of David." That's a vague phrase. It can mean the songs are by him, about him, or merely dedicated to him. David did write songs, including a funeral song for King Saul (2 Samuel 1:17). A Psalms scroll dating to about the time of Jesus and found among the Dead Sea Scrolls said David wrote 3,600 songs.

THANK GOD. Psalms is the go-to book for anyone who can't find the words to tell God how much he means to them. What many can only feel, poets express.

:: "You are my mighty rock, my fortress, my protector" (Psalm 18:2 CEV).

:: "He lifted me out of the pit of despair, out of the mud and the mire. He set my feet on solid ground and steadied me as I walked along" (Psalm 40:2). ▼

Defensive tower along the walls of the fortress city of Jerusalem. The psalm writer calls God "my fortress," rock-solid protection.

THE MOST FAMOUS PSALM. One of the most famous psalms describes God as a shepherd. The lyrics are so tender and comforting that people often read them at the bedside of the dying. "Even when I walk through the darkest valley, I will not be afraid, for you are close beside me" (Psalm 23:4).

NO RHYME, JUST REASON. Psalm lyrics are poems. Hebrew poetry doesn't rhyme. Instead of repeating sounds, it repeats ideas. Line one: "You've got me surrounded; you're blazing my trail ahead while covering my back." Line two, in this case, repeats the first: "You keep me within reach, protected by your mighty hand" (Psalm 139:5 AUTHOR'S PARAPHRASE).

FORGIVE ME. Of the many songs asking for God's forgiveness, perhaps the most haunting is the one introduced as a song King David wrote after committing adultery with Bathsheba: "God, be merciful to me. . . . Take away my sin, and I will be clean. Wash me, and I will be whiter than snow" (Psalm 51:1, 7 CEV) Another song expresses the pain of sin and the joy of forgiveness: "Though we are overwhelmed by our sins, you forgive them all. What joy" (Psalm 65:3–4).

PROVERBS

LIFE LESSONS FIT FOR A FORTUNE COOKIE

IN ONE SENTENCE

Grandfatherly grads from the school of hard knocks offer practical advice for everyday living—wisdom packaged as snappy one-liners, easy to remember.

SOUND BITE

"If you build a fire in your pants, what makes you think you won't get burned?"
—*A sage, warning young men away from adultery*
PROVERBS 6:27 AUTHOR'S
PARAPHRASE

ON LOCATION

TIME. Many proverbs are attributed to King Solomon, who reigned from about 970–930 BC.

PLACE. Israel.

NEWSMAKERS

SOLOMON, king of Israel. He is said to have written 3,000 proverbs (1 Kings 4:32), including most of those in the book of Proverbs.

YOUNG JEWISH MEN. Elderly sages tailor their insights to young men, hoping the next generation will learn from them.

LOOSE WOMEN, married or not. Many proverbs warn young men to stay away from shady ladies or suffer the rotten consequences.

USE A LITTLE COMMON SENSE. Some proverbs sound more street savvy than sacred. But the sages treat life as sacred and common sense as rare. They don't skip the obvious.

:: **DON'T COMMIT A FELONY.** "If sinners entice you. . . 'Let's hide and kill someone!'. . . . Don't go along with them!" (Proverbs 1:10–11, 15).

:: **COMPROMISE.** "Drawing straws is one way to settle a difficult case" (Proverbs 18:18 CEV).

:: **TRY A LITTLE KINDNESS.** "A kind answer soothes angry feelings, but harsh words stir them up" (Proverbs 15:1 CEV).

GIVE GOD THE BENEFIT OF THE DOUBT. When hard times come, count on God.

:: **GOD KNOWS.** "Trust GOD from the bottom of your heart; don't try to figure out everything on your own" (Proverbs 3:5 MSG).

:: **LISTEN UP.** "Listen for GOD's voice in everything you do, everywhere you go; he's the one who will keep you on track" (Proverbs 3:6 MSG).

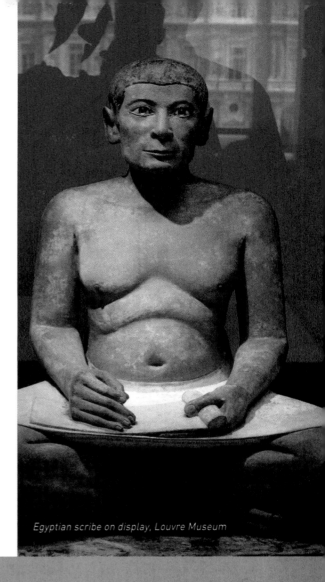

Egyptian scribe on display, Louvre Museum

RECYCLED: WISE SAYINGS FROM EGYPT. Many Bible experts agree that Proverbs 22:17–24:22 reads like a makeover of excerpts from an Egyptian book written by a scribe named Amenemope perhaps several hundred years before Solomon: Instruction of Amenemope (1300–1075 BC). A sampling

TOPIC	PROVERBS	AMENEMOPE
Poor	"Don't rob the poor . . . or exploit the needy" (22:22).	"Don't rob the poor or exploit the disabled" (2:1–2).
Hotheads	"Don't make friends with anyone who has a bad temper. You might turn out like them" (22:24–25 CEV).	"Don't associate with an emotional terrorist because it could destroy your mind, too" (10:1–2).
Money	Don't wear yourself out trying to get rich. . . . In the blink of an eye wealth. . .will sprout wings and fly away like an eagle" (23:4–5).	Don't work so hard trying to get rich. Underhanded money doesn't last. It takes off like geese on the wing (7:17–18).

DON'T BUILD A FIRE IN YOUR PANTS. Parts of Proverbs read like one of those have-to conversations between a dad and his son—the sex talk. ▲

:: **ADULTERY: DUMB.** "Adultery is a brainless act, soul-destroying, self-destructive; expect a bloody nose, a black eye, and a reputation ruined for good" (Proverbs 6:32–33 MSG).
:: **LOOSE LADY: DANGER.** Lips "sweet as honey." Mouth "smoother than oil." Path "straight to the grave" (Proverbs 5:3, 5).

LAZY IS LOONEY. Hard work is the key to success, sages insist—in a dozen proverbs. Laziness, they add, is a shortcut to the poorhouse.

:: **SNOOZE TO LOSE.** "A nap here, a nap there, a day off here, a day off there, sit back, take it easy—do you know what comes next? Just this: You can look forward to a dirt-poor life, poverty your permanent houseguest!" (Proverbs 6:10–11 MSG).
:: **HELP WANTED.** "Having a lazy employee is about as much fun as sucking on a vinegar Popsicle" (Proverbs 10:26 AUTHOR'S PARAPHRASE).

◄

Worker ant totes a leaf clipping. "Take a lesson from the ants, you lazybones" (Proverbs 6:6).

KEEP IT HONEST. Lying to make a quick buck might make you a quick buck, sages admit. But it'll make you enemies, too. God among them.

:: **HOW TO MAKE GOD SICK TO HIS STOMACH.** "God can't stomach liars" (Proverbs 12:22 MSG).

:: **IT'S GOOD BUSINESS**. "If you do the right thing, honesty will be your guide. But if you are crooked, you will be trapped by your own dishonesty" (Proverbs 11:3 CEV).

CRANK IT SHUT. When in doubt about what to say, shut your yap. That's what sages tell their students: "Keep your mouth shut, and you will stay out of trouble" (Proverbs 21:23).

:: **A FOOLISH COMEBACK**. "Don't make a fool of yourself by answering a fool" (Proverbs 26:4 CEV).

:: **WORD POLLUTION**. "The speech of a good person clears the air; the words of the wicked pollute it" (Proverbs 10:32 MSG). ◀

ARE ALL PROMISES IN PROVERBS DEPENDABLE?
No, most Bible experts agree. They're general observations from older men reflecting on life. They're not guarantees. "Hard workers get rich" (Proverbs 10:4). Sell that jingle to a single mom working three jobs.

HOW TO DEAL WITH WORD ABUSE
:: Gossips. "Never confide in blabbermouths" (Proverbs 20:19 MSG).
:: Complainers. "Kick out the troublemakers and things will quiet down; you need a break from bickering and griping!" (Proverbs 22:10 MSG).

Safe at home in Jerusalem

◀ RAISING KIDS. The sages of Proverbs are grand-dads, most likely. So they're offering tried-and-true advice to the next crop of dads.

:: TRUE NORTH. "Point your kids in the right direction. Even if they wander off for a while, in time they'll find their way back to the right trail" (Proverbs 22:6 AUTHOR'S PARAPHRASE).

:: TEACH THEM RIGHT FROM WRONG. "Correct your children while they're still young. Let it slide and it'll soon be too late to do anything but watch them make tragic choices" (Proverbs 19:18 AUTHOR'S PARAPHRASE).

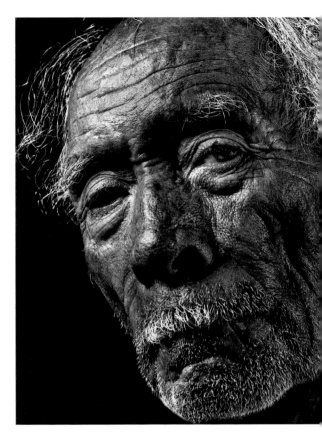

On the streets in Irapuato, Mexico

SPANK, OR NOT? Some say the Bible demands it. A few Bible translators agree:

:: "Those who spare the rod hate their children" (Proverbs 13:24 TNIV).

:: "A spanking won't kill them" (Proverbs 23:13 MSG).

Most Bible translations, however, focus on the need for discipline, not on the method.

Shepherds add their insight. They say they don't use their rod to club sheep. They use it to gently nudge them out of harm's way when the little critters start nibbling themselves into trouble.

SHOW A LITTLE COMPASSION. When we help the needy, sages say, we're double-dipping into goodness. We're helping the helpless. And we're helping ourselves.

:: IT'S A TWO-WAY STREET. "If you won't help the poor, don't expect to be heard when you cry out for help" (Proverbs 21:13 CEV).

:: PAYBACK. "Give freely and become more wealthy. . . . Whoever gives to the poor will lack nothing" (Proverbs 11:24; 28:27). Not a guarantee, most scholars say. A general observation from a lifetime on the planet. ▲

ECCLESIASTES

WHY ON EARTH DID GOD MAKE HUMANS?

IN ONE SENTENCE

King Solomon—the wisest man "who has ever lived or ever will live" (1 Kings 3:12 CEV)—searches for an answer to humanity's toughest question: What's the point of living?

SOUND BITE

"Eat, drink, and be merry."
—*Teacher's advice*
ECCLESIASTES 8:15 NKJV

ON LOCATION

TIME. Many proverbs are attributed to King Solomon, who reigned from about 970–930 BC.

PLACE. Israel.

NEWSMAKER

TEACHER. Code name for the writer, implying Solomon: "These are the words of the Teacher, King David's son, who ruled in Jerusalem" (Ecclesiastes 1:1).

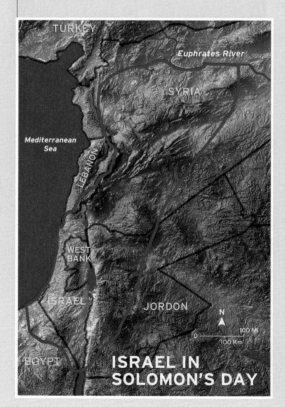

TURKEY

Euphrates River

SYRIA

Mediterranean Sea

LEBANON

WEST BANK

ISRAEL

JORDON

N

100 Mi

100 Km

EGYPT

ISRAEL IN SOLOMON'S DAY

FIRST IMPRESSION: LIFE MAKES NO SENSE. Solomon attacks the mystery of life as though it's a science experiment. First test: personal observation. As far as he can tell, life is meaningless. Humans change nothing. We come. We go. When we're gone, the sun still rises, the wind blows, and rivers rumble to the sea. Everything we do under God's heaven is a rerun—though some wonder if Solomon would change his tune if he saw the destruction we're capable of today. *(Ecclesiastes 1)*

WASTE OF TIME. Solomon tries his hand at several endeavors people like to pursue. Each trial ends in disappointment—no lasting value to any of them:

:: **WISDOM.** The more you know, the more you know you don't know. Frustrating.

:: **WORK.** You die and someone else gets all your stuff.

:: **WEALTH.** Like a light attracting bugs, money draws people who want to help you spend it.

:: **PLEASURE.** Big homes. Trophy wives. Great music. Fun, but nothing more.

:: **POLITICAL POWER.** You can have a crown on your head one day and your head on a pole the next. *(Ecclesiastes 1–2, 4, 7)*

THE GOOD DIE YOUNG. Sounding a tad cynical, Solomon says there's no reason to knock ourselves out being good, since he has seen good people die young and rotten people live too long. His preliminary conclusion: "Avoid both extremes" (Ecclesiastes 7:18). As in a spiritual C student? He'll tweak that advice by the end of his quest.

SEASONS: CYCLES OF LIFE. Solomon says we live through seasons of life that we can't control—any more than we can control seasons on the calendar. They'll come: birth/death, killing/healing, crying/laughing, hugging/releasing, finding/losing, tearing/mending, and loving/hating. We can't stop the seasons, Solomon says, but we can decide how to live through each of them. (*Ecclesiastes 3*)

BEST ADVICE: LOVE GOD, LOVE LIFE. Solomon's experiment fails. He might be the wisest person who would ever live, but he can't figure out why God plastered us high and low all over Planet Earth. Yet Solomon's experiment isn't a total loss. If he figures out nothing else, he does seem certain that it's God who put us here—and that life is God's gift to us. For that reason alone, Solomon advises, we should enjoy life and obey the giver of life. (*Ecclesiastes 5:1–7; 12*) ▶

Indonesian naval cadets try their sea legs on a tall ship used as a sail training vessel.

Figurine of woman from Gilgamesh's era

HOLY BARMAID. Parts of Ecclesiastes track nicely with advice a barmaid gave to a hero named Gilgamesh, in a story written more than 1,500 years before Solomon: *Epic of Gilgamesh.* Many students of the Bible say no problem. God can put the words of a barmaid to good use.

ECCLESIASTES 9:8–9 CEV	GILGAMESH TABLET 10
"Dress up, comb your hair, and look your best."	Take a bath, wash your hair, wear sparkling fresh clothes.
"You love your wife, so enjoy being with her."	Let your wife enjoy being with you.
"This is what you are supposed to do as you struggle through life on this earth."	This is what people are supposed to do.

SONG OF SONGS

THE GOSPEL OF LOVIN'

IN ONE SENTENCE

A man and a woman in love whip out unapologetically sensual words to express their passionate desire for each other.

SOUND BITE

" 'I'm going to climb that palm tree! I'm going to caress its fruit!' Oh yes! Your breasts will be clusters of sweet fruit to me."
—*Unnamed man, comparing his lady to a loaded tree, ripe and ready to pluck*
SONG OF SONGS 7:8 MSG

ON LOCATION

TIME. Many proverbs are attributed to King Solomon, who reigned from about 970–930 BC.

PLACE. Israel.

NEWSMAKERS

WOMAN. Unidentified dark-skinned woman from the countryside.

MAN. Unidentified man, the woman's love. Some suggest he was a country boy whom his lady said was as wonder- ful as the king (Song of Songs 3:7). Others guess he actually was King Solomon, or that someone wrote this song for one of Solomon's thousand weddings.

The song isn't all about sex. Just mostly. In the finale, the lady hits the high note. She wants more. She wants a relationship. An exclusive commitment to her. Forever. In Song of Songs 8:6, she says the passion of her love "is more powerful than death, stronger than the grave" (CEV). And as a sign of undying love, she asks the man to "wear my ring on your finger" (MSG). *(Song of Songs 8)* ▼

Before the wedding, the author's son, Brad Miller, gets a first look at his bride, Jill, in her wedding gown.

BODY LANGUAGE. Two lovers juiced on hormones know how to stoke passion from a spark of desire.

SHE: "Kiss me—full on the mouth!" (Song of Songs 1:2 MSG).

HE: "Your lips are jewel red. . . . Your breasts are like fawns. . . . You're a secret garden" (Song of Songs 4:3, 5, 12 MSG).

SHE: "Let my lover enter his garden! Yes, let him eat the fine, ripe fruits" (Song of Songs 4:16 MSG).

HE: "I'm going to climb that palm tree" (Song of Songs 7:8 MSG). ▲

DOES LOVE OUTLAST LIFE ON EARTH? Ask any widow who loved her husband. As for marriage in the afterlife, Jesus said, "We're beyond marriage" (Matthew 22:30 MSG).

WHERE'S GOD? He's a no-show. Until the 1800s, Bible scholars said this song was a metaphor. Jews said it describes God's love for Israel. Christians said it describes Christ's love for the church. Only in recent centuries did scholars start warming up to the idea that this is a love song about sex—natural and God-approved.

ISAIAH

PREDICTING ISRAEL'S DEATH, SAVIOR'S BIRTH

The prophet Isaiah predicts the invasion and fall of both Jewish nations—Israel in the north, Judah in the south—followed by good news of a coming savior and a second chance for the Jews.

SOUND BITE

"A child is born to us, a son is given . . . . He will be called: Wonderful Counselor, Mighty God, Everlasting Father, Prince of Peace."
—*Isaiah, predicting a time of glory in Galilee (future home of Jesus)*
ISAIAH 9:6

ON LOCATION

TIME. Chapters 1–39 are set in the time of Isaiah's ministry, about 740–700 BC. Chapters 40–66 seem to describe events some 200–300 years later.

PLACE. Isaiah lived in Jerusalem. His prophecies target both Jewish nations, Judah and Israel, along with their neighboring nations.

NEWSMAKERS

ISAIAH, a prophet. One of Israel's most famous prophets, his ministry spans the reigns of four kings.

HEZEKIAH, king of Judah. He's the most righteous of the Jewish kings, many say, and the most famous among the four Isaiah advises.

TWO NATIONS: ISRAEL AND JUDAH

HEAVEN'S UNHOLY GUEST. Isaiah has a vision that sounds like the nightmare of a speaker standing naked before an audience. Isaiah finds himself in heaven, standing unholy before the holy God. "I am doomed," he moans. An angel purifies him, touching hot coals to his lips. God commissions Isaiah to deliver messages to the Jews, but God warns that they won't listen. When Isaiah asks how long they'll refuse, God says, "Until the land is destroyed and left empty." *(Isaiah 6 NCV)* ▲

CALL THIS BOY "GOD WITH US." Syria and Israel threaten Judah with war. Isaiah tells Judah's king to trust God. Isaiah says God will give them a sign of his protection: "The virgin will. . .give birth to a son and will call him Immanuel (which means 'God is with us')." Isaiah adds that by the time the boy is old enough to eat solid food, Syria and Israel will be deserted. Assyrians invade and conquer both nations in 722 BC. *(Isaiah 7)*

THE VIRGIN WASN'T MARY? Mary was virgin number two, most scholars agree. The word for "virgin" in Hebrew could mean "young woman." Isaiah was talking about a woman in his time, perhaps his wife or the queen, many scholars speculate. But New Testament writers saw in the birth of Jesus a second fulfillment of this prophecy. There, the Greek word for "virgin" means a woman who hasn't had sex.

GOOD-BYE ISRAEL, HELLO IRAQ. Nothing but core-rotten kings is what the northern Jewish nation of Israel endures for all of its 200 years. From the very beginning, they've worshiped idols and ignored God. Justice is a joke. Isaiah says the kingdom will soon fall, and he lives to see it. About halfway through his 40-year ministry, Assyrians from what is now Iraq overrun Israel and take survivors home as captives. *(Isaiah 9, 28)*

DOOMSDAY FOR ENEMIES OF THE JEWS. Assyria's army thinks it's the Mean Machine—Dominator of the Middle East, to paraphrase Isaiah. It should think again. It's no machine. Just a tool. God used Assyrians to punish Israel. But Isaiah says God will soon pitch them in the trash. Isaiah adds that God will do the same to other regional enemies of the Jews: Arabia, Babylon, Damascus, Edom, Egypt, Ethiopia, Moab, Philistia, and Tyre. *(Isaiah 1, 10–23, 28)* ▼

ASSYRIAN EMPIRE

Carchemish warrior

◄ *TEARING UP THE TERRORISTS.* Every nation and empire Isaiah dooms falls. The Assyrian Empire, which terrorized and looted the Middle East, gets snuffed out at the Battle of Carchemish in 605 BC by Babylonians from southern Iraq. The Babylonian Empire gets manhandled in 539 BC by the Persian Empire headquartered in Iran.

JUDAH DOOMED, TOO. Isaiah lives in this southern Jewish nation. He says God will eventually wipe it off the map, as well—punishment for persistent sin. Babylonian invaders handle the job in 586 BC, deporting Jewish survivors to what is now Iraq.

Jerusalem 1800s, viewed from the Mount of Olives

JERUSALEM: RIP. More than a century after Assyrians turn the northland Jewish nation of Israel into a scattering of ghost towns, Babylonians ditto that to Judah in the south. Isaiah doesn't live to see it. But he predicts it as a done deal: "Your country lies in ruins. . .towns are burned" (Isaiah 1:7). Babylonians level Judah's cities, saving Jerusalem for last. In the summer of 586 BC, Babylon rips the Jewish nation off the world map. *(Isaiah 1, 22)*

JEWS GET A DO-OVER. After promising the end of the Promised Land—annihilation of both Jewish nations—Isaiah keeps talking. Good news for a change. Though Jews in the foreseeable future should expect the worst, Isaiah says, Jerusalem will "Rise from the dust . . .[to] sit in a place of honor" (Isaiah 52:2). From the dead-stump dynasty of King David, a shoot will sprout up. This is a promise some Jews say points to a messiah. *(Isaiah 11, 32, 45, 52, 55, 60)*

WOLF AND LAMB, BFF. Isaiah predicts a future peace that some Jews take literally, as a description of what life will be like when the messiah comes: "In that day the wolf and the lamb will live together. . . . A little child will lead them" (Isaiah 11:6). Many Christians read it figuratively, some as a description of how the grown-up Christ Child leads enemies into peace.

FINDING JESUS 700 YEARS BEFORE HIS BIRTH.
Many Christians see Jesus in Isaiah's description of a mysterious man whose death will save others.

:: **DESPISED.** "He was despised and rejected."

:: **INNOCENT.** "He had done no wrong."

:: **WHIPPED.** "He was whipped so we could be healed."

:: **NAILED.** "He was pierced for our rebellion."

:: **PUNISHED.** "The LORD laid on him the sins of us all."

:: **SACRIFICED.** "His life is made an offering for sin."

:: **SLAUGHTERED.** "Led like a lamb to the slaughter."

:: **CHILDLESS.** "He died without descendants."

:: **BURIED.** "He was [buried] in a rich man's grave." *(Isaiah 53)*

DEAD SAVIOR. Most Jews in Jesus' time overlooked the possibility that their messiah might have to suffer like this. They expected a warrior king on a horse— someone like David who would restore Israel's lost glory. What they got was a pacifist rabbi on a slab. Until Sunday. Then all glory broke loose, as New Testament writers tell it.

THE JEWISH TAKE. Most Jews say they don't see Jesus in this prophecy. Many say they see the Jewish nation suffering through the 50-year Babylonian exile in what is now Iraq. That's where most captives were taken after Jerusalem's fall. Others say the suffering man represents Judah's innocent minority of Jews who lost their lives because of the sins of the many.

DEAD SEA SCROLLS. Some critics wondered if someone edited Jesus into the Book of Isaiah after the fact. But a complete copy of Isaiah was found in the Dead Sea Scrolls. It's dated about a century before Jesus.

JEREMIAH

WATCHING THE LIGHTS GO OUT IN JERUSALEM

IN ONE SENTENCE

The prophet Jeremiah delivers the worst news in ancient Jewish history, on a scale with the modern Holocaust: invaders are about to wipe off the map the last fragment of the Jewish nation.

SOUND BITE

"Can a leopard remove its spots?"
—*Jeremiah, predicting that the Jews won't change their sinful ways*
JEREMIAH 13:23 CEV

ON LOCATION

TIME. Jeremiah ministers for about 40 years, 627–586 BC.

PLACE. Judah, the southern Jewish nation.

NEWSMAKERS

JEREMIAH, a Jerusalem prophet. He lives to see Babylonian invaders destroy his sacred hometown.

ZEDEKIAH, Judah's last king. He ignores Jeremiah's plea to surrender.

NEBUCHADNEZZAR, the king of Babylon. His soldiers level Jerusalem.

"I'M ONLY A BOY." That's what Jeremiah says when God appears to him—perhaps in a dream or a vision—and appoints him as a prophet to deliver God's messages to Jews in the only surviving Jewish nation. Assyrians overran and dismantled the northern Jewish nation of Israel a century earlier. God tells Jeremiah, probably just a young teen, not to worry: "I will be with you and will protect you." *(Jeremiah 1)*

CRACKED-POT JEWS. Like a lawyer making an opening statement, Jeremiah lays out God's main complaint against the Jews. Like fools, they traded in God—the constantly flowing source of life-giving water—for what amounts to water in a cracked pot. It's one of many word pictures Jeremiah uses to charge the Jews with breaking their ancestral agreement to obey God in exchange for his care, and turning instead to idols that give only the illusion of care. *(Jeremiah 2)* ▼

THE RELUCTANT PROPHETS' CLUB. Jeremiah wasn't the only prophet who tried to get out of the thankless job of telling people what they were doing wrong.

:: **Moses** offered excuses, calling himself a poor speaker and a nobody whom the Jews wouldn't believe (Exodus 3–4).

:: **Isaiah** felt too unholy, and doomed because of it (Isaiah 6).

:: **Jonah**, assigned to go east to Assyria in what is now Iraq, caught a boat going west toward Spain (Jonah 1).

GOD STOPS LISTENING TO PRAYER. A drought has blistered the land. Jews, in desperation, turn to God. But God tells Jeremiah he's done listening to their prayers and accepting their sacrifices. When it comes to worship, God says the Jews don't really mean it. They're just going through the motions, as though prayers and sacrifices are magical incantations and rituals rather than heartfelt expressions of sorrow for sin. *(Jeremiah 14)*

PROPHECY THEATER. Jeremiah acts out some of his prophecies, to help make God's point.

:: **HE DOESN'T MARRY.** Point: Jerusalem's children will die and "lie scattered on the ground like manure" (Jeremiah 16:4).

:: **HE BREAKS A CLAY JAR IN FRONT OF JUDAH'S LEADERS.** Point: God will shatter Judah "beyond repair" (Jeremiah 19:11 CEV).

:: **HE WEARS A WOODEN YOKE AROUND HIS NECK.** Point: "You must submit to Babylon's king and serve him; put your neck under Babylon's yoke!" (Jeremiah 27:8). ▶

JEREMIAH'S POTTERY LESSON. On God's order, Jeremiah goes to a pottery shop. There, he watches a potter shape a lump of clay into a jar. But the potter doesn't like the looks of the jar. So he crushes it into a lump and starts over. God can do the same thing with the Jews, he tells Jeremiah. The smashing isn't inevitable. If the nation repents, God says, he won't destroy it. *(Jeremiah 18)* ▶

ISRAEL'S SENTENCE: 70 YEARS. Time's up. The Jews refuse to honor their ancient agreement to serve God in return for peace and prosperity in the Promised Land. God invokes the penalty clause for breach of contract: eviction. "This country will be as empty as a desert, because I will make all of you the slaves of the king of Babylonia for seventy years." *(Jeremiah 25 CEV)*

TWENTY YEARS OFF FOR GOOD BEHAVIOR? Jews endured only about 50 years in exile, not the 70 that Jeremiah predicted. Jerusalem fell in 586 BC. Persians from what is now Iran defeated Babylon and freed the Jews in 538 BC. Some scholars, however, start the clock about 20 years earlier. Babylonians took some Jerusalem Jews in 605 BC, among them: the prophet Daniel of the lions' den fame.

WATCHING JERUSALEM DIE. Judah's king, Zedekiah, decides to declare independence by withholding taxes from the current Middle Eastern bully: the Babylonian Empire, in what is now Iraq. Babylon's king, Nebuchadnezzar, comes to collect. Not just taxes. Everything. Jeremiah advises his king to surrender—an act the Babylonians will reward by freeing Jeremiah after they overrun the city. They kill many. Most survivors get deported to Iraq. Only the poorest Jews remain—to tend the crops that will provide tax revenue for the empire. At least that's the plan. Ever the rebels, even those Jews rebel. They murder the new governor appointed by the king. Then they run for their lives to Egypt, forcing Jeremiah to go with them though he warned that every one of them would die in Egypt of sickness, starvation, or murder. Jeremiah is never heard from again. *(Jeremiah 39, 42, 52)*

▶

Babylon's King Nebuchadnezzar—Jerusalem's destroyer

SEAL OF JEREMIAH'S SCRIBE. Jeremiah didn't write his prophecy. He dictated it. A professional scribe did the writing: "Baruch son of Neriah" (Jeremiah 32:12). Some archaeologists say they found the impression of Baruch's seal. Scribes sealed letters with a glob of wax or clay stamped with their imprint. One of 250 seals found in 1975 reads like the full names of Baruch and his father: "Belonging to Berekyahu son of Neriyahu the scribe." Many say it's a forgery. Others disagree.

LAMENTATIONS

THE DAY JERUSALEM DIED

IN ONE SENTENCE

Saddest book in the Bible, and perhaps one of the saddest songs ever sung blue, Lamentations survives as an eyewitness account of the horrifying siege and fall of Jerusalem—and the end of the Jewish nation.

ON LOCATION

TIME. The writer describes Babylon's siege of Jerusalem. It lasted two and a half years, from January 15, 588 BC until the city fell on July 18, 586 BC.

PLACE. Jerusalem.

SOUND BITE

"Great is his faithfulness."
—*Songwriter, hopeful that God will show mercy to Jewish survivors*
LAMENTATIONS 3:23

NEWSMAKER

UNIDENTIFIED SONGWRITER. An eyewitness to the suffering of Jews inside Jerusalem during Babylon's siege.

CANNIBAL MOMS IN JERUSALEM. In heart-ripping detail, the writer describes what he saw during Babylon's two-and-a-half-year siege of Jerusalem, cutting off all supplies.

:: **BABIES DYING IN THE STREETS.** "Even the jackals feed their young, but not my people" (Lamentations 4:3).

:: **EMACIATED NOBLES, UNRECOGNIZABLE.** "Their skin sticks to their bones; it is as dry and hard as wood" (Lamentations 4:8).

:: **CANNIBAL MOTHERS.** "Tenderhearted women have cooked their own children. They have eaten them to survive the siege" (Lamentations 4:10). ▶

PRAYER STRATEGY: SOB UNTIL GOD LISTENS. The songwriter says he's pleading with God for help, but that God isn't listening. So the writer vows, "I'll cry until he notices my tears" (Lamentations 3:50 NIrv). He can't believe God enjoys punishing his chosen people. Confident that God's mercies "begin afresh each morning," he pleads: "Restore us, O Lord, and bring us back to you again! Give us back the joys we once had!" (Lamentations 3:23; 5:21).

WHEN ALL IS LOST. With the Jewish nation decimated and looted—its cities dismantled into rock piles—there's nothing much left for the survivors. "The Lord is my inheritance," the songwriter sings, in a surprisingly upbeat note. "I will hope in him!" (Lamentations 3:24).

SUFFERING FROM A TO Z. With one exception, every chapter in Lamentations has 22 verses—one for every letter in the Hebrew alphabet. Chapter 3 has three sets of 22, for 66 verses. Every verse starts with a different letter, working through the entire alphabet. It's as though the writer is saying the Jews have suffered everything from A to Z, many times over.

EZEKIEL

NIGHT TERROR: GOD LEAVES TOWN

IN ONE SENTENCE

Exiled in what is now Iraq, Ezekiel sees visions of God leaving the Jerusalem Temple and invaders wiping the Jewish nation off the map—followed eventually by God raising Israel from the graveyard of dead nations.

SOUND BITE

"Dry bones, hear the word of the LORD."
—*Ezekiel, in a vision, talking to human bones scattered in a valley*
EZEKIEL 37:4 NCV

ON LOCATION

TIME. Ezekiel ministers for 22 years: 593–571 BC. Babylon destroys Jerusalem about seven years into Ezekiel's ministry: 586 BC.

PLACE. Babylon, a city in what is now ruins south of Baghdad, Iraq.

NEWSMAKER

EZEKIEL, exiled prophet. He's a Jewish priest exiled to Babylon, where God calls him at about age 30 to become a prophet.

Babylon

EZEKIEL'S CLOSE ENCOUNTER. It reads a bit like a UFO sighting. In a vision, Ezekiel sees winged, humanoid creatures flying toward him, apparently on vehicles equipped with what sounds like gyros—described as "a wheel within a wheel." They're escorting the throne of God. Many scholars say these images are symbols fit for a priest, which Ezekiel is. The images, in theory, represent God's throne in the Temple: the Ark of the Covenant, a golden chest that holds the 10 Commandments. Winged angels decorated the lid of the chest. In this vision, God assigns Ezekiel the job of prophet. On God's order, Ezekiel eats a scroll, apparently to symbolize that from now on the words he speaks will be God's words. Ezekiel says the scroll tastes "sweet as honey." *(Ezekiel 1–3)* ▼

A PROPHET ACTING ODDLY. Ezekiel acts out some of his prophecies, just as Jeremiah does in Jerusalem. They're both on the job at about the same time.

:: Trim and a shave. Ezekiel cuts his hair and beard and divides it three ways. He burns one pile, to symbolize Jews who'll die during Babylon's siege of Jerusalem. He cuts one pile, representing Jewish captives the Babylonians will execute. He scatters the remainder, representing Jews the Babylonians will deport.

:: Dung-fired bread. He rations himself to eight ounces (228 grams) of grain per day. He uses it to cook bread over a fire of animal dung. The point: food and fuel will grow scarce during Babylon's two-and-a-half-year siege of Jerusalem.

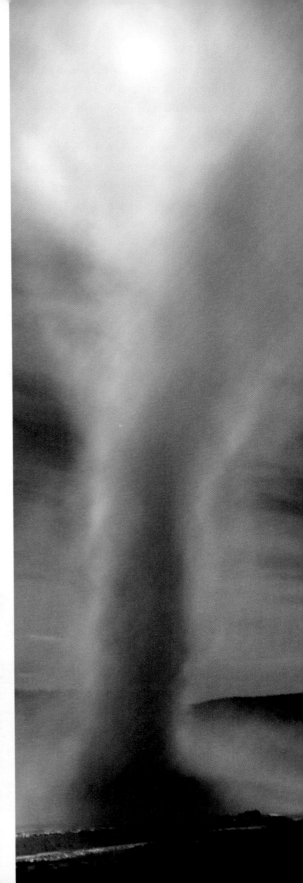

GOOD-BYE, GOD. A celestial hand grabs Ezekiel by the hair and flies him to Jerusalem's Temple. It's another vision, in 592 BC. There, Ezekiel sees Jews worshipping idols and turning their backs on God's Temple to worship the rising sun, east of the Temple. Suddenly, the "cloud of glory. . .the glory of the LORD" leaves the Temple and soars away. God has left the building, the city, and the country. Jews have driven him away. *(Ezekiel 8–10)*

CITY OF THE DAMNED. God tells Ezekiel to act as his prosecutor by leveling charges against Judah's capital city, Jerusalem: "city of murderers, doomed and damned—city of idols, filthy and foul." A sampling:

:: **EXPLOITATION.** "You cheat foreigners, orphans, widows."

:: **DESECRATION.** "You show no respect for my sacred places."

:: **ABANDONMENT.** "You have forgotten me, the LORD God." *(Ezekiel 22 CEV)*

Old Faithful geyser, under a full moon, produces a pillar of light

GOD IN A CLOUD. Ezekiel isn't the only one to see God in a cloud of glory. When Solomon dedicated the Temple, a thick cloud of glory filled the sanctuary (1 Kings 8:10–11). Centuries earlier, God led the Exodus Jews with a pillar of cloud by day and a pillar of fire by night (Exodus 13:21). ▶

THEM DRY BONES. Jerusalem is now a rock pile, Israel a footnote in history, and the Jews a race of refugees in what is now Iraq. In a vision, Ezekiel sees a valley littered with bones. Suddenly, the valley thunders with the rattling of bones snapping together, forming skeletons. Muscle and flesh erupt. Wind breathes life into the corpses. Reanimated, the bodies stand. "These bones represent the people of Israel," God says. "I will open your graves of exile and cause you to rise again. Then I will bring you back to the land of Israel." *(Ezekiel 37)* ▶

Caught in the eruption of Mount Vesuvius in AD 79, this man died in the street of Herculaneum (Ercolano), Italy.

GOD COMES HOME. Thirteen years after Babylon exiled the Jews, Ezekiel gets great news in another vision. God is going to rebuild the demolished Temple. A celestial being measures the new Temple, reporting the size of each room. Then Ezekiel sees "the glory of the God of Israel" (Ezekiel 43:2). He's back. And he's filling the Temple with his presence. *(Ezekiel 40–44)*

Relaxing by Dead Sea salt formations

REVIVING THE DEAD SEA. Fish can't survive in the Dead Sea and swimmers can't sink. That's because the water is about eight times more salty than the ocean. The lowest spot on earth and the region's drainage tank, the Dead Sea lies a quarter-mile below sea level: 1,300 feet (396 meters). Ezekiel sees a vision of a freshwater river diluting the Dead Sea enough for fish to thrive. A symbol, some say, of new life in Israel. Others take the vision more literally.

D A N I E L

PROPHET, DREAMER, LION-TAMER

From Jerusalem, Daniel is taken captive to Babylon where he ends up serving as a trusted advisor, dream interpreter, and prophet for the king—and later for Babylon's conqueror, the king of the Persian Empire.

"My God knew that I was innocent, and he sent an angel to keep the lions from eating me."
—*Daniel, in a pit, assuring the king he survived the night with lions*
DANIEL 6:22 CEV

TIME. Daniel's 60-year story starts around 600 BC.

PLACE. Daniel served two empires: Babylon in Iraq and Persia in Iran.

DANIEL, a prophet. He's a noble in Jerusalem when Babylonians deport him and other leading citizens to what is now Iraq. There, God uses him as a prophet.

SHADRACH, MESHACH, AND ABEDNEGO. Daniel's colleagues get tossed into a burning furnace; they survive.

NEBUCHADNEZZAR, king of Babylon. The most powerful of Babylon's kings, he conquers the Jewish homeland and deports the citizens. Reigned 605–562 BC.

DANIEL: A KOSHER VEGAN IN IRAQ. Jewish political prisoners in Babylon, Daniel and three of his friends get tapped to serve King Nebuchadnezzar as advisors. First, they have to finish a three-year course of study, learning the language and customs. They agree, but they refuse to eat the king's food. They want to stay kosher, eating only food allowed by Jewish law. Afraid they might be served non-kosher meat, they decide to eat only veggies. *(Daniel 1)*

DREAMS OF KINGDOMS TO COME. King Nebuchadnezzar has an odd dream. And he wants to know what it means. But he's apparently afraid his dream interpreters will fake what they can't figure out. So he demands they confirm their abilities by first telling him what he dreamed. Only Daniel can do it. The king saw a statue: gold head, silver chest, bronze belly, iron legs, and iron/clay legs. Daniel says it represents four kingdoms: Golden Babylon followed by later kingdoms, each one increasingly inferior. *(Daniel 2)* ▼

DREAMS: WINDOWS TO THE FUTURE. Jews and other ancient Middle Eastern cultures taught that dreams were messages from beyond—from God, gods, or the future. One Jew from Babylon wrote in the Talmud, an ancient Jewish collection of history and commentary: "A dream not interpreted is like a letter not read" (Berakhot 55a).

Inside a kiln

INFLAMMABLE: THREE JEWS IN A KILN.

Shadrach, Meshach, and Abednego—Daniel's friends—refuse to bow to a golden statue King Nebuchadnezzar commissioned, perhaps a statue honoring his previous dream. He orders all three men thrown into a furnace. They don't burn. When the king sees what looks like a fourth man with them, he calls them out, promotes them, and orders that no one criticize their God. *(Daniel 3)*

Crematorium, Dachau, Germany

JEWS NOT FIREPROOF. Some six million Jews were slaughtered in racial cleansing during World War II. Many were cremated in furnaces—an estimated 433,000 souls died at Auschwitz, Germany, alone. Dachau served as another execution site. Cremation is why the genocide got tagged *Holocaust*. The word means "consumed by fire."

NEBUCHADNEZZAR: KING GONE WILD.
Nebuchadnezzar dreams about a huge tree loaded with fruit that feeds the world. He hears a voice ordering the tree cut down. He asks Daniel what it means. Daniel says the king is the tree. Unless the king repents of his sins, he'll go crazy. A year later he goes insane for at least several months, living with animals. When he comes to his senses, he worships God as "King of heaven." *(Daniel 4)* ▶

GOD'S GRAFFITI. At the last party a Babylon king would throw, revelers drink from sacred cups looted from Jerusalem's Temple. Suddenly, a disembodied hand writes on the palace wall: "Numbered. Numbered. Weighed. Divided." Daniel says it means that God has the king's number— and his number's up. The king's a lightweight, so his kingdom has been divided among invaders. The Bible says King Belshazzar dies that night, perhaps in the attack by coalition forces of Medes and Persians. *(Daniel 5)*

LION TAMER. Daniel spends the night in a pit with lions—oddly enough, because the Persian king likes him. Daniel's jealous political rivals convince the king to pass an irrevocable law requiring everyone to pray to only the king for a month, or face lions. They know Daniel will pray to God, forcing the king to send Daniel to the lions. The king rushes to the lion pit the next morning. When he sees that God protected Daniel, he orders the rivals into the pit. Cat food. *(Daniel 6)*

HOW BABYLON FELL. Two versions show up in ancient documents.

:: Water wonder. Greek historian Herodotus, writing a century after Babylon fell, said Persians diverted the Euphrates River that flowed into the city, allowing the army to march in on the riverbed.

:: Welcome mat. The Persian commander who led the invasion, Cyrus the Great, said the citizens welcomed him as a liberator, opening the city gates.

DANIEL SEES THE END. But the end of what? That's the question. Daniel reads Jeremiah's prophecy that God will punish the Jews by exiling them from Israel for 70 years. Depressed, Daniel goes into mourning. The angel Gabriel comes to cheer him up with visions of end times. Gabriel says the suffering will end after "a period of seventy sets of seven." Some take this number as a cryptic symbol—*seven* symbolizes completion, since God rested on day seven after creation. So *70 x 7* means Jews will suffer the complete measure of God's punishment. Others take the numbers literally: 490 years. They use this number with other info in Daniel's prophecies to work up theories pointing to events in history or in a day yet to come. Some say the end of suffering Daniel talks about marks the Second Coming of Jesus. *(Daniel 9–12)* ▼

Ptolemy, ruler of Egypt

TRACKING PERFECTLY WITH HISTORY. Many of Daniel's prophecies track with history hundreds of years later—leading many experts to conclude someone else wrote them as history. Other scholars defend Daniel as a prophet who could tell the future in remarkable detail.

One example of a prophecy that could read like history:

"The daughter of the king of the south will be given in marriage to the king of the north to secure the alliance, but she will lose her influence over him" (Daniel 11:6).

The match with history:

South king: Ptolemy II, ruling the Greek's Ptolemy Empire in Egypt, 285–246 BC.

North king: Antiochus II Theos, ruling the Greek's Seleucid Empire in Syria, 261–246 BC.

South daughter marries north king: Northern king Antiochus exiles his wife, Laodice, so he can marry southern king Ptolemy's daughter, the princess Berenice.

South daughter loses influence. Southern bride Berenice loses her influence after Laodice poisons her ex and declares her own son the new king.

HOSEA

THE PROPHET WHO MARRIED A HOOKER

IN ONE SENTENCE

In a match made in heaven, God orders the prophet Hosea to marry a hooker—as a living parable to show the Jews how they have committed spiritual adultery.

SOUND BITE

"If you plant the wind, you'll harvest a hurricane."
—*God, comparing Israel's sin to sowing seeds of trouble that's about to produce a bumper crop of misery*
HOSEA 8:7 AUTHOR'S PARAPHRASE

ON LOCATION

TIME. Hosea ministers about 28 years, from 750 BC until Assyrian invaders overrun his nation in 722 BC.

PLACE. Northern Jewish nation of Israel.

NEWSMAKERS

HOSEA, a prophet. His family becomes a living parable of how the Jews treated God.

GOMER, Hosea's wife. She's a former prostitute.

ISRAEL
HOSEA'S HOME

ROCKY MARRIAGE. "Find a whore and marry her," God tells Hosea. "This whole country has become a whorehouse, unfaithful to me." Hosea's bride, Gomer, gives birth to three kids—none of which appears to be Hosea's. Like the marriage, each child's name sends a message.

:: **JEZREEL.** God is going to punish Israel for a bloody massacre that took place at Jezreel.

:: **NO MERCY.** God has run out of it.

:: **NOBODY.** Israel is nothing special to God anymore. *(Hosea 1 MSG)*

THE MRS. ON THE RUN. Gomer runs away. Hosea tracks her down and buys her freedom—perhaps from slavery or a pimp. Hosea takes her home, orders her to give up prostitution, and refuses to have sex with her for a time. It's part of a message. Israel will go without for a while—no king. In fact, no country. But when the Jews give up their sinful lifestyle, they'll get back everything they lost. *(Hosea 3, 14)*

REALITY STORY OR PARABLE? Many rabbis and church leaders in ancient times said they couldn't believe that God would ask a holy man to marry a hooker. They said Hosea probably experienced this in a vision—or that maybe he was telling a parable.

JOEL

LOCUST ALERT

IN ONE SENTENCE

Locusts swarm into Israel and devastate the country, but Joel warns that it's a minor inconvenience compared to what the coming swarm of soldiers will do when God sends them to punish the Jewish nation.

SOUND BITE

"Hammer your plows into swords."
—*God, promising payback for enemies of the Jews*
JOEL 3:10

ON LOCATION

TIME. Unknown. Guesses stretch over 500 years, from about 800–300 BC.

PLACE. Unknown. Joel mentions both Jewish nations, Israel in the north and Judah in the south.

NEWSMAKER

JOEL, a prophet. He warns that God is going to step into Jewish history—but this time, it's not to help the Jews. It's to punish them.

TWO NATIONS: ISRAEL AND JUDAH

Desert locust

INVASION. It's Judgment Day. God has sentenced the Jewish nation to death. Joel says the executioner is coming: an invasion force—perhaps Babylonians from what is now Iraq, who destroyed Jerusalem and the last surviving Jewish nation of Judah in 586 BC. "A great and mighty army appears. Nothing like it has been seen before or will ever be seen again." Yet even in this final moment, Joel says God may yet grant the people a reprieve—if they repent. Joel seems to know they won't. He offers consolation: one day, God will restore the nation. But not today. *(Joel 2–3)*

"They run like war horses. . .rumbling over the tops of the mountains" (Joel 2:4–5 NCV).

AMOS

NOTE TO THE RICH: YOUR TURN TO EAT DIRT

IN ONE SENTENCE

A small-town farmer turned temporary prophet goes to the big city and gives the rich and powerful Jews of Israel what for—warning they'll soon get what they deserve for helping themselves to the helpless.

NEWSMAKER

AMOS, a shepherd and farmer. Not a full-time prophet, Amos has visions that he says contain messages from God for the Jewish people and some of their neighbor nations.

SOUND BITE

"They walk on poor people as if they were dirt, and they refuse to be fair."
—*Amos, criticizing the rich and powerful*
AMOS 2:7 NCV

ON LOCATION

TIME. Anywhere from 20 to 70 years before Israel fell to Assyrian invaders in 722 BC; Amos ministers during the reign of Judah's King Uzziah (about 792–742 BC).

PLACE. Amos lives in the village of Tekoa in the southern Jewish nation of Judah. But he takes his message to Samaria, capital of the northern Jewish nation of Israel.

PROPHET FROM TEKOA

A PLAIN-SPOKEN FARMER. In the tiny village of Tekoa, a half-day's walk south of Jerusalem, a fig farmer and shepherd has visions that he feels compelled to take north to Israel's leaders. On behalf of God, he condemns the rich and powerful for a wagonload of sins, including:

:: selling the poor into slavery to recoup tiny debts: the cost of a pair of sandals (Amos 2:6)
:: bribing judges (Amos 5:7, 12)
:: mixing bags of grain with filler dirt to increase their profit margin (Amos 8:6).

SHE'S NO LADY, SHE'S A COW. For a farmer, Amos is quite the public speaker—gifted at helping his increasingly angry listeners paint mental pictures. In a warning that the butcher's coming, Amos compares the wives of Israel's rich men to livestock fattened in well-known lush pastures: "cows of Bashan" (Amos 4:1 MSG). Israel, he says, is a crooked wall. God's plumb line proves it. And God's going to do to Israel what builders do to crooked walls. Tear it down. *(Amos 4, 7–9)* ▶

Funeral portrait of woman from Bible times

FIG FARMER. Amos farmed an orchard of sycamore trees that produce sweet figs.

AMOS' LAST WORD: GOOD NEWS. Like most prophets who warn that God is about to let invaders crush Israel and deport the Jews, Amos ends on a note of hope. Quoting God, he says: "I will bring my exiled people of Israel back from distant lands, and they will rebuild their ruined cities" (Amos 9:14).

OBADIAH

NOTE TO WAR CRIMINALS: PAYBACK'S COMING

IN ONE SENTENCE

Obadiah condemns the neighbor nation of Edom for murdering Jewish war refugees, arresting and turning others over to the Babylonian invaders from what is now Iraq, and looting the war-torn Jewish homeland.

NEWSMAKER

OBADIAH, a prophet. He warns the people of Edom that God is going to wipe out their nation because they murdered Jewish war refugees.

SOUND BITE

"As you have done to Israel, so it will be done to you."
—*God's warning to Edom*
OBADIAH 15

ON LOCATION

TIME. Sometime during a 33-year stretch between the fall of Jerusalem in 586 BC and the fall of Edom in 553 BC.

PLACE. Edom, south of the Dead Sea in what is now part of the Arab country of Jordan.

Ruins of Petra

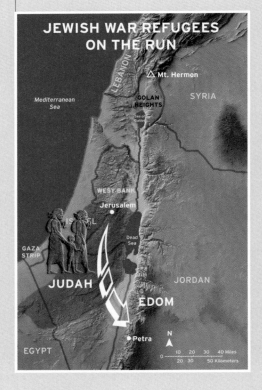

JEWISH WAR REFUGEES ON THE RUN

ROCK CITY. "You thought you were so great, perched high among the rocks. . . . Thinking to yourself, 'Nobody can get to me!'" (Obadiah 1:3 MSG). God can, the prophet Obediah says. Citizens of Edom are going to get what they deserve for arresting, murdering, and robbing Jewish refugees who ran to them for help when Babylonian invaders wiped the Jewish nation off the world map.

Sky-high view of Petra, natural fortress city of Edom with access only through a narrow canyon.

PROPHECY FULFILLED. Payback came about 33 years after Jerusalem fell. Babylonian invaders returned to the region. This time they crushed Edom: 553 BC. Ironically, Edom's refugees fled to what is now Israel. They regrouped about a day's walk south of Jerusalem and became known as the Idumeans. The Bible's most famous Idumean was Herod the Great, the king who tried to kill Baby Jesus in Bethlehem.

JONAH

THE PROPHET IS FISH BAIT

IN ONE SENTENCE

Assigned by God to personally deliver a message of doom to Assyria's capital in what is now Iraq, Jonah sets sail in the opposite direction and gets thrown overboard, swallowed by a fish, and spit up on shore—convincing him to do as he was told.

SOUND BITE

"God, if you won't kill them, kill *me*! I'm better off dead!"

—*Jonah, expressing humiliation after his prediction of Nineveh's destruction didn't come true*

Jonah 4:3 msg

NEWSMAKER

JONAH, a prophet. He warns Assyrians in Nineveh that God will destroy their city in 40 days.

ON LOCATION

TIME. During the reign of Israel's King Jeroboam II (about 793–753 BC), which is a few decades before Assyrians wipe Israel off the political map in 722 BC.

PLACE. Jonah lives in the northern Jewish nation of Israel. He travels roughly a thousand miles (1,600 km) along caravan routes to Nineveh in what is now northern Iraq—but only after trying to flee to Tarshish (possibly in Spain).

JONAH'S SCENIC ROUTE TO NINEVEH

MAN OVERBOARD. God tells Jonah to go to Nineveh in what is now northern Iraq and warn the Assyrians that God is about to destroy the city. Assyrians are vicious. They impale their enemies. Jonah boards a ship in Joppa, sailing in the opposite direction. God stirs up a storm. Jonah admits his sin to the sailors. They toss him overboard to appease God. A big fish swallows Jonah, swims him back to shore for three days, and spits him out. Jonah heads for Nineveh. *(Jonah 1–2)* ▼

SAVING NINEVEH BY DOOMING NINEVEH. God is going to destroy Nineveh in 40 days, Jonah tells the Assyrians. The king goes into mourning. He orders everyone to stop their violence, and to fast and pray to Jonah's God. The Lord forgives them and calls off the doom. Anything but happy about saving Nineveh, Jonah is bummed. He pouts, complaining that God hung him out to dry. *(Jonah 3–4)*

THE POINT? Jonah's prophecy, like any Bible prophecy, isn't about predicting the future, many scholars say. It's about confronting people with their sin in the hope of turning them to God. If they repented, God forgave them and waived the punishment. The shocker is that Jonah considered himself a failure, when he was one of the few Bible-prophet success stories.

REAL LIFE OR PARABLE? Perhaps most Christians read the story as history. Some, however, see a fictional parable in the details: the big fish, along with the abrupt, thought-provoking conclusion that's common in a parable.

MICAH

BIG NEWS FOR A LITTLE TOWN: BETHLEHEM

IN ONE SENTENCE

Though Micah predicts the fall of both Jewish nations—Israel in the north and Judah in the south—the small-town prophet is most famous for predicting a small-town Messiah.

SOUND BITE

"You, Bethlehem, David's country, the runt of the litter—from you will come the leader who will shepherd-rule Israel. . . . Peacemaker of the world!"
—*Micah, predicting the birth of a savior*
MICAH 5:2, 4 MSG

ON LOCATION

TIME. Micah's ministry spans about 65 years and three kings of Judah—Jotham, Ahaz, Hezekiah—from roughly 750–686 BC. He lives to see the northern Jewish nation of Israel fall in 722 BC.

PLACE. Micah comes from Moresheth, a village in the southern Jewish nation of Judah, about a day's walk southwest of Jerusalem—roughly 20 miles (32 km).

NEWSMAKER

MICAH, a prophet. He predicts the fall of both Jewish nations—followed by the restoration of Israel and the end of wars.

PREDICTING BIG THINGS FOR LITTLE BETHLEHEM

O LITTLE TOWN OF PEACE ON EARTH. Some 700 years before Jesus is born in Bethlehem, Micah predicts that out of this hilltop village—the hometown of King David—there will come a ruler who will change Israel for the better: "He will be the source of peace" (Micah 5:5). In time, Micah says, nations will worship in Jerusalem. And they will "hammer their swords into plow blades. . . . They will not train for war anymore" (Micah 4:3 NCV). *(Micah 4–7)* ▼

EVICTION NOTICE—JEWS GET THE BOOT. Micah levels charges against both Jewish nations, especially against their rich leaders. Then he announces the sentence they can all expect.

:: **HOME WRECKER.** "When you want a piece of land, you find a way to seize it. . . . You have evicted women from their pleasant homes" (Micah 2:2, 9). *God will evict you.*

:: **MONEY GRUBBER.** "You rulers make decisions based on bribes" (Micah 3:11). *A plowed field will be all that's left to rule of Jerusalem.*

:: **STRONG-ARMING THE WEAK.** "The rich among you have become wealthy through extortion and violence" (Micah 6:12). *God will get violent with you.*

A WISE MAN'S GPS. In Jesus' day, King Herod's Bible experts directed the Magi to Bethlehem because of Micah's prediction (Micah 5:2). That's where Jewish scholars said that Israel's greatest king would be born. ▲

JERUSALEM, WHERE THE WORLD WORSHIPS. It's a worship center for three major world religions: Jews, Christians, and Muslims—as Micah predicted: "People from all over the world will stream there to worship" (Micah 4:1).

N A H U M

NOTE TO IRAQI EMPIRE: LIGHTS OUT

IN ONE SENTENCE

Prophet Nahum tells his fellow Jews that the Assyrian Empire—which wiped the northern Jewish nation of Israel off the world map several decades earlier—is about to find out what that feels like.

SOUND BITE

"I will lift your skirts and show all the earth your nakedness."
—*God, to the Assyrian Empire that conquered and terrorized much of the Middle East*
NAHUM 3:5

NEWSMAKER

NAHUM, a prophet. He predicts the fall of the Middle East's first superpower, the Assyrian Empire.

ON LOCATION

TIME. After Assyria conquers Egypt's capital of Thebes in 663 BC (Nahum mentions it), but before Babylon conquers Assyria in 612 BC (Nahum predicts it).

PLACE. Nahum lives in Elkosh, location unknown. He targets the Assyrian Empire's capital of Nineveh.

ASSYRIAN EMPIRE

Assyria's capital of Nineveh: the "before" picture. "After" is a rock pile, courtesy of Babylonians. Today, Nineveh is a mound of dirt and rocks on the outskirts of Mosul, Iraq.

DOWN TOWN. Assyria's capital—Nineveh—is a town going down. The prophet Nahum paints a picture of the city's future:

:: "Your enemy is coming to crush you."

:: "Their glittering chariots move into position. . .spears waving above them."

:: "Soon the city is plundered, empty, and ruined."

(Nahum 2)

BAD-BOY EMPIRE. Suitable for framing in Assyria's palace at Nineveh were sculpted pictures of Shish Kabobbed captives—impaled on sharpened fence posts. Dark. But Assyrians balanced their dark side with some enlightenment. They maintained a library of 22,000 clay tablets covering history, medicine, and astronomy. ▶

HABAKKUK

SACRED ETIQUETTE: HOW TO TELL GOD OFF

IN ONE SENTENCE

Prophet Habakkuk can't believe God is going to let the evil Babylonians punish the comparatively righteous Jews, yet Habakkuk vows to keep trusting God no matter what.

SOUND BITE

"You can't be serious!"
—*Habakkuk to God, after learning God is going to let Babylonian invaders punish the Jews*
HABAKKUK 1:13 MSG

ON LOCATION

TIME. Many scholars guess it's after Babylon defeated Assyria in 612 BC, but before Babylon destroyed Jerusalem about 26 years later, in 586 BC.

PLACE. The threat comes from the Babylonian Empire, based in what is now southern Iraq. Its target is Judah, the last surviving Jewish nation, located in what is now southern Israel.

NEWSMAKER

HABAKKUK, a prophet. Like most Bible prophets, he's a mystery. The Bible reveals almost nothing about him personally.

BABYLONIAN EMPIRE

Babylon entrance

GIVING GOD WHAT-FOR. In a vision, Habakkuk shows up at God's complaint desk with one gripe that leads to another. *First gripe:* Why don't you do something about all the violence and injustice in this country? God says okay, he'll let the Babylonians punish the Jews. *Second gripe:* Babylonians? They're worse than us! Why on earth would you string us up like dead fish on their hooks? *(Habakkuk 1)* ▲

WHEN FAITH SOUNDS WACKED. God doesn't explain himself. He simply says: "Righteous people live their lives by trusting in me." Habakkuk says that's good enough for him: "Let the fig trees fall, the olive crops fail, and the fields lie dead in the dirt. Let the sheep die in the pastures and the cattle barns go empty. I'm living full. Full of joy in God. He's my salvation. He's my strength. And he'll get me safely over the mountains ahead." *(Habakkuk 2–3 AUTHOR'S PARAPHRASE)*

Martin Luther

HABAKKUK, FATHER OF THE PROTESTANT MOVEMENT. Catholic priest Martin Luther—the monk who inspired the Protestant breakaway from the Catholic Church—owes Habakkuk for the idea. Luther said we're not saved through the church. We're saved by trusting in God: "Only those who live by faith are acceptable to me" (Habakkuk 2:4 CEV).

ZEPHANIAH

ENDANGERED SPECIES: HUMANS

IN ONE SENTENCE

Though Zephaniah says God is going to hit the creation REWIND button, taking humanity and all life on earth back to zero, many scholars say he's using exaggeration to give the Jews a clue about what it's going to feel like when invaders decimate their homeland and deport the survivors.

NEWSMAKER

ZEPHANIAH, a prophet. He predicts the end of Judah and possibly the world.

SOUND BITE

"I will wipe out the entire human race."
—*God*
ZEPHANIAH 1:3 CEV

ON LOCATION

TIME. Sometime during the reign of King Josiah (640–609 BC), a couple of decades or more before Babylonian invaders level Jerusalem.

PLACE. Southern Jewish nation of Judah.

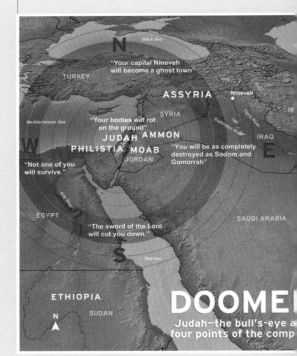

N

Black Sea

"Your capital Nineveh will become a ghost town"

TURKEY

ASSYRIA   Nineveh

SYRIA

Mediterranean Sea   "Your bodies will rot on the ground"

JUDAH AMMON

PHILISTIA MOAB   "You will be as completely destroyed as Sodom and Gomorrah"

IRAQ

W   E

JORDAN

"Not one of you will survive."

EGYPT   "The sword of the Lord will cut you down."   SAUDI ARABIA

S   Red Sea

ETHIOPIA   DOOME

SUDAN   Judah—the bull's-eye a
four points of the comp

N

KISS THE WORLD GOOD-BYE. God vows to kill every living organism. Zephaniah lists them in the opposite order that Genesis says God created them. The last will be first: humans—followed by animals, birds, and fish. Some scholars say Zephaniah is using the common Jewish practice of hyperbole—in this case to predict the end of Judah. Others say it's a double prophecy—pointing also to an end-time doomsday. *(Zephaniah 1)* ▼

THE DAY AFTER DOOMSDAY. "Cheer up," Zephaniah says. He's talking to survivors of Judah's future destruction. Promising what sounds like heaven on earth—possibly more exaggeration, some argue—Zephaniah says God will not only bring home Jewish exiles scattered abroad, they'll come home as better people who "do no wrong . . .never tell lies. . .and sleep in safety." While nations watch, Zephaniah vows, God will restore Israel's fortunes. *(Zephaniah 3)*

◄ *TARGETING THE MIDDLE EAST.* Judah (today's Israel) isn't God's only target. It's just the bull's-eye. God also targets Judah's neighbors in all four directions, promising to punish their sins, too:

:: **North**: Nineveh (Iraq)

:: **South**: Ethiopia (Sudan)

:: **East**: Ammon and Moab (Jordan)

:: **West**: Philistia (Palestinian territory).

 All of these nations eventually fall to invaders. Nineveh, near Mosul, is still a pile of rocks.

HAGGAI

HEAVEN CAN WAIT—SO CAN THE TEMPLE

IN ONE SENTENCE

When a rotten harvest gets the attention of Jerusalem-area Jews who have returned from exile, Haggai tells them they're not going to have another decent harvest until they rebuild God's Temple—a project they jump-start within three weeks.

NEWSMAKER

HAGGAI, a prophet. His known ministry spans only four months, perhaps because he was an elderly man. If his passion for the Temple stems from having seen Solomon's Temple before Babylonians tore it down in 586 BC, he would have been about age 70, perhaps older.

SOUND BITE

"You say this isn't the right time to build a temple for me. But is it right for you to live in expensive houses, while my temple is a pile of ruins?"
—*God, to the Jews some 20 years into their rebuilding of Jerusalem after invaders leveled it*
HAGGAI 1:4 CEV

ON LOCATION

TIME. August 29–December 18, 520 BC—dates are this specific because they've been cross-referenced with surviving Persian records.

PLACE. Jerusalem.

Jerusalem

TRADING DOWN. Haggai's temple will be nothing close the grandeur of Solomon's Temple, pictured here. Old priests who remember that Temple destroyed 70 years earlier "wept aloud when they saw the new Temple's foundation" (Ezra 3:2).

FARMERS ON A CONSTRUCTION CREW. After the Jews suffer through a bad harvest, the prophet Haggai guarantees them a bumper crop next year if they do just one thing: start rebuilding the Jerusalem Temple that Babylonian invaders destroyed in 586 BC. Done deal. Haggai makes the offer on August 29, 520 BC. Jews start work three weeks later. They finish the job in less than five years. *(Haggai 1–2)*

HEROD'S UPGRADE. Haggai promised that this meager Temple would see more prosperous days: "Treasures of all the nations will be brought to this Temple" (Haggai 2:7). He was right. King Herod the Great (reigned 37–4 BC) began a massive upgrade of the Temple that took 44 years. He doubled the size of the courtyard where Jews and God lovers from neighboring nations came to worship.

ZECHARIAH

PROMISE: ISRAEL WILL RISE AGAIN

IN ONE SENTENCE

A month or two after the prophet Haggai convinces the Jews to rebuild Jerusalem's Temple, torn down by invaders, Zechariah arrives with an encouraging word: God is going to help them do it—and rebuild the nation as well.

NEWSMAKER

ZECHARIAH, a prophet. He reports visions intended to assure Jews recently returned from exile in Babylon that God will take care of them, and that better days are ahead.

◄ SOUND BITE

"Raise the roof, Daughter Jerusalem! Your king is coming! A good king who makes all things right, a humble king riding a donkey."
—*Zechariah, in a prediction New Testament writers say Jesus fulfilled on the first Palm Sunday*
ZECHARIAH 9:9 MSG

ON LOCATION

TIME. Zechariah's prophecies span at least two years—520–518 BC—near the start of King Darius's reign of Persia (522–486 BC).

PLACE. Jerusalem.

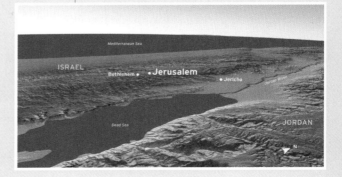

ANGELS ON PATROL. Five months into rebuilding the Temple, Jews get a morale booster, on February 15, 519 BC. In a single night, Zechariah has eight visions—each that seem intended to assure the Jews that God's taking care of them. A sampling:

:: **ANGELS ON HORSEBACK.** Patrolling the planet, they report peace on earth (1:7–17).

:: **MAN GOING TO JERUSALEM WITH TAPE MEASURE.** The city will be crowded again (2:1–5).

:: **NEW ROBES FOR THE HIGH PRIEST.** In a sacred makeover, the priest replaces his worn-out, filthy robes. It's God's promise that priests will again serve in the Temple, once it's rebuilt (3:1–10). ▼

MALACHI

STIFFING GOD

IN ONE SENTENCE

After losing their homeland to invaders—punishment for sin—the Jews are back home, rebuilding their nation, and back to sinning their way into trouble again.

NEWSMAKER

MALACHI, a prophet. God sends him messages to pass along to Jews who are rebuilding their nation.

SOUND BITE

"Are you crazy? Instead of sacrificing your best animals to God, as the law requires, you bring the crippled, diseased, and blind. You think he'll be pleased? Try giving animals like that to the governor; see if he's pleased." ▶
—*Malachi, to his fellow Jews*
MALACHI 1:7–8 AUTHOR'S PARAPHRASE

ON LOCATION

TIME. Clues in the book suggest the 400s BC, a century after the Jews return from exile in Babylon (now Iraq).

PLACE. Israel.

SIN: A JEWISH TRADITION. Half a century in exile hasn't taught the Jews much of a lesson. They distance themselves from idolatry, a key sin that got them deported. But other sins live on.

:: **SKIP TITHE.** They stop donating a tenth of their income—money used to support the Temple ministry.

:: **TEACH MAN-MADE RULES.** Priests apparently teach their opinions instead of God's law.

:: **SLEEP AROUND.** Then the Jews wonder why God isn't answering their prayers.

:: **EXPLOIT THE POOR.** They target society's helpless souls: widows, orphans, and immigrants. *(Malachi 1–3)*

MESSIAH'S ADVANCE MAN. Judgment Day is coming, Malachi warns. But before it happens, he says, Elijah will return—the prophet taken to heaven in a chariot of fire 400 years earlier. For centuries, Jews have been saying God would send a messenger to "prepare the way for the LORD" (Isaiah 40:3 NIrv). Jesus later says John the Baptist fulfills that prophecy: "He is Elijah" (Matthew 11:14). *(Malachi 4)* ◄

John the Baptist

Church tithing box

A CUP OF WINE FOR ELIJAH. Many Jews set out an extra cup of wine at the Passover meal to honor Elijah, since according to tradition he will come to announce the Messiah's arrival.

WHY EARLY CHRISTIANS DIDN'T TITHE. Christians didn't start tithing until the 1800s, historians say. That's when the American government stopped supporting churches with tax money. Preachers latched on to the Jewish tradition as a fund-raising tool. Early Christians rejected tithing, though, arguing that it was an obsolete Jewish rule—like Old Testament laws about circumcision and kosher food. See also "Tithing," page 226. ◄

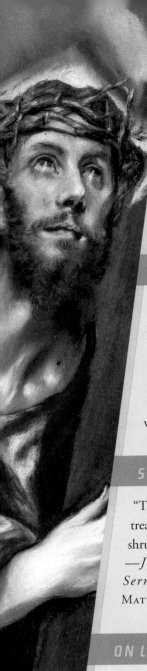

MATTHEW

STOP WAITING, THE MESSIAH HAS COME

IN ONE SENTENCE

Jesus—introduced as the Messiah predicted by prophets to bring peace to Israel—is born to a virgin, grows up to attract crowds with his healing miracles and unconventional teaching, and is crucified for those very reasons; but he doesn't stay dead.

SOUND BITE

"Treat folks the way you'd like them to treat you. That's the Bible's teaching, shrunk down to one sentence."
—*Jesus, preaching his famous Sermon on the Mount*
MATTHEW 7:12 AUTHOR'S PARAPHRASE

ON LOCATION

TIME. Lifetime of Jesus, 6 BC–AD 33, give or take a few years.
PLACE. Israel.

NEWSMAKERS

JESUS, promised Messiah and God's Son. "I have come to get sinners to follow me" (Matthew 9:13 NIrV).

TWELVE DISCIPLES, students of Jesus. They are in training to spread the teachings of Jesus.

MARY, mother of Jesus. A virgin, she becomes pregnant by the Holy Spirit.

JOSEPH, husband of Mary. Engaged to Mary, Joseph marries her after learning of her pregnancy.

PONTIUS PILATE, Roman governor of Judea. He issues the order to crucify Jesus.

HEROD THE GREAT, king of the Jews. He tries to kill young Jesus in Bethlehem.

ROTTEN APPLES IN JESUS' FAMILY TREE. A genealogy sounds like a boring way to start the story of Jesus. But why expect more of an accountant? Matthew is a former tax collector, and genealogies are legal documents establishing identity. Matthew traces Jesus' family tree to King David, since prophets said the Messiah would descend from David. Oddly, Matthew skips respected women like Abraham's wife, Sarah. But he adds shady ladies:

:: **TAMAR,** had twins by her father-in-law
:: **RAHAB,** Jericho hooker
:: **RUTH,** Arab
:: **BATHSHEBA,** committed adultery with David. *(Matthew 1:1-17)* ▼

JOSEPH'S DILEMMA: PREGNANT FIANCÉE. When Gabriel tells Mary she'll become pregnant through the power of God's Spirit, she leaves town. She visits a relative: Elizabeth, pregnant with John the Baptist. Mary returns about three months later, a little larger than life. Joseph decides to quietly back out of the wedding. But while he's sleeping off the shock, an angel appears to him in a vivid dream. "Take Mary home as your wife," the angel says (NLT). The child "is from the Holy Spirit" (CEV). Wedding: on again. *(Matthew 1:18-25)*

Jesus' family tree includes a hooker: Rahab

WHY INCLUDE THE SHADY LADIES? Lots of theories. One: it shows that God can work wonders through the most unlikely people. To some, that sounds like a perfect segue—cue the Virgin Mary.

MATTHEW'S MOTIVE. More than any of the other Bible biographers of Jesus—Mark, Luke, John—Matthew tries to prove that Jesus is the promised Messiah. He points out 60 prophecies he says Jesus fulfilled Mark comes in second, pointing out only about 30.

WISE MEN, DUMB QUESTION. "Where is the new-born king of the Jews? We saw his star as it rose, and we have come to worship him" (Matthew 2:2). Sages from the East, perhaps from what is now Iraq or Iran, ask that question in Jerusalem. But they ask it to Herod—the king who (1) didn't have a new-born son and (2) had already assassinated two of his sons because he thought they were plotting a coup. He'll execute a third son later, from his death-bed. Herod directs the sages to Bethlehem, since his advisors tell him the prophet Micah had predicted that the Messiah would be born there. Herod asks the sages to report back to him so he can honor the child. When they don't—warned in a dream to return home another way—Herod shows his take on "honor." He orders the killing of all Bethlehem boys age two and under. Joseph, warned in a dream of Herod's plan, escapes with his family to Egypt. He stays there until Herod dies. *(Matthew 2)*

Jerusalem, looking south toward Bethlehem, 7 BC

HEROD THE GREAT (ruled 37–4 BC). He wasn't a Jew by race. Decades before he was born, Jews forced his people—Idumeans in what is now southern Israel—to convert or die. Romans appointed him king. He did a lot for the Jews, including a massive makeover of the Temple. But Jews never accepted him as one of their own.

STAR OF BETHLEHEM, ONE THEORY. It was an unusual alignment of Jupiter and Saturn beside the Pisces constellation.

:: **Jupiter** represented kings.

:: **Saturn** represented Jews who worship on the day named after the god Saturn: Saturday.

:: **Pisces,** meaning "fish," represented the land beside the Mediterranean Sea, including the Jewish homeland.

Knowing the Jews were expecting a messiah king any moment, the sages concluded this was the moment.

PERFECT GIFTS: GOLD, FRANKINCENSE, MYRRH. The gifts the wise men brought for Jesus traveled well, were fit for a king, and doubled as currency—which may be how Joseph funded his family's escape to Egypt. Frankincense and myrrh were fragrant, dried tree sap. People burned it as incense or mixed it with oil to make perfume.

JESUS TAKES THE PLUNGE. Into water and ministry. Jesus goes public with his ministry the day his relative, John the Baptist, baptizes him in the Jordan River. It's a puzzler why Jesus asks John to baptize him, since John baptizes "those who repent of their sins." The Bible says Jesus "never sinned" (1 Peter 2:22). Jesus simply told John, "We must carry out all that God requires." One theory: God wanted to link John to the messenger that the prophets said would prepare the way for the Messiah. *(Matthew 3)* ▶

BAPTISM. Many ancient cultures used water for spiritual cleansing. Jews took a ritual bath after touching a forbidden object, such as a corpse.

MESSIAH. It's a title. It means "Anointed One." Often it refers to kings and priests, commissioned in a ceremony of ritual anointing with oil. Prophets said God would send a unique king from David's family to restore glory to Israel: "He will be called...Mighty God...Prince of Peace.... He will rule with fairness...for all eternity" (Isaiah 9:6–7).

HOW JESUS RESISTS TEMPTATION. Out of the water, Jesus retreats into the badlands to fast and pray. Satan shows up and tries three times to lure him off-mission. Jesus resists by quoting the Bible: Deuteronomy 8:3, 6:16, and then 6:13.

:: **FOOD:** Turn stones into bread. "People do not live by bread alone, but by every word that comes from the mouth of God."

:: **EGO:** Jump and angels will catch you. "You must not test the LORD your God."

:: **POWER:** Worship me and I'll let you rule earth. "Worship the LORD your God and serve only him." *(Matthew 4)*

DISCIPLES: LESS THAN BRAINIACS. Rabbis in Jesus' day don't go shopping for disciples any more than college profs today go on recruiting trips for doctoral students. It's the other way around—student seeks teacher. Not with Jesus. He invites a dozen men to learn from him. Average Joes. Fishermen: Peter, Andrew, James, and John. A taxman: Matthew. And possibly an anti-Roman insurgent: Simon the Zealot. Years later, Jewish scholars will describe them as "ordinary men with no special training in the Scriptures" (Acts 4:13). *(Matthew 4, 9, 10)* ▲

SERMON ON A HILLSIDE. It's the most famous sermon Jesus ever preached—for two reasons: (1) It sums him up nicely, showcasing his big ideas; (2) The big ideas are huge, sometimes parking common sense in a tow-away zone.

:: **ENEMIES.** "Love your enemies. Let them bring out the best in you, not the worst."

:: **REVENGE.** "No more tit-for-tat stuff."

:: **ASSETS.** "Don't hoard treasure down here. . . . Stockpile treasure in heaven."

(Matthew 5–7 MSG) ▼

WHICH ONE: SERMON ON THE HILL OR PLAIN? Matthew calls it the Sermon on the Mount. Luke lowers the altitude—calling it the Sermon on the Plain (Luke 6:20–49). He shortens it, too. Just a fourth of what Matthew reports. Some say there are so many jaw-dropping surprises in Jesus' message that it's probably a collection of highlights from many sermons. Some hills in Galilee gently slope into plains, forming amphitheater-style seating. So the crowd could have gathered on both a hill and a plain.

Sculpture on Israel's Mount of Beatitudes, where tradition says Jesus preached the Sermon on the Mount

DOCTOR JESUS. Jesus quickly earns a reputation as a miracle worker—a rabbi who heals the sick. Once, he heals every sick person brought to him from the fishing village of Capernaum, "no matter what their diseases" (Luke 4:40). The diseases and other complaints include:

:: **DEMON POSSESSION**
:: **BLINDNESS**
:: **LEPROSY**
:: **FEVER**
:: **PARALYSIS**
:: **LAMENESS**
:: **SPEECH PROBLEMS**
:: **DEAFNESS**
:: **SHRIVELED HAND**
:: **HEAVY MENSTRUAL PERIOD**
:: **SWOLLEN ARMS, LEGS**
:: **DISMEMBERED EAR**

(Matthew 8, 9, 12)

Mosaic of Jesus healing a paralyzed man lowered from a roof to bypass the crowd

RAISING THE DEAD. Before Jesus rose from the dead himself, Bible writers say he raised three others from the dead.

:: **BOY, DIED THAT DAY**: The son of a widow from Nain (Luke 7:11–15).
:: **MAN, FOUR DAYS DEAD**: Lazarus, brother of Mary and Martha of Bethany (John 11).
:: **GIRL, JUST DIED**: Daughter of synagogue leader in Capernaum (Matthew 9:18–19, 23–26). ▲

WAS FAITH THE CURE? Ask a corpse. Jesus raised the dead, with no help from them. Yet faith often played a role in Jesus' miracles. He told a pair of blind men they would be healed, "because of your faith" (Matthew 9:29).

But faith didn't seem to be the source of Jesus' power. Sometimes he did miracles to help people grow some faith (Matthew 8:26).

RX CENTURY ONE. A natural science writer from Jesus' day, Pliny (AD 23–79), reported some of the treatments for diseases Jesus healed.

:: **Failing eyesight:** Mix fish fat with honey. Apply to eyes.
:: **Fever:** Get a nail used in crucifixion. Wrap it in wool. Apply to neck.
:: **Excessive menstrual bleeding:** Smash a jellyfish. Apply topically. ◄

Jesus forgives woman caught in adultery

WHAT'S THE UNFORGIVABLE SIN? "Every sin and blasphemy can be forgiven," Jesus said, "except blasphemy against the Holy Spirit." Some Christians say the unforgivable sin is insulting God—like telling him to go to hell. Most scholars disagree. They say Jesus was talking to Jewish leaders who, after watching him heal a man, said the power came from Satan. They refused to acknowledge God's involvement. Many scholars say God won't forgive sinful people who ignore him. Many pastors offer this advice: If you're worried you've committed the unforgivable sin, that's proof you haven't. *(Matthew 12:22–50)* ▲

EXPLAINING GOD TO A DIRT FARMER. Jesus often teaches with stories called *parables*. In one story, a farmer throws seeds onto a field. Some seeds take root. Some don't. Simple enough. But the seed and the soil represent spiritual truths:

SEED. It's Jesus' message about how to live as citizens of God's kingdom.

PACKED DIRT. Hard-hearted people reject the message.

ROCKY DIRT. Shallow people don't let the message take root.

THORNY DIRT. Worried people let fears choke out the message.

FERTILE DIRT. Others accept the message, producing a bumper crop for God's kingdom. *(Matthew 13:1–23)* ▼

Plowing Israel

PARABLES. These are stories from everyday life, with a spiritual message woven into the story line. There are many in the Bible, including one that the prophet Nathan told King David to confront him about his adultery with Bathsheba (2 Samuel 12:1–25). But most parables (40–65 of them) come from Jesus. Scholars don't always agree on which teachings qualify. One of the most famous: a story about a good Samaritan who helps an injured Jew (see page 418).

5,000 MEN SHARE TWO FISH. Jesus gets word that John the Baptist has been executed. He sails to a remote area to grieve. Crowds follow by land. When Jesus comes ashore, 5,000 men greet him, along with women and children—perhaps over 10,000 people. Moved, Jesus heals the sick. Then he tells his disciples to feed the crowd. They scrounge up one sack lunch: five small loves and two fish. It produces 12 baskets of leftovers. *(Matthew 14)* ▲

JESUS: A ROTTEN RABBI? News about Jesus piques the curiosity of Jewish scholars in Jerusalem. Several make the week's trek north to Galilee to see if Jesus checks out kosher. He doesn't. Sure, he heals people—a godly thing to do. But he's not supposed to practice medicine on the Sabbath day of rest. Also, his disciples don't wash before they eat. These aren't Bible rules Jesus is busting. They're rules the scholars made up: their take on how to apply Bible principles. Jesus isn't impressed. *(Matthew 15)*

LOOPHOLE TARGET: 10 COMMANDMENTS. Jesus rejects the man-made rules of Jewish scholars. He cites a rule that violates one of the 10 Commandments that says to honor your father and mother. The man-made rule said that anyone who didn't want to give money to their parents could declare that money as "devoted to God" (Matthew 15:5 NIV), which in that time meant it was reserved for the Temple. Not for Mom and Dad who may have needed it more. ▶

Statue in Israel commemorating Peter's declaration

JESUS WITH A HALO, AND THEN SOME. Perhaps just a few months before his crucifixion, Jesus takes his three closest disciples with him to pray on an unidentified hilltop. All three—Peter, James, and John—fall asleep. When they wake up, Jesus is transfigured into what sounds like a celestial being: "his face shone like the sun, and his clothes became white as light." Moses and Elijah appear with him. *(Matthew 17)* ▼

Among three top contenders for the Mount of Transfiguration, Mount Tabor has the oldest tradition.

PETER TO JESUS: "YOU'RE GOD'S SON." Jesus has something extra going for him. Many have that figured out. They just don't know what it is. Herod Antipas, the Galilean ruler who ordered John the Baptist executed, feared Jesus was John reincarnated (Mark 6:14). Some said Jesus was Elijah, citing Malachi 4:5. Peter's take: Jesus is "Messiah, the Son of the living God." That doesn't mean "deity," some say—kings were called God's son (2 Samuel 7:14). But Peter certainly links Jesus to deity after the Resurrection. *(Matthew 16)* ▲

BIBLE SHINERS. Moses glowed when he came down from Mount Sinai: "his face had become radiant" (Exodus 34:29). So did the angel at Jesus' resurrection: "His face shone like lightning, and his clothing was as white as snow" (Matthew 28:3).

JESUS, THE FINANCIAL ADVISOR. Sounding like he invented the vow of poverty, Jesus offers this advice to a rich young man: "Sell all your possessions and give the money to the poor. . . . Then come, follow me" (Matthew 19:21). No dice. The rich man walks off. All he had wanted to know was how to find eternal life. He hadn't figured it might cost him the good life. *(Matthew 19)*

DEITY ON A DONKEY. The Sunday before Friday's crucifixion, Jesus takes a short donkey ride over the Mount of Olives into Jerusalem. It's an easy walk. But he knows the prophecy that many Jews associate with the Messiah's arrival: "Shout in triumph, O people of Jerusalem! Look, your king is coming. . . . He is humble, riding on a donkey" (Zechariah 9:9). Passover crowds make the connection, too. Cheering, they welcome Jesus as royalty, paving his path with palm branches. *(Matthew 21)* ▼

WHAT DID JESUS HAVE AGAINST THE RICH? Nothing. Rich people helped fund his ministry (Luke 8:3). But for some rich folks, building their own kingdom can seem more important than building God's kingdom. That may be why Jesus offered this observation, which most scholars say is a slight exaggeration—for emphasis: "It is easier for a camel to go through the eye of a needle than for a rich person to enter the Kingdom of God!" (Matthew 19:24).

Model of Jesus drawn through German streets in about AD 1200 to commemorate Palm Sundays

JESUS' PET PEEVE: RELIGIOUS SHOW-OFFS.
Anti-intellectual is what Jesus could sound like—especially to the Jewish scholars he describes as children of hell. "Don't follow their example," he tells a Jerusalem crowd. "They don't practice what they teach. . . . Everything they do is for show." They:

:: love lofty titles: Rabbi, Teacher, Father
:: flaunt their prayer clothes
:: prefer to sit at the head of a table.

Dagger inserted, Jesus gives it a twist: "The greatest among you must be a servant." *(Matthew 23)* ▼

PARABLE OF USE IT OR LOSE IT. Jesus tells a story about a boss who entrusts big bucks to three of his workers: five bags of silver to one man, two to another, and one to another. The first two men each double the investment. The last man essentially hides it under the mattress. The boss fires him and gives his silver to the top moneymaker. Jesus doesn't explain the parable. But scholars give it a try: we should use whatever talents God gave us to build his kingdom. *(Matthew 25)*

PARABLE SILVER: HOW MUCH WAS IT? The Greek word for each bag of silver is talent: 75 pounds (34 kg). Each bag was worth about 15 years of salary for the average working man.

Russian Jew wearing prayer shawl and head box containing Bible verses

ONE LAST MEAL. A few hours before his arrest, Jesus gathers his dozen disciples in Jerusalem for the annual Passover meal. For Jews, it's a meal rich in symbolism: food and rituals recalling the Exodus, when God freed their ancestors from slavery. Jesus heaps on more symbolism: bread and wine will recall the sacrifice of his body and blood, freeing everyone from slavery to sin. *(Matthew 26)* ▲

GOD'S ANSWER TO JESUS' PRAYER: NO. After the Last Supper, Jesus leads 11 of his disciples out of the city to an olive grove on the nearby ridge: the Mount of Olives. He'll spend his last minutes as a free man in prayer. Sweating huge drops, Jesus prays: "Father, if there is any way, get me out of this." Judas—the disciple who sells out Jesus for a reward—arrives with Temple officers. They arrest Jesus. *(Matthew 26 MSG)*

Raising the "host," which some Christians say is the actual body of Christ

THE RITUAL OF COMMUNION. Christians eat a piece of bread and drink a sip of grape juice or wine as a worship ritual, to commemorate the sacrifice of Jesus. The ritual goes by many names: communion, Eucharist, Mass. Most Catholics and Eastern Orthodox teach that the bread and juice become the actual body and blood of Jesus. Most Protestants say the bread and juice represent his body and blood.

JESUS, DEAD AND BURIED. Called into emergency session, Jewish council members rush to the home of Caiaphas, the high priest. By dawn, they find Jesus guilty of being disrespectful to God—he claims he's God's Son. They tell the Roman governor, Pilate, that Jesus is also an insurrectionist—he claims he's king of the Jews. Jesus is crucified by about 9 a.m. and dead about six hours later. One member of the Jewish council, Joseph of Arimathea, boldly outs himself as a follower of Jesus: He asks Pilate for permission to bury Jesus. Granted. It's almost sundown on Friday, start of the Sabbath day of rest. No work allowed, including burial. So Joseph and others quickly wrap Jesus in a shroud laced with fragrant ointment. It's to mask the stench of decay. They lay Jesus in Joseph's family tomb. Sunday morning, they'll wash his body and give him a proper burial. So they think. *(Matthew 26–27)*

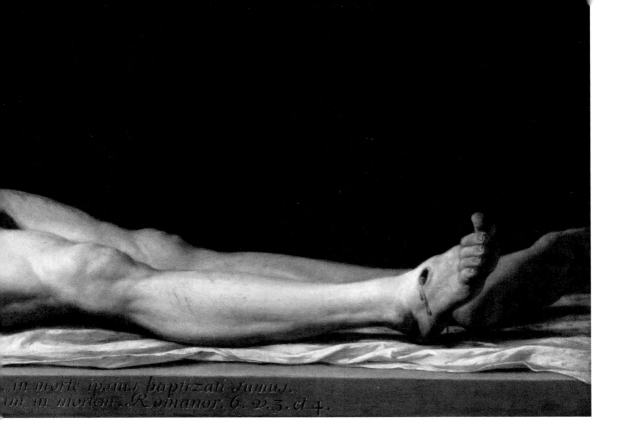

in morte ipsius baptizati sumus.
...in mortem. Romanor. 6. v. 3. et 4.

QUEST FOR THE TOMB OF JESUS. Most experts agree that what's left of Jesus' tomb is enshrined within Jerusalem's Church of the Holy Sepulchre. To get a sense of what a tomb carved out of rock looked like in Jesus' day, many tourists visit the nearby Garden Tomb and others in the area.

FIRST-CENTURY TOMB OF LEPER. DNA testing of a first-century shrouded man, buried in Jerusalem, confirms the oldest proven case of leprosy. So reports the medical journal *PLoS ONE*. Most corpses were buried twice. In the second burial, after the body's decomposition about a year later, the bones were placed in a stone box kept in the tomb. That opened up room on the slab for more burials later. But the leper was buried just once—his tomb sealed with plaster.

JESUS, UNDEAD AND WALKING.

Jewish scholars know that Jesus said he'd rise on the third day. They probably don't believe it. But they do believe his followers might steal the corpse and say he rose. They convince Pilate to post Roman guards at the tomb. Near dawn, soldiers watch in horror as a glowing angel rolls aside the massive stone blocking the tomb's entrance. They freeze, thaw, and run. They rush straight to the Jewish leaders, who bribe the guards to say that they fell asleep and the disciples stole Jesus' body. Mary Magdalene and some other woman arrive at the tomb. They're hoping to finish preparing Jesus for burial. Instead, an angel greets them: "He isn't here! He is risen." Within minutes, perhaps, Jesus appears. He asks the women to have his disciples meet him in Galilee. There, Jesus gives his followers a mission: "Go and make disciples of all the nations." *(Matthew 28)*

WHAT IF JESUS DIDN'T RISE FROM THE DEAD? In that case, Christians should find a new religion. The apostle Paul put it this way: "If Christ wasn't raised to life, our message is worthless, and so is your faith" (1 Corinthians 15:14 CEV).

DID A CHRISTIAN WRITER INVENT THE RESURRECTION STORY? If he did, experts say he should have had the sense to pick stronger witnesses than a gaggle of gals. The testimony of women was treated with skepticism:

> *Don't accept evidence from women. Rash and frivolous by nature, they shouldn't be taken seriously.*

> JOSEPHUS, FIRST-CENTURY JEWISH HISTORY WRITER

M A R K

JESUS, THE ACTION FIGURE

IN ONE SENTENCE

In the Bible's shortest, most action-packed story of Jesus, Mark skips nativity scenes with shepherds and wise men—instead, jumping right into the Jordan River baptism of Jesus, which launches a miracle-working ministry that ends with Jesus dead on a cross, but rising from the grave.

SOUND BITE

"Come with me. I'll show you how to catch people instead of fish."
—*Jesus, to fishermen brothers Peter and Andrew*
MARK 1:17 AUTHOR'S PARAPHRASE

ON LOCATION

TIME. Lifetime of Jesus, 6 BC–AD 33, give or take a few years.

PLACE. Israel.

NEWSMAKERS

JESUS, God's "dearly loved Son" (Mark 1:11).

TWELVE DISCIPLES. Jesus' handpicked students, training to spread his teachings.

PONTIUS PILATE, Roman governor of Judea. He issues the order to crucify Jesus.

ADVANCE MAN FOR JESUS. Jesus and John the Baptist are related (Luke 1:36). Both men likely know what angels told their parents about them. John: "He will prepare the people for the coming of the Lord" (Luke 1:17). Jesus: "He will be. . .called the Son of the Most High" (Luke 1:32). Before Jesus starts his ministry, John predicts, "Someone is coming soon who is greater than I am. . . . He will baptize you with the Holy Spirit!" *(Mark 1:1–15)* ▼

John the Baptist

JESUS' MISSION STRATEGY. It doesn't take long for Jesus to draw a crowd. His odd, two-part mission strategy guarantees it.

:: **HEALING.** He grabs everyone's attention by healing the sick. Not just minor illnesses. Leprosy. Paralysis. Demon possession. Astonished witnesses spread the word: "Even evil spirits obey his orders!"

:: **TEACHING.** He doesn't quote respected rabbis from generations past, as other teachers do. He speaks with the insight of a rabbi others will someday quote. *(Mark 1:21–2:12)*

Holy Spirit fills Jesus' followers at Pentecost festival

EXPLAIN: BAPTISM WITH HOLY SPIRIT. God gave people his Spirit only rarely in Old Testament times. The Spirit helped leaders like David accomplish big things. God promised that one day "I will give my Spirit to everyone" (Joel 2:28 CEV). This apparently happened after Jesus returned to heaven. His followers gathered for prayer and were "filled with the Holy Spirit" (Acts 2:4). They started teaching that Joel's prophecy had been fulfilled: God's Spirit was now available to everyone.

JESUS, DISSING THE SABBATH? One of the 10 Commandments says Jews aren't supposed to work on the seventh day of the week—the Sabbath. That's sundown Friday through sundown Saturday. What is work? Rabbis create a list of more than a thousand activities to avoid—including practicing medicine (healing) and plucking a snack of wheat kernels. Jesus rejects those rules, arguing, "The Sabbath was made for people, not people for the Sabbath" (Mark 2:27 TNIV).

JESUS TEACHES AG-ED THEOLOGY 101. Jesus knows how to talk to farmers. He grew up in Galilee, Israel's Kansas—the country's bread basket. To teach them about how big God's kingdom will become, he points out one of the tiniest seeds around: mustard. "It grows larger than any garden plant. . .big enough for birds to nest in its shade." Some scholars say Jesus was talking about his ministry. It starts with one person. It spreads throughout the world. *(Mark 4:30–34 CEV)* ▶

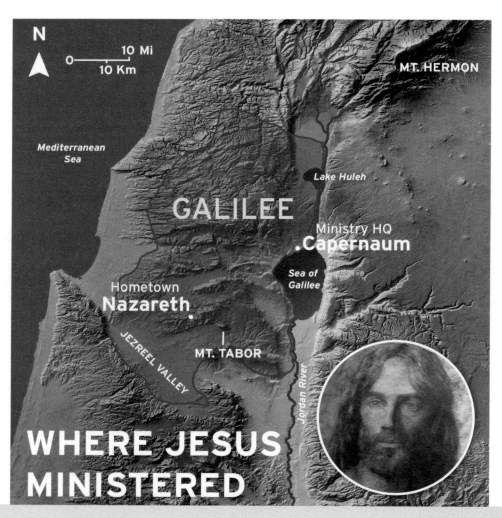

GALILEE FARMLAND. "Every inch of the soil has been cultivated by the locals," wrote first-century Jewish historian Josephus, describing Galilee in what is now northern Israel.

Farmland in Galilee's Jezreel Valley

Mustard field

MUSTARD SEED. Black mustard *(Brassica nigra)* grew on the shoreline of the Sea of Galilee. The seed measures about two millimeters. That's half the size of a BB. People crushed the seeds to produce cooking oil or to make strong-smelling mustard poultices—medicine bags placed over aching parts of the body.

EXORCIST. Jesus encounters a man loaded with demons. The demons talk: "My name is Legion, because there are many of us inside this man." A legion is the Roman army's largest unit of soldiers: 6,000 at full strength. Jesus allows the demons to enter a herd of 2,000 pigs, which rushes into the Sea of Galilee and drowns, perhaps destroying the demons, too. When the cured man spreads the word about what Jesus has done, everyone is amazed. *(Mark 5)*

JOHN THE HEADLESS. "He must become greater," John the Baptist says of Jesus. "I must become less" (John 3:30). It reads like the punch line to a joke about John's decapitation. But it refers to his job of preparing the way for Jesus: it is finished—and so is John. He condemns the marriage of Galilee's ruler, Herod Antipas, who takes his brother's ex-wife. Incest, John calls it. The Mrs. orders John's head on a platter. *(Mark 6:14–29)*

DEMON-POSSESSED PIGS? Scholars can only guess why Jesus allowed the demons to enter the herd of pigs. One theory: it symbolizes Jesus cleansing non-Jews (Gentiles), whom many Jews considered unclean—like pigs—and wouldn't touch. The story takes place in Gentile territory. Jesus cleanses a Gentile man by getting rid of "unclean spirits" as well as a herd of "unclean animals." Jews were forbidden to eat pork.

JESUS BAD-MOUTHS A LADY. Jesus takes a two-day walk north, into what is now Lebanon. A non-Jewish woman there has heard about him. She asks him to heal her daughter, who's demon-possessed. He refuses: "Jews first. It's not right to take food from God's children and toss it to the dogs." She presses: "Even the dogs get crumbs." He compliments her sharp wit and heals her daughter. *(Mark 7:14–30 AUTHOR'S PARAPHRASE)* ▼

WATER WALKER. Exhausted from ministry, Jesus retreats to the hills to pray and rest. He sends his disciples ahead, sailing to Bethsaida, a few miles east of Capernaum. They get caught in a windstorm churning huge waves. About 3 a.m. Jesus comes to their rescue—walking on water. They think he's a ghost, perhaps coming to get them. "Don't be afraid," he says, calming the water and climbing into the boat. *(Mark 6)*

WHY WAS JESUS SO NASTY? It was tongue in cheek, some explain. "Dogs" are what some Jews called non-Jews—like some Muslims today speak of non-Muslims as "infidels." Jesus went to non-Jewish territory to teach the very point the woman made: God isn't just the God of the Jews.

JESUS: "I'M GOING TO DIE." Jesus takes his disciples a day's walk north of Galilee to the foot of Mount Hermon. He tells them the Jewish leaders will soon kill him. They can't believe it. They had been expecting the Messiah to resurrect the Jewish nation, not to die trying. Jesus says he'll be the one resurrecting—after three days. They probably misunderstand. Some Jews say the spirit lingers by the corpse for three days before moving on to the afterlife. *(Mark 8:31–38)*

Bridesmaids waiting for groom's arrival

JESUS HATES DIVORCE. Jewish leaders in Jesus' day are split on divorce. Some say adultery is the only grounds. Others quote the vague grounds Moses gave: the husband finds "something wrong with her" (Deuteronomy 24:1). They argue that nearly any reason is a good reason. Jesus says no reason is a good reason: "Let no one split apart what God has joined together." Jesus sounds like his father: "I hate divorce!" (Malachi 2:16). *(Mark 10:1–12)* ▲

NO DIVORCE? EVER? Many Bible experts say Jesus wasn't forbidding divorce. He was lobbying for a sky-high view of marriage in the face of some Jews who treated it like dirt. He allowed divorce in cases of adultery (Matthew 5:32), just as he allowed the alternative: forgiveness (John 8:4–11). The apostle Paul allowed divorce in cases of abandonment (1 Corinthians 7:15). These weren't intended as the only grounds, many experts agree. They say Jesus wouldn't condemn someone to an abusive marriage.

PREPPING JESUS FOR BURIAL—BEFORE HE'S
DEAD. It's suppertime, Wednesday. In two days, Jesus will be dead. A healed leper is hosting supper in his Bethany home, on the outskirts of Jerusalem. Guest of honor: Jesus. A woman breaks open a flask of perfume worth a year's salary. She pours it on Jesus. Critics say she should have donated the cash value to the poor. But Jesus commends her for anointing him for burial. *(Mark 14:1–9)*

JESUS LOVES THE LITTLE CHILDREN OF THE
WORLD. Acting like Jesus' handlers, the disciples shoo away parents who want Jesus to place his hands on their children and bless them. "Don't push these children away," Jesus says, ticked. "Unless you accept God's kingdom in the simplicity of a child, you'll never get in." Jesus picks up a kid and starts blessing one after another. Later, he'll tell his disciples to start acting more like servant children than bossy grown-ups. *(Mark 10:13–16, 35–45 MSG)*

BURIAL PERFUME. Jews able to afford it kept scented oil for funerals. They poured it on the corpse to mask the smell of decay. They also used it to welcome guests, pouring some on their head and feet. Jesus will die at the beginning of Sabbath, sundown on Friday. His loved ones won't have time to wash and anoint his body.

Roman jug from Jesus' lifetime

ARRESTING JESUS. Judas leaves the Last Supper early. He knows Jesus is going to pray in an olive grove. And he knows the Jews want to arrest Jesus quietly, away from the Passover crowds who think he's the Messiah. Judas leads arresting officers to Jesus, for a reward of 30 silver coins—worth four months' salary. Jews rush Jesus through an overnight trial. By 9 a.m. Friday, Jesus hangs on a cross. *(Mark 14)*

HE'S ALIVE AGAIN. Dead by 3 p.m., Jesus is lying in a tomb before sundown, when Sabbath begins. His loved ones have to wait until Sunday morning to prepare his body for burial. But when women arrive at first light, they're greeted by a young man described in other reports as an angel. "He is risen from the dead!" the angel says. "Now go and tell his disciples." *(Mark 16)*

JESUS' RESURRECTION IN ROMAN HISTORY.
From the first-century book *Antiquities of the Jews*:

There was a wise man who was called Jesus, and his conduct was good. . . . Pilate condemned him to be crucified. . . . His disciples didn't abandon their loyalty to him. They reported that he appeared to them three days after his crucifixion, and that he was alive.

JOSEPHUS, JEWISH HISTORIAN (ABOUT AD 37–100)

L U K E

CALL HIM JESUS

IN ONE SENTENCE

As predicted by the angel Gabriel, Mary gives birth to Jesus—Son of God—who grows into a religion teacher and healer who's executed at the insistence of Jewish leaders, but who rises from the dead to give his followers a mission: Tell his story to the world.

SOUND BITE

"Your savior is born today in David's city. He is Christ the Lord."
—*Angel, to Bethlehem shepherds*
LUKE 2:11 CEB

ON LOCATION

TIME. Lifetime of Jesus, 6 BC–AD 33, give or take a few years.

PLACE. Israel.

NEWSMAKERS

JESUS, God's Son. He comes to save everyone—not just the Jews—from sin.

TWELVE DISCIPLES, students of Jesus. They help him in his ministry while learning from him.

MARY, mother of Jesus. She gives birth to Jesus in Bethlehem.

JOSEPH, husband of Mary. He's the legal father of Jesus.

PONTIUS PILATE, Roman governor of Judea. He orders Jesus crucified.

GABRIEL: "GREETINGS, FAVORED WOMAN!"

Mary is probably still a teenager, if her family observed marriage customs of the day. Teen or not, she gets a shocker of a visit. The angel Gabriel shows up with news. Mary, fiancée of the carpenter Joseph, is going to have a baby. "How?" Mary asks, "I am a virgin." God's Spirit. That's all the explanation Luke records. The child will be a boy: "Son of the Most High. . . . His Kingdom will never end." *(Luke 1)* ◄

BARN-BORN BETHLEHEM BABY. Joseph travels to his ancestral hometown for a census. Bethlehem was the home of his most famous forebear: King David. Mary joins Joseph on the three-day trek from Nazareth, south about 60 miles (100 km). The only shelter left in the village is with livestock, perhaps in a cave. Mary delivers Jesus there. She lays him in a feeding trough. Glowing angels flood the night sky, directing a crew of shepherds to "the Savior. . .born today in Bethlehem." *(Luke 2:1–20)* ▼

Cave below Bethlehem's Church of the Nativity, where an ancient tradition says Jesus was born

GABRIEL. One of two angels the Bible mentions by name; Michael is the other. Six centuries before Gabriel talked to Mary, he explained the meaning of a vision to the prophet Daniel (Daniel 8:16). Six months before Gabriel predicted the birth of Jesus, he predicted the birth of John the Baptist (Luke 1:13).

JESUS, THE PRE-TEEN. Adolescent Jesus talks once in the Bible. To some, he sounds like an adolescent: naïve, insolent. He's 12. His family comes to Jerusalem to celebrate the Jewish Passover festival, traveling with a group. On the trip home Joseph and Mary pitch camp and realize he's missing. Three days later, they find him in the Temple with scholars. Mary chews him out. But he says she should have known where to look. Luke quickly adds, Jesus "was obedient." *(Luke 2:41–52)* ▶

UNNEIGHBORLY NEIGHBORS: "THROW JESUS OFF A CLIFF." Ministry launched, fame rising, Jesus returns to Nazareth. Big mistake, as far as his former neighbors are concerned. He reads aloud a prophecy that Jews say describes what the Messiah will do: "Free everyone who suffers." Jesus says he's the fulfillment of that prediction—implying he's the Messiah. He's a carpenter's kid to them. And a liar. Rioting, they drag him outside to throw him off a cliff. He slips away. *(Luke 4:14–30 CEV)* ▼

Statue of boy from Roman times

Tourists at Nazareth cliff

LUKE WHO? The writer of this Gospel, according to early church leaders, was an associate of the apostle Paul: "Luke, the beloved doctor" (Colossians 4:14). Luke gives us a doc's take on Jesus' story:

:: the most detailed version of Jesus' birth

:: the only account of Jesus' parable of the Good Samaritan who helped an injured traveler

:: emphasis on Jesus' concern for the needy.

Capernaum

PARALYSIS BE GONE; SINS, TOO. Jesus adopts the fishing village of Capernaum as his ministry headquarters. He's preaching inside a packed house when some men try to carry a paralyzed buddy to Jesus for healing. Unable to fight through the crowd, they retreat and tear a hole in the roof. They lower their buddy to Jesus. Impressed at such chutzpah faith, Jesus forgives the man's sins. For scholars standing there thinking forgiveness is God's business, Jesus shows his divinity by healing the man as well. *(Luke 5:17–22)* ▲

SOLDIER NEEDS A RABBI. Actually, it's the soldier's servant in need—and not just of any rabbi. The servant needs Jesus, who can heal. Luke says the servant is almost dead. Matthew says he's a boy "paralyzed and in terrible pain" (Matthew 8:6). The soldier understands orders. He asks Jesus to simply give the order for a healing. No need to go in person. Jesus says he hasn't seen faith like that anywhere. He gives the order. The boy is healed, long-distance. *(Luke 7)* ▶

WHO'S THE SOLDIER? A Roman centurion—commander of 100 soldiers. Apparently stationed near Capernaum, he was also a friend of the Jews. He bankrolled construction of Capernaum's synagogue. Many Jews refused to go into the homes of non-Jews; it would make them ritually unclean. That may be why the soldier refused Jesus' offer to go home with him—he was trying to protect Jesus.

Roman centurion reenactment

JESUS: STORM-CHASER. Exhausted from teaching a crowd near Capernaum, Jesus retreats with his disciples to a small boat. They begin sailing across the lake to the village of Gergesa. Jesus falls into a sleep so deep that he doesn't wake up when a windstorm erupts, whipping huge waves that threaten the boat. Terrified, the disciples wake Jesus. "Silence," he says to the wind. Suddenly, it's Lake Placid. *(Luke 8:22–25)*

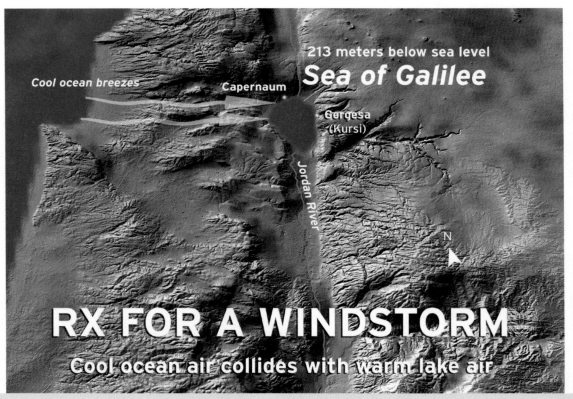

213 meters below sea level
Sea of Galilee

Cool ocean breezes

Capernaum

Gergesa
(Kursi)

Jordan River

N

RX FOR A WINDSTORM
Cool ocean air collides with warm lake air

INSTANT WINDSTORMS ON THE SEA OF GALILEE. This shallow lake is a perfect cauldron for stirring up sudden windstorms. It lies near the Mediterranean Sea, about 700 feet (213 meters) below sea level. When cool sea breezes ride the ravines down into the cauldron, colliding with afternoon or evening heat rising off the sun-baked lake, the winds that develop can stir up choppy waves.

A FEMALE THING. One woman in a crowd touches Jesus and is healed. But she feels guilty. She suffered from what sounds like excessive menstrual bleeding. Jewish law says that anyone she touches becomes ritually unclean—temporarily unfit to worship in the Temple. She's worried that Rabbi Jesus will scold her for doing this to him. "Daughter," he says, "your faith has made you well. Go in peace." *(Luke 8)*

ANCIENT RX FOR HEAVY MENSTRUAL BLEEDING. Mark's version of the story said the woman spent all her money looking for a cure (Mark 5:26). First-century Roman science writer, Pliny, lists scores of treatments for this very problem. Among them:

:: Mix ashes of a horse's head with vinegar, apply topically.
:: Mix ashes of donkey excrement with vinegar, apply with wool.
:: Smash a jellyfish; apply.

JESUS KEEPS BAD COMPANY. You can tell a rabbi by the company he keeps. So say Jewish scholars. Good rabbis keep godly company. But Jesus hangs out with hookers, tax collectors, and an assortment of other lowlifes. Jesus argues that the scholars have it backward. Rabbis are spiritual guides. Lost souls are their mission. Jesus hammers his point with three parables about lost things:

:: a sheep

:: a coin

:: a prodigal son. *(Luke 15)*

GOOD SAMARITAN FIRST AID. Jews know that their law says "Love your neighbor as yourself" (Leviticus 19:18). But many insist that only fellow Jews qualify as neighbors. One scholar asks for Jesus' opinion. Jesus answers with a parable: A Jew walking on the desolate trail between Jerusalem and Jericho gets mugged. A priest and a Temple worker each ignore him. It's a Samaritan—a man from a race hated by many Jews—who stops to help. At parable's end, Jesus asks who in the story acted like a neighbor. Everyone knows. *(Luke 10:25–38)* ▲

PRAYER: KEEP IT SHORT. Jesus isn't a fan of religious fanfare. In his famous Sermon on the Mount he says, "Don't be like the hypocrites who love to pray publicly on street corners and in the synagogues where everyone can see them" (Matthew 6:5). Pray privately. Keep it short. Then he shows his disciples how, with what becomes known as the Lord's Prayer—20 seconds of heart-to-heart with God. *(Luke 11:1–4)*

SAMARITANS. They were a mixed race descended from Jews who, 700 years earlier, married Assyrian immigrants from what is now Iraq. The animosity between Jews and Samaritans was a bit like that of Jews and Palestinians today. "Those who eat the food of Samaritans," one rabbi wrote, "are like those who eat pig" (*Shev'it* 8:10). Jewish law forbids eating pork.

MUGGER'S HEAVEN. Jesus set his parable in the Judean badlands between Jericho and Jerusalem, a barren and dangerous stretch for lone travelers. ▼

TAX COLLECTOR GETS RELIGION. Heading to Jerusalem, where he'll soon die, Jesus arrives in the garden city of Jericho. Crowds swarm him. Likely, the popular Jesus can stay anywhere he wants that night. But he invites himself into the home of Zacchaeus, the local tax collector—one of Jericho's most hated men. Jesus rubs off on him. By the next day, Zacchaeus vows to give half his money to the poor—and a quadruple tax refund to anyone he overcharged. *(Luke 19:1–10)*

Tax collectors, seldom flattered in art

WHY HATE A TAX COLLECTOR? They were Jewish traitors, getting rich off their own people. They collaborated with Roman occupiers by collecting taxes from fellow Jews—often overcharging and keeping the extra to pad their profit margin. Rabbis went on the record saying it was okay to lie to taxmen. Even big lies: "that you're a member of the king's family and exempt" (Mishnah, *Nedarium* 3:4).

JESUS' FIVE TRIALS IN 12 HOURS. Crowds waving palm branches welcome Jesus as he rides into Jerusalem on a donkey. Christians will dub the day Palm Sunday. Thursday night, Jews arrest Jesus while he's praying alone. What follows are five trials or hearings.

:: **ANNAS,** retired high priest. Officers take Jesus here first, possibly for an interrogation.

:: **CAIAPHAS,** high priest. He leads the Jewish high court in an overnight trial, convicting Jesus of blasphemy.

:: **PONTIUS PILATE,** Roman governor of Judea.

When he learns that Jesus comes from Galilee, he sends him to the Galilean ruler, in town for the Passover festival.

:: **HEROD ANTIPAS, RULER OF GALILEE.** He sends Jesus back to Pilate, dressed in a royal robe—as a joke.

:: **PONTIUS PILATE.** After resisting Jewish pressure to crucify Jesus, Pilate caves.

Jesus is hanging on the cross by about 9 a.m. on Friday, as Mark reports it. He's dead by about 3 p.m. and in a tomb before the 6 p.m. sunset. *(Luke 22–23)*

WHY DID PILATE CAVE TO JEWISH PRESSURE? To save his own skin, perhaps. Bible experts who claim Jesus died in about AD 33 say Pilate was already on shaky ground with Caesar Tiberius. That's because Sejanus, the Roman official who had recommended Pilate for the job of governing Judea, had been executed during an attempted coup in AD 31, along with many of his allies. Jews told Pilate, "If you release this man, you are no 'friend of Caesar' " (John 19:12).

WHAT WAS JESUS' CAPITAL OFFENSE? Jews leveled one charge, Romans another.

:: **Jews: Disrespecting God.** They said he claimed to be "the Son of God" (Luke 22:70).

:: **Romans: Insurrection.** When Jews realized Pilate wouldn't execute Jesus for religious reasons, they said Jesus claimed to be the Messiah, the long-awaited king of the Jews (Luke 23:2–3).

BREAKING BREAD WITH A DEAD MAN. Sunday afternoon, two of Jesus' followers are walking to the village of Emmaus about seven miles (11 km) from Jerusalem. As they walk, they lament the crucifixion. Jesus shows up, somehow disguised, and joins the conversation, reminding them that the prophets said the Messiah would suffer. By the time the men recognize him—when he blesses their food at a meal—he disappears. The two rush back to Jerusalem to tell the disciples about their Jesus sighting. *(Luke 24:13–34)* ▼

RESURRECTION: MORE THAN SPIRIT. Just as the two Emmaus followers are shocking the disciples with their eyewitness story, Jesus drops by. "Peace be with you," he says. Not a chance. They're terrified. They think he's a ghost. He's not. "Touch me," he says. He eats fish, too. Eventually calmed down, the disciples listen to him explain how prophets said he would suffer, die, and rise again. Weeks later, as Luke reports in Acts 1, they watch him ascend into the sky. *(Luke 24:36–53)*

RESURRECTION BODY. Some students of the Bible wonder if believers in the afterlife will be able to do the kinds of things Jesus did after his resurrection:

:: suddenly appear and disappear (Luke 24:13, 15, 31)

:: pass through walls of a locked house (John 20:19)

:: eat (Luke 24:42)

:: levitate (Acts 1:8–9).

JOHN

GOD, WITH A HEARTBEAT

IN ONE SENTENCE

Jesus—who existed with God the Father from the beginning of time—comes to earth on a suicide mission to save humans from the deadly effects of sin, and to show them how they can have eternal life.

SOUND BITE

"God loved the world so much that he gave his one and only Son. Anyone who believes in him will not die but will have eternal life."
—*Jesus, speaking to a Jewish leader named Nicodemus*
JOHN 3:16 NIrV

ON LOCATION

TIME. Lifetime of Jesus, 6 BC–AD 33, give or take a few years.

PLACE. Israel.

NEWSMAKERS

JESUS, Divine Son of God. He offers himself as a sacrifice for the sins of humanity.

TWELVE DISCIPLES, students of Jesus. They're working-class men handpicked by Jesus as his apprentices in ministry.

JOHN THE BAPTIST, prophet. A relative of Jesus, John baptizes him and introduces him as the Lamb of God.

PONTIUS PILATE, Roman governor of Judea. He sentences Jesus to death by crucifixion.

HOW JOHN SPOTTED THE MESSIAH. John the Baptist knows that he and his relative, Jesus, are destined for greatness. Their mothers likely compared notes about their sons' celestial birth announcements (Luke 1). But John says that only after he saw the Spirit descend on Jesus at the baptism did he realize Jesus was the Messiah. Afterward, John boldly introduces him as "the Lamb of God who takes away the sin of the world!" *(John 1:19–34)*

JESUS IN THE BEGINNING. Calling Jesus the *Word*—a term Greek philosophers used to talk about the mysterious force that powers everything in the universe—John places Jesus at the beginning of time. The Word:

:: "was with God"
:: "was God"
:: "created everything"
:: "gave life to everything that was created"
:: "became human and made his home among us." *(John 1:1–14)*

Jesus turns water into wine at a wedding in Cana.

JESUS' FIRST MIRACLE: CHEERS. Embarrassing to some Bible readers, Jesus' first miracle on record is to whip up enough wine at a wedding to get every adult in the village of Cana too drunk to drive a donkey cart. Not that it does. But it likely could have. Scholars say Cana was tiny and the Bible says wine was plentiful: at least 120 gallons (454 liters). This miracle is one of only seven reported in John's Gospel. *(John 2)* ▲

SECOND BIRTH—THIS ONE SPIRITUAL. A Jewish scholar, Nicodemus, tells Jesus that he believes the miracles of Jesus prove that his power comes from God. Jesus says that's not enough. He says that just as we're born in the flesh, we have to be born in the spirit—born again. The conversation, conducted privately at night to protect Nicodemus's reputation, produces the Bible's most famous quote: see Sound Bite, page 422. *(John 3)*

SEVEN MIRACLES, SIGNS OF DEITY. Many scholars say that each miracle John reports is intended to reveal some aspect of Jesus' deity.

1. **Turns water into wine:** creation power (John 2:1–12).
2. **Heals by long-distance:** not limited by geography (John 4:46–54).
3. **Heals on Sabbath day of rest:** not limited by time (John 5:1–17).
4. **Feeds 5,000:** He's the bread of life, physical and spiritual (John 6:1–15).
5. **Walks on water:** master of his creation (John 6:16–22).
6. **Heals the blind:** He's the light of the world, physical and spiritual (John 9:1–41).
7. **Raises Lazarus:** stronger than death (John 11:1–44).

JESUS, THE GREAT I AM. The day after Jesus feeds thousands with two fish and five slabs of bread, the crowd returns. Not for teaching, Jesus says. For food. He tells them to stop obsessing over physical things. Start searching for the spiritual. Then, he points out what he can offer them spiritually—invoking the "I AM" name of God (Exodus 3:14).

"I AM the":

:: **"BREAD OF LIFE"** (John 6:35): spiritual nourishment
:: **"LIGHT OF THE WORLD"** (John 8:12): insight
:: **"GATE FOR THE SHEEP"** (John 10:7): door to heaven
:: **"GOOD SHEPHERD"** (John 10:14): protector
:: **"RESURRECTION"** (John 11:25): source of eternal life
:: **"WAY, THE TRUTH, AND THE LIFE"** (John 14:6): highway to heaven
:: **"TRUE GRAPEVINE"** (John 15:1): spiritual nourishment.

JESUS AND THE LOOSE LADY. Five ex-husbands and a live-in lover—that's the track record of a woman Jesus meets at a well in the Samaritan village of Sychar. She's double-dip shocked he asks her for a drink, since (1) rabbis avoid women and (2) Jews avoid Samaritans. He tells her enough of her private history to convince her he's a prophet, and then he offers her "living water" for spiritual thirst. He stays two days, converting many villagers. *(John 4)* ▲

SYCHAR. It's Nablus today, some Bible scholars say. Ironically, this West Bank city in central Israel is populated mainly by Palestinians. In Jesus' day, Jews and Samaritans were about as unfriendly toward each other as many Israelis and Palestinians are today. ▶

BRING YOUR OWN BUCKET. Jesus probably had to ask for help getting a drink at the well because this well, like many, wasn't equipped with ropes or buckets. Villagers brought their own.

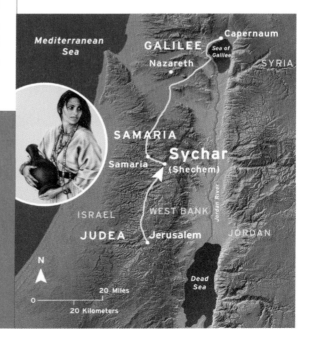

JESUS: HERE'S MUD IN YOUR EYE. Jesus treated the blind man by dabbing his eyes with dirt moistened with spit. Perhaps Jesus used the mud to help the man's faith, some say, since this was a common eye treatment in Roman times. Rx for eye inflammation:

∷ Wash eyes each morning with spit.

∷ When you wash your feet, touch your eyes three times with the muddy water.

PLINY, ROMAN SCIENCE WRITER (AD 23–79, *NATURAL HISTORY*)

BLIND MAN OPENS THE EYES OF DISCIPLES.

Jesus' disciples see a beggar who was born blind. They ask Jesus if God was punishing him or his parents. Many Jews figure that since God is just, people who suffer are getting what they deserve. Wrong. "This happened so the power of God could be seen in him," Jesus says. Then he heals the man. Miracles like this convince thousands that Jesus' power comes from God. *(John 9)*

UP. Jesus gets word that a friend is deathly sick: Lazarus, the brother of Mary and Martha. Jesus is perhaps a two-day walk away, in a city east of the Jordan River. Sounding like a terrible emergency responder, Jesus kicks back until Lazarus kicks the bucket. By the time Jesus shows up, Lazarus is four days dead and smelling like it. Four days is one day longer than Jews believe the soul lingers by its corpse. Jesus raises Lazarus with one sentence: "Lazarus, come out!" *(John 11)* ▼

Resurrection of Lazarus

JESUS ON FOOT PATROL. John skips the Last Supper (page 397). Instead, he reports something remarkable that Jesus does during the meal. Jesus wraps a towel around his waist, pours water in a bowl, and starts washing the feet of his disciples. Peter objects. Jesus insists. It's an object lesson, "an example to follow." Jesus wants these future leaders of the church to think of themselves as servants. If Jesus can take on the role of a servant, he explains, they can, too. *(John 13:1–17)* ▲

HIGHWAY TO HEAVEN, VIA JESUS. "I am the way, the truth, and the life," Jesus tells his disciples. "No one can come to the Father except through me" (NLT). What's odd about this is that Jesus adds something. He says he's not only the way to the Father, he is the living image of the Father: "Anyone who has seen me has seen the Father!" (NLT). Yet to come: "the Holy Spirit who will help you" (CEV). A trinity that's separate, yet somehow one. *(John 14 CEV)*

IS THE CHOICE JESUS OR HELL? Some Christians say yes: if we're not on the Christian road, we're headed the wrong way. Others speculate that we'll be able to accept Jesus in the afterlife. Still others say a person's eternal destiny is best left to God—that it's not our call and that God's not limited by our interpretation of the Bible.

TRYING TO FIGURE OUT THE TRINITY. Don't bother. That's what many scholars say. The best minds in early Christianity tried and failed. They decided to punt—to believe in the Trinity because the Bible teaches it.

> *We don't understand the mystery of how this can be [three Gods in one]. . . . But we trust the evidence of this truth.*
>
> AMBROSE, ITALIAN BISHOP (ABOUT AD 340–397)

GOD IS DEAD. Jewish leaders in Jerusalem manage to arrest Jesus when he's praying at night, away from admiring crowds who might have defended him. After an all-night secret trial, the Jewish high council led by Caiaphas, the high priest, convicts him of disrespecting God by claiming to be God's Son. They convince Roman governor Pilate to order him crucified immediately for a different crime—one Romans could relate to: insurrection. By claiming to be King of the Jews—Jesus was rebelling against Caesar. So said the Jews.

:: **BEATEN**. Romans often beat victims with whips embedded with chunks of metal and bone.

He [a victim of crucifixion] was whipped until his bones showed.

JOSEPHUS (ABOUT AD 37–101)

:: **MARCHED**. Jesus carries his crossbeam.

Each criminal who goes to execution must carry his own cross on his back.

PLUTARCH (AD 46–ABOUT 120)

:: **NAILED**. Soldiers nail the victim to a cross.

Anyone facing such a death would plead to die rather than mount the cross.

SENECA (ABOUT 4 BC–65 AD)

:: **LANCED**. To confirm Jesus' death, a soldier drives a spear into his side, probably upward toward the heart.

Pilate grants the request of one of Jesus' supporters on the Jewish high council—Joseph of Arimathea—allowing him to claim the body and bury it. *(John 19)*

JOHN'S REASON FOR WRITING THIS GOSPEL. Everything in this unique biography of Jesus pushes the reader toward John's one goal: "that you may believe that Jesus is the Christ, the Son of God" (John 20:31 NCV).

Removing the body of Jesus from the Cross

RESURRECTION SKEPTIC: DOUBTING THOMAS.

Jesus rises from the tomb before dawn on Sunday. Piecing together all the Gospel reports, there are three Jesus sightings that day:

:: **WOMEN**. Mary Magdalene and other women at the tomb before dawn.

:: **WALKERS GOING TO EMMAUS**. Two followers apparently returning home from the crucifixion (see page 421)

:: **10 DISCIPLES**. They're gathered in a locked house. Judas is dead—suicide. Thomas is away at the moment, perhaps buying supplies.

When the 10 tell Thomas they saw Jesus, Thomas says he'll believe it when he sees it. Eight days later, Jesus returns. He invites Thomas to touch his healed wounds. No need. Jesus replies, "Blessed are those who believe without seeing me." *(John 20)*

Honduras woman visited by a medical mission team from the United States

JESUS' PRAYER FOR BELIEVERS TODAY. At the Last Supper, hours before his arrest and execution, Jesus prays a tender prayer not only for his disciples, but for followers yet to come:

"I'm praying for everyone who will believe in me because of what these men will say and do in the days ahead. Unite them in their mission, just as you and I are united— one heart, one mind. Let the world see me in them and you in me. Like Father, like Son—and all God's children."

JOHN 17:20–21 AUTHOR'S PARAPHRASE

A meal in Emmaus

A C T S

TIME FOR CHURCH

IN ONE SENTENCE

The church is born after Jesus returns to heaven and sends the Holy Spirit in his place to give his followers death-defying boldness and miracle-working power.

SOUND BITE

"You will be my witnesses, telling people about me everywhere—in Jerusalem, throughout Judea, in Samaria, and to the ends of the earth."
—*Jesus, giving his last instructions to his disciples before he ascends into the sky*
ACTS 1:8

ON LOCATION

TIME. Spanning more than 30 years, from the early AD 30s to the AD 60s.

PLACE. Middle Eastern countries including Israel, Egypt, Syria, Lebanon, Turkey, Greece, Italy, Cyprus, and Crete.

NEWSMAKERS

PAUL, a missionary. Also known by his Hebrew name, Saul, this one-time prosecutor of Christians not only converts to the religion, he starts churches all over the empire.

PETER, leader of the disciples. His sermon to crowds in Jerusalem about two months after the crucifixion launches the Christian movement.

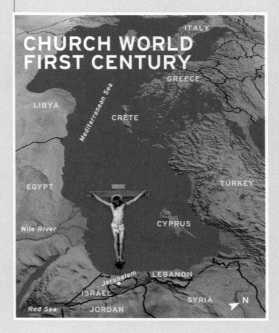

CHURCH WORLD
FIRST CENTURY

ITALY
GREECE
LIBYA
CRETE
Mediterranean Sea
EGYPT
TURKEY
Nile River
CYPRUS
Jerusalem
LEBANON
ISRAEL
SYRIA
Red Sea
JORDAN
N

GOOD-BYE, JESUS; HELLO WORLD. Six weeks after his resurrection, Jesus appears one last time to his disciples. He takes them to the Mount of Olives, a ridge across the valley beside Jerusalem. Before ascending into the sky, he tells them to wait in Jerusalem for the Holy Spirit who will give them power and guidance for their ministry ahead: spreading the story of his life and teachings "to the ends of the earth." *(Acts 1)*

GOD'S RETURN, IN SPIRIT. About 10 days later, when Jews celebrate the harvest festival of Pentecost, God's Spirit arrives. The sound of a windstorm fills the building where 120 believers have been waiting. Glowing auras, like tongues of fire, hover over each soul. Outside, crowds hear the noise and come running. Peter tells them that (1) this miracle fulfills prophecy and (2) Jesus rose from the dead. Peter's words, backed up by miracles, convince some 3,000. The church is born. *(Acts 2)*

INSTANT FOREIGN LANGUAGE SKILLS. After the Spirit arrives, the believers open their mouths to speak. To everyone's surprise the believers find themselves talking in languages they had never learned—languages spoken by Jewish pilgrims from abroad who have crowded into Jerusalem for the religious holiday. Everyone is able to hear about Jesus in their own language.

Gemini, the twins

THE CHURCH'S ASTROLOGICAL SIGN: GEMINI. The church was born near the end of May. Scholars debate both the year and the day. If the Holy Spirit arrived in AD 33, as many scholars contend, Pentecost and the first mass conversions to Christianity may have fallen on May 25. That makes the church a Gemini. In Greek mythology, the Gemini's god was Mercury—the messenger god—ironic because the church's mission is to spread Jesus' message about the real God.

TELLING THE DISCIPLES TO CORK IT. Temple guards arrest Peter and John for preaching about Jesus on Temple property. The disciples end up standing in front of the same high council that had condemned Jesus to death a few weeks ear- lier. Council leaders order the disciples to stop talking about Jesus. The disciples reply, "Do you think God wants us to obey you rather than him? We cannot stop." Reluctantly, the council releases them rather than risk a riot. (*Acts 3–4*)

After lying about her offering, Sapphira drops dead—as her husband, Ananias, had done earlier, after telling the same lie.

DONATE MONEY AND DIE. Disciples heap praise on a believer who sells some property and gives the money to the disciples to distribute among the poor. One attention-starved married couple, Ananias and Sapphira, decide they could afford a little praise. They sell some property. They keep part of the money. But they tell the disciples they're donating the full amount. Somehow, Peter knows better. When he accuses them of lying to God, they collapse. Dead. (*Acts 4–5*) ▲

DID GOD KILL THE DONORS? Probably, say many scholars who've studied the story in the original Greek language. Adding irony to oddity, *Ananias* means "God is merciful." Apparently not this day. On the other hand, some argue, this tragedy taught Christians not to mess with God or his ministers at this pivotal moment in history: the liftoff of the church.

FIRST MAN KILLED FOR BEING CHRISTIAN.
As the church's compassionate ministry program grows, the disciples appoint seven men to take care of the poor. Stephen is one of them. Christians are Jews, at this point, still worshipping in synagogues. Stephen gets in an argument at the synagogue, probably about Jesus. He ends up before the Jewish council. Politically incorrect, he accuses them and their ancestors of murdering righteous people, including the Messiah and the prophets. Proving his point, they stone him to death. *(Acts 6–7)* ▼

PAUL: HARD CASE GETS HARD SELL. The scent of Christian blood drives the Jewish leaders into a heretic-hunting frenzy. They start arresting Jerusalem-area Christians, many of whom scatter abroad—taking their religion with them. Jews send Paul to Damascus to arrest any Christian who fled there. On the way, he's blinded by a light—and he hears Jesus tell him to wait in Damascus for instructions. A Christian arrives and heals his blindness. Paul switches sides, becoming a Christian. *(Acts 8–9)*

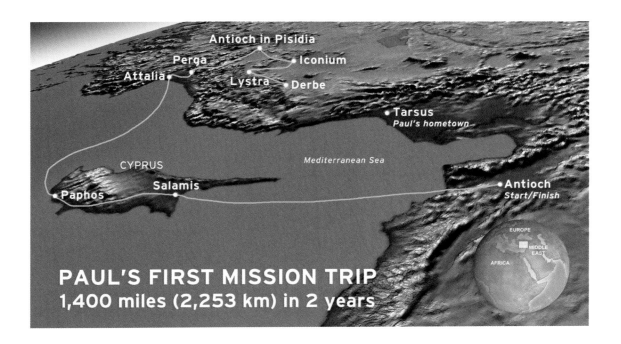

PAUL'S FIRST MISSION TRIP
1,400 miles (2,253 km) in 2 years

Pork chops—not kosher

GOD: NON-JEWS ARE KOSHER. Many Jews avoid non-Jews as much as they avoid pork on a platter. Both: non-kosher. But Peter has a vision that changes his opinion of non-Jews. God tells him to eat non-kosher animals. Then God arranges for a God-loving Roman soldier—a Gentile—to send messengers to get Peter. By the time Peter arrives, he has figured out the vision: God accepts believers of all races. The Holy Spirit fills the soldier, astonishing Jews who have accompanied Peter. *(Acts 10)*

TAKING JESUS ON THE ROAD. At first, the story of Jesus spreads like gossip. Believers travel, taking their beliefs with them. But roughly a dozen years after Jesus' ascension, Paul and Barnabas feel compelled by the Holy Spirit to take a leave of absence from co-pastoring in Antioch and carry the message of Jesus to their homelands. For the next two years, they travel some 1,400 miles (2,253 km) starting churches in Cyprus, Barnabas' home, and in southern Turkey, Paul's home. Paul skips his hometown of Tarsus, where he had already spent time as a Christian. *(Acts 13–14)* ▲

FILLED WITH THE HOLY SPIRIT. The Bible doesn't say how Peter and his associates could tell that the Roman soldier, Cornelius, received the Holy Spirit. When the Spirit came to the disciples, there was a sound of wind, a glow, and the ability to speak in unlearned human languages. But elsewhere in Paul's writings, some spoke unintelligible sounds—"the language. . .of angels" (1 Corinthians 13:1). Others prophesied.

FIRST CHURCH SPLIT. As more non-Jews join the Christian movement, some leaders insist Christianity is a branch of the Jewish faith. So they insist that non-Jewish Christians obey all Jewish laws, including the most extreme: circumcision and a kosher diet. Church leaders meet in Jerusalem and work out a compromise. The only Jewish laws required of non-Jews: Don't commit sex sins or eat food offered to idols or meat with blood in it. *(Acts 15)* ▶

HELLO EUROPE. Paul, back at his home church in Antioch of Syria, decides to hit the road again, to visit churches he and Barnabas started on their first mission trip. Barnabas and his cousin John Mark revisit Cyprus. Paul and an associate named Silas head for Turkey. Along the way Paul sees a vision. A man wants him to come to what is now Greece. Paul goes, starting churches from Philippi in the north to Corinth in the south. *(Acts 15:36–18)* ▼

DID THE CHURCH COMPROMISE WORK? No. Some Jewish Christians trailed Paul—who ministered mainly to non-Jews—and told his converts that they needed to obey Jewish laws. Paul eventually abandoned the compromise as well, telling his converts that it doesn't matter what they eat as long as they try not to offend those eating with them (Romans 14:2–3; 1 Corinthians 8).

Black Sea

Philippi
Amphipolis • Neapolis
Thessalonica
Berea • Apollonia
GREECE
Troas
• Mytilene
Aegean Sea
Ephesus
Corinth • Athens
Antioch in Pisidia
Lystra
Derbe
Tarsus
Rhodes
Patara
CRETE
Mediterranean Sea

TURKEY
Iconium

Antioch
SYRIA
CYPRUS
LEBANON
• Damascus
• Tyre
• Ptolemais
• Caesarea
West Bank
JORDAN
• Jerusalem
ISRAEL

—— Outbound route
—— Return route

PAUL'S MISSION TRIP 2
2,700 MILES (4,345 KM), 3 YEARS

PAUL'S LAST MISSION TRIP. Paul causes trouble just about everywhere he goes. It's because his preaching messes with the status quo, attracting Jews and idol worshippers to the Christian faith. On this third mission trip, which covers much the same territory as the second, Paul spends about three years in Ephesus—until idol makers run him out of town because he's hurting their business. *(Acts 19–21)*

PAUL'S SHIP VS. TYPHOON. When Paul returns to Jerusalem, Jews get him arrested on false charges. Paul exercises his right as a Roman citizen to appeal for a trial in Caesar's court. The governor sends him to Rome, with a military escort. It's autumn, a risky season to sail. A typhoon engulfs the ship mid-journey, pummeling it for two weeks—finally splintering it near the island of Malta, south of Italy. No one dies. In a cliffhanger, the story ends with Paul reaching Rome and waiting two years for trial. *(Acts 27–28)* ▼

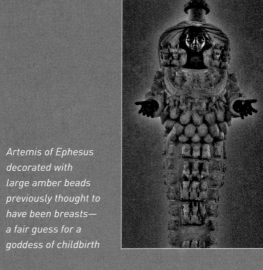

Artemis of Ephesus decorated with large amber beads previously thought to have been breasts— a fair guess for a goddess of childbirth

RIOT-MAKER ON THE RECORD. Acts says an idol manufacturer named Demetrius provoked the riot that drove Paul out of Ephesus. It started with a guild meeting about how to protect the city's patron goddess, Artemis. Archaeologists found Demetrius's name inscribed on a list of men honored as protectors of the Temple of Artemis. They also found an inscription about a silversmith guild in the city: "May the guild of the silversmiths prosper!"

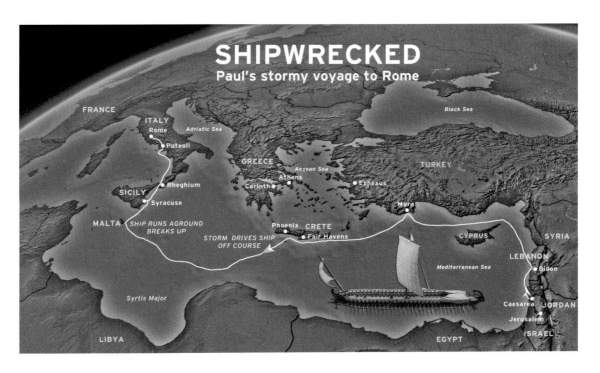

SHIPWRECKED
Paul's stormy voyage to Rome

FRANCE

ITALY
Rome

Adriatic Sea

Black Sea

Puteoli

GREECE

Aegean Sea

TURKEY

Athens

SICILY

Rheghium

Corinth

Ephesus

Syracuse

Myra

MALTA SHIP RUNS AGROUND
BREAKS UP

Phoenix CRETE

CYPRUS

SYRIA

STORM DRIVES SHIP
OFF COURSE

Fair Havens

LEBANON

Sidon

Mediterranean Sea

Caesarea JORDAN

Syrtis Major

Jerusalem

ISRAEL

LIBYA

EGYPT

ROMANS

HERE'S WHAT CHRISTIANS BELIEVE

IN ONE SENTENCE

Expecting to visit Rome, Paul writes a letter to Christians there to introduce himself by outlining his Christian beliefs—and in the process, creating Christianity's first known theology book, which reads like Christianity 101.

SOUND BITE

"Everyone has sinned. No one measures up to God's glory. The free gift of God's grace makes all of us right with him. Christ Jesus paid the price to set us free."
—*Paul, writing to Christians in Rome*
ROMANS 3:23–24 NIrV

NEWSMAKER

PAUL, a traveling preacher. A hardworking church planter, he's also a tireless writer, credited with writing almost half the books in the New Testament.

ON LOCATION

TIME. Paul wrote in about AD 57, near the end of his last known missionary trip, before his arrest in Jerusalem.

PLACE. Paul writes to Christians in Rome, a city he hopes to visit.

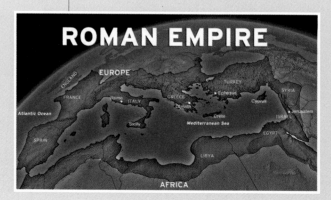

ROMAN EMPIRE

CREATION HAS A CREATOR. Even atheists know better than to doubt the existence of God, Paul writes. "They know the truth about God because he has made it obvious to them. For ever since the world was created, people have seen the earth and sky. Through everything God made, they can clearly see his invisible qualities—his eternal power and divine nature. So they have no excuse for not knowing God." *(Romans 1)*

Christian question: If life began with a bang, who pulled the trigger?

JESUS DIED SO WE CAN LIVE FOREVER. Sin and holiness can't hold hands. Sinners have no place in God's holy realm—on earth or in heaven. That's a problem, since Paul says everyone has sinned. Worse, he says that in the eyes of a holy God, sin is a capital offense. Paul offers good news, though: "God presented Jesus as the sacrifice for sin. People are made right with God when they believe that Jesus sacrificed his life, shedding his blood." *(Romans 3)*

WHAT DOES IT TAKE TO GET AN ENTRANCE PASS INTO ETERNAL LIFE? "Confess with your mouth that Jesus is Lord and believe in your heart that God raised him from the dead, you will be saved" (Romans 10:9).

Jewish scholar, New York City

FAITH TRUMPS OBEDIENCE. An ultra-conservative Jew, Paul says he used to believe that the way to please God was to obey the hundreds of Jewish rules. Paul says he doesn't believe that anymore. He says trusting God is more important. To make his case, Paul points to Abraham, father of the Jews. Centuries before God gave Moses any laws, Paul says, "God accepted Abraham because Abraham had faith in him." *(Romans 4 CEV)* ▲

SIN IS A HABIT WE CAN KICK. Paul says Christians shouldn't do what they know is wrong, as though they don't have a choice. He admits

Christians may never be perfect in this life. He says he's not. "But I press on to possess that perfection for which Christ Jesus first possessed me" (Philippians 3:12). We're free to chase that goal of godliness because Jesus frees us from "life that is dominated by sin and death." *(Romans 6–7)* ▼

LOOKING FOR MR. PERFECT. Some Christians say it's possible to live a spiritually mature life, free of sin. Others say they'll believe it when they see it. But most Christians acknowledge that as they mature, they find themselves more inclined to do what is right than what is wrong.

Christian charity: village bread distribution

JEWS AREN'T GOD'S ONLY CHOSEN PEOPLE.
Paul, a Jew himself, says the Jews were God's Chosen People. But they were chosen for a purpose, as God explained to Abraham, father of the Jews: "Everyone on earth will be blessed because of you" (Genesis 12:3 CEV). Paul says the church, which springs from Jesus' teachings, fulfills both that promise and a prophecy of Hosea: "Although they [non-Jews] are not my people, I will make them my people." *(Romans 9–11 CEV)* ▲

CHRISTIANS AREN'T NORMAL. They don't act like other folks. When in Rome, they don't do as the Romans do. Paul tells these Roman Christians: "Don't become so well-adjusted to your culture that you fit into it without even thinking. Instead, fix your attention on God. You'll be changed from the inside out. . . . Unlike the culture around you, always dragging you down to its level of immaturity, God brings the best out of you." *(Romans 12–15 MSG)* ▶

Nero, Roman emperor when Paul wrote Romans

CHRISTIAN TO-DO LIST. Paul said genuine Christians:

:: submit to rulers

:: love each other

:: work hard

:: cultivate patience

:: pray

:: help people in need

:: accept new Christians as they are, as Jesus does.

(Romans 12–15)

1,2 CORINTHIANS

CHURCH OF THE PAIN IN THE NECK

IN ONE SENTENCE

After spending a year and a half planting the church in Corinth and then moving on to start other churches, Paul hears about problems back in Corinth—power struggles, sexual sins, church folks getting drunk on communion wine—which he tries to solve by writing letters.

SOUND BITE

"God loves a cheerful giver."
—*Paul, in a fund-raising appeal for needy believers in Jerusalem*
2 CORINTHIANS 9:7 NKJV

NEWSMAKER

PAUL, a traveling preacher. Founder of the congregation in Corinth, Paul leaves to start other churches, but keeps in touch through letters that tackle questions and problems in the Corinthian church.

ON LOCATION

TIME. Paul may have written 1 Corinthians in about AD 55 and 2 Corinthians a few months later.

PLACE. Corinth, on a narrow isthmus between two seas, in what is now southern Greece.

Catholics consider Peter the first pope because Jesus implies he will build the church on Peter's leadership, adding: "I will give you the keys of the Kingdom of Heaven" (Matthew 16:19).

BATTLE FOR CHURCH BOSS. Their founder, Paul, has left town. Now, church members can't seem to agree on who's the boss. Four factions develop, each favoring a different leader:

:: **PAUL**. Perhaps because he focuses on faith instead of obeying Jewish laws.

:: **JESUS**. Maybe to justify obeying basic Jewish laws, since Jesus did.

:: **PETER**. Perhaps because Peter, leader of Jesus' original disciples, offers balance between faith and Jewish tradition.

:: **APOLLOS**. A great preacher.

Paul pleads for unity, saying it doesn't matter who continues the work he started. *(1 Corinthians 1–4)* ▲

IGNORING SEXUAL SINS IN THE CHURCH. A man in the church is sleeping with his step-mother—and still attending church. Paul tells the congregation to kindly show this man the door. For two reasons:

:: The man's sin is like spoiled yeast working its way into dough, eventually souring the entire church.

:: Excommunication might shock the man to his spiritual senses.

"Your body is the temple of the Holy Spirit," Paul adds. "You must honor God with your body." *(1 Corinthians 5, 6:9–20)*

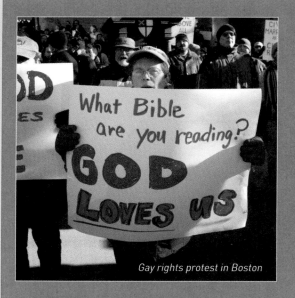

Gay rights protest in Boston

IS GAY OKAY? Not according to Paul—or at least according to how most Christians read him. He almost calls gay people *perverts*, warning they'll pay for their "unnatural" sexual relations (Romans 1:27 TNIV). Other Christians argue that Paul was talking about heterosexuals experimenting with homosexuality—doing what's "unnatural" for them. Others say Paul was giving his personal opinion, and he didn't know what he was talking about any more than he did when he insisted that only men whose kids behaved should qualify as pastors (1 Timothy 3:4–5). Christian denominations have split over this controversial topic.

TRIAL DOCKET: CHRISTIAN VS. CHRISTIAN. Corinthian church members are suing each other. Paul can't believe it. "How dare you file a lawsuit," he writes, "and ask a secular court to decide the matter instead of taking it to other believers!" It's an embarrassment to the church, he says. "Why not just accept the injustice and leave it at that?" He says that would be better than relying on pagans to become our peacemakers. *(1 Corinthians 6)*

Portrait of Italian merchant and his wife, painted in 1434

DOES CELIBACY BEAT MARRIAGE? Yes, Paul says. "It's better to stay unmarried, just as I am." He says it's about time management: "An unmarried man can spend his time doing the Lord's work and thinking how to please him. But a married man has to think about his earthly responsibilities and how to please his wife." On the other hand, Paul says it's best to get married if all you're thinking about is sex. The fewer distractions, the better. (1 Corinthians 7) ▲

SHOULD CHRISTIANS NEVER SUE FELLOW CHRISTIANS? Paul was talking about Christians in the same local church, scholars say, and probably about money—not about a violent crime. Christians interested in keeping their cases out of the secular courts sometimes turn to one of the national Christian legal services.

SINGLE LIVING DIDN'T WORK OUT SO WELL FOR THE SHAKERS. Started in 1747, this celibate break-off of the Quaker faith reached its heyday a century later: about 6,000 members. They were nicknamed "Shaking Quakers" because they danced ecstatically in church. There's just one active Shaker community left: Sabbathday Lake Shaker Village in Maine. Not a whole lot of shaking going on. Three Shakers at the moment.

Shaker woman with apples, 1907

Heads covered—as Paul preferred for women in church— women gather for worship in Papeete, French Polynesia.

WORSHIP ETIQUETTE. Worship at Corinth has spiraled into chaos. Everybody's doing their own thing. Paul's solution: Add structure. A few rules.

:: **FASHION.** Women: dress modestly, cover their heads. Men: hats off.

:: **COMMUNION.** Stop treating it like a potluck. And quit getting drunk on the wine.

:: **TONGUES.** If you speak in a heavenly language, have someone translate it for humans.

:: **WOMAN TALK.** Don't. Not in church. If you have questions, ask your husband. At home.

(1 Corinthians 11, 14)

THE BEST SPIRITUAL GIFT. Bad news for preachers. Preaching isn't the most important thing that happens in church. Not according to preacher Paul. Nor is speaking in heavenly languages—a spiritual gift the Corinthians favor.

:: **TOP GIFT: LOVE.** "So what if I speak with the eloquence of a master orator, the swaggering charisma of a rock star, and the authority of an archangel sent from God. If I don't love others, I'm just an irritating squeak in the dashboard of an old Buick" (1 Corinthians 13:1 AUTHOR'S PARAPHRASE). ▶

(1 Corinthians 12–14)

WHY DID PAUL TELL WOMEN TO SHUT UP IN CHURCH? Experts are left guessing. Some wonder if Paul's opinion helps explain why he never got married. Though he tells women to "be silent" (1 Corinthians 14:34) in church, he says it's okay for them to pray and prophesy there (1 Corinthians 11:5). It seems hard to prophesy silently, short of charades. One theory: In the "be silent" section, Paul was telling the ladies not to publicly question their husbands, potentially embarrassing them.

Peter and John rush to Jesus' tomb after hearing of his resurrection

NO RESURRECTION, NO CHRISTIANITY. Immortality of a disembodied soul—now that's an idea Christians at Corinth can handle. It's Greek, like them. But Paul preaches resurrection of a physical body of some sort—perhaps the kind Jesus had after his resurrection. Paul preached this in a sermon that sounded like standup comedy to brainiac philosophers in Athens. They laughed him out of town (Acts 17:32). "If there is no resurrection of the dead," Paul insists, "we are more to be pitied than anyone in the world." In other words, if Jesus didn't rise from the dead, Christians aren't going to rise either—and that means they picked the wrong religion. *(1 Corinthians 15)*

WHAT KIND OF RESURRECTION BODIES DO CHRISTIANS EXPECT? Christians debate this. Some offer ideas that seem more spooky than spiritual: flesh and bones with no blood—which could sound like zombie heaven. Others wonder why we should expect anything close to a physical body in a spiritual dimension. Paul simply says "our physical bodies cannot inherit the Kingdom of God. . . . Our mortal bodies must be transformed into immortal bodies" (1 Corinthians 15:50, 53).

PAUL: "I AM NOT A CROOK." After writing his first letter to Corinth, Paul pays the church a visit. Not a happy experience. Someone trash-talks him to his face. After Paul leaves, others show up at the church and accuse him of fraud, saying he's a fake apostle shaking them down for shekels. In a second letter Paul defends himself. He reminds the Corinthians of the miracles he performed, and of the fact that he paid his own way as a bi-vocational pastor, making tents. *(2 Corinthians 2–4:7)*

PAUL: "SEND MONEY." In the very letter in which Paul defends himself as anything but a minister on the take, he asks for money. This isn't a light-touch fund-raising letter. It's hard sell: "I want to find out if you really love God" (2 Corinthians 8:8 NIrV). Paul adds that he's going to compare their offering to what he gets from other churches. Implication: If they give a dinky donation, they are tightwads whose love for God can be measured in small change. *(2 Corinthians 8–9)*

Detail of a painting that portrays suffering of Palestinian children

WHY DID PAUL WANT THE MONEY? Jerusalem church leaders asked Paul to "keep on helping the poor" (Galatians 2:10). Paul hoped this offering would help heal the rift between Jewish Christians and non-Jewish Christians. The two groups argued over whether Christians should obey Jewish laws. Paul collected the offering mainly from non-Jews, and gave it to Jewish Christians in Jerusalem.

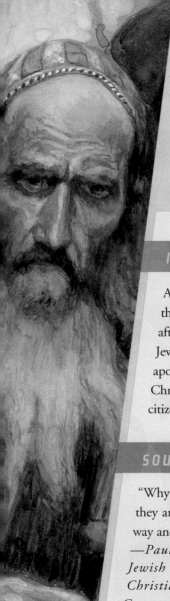

GALATIANS

APOSTLE PAUL, MAD AS ALL GET-OUT

IN ONE SENTENCE

Anger alert: Paul unloads some of the harshest language in the Bible after he's had it up to here with Jewish Christians—including the apostle Peter—treating non-Jewish Christians like they're second-class citizens of God's kingdom.

SOUND BITE

"Why don't these agitators, obsessive as they are about circumcision, go all the way and castrate themselves!"
—*Paul, writing about a group of Jewish Christians who want all Christian men circumcised*
GALATIANS 5:12 MSG

ON LOCATION

TIME. Scholars guess Paul wrote this letter sometime between AD 48 and the mid-50s.

PLACE. Paul is writing to the churches in Galatia, a Roman province in what is now central Turkey.

NEWSMAKERS

 PAUL, a traveling minister. He starts church groups throughout the Roman Empire, mainly among non-Jews.

PETER, leader of Jesus' original disciples. He works mainly among Jews in Jerusalem.

GALATIA

Peter and Paul in happier times

PAUL TO JEWISH CHRISTIANS: "CASTRATE YOURSELVES!" Some Jewish Christians show up in Galatia, insisting that non-Jewish Christians convert to Judaism—which means the men need to be circumcised. There, they start to undermine Paul's teaching that people are saved through faith in Jesus, not through obeying Jewish rules. If Paul loses this battle, Christianity could become just another branch of Judaism: a bunch of Jews who believe Jesus is the Messiah. Paul tells the Galatians: "Don't let yourselves be circumcised." *(Galatians 3–5 NIrV)*

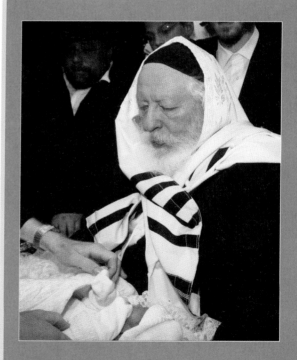

PAUL TO PETER: "YOU HYPOCRITE!" Church leaders reached a shaky agreement at a summit meeting in Jerusalem: Non-Jewish Christians didn't have to convert to Judaism. Yet some hard-nosed Jewish Christians are insisting otherwise, and making headway. When Peter visits a mainly non-Jewish church that Paul helps lead in Antioch, Peter eats with Christians—until some Jewish Christians arrive from Jerusalem. Then he follows their lead, avoiding the non-Jews. Paul chews him out. *(Galatians 1–2)* ▲

WHAT'S SO IMPORTANT ABOUT CIRCUMCISION? Cutting off the excess skin at the end of a penis is a ritual that marks a male's entry into the Jewish faith. God told Abraham, father of the Jews: "From generation to generation, every male child must be circumcised on the eighth day after his birth" (Genesis 17:12). Adult male converts are circumcised at whatever age they convert.

EPHESIANS

HOW-TO TIPS FOR CHRISTIANS

IN ONE SENTENCE

A prisoner, perhaps under the house arrest in Rome, Paul writes a gentle and loving letter to the church he started in Ephesus, giving them practical advice about how to live the Christian life.

NEWSMAKER

PAUL, a traveling minister. He writes to the church in Ephesus, where he spent more than three years starting the congregation.

ON LOCATION

TIME. Many Bible experts say Paul probably wrote this letter near the end of his life, between AD 60–62.

PLACE. "In chains" (Ephesians 6:20), perhaps in Rome, Paul writes to the church in Ephesus, a large and thriving coastal city in what is now western Turkey.

SOUND BITE

"Don't go to bed angry."
—*Paul, writing to Christians in Ephesus*
EPHESIANS 4:26 MSG

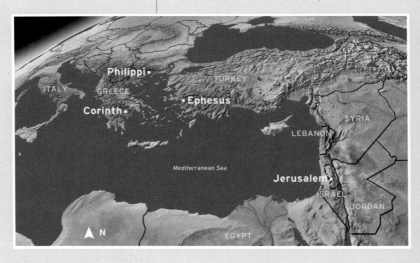

Philippi•
ITALY   GREECE   TURKEY
•Ephesus
Corinth•   SYRIA
                    LEBANON
Mediterranean Sea
                    Jerusalem•
                    ISRAEL
                    JORDAN
            N   EGYPT

© Bill Aron

Joe Martin Erber and his uncle, Meyer Gelman, hold scrolls of scripture at their synagogue in Mississippi.

GOD'S NEW AND IMPROVED CHOSEN PEOPLE.

Jews aren't God's only chosen people, Paul says. A Jew himself, Paul tells the mostly non-Jewish Christians in Ephesus that they're God's chosen people, too. He says God started with one man of faith, Abraham, growing a people of faith, the Jews. Their job: "Show people all over the world the way to be saved" (Isaiah 49:6 NCV). "Both Gentiles and Jews who believe the Good News share equally in the riches inherited by God's children." *(Ephesians 1–3)* ▲

WHAT MATURE CHRISTIANS LOOK LIKE.

"Become like Christ and have his perfection" (Ephesians 4:13 NCV). That should be the goal of every Christian, Paul says. He's still working on it himself: "I press on to possess that perfection" (Philippians 3:12). Paul offers tips for staying on track:

:: Be humble.
:: Be patient.
:: Don't get angry.
:: Don't lie.
:: Don't steal.
:: Don't talk dirty.
:: Don't tear people down with slander; build them up with compliments.
:: Don't commit sexual sins.
:: Don't be greedy.
:: Don't get drunk.

(Ephesians 1–3)

Tourists swarm ruins of the Ephesus library.

EPHESUS. A busy riverside town on Turkey's west coast, Ephesus was one of the five largest cities in the Roman Empire. Today it's a ruin, visited by tourists. The city died after the river leading to the Mediterranean Sea silted up. Ships stopped arriving and businesses moved away.

PAUL'S RX FOR HARMONY IN THE HOME.
Paul's a single guy. But he doesn't hesitate to offer up his prescription for keeping peace on the home front.

:: **HUSBANDS AND WIVES**: "Submit to one another" (NLT).
:: **CHILDREN.** "Obey your parents" (NLT).
:: **PARENTS.** "Do not provoke your children" (NLT).
:: **SERVANTS.** "Serve them [your masters] sincerely as you would serve Christ" (NLT).
:: **MASTERS.** "No abuse, please, and no threats" (MSG). *(Ephesians 5:21–6:9)*

HOLY WAR. Paul says Christians are at war. Not with unbelievers. But with the unseen world. "We are not fighting against flesh-and-blood enemies, but against evil rulers and authorities of the unseen world, against mighty powers in this dark world, and against evil spirits in the heavenly places" (Ephesians 6:12). He tells Christians to suit up in God's armor. ▶

INFERIOR WOMEN "A woman is inferior to her husband in everything. For that reason, she should obey him. . .God has put the husband in charge."
JOSEPHUS, JEWISH HISTORIAN (AD 37-101)

BODY ARMOR FOR THE BATTLEFIELD. Paul uses military metaphors to paint a picture of the spiritual resources Christians have. Creatively, he does it in a way that makes sense to two groups: (1) non-Jewish Christians who are all too familiar with Roman armor and (2) Jewish Christians who know their Bible.

PAUL'S MILITARY LINGO	JEWISH BIBLE LINKS
Belt of truth	"He will wear righteousness like a belt" (Isaiah 11:5).
Body armor of righteousness	"He put on righteousness as his body armor" (Isaiah 59:17).
Shoes of peace	"How beautiful. . .the feet of the messenger who brings. . .good news of peace" (Isaiah 52:7).
Shield of faith	God is my. . .shield and my saving strength" (2 Samuel 22:3 NCV).
Helmet of salvation	"He. . .placed the helmet of salvation on his head" (Isaiah 59:17).
Sword of God's Word	"The LORD. . . .made my words like a sharp sword" (Isaiah 49:1–2 NIRV).

PHILIPPIANS

PAUL'S THANK-YOU LETTER

IN ONE SENTENCE

Jailed, Paul gets a care package from Christians in Philippi, and he writes a thank-you letter encouraging them to hold on to their faith—no matter what happens to him, or them.

SOUND BITE

"I press on to reach the end of the race and receive the heavenly prize."
—*Paul, writing to the church in Philippi*
PHILIPPIANS 3:14

ON LOCATION

TIME. Paul may have written this letter during his two-year arrest in Rome as he waited for his trial from AD 60–62.

PLACE. Paul writes this letter to the church in Philippi, in what is now northern Greece.

NEWSMAKERS

PAUL, traveling minister. Paul starts the church at Philippi, along with many other churches throughout Turkey and Greece.

TIMOTHY, Paul's associate. He travels with Paul, running errands for him such as visiting churches to see how they're doing (Philippians 2:19).

Mamertine prison, Rome
Tradition says Paul and Peter were jailed in this dungeon, dropped in from a hole above.

LEARN TO GET ALONG. Paul has one persistent request, whether he's writing to a church in trouble or to a church on the grow: unity. "Make me completely happy! Live in harmony by showing love for each other. Be united in what you think, as if you were only one person" (CEV). Then he offers tips on the how-to:

:: "Don't be selfish."
:: "Don't try to impress others."
:: "Be humble; thinking of others as better than yourself." *(Philippians 2 NLT)*

THE RACE OF A LIFETIME. Paul's not perfect. He admits it. But that's his goal. He says he's like a runner racing for the trophy. "I press on to possess that perfection. . .to reach the end of the race and receive the heavenly prize for which God, through Christ Jesus, is calling us." Paul asks the Christians of Philippi to follow in his footsteps, all the way to heaven. *(Philippians 3)* ▶

OLYMPICS IN THE BIBLE? Paul started using athletic competitions to make his point after spending a year and a half in Corinth. While there, he may have seen the Isthmian Games held on the outskirts of town every two years. Or he may have seen the Olympics hosted every four years at Olympia, west about 75 miles (120 km).

COLOSSIANS

FAKES AND FLAKES IN THE CHURCH

Fake Christians weasel their way into the church at Colosse and pitch warped religious ideas that Paul rebuffs—ideas like the power of mind over matter and the importance of obeying ancient Jewish laws.

SOUND BITE

"Whatever you do or say, do it as a representative of the Lord Jesus."
—*Paul, writing the church in Colosse*
Colossians 3:17

ON LOCATION

TIME. Under arrest, Paul may have written while imprisoned in Rome, about AD 60–62.

PLACE. Paul wrote to a church in Colosse, a small town about a week's walk east of Ephesus, some 120 miles (193 km).

NEWSMAKERS

PAUL, traveling minister. There's no mention of him ever going to Colosse. But one of his colleagues started the church there. Paul spent three years in neighboring Ephesus.

EPAPHRAS, founder of church at Colosse. Paul describes him as "our beloved co-worker" (Colossians 1:7).

Russian Orthodox priests

THROW OUT THE RULE BOOK. Paul tells Christians in Colosse to build their life on Christ, not on a bunch of antiquated rules or new-fangled philosophies. He says they can skip:

:: eating only kosher food allowed by Jews
:: observing Jewish holy days
:: fasting, and other forms of self-denial
:: worshipping angels. *(Colossians 2)*

CHRISTIAN CHECKLIST—DO'S AND DON'TS. "Let every detail in your lives—words, actions . . .be done in the name of the Master, Jesus" (MSG). Paul says people should see Christ in Christians.

Do let people see in you:

:: mercy
:: kindness
:: humility
:: forgiveness.

Don't let them see:

:: anger
:: slander
:: dirty language
:: greed. *(Colossians 3–4)*

ANGEL WORSHIP. Ancient amulets engraved with incantations and the names of Gabriel and other angels suggest that some Christians called on angels to protect them from evil spirits.

COLOSSE. Once a busy trade-route city famous for producing dyed purple wool called *colossinus*, in Paul's day it was a city past its prime and off the beaten trail. Romans built a shortcut through neighboring Laodicea, bypassing Colosse. Today, Colosse's ruins remain buried under a mound of dirt.

1,2 THESSALONIANS

OBSESSED WITH THE SECOND COMING

IN ONE SENTENCE

Paul answers questions about the return of Jesus, but then bluntly warns Christians fixated on that topic to get over it and get back to work.

SOUND BITE

"The day the Lord comes again will be a surprise, like a thief that comes in the night."
—*Paul, writing the church in Thessalonica*
1 THESSALONIANS 5:2 NCV

ON LOCATION

TIME. Paul may have written these two letters during his second missionary trip and his year-and-a-half stay in Corinth—sometime between AD 49–51.

PLACE. Paul addresses the congregation in Thessalonica, about a 300-mile (480 km) walk to the north.

NEWSMAKERS

PAUL, traveling preacher. He starts the church in Thessalonica.

TIMOTHY AND SILAS, associates of Paul. They join his ministry team during his second missionary trip.

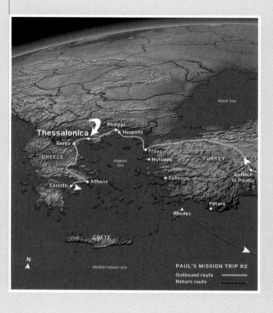

PAUL'S MISSION TRIP #2
Outbound route
Return route

Burial of a Christian martyr

COUNT ON IT: YOU'LL SUFFER. Paul survives only three weeks in Thessalonica before Jews stir up a riot and drive him out of town (Acts 17). Leaving isn't an option for converts in the church he starts there. Thessalonica is their home. Left behind, they suffer harassment and perhaps violence. Paul writes to remind them that Jesus suffered, and they'll continue to suffer as well. But he says their persistent faith inspires him. *(1 Thessalonians 1–3)*

LIVE HOLY—IT'S WHAT GOD WANTS. "God's will is for you to be holy," Paul writes. Bible experts debate what that means. Some say he's talking about perfection as a goal, since he admits he's not perfect (see page 440). He offers a few traveling tips for folks headed down the highway to holiness:

:: stay away from sexual sins
:: respect others
:: mind your own business. *(1 Thessalonians 4:1–12*

HOLINESS. It means "devoted to God," many scholars explain. A Temple lampstand, for example, was considered holy because it was devoted to God, for use only in his Temple. Jews were considered holy, too: "You are a holy people, who belong to the Lord your God" (Deuteronomy 7:6).

WHO'S THE "MAN OF LAWLESSNESS" PAUL SAYS WILL COME BEFORE JESUS RETURNS? No one seems to know. Paul says this mystery man will oppose everything godly and "will even sit in the temple of God," claiming that he himself is God" (2 Thessalonians 2:4). Some speculate this mystery man is the Antichrist, though John says there are lots of antichrists (1 John 2:18). Others point to Roman emperors, worshipped as gods. Future emperor Titus entered the Jerusalem Temple before his soldiers destroyed it in AD 70.

JESUS IS COMING BACK. Perhaps driven by their suffering, Christians ask Paul when Jesus is coming and what it'll look like. Paul says:

:: No one knows when he's coming.

:: When he does, Christians who have died will rise from their graves.

:: Those still alive will rise into the clouds to meet him.

:: Believers will live forever with him. *(1 Thessalonians 4:12–5:11)*

A WORD TO BUSYBODIES: GET BUSY. If you don't work, you don't eat, Paul tells some Christians who have stopped working. Perhaps they've taken early retirement because they figure Jesus is coming any second. Or maybe they've rounded up some sanctified sugar daddies. Whatever their excuse, Paul's not buying it: "Start working for a living." *(2 Thessalonians 3)*

Emperor Titus

SECOND COMING ITINERARY. Paul describes the Second Coming of Jesus almost as though he has seen it.

:: **Return.** "The Lord himself will come down from heaven with a commanding shout, with the voice of the archangel, and with the trumpet call of God."

:: **Resurrection.** "Christians who have died will rise from their graves."

:: **Rapture.** "Then, together with them, we who are still alive and remain on the earth will be caught up in the clouds to meet the Lord in the air."

:: **Reward.** "Then we will be with the Lord forever." *(1 Thessalonians 4:16–17)*

1, 2 TIMOTHY

HOW TO BE A GREAT MINISTER

IN ONE SENTENCE

Paul assigns his associate, Timothy, the job of pastoring perhaps the largest church on the planet, and then he sends him two letters of continuing education—down-to-earth advice from heaven, tailored for a church leader.

SOUND BITE

"Love of money is a root of all kinds of evil."
—*Paul, writing to his close friend Timothy*
1 TIMOTHY 6:10 NKJV

ON LOCATION

TIME. Perhaps in AD 63, assuming Romans found Paul not guilty during his trial reported at the end of Acts. These are likely Paul's last surviving letters, many experts say.

PLACE. Paul addresses Timothy, pastor of the church in Ephesus, located on what is now Turkey's west coast. Paul's second letter comes from jail in Rome, perhaps his second imprisonment there.

NEWSMAKERS

PAUL, traveling preacher. He starts churches throughout what is now Turkey and Greece, with the help of associates such as Timothy.

TIMOTHY, Paul's associate. After traveling with Paul during missionary trips two and three, Timothy becomes the pastor of the church in Ephesus.

TIMOTHY VS. THE BAD GUYS. When Paul tells Timothy to bail out of their mission trip and stay behind in Ephesus, he explains why: "Stop those whose teaching is contrary to the truth" (1 Timothy 1:3). Based on what Paul writes in this first letter, scholars offer guesses about what those false teachings included.

:: Christians must be Jews and obey Jewish laws.
:: We can earn God's approval by denying ourselves pleasures, like marriage.
:: Knowledge trumps faith, and lofty-sounding ideas are more important than living a godly life. *(1 Timothy 1:3–11; 4:1–5; 6:2–20)*

LADYLIKE ETIQUETTE IN THE CHURCH. A single guy, Paul seems chauvinistic to the bone—at least when it comes to women in the church. He gives Timothy much the same advice he gave church leaders in Corinth (see p. 445). Women in church should:

:: wear modest clothes
:: skip fancy hairdos
:: leave the jewelry home
:: keep quiet and learn about Jesus by listening to men talk
:: never publicly teach a man or assume authority over men. *(1 Timothy 2)* ▼

Dressed for church: jewelry off, head covered, mouth shut

see p. 445

WOULD PAUL OPPOSE WOMEN MINISTERS TODAY? Two schools of thought:

Yes. Men and women are equal partners, with different jobs: Men lead in church matters, women in domestic, such as childcare.

No. Paul targeted only churches with women-related troubles—Corinth and Ephesus—but he commended women leaders elsewhere: "Andronicus and Junia [aka Julia]. . .they are prominent among the apostles" (Romans 16:7 NRSV).

Painting of Pope John Paul II (1920–2005) and Italian priest John Bosco (1815–1888)

TIMOTHY, FAST FACTS

Born: Lystra, in what is now Turkey

Mother: Eunice, a Jew

Father: Non-Jew

Job: Paul's most trusted associate minister—a troubleshooter who carried messages to problem churches and stayed to help work out solutions.

Promotion: Paul appointed him pastor of the large congregation at Ephesus.

Death: Some church leaders said he died a martyr during a wave of Roman persecution in AD 97.

CHECKLIST FOR CHURCH LEADERS. Paul knows Timothy needs help in ministry: staff and volunteers. So he gives him a list of character traits to look for in potential church leaders. A sampling for pastoral staff:

:: respected even by non-Christians
:: enjoys houseguests
:: gentle-spirited
:: able to teach
:: not money-hungry. *(1 Timothy 3)* ▲

MINISTERING TO PROBLEM PEOPLE. A church attracts troubled souls, like a porch light draws bugs. Paul gives Timothy advice tailored to various problem groups.

:: **MEDDLING WIDOWS**. Stop it before it happens; urge young widows to remarry.
:: **GRUMPY OLD MEN**. Give them the respect you'd give your father.
:: **MINISTERS UNDER FIRE**. Two witnesses. It's the minimum for leveling any complaint against a minister.
:: **DESTITUTE WIDOWS**. If the family won't help them, the church should.
:: **SLAVES**. Tell them to respect their masters. *(1 Timothy 5—6:2)*

Portrait of man from Roman times

NO FEAR. Paul sends a second letter to Timothy. Writing from death row in a Rome prison—condemned for being a Christian—Paul preaches the Gospel of No Fear.

:: Don't be afraid to tell others about Jesus. "Be ready to suffer. . .for the sake of the Good News."

:: Don't fear death. Jesus defeated death.

:: Keep playing by God's rules, not the world's rules.

:: Expect eternal life. "If we die with him, we'll live with him" *(2 Timothy 1–2:14)* ▼

FINAL ADVICE, FROM FATHER TO SON. "Timothy, my dear son," Paul begins. What follows is fatherly advice that Paul knows may also be his last advice for Timothy:

:: "Run from temptations that capture young people."

:: "Be. . .easy to get along with."

:: "Worship with people whose hearts are pure."

:: "Stay away from stupid and senseless arguments."

:: "Be kind to everyone. . .and very patient."

:: "Keep on being faithful to what you were taught and to what you believed." *(2 Timothy 2:15–4:5 CEV)*

PAUL'S LAST REQUEST. "My death is near," Paul writes. "I have fought the good fight, I have finished the race, and I have remained faithful." Paul doesn't want to face death alone. He asks Timothy, whom he addresses as "my dear son," to make the thousand-mile (1600 km) journey to Rome. "Please come as soon as you can. . .before winter." The Bible doesn't say if Timothy arrived in time. But it's not hard for Christians to imagine that he did his best. *(2 Timothy 4:6–22)*

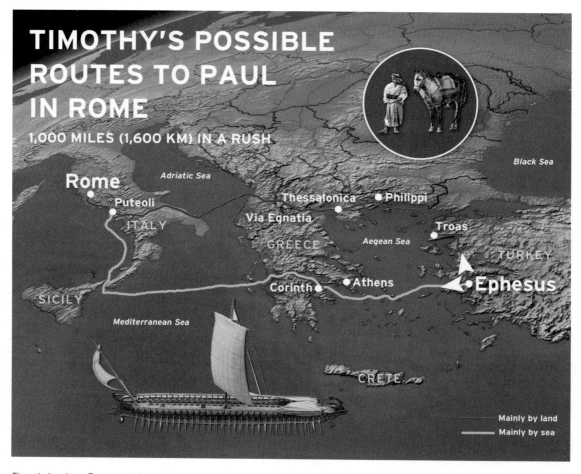

TIMOTHY'S POSSIBLE ROUTES TO PAUL IN ROME

1,000 MILES (1,600 KM) IN A RUSH

Black Sea

Rome
Puteoli
ITALY
Adriatic Sea
Thessalonica • Philippi
Via Egnatia
GREECE
Aegean Sea
Troas
TURKEY
Corinth • Athens
Ephesus
SICILY
Mediterranean Sea
CRETE

Mainly by land
Mainly by sea

Timothy's trip to Rome could have taken a month or two by land, but just a couple of weeks by sea.

HOW PAUL DIED. Romans beheaded him with a sword. So say early church reports written three centuries later, said to preserve earlier accounts.

Romans executed him on February 22 at mile marker three on the outskirts of Rome, the reports add. A church marks the site today: Saint Paul of the Three Fountains, built in the AD 400s, shortly after Rome legalized Christianity.

Peter died the same day, the reports say, crucified as part of Nero's persecution of Christians for allegedly starting the fire on July 19, AD 64 that destroyed two-thirds of Rome. ▶

A church with a statue of Paul holding a sword marks the location outside Rome where tradition says he was executed.

T I T U S

HOW TO PASTOR BOTTOM-DWELLERS

IN ONE SENTENCE

Assigned the tough job of starting churches on the island of Crete—once a pirate haven—Titus gets advice from Paul on what to look for in pastors and how to minister to this rough crowd.

SOUND BITE

"The people of Crete are all liars, cruel animals, and lazy gluttons."
—*Paul, writing to his colleague Titus, and quoting a poet from Crete*
TITUS 1:12

ON LOCATION

TIME. Paul may have written this letter the same time he wrote the similar letter of 1 Timothy, in about AD 63.

PLACE. Paul addressed Titus, ministering on the island of Crete about 100 miles (160 km) south of Greece.

NEWSMAKERS

PAUL, traveling preacher. He and his associates start churches throughout the Mediterranean world.

TITUS, Paul's associate. Paul gives him the job of appointing church leaders on the island of Crete.

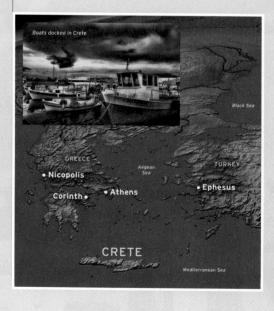

Boats docked in Crete

Black Sea

GREECE

Nicopolis

Aegean Sea

TURKEY

Corinth

Athens

Ephesus

CRETE

Mediterranean Sea

THE HAVE-TO TRAITS OF A MINISTER. After quoting a Cretan writer who essentially says Cretans are lazy, lying bone bags, Paul tells Titus to find a few exceptions to the rule—exceptional men who live "a blameless life." They'll pastor the churches that Paul and Titus started, apparently on a recent mission tour of the island. Paul tells Titus to look for men who have many of the same qualifications Paul wrote about to Timothy (see page 464). *(Titus 1)* ▶

A MINISTER'S HOW-TO GUIDE. Paul also tells Titus what he should teach to the different groups in Crete:

- :: **ELDERLY MEN**. They need to learn patience and love.
- :: **ELDERLY WOMEN**. Don't gossip or get drunk.
- :: **YOUNG MEN**. Self-control.
- :: **YOUNG WOMEN**. Follow the example of godly older women.
- :: **SLAVES**. Obey your masters.
- :: **EVERYONE**. Be kind and respectful. Obey your rulers. *(Titus 2–3)*

CRETE: PIRATE PARADISE. A century before Titus's time, pirates and mercenaries used Crete as their island port. Located in the heart of the Mediterranean Sea, Crete was the perfect spot for launching attacks on loaded merchant ships. Rome conquered the island in 67 BC and restored peace.

Shopping in Rethymnon, Crete

PHILEMON

RUNAWAY SLAVE RETURNS TO HIS MASTER

A runaway slave meets Paul, gets converted, and at Paul's urging returns to his master, Philemon, carrying Paul's letter that reads like a plea for Philemon to free the slave.

SOUND BITE

"He is no longer like a slave to you . . . . He is a beloved brother. . . . Welcome him as you would welcome me." —*Paul, telling Christian slave owner Philemon how to react to the return of his runaway slave*
PHILEMON 16–17

ON LOCATION

TIME. Paul probably writes this while under house arrest in Rome, from AD 60–62.

PLACE. Paul is a prisoner, probably in Rome. He's writing to Philemon, who lives in Colosse, more than 1,000 miles (1,600 km) away in what is now Turkey.

NEWSMAKERS

PAUL, traveling preacher. He apparently converts runaway slave Onesimus to Christianity and then sends him back to his master.

ONESIMUS (oh-NESS-uh-muhs)—a runaway slave. He returns to his master in Colosse, with a letter from Paul.

PHILEMON (fi-LEE-mon)—Onesimus's slave owner. Christians in Colosse meet in his home.

RUNAWAY SLAVE
Onesimus: Good-bye Colosse

HOW TO FREE A SLAVE. Paul converts the runaway slave Onesimus, and then sends him back to his slave master: Philemon—a church leader who uses his home as a worship center. Paul urges Philemon to welcome the young man not as a slave, but as a brother. Paul hints that he wants Onesimus freed: "I wanted to keep him here. . . . But I didn't want to do anything without your consent." As in, "Give me your consent." *(Philemon 1)* ▶

BISHOP ONESIMUS. Many Bible experts say Philemon probably freed this slave. Paul addressed his letter to the congregation that met in Philemon's home. So Philemon would have felt intense peer pressure to obey Paul, recognized there as the father of the Christian movement. About 50 years later, church leader Ignatius (died between AD 98–117) wrote a letter to the church leader in Colosse's neighbor city of Ephesus: Bishop Onesimus. Perhaps the former slave.

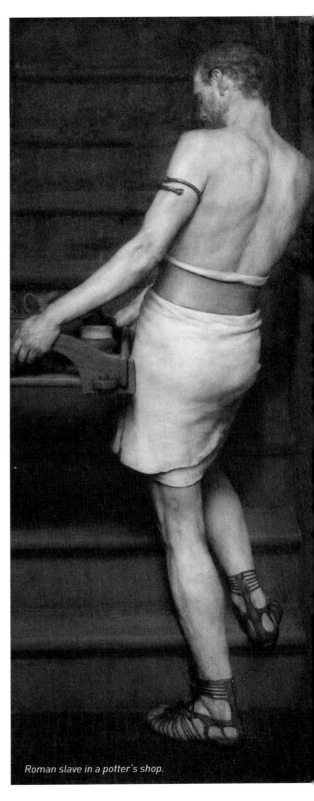

Roman slave in a potter's shop.

HEBREWS

EVERY GOOD JEW BELONGS IN CHURCH

IN ONE SENTENCE

With Jewish Christians dropping out of the persecuted Christian movement and retreating back to synagogues in the safer Jewish faith, one anonymous writer argues that there's nothing to go back to—that the Jewish religion is obsolete, replaced by Christianity.

SOUND BITE

"Faith makes us certain that what we hope for will happen. It lets our spirit see what our eyes can't."
—*Anonymous writer of Hebrews*
HEBREWS 11:1 AUTHOR'S PARAPHASE

ROMAN EMPIRE

[Map showing EUROPE, ENGLAND, FRANCE, Rome, ITALY, GREECE, Corinth, TURKEY, Ephesus, SYRIA, Cyprus, Crete, ISRAEL, Jerusalem, Atlantic Ocean, SPAIN, Sicily, Mediterranean Sea, EGYPT, LIBYA, AFRICA]

NEWSMAKER

JESUS, Son of God. He's portrayed as God's Son—superior to angels, Abraham, Moses, and priests.

ON LOCATION

TIME. Many scholars say it was probably written after Nero started persecuting Christians in AD 64, since persecution seems to lie in the background. Also, it was probably written before Romans destroyed Jerusalem and the Temple in AD 70. If the Temple had been destroyed, the writer likely would have mentioned it since he argued that Christian Jews should consider the Jewish religion obsolete. The first person known to quote the letter was church leader Clement, in about AD 97.

PLACE. Hebrews reads like an open letter to Jewish Christians throughout the Roman Empire.

JESUS: BETTER THAN MOSES. Jews in Bible times revere no human more than Moses. He's humanity's top-of-the-line model. Almost an angel on earth, Moses was holy enough to look God in the eye: "The LORD would speak to Moses face to face, just like a friend" (Exodus 33:9 CEV). Jesus trumps Moses. Moses did a good job as a servant in God's house, the writer says. But Jesus "is in charge of God's entire house." *(Hebrews 3)* ▼

Angels celebrate Jesus' birth.

CHRISTIANITY: JUDAISM 2.0. God promised that one day he would replace his covenant agreement with Israel, the writer says, quoting a prediction in Jeremiah 31:33. Instead of following the hundreds of Jewish laws, God's people would follow the guidance of God's Spirit inside them. "When God speaks of a 'new' covenant, it means he has made the first one obsolete. It is now out of date and will soon disappear" (Hebrews 8:13). The Jewish sacrificial system died in AD 70, when Romans leveled the Temple—the only place Jews were allowed to offer sacrifices.

Praying at the holiest Jewish site: Jerusalem's Western Wall—all that remains of the ancient Temple destroyed by the Romans.

JESUS: BETTER THAN AN ANGEL. Arguing that Christianity replaces Judaism, the writer builds his case that Jesus is better than the best Jews have to offer. Many Jews believe that angels are the next thing to God—holy enough to stand in his presence and trusted enough to deliver his messages. Jesus is better than any angel, the writer says. Quoting a sack full of prophecies about a coming savior, the writer presents Jesus as the fulfillment. Two of many:

:: "Let all of God's angels worship him."
:: "He will be my Son." *(Hebrews 1)*

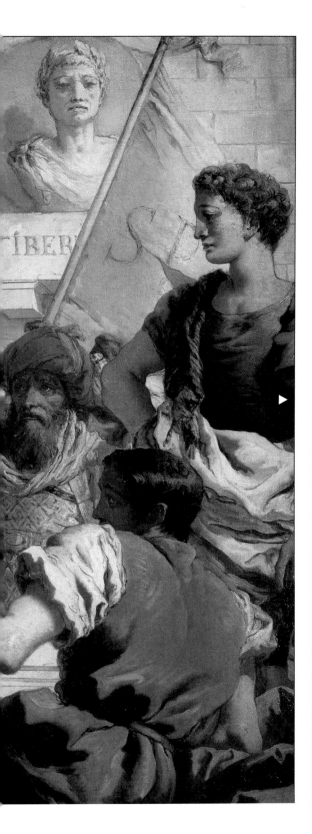

JESUS: BETTER THAN THE HIGH PRIEST. Pope of the Jews—that's the high priest in Bible times. He's the boss of all things Jewish. But Jesus out-popes him. The writer says Jesus is higher than the highest priest, including the mysterious Melchizedek—portrayed in Genesis as the spiritual superior of Abraham, father of the Jews. Two of several examples:

HIGH PRIEST	JESUS
Ministers in a man-made temple.	Ministers in God's presence in heaven.
His ministry ends when he dies.	His ministry never ends.

(Hebrews 4–9)

JESUS: THE BEST SACRIFICE OF ALL. Animal sacrifices are only temporary fixes for sin. They work a bit like an apology. But the Hebrews writer says they don't take away sin. A sacrifice "only reminds people of their sins from one year to the next" (Hebrews 10:4 CEV). Jesus' sacrifice is different. It's just one sacrifice. But it covers all sins. For everyone. Forever. Best of all, the writer says, it washes sins away. Repentant folks aren't just forgiven. In God's eyes, they're holy. That's one sin-buster of a sacrifice. *(Hebrews 9–10)*

HOW DOES THE DEATH OF JESUS MAKE US HOLY? It doesn't make us holy, as in perfect, some Bible experts say. But it gets us onto the holiness tollway, thanks to the toll Jesus paid. We live our lives traveling this highway to heaven, constantly seeking God's will and following the road wherever it leads—believing that at the end of the trail, the destination will have been worth the journey.

JAMES

CHRISTIANITY: A DO-SOMETHING RELIGION

James—possibly Jesus' brother and leader of the persecuted church in Jerusalem—gives Christians a to-do list; keeping their religion to themselves isn't on it.

"You call it 'faith' because you believe in God. How dumb is that? Demons believe in God. That kind of faith might buy you a front-row seat at your own barbecue. But it's not going to get you into heaven. Don't just say you believe in God. Act like it."
—*James, writing to fellow Christians*
JAMES, 2:19–20 AUTHOR'S PARAPHRASE

JAMES, author of this letter. Many scholars guess he was James the brother of Jesus and leader of the Jerusalem church.

TIME. If the writer was the brother of Jesus, he wrote this letter before Jews stoned him to death in the early to middle AD 60s. If the writer was James the disciple, he probably wrote it even earlier—before King Herod Agrippa I, grandson of Herod the Great, beheaded him in about AD 44.

PLACE. James addresses his short letter to "Jewish believers scattered abroad" (James 1:1), throughout the Roman Empire.

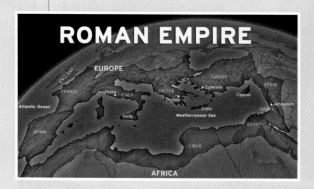

ROMAN EMPIRE

GOOD NEWS: SUFFERING AHEAD. James isn't being sarcastic. A positive thinker, he sees the good side of suffering. "When troubles come your way, consider it an opportunity for great joy. For you know that when your faith is tested, your endurance has a chance to grow." So does patience, he adds. And, perhaps implied, the admiration people will have for such a strong-hearted soul and the message of faith that empowers them. *(James 1:2–18)*

"LEAD US NOT INTO TEMPTATION." It's part of the Lord's Prayer (Matthew 6:13 NIV). James said God would never do such a thing: "Don't blame God when you are tempted! . . . We are tempted by our own desires that drag us off and trap us" (James 1:13–14 CEV). God might have to strengthen our faith by leading us through hard times, as some interpret *temptation* in the Lord's Prayer. But he'd never lure us into evil.

TREAT THE POOR LIKE THEY'RE RELATIVES WITH MONEY. In fact, Christians should treat everyone with that kind of honor, James says. "How can you claim to have faith," he asks, "if you favor some people over others?" He's talking about so-called Christians who diss the poor while giving rich folks the VIP treatment: "You give. . .a good seat to the rich person, but you say to the poor. . .'sit on the floor.'" Poetic injustice. *(James 2:1–13)*

Homeless in Italy

Mission team member Lara Tresch, left, and missionary Cindy Ceballos treat a Honduran girl who has lice.

IF YOU'RE A CHRISTIAN, PROVE IT. Words aren't good enough. Not for James. Anyone can talk. All they need is a set of vocal cords, a two-ounce (60-gram) tongue, and a chest full of hot air. Real Christians walk the talk. Christians wouldn't tell a starving person, "God be with you," and then walk away. For anyone with the gall to do that, James says, "Your words are worth nothing." So is your faith. *(James 2:14–26 NCV)* ▲

MOUTH SHUT: MANUFACTURER'S RECOMMENDED DEFAULT SETTING. "The tongue is a flame," James warns. "It can set your whole life on fire," at the speed of a syllable. James says no one can tame the tongue; it's a wild thing. But we can cage it. When we're tempted to "criticize and judge each other," we can choose to keep our mouths shut. We can't be perfect. But we can be careful. *(James 3:1–12; 4:11–12)*

PAUL: "WE CAN'T 'GOOD-DEED' OUR WAY INTO HEAVEN." Sounding like the opposite of James, Paul seems to tell Christians they don't have to ask God how high to jump to get into heaven. "Your salvation doesn't come from anything you do," he says. It's God's gift, "because of your faith in Christ" (Ephesians 2:8 NIrV). Scholars add, however, that Paul wasn't just a thinker. He was a doer. He put his faith into action, starting dozens of churches throughout the Roman Empire.

HOW CAN CHRISTIANS GET WHAT THEY WANT?

Short answer: Want what God gives. "You want what you don't have," James says of some folks, "so you scheme and kill to get it." That's not the Christian way. "You don't have what you want because you don't ask God for it," James explains. "And even when you ask, you don't get it because your motives are all wrong—you want only what will give you pleasure." *(James 4:1–3)*

PRAYER WORKS WONDERS, SOMETIMES. "Suffering hardships?" James asks. "Are any of you sick?" Pray. Ask God for help. James says prayer can work wonders. If you're sick, he says, "You should call for the elders of the church to come and pray over you, anointing you with oil in the name of the Lord. Such a prayer offered in faith will heal the sick." Not always; everyone dies. But James says prayer has the power to change things. *(James 5)* ▲

WHEN JESUS DIDN'T GET WHAT HE WANTED. Facing crucifixion, Jesus prayed: "My Father, if it is possible, take this cup of suffering away from me. But let what you want be done, not what I want" (Matthew 26:39 NIrV). Within minutes, perhaps, he's arrested. By morning, he's nailed to a cross. He's dead by sundown.

1,2 PETER

SURVIVAL MANUAL FOR CHRISTIANS UNDER FIRE

IN ONE SENTENCE

Peter encourages persecuted Christians in what is now Turkey, reminding them that Jesus suffered, too—and that life doesn't end with a hole in the ground.

SOUND BITE

"A day is like a thousand years to the Lord, and a thousand years is like a day."
—*Peter, to Christians wondering why Jesus hasn't come back yet*
2 PETER 3:8

NEWSMAKER

PETER, leader of Jesus' 12 disciples. Peter became one of the top leaders of the first generation of Christians.

ON LOCATION

TIME. Many Bible experts say Peter wrote these letters shortly before Romans executed him, sometime around AD 64.

PLACE. Peter addresses his first letter to Christians in five Roman provinces—Pontus, Galatia, Cappadocia, Asia, and Bithynia—in what is now Turkey.

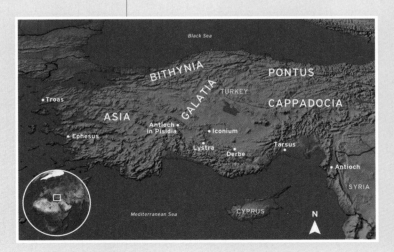

SUFFER NOW, LIVE FOREVER. Christians in what is now Turkey are experiencing violent persecution—exactly what, Peter doesn't say. "Don't jump to the conclusion that God isn't on the job," Peter writes. "Instead, be glad that you are in the very thick of what Christ experienced. This is a spiritual refining process, with glory just around the corner." Peter says Jesus suffered, died, and rose again—and Christians will, too. *(1 Peter 1:1–12; 3:13–4:19 MSG)* ▶

RESPECT THE FOLKS IN CHARGE. Don't buck the system, Peter tells Christians. "Respect all human authority" (NLT). Even Nero, the first Roman emperor to systematically persecute Christians. Nero falsely accuses Christians of setting the fire that destroys much of Rome in AD 64. Peter explains why Christians should respect leaders like this: "It is God's desire that by doing good you should stop foolish people from saying stupid things about you." *(1 Peter 2:13–25 NCV)* ▼

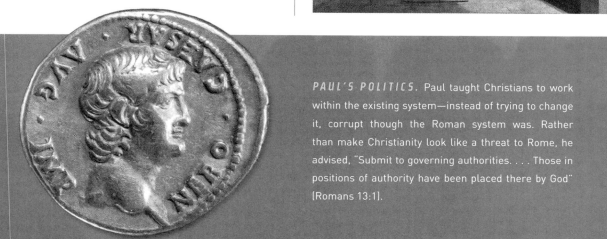

PAUL'S POLITICS. Paul taught Christians to work within the existing system—instead of trying to change it, corrupt though the Roman system was. Rather than make Christianity look like a threat to Rome, he advised, "Submit to governing authorities. . . . Those in positions of authority have been placed there by God" (Romans 13:1).

BECOME A GREAT MINISTER. Peter pleads with ministers to take good care of the congregation God has entrusted to them.

:: Don't do it for money. Do it for God.

:: Don't be bossy. Lead by example.

:: Don't get full of yourself. Keep it humble.

:: Don't worry. Give your worries to God.

(1 Peter 5:1–7)

BECOME A GREAT CHRISTIAN. Peter will die soon. He says Jesus has made that clear to him. In his final letter, Peter sounds like a godly father advising his children—offering his prescription for spiritual growth.

:: "Add goodness to your faith."

:: "To goodness, add knowledge."

:: "To knowledge, add the ability to control yourselves."

:: "To the ability to control yourselves, add the strength to keep going."

:: "To the strength to keep going, add godliness."

:: "To godliness, add kindness to believers."

:: "To kindness to believers, add love."

(2 Peter 1 NIrV) ▼

Portrait from Roman times

HOW DID PETER DIE? The Bible doesn't say. Church leader Origen (about AD 185–254) wrote that "Peter was crucified at Rome with his head downward, as he himself had desired to suffer." As the story goes, Peter didn't feel worthy to be crucified head up, as Jesus had died.

HOW TO SPOT A FRAUDULENT PREACHER.

Peter warns that fraudulent ministers are going to worm their way into churches: "predators on the prowl." So he gives his readers a heads-up on how to spot them. "Brute beasts," as Peter calls them, they:

:: brag about themselves

:: lie to get money

:: sleep around, preaching the Gospel of Party Hearty

:: promise freedom, but shackle themselves to sin. *(2 Peter 2)* ▶

SECOND COMING: WHAT'S TAKING JESUS SO LONG?

Jesus left the planet about 30 years before Peter writes this letter. In the years between, preachers like Paul have been promising, "The Lord is coming soon" (Philippians 4:5). Peter figures it's about time to address the delay. He quotes a psalm that says with God "a thousand years are as a passing day" (Psalm 90:4). And he adds that the longer Jesus delays, the more time people have to get saved. In the meantime, Peter says, people should live in a way that would please God. *(2 Peter 3)*

FIRING PLANET EARTH. Peter's description of the end of the world sounds a bit like one scientific theory. Peter: "The sky will vanish with a roar, the elements will melt with intense heat" (2 Peter 3:10 THE VOICE). Science: The sun will swell into a red giant that engulfs the earth—fortunately for us, in five billion years. That's about the age of the earth, say many geophysicists.

1–3 JOHN

HERETICS AND ANTICHRISTS AT WORK

IN ONE SENTENCE

John attacks problems in churches throughout Turkey, including what appears to be a group of heretics passing Jesus off as some kind of spirit being who only pretended he was human.

SOUND BITE

"Count on God. He's fair and he's reliable. If we ask him to forgive us, he'll forgive us."
—*John, writing to fellow Christians*
1 JOHN 1:9 AUTHOR'S PARAPHRASE

ON LOCATION

TIME. Written as late as the AD 90s.

PLACE. Probably written from Ephesus to churches in the area, in what is now western Turkey. Early church leaders said John and other disciples left Jerusalem in AD 67 after Jews revolted against Rome. John reportedly moved to Ephesus.

NEWSMAKERS

JESUS, God's Son. He came to earth in a human body to save humanity from sin.

JOHN, disciple of Jesus. Presumed writer of these letters. He says he saw and touched Jesus (1 John 1:1).

GAIUS, a church leader. He shows kindness to Christians passing through town.

DIOTREPHES, a control-freak pastor. He abuses his authority by ignoring the apostles and by kicking out

church members who welcome traveling Christians he considers outsiders.

ANTICHRIST IN BIBLE TIMES. John is the Bible's only writer to use the word *antichrist*. When he uses it, he's not talking about the future. He's talking about fraud Christians in his day who are trying to pass Jesus off as something other than the Son of God who came in flesh and blood. One emerging heresy says Jesus was a spirit who only pretended he was human. Another says Jesus was a human who morphed into a spirit being—and that we can do the same. Here's every verse in the Bible that uses the word *antichrist*.

:: **THEY'RE EVERYWHERE**. "You heard that Antichrist is coming. Well, they're all over the place, antichrists everywhere you look" (1 John 2:18 MSG).

:: **THEY DENY THE DEITY OF JESUS**. "This is what makes an antichrist: denying the Father, denying the Son. . . . It's the person who denies that Jesus is the Divine Christ" (1 John 2:22 MSG).

:: **THEY DENY JESUS CAME IN A REAL BODY**. "Many deceivers have gone out into the world. They deny that Jesus Christ came in a real body. Such a person is a deceiver and an antichrist" (2 John 1:7).

:: **THEY LIVE IN JOHN'S DAY**. "But if someone claims to be a prophet and does not acknowledge the truth about Jesus, that person is not from God. Such a person has the spirit of the Antichrist, which you heard is coming into the world and indeed is already here" (1 John 4:3).

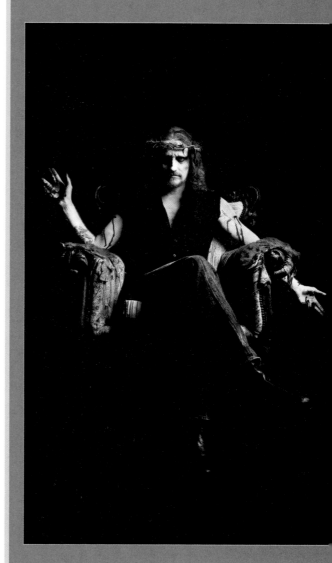

For centuries, artists have often portrayed the antichrist as Jesus' evil twin—anti everything Jesus stands for.

WHERE DID PEOPLE GET THE IDEA THAT AN END-TIME ANTICHRIST IS COMING? Bible historians say it happened several hundred years after Jesus. Christians began connecting disconnected Bible passages, forming a portrait of a future demonic leader—a bit like piecing together a jigsaw puzzle. They linked John's antichrist with the "man of sin" that Paul said was coming, and with Revelation's "beast" (2 Thessalonians 2:3–4; Revelation 13:7–8).

Some Christians view with suspicion door-to-door solicitors for Jehovah's Witnesses—shunning them as heretics. Others welcome them and compare notes about their faith.

HOW TO HANDLE A HERETIC. Love one another, but kindly show a heretic the door. In a sentence, that's the letter of Second John. "Many deceivers have gone out into the world," John writes. "They deny that Jesus Christ came in a real body. . . . If anyone comes to your meeting and does not teach the truth about Christ, don't invite that person into your home or give any kind of encouragement. Anyone who encourages such people becomes a partner in their evil work." *(2 John)*

WHEN IT'S RIGHT TO SAY A MINISTER'S WRONG. It's right, John says, when ministers start taking themselves more seriously than they take the teachings of Jesus. John is writing to a man named Gaius (GAY-us), encouraging him to ignore a control-freak pastor with bad manners. The pastor, Diotrephes (di-OTT-re-fez), excommunicates anyone who welcomes traveling Christians—as though the visitors are intruders threatening his authority. John promises to deal with this pastor. *(3 John)*

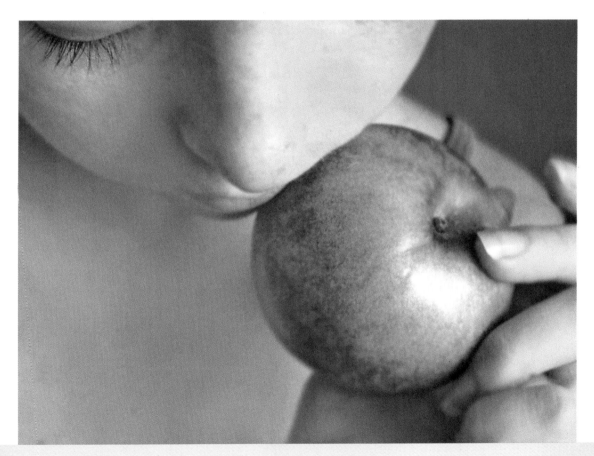

POPULAR HERESY: "IT'S OKAY TO SIN." One of the popular heresies apparently taught that physical beings can't live good lives—but that the spirit within us can achieve holiness, even while our body is sinning like crazy. In that sense, as the heresy goes, we can sin and still say we're sin-free. John's counterpoint: "If we say we're sin-free, we're only kidding ourselves into believing that nonsense is reasonable—or we're bold-faced lying" (1 John 1:8 author's paraphrase).

JUDE

HERESY: SINNING'S OKAY, WE'VE BEEN FORGIVEN

IN ONE SENTENCE

When fraud Christian teachers say it's okay to commit sins—even sexual sins—because God's "marvelous grace" constantly forgives us, Jude offers a short history lesson on God's justice, reminding readers that God punishes sin: Cain, Sodom and Gomorrah, and rebellious angels.

SOUND BITE

"These so-called Christians are like garbage at a Sunday potluck, stinking up the place with their rotten morality."
—*Jude, talking about false teachers worming their way into the church*
JUDE 12 AUTHOR'S PARAPHRASE

NEWSMAKER

JUDE, author of this letter. Early church leaders said he was one of Jesus' brothers.

ON LOCATION

TIME. Written as late as the AD 90s.

PLACE. Probably written from Ephesus to churches in the area, in what is now western Turkey. Early church leaders said John and other disciples left Jerusalem in AD 67 after Jews revolted against Rome. John reportedly moved to Ephesus.

Sculpture of Roman man from first Christian century

HOW TO SPOT A HERETIC. Jude warns Christians about heretics passing themselves off as Christians. He says they're easy to spot. They:

:: Deny Jesus, perhaps saying he wasn't divine.
:: Treat God's forgiveness as a license to sin.
:: Preach sexual immorality, and practice what they preach.
:: Defy authority.
:: Scoff at supernatural beings.
:: Brag loudly about themselves.
:: Flatter others to get what they want.

God forgives sins of the repentant. But Jude warns that God has a long history of punishing those who keep on sinning as though sin is kosher. It's not. *(Jude 8, 16)*

REVELATION

HIGHWAY TO HEAVEN, PAVED IN BLOOD

IN ONE SENTENCE

John sees visions of eternal life in heaven, preceded by what many interpret as a terrifying future for Earth, though others say these visions symbolize the persecution of Christians in John's day.

SOUND BITE

"I saw a new heaven and a new earth .... 'God's home is now among his people! . . . He will wipe every tear from their eyes, and there will be no more death or sorrow or crying or pain.' "
—*John, reporting his final vision*
REVELATION 21:1, 3–4

ON LOCATION

TIME. Written as late as the AD 90s.

PLACE. Probably written from Ephesus to churches in the area, in what is now western Turkey. Early church leaders said John and other disciples left Jerusalem in AD 67 after Jews revolted against Rome. John reportedly moved to Ephesus.

NEWSMAKERS

JOHN, the author. Exiled on Patmos Island, John sees visions, which he records in Revelation. Most early church leaders said this John was the disciple of Jesus. Others, like many scholars today, said it was another John partly because of the different writing style and a reference to the apostles as though he's not one of them (Revelation 21:14).

JESUS, Son of God. He returns to Earth to judge the people, punish sinners, and reward the faithful with everlasting life.

SATAN, a fallen angel. He ends up in a lake of fire, with demons and sinful humans.

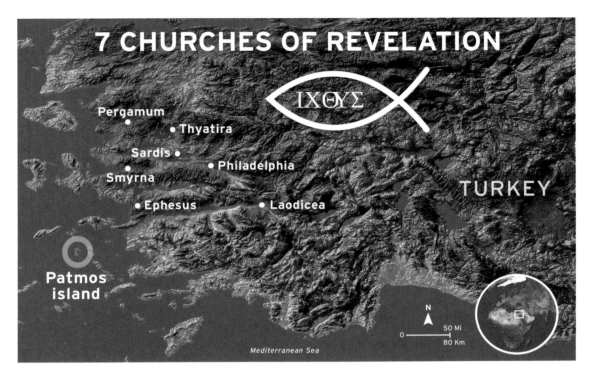

7 CHURCHES OF REVELATION

ΙΧΘΥΣ

Pergamum

Thyatira

Sardis

Philadelphia

Smyrna

Ephesus

Laodicea

TURKEY

Patmos island

Mediterranean Sea

N

50 Mi
0   80 Km

LETTERS FROM JESUS. Worshipping on a Sunday, John sees a vision. The "Son of Man"—Jesus' favorite way of referring to himself—tells him to write a book about everything he's going to see. John is to send it to seven churches on Turkey's west coast. In the Bible, seven often represents completion (see next page). So some scholars say these seven churches represent the entire Christian church. John's book begins with letters Jesus dictates to each of the churches—letters of praise and complaint, which some see as reminders to the church at large of what Jesus expects of his people.

CHURCH	COMPLIMENT	COMPLAINT
EPHESUS	You don't tolerate warped teachings.	Your love for God is fading.
SMYRNA	You're money-poor but spiritually rich.	None.
PERGAMUM	You've stayed true to the faith.	You tolerate false teachings.
THYATIRA	You're growing in faith and service.	You tolerate a false prophet.
SARDIS	You have a few Christians left.	You're nearly dead.
PHILADELPHIA	You're strong and persevering.	None
LAODICEA	None	You're wishy-washy.

(Revelation 1–3)

APOCALYPTIC LIT 101. John wrote Revelation in what many Bible experts say was code language—a genre of writing as unique as poetry or parables. It's called apocalyptic (up-POC-uh-LIP-tick). Writers often used this literary style in times of persecution or enemy occupation. Symbols that show up—like the 666 Mark of the Beast—were understood by insiders but not by the enemy, scholars say. If the enemy intercepted the letter, it would sound like nonsense. So they wouldn't bother arresting the writer or the recipient.

YOU'VE GOT MAIL: SEVEN SEALS OF DOOM.
Still in heaven, John watches as Jesus snaps seven plugs of clay or wax that seal a sacred scroll containing God's plan for the world. Each snap cues a disaster—the first four unleashing the four horsemen of the apocalypse: war, slaughter, death, and more death. In the last three, Christians are martyred, the earth quakes while stars fall and the sky grows dark, then heaven falls silent—a calm before the next storm. *(Revelation 4–7)* ▶

SEVEN TRUMPETS OF DOOM. With all seven seals broken and God's scroll finally opened, seven angels appear—each blowing a mean horn, with each horn signaling a new disaster. By the time the last note sounds, a third of the planet is burned, a third of the water polluted, and a third of humanity dead. *One third,* many scholars say, shouldn't be taken literally, but as a symbol of partial destruction. *(Revelation 8–11)* ▼

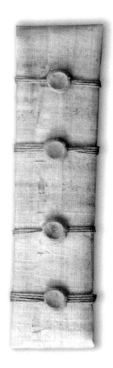

Reconstruction of ancient letter secured with four clay seals

SEVEN, A NUMBER REPRESENTING "THE MAX." God rested on the seventh day of creation. That's why Bible writers often use that number to symbolize fullness or completion. Seven seals and trumpets of doom, along with seven bowls of wrath (Revelation 15–16), for example, could imply suffering to the max.

HISTORY OR PROPHECY? Many scholars say they see Roman history throughout Revelation—in the many disasters, for example. Trumpet five cues a horde of locusts to attack and torture God's people "for five months" (Revelation 9:5). That's how long the Roman army laid siege to Jerusalem in AD 70, before breaking through the walls and leveling the city. The prophet Joel once compared invaders to a swarm of locusts (Joel 1:6). Yet some scholars say they see this particular vision as a prediction of famine and economic disaster ahead.

ANGELS ON THE WARPATH. In perhaps the most bizarre vision in all of Revelation, John describes three odd scenes:

:: A red dragon waits for a woman to give birth so it can gobble up her newborn baby boy.

:: War breaks out in heaven—with angels fighting angels.

:: In a flashback, the dragon is now after the baby boy's family. The baby himself has been air-lifted into God's protective custody in heaven.

Some Bible experts who read history into Revelation say the dragon is Satan opposing Jesus' ministry on earth. But Satan loses, symbolized by falling out of heaven. Jesus ascends to heaven, leaving Satan to go after Christians, the Baby's family. Yet others interpret the scenes as future events during the reign of a tyrannical antichrist. *(Revelation 12)*

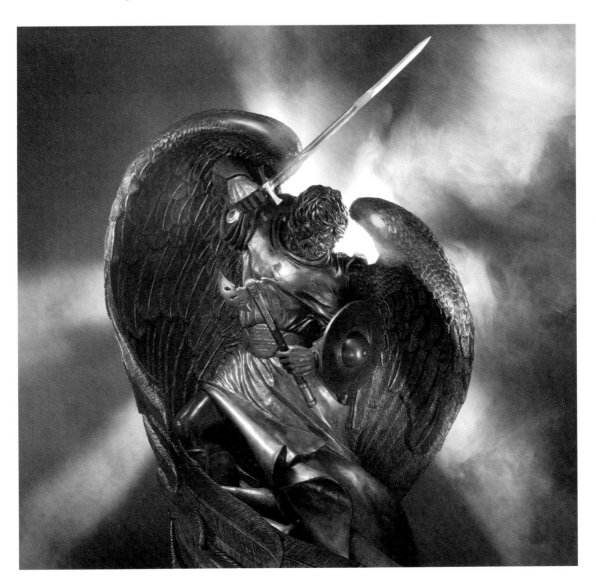

BEASTLY TAG-TEAM. There isn't just one beast. John sees two. One comes by sea, the other by land. Both represent the Roman Empire, many scholars say. Others insist the beasts are yet to come, and one of them will be the demonic Antichrist (see page 485). Some of the possible links to Roman Empire:

:: Sea beast has seven heads, which "represent the seven hills of the city" (Revelation 17:9). Rome was built on seven hills.

:: People worship the beast. Some Romans worship the Roman emperors.

:: The beast rules over the world. Romans controlled most of the civilized world.

(Revelation 13)

Reenacting Romans on the march

MARK OF THE BEAST. The second beast, this one from the land, "exercised all the authority of the first beast" from the sea. John gives a clue about his identity: "His number is 666." In some ancient copies of Revelation, the number is 616. Both numbers work with *Nero Caesar*, many scholars insist, the first Roman emperor to persecute Christians. Start with the words on a Roman coin: Nero Caesar. In Bible times, each letter had a number value.

When translating *Nero Caesar* from Rome's language of Latin into the Jewish language of Hebrew, the Hebrew letters total 616. When translating *Nero Caesar* from the international language of the day—Greek—to Hebrew, the total is 666. Though most Bible experts say they see this link to Nero, who died some 20 years before John's vision, many say the vision also points to a future Nero-like tyrant, possibly the Antichrist. *(Revelation 13:11-18)*

N	E	R	O	N		C	A	E	S	A	R	Greek
נ	ר	ו	נ		ק		ס		ר			Hebrew
50	200	6	50		100		60		200		=	666
N	E	R	O			C	A	E	S	A	R	Latin
נ	ר	ו			ק		ס		ר			Hebrew
50	200	6			100		60		200		=	616

Jews skipped writing most vowels as shorthand.

Jezreel Valley from the south side ridge of hills, looking north

ARMAGEDDON. The number *seven* shows up again, with seven bowls of wrath. The bowls pour out seven final disasters, including deadly skin sores, bloody seas and rivers, a solar blast, earthquakes, and a drought. This drought sets up Armageddon, which many speculate will be an end-time battle between the army of a world-dominating tyrant and the army of Christ.

Surprisingly, though John describes some battles, many scholars say the Battle of Armageddon isn't one of them. John says the drought evaporates the Euphrates River that courses through Syria and Iraq. He says "kings from the east" cross the dry riverbed and gather for a battle at an otherwise unknown place called *Armageddon.* End of story. No mention of the battle.

Some scholars, however, say the other battles John reports describe the Battle of Armageddon:

:: The army consisted of "200 million mounted troops" (Revelation 9:16).

:: Invaders attack "the city that his [God's] people love" (Revelation 20:9 CEV), possibly Jerusalem.

:: "Blood flowed. . .as high as a horse's bridle" (Revelation 14:20).

WHERE IS ARMAGEDDON? Armageddon doesn't show up anywhere else in ancient writings. Many Bible students speculate that the word refers to *Har Megiddo* (hill of Megiddo). Megiddo was an ancient hilltop fortress guarding an important pass through the Carmel Mountains into Jezreel Valley. Over the past 3,000 years, armies have fought more than 30 major battles in this valley that Napoleon once called the "perfect battlefield."

THE HUNT FOR ARMAGEDDON

JUDGMENT DAY. Riding on a white horse, a being that John calls "the Word of God" leads a cavalry of angels to earth. *Word,* most scholars agree, is likely a coded reference to Jesus, head of the Christian movement that Rome has outlawed. The Word and his army crush an international coalition of armies allied with "the beast and his false prophet."

An angel arrests Satan and tosses him into a bottomless pit for a thousand years. Afterward, Satan is released. He rallies nations for one more battle. Some speculate this is the Battle of Armageddon, or perhaps a later battle—one last stab at God.

Fire from the sky incinerates Satan's army. Defeated, Satan gets pitched into a lake of fire, along with "anyone whose name was not found recorded in the Book of Life." *(Revelation 19–20)*

Satan on ice

Hell on earth is a walk in the park—in Hinnom Valley on Jerusalem's west side.

▲ **HELL.** Another term for "the lake of fire," some scholars say—a place of eternal punishment for Satan and his followers, demons and humans alike.

The Greek word is *Gehenna*, a valley outside Jerusalem's city walls. Jews call it Hinnom Valley. They link the site to God's judgment because their ancestors once sacrificed to idols there. And their scriptures say God punished them for it by allowing Babylonian invaders in 586 BC to defeat them and destroy Jerusalem.

Modern theories about hell:

:: It's is a literal place of eternal torture.

:: It's separation from God, where people who wanted nothing to do with him in life get their wish in the afterlife.

:: It's annihilation. Sinners won't suffer forever, but their destruction will last forever.

:: People get a second chance in the afterlife. God will welcome sinners because through Christ, "He made peace with everything in heaven and on earth" (Colossians 1:20).

BOOK OF LIFE. A book of names or perhaps just a symbol of all the people in history whom God "counted among the righteous" (Psalm 69:28).

TOURING HEAVEN. In the Bible's climax, John sees "a new heaven and a new earth. The first heaven and the first earth were completely gone. . . . I saw the Holy City, the new Jerusalem. It was coming down out of heaven" (Revelation 21:1–2 NIrV).

Some Bible experts read this and say John is talking about a new universe, with Earth 2.0. Others say it's just another way of talking about heaven.

Whatever it is, John sees what sounds like a return to paradise lost: Eden, with the sin mess cleaned up. No more toxic spiritual pollution.

In the Genesis story, there's a river feeding life throughout Eden. In Revelation, John sees a river feeding life in New Jerusalem, which may be another name for heaven. This river comes from the throne of God. It's "the water of life" that nourishes the "tree of life," which grows leaves used to "bring healing to the nations."

Having seen this future, John closes the book on the Bible with a benediction:

"Come, Lord Jesus!" *(Revelation 21–22 NIrV)*

ISAIAH SAW A NEW HEAVEN AND EARTH. Some 800 years before John, Isaiah quoted God, "Look! I am creating new heavens and a new earth. . . . I will create Jerusalem as a place of happiness. . . . And the sound of weeping and crying will be heard in it no more" (Isaiah 65:17–19).

AND THE POINT IS? Whatever suffering Christians have to endure, and wherever it shows up on history's timeline—past, present, or future (depending on which Bible experts got it right)—there's a better day coming. And it will last forever.

BUILDER'S GRADE

Foundation stones in New Jerusalem

JASPER   SAPPHIRE   AGATE   EMERALD

ONYX   CARNELIAN   CHRYSOLITE   BERYL

TOPAZ   CHRYSOPRASE   JACINTH   AMETHYST

CELESTIAL UPGRADE. Gems on earth are nothing but foundation blocks in New Jerusalem. Some Christians take John's description of heaven literally. Others say his vision is a symbolic way of describing heaven—as a place so wonderful that by comparison, earth's greatest treasures seem as mundane as a cement block.

bold numbers: featured
regular numbers: mentioned
color numbers: image

A

Aaron, 254, 257, 261, 269, 270, 307
Abednego, 356, 358
Abortion, **69–72**
Abraham, 90, 123, 130, 145, 199, 240, 242, **249–250**, 307, 316, 319
    father of Jews, 91, 440, 441, 449, 451, 475
    marries Sarah, 147
    moves, 25, 249
    map of migration, 249
    near-sacrifice of Isaac, **250**
Absalom, 56, 124, 194, 223, 297
Abstinence, 142, 143
Abuse, **72–73**, **112**, 157, 177, 234, 452
Acacia
    Grove, 277
    map, 277
    wood, 81, 204
Acts, book of, **430–437**
Adam (man), 69, 75, 85, 91, 103, 178, 212, 214, 217, 242, 244, 245, 246, 247, 307
Adam (place), 171, 277
Addiction, **73**, 128, 142, 188–189
Advice, 73, 104, 177, 183, 218, 334
Adultery, **55–56**, **73–74**, **328**
Afterlife, see Eternal life
Agnostic, **83**, 85, 218
Ahab, 298, 302, 303
Aijalon, 279
Alcohol, see Drinking and Drugs
Allah, 30
Almond, 270
Amazing Grace, 50
Ambrose, 71, 427
Amenemope, 327
Amish, 23
Ammon, 284, 379
    map, 378
Amnon, 56, 124, 165, 194, 297
Amos, **366–367**
Ananias, 34, 433
Angels, 22, **74–76**, 75, 105, 107, 108, 118, 136, 383, 411, 446, 473, **493**
    worship of, 457
    fallen, 140, 162, **208**, 319
Anger, 54, 55, 56, **76–77**, 80, 135, 327
Anglican, 28–29, 32
Annas, 420
Anointing, 61, 79, 135, 150, 169, 206, 291, **410**, 479
Antichrist, **77–78**, 460, **485**, 494
Antioch, Syria, 80, 94, 435, 436, 449
    map, 435, 436
Antioch in Pisidia
    map, 435, 436
Antiochus, 361
Apocalyptic lit, 22, 208, **491**
Apocrypha, 30, 90

Apollos, 116, 443
Apostle, **78–79**
Apostle's Creed, 36, 274
Appearance, physical, **79**, 172–173
Aquinas, Thomas, 32
Arabia, 301, 340
    map, 340
Artaxerxes, 313
Artemis, 437
Arguments, **79–80**, 444, **455**, 464, 478
Aristotle, 71
Arminius, Jacobus, 191
Ark of the Covenant, **81**, 204, 270, 300, 353
Armageddon, **82**, 293, **495**, 496
Asa, 308
Ascension, **82**, 88, 195, **431**, 435
Asia, 105
    map, 480
Assyrians, 24, 304, 305, 308, 339, 340, 345, 370, 371, 418
    vicious, 371, 375
    doomed, 43, 340
    map, 340, 374
Astrology, **82–83**, 432
Athaliah, 303
Athanasius, 16, 32
Atheism, 31, **83–85**, 125, 218, 439
    questions asked by, **39–51**
Athens, 446
    map, 436, 437, 442, 466
Atonement, **85**, 125, 137
Attitude, **85–86**
Augustine, 129, 222, 227

B

Baal, 302
Babylon, Babylonians, 14, 25, 305, 307, 347, 348–349, 352, 360, 365, 377
    map, 309, 340, 350, 374, 376
Backsliding, **86–87**, 119
Balaam, 271
Baptism, 30, 34, 35, **87–88**, 103, 200, 389
Baptist, 29, 32, 34, 86, 118, 191, 212, 227
Barnabas, 105, 126, 435, 436
Baruch, 14, 348
Bashan, 367
    map, 366
Bathsheba, 62, 124, 189, 288, **296**, 325, 387, 392
Beast, of Revelation, 78, 140, 209, 485, 491, **494**
Beatitudes, 85, **89**, 135, 157, 169, 390
Beauty, see Appearance, physical
Beggar, 189, 426
Belief, 32, **89–90**, 438
Belshazzar, 359
Benjamin, 148, **285**
Bethlehem, 286, 287, 290, 311
    birthplace of Jesus, 47, 75, 170, 372, 373, 386, 388, 412, 413
    star of, 82, **388**
    map, 286, 372, 382
Bethsaida, 408
Betrayal, 47, 53, 54–56, 78, 383
Blasphemy, **90–91**, 420
    against Holy Spirit, 213, 231, 392
Blessings, **91**, 100, 144, 250

Sistine Chapel, 33, 69

Slavery, 50, 194

    of Jews in Egypt, 255, 258

    in Roman Empire, 60, 464, 470–471, 471

Smoking, **214–215**

Smyrna

    map, 491

Snake, 45, 46, 209, 245, 271

Sodom, **249**, 486

Solomon, 57, 298, 299, 300, 301, 302, 306, 307, 308, 326, 332, 333, 336

Son of God, 30, 47, 147, 150–151, 420

Son of Man, 90, 158, 161, **215**

Song of Songs, **336–337**

Soul, **215–217**

Spanish Inquisition, 33, 41

Spanking, 331

Spirit, **217**, 473

Spirit beings, 177–178, 215–217

Spiritual, **217–218**

Spiritual gifts, **218–219**, **445**

Spiritual growth, 65–67, 440, 451

Spiritual troubles, **62–67**

Spiritual warfare, **452–453**

Stealing, **219**

Stephen, **434**

Stewardship, see Tithing

Stonehenge, 25

Success, **219–220**

Suffering, **40–42**, **66–67**, 144, **220–221**

    for being a Christian, **459**, **477**, 481

    in joy, 153

Suicide, **221–223**, 294

Sumerians, 246

Sunday, **27**, 201–202

Susa, 312, 314

    map, 309

Sychar, 425

    map, 425

Synagogue, 14, 146, 152, 172, 236, 391, 415, 435, 451, 472

Swearing, see Cursing

T

Tamar, 124, 194, 297, 387

Tarshish

    map, 370

Tarsus

    map, 435, 436

Tattoos, **223**

Taurus Mountains, 197

Taylor, Hudson, 32

Tax collector, 78, 144, **224**, 240, 387, **419**

Taxes, **224**, 419

Tekoa

    map, 366, 372

Temper, 76–77, **225**

Temple, Jewish, 111, 226, 228, 300, 307, 308, 354, 381, 433

Temptation, **225**, 465, **477**

    of Eve, 46

    of Jesus, **389**

Ten Commandments, 14, 81, 103, 180, 203, **225**, **260**

    loophole, 393

Tertullian, 71

Thessalonica, 459

    map, 436, 458, 466

Thessalonians, books of, **458–461**

Thomas, 78, 113, 429

Thutmose III, 257

Thyatira

    map, 491

Tigris River

    map, 246, 249, 309, 340

Timothy, books of, **462–467**

    the man, 109, 454, 458, 462, 463, **464**

Tithing, **226–228**, **385**

Titus, the book, **468–469**

    the man, 161, 460, 468

Tolerance, 181–182, **228**

Tomb, 48, 95, **398–399**, 400, 411, 420, 429, 446

Tongues, Speaking in, **229–230**, 432, 435

Trinity, **46–47**, **129**, 130, **230**, **427**

Troas

    map, 436, 466

Trust, see Faith

Truth, 144, 425, 453

Tyre, 300

    map, 340

U

Universe, 84, 101, **244**, 439

Unpardonable Sin, **213**, **231**, **392**

Ur, 147

    map, 249

Uriah, **296**

Utnapishtim, 248

V

Vashti, 314, 315

Via Appia, 36

Virgin birth, 37, 45, **231–232**, 387, 413

Virginity, see Abstinence

Visions, 22, 40, 78, 125, 158, 308, 339, 355, 361, 490, 493, 494, 498–499

W

War, **232–233**, 233, 292, 304, 305

    spiritual, **453**, **493**

    map, 279, 294

Weakness, **234**

Wealth, 174, **234–235**, 327, 333, **395**

Weight, see Obesity

Wesley, John, 33, 66, 191, 192, 227

Wesleyan, 118, 191, 206

West Bank, 203, 276

    map, 364, 425,

Western (Wailing) Wall, 473

Widows, 110, 121, 122, 131, 287, 385, 391, 464

Wilderness of Paran,

    map, 268

Wilderness of Zin,

    map, 268

Wine, 36, 97, **113–115**, 115, 116, 159, 199, 313, 385, 397, 424

Wisdom, **236**, 333

Wise men, 82, 373, **388**

Witchcraft, see Occult

ART CREDITS

Abbreviations: AR=Art Resource; BAL=Bridgeman Art Library; BB=Balage Balogh; BMM=Bradley M. Miller; DA=DeviantArt.com; DW=Dave Webster; FL=Flickr; GI=Getty Images; GS=GoodSalt; IS=iStockphoto; KR=Kevin Rolly; LJ= Lars Justinen; LOC=Library of Congress; PD=Public domain; RC=Rani Calvo; SMM=Stephen M. Miller; THP=Tyndale House Publishers; TP=Tom Patterson; WM=WikiMedia; WP=WikiPedia

Front Matter

5 Hebrew lettering: Chris Pilon/FL; cathedral: Trey Ratcliff/stuckincustoms.com; book: brewbooks; 6 woman: Patrick Sheandell O'Carroll/PhotoAlto/Corbis; Mary and Jesus: DW; Saturn: NASA; 8 Shutterstock

Bible Fast Pass

10 Chris Pilon/FL; 11 planets: NASA; Moses with tablets: DMY/WM; Joshua: Ondra Havala/FL; musicians: Lawrence Lew, O.P.; 12 bearded men: WM/Giacomo Raffaelli; Jesus and disciples: Geoff Robinson/FL/Robert Bayne; Pentecost: DW/FL; 13 Paul writing: LJ/GS; man looking up: Ondra Havala/FL; three men: GS; stained glass: DW; 15 AR; 16 map: TP/rendered by SMM; 17 Time & Life Pictures/GI; 18 CEV cover: American Bible Society; NCV, NKJV covers: Thomas Nelson, Inc.; NLT cover: THP; ESV cover: Crossway; The Message cover: NavPress; KJV cover: Barbour Publishing; 20 Chris Pilon/FL; 21 Crossway; 23 Trey Ratcliff/stuckincustoms.com; 24 Noah's ark: Creation Museum, Petersburg, Kentucky, www.creationmuseum.org; pyramids: WM; map: RC/Geological Survey of Israel/rendered by SMM; Jesus' crucifixion: WM/Diego Velázquez; Peter's crucifixion: WM/Caravaggio; 25 Rameses: agefotostock/SuperStock; Stonehenge: Simon Wakefield/WM; Nativity: WM; runners: PD; Pilate: William Storage; John of Revelation: WM/Diego Velázquez; Roman soldiers: Peter Cracknell/FL

Christianity Fast Pass

26 Trey Ratcliff/stuckincustoms.com; 28 Anglican priest: Studio Woolslayer; Orthodox priest: Ian Corbridge/FL; 29 Protestant minister: IS; Catholic priest: IS; 30 Christian: IS; Muslim: IS; 31 Hindu: Sukanto Debnath/FL; Buddhist: IS; 32 baby Jesus: DW; adult Jesus: LJ/GS; Jesus' crucifixion: WM/Diego Velázquez; Athanasius: Molly Eyres; crusader: Vlados7/DA; Wycliffe: PD; Henry VIII: WM/Hans Holbein the Younger; Chinese junk: WP; Bonhoeffer: PD; 33 map of Paul's first mission: TP/rendered by SMM; Constantine: Camille King/FL; Jerome: WM; map of church split: TP/rendered by SMM; Gutenberg Bible: NYC Wanderer/FL; Inquisition: Claudia Gold/FL; Sistine Chapel: Roberto Ricci; Bible translators: Ondra Havala/FL; John Wesley: Nick Thompson/FL; Billy Graham: Hulton Archive/GI; Martin Luther King, Jr.: Cecil Stoughton, White House Press Office/WM; 35 ExactoStock/SuperStock; 36 Nicolò Musmeci/WM

Ten Tough Questions

38 brewbooks; 39 courtesy of Kim Hager and Neal Prakash, UCLA; 41 Eneas De Troya/FL; 43 Igor Kamenev; 45 Bill Aron; 46 Manchester Art Gallery/John Stanhope; 47 Andrew Dupont/FL; 48 James Emery/FL; 49 GI; 51 Corbis

Bible Survival Guide

52 Patrick Sheandell O'Carroll/PhotoAlto/Corbis; 53 IS; 54 MultiCurious/DA; 55 IS; 57 Richard T. Nowitz/Corbis; 59 Trey Ratcliff/stuckincustoms.com; 61 woman with hives: Elle Moss/GI; deathbed scene: SMM; 63 Sollina Images/Blend Images/Corbis; 65 DW; 66 KR

What the Bible Says About

68 DW; 69 Sebastian Bergmann/FL; 70 Patricia Dominguez/epa/Corbis; 71 PD; 73 KR; 74 Francisca Ulloa/FL; 75 Mark Patrick/MarkPatrickStudio.com; 76 Emery Way/WM; 77 LJ/GS; 79 David Ross/Corbis; 80 Corbis; 81 Sunset Boulevard/Corbis; 82 map: RC/Geological Survey of Israel/rendered by SMM; Jezreel Valley: Vad Levin/FL; 83 Faceout Studio; 84 NASA/WMAP Science Team; 87 STR/Reuters/Corbis; 88 Corbis; 91 IS; 93 Ulises Rodriguez/epa/Corbis; 95 Tad Green; 97 Atef Hassan/Reuters/Corbis; 99 Emilio Labrador/FL; 101 NASA; 102 KR; 105 L.C.Nøttaasen/FL; 106 Keith Dannemiller/Corbis; 108 Ferdinand Bol/PD; 111 John Rensten/Corbis; 114 WM; 115 Stefan Krause/WM; 116 Polihale/WM; 117 Charles Sprague Pearce/PD; 118 PD; 120 PD; 122 Luke Kramer/IS; 124 Molly Eyres/FL/Giuseppe Bartolomeo Chiari; 127 H. Kopp-Delaney/FL; 128 WM/Georges Croegaert; 130 PD; 131 Liyana H. (naaera)/DA; 133 Warren K. Leffler/LOC; 135 LJ/GS; 136 Viktor Vasnetsov/PD; 137 Alexander Mossin/FL; 138 GI; 139 Ron Almog/FL; 141 Konstantin Apollonovich Savitsky/PD; 143 Steven Rainwater/FL; 144 Mary Harrsch/FL; 147 Dennis Hill/FL; 148 Daniel Lobo/FL; 149 Trey Ratcliff/stuckincustoms.com; 151 El Greco/PD; 153 Munkácsy Mihály/PD; 155 Ted Soqui/Sygma/Corbis; 156 Ed Yourdon/FL; 158 Pierre J./FL; 159 Pavel Popov; 160 benjamint444/WM; 161 BAL; 163 Ed Yourdon/FL; 164 Bill Aron; 166 Rob Unreall/FL; 167 WM/Grigory Sedov; 168 Tatiana Yushmanova/PD; 169 National Museums of Scotland/BAL; 170–171 Christopher Belsten/FL; 172 LJ/GS; 173 Nuno Castro/FL/Edward Burne-Jones; 175 Michael Philip/WM/Ernst Josephson; 176 Granger Collection; 177 Barry M/FL; 178 Sailko/WM/Edward Burne-Jones; 180 WM/Charles Sprague Pearce; 182 Bill Aron; 183 Trey Ratcliff/stuckincustoms.com; 184 Adrian Tecson/FL; 185 Israelimages/Itsik Marom; 186 PD; 187 Jeff Preston/GS; 189 Rohit Markande; 191 PD; 192 Derrick Coetzee/WM/William Hamilton; 193 Ammar Awad/Reuters/Corbis; 195 Salvador Dali; 197 Richard T. Nowitz/Corbis; 198 Aidan McRae Thomson/FL; 200 Michael Jacobs/FL; 202 Ted Spiegel/Corbis; 203 Israelimages/Yasha Mazur; 204 Thomas Schuman/FL; 205 Sergei Kirillov; 206 Eric Jusino/FL; 207 Shane Gorski/FL; 208 photo illustration by SMM/clouds photo: Ordale/statue photo: Thermos/WM; 210 Faraz Shanyar/DA; 211 Pavel Svedomsky/WM; 213 Federal Bureau of Investigation/PD; 214 PD; 216 Terra Catozzi/FL; 218 Jeff Raune; 219 Duccio di Buoninsegna/PD; 221 SMM; 222 Yair Talmor/WM/Elie Marcuse; 223 Ghetttoman4bet/WM; 224 Joe Geranio/FL; 226 LJ/GS; 227 Nick Thompson/FL; 229 DW/FL; 231 ExiledFruit/DA; 233 PD; 235 Sir Lawrence Alma-Tadema/PD; 237 LOC/Matson Photograph Collection; 238–239 George Nutulescu/FL

Bible Snapshots

241 NASA

Genesis

242 creation: NASA; God: Igor Kamenev; Adam and Eve: Melanie B. Hyams/FL; Noah: GS; Abraham: PD; Jacob: GS; 243 Hennie van Heerden/FL; 244 NASA; 245 Molly Eyres/FL; 246 map: Tom Patterson/rendered by SMM; hand with apple: D is for Duck/DA; 247 Wendell Jacinto/FL; 248 Noah's ark: WM; Epic of Gilgamesh: Mike Peel/WM; 249 RC/Geological Survey of Israel/rendered by SMM; 250 Abraham and Isaac: Kelley Burke/FL; Jacob and Esau: AR; 251 AR; 252 Joseph sold: Lawrence Lew/FL; Potiphar's wife: AR; 253 Joseph as ruler: BAL; map: NASA/rendered by SMM; map art of travelers: BB

Exodus

254 Moses, left: David Smith/PD; Moses, portrait: Jacob de Wit/PD; Aaron: AKG; Pharaoh: Piotr Naszarwkowski/DA; map: NASA/rendered by SMM; 255 Exodus from Egypt: PD; bricks: Danel W. Bachman/FL; baby Moses and mother: BAL; 256 traveler with camel: H. Kopp-Delaney/FL; tree: Eric Vondy/FL; 257 Rameses II: Shd-stock/DA; frogs: THP; 258 unleavened bread: Musicpb/FL; refugees: THP; 259 Egyptian soldiers in Red Sea: BAL; Red Sea reef: Dawn Knox/FL; 260 catching quail: Joe Carnegie/Libyan Soup/FL; collecting sap: Corbis; Moses with tablets: Adam Fagen/FL; 261 tabernacle: BB; priests: AKG

Leviticus

262 Moses, left: DMY/WM; Moses, portrait: David Smith/DA; Aaron: AKG; map: NASA/rendered by SMM; 263 temple sacrifices: BB; sheep: Meirion Matthias; 264 pigeon: Rob Elsas/FL; bread: IS; goat: IS; bull: Kathy McEldowney/FL; ram: IS; 265 prime rib: IS; man with ram's horn: Israelimages

Numbers

266 travelers, left: GS; Moses, portrait: Jacob de Wit/PD; Aaron: AKG; Joshua: Johnny Shumate/WM; map: NASA/rendered by SMM; 266 tabernacle: LJ/GS; warrior: Giorge Roman/DA; 268 map: NASA/rendered by SMM; map art: PD; 269 mummy: British Museum; rebels: THP; 270 almond: Tomás Martínez/FL; oasis: Zev Radovan; 271 snake: Böhringer Friedrich/FL; donkey: Dennis Macwilliam/FL

Deuteronomy

272 Moses, left: David Smith; Moses, portrait: Jacob de Wit/PD; Joshua: Johnny Shumate/WM; map: TP/rendered by SMM; 273 Moses: PD; Code of Hammurabi: Philip Rickerby/FL; 274 LOC/G. Eric and Edith Matson Photograph Collection; 275 family tree: Israelimages/Erez Ben Simon; water from rock: THP

Joshua

276 Joshua, left and portrait: KR; Rahab: KR; 277 map: NASA/rendered by SMM; map art of priests: AR; Rahab: KR; 278 BB; 279 hail: Erez Mayerkevitch/FL; map: RC/Geological Survey of Israel/rendered by SMM; 280 Guillaume Blanchard/WM; 281 Joshua: DM/WM; map: RC/Geological Survey of Israel/rendered by SMM

Judges
282 wounded man, left: KR; Samson: WM/Albrech Durer; Delilah: Sabah J Sadoun/DA; Gideon: THP; Deborah: DW/FL; **283** Mount Tabor: Micah Sadrinas/FL; Jael: KR; **284** camel and man: Ollie Harridge; woman with tambourine: KR; **285** dead woman: KR; Delilah: Sabah J. Sadoun/DA

Ruth
286 Ruth, left: DW/FL; Ruth, portrait: Claudia K. Harvey/FL; Naomi: PD; Boaz: PD/Peter Paul Rubens: map: TP/rendered by SMM; **287** LOC

1, 2 Samuel
288 donkey herder, left: Meirion Matthias/FL; David: Maziar Boostan/FL; Saul: Kimberly Katiti/DA; Samuel: PD/Peter Paul Rubens; Bathsheba: PD/Rosalba Carriera; Nathan: PD/Peter Paul Rubens; **289** Darrel Tank/GS; **290** donkey: Ben Heine/FL; anointing oil: Eddie Chui/FL; **292** stones: Oriental Institute; David with Goliath's head: Johann Zoffany/BAL; coat of mail: GI; **293** David playing harp: PD/Nikolai Petrovich Zagorsky; Jonathan: PD/Frederic Leighton; **294** map: RC/Geological Survey of Israel/rendered by SMM; death of Saul: Yair Talmor/WM/Elie Marcuse; **295** map: NASA/rendered by SMM; Jerusalem graphic: Bill Latta; **296** David on roof: BB; Bathsheba: KR; **297** rapist Amnon: KR; Absalom: BAL

1, 2 Kings
298 Solomon, left and portrait: LJ/GS; Elijah: Diego Velazquez/FL; Jezebel: Travis Anthony Soumis/model: Cherie Roberts/DA; map: RC/Geological Survey of Israel/rendered by SMM; **299** AR; **300** temple: Peter V. Bianchi/National Geographic; cedars: Jennifer Hayes/FL; **301** woman on dunes: Saudi Aramco World/SAWDIA; harem: PD/Theodore Chasseriau; **302** map: TP/rendered by SMM; Baal: BAL; **303** Elijah: National Gallery of Art/Giuseppe Angeli; Jezebel: Travis Anthony Soumis/model: Cherie Roberts/DA; **304** attack on Samaria: Don Lawrence/BAL; Assyrian ruler: William Storage; **305** soldiers leading prisoners: Kenneth Inns/BAL; Nebuchadnezzar: Alexander Jubran/DA; siege tower: Capillon/WM

1, 2 Chronicles
306 David, left and portrait: Maziar Boostan/FL; Solomon: LJ/GS; Hezekiah: PD; **307** Babylon gate: BB; floating cedars: BB; **308** BAL; **309** map: TP/rendered by SMM; map art of soldier: BMM; Zedekiah fleeing: BAL

Ezra
310 ruins, left: BAL; Ezra: PD/Peter Paul Rubens; Cyrus: Dynamosquito/FL; map: TP/rendered by SMM; map art of soldier: BMM; **311** Corbis

Nehemiah
312 building walls, left: BB; Nehemiah: Petrus. agricola/FL; Sanballat: Shifa/DA; Ezra: PD/Peter Paul Rubens; **313** building walls: BB; Nehemiah: Petrus.agricola/FL

Esther
314 Esther, left and portrait: PD; Xerxes: PD; Mordecai: Nasib Bitar/WM; Haman: Ofir Abe/DA; Vashti: Bryan Crump/DA; **315** PD/Minerva Teichert; **316** PD/Ernest Normand; **317** Stav Gertz, Israel/FL

Job
318 Job and family, left: PD/William Blake; Job portrait: PD/Marinus Van Reymerswaele; Job's wife: Hamed Saber/FL; Job's friends: Marie-Lan Nguyen/WM/Jacob Jordaens; God: Igor Kamenev; **319** Satan: WM/Egon Schiele; man with camel: Manoj Vasanth/FL; **320** Job's friends: Ilya Repin; **321** Yosemite: Darvin Atkeson

Psalms
322 harpist, left: DW/FL; God: Igor Kamenev; David: Maziar Boostan/FL; map: NASA/rendered by SMM; **323** David: Lawrence Lew, O.P./FL; **324** shepherd and sheep: Raja Selvaraj/WM; fortress: BB; **325** DW/FL

Proverbs
326 old men, left: Bill Aron; Solomon: LJ/GS; young man portrait: WM; loose woman portrait: Sergio Andreu Atance/DA; **327** BMM; **328** veiled women: Sergio Andreu Atance/DA; ant: Shutterstock; **329** Miklós Szabó, Miki3d/DA; **330** Yoram Biberman/FL; **331** child: Jill Greenberg/GI; man: Alfredo11/FL

Ecclesiastes
332 children, left: Neils Photography/FL; teacher: LJ/GS; map: RC/Geological Survey of Israel/rendered by SMM; **333** PD/Anne-Louis Girodet; **334** figurine: Scala/AR; sailors: Bert Kaufmann/FL

Song of Songs
336 woman, left: KR; woman portrait: Kirill Gorbunov; man portrait: PD; **337** running couple: PD/Pierre-Auguste Cot; wedding couple: Carson Swisher Photography/BMM

Isaiah
338 virgin, left: ExiledFruit/DA; Isaiah: PD/Juan Carreño de Miranda; Hezekiah: PD; map: TP/rendered by SMM; **338** Isaiah's cleansing: Alex Bakharev/WM/Mikhail Vrubel; Mary: DW/FL; **340** map: TP/rendered by SMM; map art of Assyrian: William Storage; Carchemish warrior: BAL; **341** Jerusalem: PD/Charles Théodore Frère; wolf: Gary Kramer/WM; **342–343** Giovanni Battista Tiepolo

Jeremiah
344 wall, left: PD; Jeremiah: Francisco Collantes; Zedekiah: Giandomenico Tiepolo; Nebuchadnezzar: Alexander Jubran/DA; **345** Saudi Aramco World/SAWDIA; **346** KR; **347** Yann/WM; **348** seal: Zev Radovan; **349** Nebuchadnezzar: Alexander Jubran/DA

Lamentations
350 graves, left: Greg Schneider; songwriter: Ofir Abe; map: TP/rendered by SMM; map art of ziggurat: BMM; **351** Yorck Project/WM/Egon Schiele

Ezekiel
352 Ezekiel, left: LJ/GS; Ezekiel portrait: Micah Christensen; Babylon: Alexandre Jubran/DA; **353** Mahmoud Farshchian/DA; **354** William Storage; **355** bones: Corbis; Dead Sea: Albatross

Daniel
356 lion, left: GS; Daniel: Ribera del Duero; Shadrach, Meshach, and Abednego: WM/Giacomo

Raffaelli; Nebuchadnezzar: Alexandre Jubran/DA; **357** statue: LJ/GS; **358** kiln: WM; crematorium: Bukephalos/WM; **359** crazy Nebuchadnezzar: PD/William Blake; Belshazzar: Olpl/WM/Rembrandt; **360** GS; **361** Jesus in clouds: LJ/GS; Ptolemy: Phgcom/WM

Hosea
362 woman, left: PD/Edward Burne-Jones; Hosea: PD; Gomer: Ofir Abe/DA; map: TP/rendered by SMM; **363** PD/Edward Burne-Jones

Joel
364 locust, left: Scott Thompson/FL; Joel: PD; map: TP/rendered by SMM; map art of locust: Asadbabil/FL; **365** Petrus Agricola (photographer), Antonio Pisanello (artist)

Amos
366 woman, left: WM; Amos: PD/Peter Paul Rubens; map: TP/rendered by SMM; **367** woman: WM; fig: Ofer Sabban/FL

Obadiah
368 Petra, left: Greg Schneider; Obadiah: PD/Peter Paul Rubens; map: RC/Geological Survey of Israel/rendered by SMM; map art of refugees: AR **369** Blackxx/DA

Jonah
370 fish, left: Citron/WM; Jonah: PD; map: TP/rendered by SMM; **371** Martin Beek/FL

Micah
372 wise man, left: DW/FL; Micah: PD/Peter Paul Rubens; map: TP/rendered by SMM; **373** Bethlehem: BB; wise man: DW/FL

Nahum
374 Nineveh, left: BAL; Nahum: DW/FL; map: TP/rendered by SMM; map art of Assyrian: William Storage; **375** Nineveh: BAL; Assyrian impalers: AR

Habakkuk
376 Babylon, left: BB; Habakkuk: PD/Peter Paul Rubens; map: TP/rendered by SMM; map art of ziggurat: BMM; **377** Babylon: BB; Martin Luther: Nicholas Morieson/FL

Zephaniah
378 comet and earth: NASA/photo illustration by SMM; Zephaniah: PD; map: TP/rendered by SMM; **379** Alexandre Jubran/DA

Haggai
380 temple, left: National Geographic; Haggai: PD/Peter Paul Rubens; Jerusalem: BB; **381** National Geographic

Zechariah
382 donkey, left: Dennis Macwilliam/FL; Zechariah: PD/El Greco; map: RC/Geological Survey of Israel/rendered by SMM; **383** Abbott Henderson Thayer

Malachi
384 God, left: WM/Michelangelo; Malachi: AR; cows: Sunny Ripert/FL; **385** John the Baptist: Juan Martínez Montanés; tithing box: Lynsey P. Tamborello

Matthew
386 Jesus, left: PD/El Greco; Jesus, portrait: PD/
El Greco; twelve disciples: DW/FL; Mary: Siona/
DA; Joseph: PD/Raphael; Pontius Pilate: William
Storage; Herod the Great: William Storage; **387**
KR; **388** magi: Juan Bautista Maíno; star map:
Hans-Peter Scholz/WM; **389** PD/El Greco; **390**
Jesus with disciples: Pavel Popov; Jesus sculpture:
Etai Adam/FL; **391** mosaic: WM; fish: Tomás
Castelazo/WM; **392** Jesus with woman: BAL;
plowing: Ricki Rosen/CORBIS SABA; **393** loaves
and fish: Viktor Matorin; Jewish scholar: WM; **394**
statue: SMM; map: RC/Geological Survey of Israel/
rendered by SMM; map art: WM/Raphael; **394**
rich men: Frank Vincentz/WM; Jesus on donkey:
Andreas Praefcke/WM; **396** Bill Aron; **397** Last
Supper: Wolfgang Moroder/WM/Peter Nocker;
priest: **398–399** Jesus: Ondra Havala/FL/
Philippe de Champaigne; tomb: Brian Morley; **400**
PD/El Greco; **401** DW/FL

Mark
402 Jesus, left: GS; Jesus, portrait: PD/El Greco;
twelve disciples: DW/FL; Pontius Pilate: William
Storage; **403** John the Baptist: PD/El Greco;
Pentecost: PD/El Greco; **404** map: RC/Geological
Survey of Israel/rendered by SMM; map art: Patrick
Devonas; **405** Jezreel Valley: Albatross; girl in
mustard field: source unknown; **406** Herodias:
Molly Eyres/FL/Henri Alexandre Georges Renault;
pigs WM; **408** LJ/GS; **409** Jeff Gardner/FL; **410**
Jesus with children: LJ/GS; woman: GS; jug: AR;
411 Jesus on trial: WM/Mihaly Munkacsy; women
and angel: BAL

Luke
412 angel, left: DW/FL; Jesus: PD/El Greco;
twelve disciples: DW/FL; Mary: Siona/DA; Joseph:
PD/Raphael; Pontius Pilate: William Storage;
413 the annunciation: PD/El Greco; Church
of the Nativity: Israelimages/Garo Nalbandian;
414 Roman boy: William Storage/FL; tourists at
Nazareth: photo courtesy of jkramerbob/FL; **415**
Capernaum: BB; centurion: Dan Baillie/Baillie
Photography/FL; **416** Jesus calming storm: Stephen
Gjertson; map: TP/rendered by SMM; **417** Stephen
Gjertson; **418** Good Samaritan: WM/Vincent van
Gogh; Judean badlands: Israelimages/Duby Tal/
Albatross; **419** AR; **420** KR; **421** DW/FL

John
422 Jesus, left and portrait: LJ/GS; twelve disciples:
DW/FL; John the Baptist: PD/Jusepe de Ribera;
Pontius Pilate: William Storage; **423** waterfall:
WM; sheep: Phil Hearing/FL; **424** AR; **425** Jesus
and woman: WM/Jacek Malczewski; map: RC/
Geological Survey of Israel/rendered by SMM; map
art: Darrel Tank/GS; **426** healing blind man: WM;
raising Lazarus: National Gallery of London/WM/
Sebastiano del Piombo; **427** Jesus washing feet: PD/
Jacopo Tintoretto; trinity: PD/Jusepe de Ribera;
428 Molly Eyres/FL; **429** Honduran woman: Amy
Bible; Jesus at Emmaus: Moira Burke/WM

Acts
430 woman, left: WM; Paul: WM; Peter: PD/
Eugene Burnand; map: TP/rendered by SMM; map
art: José Manuel/WM/Diego Velázquez; **431** Molly
Eyres/FL; **432** Pentecost: PD/El Greco; Gemini
chart: SMM; **433** Ondra Havala/FL; **434** BAL;
435 map: TP/rendered by SMM; pork chops: Stu

Spivack/FL; **436** men shouting: LJ/GS; map: TP/
rendered by SMM; **437** Artemis: Jastrow/WM;
map: TP/rendered by SMM

Romans
438 Jesus, left: Alanso Cano; Paul: WM; map:
TP/rendered by SMM; map art of soldier: Rachel
White/FL; **439** history of universe: NASA, ESA,
and A. Feild (STScI); Jesus: AR; **440** Bill Aron;
441 bread distribution: Ophelia2/WM/Frans van
Leemputten; Nero: WM

1, 2 Corinthians
442 Paul, left: LJ/GS; Paul, portrait: WM; map:
TP/rendered by SMM; **443** Jesus and Peter: AR;
gay rights parade: Corbis; **444** couple portrait:
WM/Jan van Eyck; Shaker woman: LOC; **445**
women in church: Corbis: statue: William Storage;
446 Peter and John: PD/Eugene Bernand; angel
at tomb: DW/FL; **447** Paul: LJ/GS; Palestinian
children: Jose Mesa/FL

Galatians
448 Paul, left: BAL; Paul, portrait: WM; Peter:
PD/Eugene Bernand; map: TP/rendered by SMM;
449 Peter and Paul: PD/El Greco; circumcision:
Vatsnews/WM

Ephesians
450 man, left: Neils Photography/FL; Paul: WM;
map: TP/rendered by SMM; **451** men with scrolls:
Bill Aron; Ephesus ruins: Rui Omelas/FL; **452** PD;
453 GS

Philippians
454 writing, left: LJ/GS; Paul: WM; Timothy:
WM; map: TP/rendered by SMM; map art:
Riccardo Cuppini/WM; **455** André Durand/
durand-gallery.com/FL

Colossians
456 man, left: Lawrence Lew/FL; Paul/WM;
Epaphras: William Storage; map: TP/rendered by
SMM; **457** priests: PD; angel: Cornelia Kopp/
FL; map: RC/Geological Survey of Israel/rendered
by SMM

1, 2 Thessalonians
458 people, left: Faraz Shanyar/DA; Paul: WM;
Timothy and Silas: WM; map: TP/rendered by
SMM; **459** Alejandro Ferrant y Fischermans; **460**
painter: PD/Alexander Yanov; Titus: William
Storage; **461** Faraz Shanyar/DA

1, 2 Timothy
462 preacher, left: IS; Paul: WM; Timothy:
WM; map: TP/rendered by SMM; **463** William
Whitaker; **464** pope and priest: Lawrence Lew/FL;
Timothy: WM; **465** LJ/GS; **466** map: TP/rendered
by SMM; map art of ship: Eric Gaba/WM; map art
of traveler: LOC; **467** WM

Titus
468 Titus, left and portrait: British Museum;
Paul: WM; map: TP/rendered by SMM; map art:
Theophilos Papadopoulos; **469** old man: Tsigasp/
FL; shopping: Tomasz/FL

Philemon
470 person, left: BAL; Paul/WM; Onesimus:
DW/FL; Philemon: William Storage/FL; map:

TP/rendered by SMM; map art: PD/William
Bouguereau; **471** mosaic: Nick Thompson/FL;
slave: Ondra Havala/Sir Lawrence Alma-Tadema

Hebrews
472 man in prayer shawl, left: Bill Aron; Jesus:
PD/El Greco; map: TP/rendered by SMM; **473**
birth of Christ: PD/El Greco; Western Wall: Peter
Mulligan/FL; **474–475** Giandomenico Tiepolo

James
476 hands, left: Shutterstock; James: PD/El Greco;
map: TP/rendered by SMM; **477** Trey Ratcliff/
stuckincustoms.com; **478** Amy Bible; **479** woman
praying: Andrei Drozdov; Jesus praying: Osby
Maleri/WM

1, 2 Peter
480 man, left: BMM; Peter: PD/Eugene Burnand;
map: TP/rendered by SMM; map inset: WorldSat;
481 coin: Trustees of the British Museum; heaven-
bound man: Ondra Havala/FL/Nicolas Poussin;
482 Roman portrait: Erik Möller/WM; Peter's
crucifixion: BAL/Francisco de Zurbaran; **483** man:
WM/Egon Schiele; solar system: NASA

1, 2, 3 John
484 Antichrist, left: Ofir Abe/Orphaned Land;
Jesus: PD/El Greco; John: PD/Peter Paul Rubens;
Gaius: William Storage; Diotrephes: William
Storage; **485** Ofir Abe/Orphaned Land; **486**
Cayusa/FL; **487** Julia Dunin-Brzezi ska/DA

Jude
488 woman, left: PD/Franz von Stuck; Jude: Jan
Tendaj/FL; map: TP/rendered by SMM; **487** The
J. Paul Getty Museum, Villa Collection, Malibu,
California, Gift of Milton and Pat Gottlieb

Revelation
490 walking man, left: Vinoth Chandar/FL;
John: PD/Duccio di Buoninsegna; Jesus: PD/
El Greco; Satan: PD/Franz von Stuck; **491** RC/
Geological Survey of Israel/rendered by SMM; map
inset: WorldSat; **492** seals: Zev Radovan; angels
with trumpets: Shutterstock; **493** Mark Patrick/
MarkPatrickStudio.com; **494** Roman soldiers: Peter
Cracknell/FL; coin: Natalia Bauer/Trustees of the
British Museum; **495** Jezreel valley: Xnir.com/
PhotoStock-Israel.com; map: RC/Geological Survey
of Israel/rendered by SMM; **496** PD/Franz von
Stuck; **497** WKeown/FL; **498** Nicholas Roerich;
499 jasper: Saperaud/WM; sapphire: Daniel Torres,
Jr/WM; agate: Hannes Grobe/WM; emerald: Géry
Parent/WM; onyx: Bence Förd s/FL; carnelian:
Marie-Lan Nguyen/WM; chrysolite: Géry Parent/
WM; beryl: Orbital Joe Kienle/FL; topaz: Géry
Parent/WM; chrysoprase: Thomasin Durgin/FL;
jacinth: GI; amethyst: Orbital Joe Kienle/FL

Barbour Publishing, Inc., thanks these art suppliers
and copyright holders for permission to reproduce
their images. We have attempted to obtain
permissions to publish every image. If we have
inadvertently overlooked any, we would be happy to
hear from the copyright owners.